CIPHER SYSTEMS

Henry Beker was educated at the University of London, receiving his PhD at Westfield College in 1976. He is currently the Chief Mathematician at Racal-Comsec Ltd heading the department responsible for the cryptographic design of all the company's security equipment.

Fred Piper was educated at the University of London, receiving his PhD at Imperial College in 1964. He is currently Professor of Mathematics at Westfield College, University of London.

Both authors travel extensively, lecturing at numerous universities and other academic institutions throughout the world. Between them they have published over 50 research papers in combinatorics, geometry and cryptology.

CIPHER SYSTEMS

The Protection of Communications

Henry Beker and Fred Piper

1807 1982

A WILEY-INTERSCIENCE PUBLICATION

JOHN WILEY AND SONS
NEW YORK CHICHESTER BRISBANE TORONTO SINGAPORE

ISBN 0–471–89192–4

Printed and bound in Great Britain by
Clark Constable (1982) Ltd, Edinburgh and London

Contents

Acknowledgements

Many people have helped us during the preparation of this book. We are particularly indebted to Tony Bromfield, Cyril Garner, John Gordon, Paul Halliden, Richard Howard-Jones, Norman MacKinnon, Chris Mitchell and Mike Walker. They all read early versions of the manuscript and their criticisms and helpful suggestions were invaluable to us.

We would also like to thank Racal-Comsec Limited for their support and assistance.

Finally, our thanks to the Science Museum for permission to reproduce Figures 2.2 and 2.3, and the National Technical Information Service (United States Department of Commerce) for permission to reproduce Federal Information Processing Standard 46.

Introduction

The need to keep certain messages secret has been appreciated for thousands of years. Of course, people were not slow to realize the advantages to be gained from intercepting secret information, and this has led to a continuous, fascinating battle between the 'codemakers' and the 'codebreakers'. The arena for this contest is the communications medium which has changed considerably over the years. It was not until the arrival of the telegraph that the art of communications, as we know it today, began. But society is now highly dependent on our modern, fast and accurate means of transmitting messages. As well as the long-established forms, such as the post and courier services, we now have more technical and sophisticated media such as radio, television, telephone, telex and high speed data links. Usually the main aim is merely to transmit a message as quickly and cheaply as possible. There are, however, a number of situations where the information is confidential, and where an interceptor might be able to benefit immensely from the knowledge gained by monitoring the information circuit. In such situations, the communicants must take steps to conceal and protect the content of their message. Of course the amount of protection required will vary. On some occasions it is sufficient to prevent a casual 'listener' from understanding the message, but there are other times when it is crucial that even the most determined interceptor must not be able to deduce it. One of the main aims of this book is to illustrate the various types of protection which are available, and to stress the need for assessing the level of security offered by a given system.

If the communicants were able to use a non-interceptible means of transmission then, obviously, all their messages would be secure. But the most common forms of communication do not satisfy this requirement. The method which comes nearest to satisfying it is, probably, the use of a courier. But this is likely to be very slow, very expensive and, if the number of messages requiring transmission is large, might even be impossible. One alternative to a non-interceptible means of transmission is to conceal the content of each message by transforming it before transmission. This is the objective of a cipher system. The art (and science) of designing such systems is called **cryptography.**

There is little doubt that the problem of protecting and securing communications will continue to grow during the coming years; not only in its traditional military and political roles, but also in the public and commercial domains. The role of the cryptographer in times of war is one that has long been recognized and appreciated. But, more recently, the man in the street has been made increasingly aware of the fact that information relating to him is communicated between various data banks. Some of this information is personal in the sense that, although the knowledge would be useless to them, he would prefer other people not to know it. However some of it is confidential, and he needs to feel that unauthorized personnel will not have access to it and, possibly more important, will not be able to alter it. In such situations the communicants have no alternative but to give attention to the security of their transmissions. In fact, at the time of writing, a number of countries are introducing legislation to govern the protection of personal information.

As we shall see, the study of cryptography embraces a number of scientific fields; notably computer science, electronics, mathematics and statistics. The modern cryptographer also needs experience in practical communications. Our aim is to provide a broad introduction to the subject. The text is suitable for people with a practical interest in cryptography and/or communications, for late undergraduate students in any one of the four disciplines mentioned above and for research students. In order to make the book accessible to readers with various backgrounds, we have tried to make it reasonably 'self-contained' and to assume as little previous knowledge as possible. So, for example, we have assumed only that knowledge of mathematics which we believe most electronic engineers, computer scientists or statisticians will have. This does not mean that all the mathematics we use will be familiar to them, but we believe that any new topics are explained to a level sufficient for the understanding of our text. As a safeguard, we also provide further references for the basic material. The same principle applies to the electronics which the mathematician will need, the statistics for the computer scientist and so on. Thus, whatever the discipline of the reader, there will almost certainly be some sections which he finds very easy and others which, on a first reading, may be difficult. We recommend strongly that, during the first reading, everyone should be prepared to skip the details in any section which he finds either difficult or too easy. There is a lot to be gained from completing the book and obtaining an 'overall picture' before becoming immersed in too much detail.

We stress again that the aim of this book is to provide a comprehensive introduction to the subject of protecting and securing communications. Whether the reader intends to go on to do research in cryptography, build cryptographic equipment or simply compare and assess various pieces of equipment, this book should provide him with a suitable background with which to pursue his interest. He should be able to gain some insight into what is required of a cryptographic system, how the various pieces fit together and how the practical and theoretical sides of the subject interact. We are very much aware that a whole book could be written on almost any single chapter of this one. (In fact many have!) We do not, however, intend to exhaust any area of this expanding subject, but simply provide a firm foundation on which any reader can build.

The development of cryptography to the present day can be broken down into a number of stages. First came a number of systems, such as a simple letter substitution, that could be implemented using pencil and paper or simple mechanical machines. Almost all of these systems have been broken; i.e. it has been shown that given a sufficiently large portion of ciphered message, the complete message (and in many cases subsequent messages) can be deduced. In Chapter 1 we discuss a number of these early systems. Much of our notation is introduced in this chapter and so, in view of its importance, we have tried to make it easier than most of the others. We have deliberately avoided too much rigour and/or formality, and have tried to make it readily accessible to all readers.

The second stage of the development of cryptography dates from the beginning of the twentieth century (the time the telegraph became truly established) to the late 1950s. These systems normally used complex mechanical and electro-mechanical machines. Chapter 2 is primarily devoted to one such example, its analysis and ways in which it can be broken. Although the computational effort required to break them has often been immense, these systems have largely proved to be insecure. It is interesting to note that the breaking of one such machine during the Second World War led to the development of Colossus, one of the first dedicated calculating machines that we now know simply as computers. (Anyone attempting the examples of cryptanalysis in Chapter 2 will soon understand why!) Cryptography and **cryptanalysis** (the breaking of cipher systems) have often involved the pioneering of new techniques and abilities.

The transition from this second stage to the third stage of development is often regarded as having been due to two things. First came the revolutionary papers of C. E. Shannon in the late 1940s which showed how cryptography could be put on a sound mathematical base. The advent of microelectronics in the 1960s then provided a means for following up some of Shannon's ideas and, of course, for the introduction of new ones. It is this third stage which is the heart of our book. Chapter 3 introduces many of the theoretical concepts of Shannon and Chapter 4 relates many of these theoretical ideas to the relevant concepts of practical security. Chapters 5–9 are concerned with developing cryptographic systems.

The use of microelectronics has meant that the complexity of the functions that can now be performed by the security equipment has risen dramatically. This in turn has made the mathematics of design even more complex (the subject of Chapters 5–7). There are a few occasions, notably in Chapters 3 and 5, where we have included some mathematical proofs which may involve concepts outside the knowledge of some readers. When this happens, we include a non-mathematical synopsis of the results and the reader will in no way 'lose out' if he restricts himself to the synopses. Although it is certainly true that these more complex devices can provide a much higher level of security than was hitherto possible, it must be borne in mind that this is not always necessarily the case. It is simply not sufficient to incorporate some sophisticated security devices into a system and assume that it is 'safe'. Furthermore the cryptographer must never forget that the cryptanalyst can also benefit from this new technology. One of the reasons for the speed of development in cryptography is, of course, the presence of the cryptanalyst. In fact the protection of communications can, in many ways, be thought of as a two-player game, between the cryptographer and the cryptanalyst; with very serious consequences for the cryptographer if he loses. To play the game well, each player must make himself very much aware of the technology, and hence automation, which is available to his opponent. Thus it is impossible to develop any true skill in cryptography without recourse to cryptanalysis and *vice versa*. In this book we assume the role of the cryptographer which means that, unless the context makes it clear, words like 'good' will usually mean 'good from the cryptographic point of view'. But as the reader will see, in order to improve the systems we study, we often need to consider the situation from the cryptanalyst's point of view.

Another consequence of these recent developments is that the cost of cipher systems has been substantially reduced. This, in turn, implies that these devices are now open to users other than governments or the military. As the number of uses for cipher systems increases, it is also necessary to develop new techniques. A point we shall stress repeatedly is that the assessment of a system is not complete until every aspect of it has been considered. In other words, it is not enough merely to decide our algorithm is good, or the properties of the transmission medium are adequate, or the way the user intends to employ the system is reasonable; we must consider the suitability of the system as a whole. If a single detail is changed we must reassess the entire system. This process is discussed in Chapters 8 and 9.

Chapter 8 is concerned with a variety of applications of cipher systems, as well as questions such as key management. We consider several examples of systems and analyze them to varying depths. One of the examples we consider is a strategic telegraph system as might, for instance, be employed by military, government or high-level commercial users. We also compare the requirements of such a system with those of a portable tactical device. Another example, which we consider in some detail, is an intelligent point-of-sale terminal. This might be used at the checkout in a shop to effect the immediate electronic transfer of funds from the customer's bank account to the store's account. This is another situation where, if the customer is to be protected from unauthorized transfer of his funds, the security of communications is essential.

Chapter 9 is devoted to the problems associated with speech security.

This is an area which is currently being revolutionized by microelectronics. Until recently, analogue transmissions that were to be secure depended on bulky encryption devices. It is now possible to provide a reasonably high level of protection in a small hand-held unit or built into the radio or telephone. However, as we shall see, all these speech systems have a number of cryptographic difficulties. This chapter also highlights some of the problems arising from the transmission of voice signals, as opposed to data.

The final chapter is concerned with public-key cryptography, as proposed by Diffie and Hellman in 1976. This is a new and revolutionary type of cipher system which could overcome many of the key management problems that have plagued cipher systems since the first day of their conception. If such systems become accepted, they may well herald the start of yet another stage in the development of cryptography. However, only time, that most difficult of all tests, will tell.

We have already mentioned the desirability of reading the complete book to obtain the overall picture before working hard on any one particular chapter. It is also, perhaps, worth noting that it is not necessary to read the chapters in the order in which they appear. Apart from beginning with Chapter 1, which we consider crucial, the reader with limited mathematical knowledge or interest might prefer to read Chapters 4, 8 and 9 next. These would then convince him that some form of mathematical analysis of the security level is absolutely essential and thus motivate him to read the remaining chapters.

Finally a note about the bibliography. At the end of each chapter we list a few relevant references. Then, at the end of the book, we include a comprehensive list of books, articles, etc. on cryptography. Not surprisingly some references occur more than once. Such references have the same number throughout the book and it is this which accounts for the seemingly erratic numbering at the end of each chapter.

1.
Some Early Cipher Systems

1.1 Introduction

In this chapter we discuss some of the early cipher systems. Our aim is to be as informal as possible and to try to illustrate the basic ideas without being too technical. For this chapter virtually no previous mathematical or statistical knowledge is necessary. In order to keep the chapter moving we often use terms, e.g. secure and random, without formally defining them. The reader will have some intuitive idea of their meanings and formal definitions will be given in later chapters. (In fact the locations of all definitions are indicated by bold face numbers in the index.) For the present our aim is to acquaint the reader with some examples of ciphers and, probably more important, to make him aware of the problems facing the encipherer and some of the techniques available to the cryptanalyst. In each of the examples discussed the plaintext will be in English and the ciphertext will be a meaningless (or, rather, apparently meaningless) sequence of letters from the English alphabet.

The idea of a cipher system is to disguise confidential information in such a way that its meaning is unintelligible to an unauthorized person. The information to be concealed is called the **plaintext** (or just the **message**) and the operation of disguising it is known as **enciphering**. The enciphered message is called the **ciphertext** or **cryptogram**. The person who enciphers the message is known as the **encipherer**, while the person to whom he sends the cryptogram is called the **recipient** or **receiver**. The set of rules which the encipherer uses to encipher his plaintext is the **algorithm**. Normally the operation of this algorithm will depend on a **key** which the encipherer inputs to the algorithm together with his message. It is absolutely crucial that the recipient knows the key, and that this knowledge should enable him to determine the plaintext from the ciphertext. Thus the key and ciphertext must determine the plaintext uniquely. This process of applying a key to translate back from the ciphertext to the plaintext is known as **deciphering**. If a key is used in the way described above then the security of a well designed system should not depend on the algorithm but only on the key. A system which does not depend on a key (or, equivalently, has only one possible key) is often referred to as a **code**. We shall meet many examples of codes in this book.

One of the best known is Morse. Others, used to convert alphabetic characters into strings of 0s and 1s, are shown in Appendix 2.

Any person who intercepts a message being transmitted from the encipherer to a recipient is called, not surprisingly, an **interceptor**. An interceptor will not, in general, know the key and it is this lack of knowledge which, it is hoped, will prevent him from knowing the plaintext. **Cryptography** is the designing of cipher systems and **cryptanalysis** is the name given to the process of deducing the plaintext from the ciphertext without knowing the key. In practice the cryptanalyst will often be interested in deducing the key as well as the plaintext. If he is successful, he may then be able to decipher all other communications which he intercepts just as if he were the intended recipient. **Cryptology** includes both cryptography and cryptanalysis.

Most of the ciphers in this chapter have been in existence for many years and can be enciphered and deciphered without the assistance of a computer or any other machine. They are not, in general, used today. However, in order to trace the development of cryptographic devices and to appreciate the direction taken by the designers of such machines, it is essential to have an understanding of the principles behind many of these early 'manual' cipher systems. While it may be true that they are of no more than academic or historic interest, many of the techniques used to cryptanalyze these manual systems are still important for the cryptanalysis of a modern electronic cipher system. As we shall see later, even the well known, elementary methods of 'cracking' some of these early ciphers can often be used successfully to attack a carelessly designed electronic system which may, at first sight, appear very complex. Our use of the word 'carelessly' might be taken as implying that, with a little more thought, the designer of the system might have protected it from such methods. However it must be appreciated that the faults of a system often show up only when that system is cryptanalyzed. Thus what appears obvious with hindsight may not have been at all obvious at the design stage of the equipment.

We stress that this is not intended to be a full account of all the 'paper and pencil' ciphering methods which have ever been used. At the end of the chapter we give a short list of further reading containing books which give considerably more detail than we need, notably [2] and [5]. We have merely included some carefully chosen examples to introduce various techniques and terminology which will occur in various disguises (and perhaps surprising contexts) throughout the book. For this reason all readers, no matter what their mathematical or engineering backgrounds, are urged to read the entire chapter.

1.2 Monoalphabetic Ciphers

When schoolboys send 'secret' messages to each other they often invent a 'code' by letting each letter of the alphabet represent another one. This, in our terminology, is a **monoalphabetic cipher**. To obtain his key the schoolboy will write down the alphabet and will then write by each letter the new letter which represents it in his coded message. This choice of letters will be his key. Once the recipient has a copy of this piece of paper, he can easily decipher the message. Furthermore, it is clear that, if correctly deciphered, the secret message determines the plaintext uniquely. However if, as is usually the case with schoolboys, the rule for determining the allocation of letters is arbitrary, then the piece of paper on which the key is written is important. If it is lost or stolen the recipient will not be able to decipher the message. Its mere existence invites theft by anyone wishing to intercept the message. Clearly the system would be more secure if both encipherer and recipient could memorize the key. But to do this it is usually easier to have some rule for assigning ciphertext letters to the plaintext alphabet. Monoalphabetic ciphers are often referred to as **simple substitution ciphers** and the ordered sequence of letters which represents the alphabet is called the **substitution alphabet**.

1.2.1   Additive ciphers

One of the earliest examples of a monoalphabetic cipher was the **Caesar cipher** used by Julius Caesar in the Gallic wars. In this cipher each of the letters **a** through to **w** is represented by the letter which occurs three places after it in the alphabet. The letters **x**, **y**, **z** are represented by **A**, **B**, **C** respectively. So, if we write the ciphertext equivalent underneath the plaintext character, the substitution alphabet for the Caesar cipher is given by:

Plaintext: **a b c d e f g h i j k l m n o p q r s t u v w x y z**
Ciphertext: **D E F G H I J K L M N O P Q R S T U V W X Y Z A B C**

(Throughout this chapter we will use bold face lower case letters for plaintext and bold face capitals for ciphertext.)

The algorithm for enciphering a message is merely to replace each letter in the plaintext by the one immediately beneath it. The receiver deciphers the cryptogram by replacing each letter by the one above. For example:

Plaintext: **c a e s a r   w a s   a   g r e a t   s o l d i e r**
Ciphertext: **FDHVDU   ZDV   D   JUHDW   VROGLHU**

Clearly, the Caesar cipher is very simple and any message is so easily enciphered and deciphered that it is unnecessary to use a machine for either operation. Nevertheless, before leaving the Caesar cipher, we will describe a simple machine to implement the enciphering and deciphering algorithms. We must stress again that, in this case, the algorithm is so simple that the machine is unnecessary. But, as the algorithms we discuss become more complex, we shall see that an automatic means of enciphering and deciphering is crucial. Without it, time will be wasted and many errors may occur.

Figure 1.1 represents two concentric rings of which the outer one is free to rotate. If the outer ring is moved so that the **D** coincides with the **a**, then enciphering with the Caesar cipher is achieved by regarding the inner circle as representing the plaintext letters and replacing each letter by the one outside it.

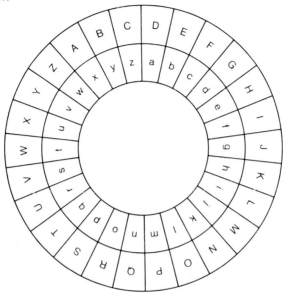

Figure 1.1
A 'machine' to implement additive ciphers

Now that we have our machine, it is clear that we can use it to obtain other ciphers. We can rotate the outside ring until any chosen letter is outside **a** to get a different substitution alphabet and then encipher our plaintext message using the same algorithm. In this way we can use our machine to get 26 different ciphers of which the Caesar cipher is merely one example. These ciphers are called the **additive ciphers** or the **translation ciphers**. (Note that in one of them, namely when **A** is outside **a**, the plaintext and ciphertext are identical. This is, of course, usually undesirable. We will often refer to this cipher as the **identity** and call any other cipher **genuine**.) It should be clear that the entire substitution alphabet of any one of these additive ciphers is determined once the ciphertext equivalent of any one plaintext letter is known. Thus we can define the key for this system as the ciphertext equivalent to the letter **a**. This then is all that has to be remembered and kept secret by the encipherer and recipient.

If the two rings are arranged so that their letters coincide, then each additive cipher is the result of rotating the outer ring anti-clockwise through a certain number of its 26 possible positions. Since rotating the outer ring through 26 positions has the same effect as leaving it alone, we can associate an integer from 0 to 25 inclusive with each of the keys. We will call this number the **shift** of the cipher. From this discussion it should now be obvious that the Caesar cipher is additive with shift 3 or, alternatively, is an additive cipher with key **D**.

For two people to communicate using a cipher, they both need to know the key and to be able to implement the algorithm. They will usually try to keep the key secret, as it is this which provides the security. In the case of our simple machine for additive ciphers, once the key is known, i.e. once one knows how far to rotate the outer ring, the implementation of the algorithm is exceptionally easy. It is probably worth noting at this stage of the discussion that, since there are only 25 genuine additive ciphers, keeping the key secret gives only very minimal security. It would not take a cryptanalyst long to try each of the 26 keys in turn and determine which one was used. As a simple illustration of how little time is involved in trying all 26 possibilities, let us put ourselves in the role of the cryptanalyst. Suppose that we intercept the following cryptogram and that we know that an additive cipher has been used. (If we knew, for instance, that the cryptographer had used one of our simple machines, then we would certainly know the cipher was additive!)

Ciphertext: **AOPZ TLZZHNL PZ H MHRL**

We will first pick one of the words in the ciphertext, say **MHRL**, and decipher it using each of the 26 ciphers in turn. In order to facilitate this procedure we first write out the substitution alphabets corresponding to the 26 keys (Table 1.1).

If a shift of 1 had been used the plaintext message would have been **lgqk**. Since there is no such word in the English language we know that the shift was not 1. The straightforward, and fairly quick, process of trying each shift in turn on **MHRL** shows that only two shifts lead to a possible plaintext word; i.e. a word in the English language. They are a shift of 7, which gives a plaintext word of **fake**, and a shift of 19 which gives **toys**. Now that we know that one of these two shifts was used, we try them both out on another word of the ciphertext. If we choose **PZ**, then a shift of 7 gives **is** while a shift of 19 gives **wg**. So clearly a shift of 7 was used and the message was: **this message is a fake**.

For this particular cryptogram there are even quicker ways to break the cipher. We could, for instance, have noted that the single letter word **H** in the ciphertext must represent **a** or **i** in plaintext. This would immediately have given us only two shifts to consider. For the moment, however, we do not wish to discuss the best method for cryptanalyzing any given message. We merely wish to illustrate that, once the algorithm is known, the fact that there are very few keys means that there is virtually no security. By this we mean that it is easy to determine the message without being told which key was used. Clearly this is an undesirable situation and, for this reason, additive ciphers are rarely used. We must now try to find algorithms which allow more choices for the key.

Plaintext		a b c d e f g h i j k l m n o p q r s t u v w x y z
Shift	0	A B C D E F G H I J K L M N O P Q R S T U V W X Y Z
,,	1	B C D E F G H I J K L M N O P Q R S T U V W X Y Z A
,,	2	C D E F G H I J K L M N O P Q R S T U V W X Y Z A B
,,	3	D E F G H I J K L M N O P Q R S T U V W X Y Z A B C
,,	4	E F G H I J K L M N O P Q R S T U V W X Y Z A B C D
,,	5	F G H I J K L M N O P Q R S T U V W X Y Z A B C D E
,,	6	G H I J K L M N O P Q R S T U V W X Y Z A B C D E F
,,	7	H I J K L M N O P Q R S T U V W X Y Z A B C D E F G
,,	8	I J K L M N O P Q R S T U V W X Y Z A B C D E F G H
,,	9	J K L M N O P Q R S T U V W X Y Z A B C D E F G H I
,,	10	K L M N O P Q R S T U V W X Y Z A B C D E F G H I J
,,	11	L M N O P Q R S T U V W X Y Z A B C D E F G H I J K
,,	12	M N O P Q R S T U V W X Y Z A B C D E F G H I J K L
,,	13	N O P Q R S T U V W X Y Z A B C D E F G H I J K L M
,,	14	O P Q R S T U V W X Y Z A B C D E F G H I J K L M N
,,	15	P Q R S T U V W X Y Z A B C D E F G H I J K L M N O
,,	16	Q R S T U V W X Y Z A B C D E F G H I J K L M N O P
,,	17	R S T U V W X Y Z A B C D E F G H I J K L M N O P Q
,,	18	S T U V W X Y Z A B C D E F G H I J K L M N O P Q R
,,	19	T U V W X Y Z A B C D E F G H I J K L M N O P Q R S
,,	20	U V W X Y Z A B C D E F G H I J K L M N O P Q R S T
,,	21	V W X Y Z A B C D E F G H I J K L M N O P Q R S T U
,,	22	W X Y Z A B C D E F G H I J K L M N O P Q R S T U V
,,	23	X Y Z A B C D E F G H I J K L M N O P Q R S T U V W
,,	24	Y Z A B C D E F G H I J K L M N O P Q R S T U V W X
,,	25	Z A B C D E F G H I J K L M N O P Q R S T U V W X Y

Table 1.1
A table of the substitution alphabets for the 26 additive ciphers

EXERCISE 1.1   We saw when deciphering **MHRL** *that* **fake** *and* **toys** *are shifts of each other. (Note that since a shift of 19 ciphers* **toys** *into* **MHRL** *a shift of 7 must cipher* **mhrl** *into* **TOYS***. Thus, since a shift of 7 also ciphers* **fake** *into* **MHRL**, *a shift of 14 will have the effect of ciphering* **fake** *into* **TOYS**.) *Find other pairs of English words which are shifts of each other.*

Exercise 1.1 is actually quite hard because there are very few such pairs of words. In fact, we know of none of length six or more.

Before moving on, we emphasize one particular aspect of the method of attack in the above example. It relies upon the fact that most combinations of letters are meaningless in the English language (and, in fact, in any language). This simple property is the basis of many of the statistical methods of attack which we will discuss in this and later chapters.

1.2.2   Affine ciphers

When discussing additive ciphers we saw that a shift of 26 was the same as a shift of 0. It was also clear that a shift of any number, no matter how large, was identical to a shift of some other number in the range 0 to 25 inclusive. To find this number we could, for instance, take our simple machine, start with **A** outside **a** and rotate it through the large number of positions. When this was done the final position of the outside ring would tell us the smaller number. For instance a shift of 84 is obtained by 3 complete revolutions (i.e. 3 consecutive shifts of 26 each, which are equivalent to a shift of $3 \times 26 = 78$) followed by a shift of 6. Thus a shift of 84 is the same as a shift of 6.

We now wish to utilize this observation to define a new 'addition' between any two positive integers. If α and β are any two positive integers then we will denote by $\alpha \oplus \beta$ the unique integer γ in the range 0 to 25 inclusive such that a shift of $\alpha + \beta$ is the same as a shift of γ. Thus, for example, since we have already seen that a shift of 84 is the same as a shift of 6 and since $21 + 63 = 84$, we have $21 \oplus 63 = 6$. (Anyone who understands modular arithmetic will realize that we are merely introducing addition modulo 26. Such readers should be able to cover the next few pages very quickly and will not, of course, need to do Exercises 1.2, 1.3 and 1.5.)

EXERCISE 1.2   Show that:
    (*i*) $15 \oplus 19 = 8$,
    (*ii*) $6 \oplus 11 = 17$,
    (*iii*) $5 \oplus (6 \oplus 19) = 4 = (5 \oplus 6) \oplus 19$,
    (*iv*) $46 \oplus 51 = 19$.

EXERCISE 1.3   If α and β are two integers such that a shift of α is the same as a shift of β, and β is in the range 0 to 25 inclusive, show that β is equal to the remainder when α is divided by 26.

Now that we have defined this new addition, we will use it to represent the additive ciphers in mathematical notation. First we represent each letter by the number of its position in the alphabet except that, instead of representing it by 26, we represent **z** by 0. Thus we have:

Letter:	**a**	**b**	**c**	**d**	**e**	**f**	**g**	**h**	**i**	**j**	**k**	**l**	**m**
Number:	1	2	3	4	5	6	7	8	9	10	11	12	13

Letter:	**n**	**o**	**p**	**q**	**r**	**s**	**t**	**u**	**v**	**w**	**x**	**y**	**z**
Number:	14	15	16	17	18	19	20	21	22	23	24	25	0

For each letter except **y**, the additive cipher with shift 1 is now obtained by adding 1 to the corresponding number to obtain the number of the ciphertext letter. Since **y** becomes **Z** and since $25 \oplus 1 = 0$, the complete cipher with shift 1 is implemented by using our new addition to add 1. Notationally we can now represent the additive cipher with shift 1 as: $\lambda \rightarrow \lambda \oplus 1$ for each integer λ in the range 0 to 25 inclusive. (In future we will simply write 'for all λ with $0 \le \lambda \le 25$' as a shorthand notation for 'for all λ in the range 0 to 25 inclusive'. This is the standard mathematical notation.)

But now, of course, we can extend this notation to represent each of the 26 additive ciphers. For any α with $0 \leq \alpha \leq 25$ we will denote the additive cipher with shift α by: $\lambda \rightarrow \lambda \oplus \alpha$ for all λ with $0 \leq \lambda \leq 25$. As an illustration of the use of this notation let us consider the additive cipher with shift 8. The plaintext letter **u**, which is number 21, will be represented by the ciphertext letter whose number is $21 \oplus 8$. But $21 \oplus 8 = 3$ so the ciphertext letter will be **C**. (The reader should look back to Table 1.1, page 19, to check that this is correct.)

EXERCISE 1.4   Use the new addition to find the ciphertext letter for **x** *under an additive cipher with shift* 19. *Use Table* 1.1 *to check your answer.*

Having defined this new addition we will use a similar idea to define a new multiplication: for any positive integers α, β we define $\alpha \otimes \beta$ to be the unique integer γ with $0 \leq \gamma \leq 25$ such that a shift of $\alpha . \beta$ is the same as a shift of γ. So, for example, if we put $\alpha = 7$ and $\beta = 13$, $7 \otimes 13$ will be the unique integer γ with $0 \leq \gamma \leq 25$ such that a shift of 7×13 is equivalent to a shift of γ. Thus, since $7 \times 13 = 91$ and $91 = 3 \times 26 + 13$, $7 \otimes 13 = 13$. (Once again we note, for those who have studied modular arithmetic that $\otimes$ merely represents multiplication modulo 26.)

EXERCISE 1.5
(*i*)   *Show that* $5 \otimes 7 = 9$ *and* $11 \otimes 20 = 12$.
(*ii*)   *Find* $11 \otimes 9$ *and* $4 \otimes 13$.

What happens if we use this new multiplication to get new ciphers? Before answering this question, we will investigate what happens if we 'multiply' each letter by 2. The letter **a**, which has number 1, will become the letter whose number is $2 \otimes 1$. But, clearly, $2 \otimes 1 = 2$ and plaintext **a** becomes ciphertext **B**. Similar calculations show that **b** becomes **D**, **c** becomes **F** etc. However, an undesirable thing happens to **n**. The letter **n** is 14, so the ciphertext equivalent has number $2 \otimes 14$. But $2 \otimes 14 = 2$ and the ciphertext equivalent of **n** is **B**. We are now in the situation where two distinct plaintext letters, namely **a** and **n**, have the same ciphertext letter, i.e. **B**. One essential prerequisite of a cipher must be that the ciphertext determines the plaintext uniquely. Otherwise deciphering can result in dangerous ambiguities. But this means that we cannot use multiplication by 2 to obtain a cipher. Fortunately this is not true for all multiplications. The reason that we failed to obtain a cipher was that we chose to multiply by 2 rather than some other more suitable number. In order to determine precisely which numbers are more suitable, we compute a complete 'multiplication' table (Table 1.2).

Straightforward verification now shows that multiplication by 1, 3, 5, 7, 9, 11, 15, 17, 19, 21, 23 and 25 are the only instances where a cipher is

Plaintext		a	b	c	d	e	f	g	h	i	j	k	l	m	n	o	p	q	r	s	t	u	v	w	x	y	z
Multiply	0	Z	Z	Z	Z	Z	Z	Z	Z	Z	Z	Z	Z	Z	Z	Z	Z	Z	Z	Z	Z	Z	Z	Z	Z	Z	Z
by	1	A	B	C	D	E	F	G	H	I	J	K	L	M	N	O	P	Q	R	S	T	U	V	W	X	Y	Z
	2	B	D	F	H	J	L	N	P	R	T	V	X	Z	B	D	F	H	J	L	N	P	R	T	V	X	Z
	3	C	F	I	L	O	R	U	X	A	D	G	J	M	P	S	V	Y	B	E	H	K	N	Q	T	W	Z
	4	D	H	L	P	T	X	B	F	J	N	R	V	Z	D	H	L	P	T	X	B	F	J	N	R	V	Z
	5	E	J	O	T	Y	D	I	N	S	X	C	H	M	R	W	B	G	L	Q	V	A	F	K	P	U	Z
	6	F	L	R	X	D	J	P	V	B	H	N	T	Z	F	L	R	X	D	J	P	V	B	H	N	T	Z
	7	G	N	U	B	I	P	W	D	K	R	Y	F	M	T	A	H	O	V	C	J	Q	X	E	L	S	Z
	8	H	P	X	F	N	V	D	L	T	B	J	R	Z	H	P	X	F	N	V	D	L	T	B	J	R	Z
	9	I	R	A	J	S	B	K	T	C	L	U	D	M	V	E	N	W	F	O	X	G	P	Y	H	Q	Z
	10	J	T	D	N	X	H	R	B	L	V	F	P	Z	J	T	D	N	X	H	R	B	L	V	F	P	Z
	11	K	V	G	R	C	N	Y	J	U	F	Q	B	M	X	I	T	E	P	A	L	W	H	S	D	O	Z
	12	L	X	J	V	H	T	F	R	D	P	B	N	Z	L	X	J	V	H	T	F	R	D	P	B	N	Z
	13	M	Z	M	Z	M	Z	M	Z	M	Z	M	Z	M	Z	M	Z	M	Z	M	Z	M	Z	M	Z	M	Z
	14	N	B	P	D	R	F	T	H	V	J	X	L	Z	N	B	P	D	R	F	T	H	V	J	X	L	Z
	15	O	D	S	H	W	L	A	P	E	T	I	X	M	B	Q	F	U	J	Y	N	C	R	G	V	K	Z
	16	P	F	V	L	B	R	H	X	N	D	T	J	Z	P	F	V	L	B	R	H	X	N	D	T	J	Z
	17	Q	H	Y	P	G	X	O	F	W	N	E	V	M	D	U	L	C	T	K	B	S	J	A	R	I	Z
	18	R	J	B	T	L	D	V	N	F	X	P	H	Z	R	J	B	T	L	D	V	N	F	X	P	H	Z
	19	S	L	E	X	Q	J	C	V	O	H	A	T	M	F	Y	R	K	D	W	P	I	B	U	N	G	Z
	20	T	N	H	B	V	P	J	D	X	R	L	F	Z	T	N	H	B	V	P	J	D	X	R	L	F	Z
	21	U	P	K	F	A	V	Q	L	G	B	W	R	M	H	C	X	S	N	I	D	Y	T	O	J	E	Z
	22	V	R	N	J	F	B	X	T	P	L	H	D	Z	V	R	N	J	F	B	X	T	P	L	H	D	Z
	23	W	T	Q	N	K	H	E	B	Y	V	S	P	M	J	G	D	A	X	U	R	O	L	I	F	C	Z
	24	X	V	T	R	P	N	L	J	H	F	D	B	Z	X	V	T	R	P	N	L	J	H	F	D	B	Z
	25	Y	X	W	V	U	T	S	R	Q	P	O	N	M	L	K	J	I	H	G	F	E	D	C	B	A	Z

Table 1.2
A table to show the effect of multiplying by each integer from 0 to 25.

obtained. (These, of course, are precisely those values which are coprime to 26.) We call these the **multiplicative ciphers** and, if α is any one of these numbers, we denote the cipher obtained by multiplying by α as: $\lambda \rightarrow \alpha \otimes \lambda$ for all λ with $0 \leq \lambda \leq 25$. Even if we include multiplication by 1, which is merely the identity cipher, there are only 12 multiplicative ciphers. Since this is even less than the number of additive ciphers, they also offer only minimal security. But now we will show how to combine a multiplicative cipher with an additive cipher to obtain a new cipher. We call these new ciphers **affine**. If $\lambda \rightarrow \alpha \otimes \lambda$ is a multiplicative cipher and $\lambda \rightarrow \lambda \oplus \beta$ is an additive cipher, then we obtain an affine cipher, which we denote by $[\alpha, \beta]$ as follows: for any plaintext letter, λ say, we first determine the ciphertext letter under $\lambda \rightarrow \alpha \otimes \lambda$. If this letter is μ, we then regard μ as a plaintext letter and find its ciphertext equivalent under $\mu \rightarrow \mu \oplus \beta$. This final letter is the ciphertext equivalent of λ under $[\alpha, \beta]$.

As an example, let us determine the ciphertext equivalent of **n** under $[7, 11]$. From Table 1.2 the ciphertext equivalent of **n** under $\lambda \rightarrow 7 \otimes \lambda$ is **T** and, from Table 1.1, the ciphertext of **t** under $\lambda \rightarrow \lambda \oplus 11$ is **E**. Thus the ciphertext of **n** under $[7, 11]$ is **E**.

In general the two parameters α and β constitute the key of the affine cipher $[\alpha, \beta]$.

*EXERCISE 1.6   Show that the ciphertext of **cat** under $[5, 17]$ is **FVM**.*

*EXERCISE 1.7   Decipher **VMWZ** if the affine cipher $[11, 2]$ was used. (Note that when deciphering the two tables must be used in the opposite order; i.e. Table 1.1 first.)*

All additive and multiplicative ciphers are affine. In fact $[\alpha, \beta]$ is additive whenever $\alpha = 1$ and is multiplicative if $\beta = 0$. There are 12 choices for α, (remember that α must be one of 1, 3, 5, 7, 9, 11, 15, 17, 19, 21, 23, 25), and 26 choices for β. Since we can combine any one of the choices for α with any of the choices for β to obtain an affine cipher, there are $12 \times 26 = 312$ affine ciphers, i.e. 312 choices for the key in an affine cipher system. Even if we ignore the identity, there are still 311 genuine affine possibilities. By modern day standards, when we have the use of computers, this does not seem a very large number. However, when all calculations had to be done by hand, it was sometimes considered large enough to deter the cryptanalyst from trying all possibilities. Even if it was not large enough to deter him, it at least ensured that he took a reasonably long time to decipher the cryptogram by systematically trying each possible key.

In all situations we would like to estimate the length of time it will take the cryptanalyst to break the particular system being used. Of course this time will depend upon many things including, for instance, the precise facilities available to him. The length of time we believe our system will resist a particular attack is normally referred to as its **cover time** for that attack. Different applications of cipher systems will require different minimal cover time. (The **minimal cover time** is the shortest cover time for any conceivable attack.) For instance within a 'tactical' network a few hours, or even minutes, may be sufficient time while within a 'strategic' system many years may be necessary.

As an indication that using affine cipher systems makes life a little awkward for the cryptanalyst, we now set two exercises. In the first it is assumed that the cryptanalyst knows that a key with $\beta = 4$ is used but does not know α. In the second we assume he knows $\alpha = 9$ but does not know β. Neither should take too long, although the former is probably more straightforward. However they should persuade the reader not to try to decipher 'by hand' knowing only that an affine cipher was employed; i.e. without knowing α or β.

*EXERCISE 1.8   Decipher **GLZOXA** knowing that an affine cipher with $\beta = 4$ was used and that the plaintext is a word of the English language.*

*EXERCISE 1.9   Decipher **QJYSV** knowing that an affine cipher with $\alpha = 9$ was used and that the plaintext is a word of the English language.*

When we discussed additive ciphers, we pointed out that the entire substitution alphabet was known once we knew the ciphertext of any one plaintext letter. It should also be clear that the same is true for multiplicative ciphers except, of course, that the ciphertext of **z** is always **Z**. For affine ciphers it is true, but not quite so obvious, that the entire substitution alphabet is determined by the ciphertext of two distinct plaintext letters. However we shall not spend any more time discussing how to attack affine ciphers, because in Section 1.2.4 we discuss the cryptanalysis of all monoalphabetic ciphers. Before doing this we will discuss briefly another system which allows many more possibilities for the key.

1.2.3 Key phrase ciphers

In these ciphers the key takes the form of a phrase together with one extra special letter. Since we may use any phrase, we now have an exceedingly large number of keys. In the resulting cipher, the first letter of the phrase will be the ciphertext equivalent of the plaintext special letter. The substitution alphabet is arrived at as follows. First, as always, the plaintext alphabet is written out. The key phrase is then written underneath beginning at the special letter, but with no letter of the phrase repeated. So, for example, if **METTLE** occurs in the key phrase we only write **METL**. The remaining ciphertext alphabet is then written after the key phrase.

As an example let us take the key phrase **MY LITTLE FINGER** with special letter **d**. First we write **MY LITTLE FINGER** omitting repeated letters to get **MYLITEFNGR**. We then write out our plaintext alphabet and write the **M** under **d** to get:

Plaintext: a b c d e f g h i j k l m n o p q r s t u v w x y z
Ciphertext: M Y L I T E F N G R

The substitution alphabet is now completed by writing the remaining ciphertext letters in alphabetic order starting with **A** under **n**. This gives:

Plaintext: a b c d e f g h i j k l m n o p q r s t u v w x y z
Ciphertext: W X Z M Y L I T E F N G R A B C D H J K O P Q S U V

Clearly, since any key phrase may be chosen, we have succeeded in obtaining a cipher where the key may be chosen so that it can be remembered easily. It is also clear that the cryptanalyst cannot possibly hope to decipher it by trying all possible key phrases. Obviously it is not practicable to attempt to quantify the number of key phrase ciphers, but the following paragraph may give some indication of the numbers involved.

If we permute the 26 letters of the alphabet in any order whatsoever and write them under the plaintext alphabet, we will have a monoalphabetic cipher. There are 26! such permutations and 26! is approximately equal to

4×10^{26}. Since absolutely any key phrase may be chosen, it is hardly surprising that a reasonable proportion of these may arise as key phrase ciphers. Even with current computer speed, it is simply impossible for a cryptanalyst to guarantee to decipher any cryptogram simply by trying all possibilities.

For many years, armed with the knowledge that the cryptanalyst could not try all possible key phrases, the cryptographer believed that this system offered reasonable security. In fact similar assumptions are often made today, but they are erroneous. Such a system is only secure if the messages transmitted are short. As soon as the message is long enough, it must be appreciated that trying every possible key is not the only way to crack a system. There are many mathematical and statistical approaches which enable the cryptanalyst to eliminate millions of keys at once. He does not need to try them all!

1.2.4 Statistical cryptanalysis

If you read any passage of English literature it is soon clear that the letter **e** occurs more often than **z**. In fact if you make comparisons between various reasonably long passages (say 1000 characters or more), taken from a number of non-technical books, newspapers, etc., you will soon observe that there is an amazingly consistent order of 'popularity' for the letters. Listed below are the frequencies with which the letters occur in the first paragraph of the Data Encryption Standard.

a 37	b 6	c 20	d 26	e 58	f 7	g 7	h 21
i 21	j 35	k 1	l 22	m 16	n 33	o 32	p 18
q 0	r 21	s 24	t 46	u 6	v 6	w 6	x 0
y 12	z 0.						

If we compare the above figures with those in Appendix 1 (page 395), taken from a sample of more than 100,000 letters, we see that the relative frequencies with which the letters occur are more or less the same. In fact no matter where the text appears, provided it is long enough and is not particularly specialized, the relative frequencies with which the letters occur are fairly predictable. (For some technical or specialized papers the relative frequencies may vary slightly, e.g. in a chemical abstract about zinc we would obviously expect **z** to occur more often than usual.)

Since these frequencies are so consistent, we are able to attach to each letter an approximate probability which represents the likelihood that a letter chosen at random from an English text will be that given letter. It is, of course, impossible to give exact values to these probabilities as they depend, to some extent, on the nature of the material from which the statistics are gathered. In this book we will use the values of the probabilities given by our statistics in Appendix 1. The statistics suggest, for instance, that the probability, p_a, of an **a** occurring is about $0 \cdot 082$; by which we mean that, on average, we would expect to find the letter **a** about 82 times in an English text of 1,000 letters. The total list of probabilities is given in Appendix 1. If we write $\sum\limits_{a}^{z} p_\lambda$ for $\sum\limits_{\lambda=a}^{\lambda=z} p_\lambda$ then we remind the reader that, as with all probabilities, $\sum\limits_{a}^{z} p_\lambda = 1$.

These probabilities are important to the cryptanalyst because they give him information about the key. For example, since p_e is so much greater than every other probability, we would anticipate that, if a monoalphabetic cipher is used, most ciphertexts will contain one letter significantly more often than any other. When this occurs it is reasonable to 'guess' that this letter is the ciphertext equivalent for **e**. There are certain letters whose probabilities are so nearly equal that, unless the text were exceptionally long, it would not make sense to distinguish between their likely frequencies. However an inspection of the statistics in Appendix 1 suggests that we can reasonably group the letters into five sets (Table 1.3).

> I   **e**,
> II   **t, a, o, i, n, s, h, r**,
> III   **d, l**,
> IV   **c, u, m, w, f, g, y, p, b**,
> V   **v, k, j, x, q, z**.

Table 1.3
The frequency groupings for letters in English plaintext

The way in which these groupings are obtained should be clear. The letter **e** is the most popular. Each letter in group II is significantly less popular than **e** but occurs much more often than those in the other groups. Any reader who plays *Scrabble* should compare our groups, or even the probabilities in Appendix 1, with the scores and the availability of the various letters. Any letter which occurs in our first three groups is frequently used in words. It is, therefore, easy to 'use' in *Scrabble* and is readily available with a low score.

Not only do the individual letters occur with reasonably constant frequencies but so do **bigrams** (pairs of consecutive letters) and **trigrams** (triples of consecutive letters). Again detailed statistics on their relative frequencies are readily available and we include some in Appendix 1, page 395. However, as before, the precise details do not concern us. As a matter of interest we give a list, in order, of the 30 most popular bigrams. It is a surprising fact that these 30 bigrams will account for over a third of all the bigrams in a standard passage of English plaintext. The bigrams are: **th, he, in, er, an, re, ed, on, es, st, en, at, to, nt, ha, nd, ou, ea, ng, as, or, ti, is, et, it, ar, te, se, hi, of**. Again in any reasonably long ciphertext from a similar source, we would expect to find about 30 bigrams occurring significantly more often than the others. We should then deduce that they were mostly the ciphertext equivalents, in roughly the same order, of those listed above.

The 12 most popular trigrams, in order of popularity, are: **the**, **ing**, **and**, **her**, **ere**, **ent**, **tha**, **nth**, **was**, **eth**, **for**, **dth**. (The frequency of **the** is nearly three times greater than **ing**. So we should be able to spot the ciphertext equivalent of **the** fairly quickly, especially as we will 'know' the ciphertext letter for **e**.) Other statistics are available. As illustrations we include in Appendix 1 the frequencies with which individual letters occur as the first or last letter of a word.

As we keep emphasizing, the longer the passage the more reliable the statistics become. For ciphertexts with only a few words the statistics are virtually meaningless and are of no help to the cryptanalyst. But, with all the statistical information available, it is straightforward to cryptanalyze any reasonably long ciphertext (provided, of course, that we know a monoalphabetic cipher was used). Before we attempt to justify this claim by deciphering a cryptogram, we make three observations:

(i) The word **the** has a tremendous effect on these statistics. It is the main reason for the high frequency of **t**, **h**, **th**, **he** and **the**. If the word **the** were deleted from the plaintext then **t** would fall below some of the other letters in group II, while **h** would fall into group III. Furthermore **th** and **he** would no longer be the most popular bigrams.

(ii) Over half the words in the English language end in **e**, **s**, **d** or **t**.

(iii) About half the words in the English language begin with **t**, **a**, **s** or **w**.

The above discussion of the statistics of the English language is based on the assumption that only the 26 letters of the alphabet are relevant. In practice the composition of a message involves a far greater selection of characters, including spaces, punctuation, numbers, etc. With an electronic means of preparing a message, even more characters are available including, for instance, carriage return, line feed and control characters. The complete set of characters available is known as the **character set** and examples can be found in Appendix 2. We will often be concerned with subsets of the character set; for example the **alphabetic characters** (letters) or the **alphanumeric characters** (letters and numbers).

Let us now put ourselves in the position of the cryptanalyst and attempt to cryptanalyze the following ciphertext knowing only that a key phrase cipher was used. Our deductions will all be based on statistical reasoning and thus, although we use words like 'know' and 'must', we must remember that nothing is 100 per cent certain and we must always be prepared to change our minds if we find we cannot obtain a meaningful message.

YKHLBA JCZ SVIJ JZB TZVHI JCZ VHJ DR IZXKHLBA VSS RDHEI DR YVJV LBXSKYLBA YLALJVS IFZZXC CVI LEFHDNZY EVBLRDSY JCZ FHLEVHT HZVIDB RDH JCLI CVI WZZB JCZ VYNZBJ DR ELXHDZSZXJHDBLXI JCZ

XDEFSZQLJT DR JCZ RKBXJLDBI JCVJ XVB BDP WZ FZHRDHEZY WT JCZ EVXCLBZ CVI HLIZB YHVEVJLXVSST VI V HZIKSJ DR JCLI HZXZBJ YZNZSDFEZBJ LB JZXCBDSDAT EVBT DR JCZ XLFCZH ITIJZEI JCVJ PZHZ DBXZ XDBILYZHZY IZXKHZ VHZ BDP WHZVMVWSZ.

The message contains 338 letters with the following frequencies:

Letter:	A	B	C	D	E	F	G	H	I	J	K	L	M
Frequency:	5	24	19	23	12	7	0	24	21	29	6	21	1

Letter:	N	O	P	Q	R	S	T	U	V	W	X	Y	Z
Frequency:	3	0	3	1	11	14	8	0	27	5	17	12	45.

This means that the order of popularity is **Z, J, V, B, H, D, I, L, C, X, S, Y, E, R, T, F, K, A, W, N, P, M, Q, U, G, O**. Since the frequency of **Z** is significantly greater than all others we deduce that **Z** must correspond to **e**.

We earlier remarked that there are many mathematical and statistical approaches which enable the cryptanalyst to eliminate millions of keys at once. We have just seen one such technique. Once we have deduced the ciphertext equivalent of **e** the number of possible keys has been reduced from 26! to 25!, i.e. by $3 \cdot 88 \times 10^{26}$. Thus $3 \cdot 88 \times 10^{26}$ keys have been eliminated!

Returning to our cryptogram the next most popular letter is **J** but, since 29 is not much larger than 27, we hesitate before assuming that **J** corresponds to **t**. However, the three letter word **JCZ** occurs eight times and this extra fact convinces us that **J** corresponds to **t** and, furthermore, that **C** is **h**. Since the single letter word **V** occurs we know that **V** must be **a** or **i**. But **a** and **i** are both in group II which means we need some extra information before deciding between them. That extra information is provided by the existence of the ciphertext word **JCVJ**. Since there is no English word **thit**, we now know **V** must be **a**.

At this stage it is worth making two observations. First the only statistics we have really used are that **e** is by far the most popular letter in the English language while **the** is the most popular trigram. Secondly, we note that **C** is the ninth most frequent letter in our ciphertext and **h** is the eighth most popular letter of the English language. So, assuming that we are correct in claiming that **C** corresponds to **h**, even in our short message the statistics are 'roughly correct'.

According to the frequencies in our ciphertext **J, V, B, H, D, I, L, C** should correspond, in some order, to the plaintext letters in group II, i.e. to **t, a, o, i, n, s, h, r**. So far we have deduced only that **J** is **t**, **V** is **a** and **C** is **h**. To find the other correspondences we merely look at suitably chosen ciphertext words. For instance, consider the fourth word **JZB**. We know **J** is **t**, **Z** is **e** and **B** is one of **o, n, r, i, s**. Trying each possibility for **B** gives plaintext words of **teo, ten, ter, tei, tes**. Clearly the plaintext word should be **ten** which indicates **B** is **n**. We now note the two letter word **VI**. Since **V** is **a**, **I** must be **s** or **n**. But we already know that **B** is **n** and this means that **I** must be **s**.

So now we know that **H**, **D**, **L** correspond to **o**, **r**, **i**, in some order. The ciphertext word **VHJ** forces **H** to be **r** and **JCLI** forces **L** to be **i**. Thus **D** must be **o**. Let us now see if we can work out the substitution alphabet key. So far we know:

Plaintext:	a	b	c	d	e	f	g	h	i	j	k	l	m
Ciphertext:	V			Z			C	L					

Plaintext:	n	o	p	q	r	s	t	u	v	w	x	y	z
Ciphertext:	B	D			H	I	J						

Before discussing the key we note that, if we had not been told the type of cipher used, the fact that three consecutive plaintext letters (i.e. **r**, **s**, **t**), correspond to three consecutive ciphertext letters is a reasonable indicator that a key phrase was employed. A longer sequence would, of course, be more conclusive.

However, in this case, we know that a key phrase cipher was used and it is clear that the special letter was **f**. Indeed this was almost guaranteed by the fact that **Z** is **e**. Since there are three gaps between **V** and **Z** in the partial substitution alphabet above and since there are only three letters between them in the alphabet, we know that **W** is **b**, **X** is **c** and **Y** is **d**. It is tempting to observe that there are two gaps between **D** and **H** and to deduce that two of **E**, **F** and **G** must be **p** and **q**. But we cannot be too confident about this as we do not know where the key phrase ends. So, for the moment, we will resist this temptation.

As we already know the plaintext equivalent of twelve ciphertext letters we will continue by looking at ciphertext words which contain some of the deciphered letters and use the fact that the plaintext equivalent must be an English word. If we start by considering **DR** then, since **D** is **o**, **R** must be one of **f**, **n**, **r** or **x**. Since we already know the ciphertext equivalents of **r** and **n**, it must be **f** or **x**. But from our statistical tables, its frequency is too high for it to be **x** so **R** 'must' be **f**. (In fact, since the ciphertext is so short, we cannot be too confident about this statistical inference. If we find ourselves unable to get a meaningful message we will come back and try putting **R** as **x**.) Similarly **WT** tells us that **T** is **y** and, after a little thought, **BDP** forces **P** to be **w**. Now that we know that **w** is **P** and **y** is **T** then, since a key phrase was used, the only plaintext letter between **w** and **y** (i.e. **x**) must be a ciphertext letter between **P** and **T**. But it cannot be **R** (since **R** is **f**) which means that **Q** or **S** is **x**. (Note this also tells us that **R** is in the key phrase.)

If we now attempt to decipher the first word we get **d–rin–**. Clearly the first – must represent a vowel and, as we already know the ciphertext for **a**, **e**, **i** and **o**, it must **u**. Thus **K** is **u** and **A** must be **g**. The message now starts **during the –ast years**. Clearly this – must be **p** or **l**. In ciphertext the – is **S**. We could look at the popularity of **S** to 'deduce' (rather dubiously!) that **S** represents **l** or (much better!) notice that there is a ciphertext word **VSS** which forces **S** to be **l**. This also means that **Q** must be **x** and that **S** is in the key phrase.

Similar considerations enable us to complete the substitution alphabet as:

> *Plaintext:*   **a b c d e f g h i j k l m**
> *Ciphertext:* **V W X Y Z R A C L O M S E**
>
> *Plaintext:*   **n o p q r s t u v w x y z**
> *Ciphertext:* **B D F G H I J K N P Q T U**

Thus we have a key phrase cipher with phrase RACAL COMSEC and special letter **f**. The message is:

during the last ten years the art of securing all forms of data including digital speech has improved manifold the primary reason for this has been the advent of microelectronics the complexity of the functions that can now be performed by the machine has risen dramatically as a result of this recent development in technology many of the cipher systems that were once considered secure are now breakable.

When breaking this message we made only minimal use of the statistical information. Two other factors were equally, or possibly more, important. One was our knowledge of the English language and the other was the format of the message. We repeatedly used the fact that we knew the lengths of the words; especially those of length three or less. The encipherer would certainly have made life much harder for us if he had written the message in letter groupings of uniform size. Since the average length of an English word is between four and five letters, it is common to send messages with the letters in groups of five. Apart from making cryptanalysis significantly harder, it has the added advantage that the cipher clerk preparing the message can easily spot if he has omitted a letter while preparing the message. Furthermore, the fact that the groups contain five letters means that the message will have approximately the same length as if it were in 'word format' so the transmission cost is not significantly altered. We will not now attempt to decipher a message transmitted in groups of five letters. Obviously it would be harder than our easy example. We would have to make more use of the statistics on bigrams and trigrams, plus the known frequencies with which groups of letters occur when we exclude space from our character set. But hopefully we have said and done enough to convince the reader that, provided the ciphertext is long enough, any monoalphabetic cipher is readily breakable.

Before leaving this example we must draw attention to our poor choice of key phrase. We made an error which is very common when keys are selected. We chose a phrase with a particular significance to us. It is generally unwise to do this; names, telephone numbers, addresses, etc., should always be avoided when choosing keys. The reason is obvious. Any cryptanalyst who discovers that he has been forced to try all possible keys is very likely to start with those which seem most relevant to the encipherer.

EXERCISE 1.10   Cryptanalyze the following ciphertext knowing only that a key phrase cipher was used:

**XNKWBMOW   KWH   JKXKRJKRZJ   RA   KWRJ   ZWXCKHI
XIH   IHNRXYNH   EBI   THZRCWHIRAO   DHJJXOHJ   JHAK
RA   HAONRJW   KWH   IHXTHI   JWBMNT   ABK   EBIOHK
KWXK   KWH   JKXKRJKRZJ   EBI   XABKWHI   NXAOMXOH
XIH   GMRKH   NRLHNU   KB   YH   TREEHIHAK   WBQHPHI
HGMRPXNHAK   JKXKRJRZJ   XIH   XPXRNXYNH   EBI
BKWHI   NXAOMXOHJ   RE   KWH   ZIUCKXAXNUJK   TBHJ
ABK   LABQ   KWH   NXAOMXOH   RA   QWRZW   KWH   DHJJXOH
QXJ   QIRKKHA   KWHA   BAH   BE   WRJ   ERIJK   CIBYNHDJ
RJ   KB   KIU   KB   THKHIDRAH   RK   KWRJ   RJ   X   TREERZMNK
CIBYNHD.**

We end this section on monoalphabetic ciphers by discussing how the analysis of a cryptogram could be carried out automatically, perhaps by a fast computer. Ideally we would like simply to be able to enter the cryptogram into the computer and for it to provide us with the plaintext message plus the cipher system used. For this to occur, we need to be able to give the computer a clearly defined set of rules as to how to proceed and how to make decisions.

A moment's thought shows that this is not a simple problem because it is quite likely to involve teaching the computer to 'spell', or to recognize words of the English language. We will then have to give it a large store of 'probable words' and it will have to try each of them in turn. When deciphering our message we often made 'guesses', and it is not at all obvious how to program the computer to do this. Nevertheless it is certainly possible to program a computer to decipher monoalphabetic ciphers. For example, one alternative to teaching the computer to spell is to devise a 'scoring' scheme which will assign a number to individual substitution alphabets, this number being chosen in some way so that it indicates the likelihood of that alphabet having been used. Clearly it is not possible to give a score to each of the 26! possibilities; there are too many. However we can use the letter frequencies of the cryptogram together with Table 1.3 (page 26) to obtain a much smaller list of likely candidates. The bigram frequencies can then be used to give more accurate scores to each of these possibilities and can measure the effect of interchanging letters. It also has the advantage that it does not depend on the word spacings and can be successfully applied to a cryptogram with five-letter groupings. This type of scoring method is the basis of a reasonably successful algorithm, due to C. J. Mitchell of Racal-Comsec Ltd, which generally gives almost correct solutions to samples of about 500 characters in size. (By 'almost' correct we mean nearly enough that the precise text would be obvious to any reader.)

1.3 Polyalphabetic Ciphers

From Section 1.2 we know that if we are to have a cipher which gives us any security from the cryptanalyst then it cannot be monoalphabetic. We have to devise cipher systems in which a given ciphertext letter may represent more than one plaintext letter. Such a cipher system is called **polyalphabetic**. However we must not forget that we need the ciphertext to determine the plaintext uniquely. We cannot, for example, have an algorithm in which a ciphertext **X** represents either plaintext **e** or **s** without having a rule to tell the decipherer precisely when it represents **e** and when it represents **s**. It is crucial that, at each position of the cryptogram, knowledge of the key uniquely defines the plaintext equivalent of each ciphertext letter.

A polyalphabetic cipher uses a sequence of monoalphabetic ciphers which are often referred to as its **substitution alphabets** or just its **alphabets**. If a polyalphabetic cipher uses a fixed number, *p* say, of alphabets in strict rotation then we say it has **period** *p*.

1.3.1 Vigenère ciphers

Perhaps the most widely known of the 'manual' polyalphabetic ciphers is that named after the French cryptographer Vigenère. It uses the encipherment array in Table 1.4, called the **Vigenère square**, which is really nothing more than Table 1.1, with the 'natural' alphabet as an extra column on the left.

Note that each letter in the extra column determines a row of the square, while each row represents an additive cipher. Thus each letter determines an additive cipher. For example e gives the additive cipher of shift 4. The basic principle behind the use of the square for enciphering is to have a sequence of letters which, in turn, determine a sequence of additive ciphers. Each of these substitution alphabets is then used, in the order of the sequence, to encipher a single letter. In the most common usage, called the **Vigenère cipher**, the method of obtaining the sequence involves choosing a keyword (or phrase). If the plaintext message is longer than the keyword then the sequence is obtained by repeating it as many times as is necessary. Thus the period is the length of the keyword. As an example we will take 'radio' as our keyword and **codebreaking** as the message. First we write the keyword, (repeated in this case), with the plaintext beneath it.

Keyword: r a d i o r a d i o r a
Plaintext: **c o d e b r e a k i n g**

Plaintext	a b c d e f g h i j k l m n o p q r s t u v w x y z
a	A B C D E F G H I J K L M N O P Q R S T U V W X Y Z
b	B C D E F G H I J K L M N O P Q R S T U V W X Y Z A
c	C D E F G H I J K L M N O P Q R S T U V W X Y Z A B
d	D E F G H I J K L M N O P Q R S T U V W X Y Z A B C
e	E F G H I J K L M N O P Q R S T U V W X Y Z A B C D
f	F G H I J K L M N O P Q R S T U V W X Y Z A B C D E
g	G H I J K L M N O P Q R S T U V W X Y Z A B C D E F
h	H I J K L M N O P Q R S T U V W X Y Z A B C D E F G
i	I J K L M N O P Q R S T U V W X Y Z A B C D E F G H
j	J K L M N O P Q R S T U V W X Y Z A B C D E F G H I
k	K L M N O P Q R S T U V W X Y Z A B C D E F G H I J
l	L M N O P Q R S T U V W X Y Z A B C D E F G H I J K
m	M N O P Q R S T U V W X Y Z A B C D E F G H I J K L
n	N O P Q R S T U V W X Y Z A B C D E F G H I J K L M
o	O P Q R S T U V W X Y Z A B C D E F G H I J K L M N
p	P Q R S T U V W X Y Z A B C D E F G H I J K L M N O
q	Q R S T U V W X Y Z A B C D E F G H I J K L M N O P
r	R S T U V W X Y Z A B C D E F G H I J K L M N O P Q
s	S T U V W X Y Z A B C D E F G H I J K L M N O P Q R
t	T U V W X Y Z A B C D E F G H I J K L M N O P Q R S
u	U V W X Y Z A B C D E F G H I J K L M N O P Q R S T
v	V W X Y Z A B C D E F G H I J K L M N O P Q R S T U
w	W X Y Z A B C D E F G H I J K L M N O P Q R S T U V
x	X Y Z A B C D E F G H I J K L M N O P Q R S T U V W
y	Y Z A B C D E F G H I J K L M N O P Q R S T U V W X
z	Z A B C D E F G H I J K L M N O P Q R S T U V W X Y

Table 1.4
The Vigenère Square

We now take our Vigenère square. Above the **c** we see an r so we encipher the **c** by using the row of the square determined by r. Thus the **c** is enciphered as **T**. Above the **o** we see a. So **o** is enciphered using the additive cipher in the first row of the square i.e., **o** is enciphered as **O**. Since we are varying the additive cipher at each letter, it should be clear that the cipher we are obtaining cannot be monoalphabetic. However, as a practical verification, we will encipher the two **e**s in the message. The first **e** is underneath i. Consequently it is enciphered by the cipher in row i to give **M**. However, there is an a above the second **e** which means this one is enciphered as **E**.

EXERCISE 1.11   Show that the complete cryptogram is:
Keyword: *r a d i o r a d i o r a*
Plaintext: **c o d e b r e a k i n g**
Ciphertext: **T O G M P I E D S W E G**

Now that we have seen the idea of using the Vigenère square, we can obviously use similar ideas to obtain many other polyalphabetic ciphers.

There is, for instance, no reason at all for restricting ourselves to writing the additive ciphers in each row. We could replace each row of the Vigenère square by any substitution alphabet and then use the new square in the way described above to obtain different ciphers. There is one particular such square, called the **Beaufort square**, which is used in Chapter 2 and included in this chapter (Table 1.5). It is, in fact, only a slight modification of the Vigenère square; the entries of each row are merely the entries of the same row of the Vigenère square written in reverse order.

Plaintext	a	b	c	d	e	f	g	h	i	j	k	l	m	n	o	p	q	r	s	t	u	v	w	x	y	z
a	Z	Y	X	W	V	U	T	S	R	Q	P	O	N	M	L	K	J	I	H	G	F	E	D	C	B	A
b	A	Z	Y	X	W	V	U	T	S	R	Q	P	O	N	M	L	K	J	I	H	G	F	E	D	C	B
c	B	A	Z	Y	X	W	V	U	T	S	R	Q	P	O	N	M	L	K	J	I	H	G	F	E	D	C
d	C	B	A	Z	Y	X	W	V	U	T	S	R	Q	P	O	N	M	L	K	J	I	H	G	F	E	D
e	D	C	B	A	Z	Y	X	W	V	U	T	S	R	Q	P	O	N	M	L	K	J	I	H	G	F	E
f	E	D	C	B	A	Z	Y	X	W	V	U	T	S	R	Q	P	O	N	M	L	K	J	I	H	G	F
g	F	E	D	C	B	A	Z	Y	X	W	V	U	T	S	R	Q	P	O	N	M	L	K	J	I	H	G
h	G	F	E	D	C	B	A	Z	Y	X	W	V	U	T	S	R	Q	P	O	N	M	L	K	J	I	H
i	H	G	F	E	D	C	B	A	Z	Y	X	W	V	U	T	S	R	Q	P	O	N	M	L	K	J	I
j	I	H	G	F	E	D	C	B	A	Z	Y	X	W	V	U	T	S	R	Q	P	O	N	M	L	K	J
k	J	I	H	G	F	E	D	C	B	A	Z	Y	X	W	V	U	T	R	S	Q	P	O	N	M	L	K
l	K	J	I	H	G	F	E	D	C	B	A	Z	Y	X	W	V	U	T	S	R	Q	P	O	N	M	L
m	L	K	J	I	H	G	F	E	D	C	B	A	Z	Y	X	W	V	U	T	S	R	Q	P	O	N	M
n	M	L	K	J	I	H	G	F	E	D	C	B	A	Z	Y	X	W	V	U	T	S	R	Q	P	O	N
o	N	M	L	K	J	I	H	G	F	E	D	C	B	A	Z	Y	X	W	V	U	T	S	R	Q	P	O
p	O	N	M	L	K	J	I	H	G	F	E	D	C	B	A	Z	Y	X	W	V	U	T	S	R	Q	P
q	P	O	N	M	L	K	J	I	H	G	F	E	D	C	B	A	Z	Y	X	W	V	U	T	S	R	Q
r	Q	P	O	N	M	L	K	J	I	H	G	F	E	D	C	B	A	Z	Y	X	W	V	U	T	S	R
s	R	Q	P	O	N	M	L	K	J	I	H	G	F	E	D	C	B	A	Z	Y	X	W	V	U	T	S
t	S	R	Q	P	O	N	M	L	K	J	I	H	G	F	E	D	C	B	A	Z	Y	X	W	V	U	T
u	T	S	R	Q	P	O	N	M	L	K	J	I	H	G	F	E	D	C	B	A	Z	Y	X	W	V	U
v	U	T	S	R	Q	P	O	N	M	L	K	J	I	H	G	F	E	D	C	B	A	Z	Y	X	W	V
w	V	U	T	S	R	Q	P	O	N	M	L	K	J	I	H	G	F	E	D	C	B	A	Z	Y	X	W
x	W	V	U	T	S	R	Q	P	O	N	M	L	K	J	I	H	G	F	E	D	C	B	A	Z	Y	X
y	X	W	V	U	T	S	R	Q	P	O	N	M	L	K	J	I	H	G	F	E	D	C	B	A	Z	Y
z	Y	X	W	V	U	T	S	R	Q	P	O	N	M	L	K	J	I	H	G	F	E	D	C	B	A	Z

Table 1.5
The Beaufort Square

The Beaufort square is then used in the same way as the Vigenère square.

1.3.2 Histograms for polyalphabetic ciphers
Listed below are two different ciphertexts for the same plaintext message.

Plaintext:	c o d e b r e a k i n g i s t h e m o s t i m p o
Ciphertext 1:	F R G H E U H D N L Q J L V W K H P R V W L P S R
Ciphertext 2:	O O B Q B P Q A I U N E U S R T E K A S R U M N A

Plaintext: r t a n t f o r m o f s e c r e t i n t e l l i g
Ciphertext 1: U W D Q W I R U P R I V H F U H W L Q W H O O L J
Ciphertext 2: R R M N R R O P Y O D E E A D E R U N R Q L J U G

Plaintext: e n c e i n t h e w o r l d t o d a y i t p r o d
Ciphertext 1: H Q F H L Q W K H Z R U O G W R G B L W S U R G
Ciphertext 2: C Z C C U N R T E U A R J P T M P A W U T N D O B

Plaintext: u c e s m u c h m o r e a n d m u c h m o r e t r
Ciphertext 1: X F H V P X F K P R U H D Q G P X F K P R U H W U
Ciphertext 2: G C C E M S O H K A R C M N B Y U A T M M D E R D

Plaintext: u s t w o r t h y i n f o r m a t i o n t h a n s
Ciphertext 1: X V W Z R U W K B L Q I R U P D W L R Q W K D Q V
Ciphertext 2: U Q F W M D T F K I L R O P Y A R U O L F H Y Z S

Plaintext: p i e s a n d t h i s i n t e l l i g e n c e e x
Ciphertext 1: S L H V D Q G W K L V L Q W H O O L J H Q F H H A
Ciphertext 2: N U E Q M N B F H G E I L F E J X I E Q N A Q E V

Plaintext: e r t s g r e a t i n f l u e n c e u p o n t h e
Ciphertext 1: H U W V J U H D W L Q I O X H Q F H X S R Q W K H
Ciphertext 2: Q R R E G P Q A R U N D X U C Z C C G P M Z T F Q

Plaintext: p o l i c i e s o f g o v e r n m e n t s y e t i
Ciphertext 1: S R O L F L H V R I J R Y H U Q P H Q W V B H W L
Ciphertext 2: P M X I A U E Q A F E A V C D N K Q N R E Y C F I

Plaintext: t h a s n e v e r h a d a c h r o n i c l e r
Ciphertext 1: W K D V Q H Y H U K D G D F K U R Q L F O H U
Ciphertext 2: R T A Q Z E T Q R F M D Y O H P A N G O L C D

Ciphertext 1 is the result of using a monalphabetic cipher while for Ciphertext 2 we used a Vigenère cipher with a keyword of three letters: may. The idea of using a polyalphabetic cipher was to invalidate the statistics which facilitate the cryptanalysis of all monoalphabetic ciphers. To illustrate visually that this has been (at least partially) achieved, we draw the histogram for the letter frequencies of each ciphertext (Fig. 1.2).

In the first histogram we see the characteristic signs of a monoalphabetic cipher. One letter occurs significantly more often than all others (obviously the ciphertext for **e**!) while three letters do not occur at all (probably the ciphertexts for three of **v**, **k**, **j**, **x**, **q** or **z**). The second histogram is much 'flatter' in the sense that no letter dominates, all letters appear and there is a much smaller difference between the most and least popular. A very crude explanation of this is that each plaintext letter will have its number of occurrences divided more or less equally between three

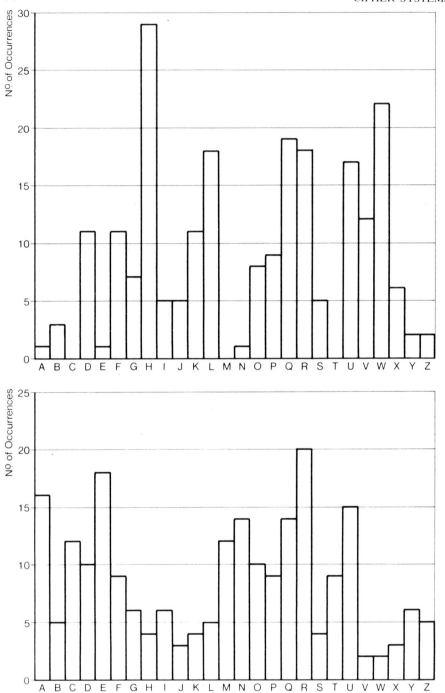

Figure 1.2
Histograms for ciphertexts 1 and 2

ciphertext letters, while each ciphertext letter will similarly represent three plaintext letters. It is now unlikely that any given ciphertext letter will have all its plaintext equivalents in any one of our frequency groupings and, consequently, there is a flattening of the histogram. An extension of this argument suggests, quite correctly, that the longer the keyword used, the flatter the resulting histogram will be.

Once we know the length of the keyword we can certainly begin an attempt to decipher a cryptogram. If the keyword has length p we write the ciphertext in p rows in such a way that the cryptogram is obtained by writing each column in order. Once this is done, if we read each row, we will obtain a sequence of ciphertext letters which is the result of a monoalphabetic cipher (in the case of the Vigenère cipher; an additive one). We can then use the statistical arguments of the last section on each row. As an illustration, we would write our Ciphertext 2 as:

OQQU
OBAN
B P I E etc.

Thus we see that a cryptanalyst needs to determine the length of the keyword used. Before seeing how he can achieve this we look at some further properties of the cryptogram.

1.3.3 Superimposing messages

If a letter is picked at random from an arbitrary sequence of letters then, since there are 26 possibilities and each is equally likely, the probability of it being any particular letter is $\frac{1}{26}$. Similarly if we pick a letter from each of two arbitrary sequences then, since the events are independent, the probability of choosing a particular (ordered) pair of letters is $(\frac{1}{26})^2$. So if we now write the two arbitrary sequences on consecutive lines, the probability of a chosen letter being above another chosen letter in a given position is $(\frac{1}{26})^2$. Thus, since there are 26 possible pairs of identical letters, the probability that identical letters appear at a given position of the two sequences is $26 \cdot (\frac{1}{26})^2 = \frac{1}{26} \simeq 0 \cdot 038$.

If we now replace the arbitrary sequences of letters by English plaintext, then, of course, the probabilities change. The complete list of probabilities is in Appendix 1 (page 395) but, for instance, the probability of finding an **a** in a given position is $p_a \simeq 0 \cdot 082$, while the probability of getting a **b** is about $0 \cdot 015$. This means that, if we write two passages of English plaintext on consecutive lines, the probability that they will both have the letter **a** in a given position is about $(0 \cdot 082)^2$, while the probability of them both having **b** is $(0 \cdot 015)^2$. Thus, in order to work out the probability of them having identical letters in a given position, we must evaluate

$$\sum_{a}^{z} (p_\lambda)^2.$$

(Recall: we want the probability that they will have two **a**s or two **b**s or … or two **z**s. To evaluate this we merely sum the probabilities of the individual events.) It is customary to denote

$$\sum_{\mathbf{a}}^{\mathbf{z}} (p_\lambda)^2$$

by χ_P. If we evaluate χ_P by using the values in Appendix 1 we get a value of about 0·065. This is nearly double the value of 0·038 obtained from two arbitrary sequences of letters.

If we now replace the two passages of English plaintext by cryptograms obtained from the same substitution alphabet, then the probability of finding any given letter in any given position of either one of them will depend on the letter. However, since the same substitution alphabet was used, each letter will have identical probabilities in the two cryptograms. For instance, if **X** is the ciphertext equivalent of **a**, then $p_\mathbf{X}$ will be $p_\mathbf{a}$ (i.e. about 0·082) in each cryptogram. This then means that the probability of both cryptograms having an **X** in a given position is about $(0·082)^2$. Thus, in order to work out the probability of the two cryptograms having identical letters in a given position, we must calculate

$$\sum_{\mathbf{A}}^{\mathbf{Z}} (p_\lambda)^2.$$

However, $p_\mathbf{A}$, $p_\mathbf{B}$, …, $p_\mathbf{Z}$ and $p_\mathbf{a}$, $p_\mathbf{b}$, …, $p_\mathbf{z}$ are the same set of numbers written in a different order. Thus

$$\sum_{\mathbf{A}}^{\mathbf{Z}} (p_\alpha)^2 = \chi_P \simeq 0·065.$$

In other words, provided the same substitution alphabet is used, the probability of two cryptograms having identical letters in a given position is the same as that for English plaintext and, consequently, significantly larger than the corresponding probability for arbitrary sequences.

This observation has several important consequences. One is that it means we have a way of getting some indication as to whether two distinct cryptograms used the same sequence of substitution alphabets. To obtain it, we simply count the number of coincidences in the various positions of the two cryptograms. Provided the cryptograms are sufficiently long we would expect about 7 coincidences per 100 letters if they used identical alphabets but only about 4 if they did not.

EXERCISE 1.12   *Show that there are grounds for believing that two of the following cryptograms were obtained by using the same sequence of substitution alphabets:*

Cryptogram 1   **TEKASRUMNARRMNRROPYODEEADERUNR**
QLJUGCZCCUNRTEUARJPTMPAWUTN.

Cryptogram 2 **KSKHKIQQEVIFLRKQUZVAEVFYZRVFBXUK GBPKYVVRQTAJKTGBQOISGHUCWIKX.**

Cryptogram 3 **GCCEMSOHKARCMNBYUATMMDERDUQFW MDTFKILROPYARUOLFHYZSNUEQMNBFHGE.**

The same type of reasoning can be applied to a single message to provide information about the cipher system. The next two sections provide examples.

1.3.4 The index of coincidence

In Section 1.3.2 we spoke, in rather vague terms, about the flatness of the histogram of a polyalphabetic cipher and related it to the number of substitution alphabets used. In this section we will endeavour to be a little more precise about what is meant by flatness, and give a method for estimating the length of the keyword in a Vigenère cipher.

In any histogram which shows, as probabilities, the frequencies of the letters in a particular sequence the average height of the bars will be $\frac{1}{26} \approx 0.038$. If each of the 26 values were actually equal to $\frac{1}{26}$ then the histogram would, literally, be flat. In the case of the identity cipher for English plaintext, $p_e - 0.038$ is almost 0.1, while $p_z - 0.038$ is about -0.037. So, in this case, the histogram is far from flat. When a poly-alphabetic cipher is used then, even for a popular ciphertext letter α, $p_\alpha - 0.038$ is much smaller than 0.1. Similarly, for an unpopular letter β, $p_\beta - 0.038$ is greater than -0.037. In other words, each bar of the histogram is nearer to the average value of 0.038. When trying to measure the flatness of the histogram we are merely trying to obtain some indication of how near to the average each p_α is. It is clearly not sufficient to evaluate

$$\sum_A^Z (p_\lambda - \tfrac{1}{26});$$

because this is the same as

$$\sum_A^Z p_\lambda - \sum_A^Z \tfrac{1}{26} = 1 - 26 \cdot (\tfrac{1}{26}) = 0.$$

The reason for this is that the negative deviations (i.e. negative differences from the average) cancel out the positive ones. From the point of view of the encipherer negative and positive deviations are equally bad, in the sense that they may give information to the cryptanalyst and certainly do not cancel each other. One possible measure of the flatness of the histogram is the **variation**; i.e.

$$\sum_A^Z (p_\lambda - \tfrac{1}{26})^2.$$

(This ensures that each term under the summation sign is positive or zero. The variation can only be small if the absolute value of each deviation is small. A large negative deviation will in no way compensate for a large positive one.) But since

$$\sum_{A}^{Z} p_\lambda = 1 \quad \text{and} \quad \sum_{A}^{Z} 1 = 26,$$

we have:

$$\sum_{A}^{Z} (p_\lambda - \tfrac{1}{26})^2 = \sum_{A}^{Z} (p_\lambda)^2 - \tfrac{2}{26} \sum_{A}^{Z} p_\lambda - (\tfrac{1}{26})^2 \sum_{A}^{Z} 1 = \sum_{A}^{Z} (p_\lambda)^2 - \tfrac{1}{26};$$

i.e. the variation is approximately

$$\sum_{A}^{Z} (p_\lambda)^2 - 0 \cdot 038.$$

As we have already noticed for an arbitrary sequence of letters, i.e. one in which each letter is equally likely, the variation is 0, while for a mono-alphabetic cipher it is roughly $0 \cdot 065 - 0 \cdot 038 = 0 \cdot 027$. If a polyalphabetic cipher is used, the value of the variation will be somewhere between these two extremes. The smaller the variation, the flatter the histogram. This means there is much less difference between the relative frequencies of the letters and, consequently, less statistical assistance available to the cryptanalyst.

To evaluate the variation we need to compute

$$\sum_{A}^{Z} (p_\lambda)^2.$$

If we have a cryptogram, then p_A is the probability that, if we look at any chosen position of the cryptogram, the entry in that position will be an **A**. If we pick two positions then, since the events are independent, the probability of finding two **A**s is p_A^2. Thus

$$\sum_{A}^{Z} (p_\lambda)^2$$

is the probability that two positions, selected arbitrarily, will contain identical letters. But to evaluate this likelihood in our given cryptogram, we need to count the total number of pairs of identical letters in the cryptogram and then divide it by the total number of possible pairs.

If the frequency of the letter **A** in our cryptogram is f_A then there are f_A positions occupied by the letter **A**. In trying to count all pairs of positions containing **A**s, we may choose the first position in f_A ways and then, having chosen the first, there are $f_A - 1$ remaining chances for the second. Thus we have $f_A(f_A - 1)$ ordered pairs of positions which contain **A**s. However, any pair of **A**s will occupy two of these ordered pairs of positions, and so the number of pairs of **A**s is $\frac{1}{2}f_A(f_A-1)$. Hence the total number of pairs of identical letters is

$$\frac{1}{2}\sum_{A}^{Z} f_\lambda(f_\lambda-1).$$

A similar count shows that, if the cryptogram has length n, the number of pairs of letters is $\frac{1}{2}n(n-1)$. Thus the likelihood of the letters in two positions being the same is $\frac{1}{2}\sum_{A}^{Z} f_\lambda(f_\lambda-1)$ divided by $\frac{1}{2}n(n-1)$ i.e.

$$\frac{\sum_{A}^{Z} f_\lambda(f_\lambda-1)}{n(n-1)}.$$

This number is called the **index of coincidence** of the cryptogram and is denoted by I_c.

From our earlier discussions we know that I_c is an approximation for

$$\sum_{A}^{Z} (p_\lambda)^2$$

and, consequently, a measure of the flatness of the histogram. This, in turn, means it provides an indication of the length of the keyword. But how?

Let us suppose that we have received a cryptogram of length n sent by using a Vigenère cipher with a keyword of length m in which all the letters are different. Then we can write our cryptogram in m rows such that two letters in the same row have been enciphered using the same additive cipher, but any two letters from different rows have definitely come from different ciphers. Thus we will have m rows with approximately $\frac{n}{m}$ letters in each. If we pick two positions in any one row then, since the same monoalphabetic cipher was used, the probability of getting identical letters is 0·065. But if we pick two positions in different rows then, since different ciphers were used, the probability is only 0·038. In order to pick a pair of positions we may choose the first one in n ways. Having chosen the first there are $\frac{n}{m}-1$ choices for the second in the same row and $n-\frac{n}{m}$ choices in other rows. Thus there are $\frac{1}{2}n\left(\frac{n}{m}-1\right)$ pairs of positions in the same row, $\frac{1}{2}n\left(n-\frac{n}{m}\right)$ pairs in different rows and $\frac{1}{2}n(n-1)$ pairs altogether. This means that, for this cryptogram, we have two ways of predicting the number of pairs of identical letters. On the one hand it is merely $\frac{1}{2}n(n-1)I_c$. But it is also

$$\frac{1}{2}n\left(\frac{n}{m}-1\right)\times 0\cdot065+\frac{1}{2}n\left(n-\frac{n}{m}\right)\times 0\cdot038.$$

Since these must be approximately equal we have

$$\frac{1}{2}n(n-1)I_c=\frac{1}{2}n\left(\frac{n-m}{m}\right)\times 0\cdot065+\frac{1}{2}n\left(\frac{nm-n}{m}\right)\times 0\cdot038.$$

But we can rearrange this to give

$$m\simeq\frac{0\cdot027n}{I_c(n-1)-0\cdot038n+0\cdot065}.$$

In other words we have a formula which gives us an approximation for the length of the keyword as soon as we know I_c.

EXERCISE 1.13   Show that the following values for I_c and m are correct:

Ciphertext 1 $I_c=0\cdot0653$ $m\simeq0\cdot99$
Ciphertext 2 $I_c=0\cdot0477$ $m\simeq2\cdot76$

These results are, of course, good because the correct values are 1 and 3 respectively and, since m must be an integer, we would have made the correct conclusions. However, it must be emphasized they are only approximations and it is often advisable to look for further evidence of their values. As a warning we point out that if the message above had been enciphered using 'key' as a keyword instead of 'may', we would have obtained an I_c of $0\cdot0516$ which gives $m\simeq1\cdot98$.

EXERCISE 1.14   Show that the values stated for I_c and m when 'key' is used are correct.

Since we know that the length was 3, this is clearly inaccurate. Another very important fact must be emphasized. When we were discussing the relation between I_c and m we assumed that the keyword did not have any repeated letters. This was crucial to our argument, and if the keyword has repeated letters our formula may well lead to a wrong answer. Nevertheless this method does give a strong indication as to the number of substitution alphabets used. The following table illustrates the relation between I_c and m, provided that the cryptogram is sufficiently long.

m	1	2	5	10	large
I_c	0·065	0·052	0·043	0·041	0·038

Table 1.6
The relation between I_c and m

If the cryptanalyst intercepts a message with no knowledge whatsoever of its origin, then he can at least evaluate I_c. If the value is near to 0.065 then he might be tempted to apply the statistical techniques for monoalphabetic ciphers. But if, for example, it is as low as 0.043 then he would probably deduce that the techniques employed against monoalphabetic ciphers were not applicable.

1.3.5 Determination of the period

In this section we will discuss, without going into too much detail, some other indicators which are used to determine the length of the keyword. It must not be forgotten that, by the time he uses these methods, the cryptanalyst will already have used the index of coincidence to obtain a tentative value for the length, and usually will be merely seeking confirmation that his first guess was correct.

Rather than discuss the general theory of our first technique we will illustrate it by applying it to Ciphertext 2. Having written down our cryptogram once, we write it a second time immediately under the first, except that on the second occasion we displace it by moving each letter one position to the right, i.e. we write the first letter underneath the second, the second beneath the third, etc. Having written them we count the number of coincidences between the two cryptograms. We then repeat this operation by displacing the cryptogram by two positions, and so on. In this way we obtain a set of statistics showing the relation between the size of displacement and the number of coincidences. When we have a displacement of 1 then, for any given position, the additive cipher used in the first line is different to that used in the second. So if we consider the position where the cryptograms overlap, we have two sequences of letters with no reason to expect a particularly high number of coincidences between them. The same is true for a displacement of 2. However, if we have a displacement of 3, since 3 is the length of the keyword, in each position where the messages overlap the letters in both sequences are the result of using the same additive cipher. Consequently we expect significantly more coincidences. The same will be true for all displacements which are a multiple of 3. (A little care is needed. What we would actually expect is for there to be a higher proportion of coincidences in the overlap of the two cryptograms. If we displace the second cryptogram too far, the size of the overlap will get too small and the actual number of coincidences will decrease.)

Thus, if we were cryptanalysts – and consequently only had a 'guess' for the length of the keyword – we would look at our table relating displacement and coincidences and expect to see significantly higher numbers for the coincidences at regular intervals in the displacement values. The gap between these displacement values would then indicate the length of the keyword and tell us whether we should have confidence in our earlier deductions. In Table 1.7 we illustrate the relation between displacement and coincidences for Ciphertext 2. The columns headed 'A' list the displacements, those headed 'B' give the number of coincidences while

A	B	C	A	B	C	A	B	C
1	9	4·054054	42	26	14·364641	83	5	3·571429
2	3	1·357466	43	6	3·333333	84	7	5·035971
3	14	6·363636	44	2	1·117318	85	5	3·623188
4	10	4·566210	45	7	3·932584	86	4	2·919708
5	13	5·963303	46	10	5·649718	87	9	6·617647
6	19	8·755760	47	9	5·113636	88	3	2·222222
7	5	2·314815	48	8	4·571429	89	9	6·716418
8	9	4·186047	49	7	4·022988	90	12	9·022556
9	11	5·140187	50	9	5·202312	91	14	10·606061
10	8	3·755869	51	3	1·744186	92	3	2·290076
1!	9	4·245283	52	5	2·923977	93	4	3·076923
12	10	4·739336	53	4	2·352941	94	2	1·550388
13	7	3·333333	54	9	5·325444	95	7	5·468750
14	10	4·784689	55	7	4·166667	96	5	3·937008
15	13	6·250000	56	9	5·389222	97	7	5·555556
16	8	3·864734	57	16	9·638554	98	4	3·200000
17	8	3·883495	58	4	2·424242	99	4	3·225806
18	10	4·878049	59	6	3·658537	100	2	1·626016
19	4	1·960784	60	15	9·202454	101	5	4·098361
20	9	4·433498	61	7	4·320988	102	16	13·223140
21	11	5·445545	62	5	3·105590	103	4	3·333333
22	8	3·980099	63	6	3·750000	104	1	0·840336
23	4	2·000000	64	7	4·402516	105	9	7·627119
24	13	6·532663	65	7	4·430380	106	6	5·128205
25	10	5·050505	66	9	5·732484	107	7	6·034483
26	10	5·076142	67	6	3·846154	108	10	8·695652
27	13	6·632653	68	7	4·516129	109	3	2·631579
28	4	2·051282	69	4	2·597403	110	4	3·539823
29	8	4·123711	70	8	5·228758	111	12	10·714286
30	12	6·217617	71	4	2·631579	112	7	6·306306
31	12	6·250000	72	11	7·284768	113	3	2·727273
32	7	3·664921	73	7	4·666667	114	6	5·504587
33	19	10·000000	74	3	2·013423	115	7	6·481481
34	7	3·703704	75	6	4·054054	116	5	4·672897
35	8	4·255319	76	1	0·680272	117	11	10·377358
36	14	7·486631	77	6	4·109589	118	2	1·904762
37	9	4·838710	78	10	6·896552	119	6	5·769231
38	7	3·783784	79	6	4·166667	120	3	2·912621
39	8	4·347826	80	3	2·097902	121	4	3·921569
40	4	2·185792	81	13	9·154930	122	8	7·920792
41	7	3·846154	82	7	4·964539	123	8	8·000000

Table 1.7
The relation between displacements and coincidences

each column 'C' gives the percentage of coincidences in the overlap. We stopped after a displacement of 124 as we did not want the overlap to be less than 100 letters.

From our discussion, since we know that a keyword of length 3 was used, we expect to see a higher rate of coincidences when the displacement is a multiple of 3. The figures, on the whole, realize this expectation. However, as we have just emphasized, the cryptanalyst will not be certain of the length of the keyword and will wish to obtain extra confidence in his guess from this table. If we denote the length of the keyword by p, then we would expect about 3·8% coincidence if the displacement is not a multiple of p and about 6·5% if it is. In other words, we would hope to deduce p by looking at the displacements with a high percentage of coincidences. Table 1.8 contains a list of all displacements which give at least 8% coincidence: the final column merely shows the factorization of the displacements.

Coincidence	Displacement	Factorization
8·76%	6	2×3
10·00%	33	11×3
14·36%	42	$7 \times 2 \times 3$
9·64%	57	19×3
9·20%	60	$5 \times 2^2 \times 3$
9·15%	81	3^4
9·02%	90	$5 \times 2 \times 3^2$
10·60%	91	13×7
13·22%	102	$17 \times 2 \times 3$
8·70%	108	$2^2 \times 3^3$
10·71%	111	37×3
10·38%	117	13×3^2
8·00%	123	41×3

Table 1.8
The displacements with a large number of coincidences

Apart from 91 all the displacements with at least 8% coincidences have a factor of 3 and, in fact, 3 is their greatest common divisor. This gives strong support for the cryptanalyst to have confidence in his assumption that the keyword length is 3. If he then finds the average percentage of coincidences when the displacement is a multiple of 3 he will see it is significantly higher than the total average.

EXERCISE 1.15   Given that the following ciphertext has been obtained by using a Vigenère cipher show that the length of the keyword is probably 5:

**UYSZNURSJPSPDPVPEGPNOUONQTYOHYDFBOVTKCB
GIVTKYMFKEAHUOPNFEQNLQKWKABCUKEJKVIGPSSE
ZQCSIROKSZVOJDAPJRZLHSGCORFCSYGSFBEPEVJEPF
JHDRTVRAIJTSOFIRZHOFUSOVHESZVOJIYUBNOUGIR
HPUFPAWLCVIOREZBWPPDDQGFIGUFUVAKEOVHSBS
BHKCSFJEQFTFUCUFUNNQYWYCSFHAPUZCJGPSWJNSP
QKQFURWGBKVAZFKVKQPWWICMVAAAURHEBONWH
YEVDAAEFBPUFRDLYJTOPVPEOJQFEJEEPEAAAU**

Our second technique looks for the encipherment of identical sequences of letters. If two identical sequences of letters occur in the plaintext then, in general, they will be enciphered differently and consequently give different ciphertext sequences. However, if the positions of the plaintext sequences are such that the first letter of each is enciphered using the same keyword letter then they will give identical ciphertext sequences. Again we will assume that there are no repeated letters in the keyword. (As always, repeated keyword letters change the situation slightly.) Thus, when considering our cryptogram, if we look for repeated sequences and count the distances between them, it is quite likely that this distance will be a multiple of the keyword length. This process of looking for repeated sequences and measuring the distance between them is called 'applying the **Kasiski Test**'. We must not, of course, forget that identical ciphertext sequences can arise from using different ciphers on distinct plaintext passages. (Note: in this context the distance between two letters is the number of letters between them plus one. Thus the distance between adjacent letters is 1.)

As an illustration of the Kasiski test we will again consider Ciphertext 2. This is a reasonably long message with a very short keyword, so there are a number of repeated sequences. Listed below are the repetitions of length 3 or more. In the case where the same sequence is repeated more than once, we have listed the distance between the first two occurrences.

Sequence	Distance	Factorization
PQA	150	$2\times5^2\times3$
RTE	42	$2\times7\times3$
ROPY	81	3^4
DER	57	19×3
RUN	117	13×3^2
UNR	12	$2^2\times3$
CZCC	114	$2\times19\times3$
MNB	42	$2\times7\times3$
ARU	42	$2\times7\times3$
UEQ	54	2×3^3

Table 1.9
The distances between repeated letter sequences

Since the highest common factor of these distances is 3 these statistics suggest that our original guess of 3 for the length of the keyword is correct. Note, however, that 6 also divides as many as 7 out of the 10 distances; so if our earlier reasoning had suggested 3 or 6, we might still feel a little nervous in choosing 3. However, if we now examine all bigrams and look at the distances between repetitions, we find that over 65% of these distances are divisible by 3 whereas less than 45% are divisible by 6. Further evidence that the keyword length is 3.

If even more evidence is needed then, as our final check, we write our cryptogram in 3 rows in the way discussed at the end of Section 1.3.2. Thus we have:

row 1 **O QQUUTAUAMRYEDUQUZUTAPPUDGE**
row 2 **O BANSESMRNOOEENLGCNERTATOCM**
row 3 **B PIERKRNRRPDARRJCCRUJMWNBCS**

row 1 **O AMYTDDFDKRYUFZUMFEFXQQQEQU**
row 2 **H RNUMEUWTIOAOHSENHIEINERGAN**
row 3 **K CBAMRQMFLPRLYNQBGLJEAVRPRD**

row 1 **X ZGZQXUAADQEFTZQMOAOD**
row 2 **U CPTPIEFVNNYIAERDHNL**
row 3 **C CMFMAQECKRCRQTFYPGC**

If a keyword of length 3 was used, then each row is the result of enciphering using a monoalphabetic cipher. So our final check is to apply the index of coincidence test to each of the three rows.

EXERCISE 1.16   *Show that the indices of coincidence for the three rows are:*
   row 1 $I_c = 0 \cdot 0717117$
   row 2 $I_c = 0 \cdot 0636801$
   row 3 $I_c = 0 \cdot 0640504.$

Each of these values is near enough to 0·065 (or above it!) to indicate that three substitution alphabets were used and, thus, that the keyword had length 3.

EXERCISE 1.17   *Use the tests of this section to substantiate the conclusion of Exercise 1.15.*

As we mentioned earlier, the Kasiski test suggests the length 6 as being almost as likely as 3.

EXERCISE 1.18   *Write the message in six rows instead of three and work out the index of coincidence for each one. Is there any evidence to reject the possibility of period 6?*

1.3.6   Reduction to monoalphabetic ciphers
Being able to determine the length of the keyword is, of course, only an intermediary step in deciphering a Vigenère cipher. The objective is to obtain the message and, if possible, to determine the keyword itself. To illustrate how this may be achieved we assume the role of the cryptanalyst. But before we discuss a statistical approach to this, a few points need emphasizing. The basic idea behind breaking a Vigenère cipher is to determine the length of the keyword, and then to regard the cryptogram as a number of messages each of which was enciphered using a monoalphabetic cipher. But, as we stressed at the time, the statistics for monoalphabetic ciphers are only meaningful for long messages. So, in this case, we

need each monoalphabetic cipher cryptogram to be long. In other words, we not only need our Vigenère cipher cryptogram to be long, but we need the length of the keyword to be short in comparison. To see why, we observe that, in the extreme case, if the keyword and cryptogram have the same length then, once we know the length of the keyword, each of our monoalphabetic ciphers has length 1. Writing it in rows so that each row is a monoalphabetic cipher message is no use to us.

So far in our discussion of Ciphertext 2, we have not made use of all the information given by the fact that a Vigenère cipher was used. We have never used the fact that each row of the square is an additive cipher; merely that it is monoalphabetic. We now utilize the special nature of additive ciphers (in particular, that there are only 26 of them). The basic idea is as follows. Suppose that we have two cryptograms and know that each has been obtained by using an additive cipher. We can certainly write them consecutively and regard the resulting ciphertext as a single cryptogram which, unless the two additive ciphers had the same shift, was not the result of a monoalphabetic cipher. We now apply each of the 26 possible additive ciphers to the first of our two cryptograms but leave the second one alone to get a total of 26 such cryptograms. But the result of taking some plaintext, enciphering using an additive cipher with shift n_1 and then enciphering the resulting ciphertext using an additive cipher with shift n_2 is merely to encipher the original plaintext with an additive cipher of shift $n_1 \oplus n_2$. Thus, in precisely one of our 26 cryptograms the entire original message will have been enciphered using the same additive cipher. Straightforward evaluation of I_c for each cryptogram should indicate which one. As soon as we know which of our 26 cryptograms is the result of a monoalphabetic cipher, we will know the difference of the shifts used for the two original cryptograms.

If the two original cryptograms of the last paragraph have length n and n', then the length of the combined cryptogram is $n + n'$. Similarly, if for each letter λ, the frequencies of λ in the two cryptograms are f_λ and f'_λ then the frequency of λ in the combined cryptogram is $f_\lambda + f'_\lambda$. Thus I_c for the combined cryptogram is:

$$\frac{\sum\limits_{\lambda}^{Z} (f_\lambda + f'_\lambda)(f_\lambda + f'_\lambda - 1)}{(n+n')(n+n'-1)} = \frac{\sum\limits_{\lambda}^{Z} (f_\lambda)^2 + \sum\limits_{\lambda}^{Z} (f'_\lambda)^2 + 2\sum\limits_{\lambda}^{Z} f_\lambda f'_\lambda - \sum\limits_{\lambda}^{Z} f_\lambda - \sum\limits_{\lambda}^{Z} f'_\lambda}{(n+n')(n+n'-1)}$$

$$= \frac{\sum\limits_{\lambda}^{Z} (f_\lambda)^2 + \sum\limits_{\lambda}^{Z} (f'_\lambda)^2 + 2\sum\limits_{\lambda}^{Z} f_\lambda f'_\lambda - n - n'}{(n+n')(n+n'-1)}$$

If we now encipher the second message using any monoalphabetic cipher then the frequencies of the letters will change. However, if for each λ we denote the new frequency by g'_λ,

$$\sum_{A}^{Z} (f'_\lambda)^2 = \sum_{A}^{Z} (g'_\lambda)^2$$

which means that, when we compute the new I_c, the only change in the terms involved is that

$$\sum_{A}^{Z} f_\lambda f'_\lambda$$

is replaced by

$$\sum_{A}^{Z} f_\lambda g'_\lambda.$$

Since the use of identical substitution alphabets results in a high value for I_c, we need to find those shifts for which

$$\sum_{A}^{Z} f_\lambda g'_\lambda$$

is largest. In order to continue our cryptanalysis of Ciphertext 2 we write it in three rows (as in Section 1.3.5), and then apply the above techniques to the three pairs of cryptograms obtained by taking any two of the three rows. In each case we apply the 26 additive ciphers to the row with the higher number.

Listed below are the values of $\sum_{A}^{Z} f_\lambda g'_\lambda$ in each case:

Shift	0	1	2	3	4	5	6	7	8
rows 1 & 2	203	261	178	194	209	168	159	178	226
rows 1 & 3	196	290	202	201	152	195	173	182	227
rows 2 & 3	238	162	240	215	280	181	153	155	197

Shift	9	10	11	12	13	14	15	16	17
rows 1 & 2	196	321	169	161	238	(396)	206	198	175
rows 1 & 3	167	195	231	(351)	232	247	179	204	218
rows 2 & 3	253	193	227	176	305	201	255	173	216

Shift	18	19	20	21	22	23	24	25	
rows 1 & 2	216	234	232	166	155	269	216	226	
rows 1 & 3	227	185	141	176	220	331	221	207	
rows 2 & 3	160	158	174	172	218	231	(325)	218	

The largest value for

$$\sum_{A}^{Z} f_\lambda g'_\lambda$$

when rows 1 and 2 are used is 396, is obtained when a shift of 14 is applied to row 2. Thus, for Ciphertext 2, it appears that the shift used for row 2 is

14 more than that for row 1. Similarly the shift for row 3 is probably 12 more than that for row 1. Note that, since $24 \oplus 14 = 12$, these two statements imply that the shift for row 3 ought to be 24 more than the shift for row 2. So, for those two statements to be correct, the maximum value for rows 2 and 3 should give a shift of 24 – otherwise our statistics would be inconsistent. This is in fact what happens and so no extra information is obtained from comparing rows 2 and 3. We merely obtain a further indication that our conclusions are correct. (If this final figure had not been consistent with the other two, we would have been much less confident about our progress.)

Now, by considering each of the 26 possibilities for the shift used for row 1, we will get 26 possible keywords. As an illustration, if the shift for row 1 had been 0, then the shifts of the additive ciphers used for rows 2 and 3 would have been 14 and 12 respectively. But the keyword is obtained by considering the effect of each additive cipher on the letter **a**. Thus, if the cipher for row 1 had shift 0, the keyword must have been AOM. Similar reasoning gives the following 26 keywords: AOM, BPN, CQO, DRP, ESQ, FTR, GUS, HVT, IWU, JXV, KYW, LZX, MAY, NBZ, OCA, PDB, QEC, RFD, SGE, THF, UIG, VJH, WKI, XLJ, YMK, ZNL. The cryptanalyst would now be able to decipher the cryptogram by trying each of these 26 keywords in turn. If he had reason to believe the keyword would be an English word he would clearly try MAY first.

We conclude by pointing out that we were extremely fortunate to find the keyword so easily. In general the maximum values for the

$$\sum_{A}^{Z} f_\lambda g'_\lambda$$

will not be consistent and the problem is to find the best possible 'fit' for the relative shifts. However, the general idea should be clear. In Chapter 2 we will meet situations where the statistics are not quite so conclusive.

EXERCISE 1.19   Use the results of this section to decipher the cryptogram of Exercise 1.15.

1.4   A Complete Example of Cryptanalysis

Suppose we intercept the following two cryptograms from the same source within a short time of each other and that we have no additional information about them:

Cryptogram 1   YHIHX RVHKK KSKHK IQQEV IFLRK QUZVA
EVFYZ RVFBX UKGBP KYVVR QTAJK TGBQO
ISGHU CWIKX OUXIH DUGIU LMWKG CHXJV
WFKIH HEHGB EXXSF DMIIL UPSLW AJKTR
WTOWP IVXBW NPTGW EKBYV SBQWS

Cryptogram 2 **PNDFF FLFAS LXSGL OEWPV SHDSN HUGYA**
QAXUG RWIHH LWFXX LXWLD MIILV TQPEJ
HXKFN AISAX QKIHH VVHAS ISYEW KSJFF
LCLVI KDTRR HMURQ

Since they were received within a short time of each other we have some justification for hoping that they were enciphered using the same system and, more importantly, using the same key. If this is the case then we have, essentially, one message and its extra length will help in the cryptanalysis. With this possibility in mind we first count the number of coincidences between the messages. As a percentage it turns out to be 6·667 which is roughly what we would expect if the same keying sequence had been used. However this evidence is far from conclusive and we need further proof.

Before continuing this discussion we must explain the format of this section. At the end of this discussion of the cryptanalysis of these two cryptograms we include the printout of an interactive computer program we used to reduce them to a single monoalphabetic cipher. (In the printout we have underlined those parts entered by the operator.) At each step of the discussion the reader should refer forward to the printout. The discussion is intended to illustrate the thoughts behind the program. This program was deliberately designed to give a large amount of printout and leave many decisions to the cryptanalyst. In practice almost all the steps can be completely automated. We have also chosen this particular program so that we can illustrate each step.

Now that we suspect that one key was used, our next step is to work out the relative frequencies in each message and calculate the indices of coincidence. (In the printout the frequencies should be read horizontally; e.g. in message 1, **A** has frequency 3, **B** has 7, **C** has 2, etc.) For message 1, $I_c \simeq 0·0439$ and for message 2, $I_c \simeq 0·0454$. Clearly both I_cs suggest polyalphabetic ciphers. For message 1, I_c suggests five or six substitution alphabets, while for message 2 (which is shorter and consequently less reliable) I_c suggests four alphabets. The joint index is about 0·0441 which indicates four or five alphabets.

For final confirmation that a polyalphabetic cipher was used we apply the Kasiski test. This, of course, should also indicate the number of substitution alphabets used. If a bigram is repeated more than once then the printout contains the distances between every pair of positions for that bigram. Unlike our example in Section 1.3.5 (page 45) the printout does not give the factorization of each distance. Straightforward verification shows that 11 of the distances for message 1 have a factor of 2, 13 have a factor of 3 and 13 also have a factor of 7. For message 2, 10 have a factor of 7 while 5 are a factor of 6 of them. Thus the Kasiski test suggests either two, three, or seven alphabets with a slight preference for seven. (The preference is only slight because, as we have already stressed, message 2 is shorter than message 1 and we must give less significance to it.) Our earlier discussions, again giving more weight to conclusions from message 1, suggest slightly more than five alphabets. So, as our first 'guess', we will opt to assume that seven alphabets were used. If this proves to be wrong we will have to try three alphabets next.

We now write our message in seven columns with the hope that each column will represent a monoalphabetic cipher. (We used rows in Section 1.3.5; but obviously this does not matter.) Evaluating the index of coincidence for each column gives:

Col.	1	2	3	4	5	6	7
I_c	0·0730159	0·0460317	0·0634921	0·0666667	0·0698413	0·0705882	0·0554622

Apart from columns 2 and 7, there are very strong indications that monoalphabetic ciphers were used. So, making a mental note to be careful of columns 2 and 7, we now assume that seven alphabets were used and attempt to find the correct position of each alphabet relative to the others. To do this we evaluate $\Sigma f_\alpha f'_\alpha$ for each pair of columns and look for the high values. When we look at the results in the printout we see that, for most pairs of columns, there is an obvious maximum value. However for many of the pairs involving column 2 there are two large adjacent values (e.g. for columns 2 and 3 there are values 81 and 83; for columns 2 and 5 there are 81 and 82). There is clearly no really significant difference between 81 and 82, and it is merely a question of trying to find the best possible fit between all the high values. The values circled are these which we choose as our first fit. They correspond to taking FNFCPQ as the starting letters for columns 2 to 7 relative to starting column 1 with A. In view of the consistency with which the number chosen for columns 2 and 3, 2 and 4, 2 and 5, 2 and 6, 2 and 7 has an equally high number on its left, we also try GNFCPQ as a starting point. On trying both as starting points we get indices of coincidence of 0·0676627 and 0·0666988 respectively. Each is higher than the value of 0·065 for a monoalphabetic cipher so we may have to try them both. However we note that, from a starting point of AGNFCPQ the word CIPHERS appears in the printout. This is strong indication that a Vigenère cipher with keyword 'ciphers' was used and, on this assumption, we obtain the final cryptogram which we hope was the result of using a monoalphabetic cipher. We leave its decipherment as an exercise.

```
              PROGRAM FOR MESSAGES 1 AND 2

ENTER MESSAGE:

YJIHX RVHKK KSKHK IQQEV IFLRK QUZVA EVFYZ RVFBX UKGBF KYVVR
QTAJK TGBQO ISGHU CWIKX OUXIH DUGIU LMWKG CHXJV WFKIH HEHGB
EXXSF DMIIL UPSLW AJKTR WIQWF IVXRW NFTGW EKBYV SRQWS

ANY MORE MESSAGES?  YES
ENTER MESSAGE:

PNDFF FLFAS LXSGL OEWFV SHDSN HUGYA QAXUG RWIHH LWFXX LXWLD
MIILV TQPEJ HXKFN AISAX QKIHH VVHAS ISYEW KSJFF LCLVI KDTRK
HMURQ
```

ANY MORE MESSAGES? <u>NO</u>

PERCENTAGE OF COINCIDENCES FOR MESSAGES 1 AND 2   6.6666667

RELATIVE FREQUENCIES FOR MESSAGE 1 :

```
 3   7   2   2   5   5   7   9  11   4  14   4   2
 1   3   4   6   5   6   5   7  10   9   8   4   2
```

INDEX OF COINCIDENCE FOR MESSAGE : 0.0438697

RELATIVE FREQUENCIES FOR MESSAGE 2 :

```
 6   0   1   4   3   8   3   9   7   2   4   9   2
 3   1   3   4   4   8   2   3   5   5   7   2   0
```

INDEX OF COINCIDENCE FOR MESSAGE : 0.0454212

JOINT INDEX OF COINCIDENCE FOR MESSAGES 1 AND 2 : 0.0440803

DO YOU WISH TO JOIN THE MESSAGES? <u>YES</u>

TYPE M FOR MONOALPHABETIC OR P FOR POLYALPHABETIC : <u>P</u>

DO YOU WISH TO TRY THE KASISKI TEST? <u>YES</u>

KASISKI TEST FOR MESSAGE 1 :

```
AJKT     63
AJK      63
JKT      63
IH       71
IH       91
HX       83
RV       30
HK        6
KI       78
EV       12
VF        5
KG       42
GB       14
GB       56
YV       92
AJ       63
JK       63
KT       63
TG       77
GB       42
BQ       84
IH       20
```

KASISKI TEST FOR MESSAGE 2 :

```
FFL      84
IHH      35
FF       85
FF       84
FL       84
```

```
AS      70
LX      35
EW      67
UG       7
AX      37
IH      35
HH      35
LV      39
IS      14
```

DO YOU WISH TO TRY TO GUESS THE PERIOD?   YES
WHICH PERIOD?   7

```
Y J I H X R V
H K K K S K H
K I Q Q E V I
F L R K Q U Z
V A E V F Y Z
R V F B X U K
G B F K Y V V
R Q T A J K T
G B Q O I S G
H U C W I K X
O U X I H D U
G I U L M W K
G C H X J V W
F K I H H E H
G B E X X S F
D M I I L U P
S L W A J K T
R W T O W P I
V X B W N P T
G W E K B Y V
S B Q W S
P N D F F F L
F A S L X S G
L O E W P V S
H D S N H U G
Y A Q A X U G
R W I H H L W
F X X L X W L
D M I I L V T
Q P E J H X K
F N A I S A X
Q K I H H V V
H A S I S Y E
W K S J F F L
C L V I K D T
R R H M U R Q
```

```
INDEX OF COINCIDENCE FOR COLUMN 1 :  0.0730159
INDEX OF COINCIDENCE FOR COLUMN 2 :  0.0460317
INDEX OF COINCIDENCE FOR COLUMN 3 :  0.0634921
INDEX OF COINCIDENCE FOR COLUMN 4 :  0.0666667
INDEX OF COINCIDENCE FOR COLUMN 5 :  0.0698413
INDEX OF COINCIDENCE FOR COLUMN 6 :  0.0705882
INDEX OF COINCIDENCE FOR COLUMN 7 :  0.0554622
```

DO YOU WISH TO TRY TO MATCH ALPHABETS? YES

```
COLUMNS 1 AND 2 :   24 26 38 56 64 (89) 69 47 45 54 58 40 38
                    31 31 49 53 56 40 69 80 78 59 39 41 32
COLUMNS 1 AND 3 :   42 82 84 53 29 43 38 18 23 49 58 56 73
                   (90) 44 39 57 60 39 29 43 32 26 55 68 66
COLUMNS 1 AND 4 :   38 63 79 66 72 (92) 57 40 39 47 35 28 34
                    27 20 48 85 79 52 65 65 45 27 34 33 26
```

```
COLUMNS 1 AND 5 :   56  79 (87) 49  50  52  68  44  28  41  31  37  52
                    57  34  42  78  84  68  32  51  34  28  27  37  50
COLUMNS 1 AND 6 :   57  31  30  66  78  63  35  44  33  31  38  37  56
                    56  79 (94) 55  44  50  60  36  22  33  41  44  47
COLUMNS 1 AND 7 :   58  72  59  57  75  69  39  23  42  32  28  27  46
                    61  68  77 (81) 50  45  47  46  28  19  30  34  47
COLUMNS 2 AND 3 :   42  34  33  49  52  49  59  81 (83) 38  44  39  38
                    38  40  44  47  52  58  58  63  55  67  53  46  34
COLUMNS 2 AND 4 :  (79) 46  34  30  33  32  46  56  51  46  58  69  63
                    62  60  39  40  32  31  31  43  57  64  66  58  70
COLUMNS 2 AND 5 :   44  52  33  38  39  42  51  65  60  45  59  60  54
                    61  37  46  32  42  42  35  48  58  81 (82) 18  42
COLUMNS 2 AND 6 :   53  41  43  37  45  40  34  55  56  71 (78) 52  38
                    42  48  33  37  36  41  53  70  70  35  47  58  47
COLUMNS 2 AND 7 :   43  35  30  36  32  49  52  47  56  67  76 (67) 41
                    37  38  39  29  31  43  55  55  62  68  57  57  58
COLUMNS 3 AND 4 :   66  41  42  74  77  53  73  55  45  27  41  33  30
                    36  56  64  52  57 (97) 64  39  37  39  29  27  42
COLUMNS 3 AND 5 :   69  57  51  65  56  65  36  58  45  23  48  37  64
                    41  58 (94) 57  53  45  68  33  35  29  55  21  57
COLUMNS 3 AND 6 :   45  50 (81) 61  45  50  53  38  36  26  45  36  46
                    87  60  36  64  57  53  35  53  45  31  42  36  49
COLUMNS 3 AND 7 :   55  49  71 (88) 51  42  45  48  24  31  26  58  38
                    54  68  74  53  64  57  42  29  38  33  28  50  44
COLUMNS 4 AND 5 :   75  72  52  28  40  35  26  50  50  51  58  65  53
                    58  36  62  46  31  29  35  36  40  64 (86) 53  65
COLUMNS 4 AND 6 :   40  30  46  40  32  30  30  57  52  56 (91) 59  60
                    87  72  48  39  32  29  33  45  58  47  41  56  50
COLUMNS 4 AND 7 :   59  42  36  48  25  32  33  37  50  57  70 (90) 60
                    51  63  49  28  20  32  34  34  42  60  70  65  73
COLUMNS 5 AND 6 :   43  42  46  63  31  36  54  31  53  42  47  60  49
                   (102) 65  44  46  42  42  35  39  41  31  63  69  44
COLUMNS 5 AND 7 :   50  66  45  61  38  32  31  37  37  54  57  48  66
                    54 (95) 40  47  26  50  31  24  38  53  48  62  70
COLUMNS 6 AND 7 :   58 (84) 47  44  44  38  32  26  40  39  44  59  61
                    51  46  58  65  40  32  34  31  47  45  44  60  56
```

SELECT STARTING ALPHABET FOR COLUMNS 2-7 RELATIVE TO COLUMN 1 : FNFCPQ

```
A F N F C P Q
B G O G D Q R
C H P H E R S
D I Q I F S T
E J R J G T U
F K S K H U V
G L T L I V W
H M U M J W X
I N V N K X Y
J O W O L Y Z
K P X P M Z A
L Q Y Q N A B
M R Z R O B C
N S A S P C D
O T B T Q D E
P U C U R E F
Q V D V S F G
R W E W T G H
S X F X U H I
T Y G Y V I J
U Z H Z W J K
V A I A X K L
W B J B Y L M
X C K C Z M N
Y D L D A N O
Z E M E B O P
```

```
MONOALPHABETIC SUBSTITUTION IS :

YEVCVCFHFXFQVRKDDLCGSFGEFOFJVVRQDJJRQSWVFUGWCFWGFR
LGVHVDGWDJGDQHPPRGVHOPKDFOEGDHGKHUGXUSHGGFFVCFPRGW
RSVDPDHVDJFZSGJVHVDRRGJUASVSORLADGRRFZJFSWDRQPIQAD
QVFVFGVDQLJRRNGCHYFIFFQYVDVVFQRRVCFWGFSKGVHVDHVDJG
DQKREFIUFINDQLHQFVCFGFHVFDQJOWFFEDQVCGIDIODRMUHSCA


RELATIVE FREQUENCIES :

  4  0 10 25  5 32 24 15  6 11  5  5  1
  2  6  6 15 19 10  0  6 28  8  2  3  2


INDEX OF COINCIDENCE FOR MESSAGE : 0.0676627


TRY AGAIN?  YES
TYPE 1 TO CHANGE NO. OF COLUMNS OR 2 TO CHANGE RELATIVE ALPHABETS : 2


SELECT STARTING ALPHABET FOR COLUMNS 2-7 RELATIVE TO COLUMN 1 : GNFCPQ

A G N F C P Q
B H O G D Q R
C I P H E R S
D J Q I F S T
E K R J G T U
F L S K H U V
G M T L I V W
H N U M J W X
I O V N K X Y
J P W O L Y Z
K Q X P M Z A
L R Y Q N A B
M S Z R O B C
N T A S P C D
O U B T Q D E
P V C U R E F
Q W D V S F G
R X E W T G H
S Y F X U H I
T Z G Y V I J
U A H Z W J K
V B I A X K L
W C J B Y L M
X D K C Z M N
Y E L D A N O
Z F M E B O P


MONOALPHABETIC SUBSTITUTION IS :

YDVCVCFHEXFQVRKCDLCGSFFEFOFJVURQDJJRPSWVFUGVCFWGFR
KGVHVDGVDJGDQHOPRGVHOOKDFOEGCHGKHUGWUSHGGFEVCFPRGV
RSVDPDGVDJFZSFJVHVDRQGJUASVRORLADGQRFZJFSVDRQPHQAD
QVFUFGVDQLIRRNGCHXFIFFQYUDVVFQRQVCFWGFRKGVHVDGVDJG
DQJREFIUFHNDQLHQEVCFGFHUFDQJOWEFEDQVCFIDIODRLUHSCA


RELATIVE FREQUENCIES :

  4  0 12 24  8 31 23 15  5 11  5  5  0
  2  8  5 17 18  8  0 10 28  5  2  2  2
```

INDEX OF COINCIDENCE FOR MESSAGE : 0.0666988

TRY AGAIN? NO

STOP

We again stress that this particular program leaves the operator to make the decision as to the number of alphabets used and their relative positions. This, of course, could also be automated by including an algorithm for choosing optimum fits. There is however a good case to be made for leaving certain choices to the operator. He can, for instance, change his mind very quickly and easily. In practice it is often difficult for a computer to replace the intuition of an operator!

The total time taken for the program to run was about ten minutes. Most of this time was, in fact, spent printing out the results and the time taken for the execution of the various tests was very small. By using a VDU (Visual Display Unit) which can print out results very quickly, printing only a hard copy of certain specifically requested information, we could, in a very short time, try a large number of possibilities if, as is quite likely, our initial tests prove inconclusive. We hope we have said and done enough to convince the reader that, even with only a comparatively unsophisticated computer, cryptanalysis of a Vigenère cipher is a straightforward, quick process.

Throughout this chapter, when we were attempting our cryptanalysis we often had to make choices between more or less equally likely possibilities. It is possible to obtain confidence levels (in terms of the standard deviation) for many of the statistical tests used. When all the calculations were performed manually by the cryptanalyst, it was important to be confident about one's assumptions before proceeding. (For example, on the two cryptograms just considered it would take hours to carry out the simple tests described.) However, with the use of a fast modern computer, the importance of being right first time has decreased. It now only takes a few seconds to retrace our steps and try another possibility. This is one of the reasons why we have not felt any need to discuss the reliability or the merits of our tests.

To make the cryptanalysis more difficult a number of variants on the use of the Vigenère square have been tried. In one, a keyword was chosen but the key only determined the shift until all its letters had been used once. From then on the plaintext itself was used to determine the shifts. To encipher using this method we would write the keyword above the plaintext message and then, if the message was longer than the key, follow it by the plaintext itself. We would then proceed in the same way as in the Vigenère cipher. As an illustration we will again use 'radio' as the key and **codebreaking** as the message.

Keyword: r a d i o c o d e b r e
Plaintext: **c o d e b r e a k i n g**

The square is used in exactly the same way as in the Vigenère cipher and the cryptogram is **T O G M P T S D O J E V**. Clearly this cipher cannot be broken by the same techniques as those we have just used for the Vigenère cipher.

Another variant was to change the square. A common method of doing this was to alter the order in which the plaintext letters are written in the top row.

There are also many other types of manual polyalphabetic ciphers. However none of them has survived. Eventually, in each case, someone would spot a flaw and then be able to use statistics as a tool for cryptanalysis. We will not discuss particular examples. It should be clear that more complex cipher systems were needed. We will now see how automation was used in an attempt to meet this requirement.

Further Reading

The following is a short bibliography of books which are especially relevant to this chapter. We particularly recommend [2] and [5] to any reader who has not previously studied cryptography.

[1] Gaines, Helen F., *Cryptanalysis, A Study of Ciphers and Their Solution*, New York: Dover, 1956.
[2] Kahn, David, *The Codebreakers, The Story of Secret Writing*, New York: Macmillan, 1967.
[3] Kullback, Solomon, *Statistical Methods in Cryptanalysis*, Laguna Hill, CA: Aegean Park Press, 1976.
[4] Pratt, Fletcher, *Secret and Urgent*, New York: Blue Ribbon Books, 1942.
[5] Sinkov, Abraham, *Elementary Cryptanalysis, A Mathematical Approach*, New York: Random House, New Mathematical Library No. 22, 1968.

2.
More Recent Mechanical Cryptographic Devices

2.1 Introduction

After a brief description of a very simple machine invented by Thomas Jefferson, this chapter is devoted to the M-209. This is a mechanical machine which was used by the U.S. Army until the early 1950s. Our discussion of the M-209 is in three parts. In the first we describe the actual design of the machine and how to use it for enciphering messages. The other two are devoted to showing how one would attempt to cryptanalyze this system.

In all the situations of cryptanalysis considered in Chapter 1, we assumed that all that the cryptanalyst had available to him was a reasonable quantity of ciphertext plus an idea as to the type of cipher system employed. Think how much easier life would have been for him if he had also had some corresponding ciphertext and plaintext, i.e. a portion of the message before and after encipherment. As we come to consider rather more complex mechanical machines, it is no longer apparent that the system can be broken even with some corresponding plaintext and ciphertext available, let alone with just ciphertext. We therefore consider these two situations separately.

It may, at the moment, seem unnaturally pessimistic for us to assume that the cryptanalyst has any corresponding ciphertext and plaintext available. But, as we shall repeatedly see (especially in Chapters 4, 8 and 9) there are many different ways in which segments of plaintext may be deduced. However, for the moment, we will not concern ourselves with how the cryptanalyst might have obtained this information. In our discussions of the cryptanalysis we do not try to give a general method, but instead concentrate on working through examples. The first, where we assume that we have nearly 500 characters of known plaintext and ciphertext equivalents, is straightforward. After cryptanalyzing it and explaining the techniques involved, we consider a more realistic example where we only know 76 characters. In both these examples we hope to bring home two important points. First, despite the complex nature of the design and the large number of possible keys, the M-209 is definitely not secure against the cryptanalyst who knows the plaintext equivalent of a reasonably long passage of ciphertext. Secondly, intelligent guessing, based on statistical information, is the basis of the approach. In this sense the method of cryptanalysis is not too dissimilar to those discussions for much simpler examples in Chapter 1.

The method of approach for the above examples is the same, so we have not included as much explanation with our description of the second one. Unfortunately this means it tends to become a sequence of tables and figures. Although this may not make particularly attractive reading it is, nevertheless, exactly what the cryptanalyst produces. The reader is urged to persevere with the first of these examples but can be forgiven for 'skipping' the second. However we must point out that this latter example gives a true picture of the drudgery involved in most cryptanalytic techniques. The cryptanalyst has no option but to 'get his hands dirty' and even an example as small as ours shows why he considers the computer an essential tool.

Finally we consider the situation where the cryptanalyst has available to him only a segment of ciphertext; albeit a rather large segment. The attack in this case is somewhat different from that when plaintext is known. For this reason it should not be overlooked.

The reader may be tempted to ask: 'why just the M-209?'. There are several reasons. First the M-209 and its derivatives have been widely used. It is therefore well known throughout most of the world and we believe that many readers will be familiar with it. Secondly, it is reasonably representative of the cryptographic machines of the mid-twentieth century. In other words, the techniques it employs also appear in many of the other machines of the same era. Thirdly, and perhaps most important, is our lack of space. In order to discuss another recent mechanical or electro-mechanical machine in any reasonable detail, we would require yet another chapter (and also a great deal of patience from the reader!). We have thus decided to restrict ourselves to a single machine.

The reader should not, on the basis of this chapter, assume that all mechanical/electro-mechanical machines can be broken in the same way and with the same quantities of plaintext and ciphertext as the M-209. Each and every cipher system must be considered and assessed in its own right before any statement regarding the security it offers can be made.

2.2   The Thomas Jefferson Wheel Cipher

In this section we give a brief description of a very simple machine which was developed by Thomas Jefferson in the 1790s. It is made by taking a cylinder, which is mounted on an axis, and dividing its surface into 26 equal parts; this division being achieved by dividing the top and bottom circumferences into 26 equal arcs and then joining these two sets of

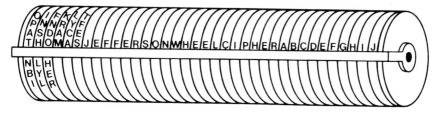

Figure 2.1
Thomas Jefferson Wheel

dividing marks by 26 parallel lines on the cylinder's surface. The cylinder is then cut into 36 smaller cylinders of equal height. The effect of this is to have 36 equal cylinders, which are all free to rotate about a common axis, whose surfaces are divided into 26 equal arcs. The machine is completed by writing one letter of the alphabet in each of the 26 divisions for every one of the 36 cylinders, and varying the order in which the letters are written for each of them.

To encipher a message using this machine, the encipherer first divides it into blocks of 36 characters each. The individual cylinders are then rotated until the first block of 36 characters appears as the entries of a prescribed row of the machine. The entries of any other chosen row can then be taken as the first 36 characters of the cryptogram. The choice of this row must be agreed beforehand by the encipherer and recipient and constitutes the key of the cipher. Thus the key is merely a number between 0 and 25. This process is then repeated for each block of 36 message characters. To decipher a block of the cryptogram the individual cylinders are rotated until the ciphertext appears in one of the rows. The plaintext will then appear in another row whose position, relative to the ciphertext, is known from the key. For instance if the key number is 7 then, when enciphering, the ciphertext is obtained from the row which is 7 positions in a given direction. Thus, when deciphering, the plaintext will be in the row which is 7 positions in the opposite direction, i.e. is 19 positions in the same direction.

Clearly we can obtain a similar machine by replacing the number 36 by any positive integer, and there seems to be no obvious reason for choosing 36. To illustrate this machine by an example we will assume that there are only 5 individual cylinders. To represent the machine we now imagine that the cylinder has been cut horizontally along one of its dividing lines and opened out to give an array with 26 rows and 5 columns. For our example, let us suppose that the allocation of the alphabet to the 5 individual cylinders is shown in Table 2.1(a).

If the message to be enciphered begins **London town** . . . then our first two blocks of 5 are **Londo** and **ntown**. Setting the machine so that first **Londo** and then **ntown** appear in the first row, we get Table 2.1(b).

A U T Z C	L O N D O	N T O W N
X R H Y G	M T I B I	O Q G V O
Y A E X K	N Q C P P	F C S U I
B B D W Z	O C B Q S	Q W A A P
Z E O V X	F W P T W	W G W C S
D Z G U L	Q G R S J	K I M E W
C X S A H	W I V R E	I H Y G J
V M A C Q	K H U O C	R Y N I E
T O W E M	I Y X Z G	J D I K C
G T M G A	R D J Y K	P V C M G
U Q Y I F	J V L X Z	H F B N K
S C N K Y	P F F W X	A L P L Z
E W I M U	H L Z V L	X P R J X
L G C N R	A P K U H	Y K V H L
M I B L D	X K Q A Q	B S U F H
N H P J B	Y S T C M	Z N X D Q
O Y R H V	B N H E A	D J J B M
F D V F T	Z J E G F	C U L P A
Q V U D N	D U D O Y	V R F Q F
W F X B O	C R O K V	T A Z T Y
K L J P I	V A G M R	G B K S U
I P L Q P	T B S N D	U E Q R R
R K F T S	G E A L B	S Z T O D
J S Z S W	U Z W J V	E X M Z B
P N K R J	S X M H T	L M E X V
H J Q O E	E M Y F N	M O D Y T
(a)	(b)	

Table 2.1
The Jefferson Wheel

If the agreed number is 6 then, by taking the row which is 6 positions below the message row, we obtain **WIVREIHYGJ** as the first 10 letters of the cryptogram. If the recipient sets the machine so that first WIVRE and then IHYGJ appear in the first row then he will find the blocks of the message in the row which is 20 rows lower.

Clearly in our example we have a polyalphabetic cipher of period 5, and it should be clear that use of the actual Jefferson machine normally results in a polyalphabetic cipher of period 36. (This assumes, of course, that the machine is 'set up' sensibly. To take an extreme case, if we assign the alphabet to the cylinders so that the order of the letters is the same for each wheel then we would only have a monoalphabetic cipher.) Since we have already discussed polyalphabetic ciphers in Chapter 1, we will not spend any time discussing how to cryptanalyze cryptograms obtained from this machine. We will, however, make one observation which will become more significant after Chapter 3 has been read. If the interceptor happens to have a Jefferson machine with the correct permutation of the letters on each cylinder, then he will almost certainly be able to decipher the message without knowing the key. Once the machine has been set so that a block of ciphertext appears in a row, there are only 26 possibilities for the message; namely the entries in each of the rows. It is extremely unlikely that more than one row of 36 letters will have any meaning in the English language and, consequently, the message will be apparent.

Now that we have so much statistical information available, the defects of the Jefferson machine are obvious. Nevertheless at the time of its invention it was an ingenious machine and its basic principle, i.e. having a number of independent, revolving wheels, is the basis of almost all mechanical or electro-mechanical cipher machines. Details of a number of these machines can be found in Kahn [2] and we will not give a historical account of their development. Instead we move straight on to one of the later mechanical machines which was used by the U.S. Army until the early 1950s. This is the **Hagelin C-36** machine or, as it is commonly known, the **M-209 Converter**.

2.3 The M-209 Converter

Figure 2.2
The M-209 (Science Museum photograph Crown Copyright)

Figure 2.3
The M-209 with lid up (Science Museum photograph Crown Copyright)

2.3.1   Physical description and method of operation

The basis of the machine comprises six wheels (often referred to as the
rotors) whose centres lie on a common axis. Each wheel has a number of
pins whose positions may be adjusted so that they are either 'active' or
'inactive'. Reading from left to right in Figure 2.3 the wheels have 26, 25,
23, 21, 19 and 17 pins respectively. The wheels are free to rotate
independently about the axis. Thus wheel 1 is labelled A to Z while wheel
6 goes from A to Q and there is a pin corresponding to each letter. Behind
these wheels is a cylinder called the **lug cage**. It comprises 27 bars which
are parallel to its axis. Each bar has two moveable projections, called **lugs**,
which can be set in any two of eight possible positions. These positions are
marked 1 0 2 3 4 5 0 6 on the number plate in Figure 2.3. If a lug is placed
in a position corresponding to zero it is non-effective. But, if it is placed in
one of the other positions, it is aligned with the corresponding wheel and is
capable of making contact with any active pins on that wheel. If the wheels
remain stationary and the lug cage is rotated, then there is only one pin in
each wheel which is in a position to make contact with the lugs. These six
pins are called the **basic pins**.

To use the machine we must set the pins on each of the six wheels; i.e. we arrange for certain of the pins on each wheel to be active. Once this is accomplished we keep the six wheels stationary and rotate the lug cage through a complete revolution. As this happens each active basic pin makes contact with every lug in the appropriate position. Whenever a lug makes contact with an active pin that bar is said to be **engaged** and, for any given setting of the pins and lugs, a complete revolution determines a unique number of engagements. As the cage rotates through a complete revolution we count the number of **bar engagements** involving the basic pins. (Note that if a bar engages with two active basic pins this only gives one bar engagement.)

We can represent the lug cage in the following way. Corresponding to each of the six wheels we denote by a 1 those bars of the lug cage that have a lug set and by a 0 those bars which do not. We then 'open up' the cylinder

Bar \ Wheel	1	2	3	4	5	6
1	0	0	0	0	0	0
2	1	0	0	0	0	0
3	1	1	0	0	0	0
4	1	0	0	1	0	0
5	1	0	0	0	0	1
6	0	1	0	0	0	0
7	0	1	0	0	0	0
8	0	1	0	0	0	0
9	0	1	0	0	0	0
10	0	1	0	0	0	1
11	0	1	0	0	0	1
12	0	1	0	0	0	1
13	0	1	0	0	0	1
14	0	1	0	0	0	1
15	0	0	1	1	0	0
16	0	0	0	1	0	1
17	0	0	0	0	1	0
18	0	0	0	0	1	0
19	0	0	0	0	1	0
20	0	0	0	0	1	0
21	0	0	0	0	1	1
22	0	0	0	0	1	1
23	0	0	0	0	1	1
24	0	0	0	0	1	1
25	0	0	0	0	1	1
26	0	0	0	0	0	1
27	0	0	0	0	0	1

Table 2.2
A Lug Cage Representation

and represent the cage as an array with 27 rows and 6 columns. In this array each entry is 0 or 1 and each row has at most two 1s. For example the cage may be set up as in Table 2.2.

Suppose, for example, that the first and fifth wheels are the only ones which contain active basic pins. As the cage rotates through a complete revolution the basic pin on the first wheel engages with bars 2, 3, 4 and 5, while that on the fifth wheel engages with bars 17, 18, 19, 20, 21, 22, 23, 24 and 25. There are no instances where both wheels engage with the same bar. Thus, for this particular example, there will be 13 bar engagements involving basic pins. As a second example suppose that the first, third and fourth wheels are the only ones which contain active basic pins. In this case, the first wheel engages with bars 2, 3, 4 and 5, the third wheel with bar 15 and the fourth wheel with bars 4, 15 and 16. There are two occasions where two wheels engage with the same bar so there will be six bar engagements.

We take this number of bar engagements as determining the substitution alphabet for the encipherment of the first plaintext letter. Once this letter is enciphered each of the six wheels is advanced by one position. This, of course, changes the basic pins and repetition of the same process will give another substitution alphabet, probably different to the first, to encipher the second letter. Continuing in this way we encipher the message.

In order to determine the substitution alphabet we take the 'natural' alphabet and write it in reverse as follows:

'natural' alphabet: a b c d e f g h i j k l m n o p q r s t u v w x y z
reversed alphabet: z y x w v u t s r q p o n m l k j i h g f e d c b a

Having done this the number of bar engagements involving the basic pins is taken as the length of a **shift** of the reversed alphabet to the right. Thus if there were three bar engagements for the basic pins, the cipher would be:

Plaintext letter: **a b c d e f g h i j k l m**
Ciphertext letter: **C B A Z Y X W V U T S R Q**

Plaintext letter: **n o p q r s t u v w x y z**
Ciphertext letter: **P O N M L K J I H G F E D**

In order to obtain an elegant expression for the encipherment of a plaintext letter λ given κ bar engagements we repeat some of Section 1.2.2 but this time use a slightly different notation.

Once again we assign the numbers 0 to 25 to the alphabet with $a = 1$, $b = 2 \ldots z = 0$. If two numbers α and β are such that a shift of α is the same as a shift of β then we will write $\alpha \equiv \beta \pmod{26}$ and say that 'α is congruent to β modulo 26'. Thus, for example, $84 \equiv 6 \pmod{26}$. As we saw in Chapter 1, every positive integer is congruent modulo 26 to an integer in the range

0 to 25 inclusive, and consequently determines a unique letter. Exercise 1.3 can be reworded as saying that if $\alpha \equiv \beta$ (mod26) and $0 \le \beta \le 25$ then β is equal to the remainder when α is divided by 26, and this enables us to determine the letter defined by any given integer. The two operations $\oplus, \otimes$ of Chapter 1 will now be called **addition modulo 26** and **multiplication modulo 26** respectively. Furthermore instead of writing, for example, $21 \oplus 63 = 6$ or $5 \otimes 7 = 9$ we will now write $21 + 63 \equiv 6$ (mod26) and $5 \times 7 \equiv 9$ (mod26).

With this change of notation, we can represent the ciphertext letter μ resulting from a message letter λ and κ bar engagements by $\mu \equiv 1 + \kappa - \lambda$ (mod26). Since this can be rearranged to give $\lambda \equiv 1 + \kappa - \mu$ (mod26), enciphering and deciphering are identical operations. This is one of the reasons for reversing the alphabet initially.

Note that using the machine in this way means that essentially we have a Beaufort cipher. However, as we shall see, the keyword is likely to be so large that the methods of Chapter 1 (e.g. the Kasiski and index of coincidence tests) will almost certainly fail. To break this system we need to develop some new techniques.

Before giving an example of the use of the M-209 and proceeding to discuss breaking the system, we should mention two operational aspects of the machine. When enciphering, all letters are printed and spaces are inserted so that the ciphertext is divided into groups of five letters each. When deciphering no such spaces are included but the letter **z** is not printed. Thus the normal method of operation is to write the letter **z** in every space of the message before enciphering it. As a result of this, the deciphered version will appear as normally spaced words except that the letter **z** will not appear. It is up to the recipient to 'spot' where a **z** has been omitted and to insert one. However the letter **z** appears very infrequently and it is usually easy to see where one is missing. Consequently there is no real danger of incorrect decipherment.

The second operational facility that we mention concerns the start of a message. In Figure 2.2 there is a clearly defined line called the **message indicator**, and the respective letters of each wheel in this position determine the set of basic pins to be used for encipherment at that instant. For example in Figure 2.2 this is set as DEGIKM. Thus an operator can set his wheels to ensure a different set of basic pins are used at the start of each message. (Of course he must transmit this information to the receiver.)

2.3.2 An example
In the example we are about to consider the lug cage setting is as in Table 2.2 and the pin settings are shown in Table 2.3.

If our plaintext message is **now is the time for all good men** then, in view of the penultimate paragraph of Section 2.3.1, we take as our plaintext the following:

Plaintext: **nowzisztheztimezforzallzgoodzmen.**

Position	1	2	3	4	5	6	7	8	9	10	11	12	13
Wheel 1	0	0	1	1	1	1	0	1	0	1	1	0	0
2	0	1	1	0	1	0	0	0	1	0	0	1	1
3	1	0	0	1	1	1	1	1	1	0	1	0	0
4	0	1	1	0	1	1	0	0	0	1	0	0	1
5	1	1	1	0	0	1	0	1	0	1	0	0	1
6	0	0	1	0	0	1	1	1	0	1	0	1	1

Position	14	15	16	17	18	19	20	21	22	23	24	25	26
Wheel 1	0	1	1	0	0	1	0	1	0	0	1	1	1
2	0	0	1	0	1	1	0	1	0	0	0	1	
3	0	1	0	1	0	1	1	0	1	0			
4	0	1	1	0	1	0	1	1					
5	0	1	0	0	0	1							
6	0	1	1	0									

Table 2.3
The pin settings

Taking the first column as representing our basic pins, we must now count the number of bar engagements involving the six pins given by 001010. Looking back to Table 2.2 we see that the pin on wheel 3 engages only with bar 15 and the pin on the fifth wheel engages with bars 17, 18, 19, 20, 21, 22, 23, 24 and 25. Since there are no double engagements, the total number of bar engagements is 10. The letter **n** is represented by the number 14, and thus its ciphertext equivalent μ is given by $\mu \equiv 1 + 10 - 14$ (mod26). Since $-3 \equiv 23$ (mod26), this gives $\mu \equiv 23$ (mod26) and thus μ is the letter **W**. After **n** has been enciphered, each wheel is rotated through one position so that each column of Table 2.3 moves one position to the left. Thus the settings for the new basic pins are 010110. There are still no double engagements. So the number of bar engagements for these basic pins is 22 and this gives **H** as the ciphertext equivalent of **o**. Continuing in this way we obtain the ciphertext: **WHDFG DPCDR FZQNR WVYFU XYESS RKHWJ BI.**

EXERCISE 2.1
 (i)   *Determine the first occasion on which a bar engages two pins simultaneously.*
 (ii) *Check that the last letter of this ciphertext is correct.*

2.3.3   Basic properties

If, as is certainly possible, the number of bar engagements for two different sets of basic pins is the same then, naturally, we will end up using the same substitution alphabet. However it should be clear that, apart from a few exceptional settings (for example, activating every pin), as the wheels are gradually rotated the substitution alphabet will vary. After 17 letters have been enciphered, the sixth wheel will have completed a revolution and will return to its original position. But, of course, the others will not have completed a revolution and, consequently, will not be in their starting positions. Clearly the sixth wheel will then return to its original position after any number of rotations which is a multiple of 17. Similarly, the fifth wheel will be in its original position after every 19 rotations. Thus when the fifth and sixth wheels return to their original position simultaneously, the number of rotations must be a multiple of both 17 and 19. But, since 17 and 19 have no common factors, any number which is a multiple of 17 and 19 must be a multiple of 17×19 which is 323. So the fifth and sixth wheels are both in their original positions after every 323 rotations.

The numbers 26, 25, 23, 21, 19 and 17 were carefully chosen so that no two of them have a common factor, and an extension of the above argument shows that the six wheels do not simultaneously return to their original positions until $26 \times 25 \times 23 \times 21 \times 19 \times 17$ rotations, i.e. until 101,405,850 rotations. Since one rotation occurs after each letter has been enciphered, this means that the pattern of substitution alphabets used must repeat itself after every 101,405,850 plaintext letters. In other words, using the machine in this way produces a polyalphabetic cipher with a period of at most 101,405,850. Clearly the actual period depends on the pin settings. For instance activating every pin produces the same number of engagements after each rotation; i.e. a monoalphabetic cipher. If we have identical settings for all the pins of any given wheel, then the number of engagements of the basic pin on that wheel will be the same after any number of rotations. Thus we have effectively nullified that wheel and will have a period of less than 101,405,850.

As an illustration of another 'bad' setting suppose we activate each alternate pin on the first wheel then, since 26 is an even number, the first wheel will appear to be in its original position after every pair of rotations and, no matter how the other wheels are set, this decreases the maximum possible period.

It should also be clear that, whatever the setting of the other pins, identical settings of the basic pins give the same substitution alphabet.

EXERCISE 2.2   Convince yourself that the pin and lug cage settings of the example in Section 2.3.2 give a polyalphabetic cipher of period 101,405,850.

The next exercise is rather difficult and the reader may find that he cannot determine the exact answer. This will not matter. The aim is to draw attention to the type of pin setting necessary to give the maximum period. For instance, as we have already seen, the maximum period will certainly not be attained unless each wheel contains at least one active pin and at least one inactive one.

EXERCISE 2.3   Count the number of different pin settings which give ciphers of period less than 101,405,850. (You may assume that there is at least one effective lug corresponding to each wheel.)

The key to the machine is, essentially, the pin and lug settings. The six wheels together have $26 + 25 + 23 + 21 + 19 + 17 = 131$ pins. Each of these pins can be made either active or inactive and the setting of each pin is obviously independent of the others. Thus, since there are 131 pins and two possible settings for each, the number of pin settings is 2^{131}. Having counted the number of pin settings, we now turn our attention to the lugs. Each individual bar of the lug cage carries exactly two lugs. Each of these lugs must occupy one of eight positions; two of which are non-effective while six correspond to the wheels. We first count the number of ways in which a particular bar may be set up, and then look at the ways of arranging all 27 of them.

The first possibility is to have no effective lugs at all on the bar. There is certainly only one way in which this can occur. If, however, a bar is to have exactly one effective lug then that lug may occupy any of the six wheel positions. Thus there are six ways of having exactly one effective lug. If we wish to count the number of ways we can arrange for a bar to have two effective lugs then we must enumerate the number of ways of occupying two positions out of six. But this is precisely the binomial coefficient $_6C_2$ or $\binom{6}{2}$, and is equal to $\dfrac{6!}{4!2!} = 15$. Thus there are $1 + 6 + 15 = 22$ ways of setting a given bar.

We must now determine the number of different ways in which the 27 bars can be set up. But since, during any encipherment, the cage makes a complete revolution, the order in which the various settings occur will not affect the outcome. Thus, for the lug cage setting as a whole, all that is relevant is how many of the individual bars are set in each of the 22 possible ways. But this means that counting the number of 'different' cage settings is equivalent to counting the number of ways in which 27 objects can be placed in 22 cells. This is a well known combinatorial problem and the answer is

$$_{48}C_{27} = \frac{48!}{27!21!} \approx 2 \cdot 23 \times 10^{13}.$$

(One way to see this is to represent the boundaries of the cells by vertical lines and the objects by asterisks. Any given allocation of the objects to the cells is then represented by a sequence of 23 straight lines and 27 asterisks. The order in which the asterisks and lines can appear is arbitrary except that, for obvious reasons, the first and last elements must both be lines. Thus we must count the number of ways of arranging 48 elements of which 27 are asterisks and 21 are lines. This is precisely $_{48}C_{27}$.)

Since we can take any pin setting with any lug setting, the total number of keys is $2^{131} \times 2 \cdot 23 \times 10^{13} \simeq 6 \cdot 075 \times 10^{52}$. As with many of the other examples we have met, trying the keys individually is out of the question. The cryptanalyst must establish alternative techniques.

We have already seen that there are a number of pin settings which should be avoided. This of course considerably reduces the number of 'good' keys. Similarly there are also certain lug cage settings that need to be avoided. We will say a little more about this at the end of the chapter. Meanwhile, for the rest of the chapter, we will assume that each wheel has at least one active pin and at least one inactive one.

2.3.4 Cryptanalysis

For the M-209, the time and work necessary for cryptanalysis depend greatly on the length of ciphertext which is known and whether any corresponding plaintext is known. In order to illustrate the principles behind this cryptanalysis we will concentrate our attention on three examples. Firstly we assume that we know the plaintext equivalent of a considerable length of ciphertext. Secondly we will discuss the case where only a short amount of plaintext is known, and finally we explore the situation where no plaintext is available. However, before we consider any examples, we will deduce relations between the shifts, pin and lug settings (i.e. the key) and the resulting substitution alphabet.

Any lug cage setting can be represented by a 27 by 6 array as in Table 2.2. Since, during any encipherment, the cage moves through a complete revolution, different settings may be equivalent (in the sense that they will result in the same ciphertext for a given plaintext letter). All that is relevant is the number of 1s in each given column and the number of rows in which each pair of columns both have 1s. The reason for this is as follows. The substitution alphabet is determined by the number of engagements between the bars of the lug cage and the basic pins during a complete revolution of the cage. But if a bar has two effective lugs and they both engage active pins simultaneously then this only counts as one bar engagement. Thus it is not merely the number of effective lugs which is important but also precisely when bars contain two effective lugs. With this in mind for any i with $1 \le i \le 6$ we let x_i denote the number of 1s in column i and for any j with $1 \le i \ne j \le 6$ we let x_{ij} be the number of rows where columns i and j both have 1s. (So x_i is the number of effective lugs corresponding to wheel i and x_{ij} is the number of positions in which wheels i and j both have effective lugs.) Clearly there are 6 x_is and, noting that x_{ij} is the same as x_{ji}, there are essentially 15 x_{ij}s. Knowledge of these 21 parameters completely determines the lug cage setting. Thus if the cryptanalyst computes these 21 parameters he will have discovered 'half' the key and will be a long way towards being able to resolve cryptograms. Before we turn our attention to the other 'half' of the key (i.e. the pin settings) we must point out that these 21 lug cage parameters are not independent. Knowing some of them definitely gives extra information about others. For instance, for any fixed i,

$$\sum_{\substack{j=1 \\ j \ne i}}^{j=6} x_{ij}$$

is an expression for the number of rows of the 27 by 6 array which contain two 1s and have one of them in column i. Clearly this cannot be larger than the total number of rows which have a 1 in column i. Thus, since this latter number is x_i, we have

$$x_i \ge \sum_{\substack{j=1 \\ j \ne i}}^{j=6} x_{ij} \quad \text{or, equivalently,} \quad x_i - \sum_{\substack{j=1 \\ j \ne i}}^{j=6} x_{ij} \ge 0.$$

(Note, by the way, that the left hand side of this inequality is the number of rows which have a single 1 in column i.) To simplify the notation slightly we will write

$$y_i = \sum_{\substack{j=1 \\ j \ne i}}^{j=6} x_{ij},$$

which means y_i is the number of double engagements involving wheel i. If every effective lug were to engage an active basic pin, then there would be

$$\sum_{i=1}^{i=6} x_i$$

engagements between lugs and basic pins. But, as we have already noted, the same bar might engage two active pins at once. So to count the number of bar engagements which determine the substitution alphabet we must subtract the number of double engagements. Since each double engagement involves two wheels,

$$\sum_{j=1}^{j=6} y_j$$

is twice the number of double engagements. Thus the maximum number of engagements is

$$\sum_{i=1}^{i=6} x_i - \tfrac{1}{2} \sum_{j=1}^{j=6} y_j.$$

However, there are only 27 bars. So the maximum number of possible engagements is 27, and we have

$$\sum_{i=1}^{i=6} x_i - \tfrac{1}{2} \sum_{j=1}^{j=6} y_j \le 27.$$

Since we are assuming that each wheel has at least one active pin, every effective lug will engage at least once. But this means that the only way in which a bar cannot be engaged at least once in a complete revolution of all the wheels is by having no effective lugs. Thus

$$\sum_{i=1}^{i=6} x_i - \tfrac{1}{2} \sum_{j=1}^{j=6} y_j = 27$$

unless there is a complete row of 0s in the array. Since we will wish to refer back to the simple inequalities just proved, we state them as a theorem.

THEOREM 2.1

    (i)   *For any i, $x_i - y_i \geq 0$;*

    (ii) $\sum_{i=1}^{i=6} x_i - \tfrac{1}{2} \sum_{j=1}^{j=6} y_j \leq 27$;

    (iii) $\sum_{i=1}^{i=6} x_i - \tfrac{1}{2} \sum_{j=1}^{j=6} y_j \neq 27$ *if and only if the 27 by 6 array has a complete row of 0s.*   □

In order to discuss the pin settings we can represent them in an array like Table 2.3. The array has six rows and each row has a different length. This means that, for the six wheels of lengths 26, 25, 23, 21, 19 and 17 respectively, we have the following variables (which all take the values 0 or 1).

$$a_1, a_2, a_3, \ldots\ldots\ldots\ldots\ldots\ldots\ldots\ldots\ldots a_{26}$$
$$b_1, b_2, b_3, \ldots\ldots\ldots\ldots\ldots\ldots\ldots b_{25}$$
$$c_1, c_2, c_3, \ldots\ldots\ldots\ldots\ldots c_{23}$$
$$d_1, d_2, d_3, \ldots\ldots\ldots\ldots d_{21}$$
$$e_1, e_2, e_3, \ldots\ldots\ldots e_{19}$$
$$f_1, f_2, f_3, \ldots\ldots f_{17}$$

Taking the first column as determining our basic pins, the shift for the first substitution alphabet is given by:

$\text{Shift}_1 = a_1 x_1 + b_1 x_2 + c_1 x_3 + d_1 x_4 + e_1 x_5 + f_1 x_6 - (a_1 b_1 x_{12} + a_1 c_1 x_{13} + a_1 d_1 x_{14} + a_1 e_1 x_{15} + a_1 f_1 x_{16} + b_1 c_1 x_{23} + b_1 d_1 x_{24} + b_1 e_1 x_{25} + b_1 f_1 x_{26} + c_1 d_1 x_{34} + c_1 e_1 x_{35} + c_1 f_1 x_{36} + d_1 e_1 x_{45} + d_1 f_1 x_{46} + e_1 f_1 x_{56}).$

To check the value for shift_1 we first note that

$$a_1 x_1 + b_1 x_2 + c_1 x_3 + d_1 x_4 + e_1 x_5 + f_1 x_6$$

counts the number of times contact is made between an active basic pin and a lug. But on each occasion that there are two effective lugs which make simultaneous contact with active pins the same bar engagement is being counted twice. Thus to compute shift_1 we must subtract from this total the number of times each bar makes contact with two active pins. If, for example, at least one of the basic pins on wheels 1 and 2 is inactive there will be no double contacts involving these wheels. If, on the other hand, they are both active the number of their double contacts will be x_{12}. Hence, in either case, the number of double contacts involving wheels 1 and 2 is $a_1 b_1 x_{12}$. A similar consideration for each pair of wheels in turn establishes the formula for $shift_1$. In fact a slight extension of the above gives the formula for the nth shift which is stated in Exercise 2.5.

EXERCISE 2.4   If the cage is set as in Table 2.2 and the pins are set as in Table 2.3 show that $shift_1 = 10$ and $shift_{15} = 22$. What is $shift_{58}$?

EXERCISE 2.5   Show that, for any n, $shift_n = a_{n_1} x_1 + b_{n_2} x_2 + c_{n_3} x_3 + d_{n_4} x_4 + e_{n_5} x_5 + f_{n_6} x_6 - (a_{n_1} b_{n_2} x_{12} + a_{n_1} c_{n_3} x_{13} + a_{n_1} d_{n_4} x_{14} + a_{n_1} e_{n_5} x_{15} + a_{n_1} f_{n_6} x_{16} + b_{n_2} c_{n_3} x_{23} + b_{n_2} d_{n_4} x_{24} + b_{n_2} e_{n_5} x_{25} + b_{n_2} f_{n_6} x_{26} + c_{n_3} d_{n_4} x_{34} + c_{n_3} e_{n_5} x_{35} + c_{n_3} f_{n_6} x_{36} + d_{n_4} e_{n_5} x_{45} + d_{n_4} f_{n_6} x_{46} + e_{n_5} f_{n_6} x_{56})$. Where $1 \le n_1 \le 26$, $1 \le n_2 \le 25$, $1 \le n_3 \le 23$, $1 \le n_4 \le 21$, $1 \le n_5 \le 19$, $1 \le n_6 \le 17$ and $n_1 \equiv n(mod\,26)$, $n_2 \equiv n(mod\,25)$, $n_3 \equiv n(mod\,23)$, $n_4 \equiv n(mod\,21)$, $n_5 \equiv n(mod\,19)$ and $n_6 \equiv n(mod\,17)$.

When discussing the cryptanalysis of the M-209 the following notation is helpful. For any i, l such that $1 \le i \le 6$ and for which wheel i has an lth pin, the (i, l)-**shifts** are those shifts to which the lth pin on the ith wheel contributes. (For example, if $i = 1$, we have $1 \le l \le 26$ while, if $i = 5$, l is restricted to $1 \le l \le 19$.) As illustrations, the $(1, 6)$-shifts are $shift_6$, $shift_{32}$, $shift_{58}$, ..., while the $(6, 15)$-shifts are $shift_{15}$, $shift_{32}$, $shift_{49}$, ... We will refer to those positions of the message which are enciphered using the (i, l)-shifts as the (i, l)-**positions**. Thus the $(1,6)$-positions are merely $6, 32, 58, \ldots$

Consider wheel i. If its lth pin is active then whenever it is in a basic position, i.e. for any of the (i, l)-shifts, there will be x_i bar engagements involving this particular pin. Thus, if r is the minimum number of bar engagements observed for all these (i, l)-positions, we have $r \ge x_i$. If, on the other hand, its lth pin is inactive then, for any of the (i, l)-shifts, each bar which has a solitary effective lug corresponding to wheel i will not be engaged during the complete revolution. So, if s is the maximum number of bar engagements observed for all these (i, l)-positions, the number of rows which have a 1 in column i and all other entries 0 is at most $27 - s$. This may be restated as $x_i - y_i \le 27 - s$. These last two inequalities are also very useful and we state them as a theorem.

THEOREM 2.2   For any given i, $1 \le i \le 6$
  (i)   *If r is the minimum number of bar engagements observed for all (i, l)-positions with the lth pin active then $r \ge x_i$.*
  (ii) *If s is the maximum number of bar engagements observed for all (i, l)-positions with the lth pin inactive then $x_i - y_i \le 27 - s$.*   □

2.3.5 An example of cryptanalysis with known plaintext

We now put ourselves in the position of the cryptanalyst and consider an example where we actually know the plaintext equivalent of about 500 ciphertext characters. In other words we know the actual shifts of roughly 500 of the substitution alphabets which were used. It is important to note immediately that we do not necessarily know the number of bar engagements for all these sets of basic pins. The reason for this is that there are only 26 possibilities for the size of the shift but, since there are 27 lug bars, the number of engagements in a complete revolution is not necessarily known even when the shift has been determined. The ambiguous cases are a shift of 0, which may arise from 0 or 26 engagements, and a shift of 1 which can come from 1 or 27. For our example we will not give the known ciphertext and corresponding plaintext. Instead we assume that we have rearranged the equation $\mu \equiv 1 + \kappa - \lambda \pmod{26}$ to give the appropriate shifts. Thus Table 2.4 gives a list of the known consecutive shifts and we mark with an asterisk those shifts which do not determine uniquely the number of engagements. The method for cryptanalysis which we discuss here is based on that of Robert Morris [7].

We begin by looking at the (i, l)-positions for all possible i and l. For each of these positions we compute the average of all the shifts except that, at this stage, we ignore all the ambiguous ones, i.e. all shifts of 0 or 1. The results are shown in Table 2.5 where, for each l, the average is given in the right hand column. Note that Table 2.4 has been transposed before being used to give Table 2.5, i.e. the rows of Table 2.4 are the columns of Table 2.5. This means that the first column of the table for wheel 1 is the first 26 entries of Table 2.4 (going along the first row and then the second) while the first column for wheel 6 is only the first 17 entries.

If we now look, for instance, at wheel 6, we see that the averages are 14·8, 13·5, 20·7, 13·3, 11·7, 19·3, 19·9, 20·6, 12·1, 20·3, 11·7, 20·1, 19·7, 12·7, 20·0, 20·0 and 13·9. Writing them in increasing order we get 11·7, 11·7, 12·1, 12·7, 13·3, 13·5, 13·9, 14·8, 19·3, 19·7, 19·9, 20·0, 20·0, 20·1, 20·3, 20·6 and 20·7. (Note that there is no value between 14·8 and 19·3.) Furthermore the averages fall into two sizeable clusters which are between 11 and 15 and between 19 and 21. There is a good reason for this division into two groups. If the lth pin on a wheel is inactive (i.e. set at 0) then the average shift which we obtain is the contribution from the five other wheels. But if the lth pin is active, the listed average shift includes a contribution from this wheel. We therefore expect the average to be smaller if the pin is inactive. Furthermore the larger the number of effective lugs corresponding to a given wheel (i.e. for wheel i the larger the value of x_i), the more distinguishable are the two clusters. To exhibit this phenomenon more clearly, we draw histograms for the six wheels. These are shown in Figure 2.4. (Note that in the column corresponding to, for instance, 19 we include all averages between 18·5 and 19·49.)

Two facts emerge quite clearly from these histograms. The first is that wheels 2, 5 and 6 all exhibit an obvious bimodality; i.e. their values occur in two very definite clusters. The second is that the values for wheels 1, 3 and 4 tend to be in one cluster rather than being scattered over a large range. Since their actual values are fairly large, this latter fact indicates that corresponding to wheels 1, 3 and 4 there are probably very few effective lugs (i.e. x_1, x_3 and x_4 are small), while the former enables us to guess the pin settings for wheels 2, 5 and 6. To make this guess we assume merely that averages in the cluster with the larger values correspond to a 1 (an active pin), and that those in the other cluster have a 0 (an inactive pin). Since this is based on a very crude statistical analysis, if we tried to resolve all pins there would probably be a few errors and so we should do everything possible to draw attention to positions where errors would be most likely to occur. With this in mind we will mark with a ? any position where the average value is not really in either of the two clusters. For wheel 6 there are no such positions but for wheel 2 the averages of 16·5 and 17·3 clearly come under this category. Thus our first guess at some of the pin settings is:

> *Wheel 2*   0110100?1?011001011010001
> *Wheel 5*   11?0010101001010001
> *Wheel 6*   00100111010110110

Since our guess for wheel 6 does not contain any question marks, we will assume it is correct and proceed using that assumption. It is important to stress here that we are only working through one particular example and not attempting to give a rigorous method for cryptanalyzing the M-209. In this example we have been 'lucky' in the sense that we have a wheel with no question marks. Our attitude when working any example will be to utilize any 'luck' which we have, and not worry about what we should do in a 'worse' situation. Nevertheless the reader should be aware of problems which might arise in other examples and decide for himself how he might cope with them.

On the assumption that wheel 6 is correct we can now use its setting to determine the actual number of bar engagements corresponding to the ambiguous shift values 0* and 1*. (To do this we assume that any ambiguous shift value of 0* or 1* in positions which occur in a high average cluster should be 26 or 27 while those in the low average cluster should be 0 or 1.) Once we have done this we can recalculate the averages for all wheels, draw new histograms and, if it seems necessary, revise our guesses. We will not give a list of the new averages for this example but they do not contradict our guess and, in fact, appear to resolve the ? positions on wheels 2 and 5 to give:

> *Wheel 2*   0110100010011001011010001
> *Wheel 5*   1110010101001010001

```
10  22   0*   5  15  22  15  22  11  22   5  19  25   0*  22  22
 1*  13  23  20  24  10  16  18  25   6  25  11  22  22   6  22
14  24   0*   6  22  20  12  19   0*  18  11  25   6  23  18  12
14  22  14  15  20  15  15   4  22  22  23  15  15  15   0*  14
12  21  21  15  13  10  21   9   6  15  20  22  23   0*  12  20
18  13  18  26   0*  15  13  22  15   3  24  14  22  15  18  20
22  19   6  21  19  15  23   6  25   0*   6  22  22  22   3  22
10  22  22  20  18  21  14  15  13  19   6  10  22  16  23  15
22  14  16  16  13   0*  22  15  11  13  20   4  24  16  24  21
 5   0*   3  18  18  13  17  25  22  13  23  17   3  10  21  22
17  24  21   4  20  22  15  21  20   3  24  14  20  12  13  15
25  21   9  22  15  17  16  22  18  22  13  15   3  22  22  15
 0*  21  16  19  17  13  16  23   5  21   0*   3  22   5  18   5
22  20  22   0*  15  18  12  22  18  14  25  16  10  10   6  22
13   3  22  25  22  22  20   4  18   0*   1*  20  22  23   5   4
25   4  19  22  18  21  12  18  15   0*  16  13  25  16  24   0*
12  18  14  14  15  25  21   5  18  22  20   0*  19  18  21  12
 3   9  22  15  11  21  22  20  14  15   3  22  22  15  24  25
 6   4  24  17  22  15  19  22  18  10  16  22  17  21  11  20
 0*  10  15   1*  21  15   4   0*  19  20   6  22  15  22  24   6
21  17  14   9  22  19  14  15  19  21  22   0*  22  10  16  22
14   0*  16   0*  15  15  25  23   9  22  14  21   6  24   3  25
22   6  23  16  15   0*  15  16   9  24   0*  22  15  10  22  13
 0*  18  19  18  16  14  15  10  21  13   5   0*  20  18  15  21
 5  18  20  24  17  22  13   1*  24  22  14  15  15  18  20  23
22  22  19  16  24  18  18   1*  24   1*  18  22  11  22  18  21
 3  24  24  22   0*   6  16  21  13  15  13  23   1*  13  22  17
20  11  18   3  25  25   9  22  22   5  22  13  22  15  15  18
14  25   3   0*  13  16  19  12  22  21  22   0*   6  25  13  12
16   0*  18  15  24   0*   0*  18   4  17  25  13  22  24  18  13
 9  16  22  22  12  16  14  25  18  10  20  18  15  23   9  25
13   6  18
```

Table 2.4
The known shift values

WHEEL 1

																				Average
10	25	20	12	25	16	3	16	22	1*	15	24	19	16	15	13	3	22	24	9	16·3
22	11	15	20	0*	16	10	22	20	20	25	25	20	0*	10	1*	24	13	0*	25	18·6
0*	22	15	18	6	13	21	18	22	22	21	6	6	15	22	24	24	22	0*	13	17·2
5	22	4	13	22	0*	22	22	0*	23	5	4	22	15	13	22	22	15	18	6	15·3
15	6	22	18	22	22	17	13	15	5	18	24	15	25	0*	14	0*	15	4	18	16·0
22	22	22	0*	22	15	24	15	18	4	22	17	22	23	18	15	6	18	17		17·9
15	14	23	15	3	11	21	3	12	25	20	22	24	9	19	18	16	14	25		16·2
22	24	15	13	22	13	4	22	22	4	0*	15	6	22	18	20	21	25	13		16·7
11	0*	15	22	10	20	20	22	18	19	19	19	21	14	16	23	13	3	22		16·4
22	6	15	15	22	4	22	15	14	22	18	22	17	21	14	22	15	0*	24		17·7
5	22	0*	3	22	24	15	0*	25	18	21	18	14	6	15	22	13	13	18		16·8
19	20	14	24	20	16	21	21	16	21	12	10	9	24	10	19	23	16	13		16·3
25	12	12	14	18	24	20	16	10	12	3	16	22	3	21	16	1*	13	9		15·8
0*	19	21	22	21	21	3	19	10	18	9	22	19	25	13	24	13	12	16		16·2
22	18	15	15	14	5	24	17	6	15	22	17	14	22	5	18	22	22	22		17·6
22	0*	13	18	15	0*	14	13	22	0*	15	21	15	6	0*	18	17	21	22		16·8
1*	11	10	20	13	3	20	16	13	16	11	11	19	23	20	1*	20	22	12		15·5
13	25	21	22	19	18	12	23	3	13	21	20	21	16	18	24	11	0*	0*		16·4
23	6	9	19	6	18	13	5	22	25	22	0*	22	15	15	1*	18	6	16		16·5
20	23	6	6	10	13	15	21	25	16	20	10	0*	0*	21	18	3	14	14		17·2
24	18	15	21	22	17	25	0*	22	24	14	15	22	15	5	22	25	25	25		17·2
10	12	20	19	16	25	21	3	22	0*	15	1*	10	16	18	11	25	13	18		16·1
16	14	22	25	23	22	9	22	20	12	3	21	16	9	20	22	9	12	10		15·9
18	22	23	23	15	13	22	5	4	18	22	15	22	24	24	18	22	16	20		17·9
25	14	0*	6	22	23	15	18	18	14	22	4	14	0*	17	18	22	18	18		18·1
6	15	17	14	17	5	0*	22	0*	14	15	0*	22	15	5	5	15	23			14·5

WHEEL 2

																				Average
10	6	14	22	19	16	17	15	5	3	16	15	17	19	3	10	22	15	3	13	13·0
22	25	15	23	15	23	25	25	21	22	13	11	21	14	25	21	22	13	0*	22	19·9
0*	11	20	0*	23	15	22	21	0*	25	25	21	11	15	22	13	19	23	13	24	19·0
5	22	15	12	6	22	13	9	3	22	16	22	20	19	6	5	16	1*	16	18	14·1
15	22	15	20	25	14	23	22	22	22	24	20	0*	21	23	0*	24	13	19	13	19·8
22	6	4	18	0*	16	17	15	5	20	0*	14	10	22	16	20	18	22	12	9	14·8
15	22	22	13	6	16	3	17	18	4	12	15	15	0*	15	18	18	17	22	16	14·9
22	14	22	18	22	13	10	16	5	18	18	3	1*	22	0*	15	1*	20	21	22	16·5
11	24	23	0*	22	0*	21	22	22	0*	14	22	21	10	15	21	24	11	22	22	19·2
22	0*	15	0*	22	22	22	18	20	1*	14	22	15	16	16	5	1*	18	0*	22	17·3
5	6	15	15	3	15	17	22	22	20	15	15	4	22	9	18	18	3	6	16	13·3
19	22	15	13	22	11	24	13	0*	22	25	24	0*	14	24	20	22	25	25	14	19·7
25	20	0*	22	10	13	21	15	15	23	21	25	19	0*	0*	24	11	13	13	25	19·2
0*	12	14	15	22	20	4	3	18	5	5	6	20	16	22	17	22	9	9	18	13·7
22	19	12	3	22	4	20	22	12	4	18	4	6	0*	15	22	18	22	12	10	14·3
22	0*	21	24	20	24	22	22	22	25	22	24	22	15	10	13	21	22	16	20	20·6
1*	18	21	14	18	16	15	15	18	4	20	17	15	15	22	13	3	5	0*	18	15·1
13	11	15	22	21	24	21	0*	14	19	0*	22	22	25	13	1*	24	22	18	15	19·0
23	25	13	15	14	21	20	21	25	22	19	15	24	23	0*	24	24	13	15	23	20·3
20	6	10	18	15	5	3	16	16	18	18	19	6	9	18	22	22	22	24	9	13·9
24	23	21	20	19	0*	24	19	10	21	21	22	21	22	19	14	0*	15	0*	25	19·7
10	18	9	22	6	3	14	17	10	12	12	18	17	14	18	15	6	15	0*	13	14·0
16	12	6	19	10	18	20	13	6	18	3	10	14	21	16	18	16	18	18	6	13·0
18	14	15	6	22	18	12	16	22	15	9	16	9	6	14	20	21	14	4	18	14·5
25	22	20	21	22	13	13	23	13	0*	22	22	22	24	15	23	13	25	17	18	20·2

Table 2.5
The average shift for each (i, l)-position

WHEEL 3

																					Average
10	18	18	10	22	20	20	24	18	5	20	16	22	14	22	0*	1*	18	25	6	22	17·0
22	25	12	21	15	4	4	21	22	22	4	24	17	9	14	18	24	21	9	25	12	17·3
0*	6	14	9	18	24	24	4	13	20	18	0*	3	22	21	19	22	3	22	13	16	16·4
5	25	22	6	20	16	16	20	15	0*	12	12	24	19	6	18	14	24	22	12	14	16·0
15	11	14	15	22	24	24	22	3	1*	24	18	20	14	24	16	15	15	5	16	25	16·6
22	22	15	20	19	24	21	15	22	20	22	14	0*	15	3	18	15	22	22	0*	18	17·1
15	22	20	22	6	21	5	21	22	22	18	14	10	19	25	14	18	13	13	18	10	16·0
22	6	15	23	21	19	0*	20	15	23	22	14	15	21	22	15	20	22	22	15	20	16·7
11	22	15	0*	19	6	3	3	0*	5	23	15	25	22	6	10	23	15	15	24	18	15·9
22	14	4	12	15	10	18	24	21	4	21	24	5	23	16	21	22	16	18	0*	15	17·0
5	24	22	20	23	3	18	14	16	25	15	5	18	16	15	13	13	22	14	0*	23	17·1
19	0*	22	18	25	17	18	20	13	4	24	4	14	15	0*	22	22	17	13	18	9	15·8
25	6	23	13	22	25	13	12	20	19	25	10	16	13	20	6	11	24	25	4	25	16·8
0*	22	15	18	14	22	17	13	19	22	3	16	16	18	16	4	20	23	3	17	13	16·9
22	20	22	0*	22	16	25	15	24	20	22	15	9	24	15	19	18	1*	13	25	6	16·4
22	12	20	6	16	13	22	25	20	18	16	18	21	5	18	21	18	13	16	13	18	16·1
1*	19	15	0*	22	16	13	23	12	21	6	21	24	0*	15	18	24	22	22			17·9
13	0*	14	15	22	13	17	9	18	15	22	15	5	18	20	24	17	19	12	24		17·0
23	18	12	13	3	17	22	22	24	22	15	22	0*	18	24	1	20	12	18			15·6
20	11	21	22	22	10	16	24	22	24	19	24	18	20	1	18	11	22	13			16·4
24	25	21	3	25	21	22	15	18	6	22	15	24	17	18	22	22	21	9			16·9
10	6	15	10	22	22	16	10	22	21	11	10	17	22	3	11	18	9	16			16·1
16	23	13	14	22	13	17	22	13	18	25	15	16	13	9	13	17	16	22	0*	22	17·8

WHEEL 4

																							Average
10	11	14	0*	0*	23	18	20	22	22	4	25	9	19	22	14	0*	5	23	0*	5	13	22	15·5
22	25	12	15	6	15	18	3	22	0*	18	16	22	22	15	0*	15	0*	22	22	6	12	12	16·0
0*	6	21	13	22	22	13	24	15	12	0*	24	15	18	22	16	16	20	19	21	16	16	16	17·4
5	23	21	22	22	14	17	14	0*	18	1*	0*	11	10	24	0*	9	18	16	13	21	0*	14	17·3
15	18	15	22	22	16	25	20	21	12	20	12	21	16	6	15	24	15	24	15	13	18	25	16·7
22	12	13	3	3	16	22	12	16	22	22	18	22	22	21	15	0*	21	16	13	15	15	18	17·1
15	14	10	24	22	13	13	13	19	18	23	14	20	17	17	25	22	5	18	15	13	15	10	16·6
22	22	21	14	10	0*	23	15	17	14	5	14	14	21	14	23	15	18	18	18	23	24	20	17·2
11	14	9	22	22	22	17	25	13	25	4	15	14	14	9	9	10	18	1*	18	1*	0*	18	16·1
22	15	6	15	22	15	3	21	25	13	25	25	3	20	22	9	20	20	24	23	13	18	15	16·4
5	20	15	18	20	11	10	9	23	16	25	21	22	0*	19	14	13	24	1*	13	22	4	23	15·3
19	14	20	20	18	13	21	22	5	10	19	5	22	10	14	21	0*	17	18	22	17	17	9	15·8
25	24	23	22	21	20	22	15	21	6	22	18	15	15	15	6	18	13	22	20	20	25	25	18·5
0*	0*	19	14	4	24	17	17	0*	22	18	22	24	1*	19	24	19	22	11	11	11	13	13	16·5
22	22	0*	6	15	24	15	22	3	13	21	20	25	21	21	3	18	24	22	18	18	22	13	16·7
22	22	12	21	13	16	24	16	22	18	20	0*	6	15	22	25	16	22	18	3	25	24	6	17·3
1*	20	12	19	19	24	4	18	22	5	12	19	4	4	0*	22	14	14	3	25	9	18	18	16·9
13	12	20	15	23	10	5	22	5	22	18	18	24	15	22	6	15	15	25	25	0*	13	13	16·5
23	19	18	15	23	5	22	18	22	13	15	21	17	19	10	23	10	15	3	9	16	9	9	15·6
20	0*	18	6	22	0*	15	15	22	22	16	12	22	20	16	16	21	18	24	22	22	6	16	17·3
24	18	0*	0*	16	3	21	3	20	20	13	3	15	6	22	15	13	20	22	22	22	25	22	16·6

Table 2.5

The average shift for each (i, l)-position (*cont.*)

WHEEL 5

																				Average
10	20	12	22	23	22	20	0*	22	14	22	20	22	18	20	15	0*	9	25	24	19·0
22	24	19	23	0*	20	22	22	13	20	15	22	22	15	0*	24	10	22	23	0*	19·9
0*	10	0*	15	12	19	18	15	23	12	0*	0*	20	0*	19	25	15	19	9	22	17·7
5	16	18	15	20	6	21	11	17	13	21	15	4	16	18	6	1*	14	22	15	14·6
15	18	11	15	18	21	14	13	3	15	16	18	18	13	21	4	21	15	14	10	13·8
22	25	25	0*	13	19	15	20	10	25	19	12	0*	25	12	24	15	19	21	22	19·3
15	6	6	14	18	15	13	4	21	21	17	22	1*	16	3	17	4	21	6	13	13·8
22	25	23	12	0*	23	19	24	22	9	13	18	20	24	9	22	0*	22	24	0*	19·3
11	11	18	21	15	19	6	16	17	22	16	14	22	0*	22	15	19	0*	3	18	15·5
22	22	12	21	13	6	10	24	24	15	23	25	23	12	15	19	20	22	25	19	19·6
5	22	14	15	22	25	22	21	21	17	5	16	5	18	11	22	6	10	22	18	15·1
19	6	22	13	15	0*	16	5	4	16	21	10	4	14	21	18	15	16	6	16	14·0
25	22	14	22	22	22	23	0*	20	22	0*	10	25	14	22	10	22	22	23	14	19·6
0*	14	15	15	3	22	15	3	22	18	22	6	4	15	20	16	24	14	16	15	14·0
22	24	20	9	24	15	22	18	15	22	5	13	19	25	14	22	6	0*	15	10	19·0
22	0*	15	6	14	3	14	18	21	13	18	3	18	5	15	17	16	16	0*	21	14·9
1*	6	15	15	22	16	16	13	20	15	13	22	21	18	3	21	0*	0*	15	13	14·7
13	22	4	20	15	10	16	17	3	3	5	22	21	18	22	11	17	15	16	5	13·5
23	20	22	22	18	22	13	25	24	22	22	25	12	22	22	20	14	15	9	0*	20·0

WHEEL 6

																															Average
10	13	0*	15	13	15	15	23	15	11	13	24	15	22	10	5	0*	3	4	15	9	15	0*	15	1*	24	15	22	0*	22	23	14·8
22	23	6	20	20	10	13	13	3	23	23	14	3	5	6	4	12	9	24	1*	22	1*	15	10	24	22	1*	13	6	24	9	13·5
0*	20	22	15	15	21	22	6	22	18	17	20	22	18	22	25	18	22	17	21	19	25	16	21	22	18	18	22	25	18	25	20·7
5	24	20	15	15	9	15	0*	12	5	3	12	22	5	13	4	14	15	22	15	14	23	13	14	22	1*	15	13	13	13		13·3
15	10	12	4	4	6	3	6	13	15	10	13	15	22	3	19	14	11	15	4	15	9	24	5	11	13	13	15	12	9	6	11·7
22	16	19	22	15	24	24	4	15	0*	24	15	0*	20	22	22	0*	21	19	0*	4	22	0*	0*	22	15	15	18	16	16	18	19·3
15	18	0*	22	22	20	14	22	21	20	14	22	21	16	22	18	19	20	19	21	15	14	22	19	18	22	18	14	0*	22		19·9
22	25	18	23	23	22	22	16	22	16	24	22	16	0*	22	21	21	20	18	20	21	21	15	18	18	18	17	14	22	22		20·6
11	6	15	23	22	22	23	16	17	21	17	21′	16	20	15	22	5	14	10	6	0*	6	10	15	21	17	20	3	15	12		12·1
22	25	25	15	15	0*	18	24	9	19	21	5	24	9	19	15	22	18	16	22	24	16	22	21	24	3	11	24	16			20·3
5	11	6	15	12	20	22	23′	22	17	13	4	15	13	12	4	5	22	3	22	15	3	5	14	3	13	0*	14				11·7
19	22	22	23	23	0*	20	15	16	23	16	18	23	18	20	18	22	16	22	24	22	25	0*	20	24	0*	18	22	25			20·1
25	22	18	14	18	19	22	3	16	18	16	22	16	23	18	20	18	21	24	24	6	19	18	16	6	25	18	20	18			19·7
0*	6	12	13	19	6	16	14	22	5	14	18	6	0*	16	24	6	15	6	6	14	19	24	0*	9	12	4	10				12·7
22	22	14	21	21	18	23	20	18	21	18	21	5	14	20	18	16	24	18	21	18	23	18	17	16	22	17	20				20·0
22	14	22	21	21	0*	18	0*	25	20	21	22	0*	16	22	21	21	25	16	18	16	16	16	25	21	22	25	18				20·0
1*	24	22	21	21	15	14	13	13	13	3	3	13	10	23	24	12	10	14	0*	15	13	14	13	1*	13	15					13·9

Table 2.5

The average shift for each (i, l)-position (cont.)

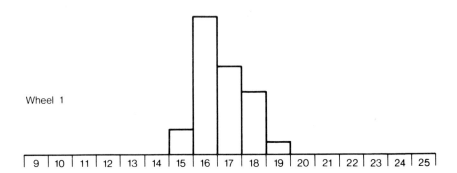

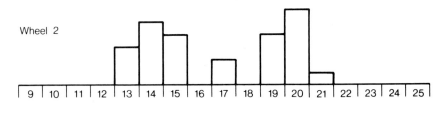

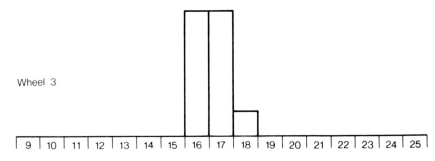

Figure 2.4
Histograms for six wheels

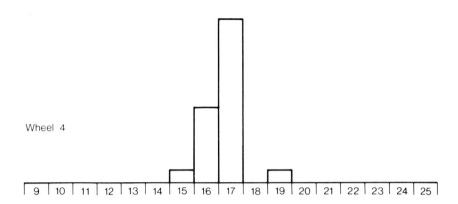

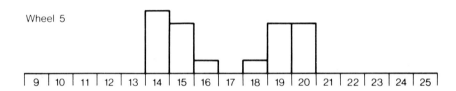

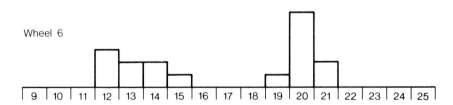

Figure 2.4
Histograms for six wheels (*cont.*)

EXERCISE 2.6   Assuming the pin settings for wheel 6 to be correct calculate the number of bar engagements for the ambiguous shifts. Use the new values to compute the new averages. Draw the new histograms and justify our guesses for wheels 2 and 5. (This is a long exercise. It is well worth doing but may be omitted if the reader is prepared to believe us!)

In this particular example, when we compute the actual numbers of bar engagements corresponding to the ambiguous shift values we find that there are never 27 engagements. Since we have a reasonably large sample, we will assume that this implies there will never be 27 engagements which, by Theorem 2.1 (iii), means that the lug cage has a row of 0s. Having made our guesses for the pin settings of wheels 2, 5 and 6, we can now see what Theorem 2.2 tells us about the lug settings corresponding to these positions. If we consider wheel 6 and look at the rows of Table 2.5 corresponding to those positions to which we have assigned a 1 (i.e. to rows 3, 6, 7, 8, 10, 12, 13, 15, 16) we see that the smallest entry is 14. Thus, from Theorem 2.2 (i), we know $x_6 \leq 14$. Similarly $x_2 \leq 10$ and $x_5 \leq 9$. If we now consider those positions to which we have assigned 0 and use Theorem 2.2 (ii), we get

$$x_6 - y_6 = x_6 - \sum_{m=1}^{m=5} x_{m6} \leq 3.$$

However, since we are assuming there is a complete row of 0s, this can be strengthened to $x_6 - y_6 \leq 2$ and implies that, in the 27 by 6 array, the sixth column has at most 14 1s and that at most 2 of the 14 corresponding rows have every other entry 0. Similar statements may be made about columns 2 and 5.

EXERCISE 2.7   Show that under our assumptions so far, $x_2 \leq 10$ and $x_2 - y_2 \leq 4$. Find similar inequalities for x_5 and y_5.

Although we have made considerable progress and know certain parts of the key, we are still a long way from determining the complete key, i.e. all the pin and lug settings. There are now two ways in which we can proceed. We can start to look at the equations of Exercise 2.5 and, under the assumptions we have already made, try to solve them simultaneously. If we are successful, this will certainly tell us the remaining pin and lug cage parameters. Alternatively, now that we know the settings for wheels 2, 5 and 6, we can try to remove their effect. This, of course, will increase the visible effect of the other wheels. Hopefully the statistics with wheels 2, 5 and 6 removed will 'spread out' the averages for the remaining wheels. They should then fall into two clusters and enable us to guess the remaining wheel settings. We will adopt the latter approach.

There are eight possibilities for the pin settings of the wheels 2, 5 and 6; namely 000, 001, 010, 011, 100, 101, 110 and 111. To remove the effect of these wheels we carry out a statistical analysis of the data for each one of the eight possibilities. With the question marks resolved our guesses for the wheel settings are:

> *Wheel 2* 0110100010011001011010001
> *Wheel 5* 1110010101001010001
> *Wheel 6* 00100111010110110

Thus, as a simple illustration, we see that the first shifts obtained when all three wheels are inactive (i.e. set at 000) are $shift_4$, $shift_{11}$, $shift_{14}$ and $shift_{17}$. Thus, by looking back at Table 2.4, the first 4 shifts with these wheels inactive are 5, 5, 0 and 1. (Note: we no longer have any ambiguous shifts. We have done Exercise 2.6 and know precisely when there were 0 engagements and when there were 26. We also know there were never 27 engagements.) In Table 2.6 we collect together the shifts for each of the eight possible settings of wheels 2, 5 and 6.

One of the most striking features of Table 2.6 is that, for each given setting, the numbers which occur are in one fairly tight cluster. This is encouraging and suggests that our guesses so far have been reasonable. When the pins are set at 000 the values attained are 0, 1, 3, 4, 5 and 6. These are all small. But, of course, this is what we expected. We have already decided that the majority of the lugs are on wheels 2, 5 and 6 and so, with all of these wheels inactive, we expect a small number of engagements. With the pins set at 001 the values are 14, 15, 16, 17, 18 which is almost the set obtained by adding 12, 13 or 14 to each of the numbers for the 000 setting. Thus it is reasonable to assume that the contribution of wheel 6 when wheels 2 and 5 are inactive is 12, 13 or 14. We have no logical reasons for choosing between these three possibilities. As a first try, for any possible settings of the three given wheels, we will assume that the contribution of the wheels in these settings is the smallest shift observed. Thus, for example, we assume that the contribution with wheel 6 active and the others inactive is 14. Similarly, when wheel 5 is the only one of the three active the contribution is 9 and if wheels 5 and 6 are active but wheel 2 is not the contribution is 18. Thus $x_6 = 14$, $x_5 = 9$ and $x_5 + x_6 - x_{56} = 18$ which, of course, implies that $x_{56} = 5$. We stress again that our statistical analysis is very crude and our guesses, while reasonable, are speculative. Thus we could easily be led to some inconsistent conclusions (e.g. if it had turned out that we put $x_5 = 3$ this would have led to a negative value for x_{56}). Inconsistent guesses must be modified, or at least noted.

Corresponding to each of the eight possible settings of wheels 2, 5 and 6 we have decided to subtract 0, 14, 9, 18, 10, 19, 18 or 23 respectively.

EXERCISE 2.8 Show that these guesses are consistent; i.e. there are no contradictions among the eight equations to which they give rise. Furthermore show that they imply: $x_2 = 10$, $x_5 = 9$, $x_6 = 14$, $x_{25} = 0$, $x_{26} = 0$, $x_{56} = 5$. (Hint: use Exercise 2.5)

Setting

000:	5	5	0	1	6	6	0	6	6	4	6	0	3	6	6	0	6	3
	6	4	7	3	3	4	3	3	5	3	5	5	6	3	4	1	5	4
	4	0	5	3	3	6	4	1	4	6	6	0	0	6	3	6	0	5
	5	1	1	1	3	6	1	3	5	3	0	6	0	4	6			

001:	15	16	18	14	18	18	14	15	15	14	15	18	18	14	16	16	16	16
	18	17	17	17	15	17	16	18	16	17	16	18	18	16	18	18	16	16
	18	15	18	18	15	17	18	16	17	17	16	16	14	16	16	15	18	18
	16	17	15	18	16	18	18	18	16	17	18	18	18	14	16	16	18	17
	18	16	16	18	18	18												

010:	10	10	12	12	14	15	12	10	9	12	13	15	15	15	10	13	15	13
	10	15	14	12	9	15	15	13	12	10	12	15	12	14	12	9	15	14
	15	10	10	15	15	15	14	9	15	9	15	9	14	10	15	14	15	9
	15	12	12	13	9	12	10	9	13									

011:	22	22	22	22	20	22	22	19	22	22	21	22	18	22	19	19	22	22
	22	22	18	19	22	22	20	18	22	20	20	22	22	20	22	18	22	22
	20	20	18	20	22	22	19	20	20	19	19	22	22	22	21	22	22	20
	18	18	22	20	22	18	22	22	21	22	20	22	22	22	21	22		

100:	15	11	13	11	11	15	15	15	15	13	13	15	15	10	14	13	15	14
	11	13	13	13	13	15	15	14	10	13	13	14	11	15	11	14	15	10
	14	15	15	10	13	15	13	13	15	11	13	13	13	11	13	15	13	13
	15	13	14	15														

101:	19	22	22	22	22	21	21	20	20	22	22	21	22	22	21	22	21	21
	21	22	21	20	21	22	21	21	22	22	22	22	21	21	21	22	21	20
	22	22	21	21	19	22	22	21	21	22	22	21	21	20	22	19	21	22
	19	22	20															

110:	22	23	24	24	20	20	23	20	23	20	24	22	23	24	24	22	22	19
	22	22	22	23	19	24	22	19	24	22	22	22	23	24	19	24	24	23
	22	24	24	22	24	22	22	22	24	23								

111:	26	25	25	25	26	25	23	23	26	26	26	24	25	23	26	24	26	25
	25	26	23	26	26	25	25	26	25	26	25	25	26	24	25	26	26	24
	26	25	24	25	23	26	26	26	24	26	23	25	25	25	26	25	26	24
	26	25	25	25														

Table 2.6

The shifts for each setting of wheels 2, 5 and 6

Now, to remove the effects of wheels 2, 5 and 6 we run through our table of displacements (Table 2.4) and, depending on our belief of the basic pins on wheels 2, 5 and 6, we make the relevant subtraction. For instance the first position in Table 2.4 is 10 and we believe the basic pins to have been

?0??10. Thus the setting for wheels 2, 5 and 6 is 010 and we subtract 9. We can use this modified Table 2.4 to recalculate our averages for the (i, l)-positions on wheels 1, 3 and 4. The results are given in Table 2.7.

For each wheel the averages divide nicely into two clusters and lead us to conclude the following wheel settings:

> *Wheel 1*   00111101011000110010100111
> *Wheel 3*   10011111101000101011010
> *Wheel 4*   01101100010010101101011

This means that we have now assigned all the pin settings. In order to check whether these assignations are reasonable, we look at the shifts which arise as a result of each of the 64 possibilities for the basic pin settings. If we are correct then there will be a consistency between the shifts for any one setting. The results are listed in Table 2.8.

```
                            WHEEL 1                                 Average
 1  2  1  3  2  2  3  2  3  1  1  1  0  2  1  3  3  3  1  0           1·8
 3  1  1  1  0  2  1  3  2  2  2  2  2  0  0  1  1  3  0  2           1·5
 3  4  5  4  6  4  2  4  4  3  2  6  6  5  4  5  5  4  3  4           4·1
 5  3  4  4  4  3  4  4  3  4  5  4  3  6  3  3  4  5  4  6           4·1
 5  6  4  4  3  4  3  3  5  5  4  5  6  2  3  5  3  6  4  4           4·2
 4  4  4  3  4  6  5  5  4  4  3  3  3  4  4  5  6  4  3              4·1
 1  0  0  0  3  1  2  3  3  2  2  3  1  0  0  1  2  0  2              1·4
 4  5  6  6  3  3  4  4  3  4  3  5  6  3  4  4  3  2  4              4·0
 1  0  1  3  0  2  2  3  0  0  0  1  2  0  2  2  3  3  3              1·5
 4  6  5  3  4  4  3  6  4  3  4  3  3  3  5  4  6  3  5              4·1
 5  3  3  6  4  5  6  3  2  4  2  4  5  6  5  4  3  3  4              4·1
 0  1  0  3  1  2  2  2  2  2  3  1  0  1  1  3  0  2  3              1·5
 2  3  3  1  0  1  1  2  0  3  3  2  3  3  2  0  1  0  0              1·6
 0  1  2  0  2  2  3  0  1  0  0  3  1  2  3  2  3  3  2              1·6
 4  3  3  3  4  5  5  3  6  6  3  3  4  3  5  5  4  4  4              4·1
 3  4  5  5  6  3  5  4  4  3  6  2  5  6  3  4  3  3  3              4·1
 1  1  3  0  3  3  2  2  3  2  1  1  1  0  2  0  2  3  3              1·7
 3  2  1  1  1  0  3  0  3  3  2  2  2  2  0  1  1  0  2              1·5
 4  6  2  4  6  4  3  5  3  2  4  3  4  6  6  5  4  6  4              4·3
 2  0  0  1  1  3  1  2  2  2  1  1  0  0  2  1  3  2  2              1·4
 5  4  6  6  3  3  2  3  4  5  5  6  4  5  5  4  2  3  4              4·2
 1  3  1  2  2  2  2  3  3  0  1  1  0  2  0  3  2  3  1              1·7
 2  0  1  1  0  3  0  3  2  3  3  2  2  0  1  1  0  2  1              1·4
 4  3  4  5  5  4  3  5  4  4  3  6  4  5  5  4  4  3  4              4·2
 2  5  4  4  4  4  6  4  4  4  4  4  3  3  4  3  4  5              3·9
 6  5  3  6  4  3  3  5  3  5  6  3  3  4  4  2  5  5  4              4·2
```

Table 2.7
The new averages

WHEEL 3

Values	Average
1 4 4 1 3 1 2 5 4 5 2 2 1 3 5 3 3 1 4 2 6 3	3·0
3 2 3 2 5 0 4 2 4 3 4 5 2 3 0 0 4 5 2 0 2 3	2·6
3 6 0 0 0 2 5 4 3 2 4 0 4 2 3 3 0 3 3 4 3 2	2·5
5 2 3 6 1 4 2 2 5 4 3 3 1 1 1 6 4 5 1 3 3 4	3·1
5 1 5 1 4 6 1 3 3 3 1 4 5 2 4 1 2 5 5 5 2 2	3·2
4 4 5 1 1 3 2 6 4 5 2 4 1 3 5 3 5 1 4 3 3 4	3·3
1 3 1 4 6 1 5 2 3 4 3 5 3 1 1 2 5 4 3 3 4 1	3·0
4 6 1 4 2 6 3 1 6 3 4 1 3 6 2 3 1 2 6 4 5 1	3·4
1 4 5 3 1 1 3 3 3 3 5 2 4 1 4 6 2 4 2 5 1 4	3·0
4 0 4 3 5 3 0 5 2 0 4 2 6 2 0 0 3 4 3 6 0 5	2·8
5 5 4 1 4 2 4 5 2 4 2 5 1 6 4 2 5 3 3 4 3 4	3·5
0 0 4 4 6 0 3 2 0 2 4 4 2 4 0 6 3 0 6 0 4 0	2·5
2 6 0 4 2 5 3 3 3 2 0 3 6 3 2 0 2 2 3 2 4 2	2·7
0 3 6 4 0 4 2 3 4 0 3 2 4 0 4 5 0 5 0 3 3 4	2·7
4 1 1 3 6 4 3 1 2 1 4 3 5 2 4 2 6 4 1 3 2 6	3·1
3 3 5 0 4 2 4 2 0 6 2 0 3 6 3 0 2 0 3 3 4 4	2·7
1 1 3 6 3 2 4 2 5 4 3 4 3 3 2 5 5 1 4 2 3	3·1
3 3 0 3 4 4 3 0 2 3 0 2 5 6 0 3 0 5 3 0 7	2·6
4 4 3 3 3 3 3 3 3 3 6 3 1 3 5 4 1 1 2 3 4	3·1
2 1 2 6 3 4 1 6 3 3 3 3 3 1 6 1 5 4 1 4 3	3·1
5 2 3 3 0 6 2 3 3 2 2 0 4 6 2 0 3 3 4 3 0	2·7
1 6 5 1 4 1 4 2 5 4 3 3 1 2 4 4 4 1 3 3 2	3·0
2 0 3 0 4 3 3 3 4 3 2 6 2 3 0 3 3 4 2 0 4	2·6

WHEEL 4

Values	Average
1 1 1 0 0 0 0 0 1 4 4 4 2 0 1 3 4 0 5 4 3 5 3 3	2·0
3 2 2 3 6 6 5 4 3 3 3 4 2 3 3 6 3 5 3 4 6 3 3 3	3·7
3 4 6 2 3 4 4 3 5 6 5 3 5 6 4 3 2 2 2 3 2 3 2 2	3·5
5 2 0 3 3 3 4 3 5 3 4 1 0 1 1 1 0 0 0 0 3 4 3 4	2·2
5 6 4 5 6 4 2 2 2 2 3 2 3 2 2 6 5 5 6 2 3 7 4 2	3·7
4 2 3 3 3 3 2 3 3 2 3 3 4 4 3 2 6 3 2 5 6 6 5 4	3·5
1 1 0 1 1 3 4 4 3 0 0 4 4 1 3 3 2 4 5 4 3 4 1 1	2·4
4 4 3 2 0 0 3 4 1 3 4 5 5 5 2 5 4 1 0 0 0 0 0 1	2·3
1 3 5 0 3 4 4 3 2 4 2 4 1 1 1 0 0 0 1 1 1 2 3 4	2·1
4 6 5 6 5 4 6 3 2 2 2 2 2 3 2 3 3 4 5 5 3 3 4 5	3·7
5 4 1 1 0 1 1 1 4 0 0 0 4 2 3 3 1 0 3 3 1 3 4 4	2·0
0 0 1 1 1 0 3 2 3 5 1 0 5 4 1 4 3 3 4 4 3 3 3 0	2·3
2 5 5 4 4 2 2 4 6 2 6 3 4 6 6 5 6 4 3 3 2 2 2 2	3·8
0 0 4 4 1 4 4 3 3 3 4 4 3 1 1 1 1 1 0 1 1 1 0 4 4	2·2
4 6 4 3 6 6 5 5 2 3 3 2 2 2 2 2 3 4 5 4 4 3 3 6	3·7
3 3 4 3 2 3 2 2 3 3 3 3 3 6 6 4 2 2 3 4 3 4 7 4	3·3
1 1 0 1 1 1 1 4 4 5 3 0 0 4 4 0 3 5 5 2 2 3 4	2·3
3 3 6 4 5 6 2 2 4 4 2 6 4 5 3 4 6 5 7 3 2 3 3	3·9
4 1 1 4 4 1 5 3 3 5 4 3 2 3 0 0 0 1 1 1 0 0 0	2·0
2 3 5 4 6 3 3 6 5 3 3 2 3 3 2 2 2 2 4 5 4 6 2	3·5
5 4 3 3 2 2 3 2 3 2 2 3 3 5 6 4 6 3 2 4 3 2 4	3·3

Table 2.7
The new averages (cont.)

Setting

Setting															
000000:	0	0	0	0	0	0	0	0	0	0					
000001:	14	14	14	14	14	14									
000010:	9	9	9	9	9	9	9	9	9						
000011:	18	18	18	18	18	18	18	18							
000100:	3	3	3												
000101:	16	16	16	16	16	16	16	16							
000110:	12	12	12	12	12										
000111:	20	20	20	20											
001000:	1	1	1	1	1	1	1								
001001:	15	15	15	15	15	15	15	15	15						
001010:	10	10	10	10	10	10	10	10	10	10					
001011:	19	19	19	19	19	19	19								
001100:	3	3	3	3	3	3	3	3	3	3	3				
001101:	16	16	16	16	16	16	16	16	16	16	16	16	16	16	16
001110:	12	12	12	12	12	12	12								
001111:	20	20	20	20	20	20	20	20	20						
010000:	10	10	10	10											
010001:	19	19	19	19											
010010:	19	19	19	19											
010011:	23	23	23	23	23	23									
010100:	13	13	13	13	13	13	13	13							
010101:	21	21	21	21	21	21	21	21							
010110:	22	22	22	22	22	22	22								
010111:	25	25	25	25	25	25	25	25							
011000:	11	11	11	11	11	11	11	11							
011001:	20	20	20	20	20	20									
011010:	20	20	20	20											
011011:	24	24	24	24	24	24	24								
011100:	13	13	13	13	13										
011101:	21	21	21	21	21	21	21	21							
011110:	22	22	22	22	22	22	22	22							
011111:	25	25	25	25	25	25	25								
100000:	4	4	4	4	4	4	4	4	4						
100001:	17	17	17	17	17	17	17	17	17	17	17				
100010:	13	13	13	13	13	13									
100011:	21	21	21	21											
100100:	6	6	6	6	6	6	6								
100101:	18	18	18	18	18	18	18	18	18	18					
100110:	15	15	15	15	15	15	15	15							
100111:	22	22	22	22	22	22	22	22	22	22	22	22	22		
101000:	5	5	5	5	5	5	5	5	5	5	5				
101001:	18	18	18	18	18	18	18	18							
101010:	14	14	14	14	14	14	14								
101011:	22	22	22	22	22	22	22	22	22	22	22	22	22	22	
101100:	6	6	6	6	6	6	6	6	6	6	6				
101101:	18	18	18	18	18	18	18	18	18	18	18				

Table 2.8

The shifts for each possible basic pin setting

Setting

Setting													
101110:	15	15	15	15	15	15	15	15	15	15	15		
101111:	22	22	22	22	22	22	22	22	22	22	22		
110000:	13	13	13	13	13	13	13						
110001:	21	21	21	21	21	21							
110010:	22												
110011:	25	25	25	25	25	25	25						
110100:	15	15	15	15	15	15	15						
110101:	22	22	22	22	22								
110110:	24	24	24	24	24	24	24	24					
110111:	26	26	26	26	26	26							
111000:	14	14	14	14	14	14	14						
111001:	22	22	22	22	22	22	22	22	22	22	22	22	22	22
111010:	23	23	23	23	23	23	23	23					
111011:	26	26	26	26	26	26	26	26	26	26			
111100:	15	15	15	15	15	15	15	15	15	15	15	15	
111101:	22	22	22	22	22	22	22						
111110:	24	24	24	24	24	24							
111111:	26	26	26	26	26	26	26						

Table 2.8
The shifts for each possible basic pin setting (*cont.*)

As is soon apparent, the shift is a constant for each setting. This is much better than we dared to hope for and we are now fairly confident that our pin settings are correct. (If the results of Table 2.8 had not been quite so conclusive, what else could we have tried?) All that remains is to determine the lug cage parameters. But this is now comparatively easy.

If we look at Table 2.8 the shift for the setting 100000 is 4 which, of course, implies $x_1 = 4$. Similarly $x_2 = 10$, $x_3 = 1$, $x_4 = 3$, $x_5 = 9$ and $x_6 = 14$. To determine, for example, x_{34} we note that for a setting of 001100 the shift is 3. Thus $3 = x_3 + x_4 - x_{34}$. But we already know $x_3 = 1$ and $x_4 = 3$ which gives $x_{34} = 1$. In this simple way we can compute every parameter. We get:

$$x_1 = 4 \quad x_{12} = 1 \quad x_{13} = 0 \quad x_{14} = 1 \quad x_{15} = 0 \quad x_{16} = 1$$
$$x_2 = 10 \quad x_{23} = 0 \quad x_{24} = 0 \quad x_{25} = 0 \quad x_{26} = 5$$
$$x_3 = 1 \quad x_{34} = 1 \quad x_{35} = 1 \quad x_{36} = 0$$
$$x_4 = 3 \quad x_{45} = 0 \quad x_{46} = 1$$
$$x_5 = 9 \quad x_{56} = 5$$
$$x_6 = 14.$$

Thus it is now apparent that the pin and lug cage settings for this example are those given in Table 2.3 and Table 2.2 respectively.

It should be clear from this example that if sufficient plaintext is known then breaking a message enciphered with an M-209 is comparatively easy. However, as the size of known plaintext decreases the difficulty of cryptanalysis increases dramatically. It is extremely unlikely that we would be presented with such obvious candidates for our guesses, and would certainly have a lot less confidence in them. There may even be times when a sensible guess is impossible. This may lead us to consider our equations of Exercise 2.5 at a much earlier stage of the analysis. Before we proceed to consider a smaller (and more realistic!) example we make one final observation about our last example. Despite the large size of the sample, shifts of 7, 8, 12, 16 and 27 did not occur. Since our example was so large we did not need to make use of this observation. But if we had heeded this information it could have aided us in determining the lug cage parameters. In general when dealing with a smaller sample it is necessary to utilize every possible scrap of information.

As we mentioned in the Introduction, we will make no attempt to offer so much detailed description and justification for the next example. We therefore recommend that it need only be studied by the reader who is particularly interested in the application of these techniques to a smaller example. However the methods of Section 2.3.7 are sufficiently different that all readers should see them.

2.3.6 A smaller example of cryptanalysis with known plaintext

Now that we have seen the principles involved in breaking the M-209 we will look at a smaller example where we have only 76 characters of corresponding plaintext and ciphertext. We have chosen to use 76 characters as it appears that, in order to be effective, this method generally requires about 3 (i, l)-shifts, for each i and l. Since the largest value for l is 26 this implies we need about 78 characters of corresponding plaintext and ciphertext. So for this example we are assuming that we know 76 shift values and these are exhibited in Table 2.9.

22	23	13	0*	23	23	2	14	25	5	17	15	0*	13	15	7
23	15	21	12	15	24	19	3	9	23	12	24	11	19	11	10
14	25	15	1*	7	4	0*	0*	12	9	15	14	15	12	1*	7
3	12	23	25	23	7	15	15	24	14	11	22	9	19	12	20
15	12	6	19	25	22	12	16	18	24	7	7				

Table 2.9
The known shift values

Although we will tackle the cryptanalysis in the same way, the essential difference between this example and the previous one is that, since we know a much smaller number of shifts, we must exercise considerably more care in our guessing.

In the last example every guess which we made was natural in the sense that it was an obvious one. Although there was always the possibility of error the sample was large enough that, at each stage, we were able to feel reasonably confident in our predictions. In this example, because the sample is so small, there will not often be such a clear-cut difference between the various possibilities and we must be more prepared to

Wheel 1				Average
22	12	23		19·0
23	24	7		18·0
13	11	15		13·0
0*	19	15		17·0
23	11	24		19·3
23	10	14		15·7
2	14	11		9·0
14	25	22		20·3
25	15	9		16·3
5	1*	19		12·0
17	7	12		12·0
15	4	20		13·0
0*	0*	15		15·0
13	0*	12		12·5
15	12	6		11·0
7	9	19		11·7
23	15	25		21·0
15	14	22		17·0
21	15	12		16·0
12	12	16		13·3
15	1*	18		16·5
24	7	24		18·3
19	3	7		9·7
3	12	7		7·3
9	23			16·0
23	25			24·0

Wheel 2				Average
22	23	23	7	18·8
23	12	25		20·0
13	24	23		20·0
0*	11	7		9·0
23	19	15		19·0
23	11	15		16·3
2	10	24		12·0
14	14	14		14·0
25	25	11		20·3
5	15	22		14·0
17	1*	9		13·0
15	7	19		13·7
0*	4	12		8·0
13	0*	20		16·5
15	0*	15		15·0
7	12	12		10·3
23	9	6		12·7
15	15	19		16·3
21	14	25		20·0
12	15	22		16·3
15	12	12		13·0
24	1*	16		20·0
19	7	18		14·7
3	3	24		10·0
9	12	7		9·3

Wheel 3				Average
22	3	1*	22	15·7
23	9	7	12	12·8
13	23	3	16	13·8
0*	12	12	18	14·0
23	24	23	24	23·5
23	11	25	7	16·5
2	19	23	7	12·8
14	11	7		10·7
25	10	15		16·7
5	14	15		11·3
17	25	24		22·0
15	15	14		14·7
0*	1*	11		11·0
13	7	22		14·0
15	4	9		9·3
7	0*	19		13·0
23	0*	12		17·5
15	12	20		15·7
21	9	15		15·0
12	15	12		13·0
15	14	6		11·7
24	15	19		19·3
19	12	25		18·7

Wheel 4				Average
22	24	15	20	20·3
23	19	14	15	17·8
13	3	15	12	10·8
0*	9	12	6	9·0
23	23	1*	19	21·7
23	12	7	25	16·8
2	24	3	22	12·8
14	11	12	12	12·3
25	19	23	16	20·8
5	11	25	18	14·8
17	10	23	24	18·5
15	14	7	7	10·8
0*	25	15	7	15·7
13	15	15		14·3
15	1*	24		19·5
7	7	14		9·3
23	4	11		12·7
15	0*	22		18·5
21	0*	9		15·0
12	12	19		14·3
15	9	12		12·0

Wheel 5				Average
22	12	0*	14	16·0
23	15	0*	11	16·3
13	24	12	22	17·8
0*	19	9	9	12·3
23	3	15	19	15·0
23	9	14	12	14·5
2	23	15	20	15·0
14	12	12	15	13·3
25	24	1*	12	20·3
5	11	7	6	7·3
17	19	3	19	14·5
15	11	12	25	15·8
0*	10	23	22	18·3
13	14	25	12	16·0
15	25	23	16	19·8
7	15	7	18	11·8
23	1*	15	24	20·7
15	7	15	7	11·0
21	4	24	7	14·0

Wheel 6					Average
22	15	15	25	25	20·4
23	21	1*	23	22	22·3
13	12	7	7	12	10·2
0*	15	4	15	16	12·5
23	24	0*	15	18	20·0
23	19	0*	24	24	22·5
2	3	12	14	7	7·6
14	9	9	11	7	10·0
25	23	15	22		21·3
5	12	14	9		10·0
17	24	15	19		18·8
15	11	12	12		12·5
0*	19	1*	20		19·5
13	11	7	15		11·5
15	10	3	12		10·0
7	14	12	6		9·8
23	25	23	19		22·5

Table 2.10
Averages for (i, l)-positions

discover that we have guessed incorrectly. We begin, as before, by computing the averages for the (i, l)-positions, which we show in Table 2.10 and then drawing the corresponding histograms (see Figure 2.5).

With such a small sample it is not surprising that there is not quite the same strong evidence of bimodality. Clearly the wheel for which the averages come closest to falling into two clusters is wheel 6. We may feel tempted to 'see' a bimodality pattern for one or two other wheels but, with such a small example, this might prove misleading. It is better to make our guesses one wheel at a time and then remove the effect of that wheel before guessing another. In this case our guess for wheel 6 is:

Wheel 6 11001100101010001

Assuming those settings to be correct we can now resolve the ambiguous positions.

EXERCISE 2.9 Resolve all the ambiguous positions.

From Exercise 2.9 we know that in position 47 we get 27 engagements which means that our 27 by 6 array does not contain a row of all zeros. When we appeal to Theorem 2.2 we see that $x_6 \leq 15$ and

$$x_6 - \sum_{j=1}^{j=5} x_{6j} \leq 11$$

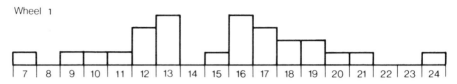

Wheel 1

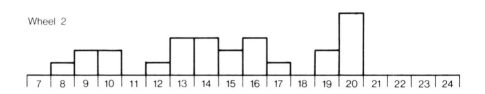

Wheel 2

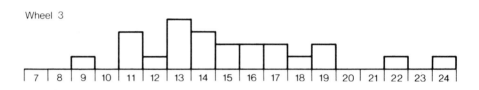

Wheel 3

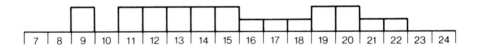

Wheel 4

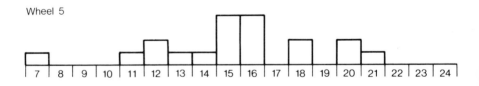

Wheel 5

Wheel 6

Figure 2.5
Histograms for six wheels

which suggests that a large proportion of the effective lugs occur in the sixth position.

In Table 2.11 we list the sequence of shifts when wheel 6 is respectively inactive and active. The smallest value when it is active is 15 which suggests that it is reasonable to proceed by subtracting 15 from those shifts where wheel 6 was active.

Setting

0:	13	0	2	14	5	15	13	15	7	12	15	3	9	12
	11	11	10	14	7	4	12	9	14	12	7	3	12	7
	15	14	11	9	12	15	12	6	12	16	7	7		
1:	22	23	23	23	25	17	26	23	15	21	24	19	23	24
	19	25	15	27	26	26	15	15	27	23	25	23	15	24
	22	19	20	19	25	22	18	24						

Table 2.11

The shifts for each setting of wheel 6

Using these new values we now compute the new averages for the (i, l)-positions. We will not give a complete list but, when this is done, it turns out that the wheel which shows the greatest tendency towards bimodality is wheel 5. Its averages are given below in Table 2.12.

				Average
7	12	11	14	11·0
8	15	11	11	11·3
13	9	12	7	10·3
0	4	9	9	5·5
8	3	0	4	3·8
8	9	14	12	10·8
2	8	0	5	3·8
14	12	12	15	13·3
10	9	12	12	10·8
5	11	7	6	7·3
2	4	3	4	3·3
15	11	12	10	12·0
11	10	8	7	9·0
13	14	10	12	12·3
15	10	8	16	12·3
7	0	7	3	4·3
8	12	15	9	11·0
0	7	0	7	3·5
6	4	9	7	6·5

Table 2.12

The new averages for wheel 5

EXERCISE 2.10 Draw the histogram for wheel 5 based on Table 2.12 and hence assign its pins.

As a result of doing Exercise 2.10 we make the following guess.

Wheel 5   1110010110011110100

Note that we appear to have been fortunate in that each of the new averages for wheel 5 seems to fall clearly into one of the two clusters. Normally we would expect to have some positions on the wheel which we would rather not guess yet. Given these wheel settings, we return to Table 2.10 and use Theorem 2.2 to get $x_5 \leq 9$ and

$$x_5 - \sum_{\substack{j=1 \\ j \neq 5}}^{j=6} x_{5j} \leq 3.$$

Now, as in the previous example, in order to remove the effect of wheels 5 and 6 we first compute shifts for each of the four possible settings for these two wheels. The results of these calculations are given in Table 2.13.

Setting														
00:	0	2	5	7	3	11	7	4	9	7	3	7	9	6
	7	7												
01:	23	17	15	21	19	23	19	15	15	15	15	24	19	20
	19	18												
10:	13	14	15	13	15	12	15	9	12	11	10	14	12	14
	12	12	15	14	11	12	15	12	12	16				
11:	22	23	23	25	26	23	24	24	25	27	26	26	27	23
	25	23	22	25	22	24								

Table 2.13
The shifts for each setting of wheels 5 and 6

We now run through the shifts in Table 2.9 and, depending on our belief for the basic pins on wheels 5 and 6, we subtract either 0, 14, 9 or 22 respectively. (Note that this fits in with our previous deduction that $x_6 \leq 15$ and $x_5 \leq 9$. It also gives x_{56} as 2.) Using this new set of values we compute a new average for each (i, l)-position. The wheel which shows the greatest tendency towards bimodality is now wheel 4 and we list its averages in Table 2.14 and illustrate the histogram in Figure 2.6.

Although the averages are more or less in two clusters, there are a number of positions where it would not be sensible to guess the setting. Our first guess for the wheel 4 pins are:

Wheel 4   0?001?01??01101100171

				Average
0	2	0	5	1·8
1	4	5	6	4·0
4	3	0	3	2·5
0	0	3	6	2·3
8	8	5	4	6·3
1	3	7	3	3·5
2	2	3	0	1·8
5	11	3	3	5·5
3	4	1	7	3·8
5	2	3	3	3·3
2	1	1	2	1·5
6	5	7	7	6·3
4	3	6	7	5·0
4	0	0		1·3
6	5	9		6·7
7	7	5		6·3
1	4	2		2·3
0	4	0		1·3
6	4	9		6·3
3	3	4		3·3
6	9	3		6·0

Table 2.14
The averages for wheel 4
(with wheels 5 and 6 removed)

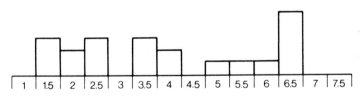

Figure 2.6
Histogram for wheel 4

Because of the question marks we cannot obtain such good bounds from Theorem 2.2. However, if we apply Theorem 2.2 to the positions we know we get $x_4 \leq 7$ and

$$x_4 - \sum_{\substack{j=1 \\ j \neq 4}}^{j=6} x_{4j} \leq 1.$$

Before proceeding to look at the other three wheels we must look carefully at those positions on wheel 4 which have a question mark. For each position we must try to find some extra information to help us make a decision. One of the undecided positions on wheel 4 is 10 and if we look at the (4, 10)-positions we find that there is a shift as small as 5 (see Table 2.10). But this means that, if $d_{10} \neq 0$, $x_4 \leq 5$ which appears to be too small. So we take this as an indication that $d_{10} = 0$. A careful inspection of the other undetermined positions on wheel 4 does not seem to help us, so our current guess for wheel 4 is:

Wheel 4   0?001?01?001101101?1

Having made our guesses for three wheels we now, as before, investigate the statistics when the effect of these three wheels is removed. The shifts corresponding to each setting of the wheels 4, 5 and 6 are given in Table 2.15. For the moment we ignore any positions that include a question mark.

Setting

000:	0	2	5	3	4	3	6		
001:	17	15	15	15	15	15	20	18	
010:	13	13	9	11	10	12	11	12	
011:	22	23	24	24	26	25	23	22	22	24
100:	7	11	7	9	7	9	7	7	
101:	23	21	23	24	19				
110:	14	15	15	15	14	12	15	14	12	12
111:	26	25	27	26	27				

Table 2.15
The shift for each setting of wheels 4, 5 and 6

Clearly, since there are at most eight possible settings for the basic pins on the other three wheels, each row cannot contain more than eight integers. (Any row with more than eight different entries would, therefore, immediately tell us that we had made a mistake.) For the setting 000 the shifts which occur are 0, 2, 3, 4, 5, 6 while for 010 we get 9, 10, 11, 12, 13. For 000 the sequence of values begins with a difference of 2 and then has 5 consecutive values. The sequence of values for 010 only has 5 consecutive values. On this rather flimsy evidence we will assume that the 9 corresponds to the 2. Using this type of reasoning we reach the following way of 'lining up' the shift sizes for each setting of the wheels 4, 5 and 6.

Setting

000:	0	2	3	4	5	6
001:	15	17	18		20	
010:		9	10	11	12	13
011:		22	23	24	25	26
100:	7	9		11		
101:	19	21			23	24
110:	12	14	15			
111:		25	26	27		

Before proceeding we stress again that the above correspondence between the various sets of shift sizes is based purely on the difference in the sizes of the values. They are, therefore, very 'suspect'. However, in order to proceed, we have to guess the contribution of wheels 4, 5 and 6 somehow, and this seems to be as reasonable a way as any. So we shall now assume that for settings 000, 001, 100, 101 and 110 the contributions of wheels 4, 5 and 6 are 0, 15, 7, 19 and 12 respectively. However, for settings 010, 011 and 111 we assume the respective contributions to be 7, 20 and 23, i.e. the number obtained by subtracting 2 from the smallest shift value with those settings. (The reason being that we believe they correspond to getting a value of 2 for the 000 setting.)

EXERCISE 2.11   *Show that the values we have decided to subtract when either exactly one or exactly two of the basic pins in these three wheels are active imply:* $x_4 = 7$, $x_5 = 7$, $x_6 = 15$, $x_{45} = 2$, $x_{46} = 3$ *and* $x_{56} = 2$. *By considering the value we have decided to subtract when all three wheels have active basic pins, show that we have an inconsistency!*

In fact, from our previous work, we should be aware that our guess for x_5 is a little low (remember $x_5 \leq 9$). We might be tempted therefore to subtract more than 7 when the setting is 010. If we did this, our solution might be a little simplified. For the purposes of our example we will not amend our guesses. Fortunately, as we shall see, this inconsistency will not stop us from breaking the system; it may just slow us down a little.

We now deduct the contributions of these three wheels and compute new averages for the remaining three wheels. The results are listed in Table 2.16.

We will not draw the histograms, but the wheel showing the greatest tendency to bimodality is wheel 1. As a result of this we now guess the following setting for wheel 1.

Wheel 1   ??101???010111100001110 0?1

EXERCISE 2.12   *Draw the histograms for the averages of Table 2.16. Do you agree with our guess for wheel 1?*

EXERCISE 2.13   *By referring to Table 2.10 and Theorem 2.2 show that* $x_1 \leq 4$ *and*

$$x_1 - \sum_{j=2}^{j=6} x_{1m} \leq 2.$$

(*Note that this question relies on Exercise 2.9.*)

If we now look back at Table 2.10 again we will see that one of the shifts corresponding to the $(1, 7)$-position is only 2. From this we will assume

Wheel 1			Average	Wheel 2			Average	Wheel 3				Average
2	3		2·5	2	4	0	2·0	2	3	4	2	2·8
4	0		2·0	5			5·0	2	0			1·0
6	4	3	4·3	6	4	3	4·3	6	4	3		4·3
0	0		0·0	0	4	0	1·3	0	0	3		1·0
4	4	5	4·3	4	3		3·5	4	4	4		4·0
3	2		2·5	4	0		2·0	4	5	0		3·0
2	2	4	2·7	2	3	5	3·3	2	3	0		1·7
2	2	2	2·0	2	2	2	2·0	2	4	0		2·0
0	2		1·0	2	4		3·0	3	3			3·0
5	4		4·5	5	0	2	2·3	5	2	0		2·3
2	0	0	0·7	2	4	2	2·7	2	2	5		3·0
3	4	5	4·0	3	0		1·5	3	0	2		1·7
3	6		4·5	3	4	0	2·3	3	4	4		3·7
6	3	5	4·7	6	6	5	5·7	6	0	2		2·7
3	6		4·5	3	3		3·0	3	4	2		3·0
0	2	0	0·7	0	5		2·5	0	6			3·0
3	0		1·5	3	2	6	3·7	3	3	0		2·0
0	2		1·0	0	0	0	0·0	0	5			2·5
2	0	0	0·7	2			2·0	2	2			2·0
5			5·0	0	2		1·0	0	5			2·5
3	4	3	3·3	3	5	0	2·7	3	6			4·5
4	4		4·0	4	4		4·0	4	0	0		1·3
3	0		1·5	3			3·0	5				5·0
3	0	0	1·0	3	3	4	3·3					
2			2·0	2	0	0	0·7					
4	5		4·5									

Table 2.16
The averages with wheels 4, 5 and 6 removed

that $a_7 = 0$ and amend our settings for wheel 1 to:

Wheel 1   ??101?0?0101111000011100?1

We must, of course, not forget that there are still some unresolved positions on wheel 4. In order to assess our progress we now write down, for each of the 76 shifts, the assumed wheel settings so far (Table 2.17).

If we now proceed by trying to remove the effects of wheels 1, 4, 5 and 6 we will find that, because there are so many shifts where at least one of the four pin settings is still undetermined, the number of values we obtain is so much smaller than the original 76 that it would be dangerous to draw any conclusions from them. It is, therefore, important that we now fill in some of the unresolved positions. To do this we first compute the values of the shifts for each of the 16 settings for wheels, 1, 4, 5 and 6; see Table 2.18. (Again we note that there must be at most four values for each setting. If there are ever more than four we know we have gone wrong.)

Position	Shift size	Basic pin settings wheel		Position	Shift size	Basic pin settings wheel	
			123456				123456
1.	22		011	39.	26	1	011
2.	23		11	40.	26	1	111
3.	13	1	010	41.	12	1	10
4.	0	0	000	42.	9	0	100
5.	23	1	101	43.	15	0	001
6.	23		11	44.	14	0	10
7.	2	0	000	45.	15	0	001
8.	14		110	46.	12	1	010
9.	25	0	11	47.	27	1	111
10.	5	1	000	48.	7	1	00
11.	17	0	001	49.	3	0	000
12.	15	1	110	50.	12	0	110
13.	26	1	111	51.	23		11
14.	13	1	010	52.	25	1	011
15.	15	1	110	53.	23		011
16.	7	0	100	54.	7		100
17.	23	0	011	55.	15	1	110
18.	15	0	001	56.	15	0	001
19.	21	0	101	57.	24	1	101
20.	12	1	10	58.	14		110
21.	15	1	110	59.	11	0	010
22.	24	1	011	60.	22		011
23.	19	0	01	61.	9	0	100
24.	3	0	000	62.	19	1	01
25.	9		010	63.	12	0	110
26.	23	1	101	64.	20	1	001
27.	12		10	65.	15	1	10
28.	24		011	66.	12	1	010
29.	11	1	100	67.	6	1	000
30.	19	0	01	68.	19	0	101
31.	11	1	010	69.	25	0	11
32.	10		010	70.	22	0	011
33.	14	0	110	71.	12	0	110
34.	25		111	72.	16	1	10
35.	15	0	001	73.	18	1	001
36.	27	1	111	74.	24	1	011
37.	7	0	100	75.	7	0	100
38.	4	1	000	76.	7	0	100

Table 2.17
The situation so far

Now let us see how we can settle some of the unresolved positions. Since wheel 1 begins with ? we will try to find a_1. We know that $\text{shift}_1 = 22$ and the basic pin settings are a_1 ??011. Similarly $\text{shift}_{27} = 12$ with a setting a_1 ???10 and $\text{shift}_{53} = 23$ with settings a_1 ??011. But, by looking at Table 2.18, we

Setting

0000:	2	2	3	3	
0001:	17	15	15	15	15	15
0010:	11				
0011:	23	22			
0100:	7	7	9	9	7	7
0101:	21	19			
0110:	14	12	12	12	
0111:					
1000:	5	4	6		
1001:	20	18			
1010:	13	13	11	12	12
1011:	24	26	25	24	
1100:	11				
1101:	23	23	24		
1110:	15	15	15	15	
1111:	26	27	26	27	

Table 2.18

The shifts for each setting of wheels 1, 4, 5 and 6

know that the pin settings 0??011 give shifts of 22 and 23. This result, clearly, is consistent with putting $a_1 = 0$ in the above. Also from Table 2.18, the pin setting 1??011 gives shifts of 24, 25 and 26. Therefore it appears that we must put $a_1 = 0$. A similar argument settles the remaining settings on wheel 1 as $a_2 = 0$, $a_6 = 0$, $a_8 = 0$ and $a_{25} = 0$. For wheel 4 we find that $d_2 = 1$, $d_9 = 1$, $d_{20} = 0$, but run into difficulties when trying to decide d_6. There are four shifts corresponding to d_6. They are: $shift_6 = 23$ with setting 0??$d_6$11, $shift_{27} = 12$ with setting 0??$d_6$10, $shift_{48} = 7$ with setting 1??$d_6$00 and $shift_{69} = 25$ with setting 0??$d_6$11. The shifts 27 and 69 clearly indicate that $d_6 = 1$ whereas $shift_{48}$ equally implies $d_6 = 0$. This inconsistency may imply that we have made an error somewhere. Anyway, for the moment, rather than risk making any further errors we will leave d_6 as unresolved. This means we have:

Wheel 1   00101000010111100001110001
Wheel 4   01001?011001101100101

EXERCISE 2.14   Use Table 2.18 to confirm $a_2 = 0$, $a_6 = 0$, $a_8 = 0$, $a_{25} = 0$, $d_2 = 1$, $d_9 = 1$, $d_{20} = 0$. Note, also, that we could have used Table 2.15 to try to resolve wheel 4 before we made any guesses for wheel 1. See what conclusions you can draw from Table 2.15.

In view of Exercise 2.14 we remark that we had no particular reason for guessing wheel 1 before trying to settle the remaining positions on wheel 4. It was an arbitrary choice to proceed as we did. Having resolved (well almost!) four wheels we now carry on as before. That is, we try to remove the effect of these four wheels and look at the resulting statistics for the remaining two. First we recompute the shifts for each of the 16 possible settings of the four wheels. The result is in Table 2.19. It is important to realize that the reason for the list in Table 2.19 containing so many more entries than Table 2.18 is that we have now resolved eight positions which were not known for Table 2.18. In fact Table 2.19 has 72 entries. The four which are missing being those which involve the unresolved position on wheel 4. Since this is position 6, the missing values are those corresponding to the (4,6)-positions i.e. shift_6, shift_{27}, shift_{48} and shift_{69}.

Setting							
0000:	0	2	3	3			
0001:	17	15	15	15	15	15	
0010:	9	10	11				
0011:	22	23	24	23	22	22	
0100:	7	7	9	7	9	7	7
0101:	21	19	19	19			
0110:	14	14	14	12	14	12	12
0111:	23	25	25	23			
1000:	5	4	5	6			
1001:	19	20	18				
1010:	13	13	12	11	12	12	12	12
1011:	24	26	25	24			
1100:	11						
1101:	23	23	24				
1110:	15	15	15	15	15	16	
1111:	26	27	26	27			

Table 2.19
The shifts for each setting of wheels 1, 4, 5 and 6
after determining the unresolved positions

We now have to use Table 2.19 to decide the contribution of the wheels 1, 4, 5, 6 from each of their 16 settings. As before this is by no means a precise calculation. We will assume the following values: 0, 15, 9, 22, 7, 19, 12, 23, 4, 18, 11, 24, 9, 22, 14, 25. (The order in which they are listed coincides with the order of the settings in Table 2.19.) Before continuing the reader should decide which set of values he would use. After subtracting these values for the contributions of the four wheels we compute our new averages (Table 2.20).

From these values we feel it is better to guess wheel 2 and our guess is:

Wheel 2   00100011101001?010100?010

EXERCISE 2.15   Check that you agree with our guess for wheel 2 and show

$$x_2 \le 2 \text{ and } x_2 - \sum_{\substack{j=1 \\ j \ne 2}}^{j=6} x_{2j} \le 1.$$

Wheel 2				Average
0	1	0	0	0·3
0	1			0·5
2	2	1		1·7
0	2	0		0·7
1	0	1		0·7
0	0			0·0
2	1	2		1·7
2	2	2		2·0
2	2	2		2·0
1	0	0		0·3
2	2	2		2·0
1	0	1		0·7
1	0	0		0·3
2	2	2		2·0
1	1	1		1·0
0	1	1		0·7
1	2	2		1·7
0	0	0		0·0
2	2			2·0
1	0	0		0·3
1	1	0		0·7
0	2	2		1·3
0	0			0·0
3	3	0		0·0
0	0	0		0·0

Wheel 3				Average
0	3	2	0	1·3
0	0	0		0·0
2	1	3	2	2·0
0	0	0		0·0
1	2	0	0	0·8
2	1	0		1·0
2	0	1	0	0·8
2	0	0		0·7
2	1	1		1·3
1	2	0		1·0
2	2	2		2·0
1	0	2		1·0
1	2	2		1·7
2	0	0		0·7
1	0	2		1·0
0	2	1		1·0
1	1	0		0·7
0	1	2		1·0
2	2	1		1·7
1	0	1		0·7
1	2	2		1·7
0	0	0		0·0
0	1			0·5

Table 2.20
The averages for the last two wheels

EXERCISE 2.16   Refer back to Table 2.10 to see that b_{22} gives rise to a shift of 27. Deduce that this implies $b_{22} = 1$.

In view of Exercise 2.16 we have:

Wheel 2   00100011101001?0101001010

Given this setting we now compute the displacements for each of the 32 possible settings for these five wheels. This is shown in Table 2.21.

We must now try to resolve our two undetermined parameters: b_{15} and d_6. We begin with d_6. The four shifts involving this position are:

$$\text{shift}_6 = 23 \quad \text{setting } 00?d_611$$
$$\text{shift}_{27} = 12 \quad \text{setting } 00?d_610$$
$$\text{shift}_{48} = 7 \quad \text{setting } 10?d_600$$
$$\text{shift}_{69} = 25 \quad \text{setting } 01?d_611$$

If $d_6 = 1$ then, from Table 2.21, shift_6 should be 23, shift_{27} should be 12, shift_{48} should be 11 and shift_{69} should be 25. Thus three of the four are consistent with $d_6 = 1$. If $d_6 = 0$ then shift_6 should be 22, shift_{27} should be 9,

Setting

Setting					
00000:	0				
00001:	15	15	15	15	15
00010:	9				
00011:	22	22	22		
00100:	7	7	7	7	7
00101:	19	19	19		
00110:	12	12	12		
00111:	23	23			
01000:	2	3	3		
01001:	17				
01010:	10	11			
01011:	23	24	23		
01100:	9	9			
01101:	21				
01110:	14	14	14	14	
01111:	25	25			
10000:	5	4			
10001:	19	18			
10010:	12	11	12	12	12
10011:	25				
10100:	11				
10101:	23	23			
10110:	15	15	15		
10111:	26				
11000:	6				
11001:	20				
11010:	13	13			
11011:	24	26	24		
11100:					
11101:	24				
11110:	16				
11111:	27	27			

Table 2.21
The shifts for each setting of wheels 1, 2, 4, 5 and 6

shift$_{48}$ should be 4 or 5 and shift$_{69}$ should be 23 or 24. (In case it is not clear how these conclusions are reached we elaborate on one case. Suppose $d_6 = 0$. Then for shift$_{48}$ the setting will be 10?000 and so, looking for the values corresponding to 10000 in Table 2.21, we get that shift$_{48}$ must be 4 or 5.) Clearly neither $d_6 = 0$ nor $d_6 = 1$ leads to consistency. However it is clear that $d_6 = 1$ is much more likely than $d_6 = 0$. We are forced to conclude that $d_6 = 1$ and that we have made an error somewhere. Furthermore that error must involve one of the pin settings involved in shift$_{48}$. We know that shift$_{48} = 7$ so we now look at Table 2.21 to see which pin settings give rise to a 7. Fortunately there is only one possibility, i.e. 00100. Since we know that $d_6 = 1$, this suggests that our setting on wheel 1 should be 0 for shift$_{48}$ (and not a 1 as we have guessed). But, since $48 \equiv 22 \pmod{26}$, this setting is a_{22}. So we now suspect that a_{22} should be 0 and not 1. Of course we cannot simply alter a_{22} from 1 to 0. We must check that such a change does not lead to even more inconsistencies. The shifts involving a_{22} are shifts 22, 48 and 74. Changing a_{22} to 0 we have:

$$\text{shift}_{22} = 24 \quad \text{setting } 01?011$$
$$\text{shift}_{48} = 7 \quad \text{setting } 00?100$$
$$\text{shift}_{74} = 24 \quad \text{setting } 01?011$$

Since the shifts corresponding to 01011 are 23 or 24 this fits in nicely with Table 2.21. In fact it is even a slight improvement since previously, with $a_{22} = 1$, the setting 11?011 gave rise to shifts of 24 and 26, and this was the

Setting

Setting						
00000:	0					
00001:	15	15	15	15	15	
00010:	9					
00011:	22	22	22			
00100:	7	7	7	7	7	7
00101:	19	19	19			
00110:	12	12	12	12		
00111:	23	23	23			
01000:	2	3	3			
01001:	17					
01010:	10	11				
01011:	23	24	24	23	24	
01100:	9	9				
01101:	21					
01110:	14	14	14	14		
01111:	25	25	25			
10000:	5	4				
10001:	19	18				
10010:	12	11	12	12	12	
10011:	25					
10100:	11					
10101:	23	23				
10110:	15	15	15	15	15	
10111:	26	26				
11000:	6					
11001:	20					
11010:	13	13				
11011:	26					
11100:						
11101:	24					
11110:	16					
11111:	27	27				

Table 2.22
Table 2.21 revised

only occasion on which a pin setting gave 2 values more than one digit apart. If we now consider b_{15} in the standard way it appears likely to be 0 and we now have:

Wheel 1 001010000101111100001100001
Wheel 2 00100011101001001010010101010
Wheel 4 0100110110011011100101

Table 2.22 incorporates this new information.

Our outstanding tasks are to determine the settings for wheel 3 and then find the lug cage parameters. In order to resolve wheel 3 we could proceed as before by removing the effect of the other five wheels. However, we note that for each setting of Table 2.22 for which we have two possible shifts (i.e. for each setting of the other five wheels for which there are two possible shift values) the smaller value must correspond to a 0 on wheel 3 while the larger value corresponds to a 1. This fact alone tells us a lot about wheel 3.

For instance from Table 2.23 (which shows the situation so far) we see that position 7 in conjuction with Table 2.22 implies that c_7 is a 0 whereas there is no immediate implication from positions 1 to 6. To determine c_1 note position 22. Continuing in this way we get:

$$\textit{Wheel 3} \quad 1?101?0001??1?0101?1?11$$

This means that we are able to produce an improvement to Table 2.23 and get a more complete picture of the basic pin settings for each of the 76 shifts (Table 2.24).

We now repeatedly use Exercise 2.5 to determine the lug cage parameters. Naturally we start with the easiest equations. For instance the setting for shift$_7$ is 010000 which implies that shift$_7$ is equal to the number of effective lugs corresponding to wheel 2. Thus $x_2 = 2$. Similarly, by locating the other shifts with only one active pin, we have $x_1 = 4$ and $x_4 = 7$. Having determined these 3 parameters there are many ways to proceed. We have to solve a large number of equations as 'painlessly' as possible. We give one reasonable way of doing it, but urge the reader to find his own and check his answers with ours. We next look at those shifts which have two pins active where one, at least, is in position 1, 2 or 4.

Shift$_{10} = 5 = x_1 + x_3 - x_{13}$ which, since $x_1 = 4$, gives $x_3 - x_{13} = 1$. Similarly from shift$_{16}$ we get $x_3 - x_{34} = 0$. But if $x_3 = x_{34}$, we must have $x_{3j} = 0$ for all $j \neq 4$.

$$\left(\text{Recall that, from Theorem 2.2,} \quad x_3 \geq \sum_{\substack{j=1 \\ j \neq 3}}^{j=6} x_{3j}. \right)$$

Thus $x_3 = x_{34} = 1$ and $x_{31} = x_{32} = x_{35} = x_{36} = 0$. We merely list some calculations without giving the explanations.

Position	Shift size	Basic pin settings wheel 123456	Position	Shift size	Basic pin settings wheel 123456
1.	22	00 011	39.	26	11 011
2.	23	00 111	40.	26	10 111
3.	13	11 010	41.	12	10 010
4.	0	00 000	42.	9	01 100
5.	23	10 101	43.	15	00 001
6.	23	00 111	44.	14	01 110
7.	2	01 000	45.	15	00 001
8.	14	01 110	46.	12	10 010
9.	25	01 111	47.	27	11 111
10.	5	10 000	48.	7	00 100
11.	17	01 001	49.	3	01 000
12.	15	10 110	50.	12	00 110
13.	26	10 111	51.	23	00 111
14.	13	11 010	52.	25	10 011
15.	15	10 110	53.	23	01 011
16.	7	00 100	54.	7	00 100
17.	23	01 011	55.	15	10 110
18.	15	00 001	56.	15	00 001
19.	21	01 101	57.	24	11 101
20.	12	10 010	58.	14	01 110
21.	15	10 110	59.	11	01 010
22.	24	01 011	60.	22	00 011
23.	19	00 101	61.	9	01 100
24.	3	01 000	62.	19	10 001
25.	9	00 010	63.	12	00 110
26.	23	10 101	64.	20	11 001
27.	12	00 110	65.	15	10 110
28.	24	01 011	66.	12	10 010
29.	11	10 100	67.	6	11 000
30.	19	00 101	68.	19	00 101
31.	11	10 010	69.	25	01 111
32.	10	01 010	70.	22	00 011
33.	14	01 110	71.	12	00 110
34.	25	01 111	72.	16	11 110
35.	15	00 001	73.	18	10 001
36.	27	11 111	74.	24	01 011
37.	7	00 100	75.	7	00 100
38.	4	10 000	76.	7	00 100

Table 2.23
An improved version of Table 2.17

Position	Shift size	Basic pin settings wheel **123456**	Position	Shift size	Basic pin settings wheel **123456**
1.	22	001011	39.	26	111011
2.	23	00 111	40.	26	100111
3.	13	111010	41.	12	101010
4.	0	000000	42.	9	01 100
5.	23	101101	43.	15	001001
6.	23	00 111	44.	14	01 110
7.	2	010000	45.	15	001001
8.	14	010110	46.	12	101010
9.	25	010111	47.	27	111111
10.	5	101000	48.	7	00 100
11.	17	01 001	49.	3	011000
12.	15	10 110	50.	12	000110
13.	26	101111	51.	23	001111
14.	13	11 010	52.	25	10 011
15.	15	100110	53.	23	010011
16.	7	001100	54.	7	000100
17.	23	010011	55.	15	100110
18.	15	001001	56.	15	001001
19.	21	01 101	57.	24	11 101
20.	12	101010	58.	14	01 110
21.	15	10 110	59.	11	011010
22.	24	011011	60.	22	00 011
23.	19	001101	61.	9	010100
24.	3	011000	62.	19	101001
25.	9	00 010	63.	12	000110
26.	23	101101	64.	20	111001
27.	12	000110	65.	15	10 110
28.	24	011011	66.	12	101010
29.	11	10 100	67.	6	11 000
30.	19	000101	68.	19	001101
31.	11	100010	69.	25	011111
32.	10	010010	70.	22	001011
33.	14	011110	71.	12	00 110
34.	25	01 111	72.	16	111110
35.	15	00 001	73.	18	100001
36.	27	111111	74.	24	011011
37.	7	00 100	75.	7	00 100
38.	4	100000	76.	7	000100

Table 2.24
An improved version of Table 2.23

$$\text{shift}_{18} = 15 = x_3 + x_6 - x_{36} \quad \text{so} \quad x_6 = 14$$
$$\text{shift}_{27} = 12 = x_4 + x_5 - x_{45} \quad \text{so} \quad x_5 - x_{45} = 5$$
$$\text{shift}_{30} = 19 = x_4 + x_6 - x_{46} \quad \text{so} \quad x_{46} = 2$$
$$\text{shift}_{31} = 11 = x_1 + x_5 - x_{15} \quad \text{so} \quad x_5 - x_{15} = 7$$
$$\text{shift}_{32} = 10 = x_2 + x_5 - x_{25} \quad \text{so} \quad x_5 - x_{25} = 8$$
$$\text{shift}_{73} = 18 = x_1 + x_6 - x_{16} \quad \text{so} \quad x_{16} = 0$$
$$\text{shift}_1 = 22 = x_3 + x_5 + x_6 - x_{35} - x_{36} - x_{56} \quad \text{so} \quad x_5 - x_{56} = 7$$
$$\text{shift}_8 = 14 = x_2 + x_4 + x_5 - x_{24} - x_{25} - x_{45} \quad \text{so} \quad x_5 - x_{24} + x_{25} - x_{45} = 5.$$

But, from an earlier equation, we know $x_5 - x_{45} = 5$. So we now have $x_{24} = x_{25} = 0$. Since $x_5 - x_{25} = 8$ this gives $x_5 = 8$, and $x_5 - x_{15} = 7$ now implies $x_{15} = 1$. Similarly $x_{45} = 3$ and $x_{56} = 1$. So x_{12}, x_{14} and x_{26} are the only unknown parameters. Shift$_{15}$ gives $x_{14} = 0$, shift$_{17}$ gives $x_{26} = 0$ and, finally, shift$_{55}$ gives $x_{14} = 0$. This gives the lug cage parameters as:

$$
\begin{array}{llllll}
x_1 = 4 & x_{12} = 1 & x_{13} = 0 & x_{14} = 0 & x_{15} = 1 & x_{16} = 0 \\
x_2 = 2 & x_{23} = 0 & x_{24} = 0 & x_{25} = 0 & x_{26} = 0 \\
& x_3 = 1 & x_{34} = 1 & x_{35} = 0 & x_{36} = 0 \\
& & x_4 = 7 & x_{45} = 3 & x_{46} = 2 \\
& & & x_5 = 8 & x_{56} = 1 \\
& & & & x_6 = 14.
\end{array}
$$

It is now a simple matter to resolve the remaining pins on wheel 3.

Wheel 3   11101100011111010111111

All that remains is to check that our lug cage and pin settings are consistent with our data. But this is easily verifiable and we will not do it here.

2.3.7 Cryptanalysis with ciphertext only

We now turn our attention to the situation where we have intercepted some ciphertext but do not know any equivalent plaintext. In this case we need considerably more ciphertext than for the earlier examples. However, since it is only ciphertext that we require, it is quite plausible that our sample of data is fairly long. In fact the sample of ciphertext we will consider is shown in Table 2.25. This example consists of a lengthy passage of ciphertext from a single enciphered message. After using this example to illustrate the general principles involved we will be able to consider the situation where the ciphertext consists of several shorter messages.

To begin our analysis of this cryptogram we might apply the index of coincidence test. If we did, we would find $I_c = 0 \cdot 0392$ and hence using our formula from Section 1.3.4 the number of alphabets is about 22. In fact it would be dangerous to be any more accurate than to guess that between 15 and 30 substitution alphabets had been used. Of course this is precisely what we would expect from a cryptogram produced on the M-209, since we

```
YUABR GZJOJ WYTJM AVSPD ZWIAE HXWBH ZMWHM KMTED AVUKN KHDSE
ZXRVM TYRHR AXAAK ADFVJ XJBLV ZUPAC GEGQL IZUUY PHOBZ TSOBS
TGEZQ IXJBT XSSBA XFTLR WQUOL TAYDX VQLHX TKZTA SYPSQ VHAPF
JFFBC YNPLI STDKA LBTDY ISONL MFYYF PFONQ IKXAS ZITLZ HWUBT
YXJZL VYJCN FAAUG TZDER KCFOF AJCTS JPYNB CDYLQ FVSQN RYOHW
SJERX KDUMK VVPJA FJKPH PUUXK BAMEE RGGNA NMRBT SPCJO 8BOLR
OZFZK MHIMI SGFCT OCJRL UJZQB FOZME TVRVZ TJZKU EEZVG UJJTM
HUMLG WPYIK ARQFN TKWKY UXBJK DCJGV SJAVL WDSQJ JIZUE SJTZP
LBUZT MDUPW BEXSS MTGON JOMBO BXTNN SLZFX KLNTX FFJFR VJKXY
XZVOT NZFMA MJSIK YUHHQ MUBJC WLSRF ADPIF HXONB RHKDP GBMZK
RPTRW BNFEM DETBD BMYLF ZMUCV DOEUN MTVLX GIXWR PHKMQ EZWFT
XLVFD HTLSA WEBGL FBQPS GZWNP GLTPL GGXMN AYGZY WBSUZ TREDP
BSFMF ZJWMJ FEIKG NPVJU AGNLJ TZKAI MDTVM UNQCE QIHAN DEIGG
OLWNG CCRQN RMTYC SRCDJ QVEAZ XBTGF EKLPR OHRML AELOP WJXUF
BDWGS XZSSM FRMJA RKXLT IACEY DFQSH GXLMQ LFWJS FEECB LQWHP
EBBFT NCFEW ZJRET ANIAS AHRTY XTGZX ALFDZ GPVXQ AYCBM UFLNC
WYBRF NCSQR FXMIZ RNJFP VRDDD WPKSM FTGSN HKIBN IPGCE DZZPU
ARIXG SNDDL QWTNY RIGQP MYGMF ASVEH BRAJI RLLSM FEJSJ PATQT
BCTVD NSTZZ RMBVF XZCCT IJSJI PDNCU TGJPA ZADHK RJCZO MHEJR
FUUPK AVMYM OQBZH LXMNI KTIVI YCRHS UBHTZ NQXPA SNWXD LYRIS
TADIM BLZVK ZKVVQ BWKEJ NUZUV CHAVB QGDCI FZYQY KIGZY YYLJI
ULJBU XZIWF IRMKC MVKPL YGTZO GMLCN YGVRS RUXQP HDTBM TELYT
KXXAS ADHAS ANTQT QEAKT QEYSY PMXLY DYIVJ MEQMG RXVZX UKXSD
JJRZJ ZUBOD PEFVD GBFRZ ANRBO NRGJK QEHWS UMVRD FJGSI BLLIK
YAGFC FPWKS QSQHZ BKKNM ARCAY MPZMA GQXMQ OKYCK GLCSK FELHQ
ADIHL GDDZJ HYXKU JSDQO CEWRW NEPJL STGKK DSXBV UTTMJ QKAIV
TNXDG LLGNQ KGRXX HXGFL UJIRC ARKMK PZYNW ZDBGR ZCCXM TEJRW
UPDJT FZSSD UHFML LBPHN OSGKU UYGKH VFAPS FUPOU LAGPF WSZWB
RVWZQ PMKAR KSYYQ IYWLS YWDEL PTFRS RGSBW LYEDS EHJYA WQYYW
FMTFG GBEWL EQJDY LBZOH CSLVT KVGEI HXXHT XZUDK VBFEG ZPRUO
XOHGN REQND LAHKA QKACI DCFPA UJEZD GSFAM QNXWW JOTNJ ZXEBL
SSNKR GODGM TMPFS UZCEB UPPTQ CGOFM MOPCP RDOJX YADVN PIAKR
CKWJQ QXWBG BIUMM RAAJT MIWGJ YOBAE VIWEZ TRXHE HCWBX NQLUJ
NMBUP WVIRQ NXCSE QKUNL GLLUG WWRXG TQREM UGFGP ZQZHV XIRXR
QBVTF LWRHV TEZMR HSGEY TKXBH UOUML EWFNO ETTGE MXDIL ZRVIL
EULLH BKTVQ VZEKZ HEXYA LNYBS LGANL BHTZB PQFCH SNDQO PDXGW
OILNC XDPUD HGVNR LMKLT UQMXO EQXSS ZJMZI NFWBD XJSHM GATWB
GLWIB QHUVF MAPIB EVIPQ JEYMI LYSMF LVKDB XTPIT QVCWQ FKJEI
ZNVNX GOEPG QQLVG PXJEP RXFYY KQBUI SIYFF LTXRR OPZKH TIVOO
YWQEQ EKFWC ZHCRU RBXJP EXIDM XAYEC ZVFXM FXRMF NMOMV FHMIS
MMXEY DQPJN AMSJD DVRAC RFSCP PFOJK AEAYJ SJZJX YKLIB OSDNB
TSQFN TGIQK QFTOJ SDWHX LVATI FPTFD ZCKFY QOCIU ANCLZ ZKPSW
DKRDM KDYQY NLELB VCKKJ HUYZV YFTBW IOQTS XWCJS GAFUM XEKNX
DTDTA OBZII TYWAM NEWGE WDLRV TAEFD XSVSW XELGL REUUT KASBS
SPDXB UAGPS XTXFS GEQRL YMDAI GULED CYEPP PVGLE AIPNO FJUBH
URTON LFUTJ HTAFT ZITQE DWIWL NTQIE LMNGA RPAGZ JHUSO WRUBC
UZFWN ZMGRT UURPA ULHPA KQMMX JQZOJ GUZLO WGDVG HLPWG JYFKZ
VTOKP HRFSI MMXOY JGPQT WHZQH TZJUW ALCFX IEBMJ ZQBZQ CMRCS
OVWDF EZROM OSAYF LLBXE UDFZR UPJIF YNWCF SDUEV NLZXE QSYJL
AVRAK NOXPW HAGNK UDMQI NDPJQ MEHII JFYHM BKTJQ ELBGY JLXRP
RXVNN QXUFA GAPEZ BMTXQ TQWXT TSGRX MQGGJ FCWBE OJJDL IDIZV
JUOTK SXYMS POVWV NEPTH LPSOV SVOUM VEPQI BHVJA MYYDH BLTRN
GCZHQ TMTUZ KVMWX HHXSM VRFMA ZIVGD SDXPJ RKUSO ZVXEU BCGBM
LFXQQ UJZVF GZTMU ABTJG DYJYC XZWHK ZKHXS SGPJS PFWQT MCSLG
DRKFP VHKIH NLRQU PMFAY PIALE GFPSF EVKLJ BQBGG BJAAF MMJIR
TQGBH GQVIL LEQQU AUBKX NBHIC CQFWM BRPVX LXIHT YMPWJ ZUTQX
ULBMS NJMKX UHEGP BCPFG IEEWS HIQLQ SCERQ KRTCI SDZXA ESLTR
WMSPM EATRQ HCMHY IZFDR XETZJ GMJEX NCARF TJCZJ HNDUJ KENAP
YMWMS IHNHP BJQMY FIJQE KVTYD ZNWVC FGWNL JESAE MDBQM ATOPP
REJNG CZWVA OFGLI MPMUP TNXZL YYJRW RQPYC XRLMU UISVF MNJON
```

Table 2.25
An intercepted ciphertext

hope to use most of the 26 possibilities. So if we had some reason for suspecting that the M-209 was used to encipher this message but were not absolutely certain, the index of coincidence test might help us resolve the situation. Now, before proceeding with our example, we will look at the consequences of having the machine settings as in Tables 2.2 and 2.3. By doing this we will exhibit certain 'patterns' which we will then be able to exploit in our cryptanalysis.

If wheel i has an lth pin then the (i, l)-positions of the ciphertext are the only ones affected by the setting of this particular pin. If we now fix on a particular pin then, whenever it is in a basic position, there are 32 possibilities for the settings of the other five basic pins. In order to illustrate what happens we will concentrate on a pair of particular values for i and l. Let us take $i = 6$ and $l = 1$. We know from Table 2.3 that the $(6, 1)$ pin is inactive. If the pin settings of the other five wheels are 00000 (taking wheel 1 first), then the shift used to determine the substitution alphabet is obviously 0. If they are set at 00001 then, using Table 2.2, the shift is 9. It is straightforward to try each possible key setting and to determine all possible values for the shifts.

EXERCISE 2.17   Each setting for the wheels 1 to 5 may be regarded as the binary representation of an integer from 0 to 31. Show that when the settings are considered in numeric order the 32 possible shifts for the $(6, 1)$-positions are: 0, 9, 3, 12, 1, 10, 3, 12, 10, 19, 13, 22, 11, 20, 13, 22, 4, 13, 6, 15, 5, 14, 6, 15, 13, 22, 15, 24, 14, 23, 15, 24.

The calculations involved in solving Exercise 2.17 will clearly be the same for any inactive pin on the sixth wheel. However active pins result in a different set of shift values.

EXERCISE 2.18   Show that, under the conditions of Exercise 2.17, the 32 possible shifts for the $(6, 3)$-positions are: 14, 18, 16, 20, 15, 19, 16, 20, 19, 23, 21, 25, 20, 24, 21, 25, 17, 21, 18, 22, 18, 22, 18, 22, 21, 25, 22, 26, 22, 26, 22, 26.

In general, for any given setting of the lug cage and any particular i and l, the (i, l)-positions of a sufficiently long ciphertext passage will be the result of using 32 shifts, and hence 32 substitution alphabets. They are, of course, not necessarily distinct. For any fixed i there will be only two possibilities for the values of these 32 shifts; one corresponding to the active pins and the other to those which are inactive. It is this observation which forms the basis of the attack we are about to describe.

Let us now return to our example in Table 2.25. We begin the cryptanalysis by trying to determine the pin settings. Since there are so many pins and so much ciphertext we will use a computer. But it must be stressed that this is not because the calculations are particularly difficult. They are merely very long and too time consuming to be performed by hand.

As our preliminary discussion indicated, the first step is to consider all possible (i, l)-positions. Unlike our earlier examples each sequence of (i, l)-positions merely gives us some ciphertext. Our aim is to deduce each pin setting from the corresponding ciphertext. To do this, of course, we need each of these ciphertext sequences to be reasonably long; one obvious reason why we need the original ciphertext to be so lengthy. Since wheel 1 has 26 positions and our example has about 3000 letters, the passage corresponding to any given $(1, l)$-position is about $\frac{3000}{26}$ letters. Every other wheel has fewer positions than wheel 1 so their passages will be even longer.

We now choose one particular wheel; we take wheel 6 as our first choice. (We must stress there is no particular reason for this choice. All wheels will eventually be considered.) Each set of $(6, l)$-positions is the result of a rather complex polyalphabetic cipher utilizing 32 substitution alphabets which, of course, are not all distinct. If we were to draw the frequency histograms for each one we would find that, although they do not exhibit the characteristic properties of simple substitutions, they are most certainly not flat. However, as we saw when discussing the settings of Tables 2.2 and 2.3, we expect the histograms corresponding to positions with an active pin to have a certain similarity. Those corresponding to an inactive pin should also have common similarities but are likely to be very different to those of the active pins. Of course the bigger the sample the more striking we would expect these similarities and dissimilarities to be. This example has been chosen so that it is long enough for us to distinguish them. Our aim, then, is to divide the pins on each wheel into two classes; the active ones and the inactive ones. But before we do it we must point out that, even if we succeed, we will not know which of the two sets of pins is active.

One way in which we might achieve this division would be actually to draw the 131 histograms, compare every pair corresponding to each wheel and make the division according to the 'pictorial evidence'. But with a sample of our size this would be very crude. It is extremely unlikely that the histograms would be sufficiently distinctive for us to achieve our goal. Nevertheless we recommend that the interested reader draws some of the histograms for a given wheel, wheel 6 say, and attempts the division. The results can then be compared with those we will obtain by calculation.

Our method is based on the technique of matching alphabets introduced in Section 1.3.6. In that earlier section we had two cryptograms and knew the frequency with which each letter occurred in them. We had reason to believe that an unknown shift of one would result in a cryptogram using the same substitution alphabets as the other. So, if f_α and f'_α denote the frequency of α in each cryptogram ($\alpha = $ **A**, **B**, ... **Z**), we computed

$$\sum_{\mathbf{A}}^{\mathbf{Z}} f_\alpha f'_\alpha$$

for every possible shift and decided that the shift which maximized

$$\sum_{A}^{Z} f_\alpha f'_\alpha$$

was the one we wanted.

The same principle applies here. Suppose that, for a particular wheel, we are considering three positions with letter frequencies f_α, g_α and h_α, $\alpha = A$, $B, \ldots, Z$. Suppose also that for some reason we know that the first of these positions used exactly the same set of substitution alphabets as one of the other two. If we were to compute

$$\sum_{A}^{Z} f_\alpha g_\alpha \quad \text{and} \quad \sum_{A}^{Z} f_\alpha h_\alpha$$

then for precisely the same reasons as were given in Section 1.3.6, we would expect the larger of these two values to correspond to the matching positions.

Returning to our example, if we consider wheel 6 then we have 17 positions to consider which means there are $\frac{17 \cdot 16}{2}$ ($= 136$) comparisons to make, i.e. 136 different summations

$$\sum_{A}^{Z} f_\alpha f'_\alpha$$

for pairs of ciphertext passages to compute. On the assumption that about half the pins were active (which is certainly what many users recommend), we would expect those values of

$$\sum_{A}^{Z} f_\alpha f'_\alpha$$

which are above the average to indicate matching positions. Of course we would be very fortunate if this were always the case. In practice it is quite likely that the crude division of taking values of

$$\sum_{A}^{Z} f_\alpha f'_\alpha$$

above the average as indicating matching positions will lead to the contradiction that, for some j, k, l, positions $(6, l)$ and $(6, j)$ match while $(6, k)$ matches with $(6, l)$ but not $(6, j)$. This type of contradiction will need resolving and we must think of a better way of separating the positions.

EXERCISE 2.19   Find an efficient way of using the 136 comparisons to separate the $(6, l)$-positions into two groups.

This exercise is included merely to emphasize the problem. There is no obvious 'best' answer although there are many techniques available. One approach, for instance, is to look at several of the highest and lowest values and, assuming they do not already give a contradiction, suppose that they are correct. Thus we assume that any pair of positions involved in one of these high values is in the same group and those involved in low values lie in different groups.

EXERCISE 2.20   Suppose the six highest values come from comparisons of positions 1 and 3, 6 and 11, 1 and 5, 9 and 11, 8 and 15, 2 and 5 respectively, while the six lowest values come from comparisons of 8 and 11, 3 and 17, 15 and 17, 1 and 9, 11 and 15, 3 and 5 respectively.

  (*i*)   *Show that taking the five highest and lowest values leads to two groups one of which contains 1, 3, 5, 8 and 15, while the other contains 6, 9, 11 and 17.*
  (*ii*) *Show that taking the six highest and lowest values leads to a contradiction.*

We could then try to resolve the group of every other position by comparing it with our groupings so far.

A second method, which often seems rather more effective, is to take each position in turn and resolve every other position relative to this one. For instance let us fix on position 1 of wheel 6 and try to resolve the other 16 positions relative to position 1. To do this we might use a scoring system. For example suppose we want to decide if position 2 is in the same group as position 1. The first thing to look at would clearly be $\Sigma f_\alpha f'_\alpha$ for positions 1 and 2. If this is above the average we might score 2 points (we might even score varying amounts of points depending on how far it is from the average). The next step might be to consider 1 and 2 relative to each of the other 15 positions.

EXERCISE 2.21   Pick an integer l with $3 \le l \le 17$. Show that if $\Sigma f_\alpha f'_\alpha$ for positions 1 and l and 2 and l are either both above average or both below average then this indicates that positions 1 and 2 are in the same group. Furthermore show that the other two possibilities indicate that they are in different groups.

In view of Exercise 2.21 we might let *l* vary from 3 to 17 and score 1 point each time we get an indication that 1 and 2 are in the same group. Thus our final score will lie somewhere between 0 and 17. Clearly if the score is 0 we would assume 1 and 2 are in different groups whilst if it is 17 we would assume them to be in the same group. In fact, if the score is more than about 10 we might take it as an indication they are in the same group. Similarly if it is less than about 7 this may indicate they belong in different groups. If the value is 8 or 9, however, we might be very reluctant to make a decision. In this case we need a third group: the 'don't knows'.

We could now continue by resolving positions 3 to 17 relative to 1. Similarly we could resolve the positions relative to 2 and so on. In this way we will eventually have 17 different (although hopefully not too different) ways of splitting the positions into two groups. In order to achieve our final groupings we might then do a majority vote. In each of our different groupings we have two groups plus the 'don't knows'. We try to 'line up' our 17 groupings so that there are as few disagreements as possible. We then decide which group each position is in most often. Again, when the voting is too close, we may wish to have a 'don't knows' group.

For our purposes we have said enough about this particular problem. It should be clear that, by one of the above techniques or some variation, we can split the pins into two or three groups. Of course, and we must re-emphasize this, we will have no idea which of the two sets of pins is active.

If we do this for each wheel in turn then we will probably feel a great deal more confidence in some of our 'guesses' than in others. The idea now is to take the wheel (or wheels) which we consider to be our 'best' guess and to make another attempt at reconciling the other wheels on the assumption that our best guess is correct.

For our particular example, the initial guess is shown in Table 2.26. The two groups are represented by Xs and Ys and ?s are used to represent the 'don't knows'.

```
WHEEL: LENGTH 17 IS GUESSED TO BE
Y Y ? X Y X X Y Y Y Y X ? X Y Y Y

WHEEL: LENGTH 19 IS GUESSED TO BE
Y X Y X Y X Y X Y X Y X X Y X ? X X Y

WHEEL: LENGTH 21 IS GUESSED TO BE
Y Y X Y X X X Y Y Y X Y X X X X Y X Y X Y

WHEEL: LENGTH 23 IS GUESSED TO BE
? ? ? ? X ? X Y ? Y X X Y ? X ? ? ? Y ? ? X X

WHEEL: LENGTH 25 IS GUESSED TO BE
Y ? Y X X ? X Y X X Y X Y X ? X X Y X X Y X Y ? Y

WHEEL: LENGTH 26 IS GUESSED TO BE
Y X X ? Y X ? X X Y X X ? Y X Y Y X Y ? ? X ? X Y ?
```

Table 2.26
Our original guess for the pin groupings

In order to illustrate the chain of events involved in reassessing some wheel on the assumption that others are correct, we will revert to the situation where the machine was set using Tables 2.2 and 2.3. We will assume that we have guessed wheel 1 correctly and that we wish to use this guess to determine the settings on wheel 6. If we now consider the $(6, l)$-positions then for each of them we know whether the basic pin on wheel 1 was active or inactive.

EXERCISE 2.22
> (i) *Show that if wheel 1 is active and wheel 6 is inactive then the 16 possible shifts are:* 0, 9, 3, 12, 1, 10, 3, 12, 10, 19, 13, 22, 11, 20, 13, 22.

(ii) *Show that if wheel 1 is active and wheel 6 is inactive then the 16 possible shifts are:* 4, 13, 6, 15, 5, 14, 6, 15, 13, 22, 15, 24, 14, 23, 15, 24.

(iii) *Compare the shifts in* (i) *and* (ii) *with the shifts obtained in Exercise 2.17.*

(iv) *Find the two sets of possible shifts when wheel 1 is inactive.*

From the solution of Exercise 2.22 it should be clear that, once we know the settings for wheel 1, if the basic pin on any other wheel is active there are only 16 possible shifts for any of its positions, and another 16 if the basic pin is inactive. This means that, for any given position, instead of having one ciphertext passage using 32 substitution alphabets we now have two passages each using 16. This makes the matching easier. If, in our example, the frequences of the two passages in the (i, l)-positions are f_α and f_α^* and those in the (i, j)-positions are g_α and g_α^* $(\alpha = \mathbf{A}, \ldots, \mathbf{Z})$, then we now look for high values of

$$\sum_{\mathbf{A}}^{\mathbf{Z}} (f_\alpha g_\alpha + f_\alpha^* g_\alpha^*).$$

Reapplying whichever of the matching techniques was chosen earlier will enable us to reassess every other wheel.

Table 2.27 shows the computer printout after a series of successive reassessments for our particular example. It illustrates one important point. Each setting after the first depends on the assumption that our original 'best guess' was correct. This, of course, is dangerous and it is advisable to reassess each wheel, including the so-called 'best', more than once. In this case we reassessed our wheels 6 and 4 after we had guessed four wheels.

We still do not know which of the two groups on any given wheel represent the active pin. (In case it is not clear, we stress that we labelled the groups on each wheel X and Y in a completely arbitrary manner. So, and this is what we must stress, the group labelled X is likely to be active on some wheels and inactive on others.) We must now resolve the pin settings and the lug cage parameters. There are a number of ways to proceed. In general, however, assuming that there is a reasonably long ciphertext passage and that most of the pins are in the correct groups, the simplest way to deduce the lug cage parameters is to use the equations of Exercise 2.5.

It should be clear that if we consider the (i, l)-positions corresponding to a particular setting of the basic pins, then the cipher system used for these characters is monoalphabetic (with the substitution alphabet obtained by reversing the natural alphabet and 'shifting' it).

But this means that, once the pin settings are known, we can break up our ciphertext into 64 passages each of which corresponds to a given setting of the basic pins and, as a consequence, is the result of the same simple substitution. Furthermore we can decide which of the 26 shifts was

```
WHEEL: LENGTH 21 IS ASSUMED TO BE
Y Y X Y X X X Y Y Y X Y X X X X Y X Y X Y

WHEEL: LENGTH 17 IS GUESSED TO BE
Y Y Y X Y X Y X Y X Y X Y Y Y Y Y

WHEEL: LENGTH 19 IS GUESSED TO BE
Y X Y X Y X Y X Y X Y X X Y X Y X X Y

WHEEL: LENGTH 23 IS GUESSED TO BE
? X Y ? X X ? Y X ? X X Y X ? X Y Y X Y X Y X

WHEEL: LENGTH 25 IS GUESSED TO BE
Y Y Y X X X X Y X X Y X Y X Y Y Y X Y X X Y X Y X X

WHEEL: LENGTH 26 IS GUESSED TO BE
Y Y ? ? ? X ? ? ? Y X X X Y ? Y ? ? Y ? X ? ? ? Y ?
```

```
WHEEL: LENGTH 17 IS ASSUMED TO BE
Y Y Y X Y X Y X Y X Y X Y X Y Y Y Y

WHEEL: LENGTH 21 IS ASSUMED TO BE
Y Y X Y X X X Y Y Y X Y X X X X Y X Y X Y

WHEEL: LENGTH 19 IS GUESSED TO BE
Y X Y X Y X Y X Y X Y X X Y X Y X X Y

WHEEL: LENGTH 23 IS GUESSED TO BE
Y X Y X X X X Y X Y X X Y X Y Y Y X ? X Y X

WHEEL: LENGTH 25 IS GUESSED TO BE
Y Y ? X X Y X Y X X Y X Y X Y Y X Y X X Y X Y X X

WHEEL: LENGTH 26 IS GUESSED TO BE
Y X Y X Y X Y Y Y Y Y X X X Y X Y X ? Y X X X X Y Y Y
```

```
WHEEL: LENGTH 17 IS ASSUMED TO BE
Y Y Y X Y X Y X Y X Y X Y X Y Y Y Y

WHEEL: LENGTH 19 IS ASSUMED TO BE
Y X Y X Y X Y X Y X Y X X Y X Y X X Y

WHEEL: LENGTH 21 IS ASSUMED TO BE
Y Y X Y X X X Y Y Y X Y X X X X Y X Y X Y

WHEEL: LENGTH 23 IS GUESSED TO BE
Y X Y X X X X Y X Y X X Y X Y Y Y Y X Y X Y X

WHEEL: LENGTH 25 IS GUESSED TO BE
Y Y ? X X Y X Y X X Y X Y X Y Y Y X Y X X Y X Y X X

WHEEL: LENGTH 26 IS GUESSED TO BE
Y X Y X Y X Y X Y Y Y X X X Y X Y X X X Y X X Y X Y Y Y
```

Table 2.27
The reassessment process

```
WHEEL: LENGTH 17 IS ASSUMED TO BE
Y Y Y X Y X Y X Y X Y X Y Y Y Y

WHEEL: LENGTH 19 IS ASSUMED TO BE
Y X Y X Y X Y X Y X Y X X Y X Y X X Y

WHEEL: LENGTH 21 IS ASSUMED TO BE
Y Y X Y X X X Y Y Y X Y X X X X Y X Y X Y

WHEEL: LENGTH 23 IS ASSUMED TO BE
Y X Y X X X X Y X Y X X Y X Y Y Y Y X Y X Y X

WHEEL: LENGTH 25 IS GUESSED TO BE
Y Y Y X X Y X Y X X Y X Y X Y Y X Y X X Y X Y X X

WHEEL: LENGTH 26 IS GUESSED TO BE
Y X Y X Y X Y X Y X X X X Y X Y X X Y X X Y X Y Y Y
```

```
WHEEL: LENGTH 19 IS ASSUMED TO BE
Y X Y X Y X Y X Y X Y X X Y X Y X X Y

WHEEL: LENGTH 23 IS ASSUMED TO BE
Y X Y X X X X Y X Y X X Y X Y Y Y Y X Y X Y X

WHEEL: LENGTH 25 IS ASSUMED TO BE
Y Y Y X X Y X Y X X Y X Y X Y Y X Y X X Y X Y X X

WHEEL: LENGTH 17 IS GUESSED TO BE
Y Y Y X Y X Y X Y X Y X Y X Y ? Y

WHEEL: LENGTH 21 IS GUESSED TO BE
Y Y X Y X Y X Y Y Y X Y X X X X Y X Y X Y

WHEEL: LENGTH 26 IS GUESSED TO BE
? ? Y X Y X Y X Y ? X X X Y ? Y X X Y X X Y ? Y Y Y
```

```
WHEEL: LENGTH 19 IS ASSUMED TO BE
Y X Y X Y X Y X Y X Y X X Y X Y X X Y

WHEEL: LENGTH 21 IS ASSUMED TO BE
Y Y X Y X Y X Y Y Y X Y X X X X Y X Y X Y

WHEEL: LENGTH 23 IS ASSUMED TO BE
Y X Y X X X X Y X Y X X Y X Y Y Y Y X Y X Y X

WHEEL: LENGTH 25 IS ASSUMED TO BE
Y Y Y X X Y X Y X X Y X Y X Y Y X Y X X Y X Y X X

WHEEL: LENGTH 17 IS GUESSED TO BE
Y Y Y X Y X Y X Y X Y X Y X Y Y Y

WHEEL: LENGTH 26 IS GUESSED TO BE
Y X Y X Y X Y X Y X X X X Y X Y X X Y X X Y X Y Y Y
```

Table 2.27
The reassessment process (*cont.*)

used for each passage by comparing its frequency distribution with the expected one. Remembering that the M-209 uses z as a space we can use Appendix 1 to write down the frequency distribution against which we should compare each of the 64 passages.

As a reminder of the way in which Exercise 2.5 is used we set a straightforward exercise.

EXERCISE 2.23   Show that if the shift corresponding to an active pin setting of 100000 is 10 then x_1 is probably 10. If the shift corresponding to 010000 is 5 and that of 110000 is 14 show also that x_2 is probably 5 and x_{12} is probably 1.

Thus once we know the actual pin settings it is fairly straightforward to resolve the lug parameters. But, of course, we still do not know the actual pin settings. Our groupings of the pins on each wheel into two sets allows 64 possibilities for the actual pin settings. We now merely try each one in turn to see which leads to the most consistent setting for the lug cage. (Note that for a number of the settings the values for the lug cage parameters will not satisfy the inequalities of Theorem 2.1 and consequently not make sense.) Our final choices for the pin and lug settings are shown in Tables 2.28 and 2.29 respectively.

```
1 0 1 0 1 0 1 0 1 0 0 0 0 1 0 1 0 0 1 0 0 1 0 1 1 1
1 1 1 0 0 1 0 1 0 0 1 0 1 0 1 1 0 1 0 0 1 0 1 0 0
1 0 1 0 0 0 0 1 0 1 0 0 1 0 1 1 1 1 0 1 0 1 0
0 0 1 0 1 0 1 0 0 0 1 0 1 1 1 1 0 1 0 1 0
0 1 0 1 0 1 0 1 0 1 0 1 1 0 1 0 1 1 0
1 1 1 0 1 0 1 0 1 0 1 0 1 0 1 1 1
```

Table 2.28
The pin settings

$$x_1 = 8 \quad x_{12} = 1 \quad x_{13} = 1 \quad x_{14} = 0 \quad x_{15} = 0 \quad x_{16} = 0$$
$$x_2 = 2 \quad x_{23} = 0 \quad x_{24} = 0 \quad x_{25} = 0 \quad x_{26} = 0$$
$$x_3 = 4 \quad x_{34} = 0 \quad x_{35} = 0 \quad x_{36} = 1$$
$$x_4 = 1 \quad x_{45} = 0 \quad x_{46} = 0$$
$$x_5 = 11 \quad x_{56} = 3$$
$$x_6 = 7$$

Table 2.29
The lug cage parameters

Given all the parameters it is a simple matter to decipher the message and get the plaintext shown in Table 2.30.

It is worth noting that, although this particular cryptogram had 3000 characters, our algorithm generally works for samples of about 2500 characters and often with as few as 2000. This algorithm is completely

```
A GREAT DEAL OF INTEREST HAS BEEN SHOWN RECENTLY IN ELECTRONIC FUND T
RANSFER SYSTEMS MUCH OF THE ATTRACTION OF SUCH A SYSTEM IS THAT IT OFFER
S AN ALTERNATIVE TO THE GROWING PROBLEMS OF PAPERBASED TRANSACTIONS  FUR
THERMORE WITH CAREFUL DESIGN AN ELECTRONIC FUND TRANSFER SYSTEM CAN OFFE
R ITS USERS A HIGHER DEGREE OF SECURITY THAN THEY HAVE HITHERTO HAD AVAI
LABLE    MANY ARTICLES HAVE APPEARED DISCUSSING BOTH THE ECONOMICS AND E
RGONOMICS OF THESE SYSTEMS IN THE PRESENT PAPER THE DISCUSSION WILL BE R
ESTRICTED TO THE SECURITY ASPECTS OF ELECTRONIC FUNDS TRANSFER IN ITS RO
LE AS AN ONLINE FUND SYSTEM BY AN ONLINE SYSTEM IT IS MEANT THAT ALL VER
IFICATION AND AUTHORIZATION TAKES PLACE WITHIN A COMPUTER NETWORK THAT I
S REMOTE FROM THE TERMINAL    TO EXAMINE THE TYPE OF SECURITY THREATS WI
TH WHICH AN ELECTRONIC FUNDS TRANSFER SYSTEM MIGHT HAVE TO COPE CONSIDER
 FIRST THE WAY IN WHICH A TYPICAL SYSTEM MIGHT WORK SUPPOSE A TYPICAL SY
STEM CONSISTS OF TERMINALS AT THE POINT OF SALE IN A RETAILER AND THAT T
HESE TERMINALS COMMUNICATE VIA A COMMUNICATIONS NETWORK WITH A CENTRAL C
OMPUTER WHOSE FUNCTION IT IS TO RATIFY THE TRANSACTION AND RETURN A SIGN
AL TO THE TERMINAL WHICH MAY EITHER AUTHORISE IT OR NOT    A CUSTOMER WI
SHING TO USE THIS SYSTEM WOULD NORMALLY BE ISSUED WITH A PLASTIC CARD BE
ARING A MAGNETIC STRIPE THE MAGNETIC STRIPE WOULD CONTAIN SOME IDENTIFIC
ATION OF THE CUSTOMER FOR EXAMPLE AN ACCOUNT NUMBER TOGETHER WITH VARIOU
S OTHER INFORMATION TYPICALLY SOME CARDISSUER IDENTIFICATION AND AN EXPI
RY DATE IN ADDITION THE CUSTOMER WOULD BE ISSUED WITH SOME PERSONAL IDEN
TIFICATION DATA THAT WOULD BE KEPT SECRET    IDEALLY THIS DATA IS KNOWN
ONLY TO THE CUSTOMER AND THE CARDISSUER BETTER STILL IF IT IS ONLY THE CA
RDISSUERS COMPUTER THAT HAS THIS INFORMATION    TO USE THE SYSTEM THE FO
LLOWING SEQUENCE OF EVENTS WOULD TAKE PLACE FIRST THE RETAILER ENTERS ON
 THE TERMINAL THE AMOUNT OF THE TRANSACTION THE CUSTOMERS CARD IS THEN R
EAD BY THE TERMINAL THE CUSTOMER ON AGREEING THE AMOUNT ENTERS HIS PERSO
NAL IDENTIFICATION DATA WHICH WOULD IDEALLY BE VIA A SEPARATE KEYBOARD T
HUS THE TERMINAL NOW KNOWS THE AMOUNT OF THE TRANSACTION THE CUSTOMER ID
ENTIFICATION AND THE PERSONAL IDENTIFICATION DATA AS WELL AS OTHER INFOR
MATION SUCH AS THE CARD EXPIRY DATE TERMINAL IDENTIFICATION ETC    IT MU
ST NOW VIA THE COMMUNICATIONS NETWORK COMMUNICATE WITH THE CARDISSUERS C
OMPUTER THIS HAS A RECORD OF THIS CUSTOMERS DATA WHICH CAN BE ACCESSED V
IA THE CUSTOMER IDENTIFICATION AND CAN THUS VERIFY THAT THE USER HAS ENT
ERED THE CORRECT DATA CORRESPONDING TO HIS MAGNETIC CARD IN THIS WAY THE
 DATA ACTS AS A SIGNATURE    SO PROVIDED THE COMPUTERS RECORDS SHOW THAT
 THE FUNDS ARE AVAILABLE THE TRANSACTION CAN BE AUTHORISED THIS AUTHORIS
ATION OR NONAUTHORISATION INFORMATION IS THEN COMMUNICATED TO THE TERMIN
AL AND THE COMPUTER AWAITS A CONFIRMATION THAT THE TRANSACTION HAS TAKEN
 PLACE UPON WHICH IT CAN MAKE THE TRANSFER OF FUNDS    IN SOME SYSTEMS T
HE TRANSFER OF FUNDS MAY NOT TAKE PLACE IMMEDIAT
```

Table 2.30
The plaintext message

automated and if we remove some of the automation then about 1500 characters can be handled.

Throughout this discussion we assumed that we had intercepted one single enciphered message. If we obtain several shorter messages then the cryptanalysis will depend on how the machine is set up for each of the individual messages. If, at one extreme, the machine was not altered between transmissions then we could proceed as if we had only one message. But it is more customary to change the wheel settings at the start of each new message. (The reader should look back to the last paragraph of Section 2.3.1 if the role of the message indicator has been forgotten.) If these new wheel settings are transmitted in clear, an interceptor can deduce the relative positions of the wheels in the various messages and can assemble all the data for his attack. However a little extra work is necessary to do this. In general if the interceptor knows how the machine settings are altered at the start of each message he may be able to combine all the intercepted messages for a single attack.

We end this discussion of the M-209 with an extremely important observation. Throughout the chapter we have assumed that any pin and lug setting is possible except that every wheel must have at least one active pin and at least one inactive. In other words that just about every key was possible. In practice there are many keys which do not yield 'good' ciphertext. We saw one example of this in Section 2.3.5 when the key employed did not allow all 28 possibilities for the shift. The use of one of these 'bad' keys may make the cipher system very insecure. This has resulted in a number of users writing down certain rules for the way in which the key must be chosen. For example they suggest that the percentage of active pins on each wheel should lie between 40% and 60% and that no wheel should ever have six consecutive pins in the same state. They have also listed certain preferred lug cage settings. It must not be forgotten that obeying such rules considerably decreases the number of possible keys, and that knowledge of the rules gives considerable help to the cryptanalyst. Our attacks might have been much shorter if we had known such rules were being followed!

Further Reading

[6] is a simple introduction to the M-209, and [7] is the basis of our 'known-plaintext' attack in Sections 2.3.5 and 2.3.6. In [2] further examples of recent mechanical and electro-mechanical machines can be found.

[6]   Barker, Wayne G., *Cryptanalysis of the Hagelin Cryptograph*, Laguna Hill, CA: Aegean Park Press, 1977.
[2]   Kahn, David, *The Codebreakers, The Story of Secret Writing*, New York: Macmillan, 1967.
[7]   Morris, Robert, 'The Hagelin Cipher Machine (M-209). Reconstruction of the Internal Settings', *Cryptologia*, Volume 2, Number 3, 1978, 267–289.

3.
A Theoretical Approach to Cryptography

3.1 Introduction

There can be little doubt that C. E. Shannon's work on cryptology in the 1940s has had a fundamental influence on the subject. In this chapter we discuss some of his original ideas and concepts. Thus we regard a cipher system as a number of transformations from the set of all possible messages into the set of all possible cryptograms. Without getting too deeply involved in either the mathematics or the statistics, we then explore how various desirable properties for a cipher system are reflected in the behaviour of the transformations. Although we keep very close to Shannon's approach, whenever a mathematical concept is introduced we also include a non-mathematical definition or explanation. Thus the basic ideas and crucial definitions should be clear even if the reader has to skip a few proofs.

Primarily we will be concerned with the notions of secrecy in a cipher system and redundancy in a language. Particular emphasis is given to redundancy. As we saw in Chapter 1, the statistics of the language, i.e. the frequencies of individual letters, bigrams etc., can be used to cryptanalyze many cryptograms. For instance, if a monoalphabetic cipher is used then, provided the cryptogram is long enough, one letter will occur significantly more often than any other and that letter will probably be the substitute for **e**. Yet it is a fact that if we removed the letter **e** completely from any English sentence, we would almost certainly be able to deduce the sentence. For instance removing the **e**s from the end of the last sentence gives **b abl to dduc th sntnc**. If we now try adding **e**s to give a meaningful phrase we obviously get the correct one. So, in some sense, the letter **e** is redundant and omitting it from all messages would certainly make the cryptanalyst's job harder. Shannon expanded this simple observation and gave various criteria for measuring the redundancy of a language.

Any reader who is interested in seeing a more rigorous mathematical and statistical approach should consult either Shannon's original papers [13, 14] or Khinchin [11].

3.2   Definition of a Cipher System

Figure 3.1 illustrates a **cipher system** or, as it is often called, a **secrecy system**. (Of course, the interceptor is not part of the system! He is included in the diagram merely to show where the interception is most likely to take place.) Before any message is sent, the two parties concerned, namely the **encipherer** and **recipient**, agree on their **key**. In other words they choose one particular key from the set available. For instance if an additive cipher is used as the enciphering algorithm, then the set of all keys is the 26 possible shifts. In this case they merely agree on the shift to be used. Once the two parties have agreed on a key it is kept secret, and it will always be assumed that although he knows the enciphering algorithm an interceptor does not know the particular key used. This is a fairly realistic assumption. In practical terms it means that the interceptor knows the machine used for enciphering but does not know precisely how. Once the key is agreed, the encipherer decides on the message that he wishes to send and then, using the key and the algorithm, enciphers it before transmission.

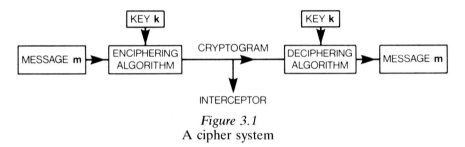

Figure 3.1
A cipher system

The set of all possible messages which the encipherer can send is called the **message space** and we will usually denote it by **M**. The set **C** of all cryptograms is called the **cryptogram space** and the set of all keys is usually denoted by **K**. In any practical situation **M**, **C** and **K** will be finite sets but, of course, much too large for us to list their elements explicitly. The procedure so far can be restated as follows: The encipherer and recipient choose an element $\mathbf{k} \in \mathbf{K}$. The encipherer first selects $\mathbf{m} \in \mathbf{M}$ and then uses the enciphering algorithm **f** to determine a unique $\mathbf{c} \in \mathbf{C}$. (The element **c** of **C** depends on both **k** and **m**. We write $\mathbf{c} = \mathbf{f}(\mathbf{m}, \mathbf{k})$.)

There is an alternative, but equivalent, way of viewing this chain of events. This is to regard the algorithm as a set of transformations from **M** into **C**. Before considering this approach we include a brief discussion of transformations.

If **A** and **B** are any two sets, not necessarily different, a **transformation** α from **A** into **B** is a rule which assigns to each element $\mathbf{a} \in \mathbf{A}$ a unique element, denoted by $\alpha(\mathbf{a})$ or $\alpha\mathbf{a}$, of **B**. We call $\alpha(\mathbf{a})$ the **image** of **a** under α. (Transformations are also often called **mappings** or **functions**.) We will write $\alpha: \mathbf{A} \rightarrow \mathbf{B}$ as a shorthand for 'α is a mapping from **A** into **B**'. For any sets **A**, **B**, **C** and transformations $\alpha: \mathbf{A} \rightarrow \mathbf{B}$ and $\beta: \mathbf{B} \rightarrow \mathbf{C}$, we can define a transformation γ: $\mathbf{A} \rightarrow \mathbf{C}$ by $\gamma(\mathbf{a}) = \beta(\alpha(\mathbf{a}))$ for each $\mathbf{a} \in \mathbf{A}$. (Note that $\alpha(\mathbf{a})$ is an element of $\mathbf{B}$.) We will write $\gamma = \beta\alpha$ and call γ the **product** of α with β. For any set $\mathbf{A}$ the **identity transformation** of $\mathbf{A}$ is the transformation $\mathbf{I_A}$: $\mathbf{A} \rightarrow \mathbf{A}$ defined by $\mathbf{I_A}(\mathbf{a}) = \mathbf{a}$ for all $\mathbf{a} \in \mathbf{A}$. Clearly any non-empty set has an identity transformation. If, for a given α: $\mathbf{A} \rightarrow \mathbf{B}$, there exists β: $\mathbf{B} \rightarrow \mathbf{A}$ with $\beta\alpha = \mathbf{I_A}$, then we say that α is **reversible** and call β an **inverse** of α. It is certainly possible for a reversible transformation to have more than one inverse. However, if α has a unique inverse β then we say that α is **uniquely reversible** and write $\beta = \alpha^{-1}$. An understanding of transformations is important for certain parts of this chapter and any reader who is not familiar with them should do the following exercises.

EXERCISE 3.1   If $\mathbf{A} = \{a_1\ a_2\}$, $\mathbf{B} = \{b_1, b_2, b_3\}$ and $\mathbf{C} = \{c_1, c_2, c_3, c_4\}$ then:

   (i)   *show that there are only nine transformations from $\mathbf{A}$ into $\mathbf{B}$ and list them. (Note: to write down a transformation α: $\mathbf{A} \rightarrow \mathbf{B}$ you merely have to state the images $\alpha(a_1)$ and $\alpha(a_2)$. Thus $\alpha(a_1) = b_1$, $\alpha(a_2) = b_3$ is a transformation from $\mathbf{A}$ into $\mathbf{B}$),*

   (ii) *show that there are only eight transformations from $\mathbf{B}$ into $\mathbf{A}$ and list them,*

   (iii) *show that if α: $\mathbf{A} \rightarrow \mathbf{B}$ is defined by $\alpha(a_1) = b_3$, $\alpha(a_2) = b_2$ and, β: $\mathbf{B} \rightarrow \mathbf{C}$ is defined by $\beta(b_1) = c_2$, $\beta(b_2) = c_2$, $\beta(b_3) = c_4$ then $\beta\alpha$ is defined by $\beta\alpha(a_1) = c_4$, $\beta\alpha(a_2) = c_2$,*

   (iv) *show that if α: $\mathbf{A} \rightarrow \mathbf{B}$ is defined by $\alpha(a_1) = b_1$, $\alpha(a_2) = b_3$ then α has two inverses, namely β: $\mathbf{B} \rightarrow \mathbf{A}$ defined by $\beta(b_1) = a_1$, $\beta(b_2) = a_1$, $\beta(b_3) = a_2$ and γ: $\mathbf{B} \rightarrow \mathbf{A}$ defined by $\gamma(b_1) = a_1$, $\gamma(b_2) = a_2$, $\gamma(b_3) = a_2$,*

   (v) *show there are no reversible transformations from $\mathbf{B}$ into $\mathbf{A}$.*

EXERCISE 3.2   For any finite set $\mathbf{X}$ we let $|\mathbf{X}|$ denote the number of elements in $\mathbf{X}$. If $\mathbf{A}$ and $\mathbf{B}$ are finite sets with $|\mathbf{A}| = n$ and $|\mathbf{B}| = m$, show

   (i)   *there are m^n transformations from $\mathbf{A}$ into $\mathbf{B}$ and n^m transformations from $\mathbf{B}$ into $\mathbf{A}$,*

   (ii) *if $n < m$ then some, but not all, of the transformations from $\mathbf{A}$ into $\mathbf{B}$ are reversible, but there are no reversible transformations from $\mathbf{B}$ into $\mathbf{A}$,*

   (iii) *there is a uniquely reversible transformation from $\mathbf{A}$ into $\mathbf{B}$ if and only if $n = m$.*

EXERCISE 3.3   If $\mathbf{A}$ is a finite set and α: $\mathbf{A} \rightarrow \mathbf{A}$ is uniquely reversible show that $\alpha\alpha^{-1} = \mathbf{I_A}$. (Note the fact that α is uniquely reversible implies only that $\alpha^{-1}\alpha = \mathbf{I_A}$. You must show that α^{-1} is uniquely reversible and that its inverse is α.)

Suppose now that $\mathbf{K}$ consists of a finite number of keys $k_1, k_2, \ldots, k_h$ and that the probability of choosing the key k_i is p_i for $i = 1, 2, \ldots, h$. Each key $\mathbf{k}$

of $\mathbf{K}$, together with the enciphering algorithm, determines a transformation $\mathbf{t_k}: \mathbf{M} \rightarrow \mathbf{C}$. Thus we may regard the enciphering algorithm as a set $\mathbf{T}$ of transformations from $\mathbf{M}$ into $\mathbf{C}$. There is no reason why two distinct keys should not determine the same transformation. In practice, there is often not a unique key associated with a given transformation. For instance, there may be more keys than transformations. If the keys are equiprobable and there are more keys than transformations, then this may force the transformations to have unequal probabilities. We have already seen examples where different keys give rise to the same transformation. As a trivial example, consider the M-209. If each pin is inactive then the lug cage settings are irrelevant. Thus the various different keys with each pin inactive, but varying lug settings, all give rise to the same transformation. However it is clearly desirable for different keys to determine distinct transformations and, unless we state otherwise, we will assume that this is the case. Although this is a somewhat unrealistic assumption, it has the advantage of simplifying the discussion and is adequate for this chapter. Under this assumption if $\mathbf{K} = \{\mathbf{k}_1, \mathbf{k}_2, \ldots, \mathbf{k}_h\}$ then we will usually write $\mathbf{t}_i$ for $\mathbf{t_{k_i}}$, the transformation determined by the key $\mathbf{k}_i$. Thus the probability of the transformation $\mathbf{t}_i$ being used is p_i. In our example of additive ciphers we have 26 keys. Each key uniquely determines one of the 26 possible substitution alphabets. The image of any message under the transformation determined by a key is obtained, as we saw in Chapter 1, by applying the substitution alphabet to the message. Thus each transformation is uniquely defined by one of the 26 substitution alphabets which, of course, means there are only 26 transformations. Furthermore the probability of any given transformation being used is $\frac{1}{26}$. In general, if $p_i = \dfrac{1}{h}$ for each i, where $h = |\mathbf{K}|$, then we will not bother to state the probabilities. From now on, if no probabilities are listed each key should be assumed to be equally likely. Again this is a slightly unrealistic assumption. With the M-209, for instance, we noted that some users recommended certain 'good' pin and lug settings, which had the effect that these keys were used more often than others. Nevertheless we will make it in order to simplify our discussions. Since each key uniquely determines a transformation, we will usually regard keys and transformations as being the same. As well as assuming that $\mathbf{K}$ is finite, we also assume that there are only a finite number of messages and that each message $\mathbf{m}_i \in \mathbf{M}$ has an associated probability q_i of being transmitted. (Note: of course we are not assuming that finite means small!) If it is impossible for a particular key or message to be chosen, then we will not include it in $\mathbf{K}$ or $\mathbf{M}$ respectively.

One crucial requirement of a cipher system is that knowledge of the cryptogram, key and algorithm must enable the recipient to determine the message uniquely. Thus if $\mathbf{c} = \mathbf{t}(\mathbf{m})$, then $\mathbf{m}$ must be uniquely determined by $\mathbf{c}$ and $\mathbf{t}$. In other words, $\mathbf{t}$ must be reversible and $\mathbf{m}$ must be the image of $\mathbf{c}$ under $\mathbf{t}^{-1}$. We can now give Shannon's definition of a cipher system. A **cipher system** is a finite family $\mathbf{T}$ of reversible transformations from a (usually finite) set of messages **M** into a set of cryptograms **C**. For each $t_i \in$ **T** there is an associated probability p_i which represents the probability of t_i being chosen. Similarly each message also has an associated probability.

In this terminology the difference between the recipient's and interceptor's knowledge is that the recipient knows which t_i was used, while the interceptor knows only the *a priori* probabilities of the various transformations. If, as in the example using additive ciphers, each key is equally likely then the interceptor merely has a list of all possible transformations.

The definition of a cipher system allows for the keys and messages to have different probabilities, and it is important to realize that this can, and indeed does, occur. However, in many of the examples which we have either met already or will discuss later, each key is equally likely. Not surprisingly the mathematics involved in studying 'equiprobable' systems is considerably simpler than that necessary to discuss arbitrary systems. Having given the 'correct' definition we will, in the next two sections and at various other times, use a slightly 'weaker' definition. Unless the context makes it clear that we are doing otherwise, we will assume that in a cipher system each key is equally likely. However, in order to remind the reader that we are over-simplifying the situation and also to indicate the type of calculations we are avoiding, we include examples where the key probabilities are different. When we do this we will draw special attention to the fact and will say that the system is **variant**.

Similarly we do not wish to keep referring to the message probabilities, although in this case it is very unlikely that they will all be equal. The reader should therefore, unless they are explicitly stated, use his own judgement regarding their values. This is more or less what we did in Chapter 1.

Any cipher system with a finite number of messages and cryptograms may be represented pictorially in the following way. On the left we write a column of dots; each dot representing a possible message. A second column of dots, representing all possible cryptograms, is written on the right. If a given key **k** transforms message **m** to cryptogram **c** then a line, labelled **k**, is drawn from the dot of **m** to the dot of **c**. For example suppose **M** = {m_1, m_2, m_3}, **C** = {c_1, c_2, c_3, c_4}, **K** = {k_1, k_2, k_3} and **T** = {t_1, t_2, t_3} where $t_1(m_1) = c_1$, $t_1(m_2) = c_2$, and $t_1(m_3) = c_3$; $t_2(m_1) = c_1$, $t_2(m_2) = c_4$ and $t_2(m_3) = c_2$; $t_3(m_1) = c_4$, $t_3(m_2) = c_3$ and $t_3(m_3) = c_1$. Then remembering that t_i is the transformation determined by key k_i, and $i = 1, 2, 3$, the diagram is as shown in Figure 3.2.

Figure 3.2 may be taken as representing a graph with the messages and cryptograms as vertices and the lines as edges. By its definition, this graph has the property that there is no edge joining two messages or two cryptograms. Any graph in which the vertices may be divided into two disjoint sets such that there is no edge joining any two vertices in the same set is called **bipartite**. Thus any cipher system may be regarded as a bipartite graph. Clearly for each message m_i there will be exactly one edge

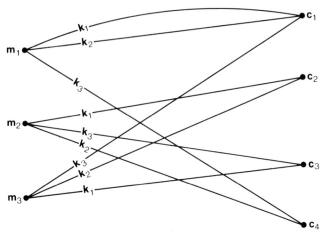

Figure 3.2
A graph of the example

emerging for each different key. (This merely reflects the property that each key must enable all messages to be enciphered.) Furthermore, since each transformation is reversible, the same key cannot join different messages to the same cryptogram. Thus each cryptogram has at most one edge entering it for each key. If, as is not the case in our example, there is also exactly one edge entering each cryptogram for each key then each transformation is uniquely reversible and the cipher system is called **closed**. Figure 3.3 gives a very simple example of a closed cipher system.

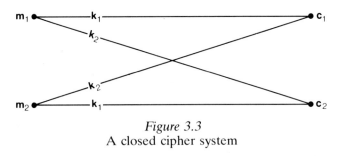

Figure 3.3
A closed cipher system

3.3   Some Examples

Unless otherwise stated, when we discuss specific examples in this section the message and cryptogram spaces are all possible finite sequences of the letters of the English alphabet. In practice, of course, the message space may be restricted to those sequences which, allowing for an occasional error, have some meaning in the language.

3.3.1 Monoalphabetic ciphers

Our first example of a cipher system was a monoalphabetic cipher. Here a typical message $\mathbf{m}$ is given by $\mathbf{m} = \mathbf{m}_1\mathbf{m}_2\mathbf{m}_3\ldots$ where each $\mathbf{m}_i$ is a letter of the alphabet. The algorithm replaces each letter by a uniquely determined substitute, and the keys are the various ways of assigning the substitutes to the message letters. Thus, as we saw in Chapter 1, there are 26! keys. Once we have chosen a key $\mathbf{k}$ with associated transformation $\mathbf{t}$ then, for any $\mathbf{m}$ in the message space $\mathbf{M}$, the method described in Chapter 1 for determining the cryptogram $\mathbf{c} = \mathbf{t}(\mathbf{m})$ may be interpreted as follows.

We first write out the plaintext alphabet and underneath each letter we write its ciphertext equivalent. Thus we get:

Plaintext:	**a**	**b**	**c**	**d**	$\ldots$
Ciphertext:	$\mathbf{t(a)}$	$\mathbf{t(b)}$	$\mathbf{t(c)}$	$\mathbf{t(d)}$	$\ldots$

The rule for enciphering is then merely to write out the message $\mathbf{m} = \mathbf{m}_1\mathbf{m}_2\mathbf{m}_3\ldots$ and replace each letter by the relevant one in the substitution alphabet. Thus if $\mathbf{c} = \mathbf{t}(\mathbf{m})$ and $\mathbf{c} = \mathbf{c}_1\mathbf{c}_2\mathbf{c}_3\ldots$ then $\mathbf{c}_i = \mathbf{t}(\mathbf{m}_i)$ for all i. In other words $\mathbf{t}(\mathbf{m}_1\mathbf{m}_2\mathbf{m}_3\ldots) = \mathbf{t}(\mathbf{m}_1)\mathbf{t}(\mathbf{m}_2)\mathbf{t}(\mathbf{m}_3)\ldots$

We will refer to these 26! transformations as the **monoalphabetic transformations** or **simple substitutions**. Of course it may happen that the particular cipher system being used only allows a small subset of these 26! transformations, e.g. the additive ciphers.

3.3.2 Vigenère ciphers

As an example of a polyalphabetic cipher we will discuss the Vigenère cipher. Although the message and cryptogram spaces are the same as in Section 3.3.1, the number of keys is increased dramatically. Each keyword is a key and determines a transformation $\mathbf{t} : \mathbf{M} \rightarrow \mathbf{C}$. This transformation may, in this case, be regarded as a sequence of monoalphabetic transformations from $\mathbf{M}$ into $\mathbf{C}$. If $\mathbf{t}$ determines the sequence $\mathbf{t}_1\mathbf{t}_2\mathbf{t}_3\mathbf{t}_4\ldots$ of simple substitutions from $\mathbf{M}$ into $\mathbf{C}$ and if $\mathbf{m} = \mathbf{m}_1\mathbf{m}_2\mathbf{m}_3\mathbf{m}_4\ldots$, where each $\mathbf{m}_i$ is a letter, then $\mathbf{t}(\mathbf{m}) = \mathbf{t}_1(\mathbf{m}_1)\mathbf{t}_2(\mathbf{m}_2)\mathbf{t}_3(\mathbf{m}_3)\mathbf{t}_4(\mathbf{m}_4)\ldots$ For example if the keyword is 'may' and if $\mathbf{t}_1, \mathbf{t}_2, \mathbf{t}_3$ are the transformations from $\mathbf{M} \rightarrow \mathbf{C}$ determined by additive ciphers with shifts $12, 0, 24$ respectively then $\mathbf{t}$ is the sequence $\mathbf{t}_1\mathbf{t}_2\mathbf{t}_3\mathbf{t}_1\mathbf{t}_2\mathbf{t}_3\mathbf{t}_1\mathbf{t}_2\mathbf{t}_3\mathbf{t}_1\ldots$

3.3.3 Weighted sums

If we have two cipher systems $\mathbf{T}$ and $\mathbf{R}$ then there are certain circumstances under which we can combine them to obtain a third system $\mathbf{S}$. Before discussing some of those methods, we will clarify what we mean by the statement 'two systems are equal' or 'two systems are different'. Two cipher systems will be called **equal** (or the same) if they have the same message and cryptogram spaces plus the same transformations. (If the assumption that each key is equally likely is dropped, then, for two systems to be equal, each transformation must have the same probability in each system.) In this method for combining systems, and also in many others, even if one starts with two systems in which the keys are equally likely there is no guarantee that the resulting system will not be variant. Consequently we will discuss this method by combining variant systems, and thus illustrate some of the extra difficulties which arise when the keys are not all equally likely.

If $\mathbf{R}$ and $\mathbf{T}$ are any two variant cipher systems with the same message space $\mathbf{M}$ and if p and q are non-negative real numbers with $p + q = 1$, then we can combine the transformations of $\mathbf{R}$ and $\mathbf{T}$ to obtain a new variant cipher system $\mathbf{S}$, called a **weighted sum** of $\mathbf{R}$ and $\mathbf{T}$ and written $\mathbf{S} = p\mathbf{R} + q\mathbf{T}$, with message space $\mathbf{M}$. To encipher using $\mathbf{S}$ we must first choose between the systems $\mathbf{R}$ and $\mathbf{T}$ (the probability of choosing $\mathbf{R}$ being p). Having chosen between $\mathbf{R}$ and $\mathbf{T}$, we then choose which particular transformation to use. Thus if the transformations of $\mathbf{R}$ are $\mathbf{r}_1, \mathbf{r}_2, \ldots, \mathbf{r}_m$ with probabilities $p_1, p_2, \ldots, p_m$ respectively, and the transformations of $\mathbf{T}$ are $\mathbf{t}_1, \mathbf{t}_2, \ldots, \mathbf{t}_n$ with respective probabilities $q_1, q_2, \ldots, q_n$, then the transformations of $\mathbf{S}$ are $\mathbf{r}_1, \mathbf{r}_2, \mathbf{r}_3, \ldots, \mathbf{r}_m, \mathbf{t}_1, \mathbf{t}_2, \ldots, \mathbf{t}_n$ with probabilities $pp_1, pp_2, \ldots, pp_m, qq_1, \ldots, qq_n$ respectively. Of course there is no reason why $\mathbf{R}$ and $\mathbf{T}$ should not have some common transformations. If this occurs then the number of transformations of $p\mathbf{R} + q\mathbf{T}$ will be less than $m + n$. In this case if, for example, $\mathbf{r}_i$ is the same as $\mathbf{t}_j$ then the probability of $\mathbf{r}_i$ in $p\mathbf{R} + q\mathbf{T}$ will be $pp_i + qq_j$; i.e. the weighted sum of the probabilities of $\mathbf{r}_i$ and $\mathbf{t}_j$.

As an illustration of a weighted sum, suppose that $\mathbf{R}$ and $\mathbf{T}$ are the systems of genuine additive and multiplicative ciphers respectively. Recalling that genuine means non-identity, this means that $\mathbf{R}$ has 25 transformations while $\mathbf{T}$ has 11. If the transformations of $\mathbf{R}$ are $\mathbf{r}_1, \mathbf{r}_2, \ldots, \mathbf{r}_{25}$, then each has probability $\frac{1}{25}$ and if those of $\mathbf{T}$ are $\mathbf{t}_1, \mathbf{t}_2, \ldots, \mathbf{t}_{11}$ then each has probability $\frac{1}{11}$. If $\mathbf{S}$ is the cipher system whose transformations are $\mathbf{r}_1, \mathbf{r}_2, \ldots, \mathbf{r}_{25}, \mathbf{t}_1, \mathbf{t}_2, \ldots, \mathbf{t}_{11}$ with all probabilities equal then $\mathbf{S} = \frac{25}{36}\mathbf{R} + \frac{11}{36}\mathbf{T}$. But now suppose that $\mathbf{A}$ and $\mathbf{B}$ are the systems of all additive and multiplicative ciphers. Then $\mathbf{A}$ and $\mathbf{B}$ have the identity transformation $\mathbf{I}$ in common. Let the transformations of $\mathbf{A}$ be $\mathbf{I}, \mathbf{a}_1, \mathbf{a}_2, \ldots, \mathbf{a}_{25}$ and those of $\mathbf{B}$ be $\mathbf{I}, \mathbf{b}_1, \mathbf{b}_2, \ldots, \mathbf{b}_{11}$. For any non-negative p and q with $p + q = 1$, $p\mathbf{A} + q\mathbf{B}$ has transformations $\mathbf{I}, \mathbf{a}_1, \ldots, \mathbf{a}_{25}, \mathbf{b}_1, \ldots, \mathbf{b}_{11}$. The probability of $\mathbf{I}$ is $\dfrac{p}{26} + \dfrac{q}{12}$, the probability of $\mathbf{a}_i$ is $\dfrac{p}{26}$ and the probability of $\mathbf{b}_j$ is $\dfrac{q}{12}$ for each i and j. In this case, although $\mathbf{A}$ and $\mathbf{B}$ both have each of their keys equally likely, their weighted sum has one key which is more likely than any other; i.e. the weighted sum of two non-variant cipher systems can be variant.

More generally, if $\mathbf{T}_1, \mathbf{T}_2, \ldots, \mathbf{T}_s$ are any number of variant systems with the same message space and if $p_1, p_2, \ldots, p_s$ are any non-negative real numbers with

$$\sum_{i=1}^{s} p_i = 1$$

we may form, in the obvious way, the weighted sum

$$\mathbf{S} = p_1\mathbf{T}_1 + p_2\mathbf{T}_2 + \ldots + p_s\mathbf{T}_s.$$

We now note that if $\mathbf{T}$ is any variant system with transformations $\mathbf{t}_1, \mathbf{t}_2, \ldots,$ $\mathbf{t}_h$ and probabilities $p_1, p_2, \ldots, p_h$ then, since one transformation gives a system and $\sum_{i=1}^{h} p_i = 1$, $\mathbf{T} = p_1\mathbf{t}_1 + p_2\mathbf{t}_2 + \ldots + p_h\mathbf{t}_h$. This means that any cipher system is a weighted sum of its individual transformations. In defining weighted sums we have not mentioned the cryptogram spaces. However it should be clear that, for any $\mathbf{R}$ and $\mathbf{T}$ with the same message space $\mathbf{M}$, a weighted sum $\mathbf{S} = p\mathbf{R} + q\mathbf{T}$ can be defined no matter what cryptogram spaces $\mathbf{R}$ and $\mathbf{T}$ have. The cryptogram space of $\mathbf{S}$ is merely the union of their two cryptogram spaces.

3.3.4 Superenciphering

A second way of combining two cipher systems is by forming their product. Suppose that $\mathbf{R}$ and $\mathbf{T}$ are two cipher systems such that the cryptogram space $\mathbf{C}$ of $\mathbf{T}$ is the message space of $\mathbf{R}$. (In fact, as will be apparent, it is sufficient to assume that $\mathbf{C}$ is contained in the message space of $\mathbf{R}$. However for our purposes we will assume equality.) Let $\mathbf{M}$ be the message space of $\mathbf{T}$. For any $\mathbf{m} \in \mathbf{M}$ and any transformation $\mathbf{t}$ of $\mathbf{T}$, the cryptogram $\mathbf{c} = \mathbf{t}(\mathbf{m})$ is in $\mathbf{C}$. Thus, for any transformation $\mathbf{r}$ of $\mathbf{R}$, $\mathbf{r}(\mathbf{c}) = \mathbf{r}(\mathbf{t}(\mathbf{m}))$. This means that we can encipher $\mathbf{m}$ by first using any transformation of $\mathbf{T}$ and then using any transformation of $\mathbf{R}$ on the resulting cryptogram. The resulting cipher system, which has $\mathbf{M}$ as its message space and the cryptogram space of $\mathbf{R}$ as its cryptogram space, is called the **product** of $\mathbf{T}$ and $\mathbf{R}$ and is written $\mathbf{RT}$. The process of enciphering by using the product of two transformations is called **superenciphering**. We have already met an example of superenciphering; namely when we discussed affine ciphers in Chapter 1. To illustrate this we repeat some of Section 1.2.2, but with the notation of Chapter 2.

With this change of notation, the additive cipher with shift β is the transformation $\lambda \to \lambda + \beta \pmod{26}$ for all λ with $0 \le \lambda \le 25$. Similarly, if α is one of 1, 3, 5, 7, 9, 11, 15, 17, 19, 21, 23 or 25, the multiplicative cipher defined by α is the transformation $\lambda \to \alpha\lambda \pmod{26}$. Finally, the affine cipher $[\alpha, \beta]$ is the transformation $\lambda \to \alpha\lambda + \beta \pmod{26}$. Let $\mathbf{T}$ be the cipher system of all the multiplicative ciphers and let $\mathbf{R}$ be the system of all additive ciphers. So $|\mathbf{T}| = 12$ and $|\mathbf{R}| = 26$. If $\mathbf{t}$ is any transformation of $\mathbf{T}$ then $\mathbf{t} = [\alpha, 0]$, for one of the twelve appropriate values of α, while if $\mathbf{r}$ is a transformation of $\mathbf{R}$ then $\mathbf{r} = [1, \beta]$ for some β with $0 \le \beta \le 25$. For any letter λ, i.e. for any integer λ with $0 \le \lambda \le 25$, $\mathbf{t}(\lambda) = \alpha\lambda \pmod{26}$ and $\mathbf{r}(\mathbf{t}(\lambda)) = \mathbf{r}(\alpha\lambda) = \alpha\lambda + \beta \pmod{26}$. Thus $\mathbf{rt}$ is $[\alpha, \beta]$. This shows that the effect of superenciphering a multiplicative cipher by an additive cipher is to obtain an affine one. It is now easy to see that $\mathbf{RT}$ is the system of all affine ciphers.

In general let $\mathbf{T}$ be a variant cipher system with message space $\mathbf{M}$, cryptogram space $\mathbf{C}$ and transformations $\mathbf{t}_1, \ldots, \mathbf{t}_h$ with probabilities $p_1, \ldots, p_h$ respectively, while $\mathbf{R}$ has message space $\mathbf{C}$, cryptogram space $\mathbf{E}$ and transformations $\mathbf{r}_1, \ldots, \mathbf{r}_m$ with respective probabilities $q_1, \ldots, q_m$. Then $\mathbf{RT}$ is a variant cipher system with message space $\mathbf{M}$ and cryptogram space $\mathbf{E}$. Each transformation $\mathbf{r}_i \mathbf{t}_j$ from $\mathbf{M}$ into $\mathbf{E}$ is a transformation of $\mathbf{RT}$. However there is no reason whatsoever why $\mathbf{r}_i \mathbf{t}_j$ and $\mathbf{r}_l \mathbf{t}_k$ should not be the same transformation, even if $i \neq l$ and $j \neq k$. Thus $\mathbf{RT}$ need not have hm distinct transformations. The probability of $\mathbf{r}_l \mathbf{t}_k$ is the sum of all the probabilities $\mathbf{p}_i \mathbf{q}_j$ for i and j with $\mathbf{r}_i \mathbf{t}_j = \mathbf{r}_l \mathbf{t}_k$. As a simple example let $\mathbf{R}$ and $\mathbf{T}$ both be the systems illustrated in Figure 3.4.

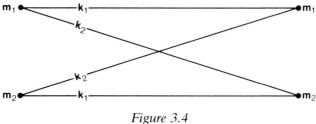

Figure 3.4
The graphs for $\mathbf{R}$ and $\mathbf{T}$

In this case $\mathbf{M} = \mathbf{C} = \mathbf{E} = \{\mathbf{m}_1, \mathbf{m}_2\}$, $\mathbf{r}_1 = \mathbf{t}_1$, $\mathbf{r}_2 = \mathbf{t}_2$ and $p_1 = p_2 = q_1 = q_2 = \frac{1}{2}$. To determine $\mathbf{RT}$ we must work out the transformations $\mathbf{r}_1 \mathbf{t}_1$, $\mathbf{r}_1 \mathbf{t}_2$, $\mathbf{r}_2 \mathbf{t}_1$ and $\mathbf{r}_2 \mathbf{t}_2$. But $\mathbf{r}_1 \mathbf{t}_1(\mathbf{m}_i) = \mathbf{r}_1(\mathbf{t}_1(\mathbf{m}_i)) = \mathbf{r}_1(\mathbf{m}_i) = \mathbf{m}_i$ for $i = 1, 2$. Thus $\mathbf{r}_1 \mathbf{t}_1 = \mathbf{r}_1 = \mathbf{t}_1$. Similarly $\mathbf{r}_2 \mathbf{t}_2(\mathbf{m}_1) = \mathbf{r}_2(\mathbf{t}_2(\mathbf{m}_1)) = \mathbf{r}_2(\mathbf{m}_2) = \mathbf{m}_1$ and $\mathbf{r}_2 \mathbf{t}_2(\mathbf{m}_2) = \mathbf{r}_2(\mathbf{t}_2(\mathbf{m}_2)) = \mathbf{r}_2(\mathbf{m}_1) = \mathbf{m}_2$. Thus $\mathbf{r}_2 \mathbf{t}_2 = \mathbf{r}_1 = \mathbf{t}_1 = \mathbf{r}_1 \mathbf{t}_1$. Straightforward verification also gives $\mathbf{r}_1 \mathbf{t}_2 = \mathbf{t}_2 = \mathbf{r}_2 = \mathbf{r}_2 \mathbf{t}_1$. In $\mathbf{RT}$ the probability of $\mathbf{t}_1$ is the sum of the probabilities of $\mathbf{r}_1 \mathbf{t}_1$ and $\mathbf{r}_2 \mathbf{t}_2$, which is $\frac{1}{4} + \frac{1}{4} = \frac{1}{2}$. Similarly the probability of $\mathbf{t}_2$ in $\mathbf{RT}$ is $\frac{1}{2}$ and so $\mathbf{RT} = \mathbf{T}$.

In the small example above, and in all our earlier examples using the English alphabet, each cipher system has its message and cryptogram spaces equal. (Such systems are called **endomorphic**). If $\mathbf{T}$ is any endomorphic cipher system then we can form the product $\mathbf{TT}$, which we write as $\mathbf{T}^2$, and can repeat the process to form $\mathbf{T}^n$ for any positive integer n. In the above small example, since $\mathbf{R} = \mathbf{T}$, we have shown that $\mathbf{T}^2 = \mathbf{T}$ and so, of course, $\mathbf{T}^n = \mathbf{T}$ for all positive integers n. Any cipher system $\mathbf{T}$ with $\mathbf{T}^2 = \mathbf{T}$ is called **idempotent**. Idempotency means that the encipherer gains nothing by superenciphering because, for an idempotent cipher system $\mathbf{T}$, if $\mathbf{t}_i$, $\mathbf{t}_j$ are any transformations of $\mathbf{T}$ there must exist a transformation $\mathbf{t}_k$ of $\mathbf{T}$ with $\mathbf{t}_k = \mathbf{t}_i \mathbf{t}_j$. Thus superenciphering gives no new transformations.

EXERCISE 3.4   Show that the following cipher systems, with equiprobable keys, are idempotent.
(i)   *The system of all additive ciphers.*

(*ii*)   *The system of all multiplicative ciphers.*
(*iii*)   *The system of all affine ciphers.*

Suppose that **R** and **T** are two endomorphic cipher systems with the same message space **M** and therefore, by the definition of endomorphic, the same cryptogram space **Ṁ**. Then we can define two products, namely **RT** and **TR**. If **RT** = **TR** then we say **R** and **T** **commute**. It is important to note that two systems need not commute and that even if they do commute then, although **RT** = **TR**, it does not necessarily follow that $r_i t_j = t_j r_i$, where r_i and t_j are individual transformations of **R** and **T** respectively. As an illustration of two commuting systems where individual transformations do not commute we return to our example, at the beginning of this section, where **R** and **T** are the systems of additive and multiplicative ciphers respectively. We know that **RT** is the system of affine ciphers. If **r, t** are transformations of **R** and **T** respectively then we have seen that if $r = [1, \beta]$ and $t = [\alpha, 0]$ then $rt = [\alpha, \beta]$. But for any integer λ with $0 \le \lambda \le 25$, $tr(\lambda) = t(r(\lambda)) = t(\lambda + \beta) = \alpha(\lambda + \beta) \equiv \alpha\lambda + \alpha\beta \pmod{26}$. Thus $tr = [\alpha, \alpha\beta]$ and, in general $tr \ne rt$. To show **RT** = **TR** we must show that **TR** is the system of all affine ciphers. Clearly, for any additive transformation **r** and any multiplicative transformation **t**, **tr** is affine. So we must show that every affine cipher is in **TR**, i.e. we must show that any $[\alpha, \beta]$ may be written as **tr** with **t** a transformation of **T** and **r** in **R**. Suppose $t = [\alpha, 0]$ then the transformation $\lambda \to \alpha\lambda \pmod{26}$ gives a different substitute for each of the 26 letters. Thus each letter must be the substitute for another and so, given any β with $0 \le \beta \le 25$, there exists a unique integer γ with $0 \le \gamma \le 25$ such that $\beta \equiv \alpha\gamma \pmod{26}$. (The letter of γ is then the one for which the letter of β is the substitute.) But now, for this particular γ, if $t = [\alpha, 0]$ and $r = [1, \gamma]$ we have $tr(\lambda) = t(r(\lambda)) = t(\lambda + \gamma) = \alpha\lambda + \alpha\gamma \equiv \alpha\lambda + \beta \pmod{26}$, i.e. $[\alpha, \beta] = tr$. Thus we have justified our claim that **TR** = **RT**.

The above discussion also illustrates that cipher systems need not commute. Each individual transformation of **R** or **T** above determines a cipher system. So if, for example, we let **U** be the system whose only transformation is $[1, 2]$ and **W** be the system whose only transformation is $[3, 0]$ then **UW** ≠ **WU**. We could, of course, construct larger non-commuting systems.

*EXERCISE 3.5   Suppose that **B** and **V** are the systems of all Beaufort and Vigenère ciphers respectively having keyword a given fixed length with all keys equally likely. Show that **BB** = **V** and that **V** is idempotent. Find transformations b_i, b_j in **B** with $b_i b_j \ne b_j b_i$.*

3.4   Pure Ciphers

3.4.1   Synopsis
Now that we have formally defined a cipher system, we can begin to consider how to design a system to make it secure against various methods

of attack. When doing this it is important to remember that the system includes not only the keys (or, equivalently, the transformations) but also the message and cryptogram spaces. We have already seen the importance of having enough keys that a cryptanalyst cannot try them all. However, it is certainly not sufficient merely to have a large number of keys. We note again that we have already seen illustrations of this. For example, if a monoalphabetic cipher system is used there are 26! possible keys. As soon as the cryptanalyst knows the plaintext equivalent of any single ciphertext letter he has decreased the number of possibilities to 25!. Thus this piece of information eliminates over $3·88×10^{26}$ keys. In this case, as we saw in Chapter 1, it is the statistics of the English language which are likely to lead the cryptanalyst to this type of deduction and, as a result, to break the system. So for monoalphabetic ciphers of the English language a major 'fault' in the system lies in the choice of message space. (This is in addition to any 'faults' in the key space.) In this section we begin to tackle the problem of defining a 'good' system. To do this we need to introduce a number of Shannon's ideas; the first being the concept of a pure cipher which we meet later in this section.

Clearly, if we are going to investigate the effect of trying all possible transformations, we must look at what happens when we try to decipher using the wrong one. For any given cryptogram and transformation there are only three possibilities:

(a)   correct decipherment,
(b)   incorrect decipherment, or
(c)   no decipherment possible.

If (c) occurs then that particular transformation can be discounted. Obviously we do not want too many possibilities to be eliminated too easily and so, from this particular point of view, we may find it desirable to have a system in which every cryptogram is the image of some message under every transformation. (This, of course, is precisely the definition of a closed system.) If (a) or (b) occurs then, ideally, we want the cryptanalyst to be unable to distinguish between them. If we use the English language then, for messages of any reasonable length, this simply does not happen. As we intimated in Exercise 1.1, the cryptanalyst is almost certain to be able to distinguish between (a) and (b), and it is this fact which is so helpful to the cryptanalyst who attacks polyalphabetic ciphers. Once again we have an instance where a 'fault' lies in the message space. (It was this type of observation which led Shannon to define another fundamentally important concept, namely that of redundancy in a language. We will meet this in Section 3.6.)

A cipher system is called **pure** if, whenever we encipher with one transformation, decipher with a second and then encipher again with a third, we can find a single transformation in the system which has the same effect. This probably seems a somewhat obscure and/or artificial property.

However it is worth noting that most of our earlier examples are pure. It is also a highly desirable property as it enables us to introduce some very interesting and useful concepts. Possibly the most important of these is the notion of a message residue class. For any message $\mathbf{m}$ the **message residue class** of $\mathbf{m}$, which we denote by $\mathbf{M}(\mathbf{m})$, consists of all those messages which might be obtained by enciphering $\mathbf{m}$ and then deciphering the resulting cryptogram using any other transformation of the system. Thus $\mathbf{M}(\mathbf{m})$ is the set of all messages which a cryptanalyst might 'confuse' with $\mathbf{m}$ when he tries deciphering using all possible keys. If the system is pure then two interesting things happen. The first is that the message residue class of any message in $\mathbf{M}(\mathbf{m})$ is precisely $\mathbf{M}(\mathbf{m})$ again. The second is that the sets of all cryptograms obtainable from any of the messages in the same message residue class are identical. Thus, in a pure system with equiprobable messages, any cryptanalyst will be unable to distinguish between the messages of any given message residue class. In such a system if we arrange for each class to be large then we will have protected ourselves against the 'try all possible keys' attack. In this case the cryptogram space is also divided into similar classes, called **cryptogram residue classes**, which have similar properties.

The rest of Section 3.4 is devoted to formalizing the above discussion and proving some of the assertions. It is somewhat abstract and the actual proofs are of no practical value. Thus any reader who was previously unacquainted with transformations and who feels he has 'suffered' enough may safely omit the section and proceed to Section 3.5.

3.4.2 Basic concepts

If $\mathbf{T}$ is a cipher system with message space $\mathbf{M}$, cryptogram space $\mathbf{C}$ and transformations $\mathbf{t}_1, \ldots, \mathbf{t}_h$, then each $\mathbf{t}_i$ is a reversible transformation. As we have already seen if a message $\mathbf{m}$ is enciphered using transformation $\mathbf{t}$ then by using an inverse transformation of $\mathbf{t}$ correct decipherment of cryptogram $\mathbf{c}$ is achieved. For any transformation $\mathbf{t}$ we call the set of all $\mathbf{t}(\mathbf{m})$, as $\mathbf{m}$ varies over $\mathbf{M}$, the image space of $\mathbf{t}$ and denote it by $\mathbf{t}(\mathbf{M})$. (Clearly the cryptogram space is the union of all the possible image spaces for all the transformations $\mathbf{t}$ in $\mathbf{T}$.) We denote by $\mathbf{t}^{-1}$ the transformation from $\mathbf{t}(\mathbf{M})$ into $\mathbf{M}$ given by $\mathbf{t}^{-1}(\mathbf{t}(\mathbf{m})) = \mathbf{m}$. It should be apparent that, for any $\mathbf{t}$, $\mathbf{t}^{-1}$ is unique and any inverse of $\mathbf{t}$ must agree with $\mathbf{t}^{-1}$ on $\mathbf{t}(\mathbf{M})$. Furthermore $\mathbf{t}^{-1}$ represents the process of deciphering using the key associated with $\mathbf{t}$. We will now consider what happens if a message is deciphered using the wrong transformation. If $\mathbf{c} = \mathbf{t}_i(\mathbf{m})$ we want to know what, if anything, can be said about $\mathbf{t}_j^{-1}(\mathbf{c}) = \mathbf{t}_j^{-1}(\mathbf{t}_i(\mathbf{m}))$ if $i \neq j$.

Let us consider the system illustrated in Figure 3.2. If we encipher using transformation $\mathbf{t}_1$, then $\mathbf{t}_1(\mathbf{m}_1) = \mathbf{c}_1$, $\mathbf{t}_1(\mathbf{m}_2) = \mathbf{c}_2$ and $\mathbf{t}_1(\mathbf{m}_3) = \mathbf{c}_3$. If we now try deciphering using $\mathbf{t}_2$ then $\mathbf{t}_2^{-1}(\mathbf{c}_1) = \mathbf{m}_1$, $\mathbf{t}_2^{-1}(\mathbf{c}_2) = \mathbf{m}_3$ but, as there is no message $\mathbf{m}$ with $\mathbf{t}_2(\mathbf{m}) = \mathbf{c}_3$, we cannot attach a meaning to $\mathbf{t}_2^{-1}(\mathbf{c}_3)$. Thus, even in this small example, we can see that deciphering a given cryptogram using the wrong transformation can lead to the correct message, e.g.

deciphering c_1 using t_2, but also that it may be impossible to decipher (even incorrectly!) using the wrong transformation. The more usual occurrence of course is simply to get the wrong message; e.g., in our example, deciphering c_3 using t_3 gives m_2 instead of m_3. If we look at Figure 3.2 we see that there is no edge labelled k_2 entering c_3 and this is why there is no element $t_2^{-1}(c_3)$. If the graph had the property that, for each key k_i and each cryptogram c_j, there was an edge labelled k_i entering c_j then we would be able to decipher (albeit incorrectly) any cryptogram using any transformation. But this is exactly what we defined as a closed system. Of course if T is closed then every t in T is uniquely reversible with inverse t^{-1}. Thus we see that if T is closed then, for any transformations t_i, t_j of T, $t_j^{-1}(t_i(m)) = t_j^{-1}(c_i)$ which is a message of M. Thus $t_j^{-1}t_i$ is a transformation of M into itself. But if $t_j^{-1}t_i$ is a transformation of M into itself and if t_k is another transformation of T then, for any $m \in M$, $t_k t_j^{-1}(t_i(m)) = t_k(m')$ where $m' = t_j^{-1}t_i(m)$. Thus $t_k t_j^{-1}t_i$ is a transformation from M into C. Figure 3.5 gives a closed system which illustrates that, although it is a transformation from M into C, $t_k t_j^{-1}t_i$ need not be in T. Straightforward verification shows that $t_2 t_3^{-1} t_1(m_1) = c_3$ and so, since there is no edge joining m_1 to c_3, $t_2 t_3^{-1} t_1$ is not in T. We will call a cipher system T **pure** if, for any transformations t_i, t_j, t_k in T, there exists a transformation t_s in T with $t_s = t_k t_j^{-1}t_i$. If T is not pure it is called **mixed**.

We have already met many examples of pure cipher systems. For instance the system of all additive ciphers, the system of all multiplicative ciphers, the system of all affine ciphers and the system of all Vigenère ciphers with keyword a given length (and each key equally likely). Each of the above examples is endomorphic but, as the following example of

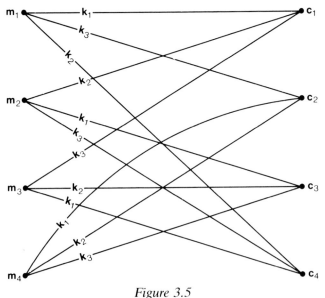

Figure 3.5
An example of a closed system

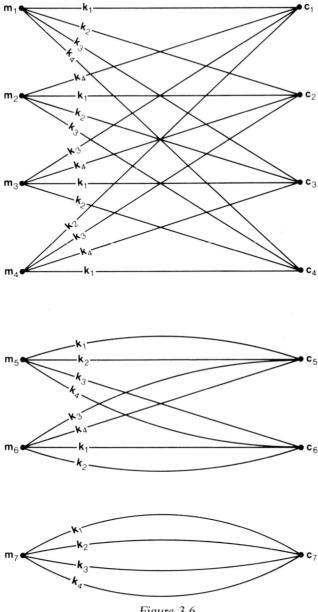

Figure 3.6
An example of a pure non-endomorphic cipher

Shannon illustrates, a system can be pure and non-endomorphic.

Before we establish some important properties of pure cipher systems we will show that an idempotent system is pure. We stress again that the proofs are somewhat abstract and may be omitted. However the results are important. Since the definition of pure is rather cumbersome, it is often difficult to establish whether or not a given system is pure. In most of the situations which we discuss we will be able to show that the systems under consideration are pure by showing that they are idempotent.

LEMMA 3.1   An idempotent cipher system with a finite key is pure.

PROOF   We must show that, for any transformations t_i, t_j, t_k in **T**, there is a transformation t_s in **T** with $t_s = t_k t_j^{-1} t_i$. Since **T** is idempotent we know that, for any t_a and t_b in **T**, $t_a t_b$ is in **T**. We also know that t_a is reversible. We do not, however, know that t_a^{-1} is in **T**. But if $t_a t_b = t_a t_c$ then $t_a^{-1} t_a t_b = t_a^{-1} t_a t_c$ i.e. $t_b = t_c$. Thus if $b \neq c$ we have $t_a t_b \neq t_a t_c$ and so, for any fixed a, the set of transformations $t_a t_b$ with $1 \leq b \leq h$, where $h = |\mathbf{T}|$, is the whole of **T**. Thus for any given t_i and t_j there is a transformation t_m in **T** with $t_j t_m = t_i$, i.e. with $t_m = t_j^{-1} t_i$. But now $t_k t_j^{-1} t_i = t_k t_m$ which, since **T** is idempotent, is in **T**. $\square$

Now suppose **T** is a pure cipher system with message space **M**, cryptogram space **C** and transformations $t_1, t_2, \ldots, t_h$. Since, for any t_i, t_j, t_k in **T**, there is a transformation t_s in **T** with $t_s(\mathbf{m}) = t_k t_j^{-1} t_i(\mathbf{m})$ for all **m** in **M**, we know that $t_j^{-1} t_i(\mathbf{m})$ is defined for all t_i, t_j in **T** and all **m** in **M**.

Thus, essentially, hidden in the definition of pure is the following.

LEMMA 3.2   A pure cipher system with a finite key is closed. $\square$

Now let $\mathbf{S_T}$ be the set of all products of the form $t_j^{-1} t_i$ with t_i, t_j in **T**. Then clearly $\mathbf{S_T}$ is a set of transformations from **M** into **M**. There are, formally, h^2 products of the form $t_j^{-1} t_i$ but of course we may have $t_j^{-1} t_i = t_c^{-1} t_d$ where $j \neq c$ and $d \neq i$. Thus $|\mathbf{S_T}| \leq h^2$. But if $t_a^{-1} t_b = t_a^{-1} t_c$ then $t_a t_a^{-1} t_b = t_a t_a^{-1} t_c$ which, using Exercise 3.3, gives $t_b = t_c$. Thus if we fix t_a and consider all products of the form $t_a^{-1} t_b$ as t_b varies over **T**, we get h distinct elements of $\mathbf{S_T}$. Thus $|\mathbf{S_T}| \geq h$. In this discussion of $\mathbf{S_T}$ we have not yet utilized the fact that **T** is pure. Since **T** is pure, for every t_i, t_j, t_k in **T** there is a t_s in **T** such that $t_s = t_k t_j^{-1} t_i$, i.e. such that $t_k^{-1} t_s = t_j^{-1} t_i$. By keeping t_i and t_j fixed and letting t_k vary over the h transformations of **T**, we get h distinct pairs t_k, t_s such that $t_k^{-1} t_s = t_j^{-1} t_i$. (Note one of them has $t_k = t_j$ and, consequently, $t_s = t_i$.) This means that each element of $\mathbf{S_T}$ occurs as at least h formal products of the form $t_j^{-1} t_i$ which, since there are only h such products, implies $|\mathbf{S_T}| \leq \dfrac{h^2}{h}$, i.e. $|\mathbf{S_T}| \leq h$. Thus we have shown that $|\mathbf{S_T}| = h$ and that, for any fixed transformation t_u in **T**, $\mathbf{S_T} = \{t_j^{-1} t_u \mid j = 1, 2, \ldots, h\}$. If we now pick any transformation, $t_i^{-1} t_u$ say, of $\mathbf{S_T}$ then, since **T** is pure, there is a transformation t_j in **T** such that $t_j = t_u t_i^{-1} t_u$. But if $t_j = t_u t_i^{-1} t_u$ then $\mathbf{I_M} = t_j^{-1} t_j = t_j^{-1} t_u t_i^{-1} t_u$. Thus $t_i^{-1} t_u$ is reversible. But this means we may regard $\mathbf{S_T}$ as an endomorphic cipher system which has message space **M** and the same number of keys as **T**. (In fact, once we have chosen a given t_u, we may regard the key $\mathbf{k}_i$ as determining both the transformation $\mathbf{t}_i$ of $\mathbf{T}$ and the transformation $\mathbf{t}_i^{-1}\mathbf{t}_u$ of $\mathbf{S}_T$.) If $\mathbf{t}_i^{-1}\mathbf{t}_u$ and $\mathbf{t}_j^{-1}\mathbf{t}_u$ are two transformations of $\mathbf{S}_T$ then, since $\mathbf{T}$ is pure, there is a transformation $\mathbf{t}_k$ with $\mathbf{t}_k = \mathbf{t}_u\mathbf{t}_j^{-1}\mathbf{t}_u$. Thus $\mathbf{t}_i^{-1}\mathbf{t}_u\mathbf{t}_j^{-1}\mathbf{t}_u = \mathbf{t}_i^{-1}\mathbf{t}_k$, which is in $\mathbf{S}_T$. This means that $\mathbf{S}_T\mathbf{S}_T = \mathbf{S}_T$, i.e. $\mathbf{S}_T$ is idempotent and, by Lemma 3.1, pure. (Note: $\mathbf{S}_T\mathbf{S}_T$ is defined as the set of all products $\mathbf{s}_i\mathbf{s}_j$ with $\mathbf{s}_i$, $\mathbf{s}_j$ in $\mathbf{S}_T$. Since $\mathbf{I}_M$ is in $\mathbf{S}_T$, $\mathbf{s}_i$ (which is equal to $\mathbf{s}_i\mathbf{I}_M$) is in $\mathbf{S}_T\mathbf{S}_T$, for all $\mathbf{s}_i$ in $\mathbf{S}_T$. Thus every element of $\mathbf{S}_T$ is in $\mathbf{S}_T\mathbf{S}_T$. The argument above shows every element of $\mathbf{S}_T\mathbf{S}_T$ is in $\mathbf{S}_T$ which now implies $\mathbf{S}_T\mathbf{S}_T = \mathbf{S}_T$.) The above discussion proves:

THEOREM 3.3 *Let $\mathbf{T}$ be a pure cipher system with message space $\mathbf{M}$, cryptogram space $\mathbf{C}$ and transformation set $\{\mathbf{t}_1, \mathbf{t}_2, \ldots, \mathbf{t}_h\}$. If $\mathbf{S}_T = \{\mathbf{t}_i^{-1}\mathbf{t}_j \mid \mathbf{t}_i \in \mathbf{T} \text{ and } \mathbf{t}_j \in \mathbf{T}\}$ then $\mathbf{S}_T$ is an idempotent endomorphic system with message space $\mathbf{M}$ and, for any fixed $\mathbf{t}_u$ in $\mathbf{T}$, the transformation set of $\mathbf{S}_T$ is $\{\mathbf{t}_1^{-1}\mathbf{t}_u, \mathbf{t}_2^{-1}\mathbf{t}_u, \ldots, \mathbf{t}_h^{-1}\mathbf{t}_u\}$.* ☐

3.4.3 Residue classes

If we pick a message $\mathbf{m}$ then, for any $\mathbf{t}_u$ in $\mathbf{T}$, the set of all images of $\mathbf{m}$ under the transformations of $\mathbf{S}_T$ is merely the set of possible messages one would obtain by deciphering $\mathbf{t}_u(\mathbf{m})$ using all possible keys. Since this is true for all choices of $\mathbf{t}_u$, if we encipher a given message using any one of the keys and then decipher using each key in turn, we will always end up with the same set of possible messages as 'candidates' to be the one actually sent. We now investigate the situation in more detail. First we make some definitions. If $\mathbf{T}$ is a pure cipher system with message space $\mathbf{M}$, cryptogram space $\mathbf{C}$ and transformations $\mathbf{t}_1, \mathbf{t}_2, \ldots, \mathbf{t}_h$ then, for any $\mathbf{m}$ in $\mathbf{M}$, let $\mathbf{C}(\mathbf{m}) = \{\mathbf{t}_i(\mathbf{m}) \mid \mathbf{t}_i \in \mathbf{T}\}$ and $\mathbf{M}(\mathbf{m}) = \{\mathbf{t}_i^{-1}\mathbf{t}_j(\mathbf{m}) \mid \mathbf{t}_i, \mathbf{t}_j \in \mathbf{T}\}$. Thus $\mathbf{C}(\mathbf{m})$ is the set of all cryptograms which may represent $\mathbf{m}$ while $\mathbf{M}(\mathbf{m})$ is the set of all messages which may be obtained if $\mathbf{m}$ is enciphered and then deciphered using all transformations in $\mathbf{T}$. We call $\mathbf{C}(\mathbf{m})$ the **cryptogram residue class** of $\mathbf{m}$ under $\mathbf{T}$ and $\mathbf{M}(\mathbf{m})$ its **message residue class**. (Note that $\mathbf{m}$ is always contained in $\mathbf{M}(\mathbf{m})$ but, since the system need not be endomorphic, not necessarily in $\mathbf{C}(\mathbf{m})$. Note also that $\mathbf{M}(\mathbf{m})$ is also the cryptogram residue class of $\mathbf{m}$ under $\mathbf{S}_T$.) These residue classes have many very important properties. We will first establish these properties and then discuss their significance.

If we pick two messages $\mathbf{m}_1$, $\mathbf{m}_2$ with $\mathbf{m}_1$ in $\mathbf{M}(\mathbf{m}_2)$, then there are transformations $\mathbf{t}_a$, $\mathbf{t}_b$ in $\mathbf{T}$ such that $\mathbf{m}_1 = \mathbf{t}_a^{-1}\mathbf{t}_b(\mathbf{m}_2)$. Thus, for any $\mathbf{t}_i$ in $\mathbf{T}$, $\mathbf{t}_i(\mathbf{m}_1) = \mathbf{t}_i\mathbf{t}_a^{-1}\mathbf{t}_b(\mathbf{m}_2)$. But, since $\mathbf{T}$ is pure, there is a transformation $\mathbf{t}_j$ which is equal to $\mathbf{t}_i\mathbf{t}_a^{-1}\mathbf{t}_b$ and we now have $\mathbf{t}_i(\mathbf{m}_1) = \mathbf{t}_j(\mathbf{m}_2)$ or $\mathbf{m}_2 = \mathbf{t}_j^{-1}\mathbf{t}_i(\mathbf{m}_1)$. Hence if $\mathbf{m}_1$ is in $\mathbf{M}(\mathbf{m}_2)$ then $\mathbf{m}_2$ is in $\mathbf{M}(\mathbf{m}_1)$. Now suppose we pick another message $\mathbf{m}_3$ in $\mathbf{M}(\mathbf{m}_2)$. Then $\mathbf{m}_3 = \mathbf{t}_c^{-1}\mathbf{t}_d(\mathbf{m}_2)$ for some $\mathbf{t}_c$, $\mathbf{t}_d$ in $\mathbf{T}$. Thus, since $\mathbf{m}_2 = \mathbf{t}_j^{-1}\mathbf{t}_i(\mathbf{m}_1)$, $\mathbf{m}_3 = \mathbf{t}_c^{-1}\mathbf{t}_d\mathbf{t}_j^{-1}\mathbf{t}_i(\mathbf{m})$. Again using the fact that $\mathbf{T}$ is pure we have $\mathbf{t}_d\mathbf{t}_j^{-1}\mathbf{t}_i = \mathbf{t}_u$, for some $\mathbf{t}_u$ in $\mathbf{T}$, and $\mathbf{m}_3 = \mathbf{t}_c^{-1}\mathbf{t}_u(\mathbf{m}_1)$ which means that $\mathbf{m}_3$ is in $\mathbf{M}(\mathbf{m}_1)$. A similar argument shows that any message in $\mathbf{M}(\mathbf{m}_1)$ is also in $\mathbf{M}(\mathbf{m}_2)$ and we have shown that, for any $\mathbf{m}_1$ in $\mathbf{M}(\mathbf{m}_2)$, $\mathbf{M}(\mathbf{m}_1) = \mathbf{M}(\mathbf{m}_2)$. Thus for any m_i, m_j, either $M(m_i) = M(m_j)$ or $M(m_i)$ and $M(m_j)$ are disjoint. We have thus established part (i) of the following:

LEMMA 3.4   *Let* T *be a pure cipher system with message space* M, *cryptogram space* C *and finite key. Then*
  (i)   *the message residue classes partition* M. (*This means that no two classes have any message in common and that every message is in one of the classes.*)
  (ii)   *the cryptogram residue classes partition* C.

PROOF   We have already proved (i).
   The proof of (ii) is similar and we will leave it as an exercise. However we draw attention to two facts. The first is that, in order to show that each message is in one of the classes, we need to observe that m is in $M(m)$ for all m. The fact that each cryptogram is in one class is built into our definition of C. We regard C as the set of all possible cryptograms and if c is in C there is, automatically, at least one m in M and t in T with $c = t(m)$. We also point out that this result is only true for pure systems. The assumption that T is pure was crucial for our proof of (i) and will be equally necessary for (ii).

EXERCISE 3.6   *Prove part* (ii) *of Lemma 3.4.*

THEOREM 3.5   *Let* T *be a pure cipher system with message space* M, *cryptogram space* C *and transformation set* $\{t_1, t_2, \ldots, t_h\}$. *Then*
  (i) $|M(m)| = |C(m)|$ *for all* m *in* M;
  (ii)   *for any* m *there is an integer* g_m *such that* $g_m|C(m)| = h$, *i.e.* $|C(m)|$ *divides* h *for all* m;
  (iii)   *if* m_i *is in* $M(m)$ *and* c_j *is in* $C(m)$ *there are exactly* g_m *transformations* t *in* T *with* $t(m_i) = c_j$.

PROOF   (i)   For any m in M we know, by Lemma 3.4, that m_u is in $M(m)$ if and only if $M(m_u) = M(m)$. Clearly $C(m) = C(m_u)$ if and only if there exist t_i, t_j in T with $t_i(m) = t_j(m_u)$; which is equivalent to $m_u = t_j^{-1}t_i(m)$ or $m_u \in M(m)$. Thus $C(m) = C(m_u)$ if and only if $M(m) = M(m_u)$, i.e. $|C(m)| = |M(m)|$.

(ii) and (iii)   Suppose there are x transformations which map m on to c_j and let these transformations be $t_{a_1}, t_{a_2}, \ldots, t_{a_x}$. Then

$$c_j = t_{a_1}(m) = t_{a_2}(m) = \ldots = t_{a_x}(m).$$

If m_i is in $M(m)$ there exist t_k, t_u such that $m = t_k^{-1}t_u(m_i)$ and so

$$c_j = t_{a_1}t_k^{-1}t_u(m_i) = \ldots = t_{a_x}t_k^{-1}t_u(m_i).$$

Thus, since T is pure, there are at least x transformations sending m_i on to c_j for any m_i in $M(m)$. If we now choose m_j in $M(m)$ so that, amongst all the messages in $M(m)$, it has the maximum number of transformations sending it on to c_j and if we let this number be y, then the same argument will give at least y transformations sending m on to c_j. Thus, for each m_v in $M(m)$, there are exactly x transformations sending $\mathbf{m}_i$ on to $\mathbf{c}_j$. But since $\mathbf{T}$ is pure it is closed (see Lemma 3.2) and so each transformation in $\mathbf{M(m)}$ sends one of the messages in $\mathbf{M(m)}$ on to $\mathbf{c}_j$. Thus the total number of transformations is $x \mid \mathbf{M(m)} \mid$. But $\mid \mathbf{M(m)} \mid = \mid \mathbf{C(m)} \mid$ and the number of transformations is h, so, if we write $g_\mathbf{m}$ for x, the theorem is proved.   ☐

If we now put ourselves in the position of the cryptanalyst who has intercepted a cryptogram where the cipher system used was pure, we will see the significance of these last two results and also get some indication of the power of pure systems. If we intercept a cryptogram $\mathbf{c}$ in the class $\mathbf{C(m)}$ then we know that the message must belong to $\mathbf{M(m)}$. However, by choosing the appropriate key, any message in $\mathbf{M(m)}$ could have been enciphered to give this cryptogram. Furthermore, so far as we can tell, each message in $\mathbf{M(m)}$ is equally likely to be the enciphered message no matter which key was used. Since the different possible keys all result in cryptograms in the same residue class $\mathbf{C(m)}$, we would have reached the same conclusions if we had intercepted any of the cryptograms in $\mathbf{C(m)}$. We say that two cryptograms in the same residue class are **cryptanalytically equivalent** if each one is equally likely to have come from any message in the appropriate message class.

As a very simple example consider $\mathbf{T}$ to be the pure cipher system consisting of all monoalphabetic ciphers with each key equally likely. Suppose we intercept the three letter cryptogram $\mathbf{XYO}$. Then the corresponding residue classes are the set of all messages of the form $\mathbf{t}_j^{-1}(\mathbf{XYO})$ and all cryptograms of the form $\mathbf{t}_i \mathbf{t}_j^{-1}(\mathbf{XYO})$, where $\mathbf{t}_i$, $\mathbf{t}_j$ are monoalphabetic ciphers. A moment's thought shows that both classes consist of all sequences of three distinct letters. (Not very informative!) In fact in this particular system, for any cryptogram $\mathbf{c}$, both classes will be identical and will be the set of all letter sequences with the same length and 'pattern' as $\mathbf{c}$. (We do not want to define a pattern formally. If $\mathbf{c}$ is, for example, **AXXEFFFT** then **COOUYYYS** has the same pattern but **UYVVTTTS** does not (because its second and third letters are different).)

If we now consider $\mathbf{T}$ to be the set of all Vigenère ciphers with keyword length h, then the classes are smaller. If, for example, we assume $h = 3$ and $\mathbf{c} = \mathbf{AXYD}$ then we know that the encipherer used the same additive cipher to obtain the $\mathbf{A}$ and the $\mathbf{D}$. This means that, in the original message, the fourth letter must occur three places 'after' the first letter. (Regarding a as coming 'after' z.) Thus **TAUW** is in both classes but **COYV** is not. In general, regarding each letter as a number from 0 to 25 inclusive in the usual way, if $\mathbf{m} = \mathbf{m}_1\mathbf{m}_2\mathbf{m}_3\ldots$ and $\mathbf{c} = \mathbf{c}_1\mathbf{c}_2\mathbf{c}_3\ldots$ then $\mathbf{c}$ is in $\mathbf{M(m)}$ if and only if $\mathbf{m}_{h+i} - \mathbf{m}_i \equiv \mathbf{c}_{h+i} - \mathbf{c}_i \pmod{26}$ for every i, (where h is the length of the keyword).

3.5 Perfect Secrecy

Now that we know what is meant by a cipher system (or secrecy system) we can begin to consider the question of how much security a system offers.

Before we do this, we observe that it is possible for two different systems to be **cryptanalytically equivalent**, in the sense that if one of the systems can be broken then so can the other. We will call two cipher systems **R** and **S** **similar** if there is a uniquely reversible transformation **f** such that $\mathbf{R} = \mathbf{f(S)}$. (Thus **f** is a transformation from the message space of **S** to the message space of **R**, the cryptogram space of **S** to the cryptogram space of **R** and the transformations of **S** to the transformations of **R**. If **m** is in the message space of **S** then **m** and **f(m)** must have equal probabilities and if **S** is variant then, for any transformation **s** in **S**, the probability of **s** is the probability of **f(s)**.) Clearly if **S** can be broken then **R** can be broken by first breaking **S** and then applying the transformation **f**. Note that $\mathbf{f}^{-1}(\mathbf{R}) = \mathbf{S}$, so one could also break **S** by breaking **R** first and then applying $\mathbf{f}^{-1}$. One simple way to obtain two similar, but unequal, systems is to take a monoalphabetic cipher and then change it by using 26 new symbols for the cryptogram alphabet. The cryptograms in each case would look different but the systems are clearly similar. Other, slightly less obvious, examples of two similar systems are the Vigenère and Beaufort ciphers with the same keyword. Here the transformation **f** is the identity on the message space and maps the transformation $\mu \equiv 1 + \kappa + \lambda \pmod{26}$ associated with the Vigenère cipher on to the transformation $\mu \equiv 1 + \kappa - \lambda \pmod{26}$ of the Beaufort cipher. We have already given enough information about **f** to determine its 'action' on the cryptograms.

If we are going to discuss how much security a system offers, then we need some way to measure security. It is not at all obvious what this 'measure' should be. One desirable property is that the interceptor should not be able to decipher a cryptogram by trying all key possibilities. However we have already seen examples to show that this does not necessarily provide much security. If we suppose that a monoalphabetic cipher is used (with each key equally likely) and that the cryptanalyst has intercepted a cryptogram of 100 characters, then even if he tries one of the 26! keys every microsecond, it will take him about $1 \cdot 23 \times 10^{13}$ years to try all possibilities. But we know, from our discussion in Chapter 1, that he can use statistical information to break the system very quickly and that, despite the time taken to try all possibilities, it is very insecure. But let us suppose we have a system where the cryptanalyst does actually have the time to try each possibility. In this case will he be able to determine the message? Again, by looking back at Exercise 1.1, we know that the answer is 'not necessarily'. If, even after he has tried all possibilities, the crypt-analyst cannot decide which message was sent, then we are some way towards providing security. As we pointed out in Exercise 1.1, if the messages are in English (and the cipher is additive) then it is extremely unlikely that there will be two meaningful possible messages if more than six or seven letters of the cryptogram are intercepted. For any given cipher system, one possible factor in measuring security might be the length of cryptogram which must be intercepted so that, by trying all possibilities, the message is uniquely obtainable. Clearly, for any cryptogram, the greater the number of meaningful messages that can be obtained by deciphering using every key, the harder it is for the cryptanalyst to decide which message was actually sent. Ideally we would like each cryptogram to give every message when deciphered using every key because, in this case, deciphering using every key would then give the cryptanalyst no information whatsoever. This leads us to introduce the concept of perfect secrecy. In our discussion of perfect secrecy we will not assume either that each message is equally likely or that the keys are equiprobable.

Suppose that we have a cipher system $\mathbf{T}$ with a finite message space $\mathbf{M} = \{\mathbf{m}_1, \mathbf{m}_2, \ldots, \mathbf{m}_n\}$, a finite cryptogram space $\mathbf{C} = \{\mathbf{c}_1, \mathbf{c}_2, \ldots, \mathbf{c}_u\}$ and transformations $\mathbf{t}_1, \mathbf{t}_2, \ldots, \mathbf{t}_h$. Suppose that, for any $\mathbf{m}_i$, the *a priori* probability of $\mathbf{m}_i$ being transmitted is $p(\mathbf{m}_i)$. If the cryptanalyst intercepts a particular cryptogram $\mathbf{c}_j$ then, for each message $\mathbf{m}_i$, he can calculate, at least in principle, the *a posteriori* probability $p_j(\mathbf{m}_i)$ that $\mathbf{m}_i$ was transmitted. (Thus $p_j(\mathbf{m}_i)$ is the probability that $\mathbf{m}_i$ was transmitted given that $\mathbf{c}_j$ was received.) The system $\mathbf{T}$ is said to have **perfect secrecy** if, for every message $\mathbf{m}_i$ and every cryptogram $\mathbf{c}_j$, $p_j(\mathbf{m}_i) = p(\mathbf{m}_i)$. Thus, if $\mathbf{T}$ has perfect secrecy, the cryptanalyst who intercepts $\mathbf{c}_j$ has obtained no further information to enable him to decide which message was transmitted. Clearly perfect secrecy is highly desirable. But is it possible and, if it is, how do we know that we have achieved it?

For any cryptogram $\mathbf{c}_j$ we will let $p(\mathbf{c}_j)$ denote the probability of obtaining $\mathbf{c}_j$, (from any message), and the probability of obtaining $\mathbf{c}_j$ if message $\mathbf{m}_i$ is transmitted by $p_i(\mathbf{c}_j)$. Thus, if as usual we let p_i be the probability of choosing transformation $\mathbf{t}_i$ or, equivalently, key $\mathbf{k}_i$, $p_i(\mathbf{c}_j) = \Sigma p_u$, where the summation is over all those u for which $\mathbf{c}_j = \mathbf{t}_u(\mathbf{m}_i)$. To establish our next theorem we need Bayes' Theorem which says that, for any $\mathbf{m}_i$ and $\mathbf{c}_j$, $p_i(\mathbf{m}_i) \cdot p(\mathbf{c}_j) = p_i(\mathbf{c}_j) \cdot p(\mathbf{m}_i)$, (see [12]).

LEMMA 3.6   A necessary and sufficient condition for perfect secrecy is that $p_i(\mathbf{c}_j) = p(\mathbf{c}_j)$ for all $\mathbf{m}_i$ and $\mathbf{c}_j$.

PROOF   Since we only include those messages which can be transmitted, $p(\mathbf{m}_x) \neq 0$ for any message $\mathbf{m}_x$ in $\mathbf{M}$. Lemma 3.6 is now an immediate consequence of Bayes' Theorem.   ⊓

Perfect secrecy means that, for any messages $\mathbf{m}_i$, $\mathbf{m}_j$ and any cryptogram $\mathbf{c}_k$, the total probability of all the keys which transform $\mathbf{m}_i$ into $\mathbf{c}_k$ is the same as that of all keys which transform $\mathbf{m}_j$ into $\mathbf{c}_k$. (Since, by Lemma 3.6, $p_i(\mathbf{c}_k) = p(\mathbf{c}_k) = p_j(\mathbf{c}_k)$.) Thus, when each key is equally likely, the number of keys which transform $\mathbf{m}_i$ into $\mathbf{c}_k$ is the same as the number which transform $\mathbf{m}_j$ into $\mathbf{c}_k$. Since $\mathbf{m}_i$, $\mathbf{m}_j$ and $\mathbf{c}_k$ were arbitrary, this means that in a system with all keys equally probable, perfect secrecy implies that there is a constant, w say, such that there are exactly w keys which send any given message $\mathbf{m}$ on to any given cryptogram $\mathbf{c}$. This discussion leads us to the following very important lemma:

LEMMA 3.7   In a system with perfect secrecy, the number of different keys is at least as great as the number of possible messages.

PROOF   For any transformation $\mathbf{t}$ and any two messages $\mathbf{m}_i$ and $\mathbf{m}_j$, $\mathbf{t}(\mathbf{m}_i)$ and $\mathbf{t}(\mathbf{m}_j)$ are distinct cryptograms. Thus the messages of $\mathbf{M}$ all give different cryptograms in $\mathbf{C}$ and, for any cipher system, the number of cryptograms is at least as large as the number of messages. But, for perfect secrecy, $p_i(\mathbf{c}_j) = p(\mathbf{c}_j) \neq 0$ for any message $\mathbf{m}_i$ and cryptogram $\mathbf{c}_j$. Thus, in this case, there is at least one transformation taking any given message $\mathbf{m}$ into any one of the cryptograms. Hence, since the same transformation cannot map $\mathbf{m}$ into two distinct cryptograms, the number of transformations is at least as large as the number of cryptograms.   □

It is certainly possible, as the following example shows, to obtain perfect secrecy with the numbers of keys equal to the number of messages. Consider the cipher system $\mathbf{T}$ with $\mathbf{M} = \{\mathbf{m}_1, \mathbf{m}_2, \ldots, \mathbf{m}_n\}$, $\mathbf{C} = \{\mathbf{c}_1, \mathbf{c}_2, \ldots, \mathbf{c}_n\}$ and with transformations $\mathbf{t}_1, \mathbf{t}_2, \ldots, \mathbf{t}_n$ with $p_i = \dfrac{1}{n}$, $i = 1, \ldots, n$. The transformations are given by $\mathbf{t}_i(\mathbf{m}_j) = \mathbf{c}_s$ where $s \equiv i + j \pmod{n}$. So, for example, if $n = 3$ then $\mathbf{t}_2(\mathbf{m}_1) = \mathbf{c}_3$, $\mathbf{t}_2(\mathbf{m}_2) = \mathbf{c}_1$ and $\mathbf{t}_2(\mathbf{m}_3) = \mathbf{c}_2$. Figure 3.7 gives the

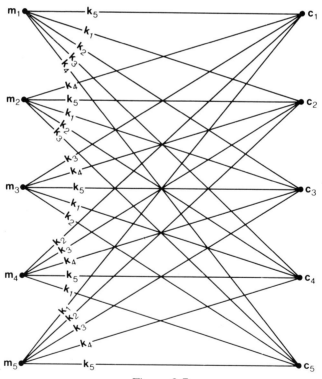

Figure 3.7
An example of perfect secrecy

complete system when $n = 5$.

To show that, for any n, $\mathbf{T}$ has perfect secrecy we will show $p(\mathbf{c}_j) = p_i(\mathbf{c}_j)$ for all $\mathbf{m}_i$ and $\mathbf{c}_j$. Since there is precisely one key which maps $\mathbf{m}_i$ on to $\mathbf{c}_j$ and n keys altogether, $p_i(\mathbf{c}_j)$ is merely the probability of choosing a particular one of the n keys, i.e. $p_i(\mathbf{c}_j) = \dfrac{1}{n}$. If we pick integers i and s in the range 1 to n inclusive we will denote by $\bar{i}$ the integer in the same range such that $s \equiv i + \bar{i} \pmod{n}$. Then for any i, $\mathbf{t}_{\bar{i}}$ is the unique transformation with $\mathbf{t}_{\bar{i}}(\mathbf{m}_i) = \mathbf{c}_s$.

So $p(\mathbf{c}_s) = p(\mathbf{m}_1)p_{\bar{1}} + p(\mathbf{m}_2)p_{\bar{2}} + \ldots + p(\mathbf{m}_n)p_{\bar{n}}$. But $p_{\bar{i}} = \dfrac{1}{n}$ for all $\bar{i}$ so

$$p(\mathbf{c}_s) = \frac{1}{n}(p(\mathbf{m}_1) + p(\mathbf{m}_2) + \ldots + p(\mathbf{m}_n)) = \frac{1}{n}.$$

$$\left(\text{Note } \sum_{i=1}^{n} p(\mathbf{m}_i) = 1. \right)$$

Thus, for any s, $p(\mathbf{c}_s) = \dfrac{1}{n} = p_i(\mathbf{c}_s)$ for all i.

We now give necessary and sufficient conditions for certain systems to offer perfect security.

THEOREM 3.8 *Let $\mathbf{T}$ be a cipher system in which the number of messages, the number of keys and the number of cryptograms are all equal. Then $\mathbf{T}$ has perfect secrecy if and only if*
 (i) *there is exactly one key transforming each message to each crypto-gram; and*
 (ii) *all keys are equally likely.*

PROOF If $\mathbf{T}$ has perfect secrecy we know, by Lemma 3.6, that there is at least one transformation sending any given message into any given cryptogram. Thus, if the number of keys equals the number of crypto-grams, (i) must hold. Further, again by Lemma 3.6, for any given crypto-gram $\mathbf{c}_j$, $p_1(\mathbf{c}_j) = p_2(\mathbf{c}_j) = \ldots = p_n(\mathbf{c}_j)$ where $|\mathbf{M}| = n$. But, as we saw in an earlier discussion, $p_i(\mathbf{c}_j)$ is the probability that we choose the unique key (or transformation) which transforms $\mathbf{m}_i$ into $\mathbf{c}_j$. Since each key must transform one of the messages into $\mathbf{c}_j$, this implies that each key is equally likely, i.e. (ii) holds.

On the other hand if (i) and (ii) hold then, since $p_i(\mathbf{c}_j)$ is merely the probability of choosing the key which maps $\mathbf{m}_i$ on to $\mathbf{c}_j$ and since all keys are equally likely, $p_i(\mathbf{c}_j) = \dfrac{1}{n}$ for all $\mathbf{m}_i$ and $\mathbf{c}_j$. Furthermore $p(\mathbf{c}_j) = p(\mathbf{m}_1)q_1 + p(\mathbf{m}_2)q_2 + \ldots + p(\mathbf{m}_n)q_n$, where q_i is the probability of choosing the key which sends $\mathbf{m}_i$ on to $\mathbf{c}_j$.

$$\text{Thus, since } q_i = \frac{1}{n} \text{ for all } i, \; p(\mathbf{c}_j) = \frac{1}{n}\left(p(\mathbf{m}_1) + p(\mathbf{m}_2) + \ldots + p(\mathbf{m}_n)\right) = \frac{1}{n}$$

and $\mathbf{T}$ has perfect secrecy.   ▯

Perfect secrecy is obviously a very desirable objective. It means that, unless he has some extra information, the cryptanalyst obtains no information whatsoever from his intercepted cryptogram, i.e. that the system is **unbreakable**. It should, however, be apparent that to ensure perfect secrecy in any practical cipher system (where one would presumably want to be able to transmit a reasonable amount of information which, of necessity, means a large message space) the amount of key which must be distributed might cause enormous management problems. Nevertheless there are situations where complete secrecy is of paramount importance and then, despite the obvious problems, such systems are used. If the message space is small then they can even be practical. For instance if only two messages, **yes** and **no** say, are necessary, then only two keys are needed to offer perfect secrecy. Such a system is shown in Figure 3.3. Figure 3.7 illustrates perfect secrecy for five messages.

If we go back to considering the situation when a monoalphabetic cipher is used to transmit a message in the English language, then we will get an illustration of a common phenomenon. If the message space is restricted to messages of one letter, then clearly we can attain perfect secrecy. As we increase the size of the message space to include longer words then, as was so apparent in Chapter 1, the security offered by the system falls rapidly. As we shall soon see, for cryptograms of more than 25 letters, there is nearly always a unique solution; although in practice one may need a longer cryptogram to find it.

There is one particular system which offers perfect secrecy and which deserves special mention; the **one-time-pad**. In this system there is an upper bound, N say, on the length of all possible messages, and the number of keys, which are all equally likely, is at least as large as N. If the message $\mathbf{m} = \mathbf{m}_1\mathbf{m}_2\ldots\mathbf{m}_n$ is to be enciphered then a random sequence $\mathbf{k}_1\mathbf{k}_2\ldots\mathbf{k}_n$ is selected. (By this we mean that each $\mathbf{k}_i$ is chosen independently of any other. Furthermore, there must be the same number of possibilities for each $\mathbf{k}_i$ as there are for each $\mathbf{m}_i$.) The enciphering is then fully described by Figure 3.8.

A commonly used mixer is a modulo 26 adder. In this case, if each $\mathbf{m}_i$ is an alphabetic character represented by one of 0-25 and each $\mathbf{k}_i$ is a number between 0 and 25 then the resulting cryptogram is $\mathbf{c} = \mathbf{c}_1\mathbf{c}_2\mathbf{c}_3\ldots$ where each $\mathbf{c}_i$ is given by $\mathbf{c}_i \equiv \mathbf{m}_i + \mathbf{k}_i \pmod{26}$.

The name 'one-time-pad' is derived from the fact that the encipherer utilizes written pads of random characters to obtain the sequence $\mathbf{k}_1\mathbf{k}_2\ldots\mathbf{k}_n$. Each page of the pad is used once and then destroyed. It is an immediate corollary of Theorem 3.8 that the one-time-pad is unbreakable

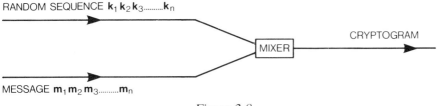

Figure 3.8
The one-time-pad

and, as we shall see in later chapters, this result greatly influenced cryptographers in their attempts to construct secure systems. Although our description is brief we cannot overemphasize the importance of this particular system.

If a system is breakable then there is a standard pattern to the method of obtaining the solution. Before any material is intercepted the cryptanalyst has a knowledge of the message space plus all the keys (and, if they are not all equally likely, the associated probabilities). As material is intercepted the cryptanalyst calculates probabilities, based on his cryptogram, of the various messages and keys. As n, the number of letters in the intercepted cryptogram, increases then the probabilities of certain messages increase while the probabilities of most of them decrease to almost 0. Eventually a situation is reached where one message has probability almost 1 while the others have probability virtually 0. As an illustration of this pattern we will consider a specific example.

Let us suppose that an additive cipher is used to encipher a message which begins with the word **consider**. The cryptogram received will be one of the 26 sequences of letters in the cryptogram residue class of **consider** and knowing the cryptogram gives no information as to which key was used, i.e. even when the cryptogram is intercepted each key is still equally likely to have been used. In this particular example the cryptogram and message spaces are identical so the only possible messages are the 26 sequences in the cryptogram class. Table 3.1, page 150, shows the *a posteriori* probabilities of each of these 26 possibilities for $n = 1, 2, 3, 4, 5$. To determine the *a posteriori* probabilities of each possibility for any given n, we merely compute the *a priori* probabilities of the first n letters of each message in the class and then divide by the sum of all these probabilities. Thus if $n = 1$ the probability of each possible message is merely the probability of its first letter occurring in the English language. (See Appendix 1.) If $n = 2$ the probabilities reflect the relative likelihood of the various bigrams which commence each message (again see Appendix 1).

From Table 3.1 it is clear that, when n is only 3, two messages are more probable than any others. For $n = 4$ there are only two messages to examine and $n = 5$ uniquely determines **consider**.

Residue class	$n = 1$	$n = 2$	$n = 3$	$n = 4$	$n = 5$
c o n s i	0·028	0·202	0·515	0·818	1
d p o t j	0·043				
e q p u k	0·127	0·044			
f r q v l	0·022	0·058			
g s r w m	0·020	0·015			
h t s x n	0·061	0·052	0·046		
i u t y o	0·070	0·001			
j v u z p	0·002				
k w v a q	0·008				
l x w b r	0·040				
m y x c s	0·024	0·028			
n z y d t	0·067	0·001			
o a z e u	0·075	0·014			
p b a f v	0·019				
q c b g w	0·001				
r d c h x	0·060	0·070			
s e d i y	0·063	0·257	0·427	0·182	
t f e j z	0·091	0·003			
u g f k a	0·028	0·052			
v h g l b	0·010				
w i h m c	0·024	0·128			
x j i n d	0·002				
y k j o e	0·020				
z l k p f	0·001	0·001			
a m l q g	0·082	0·072	0·004		
b n m r h	0·015				

Table 3.1
A posteriori probabilities

In principle we could try a similar process to break any system but, unless the number of keys was small, in practice it would be impossible. It should by now be clear that there are two different concepts which we could, for want of better terminology, call 'theoretical security' and 'practical security'. Practical considerations may make it impossible to break a system which is certainly not theoretically secure. We will discuss this further in Chapter 4. For the moment we will continue to concentrate on theoretical security. Thus we are interested in the chances of obtaining a unique solution by trying each key in turn on an intercepted cryptogram. One of our main concerns will be to determine the amount of cryptogram needed before a unique solution can be obtained. We call this the **unicity distance**. It is measured in characters of intercepted text and is usually denoted by n_o.

3.6 Random Ciphers

3.6.1 Entropy and equivocation

We will now put ourselves in the role of the cryptanalyst for the last example, and see how our ability to predict the original message changes as the length of intercepted cryptogram increases. After receiving only one letter we have a list of probabilities for the first letter of the message. (Note that this list would be the same no matter which cryptogram was transmitted!) Using this list we would, if we had to, probably guess that the message began with **e**. However there are other possible letters with comparably large probabilities. Of course if we were sure that our first intercepted letter corresponded to the first letter of a plaintext word we might guess **t** instead. (See Appendix 1.) Anyway we would certainly have no confidence in our guess. As soon as we receive the second letter the situation changes dramatically. It seems quite likely that the message begins with either **co**, **se** or **wi**. These three possible bigrams have probabilities which are significantly higher than all the others. If we were forced to make a single guess then, since it has a slightly higher probability, we would have to choose **se**, but with no confidence at all. After receiving three letters then, although it is not the only possibility, it seems more likely that the message begins **con**, and by the time we receive five letters we can be almost certain.

In any situation where we are faced with a set of possible events, each of which has an associated probability, if we have to guess the actual event we can only logically choose the one with the highest probability. (When there is not a unique event with this highest probability, then we have to make a random choice between the most likely events.) The confidence with which we make our guess varies. It depends on by how much the probability of the chosen event exceeds every other. We now introduce the concepts of entropy and equivocation which are designed to give a quantitative measure to this level of confidence. Although we give precise mathematical definitions, it is not necessary to understand why the particular functions were chosen for this purpose. All that is necessary is to appreciate the properties which the functions must have. The entropy function of a system is a way of quantifying the uncertainty of that system (or, in our case, the confidence with which we can predict that a certain event has occurred). If, for example, each event is equally likely then we are making a purely random guess. Thus we can have no confidence whatsoever and the uncertainty is as high as possible. Our entropy function should have a maximum value when all events are equally likely. If, on the other hand, one event has probability 1 and all others have probability 0, then we can be extremely confident. In this case we are almost sure and the value of the entropy function should be 0.

In a cipher system there are two statistical choices involved; those of the message and the key. The **message entropy** $H(\mathbf{M})$ of the system is defined by

$$H(\mathbf{M}) = - \sum_{\mathbf{m} \in \mathbf{M}} p(\mathbf{m}) \log p(\mathbf{m}),$$

while the **key entropy** is defined by

$$H(\mathbf{K}) = - \sum_{\mathbf{k} \in \mathbf{K}} p(\mathbf{k}) \log p(\mathbf{k}).$$

(We have deliberately not stated a base for the logarithms. Any base will do. No matter which base is chosen, it is easy to see that the entropy is 0 if and only if one event has probability 1 and all others have probability 0. It is also true, but certainly not so obvious, that, no matter which base is chosen, the entropy is a maximum when each event is equally likely. Changing the base for the logarithms alters the actual value assigned to the entropy but does not affect these fundamental properties. In most numerical situations we will work with base 10, but when discussing the theory we often, for reasons that will be obvious, choose base 2.)

The message entropy of a system reflects, in some sense, the confidence with which we can predict that a particular message will be transmitted. As cryptanalysts this is not quite what we want. We will usually be in the position of already having intercepted some ciphertext and will want to know, given the information, how confidently we can predict that a given message was sent, or a given key was used. This leads us to introduce the idea of conditional entropy or, as Shannon called it, **equivocation**. For any set of cryptograms $\mathbf{C}$ and any positive integer n, we let $\mathbf{C}_n$ denote the cryptograms of length n in $\mathbf{C}$. We define the equivocations $H_{\mathbf{C}}(\mathbf{M}, n)$ and $H_{\mathbf{C}}(\mathbf{K}, n)$ as follows:

$$H_{\mathbf{C}}(\mathbf{M}, n) = - \sum_{\substack{\mathbf{m} \in \mathbf{M} \\ \mathbf{c} \in \mathbf{C}_n}} p(\mathbf{c}, \mathbf{m}) \log p_{\mathbf{c}}(\mathbf{m})$$

and

$$H_{\mathbf{C}}(\mathbf{K}, n) = - \sum_{\substack{\mathbf{k} \in \mathbf{K} \\ \mathbf{c} \in \mathbf{C}_n}} p(\mathbf{c}, \mathbf{k}) \log p_{\mathbf{c}}(\mathbf{k}).$$

Here $p(\mathbf{c}, \mathbf{m})$ is the probability of message $\mathbf{m}$ being sent and cryptogram $\mathbf{c}$ being received, while $p_{\mathbf{c}}(\mathbf{m})$ is the *a posteriori* probability that message $\mathbf{m}$ was sent given that $\mathbf{c}$ was received. The probabilities $p(\mathbf{c}, \mathbf{k})$ and $p_{\mathbf{c}}(\mathbf{k})$ are defined analogously. Clearly both equivocations will vary as the integer n changes.

If we go back to our example at the end of the last section then, since there were only 26 possible keys, Table 3.1 gives a list of all messages $\mathbf{m}$ such that, for the received cryptogram $\mathbf{c}$, $p(\mathbf{c}, \mathbf{m}) \neq 0$. (In this example the cryptogram residue class is exactly the same as the message residue class. Consequently we can take $\mathbf{c}$ as being any one of the 26 listed messages.) We now take $\mathbf{C}_i$ to be the set of all cryptograms obtained by taking the first i letters of $\mathbf{c}$ for $i = 1, 2, 3, 4, \ldots$. Thus, for any integer n less than or equal to the length of $\mathbf{c}$, $\mathbf{C}_n$ consists of only one cryptogram. (For instance, if $\mathbf{c}$ begins **ugfka** then $\mathbf{C}_1$ contains **u** only while $\mathbf{C}_4$ consists of **ugfk**.) It is also true for this particular example that, since the probability of any one of the 26 possible messages being sent is precisely the probability of choosing the corresponding key, $H_C(\mathbf{K}, n) = H_C(\mathbf{M}, n)$ for all n. Using logarithms to base 10 we obtain the following values for the equivocations: $H_C(\mathbf{M}, 1) = 1\cdot26$, $H_C(\mathbf{M}, 2) = 0\cdot948$, $H_C(\mathbf{M}, 3) = 0\cdot394$, $H_C(\mathbf{M}, 4) = 0\cdot206$, and $H_C(\mathbf{M}, 5) = 0$. Thus, at least for this example, we can see that the equivocation gives some quantitative measure to the uncertainty in having to predict which message was sent, or, equivalently, which key was used, after intercepting n letters of the cryptogram.

We are now able to discuss another reason why this particular function was chosen to measure the entropy. Increasing n means increasing the length of cryptogram. Thus an increase in n amounts to an increase in information for the receiver. Although this extra information may not give the cryptanalyst any extra help in determining the key or message, it will certainly not make it any harder. In other words, although we cannot guarantee that it decreases, the uncertainty definitely does not increase as n increases. Our functions which give the equivocations reflect this property. (In mathematical terminology, $H_C(\mathbf{K}, n)$ and $H_C(\mathbf{M}, n)$ are non-increasing functions of n.)

EXERCISE 3.7 If $|\mathbf{K}| = h$ with each key equally likely show that $H(\mathbf{K}) = \log h$.

3.6.2 Definition of a random cipher system

We are now in a position to be able to discuss Shannon's idea of a random cipher. If we have an alphabet $\mathbf{A}$ with x letters then, for any positive integer n, the total number of distinct sequences of length n with entries from $\mathbf{A}$ is x^n. (For any one of the n positions of the sequence there are x choices for the letter.) The first property of a random cipher system $\mathbf{S}$ is that the number of messages of length n is x^n, which is also the number of possible cryptograms. Since, of course, $\mathbf{S}$ contains all possible messages of a given length n then, for any integer $q \leq n$, the first q positions of these messages must contain all sequences of length q. As we usually use binary digits then we often write $2^{r_0 n}$ instead of x^n, where $r_0 = \log_2 x$. (Note that, of course, $x = 2^{\log_2 x}$ which implies $x^n = 2^{n \log_2 x}$.) A second property of a random cipher system is that the $2^{r_0 n}$ messages of length n can be divided into two groups. In one of these groups (the '**meaningful**' messages) the messages all have approximately equal probabilities which are significantly higher than the negligible probabilities of the members of the other group. The higher probability group contains $2^{r_n n}$ messages where

$$r_n = \frac{H_C(\mathbf{M}, n)}{n}.$$

(Note that, since all messages have length n, for a random cipher $H_C(\mathbf{M}, n) = H(\mathbf{M})$. So for convenience we will denote it by $H(\mathbf{M})$.) Thus r_n is the entropy of the message source per letter and is often referred to as the **rate of the language**. To evaluate r_n, $H(\mathbf{M})$ is evaluated using logarithms to base 2.

In a random cipher system S all keys are equally likely. If S has h keys then, since the number of messages is equal to the number of cryptograms, S is closed and each cryptogram can be deciphered using h keys. A third property of a random cipher system is that, when it is represented as a bipartite graph in the usual way, the h lines from any given cryptogram c go back to a random selection of the messages.

Finally we note that, since all keys are equally likely, we know $h = 2^{H(\mathbf{K})}$ where, again, $H(\mathbf{K})$ is evaluated using logarithms to base 2 (see Exercise 3.7).

3.6.3 Redundancy and unicity distance

If we have a random cipher system S with $2^{r_0 n}$ messages of length n of which $2^{r_n n}$ are 'meaningful', then the probability that a message chosen at random will be meaningful is $2^{r_n n - r_0 n} = 2^{-n(r_0 - r_n)}$. Thus, if a message $\mathbf{m}$ is enciphered to give c and if we decipher c by choosing a key at random, then, since deciphering c using all keys leads to a random selection of messages, the probability of getting a meaningful decipherment is $2^{-n(r_0 - r_n)}$. If $r_0 = r_n$, i.e. if every message is meaningful, then this probability is 1. If, on the other hand, r_n is small compared with r_0, then this probability is small. When we were discussing deciphering in Chapter 1 where, of course, the meaningful messages were those which make sense in the English language, we were able to cryptanalyze messages precisely because most decipherments led to meaningless messages. In other words precisely because r_n, the rate, is small compared with r_0. This leads us to define the **redundancy** of the system S to be $d_n = r_0 - r_n$. So if we have redundancy d_n then the probability of obtaining a meaningful decipherment from a cryptogram is 2^{-nd_n}. Usually it is the existence of meaningless decipherments which enables cryptograms to be broken and, from the encipherer's point of view, a high redundancy is undesirable.

Since there are $2^{H(\mathbf{K})}$ keys, the expected number of meaningful decipherments when we try all possible keys is $2^{H(\mathbf{K})} . 2^{-nd_n} = 2^{H(\mathbf{K}) - nd_n}$. If there are a large number of such decipherments, i.e. if $H(\mathbf{K})$ is much larger than nd_n, then there is a high probability of obtaining a meaningful decipherment and, consequently, a low likelihood of determining the correct message. However if there were only one such decipherment (and, of course, since the cryptogram was obtained by enciphering a message there must be at least one) then as soon as a meaningful decipherment was obtained it would have to give the correct message.

In most of the practical situations which we have encountered, such as any system employing the English language, the constraints of a random cipher system are not fully satisfied. In particular messages do not all have the same length. In such circumstances it may happen that, for any n, the cipher system obtained by considering only the messages of length n satisfies the conditions of a random system. In this case we can explore what happens as n becomes arbitrarily large and it can be shown that as this happens r_n tends to a constant. In other words once n is sufficiently large we can regard r_n as fixed. This value for r_n is called the **true rate of the language** and is denoted by r. Similarly there is a corresponding value for d_n, which we denote by d. Thus $d = r_0 - r$.

If we have such a cipher system **S** with $H(\mathbf{K})$ keys and if we know the true rate of the language r then, of course, we know d. So, if we have intercepted the first q letters of a cryptogram, the expected number of meaningful decipherments for those q positions (i.e. decipherments which lead to the first q positions of a meaningful message) is $2^{H(\mathbf{K})-qd}$. This prompts us to take the **unicity distance** of a random cipher system to be

$$n_0 = \frac{H(\mathbf{K})}{d}.$$

Thus n_0 is the smallest integer which gives an expected unique meaningful decipherment.

To illustrate the above discussion we will try to evaluate n_0 for a monoalphabetic cipher. Here there are 26! keys which are all equally likely so, by Exercise 3.7, $H(\mathbf{K}) = \log_2 (26!) \simeq 88.4$. The alphabet has 26 letters so $x = 26$ and $r_0 = \log_2 26 \simeq 4.7$. In order to calculate d, we need to determine the true rate r of the English language. But, unlike the other two quantities, this is not so clearly defined. There is no way of giving a precise value to the probability of any given word appearing in a message. Different statistical surveys attach slightly varying probabilities to various words and this leads ultimately to discrepancies in their values for r. For instance Hellman [10] estimates r to be about 1.5 while Deavours [8] puts it as small as 1. If we put $r = 1.5$, we have $d = 4.7 - 1.5 = 3.2$ and $n_0 = 27.6$. (The concept of redundancy may become clearer if we use d to show what percentage of the text is redundant. For instance $d = 3.2$ says that out of every 4.7 characters there are 3.2 redundant ones. Thus $\frac{3.2}{4.7} \times 100 = 68\%$ of the English language is redundant.) Taking $r = 1$ gives $d = 3.7$ (79% redundancy) and $n_0 = 23.9$. Taking the worse of these values we would expect any cryptogram of 28 letters or more to have a unique solution. This agrees with the experimental evidence since Friedman [9] has estimated that with 25 letters there will normally be a unique solution. In practice, however, one needs many more than the 25 letters in order to determine this unique solution.

When we discussed deciphering in Chapter 1 we made extensive use of the statistical facts which are known about the English language. However we stressed at the time that our methods would only work if the intercepted cryptogram was long enough. If we only have 25 letters then there is simply not sufficient information for us to rely on these statistical arguments. Consequently the only way in which we can be sure of obtaining the unique solution is by trying all possibilities. We can formulate this in terms of unicity distances and, at the same time, draw attention to some other problems. In our discussion of random cipher systems we had a fixed integer n, rate r_n and redundancy d_n. We will now compute r_1 and r_2 for the English language and include a graph (Figure 3.9) to illustrate the behaviour of d_n for large values of n. The difficulties of the computations involved in calculating r_2 should demonstrate adequately the complexity of determining r.

If we take $n = 1$ then, using the statistics in Appendix 1 and writing $H(\mathbf{M}, n)$ for $H_C(\mathbf{M}, n)$, we get

$$H(\mathbf{M}, 1) = - \sum_{A}^{Z} p_\alpha \log_{10} p_\alpha \approx 1 \cdot 262.$$

Converting the logarithms to base 2, which merely involves dividing by $\log_{10} 2$, we get

$$r_1 = - \sum_{A}^{Z} p_\alpha \log_2 p_\alpha \approx 4 \cdot 192.$$

Thus since $r_0 = \log_2 26 \approx 4 \cdot 700$ we have $d_1 \approx 0 \cdot 508$ or about $10 \cdot 8\%$ redundancy. (Note most calculators do not have a function key for calculating logarithms to base 2. Thus it is often necessary to work with logarithms to base 10 and 'convert'.)

EXERCISE 3.8   Using the table of bigram frequencies (excluding spaces) in Appendix 1, show that $H(\mathbf{M}, 2) \approx 2 \cdot 346$. Convert the logarithms to base 2 and, remembering to divide by 2, show that $r_2 \approx 3 \cdot 896$. Hence show $d_2 \approx 0 \cdot 804$ giving about $17 \cdot 1\%$ redundancy.

EXERCISE 3.9   Show that $d_1 \approx 0 \cdot 508$ gives a unicity distance of about 174 but taking $d_2 \approx 0 \cdot 804$ makes it 'shrink' to about 110.

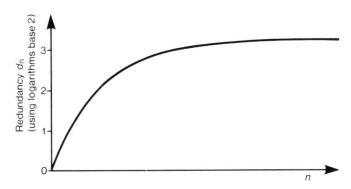

Figure 3.9
Changes in redundancy d_n with increasing n

What is happening is that the more information we use the higher the redundancy of the language becomes and, consequently, the smaller the unicity distance. Eventually, the redundancy levels off to an almost constant value which is what Hellman approximates to $3 \cdot 2$ and Deavours to 3·7 (see Figure 3.9). In the extreme, if we try every key and consider the frequencies of n-grams for all n, then we make use of all the redundancy which the language possesses.

Although it has many of the right properties, we must not forget that the system of monoalphabetic ciphers is not exactly a random cipher system. We have already mentioned some of the reasons for this when discussing the true rate. Another reason is that, when using a monoalphabetic cipher, a message has to be fairly long before it contains every letter and thus involves the entire key. Until this happens the possible decipherments of a cryptogram will not be randomly distributed amongst the messages. To see this we merely notice that all keys which differ only in the letters not appearing in the cryptogram will give the same message.

If we look again at the system of all monoalphabetic ciphers then we know now that the unicity distance n_0 is somewhere near 25. If we put $n = 40$ and take $r = 1·5$, we get an expected number of meaningful decipherments of about $1·2 \times 10^{-10}$. Thus, since we know there is at least 1, we would clearly expect a unique solution. If, on the other hand, we take a value of n which is less than n_0, say $n = 20$, then, again taking $r = 1·5$, we get an expected number of $2·2 \times 10^7$ meaningful decipherments; a very large number! In fact the expected number remains large for all values of n up to n_0 and then suddenly drops dramatically. In his paper Shannon [14] has a number of examples and graphs to illustrate this phenomenon.

Further support for Shannon's theory of random cipher systems is obtained by applying it to other known systems. For the one-time-pad we get an expected number of 2^m meaningful decipherments. Since there are 2^m meaningful messages this is what we would expect. If we take the system of all Vigenère ciphers with keyword of length h, then there are 26^h keys and $H(\mathbf{K}) = \log_2 26^h = h \log_2 26 \simeq 4·7 h$. Taking $r = 1·5$ we get

$$n_0 = \frac{4·7 h}{3·2} \simeq 1·47 h.$$

EXERCISE 3.10   Show that, assuming $d = 3·4$, the unicity distance of the M-209 is about 52.

3.6.4   Ideal systems

One of the requirements for a random system is that, for any given cryptogram $\mathbf{c}$, deciphering using all keys leads to a random selection of all the messages, i.e. a random selection of both meaningful and meaningless messages. This clearly implies that the number of meaningful decipherments is less than we could guarantee if we knew that deciphering a cryptogram, which came from a meaningful message, had to give a meaningful message. But this latter requirement demands that the cryptogram space can also be divided into two classes, namely those which arise from enciphering meaningful messages and those which do not. If it is possible to divide the cryptogram space into two such groups and if the probabilities assigned to the meaningless messages are small enough, then we can reduce the message space (and, consequently, also the cryptogram space) so that all messages are meaningful and so that every decipherment of a cryptogram (with or without the right key) results in a meaningful message. But removing the meaningless messages is equivalent to removing the redundancy from the system. Thus if we could remove all redundancy from a language then, by using that language, almost any cipher system would be satisfactory and provide a high level of security. In practice, of course, this is virtually impossible. The structure of all natural languages is too complex. However in a number of situations it may be possible to reduce the redundancy considerably, or at least to 'spread' it out, so that the cryptanalyst finds it harder to use. Applying a process of this kind to a message prior to its encipherment is called **source coding**. We shall meet examples of source coding in later chapters.

Whenever we have given an example of cryptanalyzing a cryptogram, we have been in the position where, as more text was intercepted, we were able to 'guess' the message with more confidence. This leads us to define an ideal system as one in which receiving extra information does not necessarily help. More formally a system is called **ideal** if $H_C(\mathbf{K}, n)$ does not tend to zero as n gets very large. One simple example of an ideal system is the set of monoalphabetic ciphers on an artificial language in which all letters are equiprobable and successive letters are independently chosen.

Further Reading

[13] and [14] are the classical papers of Shannon. In [10] Hellman introduces some of Shannon's concepts in a different and interesting way. [8] is a good introduction to the concept of unicity distance. [11] is a suitable introduction to Information Theory and [12] covers almost all the statistical concepts we shall require for this book.

[8]   Deavours, C. A., 'Unicity Points in Cryptanalysis', *Cryptologia*, Vol. 1, No. 1, 1977, 46-68.

[9]   Friedman, William F., *Military Cryptanalysis*, U.S. Government Printing Office, 1944.

[10] Hellman, Martin, E., *The Information Theoretic Approach to Cryptography*, Stanford University Report, 1974.

[11] Khinchin, A. I., *Mathematical Foundations of Information Theory*, Dover Publications, 1957.

[12] Lindgren, B. W., *Statistical Theory*, 3rd Edition, Macmillan Publishing Co., 1976.

[13] Shannon, C. E., 'A Mathematical Theory of Communication', *Bell System Technical Journal*, 27 July 1948, 379–423 and October 1948, 623–656.

[14] Shannon, C. E., 'Communication Theory of Secrecy Systems', *Bell System Technical Journal*, 28, 1949, 656–715.

4.
Practical Security

4.1 Introduction

In Chapter 3 we assumed essentially that the cryptanalyst has unlimited time, facilities and funds. When a system is secure under these assumptions, we say that it is **theoretically secure**. In reality, of course, the cryptanalyst is likely to be faced with a totally different situation. He will have to worry about all three of the above resources and, in a number of situations, the time taken to solve a cryptogram will be of the utmost importance to him. In Chapter 1 we introduced the concept of cover time. In many tactical environments the minimum cover time needed by the encipherer is very short and, as a consequence, a time-consuming cryptanalytical technique may be of little practical value to an interceptor. Thus it is certainly possible for a theoretically insecure system to provide adequate practical security. It is also possible for a theoretically secure system to be highly vulnerable when used in a practical situation. As an example of such a system, consider the one-time-pad which was mentioned in Chapter 3. We have certainly shown that the one-time-pad is theoretically unbreakable. However that all-embracing phrase 'theoretically unbreakable' ignores many very important practical facts. For instance, in the discussion of the one-time-pad we assumed that the transmission of the key material was not part of the cipher system. This may have been reasonable but it must not be forgotten that for this particular system the security lies in the fact that there is at least as much key material as message. The discussion completely ignored the practical problem of transmitting the immense volume of key material to the receiver and, of course, the system is only practically secure if the encipherer can find a safe way of letting the recipient know the key he has employed. Thus the user of the one-time-pad is faced with the same problems as the schoolboys in Section 1.2. There is no doubt that, for the one-time-pad, the actual 'key management' is highly vulnerable and that the system is not necessarily practically secure.

As another illustration of the need to distinguish between practical and theoretical security, we consider ideal systems. At the end of Chapter 3 we observed that one example of an ideal system is the set of monoalphabetic ciphers on an artificial language in which all letters are equiprobable and successive letters are independently chosen. Under the criteria used in Chapter 3, the proposed system provides a high level of security. But if, for instance, the system were actually used and a cryptanalyst obtained some corresponding ciphertext and plaintext, then the system would become vulnerable. Indeed if the sample of corresponding plaintext and ciphertext were long enough, a cryptanalyst could reconstruct the entire substitution alphabet, i.e. the entire key, and could then decipher the remaining ciphertext plus any other cryptograms which were enciphered using the same key. (Once again we stress that, unfortunately, this is a realistic assumption. If a system is to offer a reasonable level of practical security then it must be able to withstand 'known-plaintext' attacks.)

In order to assess the practical security of a system we must have some idea of the resources which are likely to be available to a would-be cryptanalyst. In particular, we need to have some idea of the likely computing power at his disposal. Of course this will depend on the circumstances of the particular cryptanalyst, but it is always safest for the cryptographer to assume that every cryptanalyst has the best equipment at his disposal. Suppose, for example, that we have a system which we know to be breakable, but would require at least 10^{50} storage elements or operations. In [15] it is estimated that achieving 10^{50} storage elements would require a memory covering the entire land surface of the earth to a height of 10 kilometres. Even with this volume, the memory bank would be so dense that only one atom could be allocated to each memory bit. Of course the details of this estimate are irrelevant. But the conclusion is obvious: if, to break our system, a cryptanalyst needs storage for 10^{50} elements then we can safely regard it as unbreakable. A similar conclusion holds if 10^{50} operations are needed. This suggests that such a system would be secure and, in fact, given current technology, the need for far fewer than 10^{50} storage elements or operations makes a system unbreakable in practice. Even with as 'few' as 10^{18} necessary operations and an extremely fast machine capable of executing an operation in 10^{-9} seconds, the system would have a cover time of over 30 years! (It is worth noting here that there are only 31,536,000 seconds in a year!) If we are trying to assess the practical security of a system, we must determine the number of operations or storage elements needed to break it and then decide if it provides enough cover-time for our purposes. Having said that, we must immediately point out that the number of operations needed is obviously dependent on the efficiency of the method of attack. Thus the cryptanalyst is always seeking ways of reducing the number of operations. As mentioned earlier, even when testing one key every microsecond, to solve a monoalphabetic cipher by trying every key would take about $1 \cdot 28 \times 10^{13}$ years. In practice, therefore, the cryptanalyst must try to find methods which do not entail trying every key, but which eliminate many possibilities at a time. For instance, returning to monoalphabetic ciphers, even for fairly short cryptograms he could try to deduce which letter represents **e**. By using just the simple frequency analysis, i.e. seeing which letters occur most often in the cryptogram, he may not be absolutely certain of the letter but should be able to limit the number of possibilities to 2 or 3. Just doing this eliminates many of the 26! possible keys in one operation. This, of course, is the principle of practical cryptanalysis; to attempt to remove large numbers of possibilities for the key with each single operation or statistical test which takes place. On the other hand, our objective as the cryptographer, assuming either that the system we design is not ideal or does not have perfect secrecy, is to ensure that the amount of work which the cryptanalyst needs to perform does not get too small, even if the length of cryptogram exceeds the unicity distance.

4.2 Diffusion and Confusion

The discussion at the end of the last section pinpoints yet another weakness of the monoalphabetic cipher which it is necessary for the cryptographer to avoid in other systems. When we use a monoalphabetic cipher, the encipherment of any one letter only involves using a small portion of the key – in this case, exactly the one letter which is substituted for it. Thus we can, and indeed did in Section 1.2.4 (page 25), determine the key by finding small pieces of it, and then use the portion of the key already found to determine the rest. To make a system secure, it seems desirable that a considerable amount of key should be used to encipher each character of the message. It is also probably helpful to 'spread' the statistical structure of the cryptogram by enciphering a number of message characters simultaneously.

In order to accommodate these two points and hence reduce the effectiveness of statistical attacks on cryptograms, Shannon suggests that the cryptographer uses two techniques which he calls **diffusion** and **confusion**. The idea behind diffusion is to 'spread' the statistics of the message space into a statistical structure which involves long combinations of the letters in the cryptogram. This is similar to the concept of source coding which we met in Chapter 3. An example of diffusion is, after regarding each letter as an integer modulo 26 in the normal way, to perform an 'averaging' operation on each message. So if $\mathbf{m} = \mathbf{m}_1\mathbf{m}_2 \ldots$ then we pick an integer s and replace $\mathbf{m}$ by the sequence $\mathbf{y}_1\mathbf{y}_2 \ldots$ where

$$\mathbf{y}_n = \sum_{i=0}^{s-1} \mathbf{m}_{n+i}(\mathrm{mod}\,26)$$

for $n = 1, 2, 3, \ldots$. By doing this we get a message space with the same redundancy as the original $\mathbf{M}$, but the letter frequencies of the new message space $\mathbf{Y}$ will be more equal than in $\mathbf{M}$. The effect of all this is that the cryptanalyst needs to intercept a much longer cryptogram before he can attempt statistical decipherment. In practice this means that we are enciphering a number of message characters simultaneously and dependently. One disadvantage of this type of system is that, at the receiver, each part of the message depends on a number of ciphertext characters. Thus, if one single ciphertext character is erroneously transmitted, this may cause many errors in the received message. This diffusing effect of one error in transmission causing many in decipherment is usually called **error propagation**.

The idea of confusion is to make the relation between a cryptogram and the corresponding key a complex one. This aims to make it difficult for statistics to pinpoint the key as having come from any particular area of the key space. In particular, it tries to ensure that the majority of the key is needed to obtain even very short cryptograms. This implies that every message character enciphered will depend on virtually the entire key. Hopefully, this then forces the cryptanalyst to find the whole key simultaneously and will make him solve considerably more complex equations than when he was able to find the key piece by piece.

The concepts of diffusion and confusion are the principles behind the design of most block ciphers. In a **block cipher** to encipher a message $\mathbf{m} = \mathbf{m}_1\mathbf{m}_2\mathbf{m}_3 \ldots \mathbf{m}_s\mathbf{m}_{s+1} \ldots \mathbf{m}_{2s}\mathbf{m}_{2s+1} \ldots$ we first choose an integer s. We then use a key $\mathbf{k}$ and s transformations (usually different) $\mathbf{f}_1, \mathbf{f}_2, \ldots, \mathbf{f}_s$ to encipher the first s message characters $\mathbf{m}_1\mathbf{m}_2 \ldots \mathbf{m}_s$ (called a **block**) and obtain a cryptogram $\mathbf{c}_1\mathbf{c}_2 \ldots \mathbf{c}_s$. Using the same key and functions, we then encipher the next block of s message characters, i.e. $\mathbf{m}_{s+1}\mathbf{m}_{s+2} \ldots \mathbf{m}_{2s}$. Thus the message is enciphered in blocks of s, the cryptogram is produced in blocks of s and each bit of ciphertext in a given block normally depends on the complete corresponding plaintext block. As has already been observed, a major disadvantage of such a system is the accompanying likelihood of error propagation.

4.3   Shannon's Five Criteria

Now that we have discussed cipher systems in some detail, we are in a position to discuss the merits of five criteria which Shannon suggested should be applied. It must not be forgotten that his suggestions were made in the 1940s and that technology has advanced considerably since then. His suggested important criteria were:

  (i)   *the amount of secrecy offered,*
 (ii)   *the size of the key,*
(iii)   *the simplicity of the enciphering and deciphering operations,*
 (iv)   *the propagation of errors,* and
  (v)   *extension of the message.*

Apart from (i), whose importance is obvious, we will discuss very briefly Shannon's reasons for listing these particular criteria. The reasoning and assertions in this paragraph are a summary of Shannon's statements. The key must be kept secret and, on occasion, may need to be memorized. Consequently it should be as small or simple as possible. For (iii) we quote Shannon: 'Enciphering and deciphering should, of course, be as simple as possible. If they are done manually, complexity leads to loss of time, errors, etc. If done mechanically, complexity leads to large, expensive machines.' With some cipher systems, one error occurring on a transmission can mean that, when the cryptogram is deciphered, whole portions, or even the complete message, are garbled. For most communication systems this error propagation should clearly be minimized. Finally in some cipher systems the size of the message is increased by the enciphering process. For instance, the use of **nulls** (i.e. adding extra meaningless characters to swamp the message statistics) causes a larger cryptogram than message. Such a message extension is undesirable for most communication systems.

From our discussion of cipher systems, there appears to be a certain incompatibility between the requirements for each of these five criteria when our message space consists of a natural language. It is probably not possible to satisfy all five but, if one is dropped, it may be possible to satisfy the other four. If, for example, we drop the first requirement and are not concerned with secrecy, then any monoalphabetic cipher will satisfy the other four. In fact we do not need a cipher system at all! If the size of the key is not limited then we can use the one-time-pad which, if we ignore the key management patterns, we know offers perfect secrecy.

If we drop (v) and allow unlimited message extension, then we can encipher many extra messages and use part of the key to indicate the correct one. Such a system might even be capable of attaining a high level of security, although it is not clear that it could achieve our requirements for (ii) or (iii). By dropping (iv) we can use a block cipher. But again it is not clear that our requirements for either (ii) or (iii) can be achieved in this way. Although block ciphers may lead to error propagation, this is not necessarily a bad thing. In Chapters 8 and 9 we will see examples of cipher systems where the effects of error propagation will range from being totally unacceptable to being possibly advantageous.

We have deliberately avoided discussing Shannon's third criterion regarding complexity. Today we have the advantages of electronics and do not need to bother with mechanical machines. This means that we now have reasonably cheap ways of producing reliable and extremely complex equipment for enciphering and deciphering messages. Thus Shannon's third criterion no longer concerns us. Consequently, for the rest of this book, we will assume the benefits offered by electronics. We will drop Shannon's third criterion and concern ourselves with constructing and examining cipher systems which can be implemented cheaply and easily using microelectronics. We should, however, bear in mind that the reliability of any equipment we might use is a fundamental aspect of its practical security. If a particular implementation of a cipher system is unreliable, the security afforded by the system is almost certainly reduced quite dramatically. The problem of ensuring sufficient reliability is one which can be solved and is part of the task faced by the electronic engineer. We will not concern ourselves with this problem.

In the first three chapters we have examined some of the theory of cipher systems and looked at some simple (often outdated) examples. We will now concentrate on trying to construct modern, secure systems. However before we can undertake such a project we must be absolutely sure we know what the threats to our systems might be.

4.4   Worst Case Conditions

When designing a cipher system, we must always assume that any would-be cryptanalyst has as much knowledge and 'intelligence' information as possible. It is only by making these assumptions that we will be able to assess our cover-time. Once again it is worth emphasizing that, apart from the case of the one-time-pad, we are now considering a theoretically breakable system, and our major consideration is the time needed for a cryptanalyst to break it.

In order to assess the security of a system we will make the following three assumptions, which we refer to as the **worst case conditions**.

C1   *The cryptanalyst has a complete knowledge of the cipher system.*
C2   *The cryptanalyst has obtained a considerable amount of ciphertext.*
C3   *The cryptanalyst knows the plaintext equivalent of a certain amount of the ciphertext.*

In any given situation we will attempt to quantify realistically what we mean by 'considerable' and 'certain'. This will depend on the particular system under consideration.

Condition **C1** implies that we believe there is no security in the cipher system itself, and that all security must come from the key. Naturally the cryptanalyst's task is considerably harder if he does not know the system used and it is now possible to conceal this information to a certain extent. For instance, with a modern electronic system, the function used for enciphering can be concealed in hardware by the use of microelectronics. By using Large Scale Integration, we can conceal the entire function within a 'chip' which is about one quarter the size of a fingernail. To actually 'open up' one of these chips is a delicate and time consuming process. Nevertheless it can be done, and we should not assume that the cryptanalyst has not the ability and patience to do it. Similarly any part of the function which is included as software within the machine can be disguised by a carefully written program. Once again, with patience and skill, this can be uncovered. It is even possible that, in some situations, the cryptanalyst will have the precise algorithm available to him. It should be clear that, from any manufacturer's or designer's point of view, this is an essential assumption, since it removes a great deal of the ultimate responsibility involved in keeping a system secret. In Chapter 7 we discuss a cipher system for which the algorithm has deliberately been made public.

It should be clear that **C2** is a necessary assumption which, in conjunction with **C1**, has formed the basis of many of our earlier cryptanalytic attacks. It has to be assumed that, if a cryptanalyst can intercept one communication between two parties, he is likely to be able to intercept others. Furthermore a number of these communications may have employed the same key!

C3 (in conjunction with **C1**) is the basis of the **known plaintext attack** which is probably the most important and most commonly used method of breaking ciphers. In this case the cryptanalyst has, possibly by guesswork, deduction, or even by 'planting' it in some way, obtained knowledge of some of the plaintext message prior to its encipherment. So he already knows the plaintext equivalent of part of the cryptogram. (We saw an example of this type of attack in Chapter 2.) The cryptanalyst may, for instance, know that all communications between two sources begin with a particular name and address; or even with a particular expression like **Dear John**. He may have intercepted other cryptograms between the two parties and, having broken them, knows the style in which they are written. Alternatively he may have a method of 'planting' some plaintext or of merely ascertaining the general theme of the plaintext. (This latter knowledge then tells him some particular words to expect in the message.)

One important question which the cryptographer must repeatedly ask himself is 'how difficult is it to determine part, or all, of the message knowing the cryptogram plus a small portion of its plaintext equivalent?'. Clearly the answer depends on many things, including the actual length of known plaintext.

When discussing the cryptanalysis of cryptograms from the M-209, we looked at two examples which involved known plaintext attacks. Not surprisingly the one with the larger amount of known plaintext took less time than the other. Furthermore both were considerably shorter than the ciphertext only attack. In many ciphertext only attacks, a cryptanalyst may decide to try to guess a certain amount of plaintext before trying to break the system systematically. When this occurs the total time needed depends both on the number of guesses needed to deduce the plaintext, and on the time of the known plaintext attack which he then adopts. One problem facing the cryptanalyst is to decide how much plaintext, if any, he should try to guess. It may happen, for instance, that if a certain number of characters of plaintext are known then the time needed to break the system is very small. If this is so, then the cryptanalyst must decide how many trials he needs to determine that number of characters. (We will see an example of this situation in Section 5.6.5.) If the number is large and the system is one that involves the daily transmission of only a few characters of a highly random nature, the number of guesses required is likely to be enormous and it is therefore unrealistic. On the other hand, if this is a computer data link transmitting highly formatted information, the determination of a large number of corresponding plaintext and ciphertext characters may not be out of the question.

Of course our three conditions are rather pessimistic from the cryptographer's point of view. But they are not unreasonable, and any system which is not secure against such a threat must be considered unsuitable for use in any situation where security is important.

4.5   Stream Cipher Systems

We now change our emphasis. So far, we have considered the development of ciphers up to the end of the Second World War. Each system discussed could be implemented in a reasonably short time, either by hand or by using a mechanical or electro-mechanical machine. We now begin to look at post-Second World War systems and, not surprisingly, there are dramatic changes. The most significant factors in the development of the design of cipher systems were the advent of the computer and then, in the 1960s, the expanding use of microelectronics. They meant that a whole new range of functions were available to the cryptographer. But they also compelled him to increase his mathematical knowledge. Many of these new functions could only be expressed in terms of a mathematical language which was considerably more advanced than any of the mathematical knowledge previously required.

The development of the cipher system was greatly influenced by the fact that Shannon had proved the one-time-pad to be unbreakable. Many cryptographers felt that, if they could emulate the one-time-pad system in some way, they would have a system with a guaranteed high security level. They were also encouraged by the fact that, since the 1920s, many of the mechanical and electro-mechanical machines had operated in a way similar to the one-time-pad; in the sense that they produced long sequences of displacements which were applied, character by character, to the plaintext message. However there is one fundamental difference. Unlike the situation for the one-time-pad, a sequence produced by one of these machines is not random; in fact it is completely determined by the key. Once the key has been set up, the sequence, although certainly as long as the message, is completely predetermined. Nevertheless, by careful choice of the algorithm, it was possible to produce a sequence which appeared to be random, i.e. a sequence in which there was no obvious relation between the elements. It was argued by many cryptographers that such a system would be highly secure. We shall see later that this is not necessarily the case.

The above ideas led to the introduction of the **stream cipher**, illustrated in Figure 4.1.

Thus a stream cipher is a system in which the key is fed to an algorithm which uses the key to generate an infinite sequence. (The algorithm is usually referred to as the **sequence generator** or **keystream generator**.) In

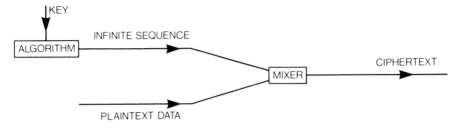

Figure 4.1
A stream cipher

all practical cases of cipher systems, the algorithm is an example of a finite state machine. (We shall consider finite state machines in Chapter 5.)

It is important to realize that a stream cipher attempts to utilize confusion, but not diffusion. This gives it a major advantage over a block cipher; namely that it is not error propagating. For this reason, stream ciphers provide probably the most important method of modern encipherment, and Chapters 5 and 6 are devoted to them. Since the majority of such systems employ electronic techniques, both the plaintext and the infinite sequence use a character set which has only two possibilities corresponding to **on** and **off**. For convenience these are labelled 1 and 0 and the resulting system is called a **binary system**. (The character symbols 0 and 1 are known as **binary digits** or **bits**.)

Normally the messages which we wish to transmit employ a larger alphabet. To overcome this problem we represent each character by a set of bits. (This, of course, is why we used logarithms to base 2 in Section 3.6.) If, for instance, we want to transmit a message using only the letters of the English alphabet then we need a character set of 26 elements. If we want the sets of bits representing each character to have the same size then we must represent each character by at least $\log_2 26$ bits. Obviously we need a whole number of bits and so, rounding up, we need at least 5 bits per character. (Note $2^5 = 32$, so using 5 bits per character leaves us a little scope to increase our character set slightly.) In Appendix 2 we list two codes which 'convert' character sets into sets of bits. One, the ITA 5, has a character set of 128 and uses 7 bits to represent each character ($2^7 = 128$). ITA 2 utilizes 5 bits per character. By using two of the 32 possible 5-bit combinations to denote 'letter shift' and 'figure shift', it incorporates a 58-character set. (In Table C1 of Appendix 2, letter shift and figure shift are denoted by 'letters' and 'figures' respectively.) Essentially there are two sets of 26 characters each, and the set from which the 5-bit combination represents a character depends on whether the last shift character was 'letters' or 'figures'. The characters 'letter shift' and 'figure shift' are accessible no matter what the shift is. Similarly 'carriage return', 'line feed', 'null' and 'space' are accessible independent of the shift. Thus we have 58 ($2\times26+6$) possible characters.

EXERCISE 4.1   Use Appendix 2 to show that LET 24 BE can be represented by:
   (i)
*1111101001100000000100100110111100101010001001111111001110000
in ITA 2*
   (ii)
*1001100100010110101000100000001100100110100010000010000101000101
in ITA 5.*

The mixer of Figure 4.1 is usually an **exclusive-or gate (XOR)**. Its effect is to add, modulo 2, the two bits entering it and, for this reason, we normally refer to it as a **modulo 2 adder** and denote it by $\oplus$.

EXERCISE 4.2   If the data begins 11010, the sequence begins 01110 and the mixer is a modulo 2 adder, show that the output sequence begins 10100.

One way of viewing our stream cipher system is as a polyalphabetic cipher whose periodicity is governed by the sequence which the algorithm produces. We will say much more about this in Chapter 5, but it is important to realize that, although the sequence has infinite length, this does not mean that the polyalphabetic cipher cannot have finite period. The infinite sequence may have the property that it is merely numerous repetitions of a finite sequence. If this occurs then we say that it is **periodic**. We call the shortest repeated sequence a **cycle** and the length of a cycle is the **period** of the infinite sequence. If we represent the sequence $s_1 s_2 s_3 \ldots$ by (s_t), then if (s_t) has period p we know $s_m = s_{m+p}$ for every m.

If the period of our output sequence is small, the system will have the same type of drawbacks as the Vigenère cipher with short keyword, which we discussed in Chapter 1. It is essential for security that our output sequence should have a large period and that the period should, as an absolute minimum, be at least as long as any message to be enciphered. For this reason, we will need theorems which tell us when the output sequence has a guaranteed minimum period. A second requirement for our output sequence, again based on our experience in attempting to cryptanalyze Vigenère-type ciphers, is that it should appear to be random and, thus, not allow the cryptanalyst to use any known statistical analysis of the language of the system. Thus our two main aims are:

A1   *The input sequence must have a guaranteed minimum length for its period. (We will then only encipher messages which are shorter than this value.)*
A2   *The ciphertext must appear to be random.*

We will give a formal definition of periodicity and discuss it in greater detail when we consider specific algorithms. We will then also need to be able to examine any given sequence to decide if it is sufficiently random. Unfortunately it is not easy to quantify randomness and we must determine some criteria with which to assess it.

4.6 The Concept of Randomness

Our first problem is to decide what we mean by randomness. Before attempting to give a formal definition, we will try to decide what we want our randomness properties to indicate. Clearly no periodic sequence is truly random. In cryptography what we normally require of our sequence is unpredictability rather than randomness. We want to know that, if a cryptanalyst intercepts part of the sequence, he will have no information on how to predict what comes next. Again this is, strictly speaking, impossible for any periodic sequence since, as soon as he knows a complete cycle, the cryptanalyst knows the entire sequence. Nevertheless it is not unreasonable to try to ensure that, if a segment of ciphertext which is considerably shorter than the period is intercepted, no further information is imparted. Any deterministic sequence satisfying these general properties is normally called a **pseudo-random sequence**.

When we were considering the cryptanalysis of ciphertext in Chapter 1, our aim was to use the statistical information available for the ciphertext language. Cryptanalysis was made more difficult when each ciphertext letter appeared more or less equally often. We discovered that if each bigram, trigram, etc. also appeared equally often then the ciphertext would appear to be random and the statistics would be useless. This is another property we will try to build into our idea of randomness.

We cannot give our definition of randomness without introducing more terminology and defining the statistical concept of an autocorrelation function. If (s_t) is any binary sequence then a **run** is a string of consecutive identical sequence elements which is neither preceded nor succeeded by the same symbol. Thus, for example, 0111001 begins with a run of one 0, contains a run of three 1s and a run of two 0s, and then ends with a run of one 1. A run of 0s is called a **gap** while a run of 1s is a **block**.

Suppose that (s_t) is a binary sequence of period p. (Recall that this implies $s_{m+p} = s_m$ for every m.) For any fixed τ, we compare the first p terms of (s_t) and its **translate** $(s_{t+\tau})$. If A is the number of positions in which these two sequences agree and $D(= p - A)$ is the number of positions in which they disagree, then the **autocorrelation function** $C(\tau)$ is defined by:

$$C(\tau) = \frac{A - D}{p}.$$

Clearly $C(\tau + p) = C(\tau)$ for all τ, so it suffices to consider only those τ satisfying $0 \le \tau < p$. When $\tau = 0$ we have **in-phase autocorrelation**. In this case, clearly, $A = p$ and $D = 0$, so that $C(0) = 1$. For $\tau \ne 0$ we have **out-of-phase autocorrelation**.

The following three **randomness postulates** for a binary sequence of period p were proposed by Golomb [16].

R1 *If p is even then the cycle of length p shall contain an equal number of zeros and ones. If p is odd then the number of zeros shall be one more or less than the number of ones.*

R2   *In the cycle of length p, half the runs have length 1, a quarter have length 2, an eighth have length 3 and, in general, for each i for which there are at least 2^{i+1} runs, $\dfrac{1}{2^i}$ of the runs have length i. Moreover, for each of these lengths, there are equally many gaps and blocks.*

R3   *The out-of-phase autocorrelation is a constant.*

In Section 4.7 we shall look at some statistical randomness tests which can be applied to binary sequences. When we do, the implications of Golomb's postulates may become clearer. For the time being we merely observe that, when applied to ciphertext sequences, **R1** reflects the property that the input characters occur equally often. Without going into details, **R2** says something like 'bigrams, trigrams, etc.' occur equally often. What does **R3** say? This is not quite so clear. Obviously it says that we cannot obtain extra information by comparing the cryptogram with translates of itself. But would we expect to? Rather than answer this, we refer the reader to the process, used in Section 1.3.5, for determining the length of the keyword used for a Vigenère cipher. That provides an example where we did get information by comparing a sequence of the ciphertext with translates of itself. Of course the situation was different, in the sense that we did not compute the autocorrelation, but it is not completely unrelated. It is certainly near enough to suggest that some property like **R3** is desirable. The most familiar example of a random binary sequence arises from tossing an unbiased coin repeatedly and writing 1 when it is heads and 0 for tails. In this context, Golomb gave the following interpretation of his postulates: 'In flipping a "perfect coin", **R1** is the postulate that heads and tails occur about equally often, and **R2** is the assertion that after a run of n heads (tails) there is a fifty-fifty chance that it will end with the next coin flip. Finally **R3** is the notion of independent trials – knowing how the toss came out on a previous trial gives no information for the current trial.'

For the time being we will accept Golomb's postulates as being a reasonable requirement for a random binary sequence, and call a sequence satisfying them **G-random**; such sequences are often referred to as **PN-sequences** (PN being the abbreviation for pseudo-noise).

4.7   Statistical Tests for Local Randomness

From our earlier discussions we know that, if they are to be used as enciphering sequences in a stream cipher system, our sequences must resemble a random sequence. With many of the sequences which we shall introduce, we will be able to show that they do indeed have some good randomness properties, e.g. an approximately equal number of zeros and ones, and a reasonably flat autocorrelation function. However these are mathematical results which can only be obtained by considering a complete period of the sequence. In practice, the sequences used in cipher systems have large periods. A period of less than 10^{10} is rarely used, and periods as long as 10^{50} are quite common. Although knowledge of properties of the entire sequence is crucial and gives us confidence in the system, it tells us little about small sections of the sequence. But if an interceptor does obtain some of our ciphertext, it will almost certainly be a relatively small section. Thus it is important to apply statistical tests to sections of our sequence and to check that they also appear to be random. This type of randomness is often referred to as **local randomness.**

We have already discussed our definition of a G-random sequence. One requirement is that each complete cycle should contain an equal number of 0s and 1s. If we now test a section of the sequence then, clearly, it would be unreasonable to expect a precise fifty-fifty split. However, equally clearly, we must not have a dominance of either digit. In this section we list five statistical tests which can be performed to provide a quantitative measure of randomness. All these tests, in their various ways, measure the relative frequencies of certain patterns of 0s and 1s in a section of the sequence. Once we have this measure it is up to us, as the cryptographer, to decide if the sequence is random enough for our purposes. We need to determine our own levels of confidence for the tests so that we can decide whether a sequence has passed or failed the test. To do this we establish statistical values corresponding to truly random sequences and then set a pass mark. As an illustration, suppose our pass mark is 95%. This means that a given sequence passes the test if its value lies in the range in which we would expect to find 95% of all truly random sequences. It is usual to denote the pass mark as $(100-\alpha)\%$, where α is called the **significance level** of the test.

There are numerous statistical tests which can be applied to a sequence. It is not our aim to discuss hypothesis testing in any detail, and the interested reader is referred to [12]. Our aim now is merely to describe five particular tests and give an indication of their usefulness. In practice the five tests might be combined to form part of a computer package and we would expect our sequence to pass all five.

Throughout the following discussions we will assume that a sample of n bits of our sequence contains n_0 zeros and n_1 ones.

Test 1: The frequency test
This is perhaps the most obvious of the tests and is applied to ensure that there is roughly the same number of 0s and 1s. For this we merely compute

$$\chi^2 = \frac{(n_o - n_1)^2}{n}.$$

Clearly if $n_0 = n_1$ then $\chi^2 = 0$, and the larger the value of χ^2 the greater the discrepancy between the observed and the expected frequencies. To decide if the value obtained is good enough for the sequence to pass, we have merely to compare our value with a table of the χ^2 distribution, for one degree of freedom. (Such tables are commonly available and give the values of χ^2 corresponding to the various significance levels.) From this table we find that the value of χ^2 for a 5% significance level is 3·84. So, quite simply, if our value is no greater than 3·84 the sequence passes. Otherwise we must reject it. (We might also decide to fail our sequence if the value of χ^2 is 0. Being too 'good' can be suspicious!)

Test 2: The Serial Test
The serial test is used to ensure that the transition probabilities are reasonable; i.e. that the probability of consecutive entries being equal or different is about the same. This will then give us some level of confidence that each bit is independent of its predecessor. Suppose 01 occurs n_{01} times, 10 occurs n_{10} times, 00 occurs n_{00} times and 11 occurs n_{11} times. $n_{01} + n_{00} = n_0$ or $n_0 - 1$, $n_{10} + n_{11} = n_1$ or $n_1 - 1$ and $n_{10} + n_{01} + n_{00} + n_{11} = n - 1$. (Note the -1 occurs because in a section of length m there are only $m - 1$ transitions.) Ideally we want $n_{01} = n_{10} = n_{00} = n_{11} \simeq \dfrac{n-1}{4}$. Good[17] has shown that

$$\frac{4}{n-1} \sum_{i=0}^{1} \sum_{j=0}^{1} (n_{ij})^2 - \frac{2}{n} \sum_{i=0}^{1} (n_i)^2 + 1$$

is approximately distributed as χ^2 with two degrees of freedom. From the appropriate tables we find that, for two degrees of freedom, the value of χ^2 corresponding to a 5% significance level is 5·99. Thus for this test we compute

$$\frac{4}{n-1} \sum_{i=0}^{1} \sum_{j=0}^{1} (n_{ij})^2 - \frac{2}{n} \sum_{i=0}^{1} (n_i)^2 + 1$$

and reject any sequence for which the value is greater than 5·99.

Test 3: The Poker Test
For any integer m there are 2^m different possibilities for a section of length m of a binary sequence. In this test we partition our sequence into blocks (or **hands**) of size m and then we count the frequency of each type of section of length m in our sequence. If the frequencies are $f_0, f_1, \ldots, f_{2^m-1}$ then

$$\sum_{i=0}^{2^m-1} f_i = F = \left[\frac{n}{m}\right], \text{ where } \left[\frac{n}{m}\right] \text{ means the largest integer which is not bigger}$$

than $\dfrac{n}{m}$. Then, as before, we evaluate

$$\chi^2 = \frac{2^m}{F} \sum_{i=0}^{2^m-1} (f_i)^2 - F.$$

Finally we compare our value with the table for χ^2 having $2^m - 1$ degrees of freedom to see if we have a 5% significance level.

We can apply this test many times for different values of m. However in certain circumstances some values of m may be more relevant than others. Suppose, for example, that if our sequence 'passes' we want to use it for encipherment of data that is converted to binary using ITA 2. Suppose also that the cipher will be reconverted to alphanumeric characters using ITA 2 before transmission. Then, in this case, as ITA 2 is a 5-bit code we may be especially interested in the poker test for $m = 5$.

There is a variation of the poker test which is occasionally useful. In this variation we evaluate the numbers $x_0, x_1, \ldots, x_m$ where, if m is the block length, and x_i is the number of m-bit blocks having i ones and $m - i$ zeros. We may then apply the χ^2 with m degrees of freedom, where

$$\chi^2 = \frac{2^m}{F} \cdot \sum_{i=0}^{m} \frac{(x_i)^2}{\binom{m}{i}} - F.$$

Test 4: The Autocorrelation Test
Suppose the sequence of n bits which we wish to test for randomness properties is $a_1, \ldots, a_n$. Then set:

$$A(d) = \sum_{i=1}^{n-d} a_i a_{i+d} \quad 0 \le d \le n - 1$$

Clearly $A(0) = \sum_{i=1}^{n} (a_i)^2 = \sum_{i=1}^{n} a_i = n_1$.

If the sequence has n_0 zeros and n_1 ones, which are randomly distributed, the expected value of $A(d)$, $(d \ne 0)$, is

$$\mu = \frac{n_1^2(n - d)}{n^2}.$$

This enables us to use standard hypothesis testing techniques to decide whether or not we believe our sequence has a 'random' distribution.

Test 5: The Runs Test
For the runs test we divide the sequence into blocks and gaps. We let r_{0i} be the number of gaps of length i and r_{1i} be the number of blocks of length i. If r_0 and r_1 are the number of gaps and blocks respectively then

$$r_0 = \sum_{i=1}^{i=n} r_{0i} \quad \text{and} \quad r_1 = \sum_{i=1}^{i=n} r_{1i}.$$

Using the notation of the serial test, it is easy to see that $n_{01} = r_0$ or $r_0 - 1$, $n_{10} = r_1$ or $r_1 - 1$, $n_{00} = n_0 - r_0$ and $n_{11} = n_1 - r_1$.

We would not be applying this test if the sequence had not already passed the serial test, so we know that the total numbers of gaps and blocks are within acceptable limits. We now expect about half the gaps (or blocks) to have length 1, a quarter to have length 2 and so on (see Golomb's postulate **R2**). We will not worry about the precise statistical test which should now be used, but refer to the interested reader to Mood [19].

Further Reading

[15] is concerned with limits of computation. [16] introduces G-randomness. [12], [17], [18] and [19] all contain material which is relevant to the randomness tests as detailed in Section 4.7.

[15]   Davies, Donald, 'Limits to Computation', Note from NPL, 1980.
[16]   Golomb, Solomon W., *Shift Register Sequences*, Holden-Day, 1967.
[17]   Good, I. J., 'On the serial test for random sequences', *Ann. Math. Statist.*, 28, 1957, 262–264.
[18]   Knuth, D. E., *The Art of Computer Programming, Volume 2: Seminumerical Algorithms*, Addison-Wesley, 1973.
[12]   Lindgren, B. W., *Statistical Theory*, 3rd Edition, Macmillan Publishing Co., 1976.
[19]   Mood, A. M., 'The distribution theory of runs', *Ann. Math. Statist.*, 11, 1940, 367–392.
[14]   Shannon, C. E., 'Communication Theory of Secrecy Systems', *Bell System Technical Journal*, 28, 1949, 656–715.

5.
Linear Shift Registers

5.1 Introduction

We have just considered some of the requirements which a cipher system must fulfil in order to be considered secure in a practical sense. In the next few chapters we will discuss how the encipherment algorithm for such a system might be implemented. We will then be able to consider the overall system which, of course, includes the coding method, mode of transmission, etc. Apart from one specific algorithm which we shall meet in Chapter 7, almost all the current cipher systems which are commercially available are based on stream ciphers. The sequence which is added to the plaintext may be generated in a number of different ways, but nearly all of these methods employ shift registers. One of the main reasons for this is that they are easily obtainable and comparatively inexpensive. In view of their importance, it is essential that the interested reader should understand how shift registers work.

In this chapter we consider a stream cipher system where the enciphering sequence is produced from an n-stage shift register with linear feedback. In particular we determine when such a system satisfies our requirements **A1** and **A2**, and then discuss whether it remains secure in our worst case situation of Section 4.4. This involves us in a reasonably detailed analysis of linear shift register sequences and will be invaluable for some of the later chapters (especially Chapter 6).

Two of the Sections, 5.4 and 5.6, might be a little tedious and/or difficult for the non-mathematician, and so we have included synopses of them. We recommend that, on a first reading, any reader who feels he might have trouble with the mathematics should restrict himself to these synopses. This will certainly enable him to complete the book. However, in view of the special importance of linear shift register theory, such readers are advised to return to this chapter later and read through Sections 5.4 and 5.6. (We define all the mathematical concepts needed, and the list of further reading at the end of the chapter contains references to suitable algebra texts.)

Finally we must point out that, in this chapter, we only present a very small part of the theory of linear shift registers. In particular we have restricted ourselves to searching for sequences with particular properties. By being less restrictive we could have obtained an abundance of interesting results (see, for example, [22]).

5.2 Finite State Machines

A finite state machine consists of a finite collection of states $\mathbf{S} = \{\mathbf{S}_i\}$ and accepts an input sequence of entries from a finite set $\mathbf{A} = \{A_i\}$, called the **input alphabet**. It then produces an output sequence with a finite set $\mathbf{B} = \{B_i\}$ as **output alphabet**. For any given state $\mathbf{S}_i$ and input A_j, the output B_k is determined by an output function μ, i.e. $B_k = \mu(\mathbf{S}_i, A_j)$. Furthermore any given state and input also completely determine the new state, i.e. there is a function δ such that $\mathbf{S}_l = \delta(\mathbf{S}_i, A_j)$. Most digital computers, calculators etc., are complex examples of finite state machines.

We will normally let (a_n), $n = 0, 1, 2, \ldots$ denote the input sequence, which merely means that a_0 is the first input, a_1 is the second and so on. If the input alphabet is $\mathbf{A}$, each a_i is in $\mathbf{A}$; i.e. $a_i = A_j$ for some j. Similarly we will let (b_n) and (s_n) denote the output sequence and sequence of states respectively. Thus, from the definitions of μ and δ we have $b_i = \mu(s_i, a_i)$ and $s_{i+1} = \delta(s_i, a_i)$ for $i = 0, 1, 2, \ldots$.

As a simple illustration, suppose we have a finite state machine which only has two states $\mathbf{S}_1$ or $\mathbf{S}_2$; i.e. $\mathbf{S} = \{\mathbf{S}_1, \mathbf{S}_2\}$. Suppose also that the input alphabet contains only two elements A_1 and A_2 while the output alphabet consists of B_1, B_2 and B_3. Thus $\mathbf{A} = \{A_1, A_2\}$ and $\mathbf{B} = \{B_1, B_2, B_3\}$. The machine is completely described if, for any given state and input, we know the output and the resultant state. This information can be displayed in many ways. One such way is by means of the following **function table**.

	A_1	A_2
$\mathbf{S}_1$	$\mathbf{S}_1, B_1$	$\mathbf{S}_2, B_3$
$\mathbf{S}_2$	$\mathbf{S}_1, B_2$	$\mathbf{S}_2, B_2$

Table 5.1
A function table

The use of the table should be clear. For instance if the machine is in state $\mathbf{S}_1$ and receives input A_2 then, by looking at the row of $\mathbf{S}_1$ and the column of A_2, we see the new state will be $\mathbf{S}_2$ and the output will be B_3.

Another way of displaying the same information is by means of a **state diagram**. In a state diagram each state is represented by a vertex of a graph; i.e. by a dot or a cross. If input A_k changes state $\mathbf{S}_i$ to $\mathbf{S}_j$ then, in the state diagram, we draw a line from $\mathbf{S}_i$ to $\mathbf{S}_j$ with an arrow in the appropriate direction and write A_k over the line. If the output resulting from input A_k and state $\mathbf{S}_i$ is B_h, then we write B_h in brackets beside the A_k. Thus we get:

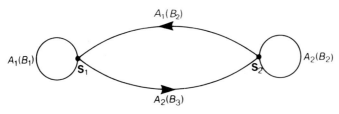

The diagram for our simple example is shown in Figure 5.1.

Figure 5.1
The state diagram for our simple example

A state diagram is nothing more than a directed graph (possibly with loops and multiple edges). For this reason we often refer to the lines representing the possible inputs as the **edges** of the diagram.

Of course, for larger or more complicated finite state machines the two functions μ and δ will be more complex and so, therefore, will the state diagram and function table.

If we are given a machine with sets **A** and **S**, then it is clearly not possible to test the machine's response to all possible input sequences. However there are certain input sequences that will be of particular interest to us. Our reasons for choosing these input sequences will vary. Sometimes we will choose them because they are the easiest to 'generate'. On other occasions, it will merely be because they are the ones for which we get the type of output we require. In this context there is a property of infinite sequences which plays an important role; this is the property of being periodic.

As we mentioned in Chapter 4, in non-technical terms an infinite sequence is periodic if it is a given finite sequence repeated over and over again. Formally, an infinite sequence (u_n) is called **periodic** if there exists an integer $p \neq 0$ such that $u_{t+p} = u_t$ for all t. If such an integer exists then (u_n) is equal to $u_0 u_1 u_2 \ldots u_{p-1} u_0 u_1 \ldots u_{p-1} u_0 \ldots$. The smallest value for p is called the **period** of the sequence and, in this case, we say that (u_n) is **generated by** $u_0 u_1 \ldots u_{p-1}$. In a sequence of period p, any p consecutive terms are said to form a **cycle** of length p. Clearly there are p different cycles to be found in a sequence (u_n) with period p: namely, one corresponding to each possible starting point. If x is any integer, then we can always divide x by p to get a quotient m and a remainder r with $0 \leq r < p$. Thus we can always write x in the form $mp + r$ with $0 \leq r < p$. If we do, then $u_x = u_r$ and the cycle of length p with u_x as its first term is $u_r u_{r+1} \ldots u_{p-1} u_0 \ldots u_{r-1}$. However, unless $r = 0$, the sequence (u_n) is not generated by $u_r u_{r+1} \ldots u_{p-1} u_0 \ldots u_{r-1}$. Thus, of the p distinct cycles of length p, only the cycle $u_0 u_1 \ldots u_{p-1}$ actually generates (u_n). We call such a cycle a **generating cycle**. Periodic sequences play a central role in shift register theory.

EXERCISE 5.1
    (i)   *If (u_n) has period p show that, for any positive integer m, $u_{t+mp} = u_t$ for $t = 0, 1, 2, \ldots$ i.e. $u_0 u_1 \ldots u_{mp-1}$ is also repeated.*
    (ii) *If (u_n) has period p and $u_{t+x} = u_t$ for $t = 0, 1, 2, \ldots$ show that $x = mp$ for some integer m.*

EXERCISE 5.2   Show that if the input sequence (a_n) of a finite state machine is constant, i.e. has period 1, then $\mathbf{s}_i = \mathbf{s}_j$ implies $b_i = b_j$ and $\mathbf{s}_{i+1} = \mathbf{s}_{j+1}$. Hence show that if $\mathbf{s}_i = \mathbf{s}_j$ then $\mathbf{s}_{i+t} = \mathbf{s}_{j+t}$ for $t = 0, 1, 2, \ldots$.

If we consider our earlier example with an input sequence (a_n) of period 3 having $a_0 = A_1$, $a_1 = A_1$, $a_2 = A_2$ and initial state $\mathbf{S}_1$ then, by straightforward use of our function table, we can deduce the complete output sequence. For instance, since an input of A_1 with a state of $\mathbf{S}_1$ gives an output of B_1 and leaves the state as $\mathbf{S}_1$, the first term of the output sequence is B_1 while the second state is $\mathbf{S}_1$. The chart below represents the beginning of the sequence of events: the first row represents successive input entries, while the second and third rows show the successive states and outputs respectively. (Note that by being told a_0, a_1, a_2 and that (a_n) has period 3, we were given the entire input sequence: it must be generated by $A_1 A_1 A_2$.)

Input	A_1	A_1	A_2	A_1	A_1	A_2	A_1	A_1	A_2	$A_1 \ldots$
State	$\mathbf{S}_1$	$\mathbf{S}_1$	$\mathbf{S}_1$	$\mathbf{S}_2$	$\mathbf{S}_1$	$\mathbf{S}_1$	$\mathbf{S}_2$	$\mathbf{S}_1$	$\mathbf{S}_1$	$\mathbf{S}_2 \ldots$
Output	B_1	B_1	B_3	B_2	B_1	B_3	B_2	B_1	B_3	$B_2 \ldots$

It should be clear that the states continue $\mathbf{S}_1 \mathbf{S}_1 \mathbf{S}_2 \mathbf{S}_1 \mathbf{S}_1 \mathbf{S}_2 \ldots$ and the output continues as $B_1 B_3 B_2$ repeated.

Since there is only one pair of consecutive entries of B_1 in the output sequence (b_n), namely b_0 and b_1, there cannot exist an integer $p \neq 0$ with $b_{0+p} = b_0$ and $b_{1+p} = b_1$. Thus (b_n) is not periodic. However, for every positive integer t, $b_{t+3} = b_t$. This means that, if we ignore the first term of (b_n), we get a sequence which has period 3. In general, a sequence (u_n) is said to be **ultimately periodic** if the sequence obtained by ignoring a finite number of terms at the beginning is periodic. We call this finite set of terms the **delay** of the sequence and define the **period** of an ultimately periodic sequence as the period of the sequence obtained by ignoring the delay.

Our simple example shows that a periodic input sequence need not give a periodic output. The best we can hope for is that the output will be ultimately periodic. This, in fact, is what does happen.

THEOREM 5.1   If the input sequence to a finite state machine is ultimately periodic then the output sequence is ultimately periodic.

PROOF Suppose that the input sequence (a_t) is ultimately periodic with period p after the first m terms, $a_0 a_1 \ldots a_{m-1}$. Then, if N is any integer with $N \geq m$, $a_r = a_{r+p}$ for all $r \geq N$. Thus $a_N = a_{N+p} = \ldots = a_{N+sp}$ for all positive integers s. But, since we have a finite state machine, $|\mathbf{S}|$ is finite and so, if $|\mathbf{S}| = n$, the $n+1$ states $\mathbf{s}_N$, $\mathbf{s}_{N+p}$, $\mathbf{s}_{N+2p}$, ..., $\mathbf{s}_{N+np}$ cannot all be distinct. Hence, there exist distinct integers x, y (with $0 \leq x < y \leq n$) such that $\mathbf{s}_{N+xp} = \mathbf{s}_{N+yp}$. Let us, for convenience, put $u = N + xp$ and $w = y - x$. Then $\mathbf{s}_u = \mathbf{s}_{u+wp}$ and so, since $a_u = a_{u+wp}$, we have $b_u = \mu(\mathbf{s}_u, a_u) = \mu(\mathbf{s}_{u+wp}, a_{u+wp}) = b_{u+wp}$. Furthermore we also have $\mathbf{s}_{u+1} = \delta(\mathbf{s}_u, a_u) = \delta(\mathbf{s}_{u+wp}, a_{u+wp}) = \mathbf{s}_{u+1+wp}$. But now since $a_{u+j} = a_{u+j+wp}$ for all j, routine induction shows that $b_{u+j} = b_{u+j+wp}$ for all j; i.e. the output sequence (b_t), with the first u terms ignored, is periodic. In other words, (b_t) is ultimately periodic. □

One particular, but very important, example of a periodic sequence is one in which each entry is the same, i.e. one with period 1. We call such a sequence a **constant sequence**. If that constant is zero then the sequence is **null**. It will often be the case that we shall use a constant sequence, especially the null sequence, as our input sequence. A special, but again important, case of Theorem 5.1 is:

COROLLARY 5.2 *If the input sequence to a finite state machine is ultimately constant then the output is ultimately periodic.* □

Let us now return to our stream cipher as defined in Chapter 4. If we assume, as is usually the case, that our algorithm is a finite state machine then, since our key is of finite length and this is the only input to our machine, we must produce a sequence that is ultimately periodic. As we saw in Section 4.5 it is essential for security that our output sequence should have certain properties. Namely:

A1 *The output sequence must have a guaranteed minimum length for its period.*
A2 *The ciphertext must appear to be random.*

In the 1960s cryptographers found a way of achieving these objectives. It was based on the theory of shift registers with linear feedback. However, as we shall soon see, the proposed system had a major flaw. In order to understand the system and its inherent problems, and also so that we can understand some of the more complex systems in later chapters, we must now study certain aspects of shift register theory. We will not attempt to give an exhaustive account of the theory, but refer the interested reader to Selmer [27] or Golomb [16].

5.3   Shift Registers

5.3.1   Basic definitions

As we have already remarked the most frequently used alphabet is $\{0, 1\}$, and any sequence (u_n) with $u_i = 0$ or 1, for each i, is called a **binary sequence**. As we explained in Section 4.5 we can define **modulo 2 addition** $\oplus$ for the set $\{0, 1\}$ by $0 \oplus 1 = 1 \oplus 0 = 1$ and $0 \oplus 0 = 1 \oplus 1 = 0$. We can also define **modulo 2 multiplication** $\otimes$ by $0 \otimes 0 = 0 \otimes 1 = 1 \otimes 0 = 0$ while $1 \otimes 1 = 1$. The set $\{0, 1\}$ with this addition and multiplication is a field which we denote by $GF(2)$. (For the reader who is not familiar with the concept of a field we remark that by referring to $GF(2)$ as a field we merely wish to imply that, with the appropriate definitions of addition and multiplication, all the 'normal' operations of arithmetic 'work'.) In electronic engineering terms $\oplus$ and $\otimes$ are merely *XOR* and *AND* respectively. The fact that $GF(2)$ is a field essentially means that we can construct any logic system using only these two operations. Anyone who is familiar with the *NAND* gate from which all logics can be constructed should note that, in our terminology, *NAND* is simply $(a \otimes b) \oplus 1$. We will represent modulo 2 adders on our diagrams by $\oplus$ and modulo 2 multipliers by $\otimes$ or $\odot$. Any computer science student will almost certainly have met $GF(2)$ and be familiar with modulo 2 addition and multiplication. These two operations occur so frequently that, provided the context makes it clear we are in $GF(2)$, it is customary to represent them by the normal symbols for addition and multiplication. For anyone not too conversant with modulo 2 addition we make one important observation. Since $1 + 1 = 0, + 1$ and -1 are the same. Thus, in modulo 2 arithmetic, $+$ and $-$ are identical and we will not, in general, write $-$.

When, in a later section, we discuss polynomials $f(x)$ whose coefficients are in $GF(2)$, we shall refer to $f(x)$ as a **polynomial over $GF(2)$** or, if it is clear that we are working over $GF(2)$, simply as a polynomial.

Figure 5.2 illustrates a general shift register with feedback. (In Figure 5.2 the signal flow is from right to left which is different from our earlier block diagrams. It is probably more convenient to have this change of direction for shift registers. However when we include a shift register in a complete system diagram we may reverse its direction so that, in line with the rest of the diagram, the flow is from left to right. See, for example, Figure 5.7, page 198.)

Each of the squares labelled $S_0, S_1, \ldots, S_{n-1}$, is a binary storage element, which might be a flip-flop (bistable), position on a delay line or some other memory device. These n binary storage elements are called the **stages** of the shift register and, at any given time, their contents are called its **state**. The state of a shift register is a binary n-tuple which we may, at various times, regard as the binary expression of an integer. Clearly a shift register with n stages has 2^n possible states. If, for each i, s_i is the entry in S_i we will either write the state as $s_0 s_1 \ldots s_{n-1}$ or as the n-tuple $(s_0, s_1, \ldots, s_{n-1})$.

At time intervals, which are determined by a master clock, the contents

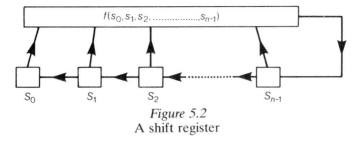

Figure 5.2
A shift register

of S_i are transferred into S_{i-1} for all i with $1 \le i \le n-1$. However to obtain the new value for location S_{n-1} we compute the value of a given function $f(s_0, s_1, \ldots, s_{n-1})$ of all the present terms in the register, and transfer this into S_{n-1}. We call $f(s_0, s_1, \ldots, s_{n-1})$ the **feedback function** of the shift register.

As drawn, our shift register has no input or output. However, we can readily arrange for some input sequence to be added to $f(s_0, s_1, \ldots, s_{n-1})$ to give the new entry in S_{n-1} and, similarly, for the entries in S_0 to give the output sequence. Our new diagram is shown in Figure 5.3.

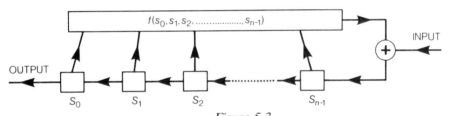

Figure 5.3
A shift register as a finite state machine

It is apparent that a shift register is a finite state machine. The set of possible states, **S**, is the set of binary expansions for the integers from 0 to $2^n - 1$ inclusive. The input alphabet **A** is $\{0, 1\}$ which is also the output alphabet **B**. If the state of the register is $(s_0, s_1, \ldots, s_{n-1})$ and the input is a_i then δ and μ are given by:

$$\delta((s_0, s_1, \ldots, s_{n-1}), a_i) = (s_1, s_2, \ldots, s_{n-1}, a_i + f(s_0, s_1, \ldots, s_{n-1}))$$

while $\mu((s_0, s_1, \ldots, s_{n-1}), a_i) = s_0$. It is worth pointing out that, in most of the cases which we shall consider, the input sequence will be the null sequence (0).

5.3.2 Linear shift registers

If the feedback function can be written in the form $f(s_0, s_1, \ldots, s_{n-1}) = c_0 s_0 + c_1 s_1 + \ldots + c_{n-1} s_{n-1}$, where each c_i is 0 or 1 and all addition is over $GF(2)$, then the shift register is called **linear**. In this case the diagram may be drawn somewhat differently, (see Figure 5.4). The constants $c_0, c_1, \ldots, c_{n-1}$ are called the **feedback coefficients**.

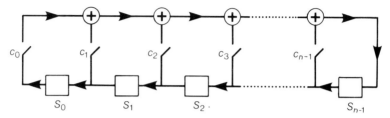

Figure 5.4
A shift register with linear feedback

In the diagram $c_i = 1$ will be represented by a closed switch while an open switch means the corresponding feedback coefficient is 0. If we now let $s_i(t)$ denote the content of stage S_i after the tth time pulse then, for any t, $s_i(t+1) = s_{i+1}(t)$ for $i = 0, 1, \ldots, n-2$, while

$$s_{n-1}(t+1) = \sum_{i=0}^{n-1} c_i s_i(t).$$

Unless we state otherwise, whenever we discuss shift registers we will assume that the input sequence is null and the feedback function is linear.

Before we carry on with our discussion of shift registers we will consider an example.

EXAMPLE 5.1   If we have a five-stage shift register with feedback function $s_0 + s_3$, then its diagram is given in Figure 5.5. However, it is customary to simplify it, by not drawing the open switches, to get Figure 5.6.

If the initial state, i.e. the state when $t = 0$, is 01010 then when $t = 1$ the new state will be $1010f(0, 1, 0, 1, 0)$. But $f(0, 1, 0, 1, 0) = 1$ and so, when $t = 1$, the state is 10101. The sequence of states is given in Table 5.2.

$t=0$	01010	$t=8$	01100	$t=16$	11100	$t=24$	10010
1	10101	9	11000	17	11001	25	00100
2	01011	10	10001	18	10011	26	01000
3	10111	11	00011	19	00110	27	10000
4	01110	12	00111	20	01101	28	00001
5	11101	13	01111	21	11010	29	00010
6	11011	14	11111	22	10100	30	00101
7	10110	15	11110	23	01001	31	01010
							etc.

Table 5.2
The first 32 states for Example 5.1

At this stage the reader is advised to draw the state diagram which represents all 32 states of the shift register of Example 5.1 and to note that it actually looks like a cycle of 31 plus a 'loop' of length 1.

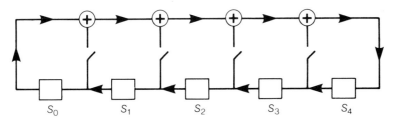

Figure 5.5
The shift register for Example 5.1

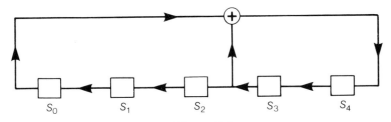

Figure 5.6
A simplified version of Figure 5.5

In this example the state when $t = 31$ is the same as when $t = 0$. Since the input is null each state completely determines the next. Hence, as soon as any state is repeated, the sequence of states will start to repeat itself (see Exercise 5.2). So, in our example, as $t = 31$ is the first occasion on which any of the states is repeated, the sequence of states must have period 31.

If we now take the same size shift register with the same initial state but with all its feedback coefficients 0, then the sequence of states will begin 01010, 10100, 01000, 10000, 00000, and every subsequent state will be 00000. In fact if we take any n-stage shift register with all its feedback coefficients 0 then, since each time pulse introduces a 0 into S_{n-1}, after n time pulses the state will be 0000...0 and, of course, will remain like that for ever. To avoid this degenerate case we will always assume that one of our feedback constants is 1. Suppose $c_j = 1$ but $c_i = 0$ for all $i < j$, and let us write the initial state as $s_0(0)s_1(0)s_2(0)...s_{n-1}(0)$. Since the feedback function does not depend on the contents of $S_0, ..., S_{j-1}$, after the jth pulse the state of the register is completely determined by the initial contents of $S_j, S_{j+1}, ..., S_{n-1}$ and the feedback coefficients. But this means that, essentially, we are only considering an $(n-j)$-stage shift register with a j-stage delay.

This is clearly going to be undesirable in most situations, since it means we are wasting hardware; we could simply forget the first j terms and use an $(n-j)$-stage register. Consequently we will usually wish to prevent this from happening and so, unless we state otherwise, we shall assume that $c_0 = 1$.

Since our shift register is a finite state machine with constant input we know, from Corollary 5.2, that the output sequence must be ultimately periodic. In fact, as we shall now show, provided $c_0 = 1$, it is actually periodic.

LEMMA 5.3 *The output sequence of a shift register with null input and linear feedback with $c_0 = 1$ is periodic.*

PROOF Suppose that (s_t) is ultimately periodic with period p and that m is the least positive integer such that $s_{m+t} = s_{m+t+p}$ for all non-negative integers t. Then, if $m \neq 0$, $s_{m-1} \neq s_{m+p-1}$. (If they were equal we would have $s_{m-1+t} = s_{m-1+t+p}$ for all non-negative t; which would be a contradiction to the choice of m.) The mth-state is $s_{m-1} s_m s_{m+1} \ldots s_{m+n-2}$ and, using the fact that $s_{m+t} = s_{m+t+p}$ for all t, the $(m+p)^{\text{th}}$-state is $s_{m+p-1} s_m s_{m+1} \ldots s_{m+n-2}$, i.e. they are identical except for the first term. Using the mth-state plus the fact that $c_0 = 1$, we see that

$$s_{m+n-1} = s_{m-1} + \sum_{i=0}^{n-2} c_{i+1} s_{m+i}.$$

but, using the $(m+p)^{\text{th}}$-state plus the fact that $s_{m+t+p} = s_{m+t}$, we have

$$s_{m+n-1} = s_{m+p-1} + \sum_{i=0}^{n-2} c_{i+1} s_{m+i}.$$

Since $s_{m-1} \neq s_{m+p-1}$, this is impossible and we must have been wrong in assuming $m \neq 0$. Hence by assuming $c_0 = 1$ our output sequence must be periodic.   □

In order to determine whether **A1** can be satisfied, our first task must be to determine all possible lengths for the period (the period will, presumably, depend on the initial state and the feedback coefficients) and, in particular, its maximum possible length. If our register has state $00\ldots0$ then, since there is a null input, every subsequent state will be the same and the sequence of states will have period 1. But this means that any sequence of states with period greater than 1 cannot contain $00\ldots0$. Thus, since we know that as soon as any state is repeated the sequence of states must start 'repeating', the period must be bounded above by the number of distinct states other than $00\ldots0$. There are precisely $2^n - 1$ of these and so we have proved:

LEMMA 5.4 *The succession of states on an n-stage linear shift register is periodic with period $p \leq 2^n - 1$.*   □

Since our Example 5.1 has period $2^5 - 1$, the conclusion of Lemma 5.4 is the best possible in the sense that we can certainly achieve $p = 2^n - 1$ for some values of n.

EXERCISE 5.3   There are eight linear feedback functions with $c_0 = 1$ for a four-stage shift register. Determine the sequence of states using each in turn with an initial state of 1010. What are the possible periods? Find the sequence of states when $c_0 = c_1 = 0$, $c_2 = c_3 = 1$ and the initial state is 1010. Make sure you understand why no linear feedback function with $c_0 = 0$ can possibly give a sequence with period $2^4 - 1$ (no matter which initial state is used!).

The sequence of entries in a given stage is called the **history** of that stage. Since any entry in S_{n-1} passes through each of the other stages in turn, the history of any stage is the same as the history of S_{n-1} except for a delay caused by the few entries before the initial entry of S_{n-1} reaches that stage. For instance, the history of S_{n-3} is $s_{n-3}(0)$, $s_{n-3}(1)$ and then from time $t = 2$ onwards it is the history of S_{n-1}, i.e. $s_{n-3}(t+2) = s_{n-1}(t)$ for all $t \geq 0$. Thus we can think of the sequence of states in terms of the history of any one stage. If the initial state is $s_0 s_1 \ldots s_{n-1}$ then the first n contents of S_0 are $s_0, s_1, \ldots, s_{n-1}$. If we now let $s_0, s_1, \ldots, s_{n-1}, s_n, \ldots$ denote the successive contents of stage S_0 then

$$s_{t+n} = \sum_{i=0}^{n-1} c_i s_{t+i}$$

for any t. (Note that if $s_0 s_1 \ldots s_{n-1} s_n \ldots$ is the sequence of contents of stage S_0, then $s_i s_{i+1} s_{i+2} \ldots$ is the sequence of contents of stage S_i for any i with $0 \leq i \leq n-1$. Furthermore, the state after the ith time pulse is $s_i s_{i+1} \ldots s_{i+n-1}$. Note also that the sequence $(s_t) = s_0 s_1 \ldots s_{n-1} s_n \ldots$ is the output sequence in Figure 5.3.) For any sequence (x_t) a relation of the type

$$x_{r+n} = \sum_{i=0}^{n-1} d_i x_{r+i}$$

for all r is called a **linear recurrence relation of order n** and (x_t) is called a **linear recurring sequence**. If we look back at Example 5.1 the linear recurring sequence which it generates has period 31 and is generated by 0101011101100011111001101001000. (Note that this sequence is obtained by taking the first entry in each of the successive states.)

If (u_t) and (v_t) are two sequences such that, for some constant τ, $v_t = u_{t+\tau}$ for all t, then we say that (v_t) is the **translate of (u_t) by τ**. We write, simply, $(v_t) = (u_{t+\tau})$. (You will recall that we mentioned this concept very briefly in Section 4.6, page 169.) If we go back to Example 5.1, it is clear that, if we had taken 01011 as our initial state, we would have obtained a different sequence of states. However, since 01011 is the third state in the example, the new sequence would merely be 2 ahead of the original one, i.e. at time t the state obtained from an initial state of 01011 is the state at time $t+2$ in our example. Thus the new sequence of states is a translate by 2 of the sequence in the example.

For any n-stage shift register with a given feedback function, the first n terms of the output sequence are the n entries of the initial state. Thus the 2^n different states will give rise to 2^n different periodic output sequences. Some, as we have seen, will merely be translates of each other. Clearly these are essentially the same in the sense that any finite sequence in one is also in the other (albeit in a different position). However, others may be fundamentally different and even have different periods. If one such sequence (s_t) has period p then $s_0 s_1 \ldots s_{p-1}$ is the generating cycle of length p. If we take each of the p different starting points for the cycle, then we will get generating cycles for p distinct sequences. These p sequences are, however, merely translates of each other.

As we have already mentioned, for every linear feedback function the sequence generated from an initial state of $00 \ldots 0$ is the null sequence (0). For any given set of feedback coefficients the remaining $2^n - 1$ initial states will give rise to $2^n - 1$ different sequences of states and, in general, amongst them there will be sequences of different periods, i.e. there will be generating cycles of different lengths. If, however, one initial state gives a generating cycle of length $2^n - 1$ then clearly every non-zero state occurs in that cycle. Thus, in this special case, the sequences obtained by using any of the $2^n - 1$ initial states are all translates of each other and, consequently, have the same period of $2^n - 1$. An output sequence of the maximum possible length, i.e. $2^n - 1$, is called an **m-sequence**.

From Example 5.1 we know that it is possible to obtain an m-sequence. We now need to know when it happens. We already know that, if it happens, any initial state other than $00 \ldots 0$ will give one. Thus we need only consider the choice of feedback constants. Once we know how to choose $c_0, \ldots, c_{n-1}$ to give an output sequence of period $2^n - 1$ we will have achieved our aim **A1**.

5.4   Characteristic Polynomials and Periodicity

5.4.1   Synopsis

In the next few sections we investigate the close relation between the feedback constants and various properties of the output sequence. To justify some of our assertions we need to apply some results using mathematical concepts for which we cannot possibly include a complete explanation, e.g. vector spaces and polynomials over finite fields. As some readers may be unfamiliar with these concepts, we give synopses of the more mathematical sections. Our aim, as in Section 3.4, is to enable any reader with insufficient mathematical background to skip the details but still be able to understand the fundamental ideas. This will then enable him to proceed to the later chapters. As always we stress that reading only the synopses and skipping the various sections will in no way hinder the understanding of the later chapters. We must, however, emphasize that the mathematics in these sections are not particularly difficult. We certainly do not wish to discourage anyone, no matter what his background, from reading them and we actually define as many of the mathematical concepts as we can.

For any n-stage register with feedback constants $c_0, c_1, \ldots, c_{n-1}$ the **characteristic polynomial** $f(x)$ is defined by

$$f(x) = c_0 + c_1 x + \ldots + c_{n-1} x^{n-1} + x^n.$$

For a given characteristic polynomial there are 2^n different possible initial settings of the register and, consequently, the polynomial can be used to 'generate' 2^n different sequences (of which one will be null). (Each of these sequences is determined completely by its first n positions and it is this which enables us to show that they can be regarded as a vector space over $GF(2)$. Any reader who has only studied real vector spaces has certainly learnt enough to study vector spaces over $GF(2)$. Apart from the fact that addition and multiplication are modulo 2, the arithmetic and behaviour of the two types of vector spaces are (for our purposes) the same.) For most choices of $f(x)$ it is possible for two non-null sequences to have different periods. The main result of Section 5.4.2 is that if $f(x)$ has the special property of being **primitive** then every one of its non-null sequences has period $2^n - 1$, i.e. it is an m-sequence. Furthermore any polynomial which can generate an m-sequence must be primitive. A precise definition of a primitive polynomial is given. However it is not particularly important. The crucial facts are that there are many primitive polynomials and that, for various values of n, lists of them are obtainable from the literature. (We include a list of those with small degrees in Appendix 3, page 404, and in Table 5.3, page 195, we give the number of primitive polynomials for all degrees up to 24.) It is important to realize that anyone, even if he knows nothing about polynomials, can arrange for a shift register to generate an m-sequence. Thus our condition **A1** is easily satisfied.

5.4.2 Basic properties

An n-stage linear shift register is determined by the feedback constants $c_0, c_1, \ldots, c_{n-1}$. If (s_t) is the output sequence generated from an initial state of $s_0 s_1 \ldots s_{n-1}$ then, as we saw in the last section, the following recurrence relation of order n is satisfied:

$$s_{t+n} = \sum_{i=0}^{n-1} c_i s_{t+i}$$

for $t = 0, 1, \ldots$. Associated with any such recurrence relation is a **characteristic polynomial** $f(x)$ defined by

$$f(x) = 1 + c_1 x + \ldots + c_{n-1} x^{n-1} + x^n.$$

(Recall that we always assume $c_0 = 1$. We will, in fact, often use the term 'characteristic polynomial' to mean a polynomial with constant term 1. Certainly all our characteristic polynomials have this property.) We shall refer to $f(x)$ as the characteristic polynomial of the shift register and shall talk of the sequences and cycles generated by $f(x)$. When discussing polynomials we will write deg $f(x)$ for the degree of $f(x)$. For any n-stage linear shift register with characteristic polynomial $f(x)$, deg $f(x) = n$.

EXERCISE 5.4   Let $f(x) = 1 + c_1 x + \ldots + c_{n-1} x^{n-1} + x^n$ and let $g(x) = x^2 f(x)$. If (s_t) is the sequence generated on an n-stage shift register with initial state $s_0 s_1 \ldots s_{n-1}$ and characteristic polynomial $f(x)$, show that the sequence generated on an $(n+2)$-stage shift register, by taking an initial state $ab s_0 s_1 \ldots s_{n-1}$ and using the polynomial $g(x)$, is (u_t), where $u_0 = a$, $u_1 = b$ and, for all integers $t \geq 2$, $u_t = s_{t-2}$, i.e. it is the sequence (s_t) with a delay of the two terms a and b.

Since there are 2^n initial states there are 2^n infinite binary recurring sequences generated by any given $f(x)$. The collection of these sequences is called the **solution space** of $f(x)$ and is denoted by $\Omega(f)$. If (u_t) and (v_t) are any binary sequences we call the output which results from feeding them into a modulo 2 adder, or *XOR* gate, the **sum** of (u_t) and (v_t). We represent this sum by $(u_t) + (v_t)$, so that $(u_t) + (v_t) = (u_t + v_t)$. Similarly, if $c = 0$ or 1, we define $c(u_t)$ to be the sequence (cu_t) obtained by inputting (u_t) and the constant sequence with each entry c into a modulo 2 multiplier or *AND* gate. With these definitions of addition of sequences and 'multiplication by a scalar' we have:

THEOREM 5.5   If $f(x)$ is a characteristic polynomial for an n-stage linear shift register then $\Omega(f)$ is an n-dimensional vector space over $GF(2)$.

PROOF   We will show that if (u_t) and (v_t) are in $\Omega(f)$ and if $c = 0$ or 1, then $(u_t) + (v_t)$ and $c(u_t)$ are both in $\Omega(f)$. The verification that the axioms of a vector space are satisfied is left as an exercise.
If $f(x) = 1 + c_1 x + \ldots + c_{n-1} x^{n-1} + x^n$, then a binary sequence (w_t) is in $\Omega(f)$ if and only if

$$w_{t+n} = \sum_{i=0}^{n-1} c_i w_{t+i}$$

for all t. Thus, since (u_t) and (v_t) are in $\Omega(f)$, we have:

$$u_{t+n} = \sum_{i=0}^{n-1} c_i u_{t+i} \text{ and } v_{t+n} = \sum_{i=0}^{n-1} c_i v_{t+i}.$$

Thus,

$$u_{t+n} + v_{t+n} = \sum_{i=0}^{n-1} c_i (u_{t+i} + v_{t+i})$$

and $(u_t) + (v_t)$ is in $\Omega(f)$. Clearly (0) is in $\Omega(f)$, thus $c(u_t)$ is in $\Omega(f)$.
To show that the dimension of $\Omega(f)$ is n we first observe that any sequence in $\Omega(f)$ is completely determined by its first n terms. Thus a set of sequences will be linearly independent if and only if their first n terms (i.e.

the initial states of the register) are linearly independent. Hence the dimension of $\Omega(f)$ is equal to the dimension of the space of initial states; i.e. n. $\square$

Since we are always assuming that $f(x)$ has $c_0 = 1$ and has degree n, where n is the size of the shift register, the polynomial 1 is not a characteristic polynomial. Nevertheless, we shall abuse our notation slightly and write $\Omega(1)$ for the 0-dimensional vector space consisting of the null sequence (0).

EXERCISE 5.5   Show that any translate of a sequence in $\Omega(f)$ is also in $\Omega(f)$; i.e. that, for any fixed τ, if $(u_t) \in \Omega(f)$ then $(u_{t+\tau}) \in \Omega(f)$.

EXERCISE 5.6   Show that if $f(x)$ has degree n and $(u_t) \in \Omega(f)$ has period $2^n - 1$ then, for any τ and ρ, $(u_{t+\tau}) + (u_{t+\rho})$ is either (0) or a translate of (u_t).

If we have a linear shift register with given feedback constants and a given initial state, then the output sequence (s_t) is completely determined. But with any infinite sequence (a_t) we can associate a **generating function**

$$G(x) = \sum_{i=0}^{\infty} a_i x^i.$$

So, if $G(x)$ is the generating function of (s_t), $G(x)$ must be completely determined by the characteristic polynomial $f(x)$ and the initial state. The following exercise illustrates an important property of the generating function of a linear shift register sequence.

EXERCISE 5.7   If (s_t) has period p show that

$$G(x) = (s_0 + s_1 x + \ldots + s_{p-1} x^{p-1})(1 + x^p + x^{2p} + \ldots).$$

In order to see how $G(x)$ is determined we need to define the concept of a reciprocal polynomial. If d is any positive integer and

$$h(x) = \sum_{i=0}^{d} h_i x^i$$

is any polynomial of degree d over $GF(2)$ then the **reciprocal polynomial** $h^*(x)$ is defined by

$$h^*(x) = \sum_{i=0}^{d} h_i x^{n-i} = x^d h\left(\frac{1}{x}\right).$$

The degree of $h^*(x)$ is at most d and is equal to d precisely when $h_0 = 1$. Thus, since we are always assuming that characteristic polynomials have constant term 1, for any characteristic polynomial $f(x)$ we have $\deg f^*(x) = \deg f(x)$. In order to familiarize himself with reciprocation of polynomials the reader should solve the following exercises.

EXERCISE 5.8 If $f(x)$ is any polynomial over GF(2) show that $(f^*(x))^* = f(x)$ if and only if $f(0) = 1$.

EXERCISE 5.9 Show that, for any polynomial $f(x)$ over GF(2) with degree at least one, $f^*(0) = 1$. Note that this implies that, for certain choices of the polynomial $g(x)$, there need not exist a polynomial $h(x)$ with $h^*(x) = g(x)$.

EXERCISE 5.10 Find two distinct polynomials $f_1(x)$ and $f_2(x)$ over GF(2) such that $f_1^*(x) = f_2^*(x)$.

EXERCISE 5.11 If $h_1(x)$ and $h_2(x)$ are any two polynomials over GF(2), show that the reciprocal polynomial of $h_1(x) \cdot h_2(x)$ is $h_1^*(x) \cdot h_2^*(x)$.

THEOREM 5.6 Let $f(x) = 1 + c_1 x + \ldots + c_{n-1} x^{n-1} + x^n$ be a polynomial over GF(2) and suppose $(s_t) \in \Omega(f)$. If

$$G(x) = \sum_{i=0}^{\infty} s_i x^i$$

then

$$G(x) = \frac{\phi(x)}{f^*(x)}$$

where

$$\phi(x) = \sum_{i=1}^{n} \left(c_i x^{n-i} \left(\sum_{j=0}^{i-1} s_j x^j \right) \right)$$

and $c_n = 1$.

PROOF $\displaystyle G(x) = \sum_{t=0}^{\infty} s_t x^t = \sum_{t=0}^{n-1} s_t x^t + \sum_{t=0}^{\infty} s_{t+n} x^{t+n}.$

But, by the recurrence relation,

$$s_{t+n} = \sum_{i=0}^{n-1} c_i s_{t+i}$$

for each i. Thus,

$$G(x) = \sum_{t=0}^{n-1} s_t x^t + \sum_{t=0}^{\infty} \left(\sum_{i=0}^{n-1} c_i s_{t+i} \right) x^{t+n}$$

$$= \sum_{t=0}^{n-1} s_t x^t + \sum_{i=0}^{n-1} \left(c_i x^{n-i} \left(\sum_{t=0}^{\infty} s_{t+i} x^{t+i} \right) \right)$$

$$= \sum_{t=0}^{n-1} s_t x^t + c_0 x^n \sum_{t=0}^{\infty} s_t x^t + \sum_{i=1}^{n-1} \left(c_i x^{n-i} \left(\sum_{t=0}^{\infty} s_t x^t + \sum_{j=0}^{i-1} s_j x^j \right) \right)$$

$$= \sum_{t=0}^{n-1} s_t x^t + c_0 x^n G(x) + \sum_{i=1}^{n-1} \left(c_i x^{n-i} \left(G(x) + \sum_{j=0}^{i-1} s_j x^j \right) \right).$$

(Before proceeding it is important to remember that our addition is over $GF(2)$ so that $+$ and $-$ are the same. Hence our justification for writing only $+$ in the last two lines!)

Rearranging our last equation we have:

$$G(x)\left(1+\sum_{i=1}^{n-1} c_i x^{n-i} + c_0 x^n\right) = \sum_{t=0}^{n-1} s_t x^t + \sum_{i=1}^{n-1} c_i x^{n-i}\left(\sum_{j=0}^{i-1} s_j x^j\right)$$

or

$$G(x)f^*(x) = \sum_{i=1}^{n} c_i x^{n-i}\left(\sum_{j=0}^{i-1} s_j x^j\right)$$

where $c_n = 1$. $\square$

As was to be expected, the polynomial $\phi(x)$ is completely determined by $f(x)$ and $s_0, \ldots, s_{n-1}$; i.e. by the feedback constants and the initial state. It is also clear that the degree of $\phi(x)$ is at most $n-1$.

Conversely if we were given $f(x)$ and $\phi(x)$ then, by Theorem 5.6, we could determine $G(x)$. In other words, the complete sequence (s_t) is determined by the feedback constants and $\phi(x)$. Furthermore, we could take any polynomial of degree at most $n-1$ as $\phi(x)$ and get a sequence (s_t). This means that, for any given $f(x)$, any sequence (s_t) of $\Omega(f)$ uniquely determines, and is uniquely determined by, a polynomial $\phi(x)$ of degree at most $n-1$. Thus, there is a one-to-one correspondence between the 2^n sequences of $\Omega(f)$ and the 2^n polynomials $\phi(x)$ of degree at most $n-1$ over $GF(2)$. So, if we identify the sequence (s_t) with its generating function

$$G(x) = \sum_{t=0}^{\infty} s_t x^t,$$

we have shown that

$$\Omega(f) = \left\{\frac{\phi(x)}{f^*(x)} \mid \phi(x) \text{ is a polynomial over } GF(2) \text{ with degree at most } n-1\right\}.$$

(Note: the fact that the degree of $\phi(x)$ is less than n guarantees that $\dfrac{\phi(x)}{f^*(x)}$ cannot have finite degree.)

We now need to use some elementary facts about polynomials. Let $f(x)$, $g(x)$ and $h(x)$ be polynomials over $GF(2)$. If $h(x) = f(x)g(x)$, then we say that $f(x)$ and $g(x)$ **divide** $h(x)$ and we write $f(x) \mid h(x)$ and $g(x) \mid h(x)$. If $f(x)$ does not divide $h(x)$, i.e. if there is no polynomial $d(x)$ over $GF(2)$ such that $f(x)d(x) = h(x)$, then we write $f(x) \nmid h(x)$. A polynomial $f(x)$ over $GF(2)$ is called **irreducible over $GF(2)$**, if the only polynomials over $GF(2)$ which divide it are 1 and $f(x)$ itself. Note that if $f(x)$ is irreducible over $GF(2)$ then $f(0) \neq 0$ and $f(1) \neq 0$ since, otherwise, $f(0) = 0$ implies $x \mid f(x)$ while $f(1) = 0$ implies $(x+1) \mid f(x)$. The basic idea which we shall want to utilize at various times is that polynomials over $GF(2)$ behave rather like the integers, with irreducible polynomials taking on the role of primes. If

$f(x)$ and $g(x)$ are any two polynomials over $GF(2)$ then the polynomial $b(x)$ is called the g.c.d. (greatest common divisor), of $f(x)$ and $g(x)$ if $b(x)| f(x)$, $b(x)| g(x)$ and if any other polynomial which divides $f(x)$ and $g(x)$ also divides $b(x)$. We write $b(x) = (f(x), g(x))$. If $(f(x), g(x)) = 1$ then $f(x)$ and $g(x)$ are called **coprime**. Similarly $a(x)$ is the l.c.m. (lowest common multiple) of $f(x)$ and $g(x)$ if $f(x)| a(x)$, $g(x)| a(x)$ and if $a(x)$ divides every other polynomial which they both divide. We write $a(x) = [f(x), g(x)]$. We need two results about polynomials which we will now quote. If they are new to the reader, he should compare them with the corresponding results for integers.

RESULT 5.1   If $f(x)$ and $g(x)$ are any two polynomials over $GF(2)$ and if $d(x) = (f(x), g(x))$ then $\dfrac{f(x)}{d(x)}$ and $\dfrac{g(x)}{d(x)}$ are coprime.

RESULT 5.2   If $a(x)$, $b(x)$, $c(x)$ are polynomials over $GF(2)$ such that $a(x)| b(x)c(x)$ and $(a(x), b(x)) = 1$ then $a(x)| c(x)$.

If $f(x)$ is any polynomial over $GF(2)$ such that $f(0) \neq 0$, then we say that $f(x)$ has **exponent** e if $f(x)| x^e + 1$ but $f(x) \nmid x^r + 1$ for any r satisfying $0 < r < e$. (Note that if $f(x) = c_0 + c_1 x + \ldots + x^n$, then $f(0) \neq 0$ if and only if $c_0 = 1$. Thus any characteristic polynomial has an exponent. Furthermore any polynomial with an exponent is a characteristic polynomial for some sequence.) It is well known that, if $f(x)$ has degree n and $f(0) \neq 0$, then $f(x)$ has an exponent which is at most $2^n - 1$, (see, for example, [20]). An irreducible polynomial of degree n over $GF(2)$ is called **primitive** if its exponent is $2^n - 1$. We will complete this section by showing that if the degree of $f(x)$ is n then a sequence (s_t) in $\Omega(f)$ has the maximum possible period, (i.e. has period $2^n - 1$), if and only if $f(x)$ is primitive.

We point out again that, although it is desirable that the reader should understand our proofs and also know a little about primitive polynomials, it is not crucial. The important thing is to realise that, by choosing $f(x)$ correctly, we can guarantee the period of all non-null output sequences. First we prove a lemma.

LEMMA 5.7   If $f(x)$ is a polynomial over $GF(2)$ with exponent e and if $(s_t) \in \Omega(f)$, then the period of (s_t) divides e.

PROOF   Since $f(x)$ has exponent e we know that $f(x)| x^e + 1$. So let $g(x)$ be the polynomial over $GF(2)$ such that $f(x)g(x) = x^e + 1$. By Theorem 5.6, $G(x) = \dfrac{\phi(x)}{f^*(x)}$ for some polynomial $\phi(x)$ with degree less than $\deg f(x)$. But since $f(x)g(x) = x^e + 1$, $(f(x)g(x))^* = (x^e + 1)^*$, i.e. $f^*(x)g^*(x) = 1 + x^e$ (see Exercise 5.11). Thus

$$G(x) = \frac{\phi(x)g^*(x)}{1 + x^e} = \phi(x)g^*(x)(1 + x^e + x^{2e} + \ldots)$$

and so, since

$$G(x) = \sum_{t=0}^{\infty} s_t x^t,$$

we have $s_{t+e} = s_t$ for all t. Thus, by Exercise 5.1, the period of (s_t) divides e. $\square$

As it stands Lemma 5.7 appears to be a step in the wrong direction. It guarantees that the period will be less than some value, namely the exponent of $f(x)$, whereas we want a guaranteed minimum. However, we can now give a condition under which the period will actually be equal to e.

THEOREM 5.8 *If $f(x)$ is an irreducible polynomial over $GF(2)$ with exponent e and if $(s_t) \neq (0)$ is in $\Omega(f)$, then the period of (s_t) is e.*

PROOF We will write per (s_t) for the period of (s_t). Let $(s_t) \in \Omega(f)$, $(s_t) \neq (0)$. Then, by Lemma 5.7, we know that per $(s_t) | e$. Let us suppose that per $(s_t) = p$ where $p < e$. Then

$$G(x) = (s_0 + s_1 x + \ldots + s_{p-1} x^{p-1})(1 + x^p + x^{2p} + \ldots) = \frac{s(x)}{1 + x^p},$$

where

$$s(x) = s_0 + s_1 x + \ldots + s_{p-1} x^{p-1}.$$

But, by Theorem 5.6, $G(x)$ is also equal to $\dfrac{\phi(x)}{f^*(x)}$. Equating these two expressions for $G(x)$ we get $(1 + x^p)\phi(x) = s(x)f^*(x)$ which, on reciprocating, gives $(1 + x^p)\phi^*(x) = s^*(x)f(x)$.

Since, by assumption, $f(x)$ is irreducible it can have no factor in common with $\phi^*(x)$. (Recall that $\phi(x)$ and, hence, $\phi^*(x)$ have lower degree than $f(x)$.) Thus, by Result 5.2, $f(x) | x^p + 1$ which contradicts the assumption that $f(x)$ has exponent e and $p < e$. Thus the period of (s_t) must be e. $\square$

Theorem 5.8 has an immediate corollary that if an irreducible polynomial $f(x)$ has degree n and exponent $2^n - 1$ (i.e. if $f(x)$ is primitive) then any non-null sequence (s_t) in $\Omega(f)$ will be an m-sequence. However, we can prove something even better. Namely that the only way to obtain an m-sequence is to use a primitive polynomial.

THEOREM 5.9 *Let $f(x)$ be a polynomial of degree n over $GF(2)$. If $(s_t) \in \Omega(f)$, $(s_t) \neq (0)$, then (s_t) is an m-sequence if and only if $f(x)$ is primitive.*

PROOF As we have already pointed out, if $f(x)$ is primitive then it has exponent $2^n - 1$ and so, by Theorem 5.8, any (s_t) in $\Omega(f)$, $(s_t) \neq (0)$, has period $2^n - 1$, i.e. is an m-sequence.

If $(s_t) \in \Omega(f)$ and (s_t) has period $2^n - 1$ then, by Lemma 5.7 and the fact that its exponent is at most $2^n - 1$, $f(x)$ has exponent $2^n - 1$. Thus, to prove

$f(x)$ is primitive, we must show that it is irreducible. Suppose that $f(x)$ is reducible. Then there exist polynomials $f_1(x)$, $f_2(x)$ over $GF(2)$ with $0 < \deg(f_i(x)) = n_i < n$ $(i = 1, 2)$ and $f(x) = f_1(x)f_2(x)$. Since $f_2(x)$ has degree $n_2 < n$, $f_2^*(x)$ has degree less than n. Hence if we put $\phi(x) = f_2^*(x)$ then, from the discussion following Theorem 5.6, $\dfrac{f_2^*(x)}{f^*(x)}$ is a generating function for a sequence in $\Omega(f)$. But, by Exercise 5.11, $f^*(x) = f_1^*(x)f_2^*(x)$. So $\dfrac{1}{f_1^*(x)}$ generates a sequence in $\Omega(f)$. But the same argument, this time choosing $\phi(x) = 1$, shows that $\dfrac{1}{f_1^*(x)}$ generates a sequence in $\Omega(f_1)$. If (u_t) is this sequence then $(u_t) \in \Omega(f)$ implies its period is $2^n - 1$ (we emphasize again that *every* non-null sequence in $\Omega(f)$ has period $2^n - 1$) while $(u_t) \in \Omega(f_1)$ implies its period is $\leq 2^{n_1} - 1 < 2^n - 1$. This contradiction shows that $f(x)$ is irreducible.   □

So now we have a way of satisfying condition **A1** and guaranteeing a minimum value for the length of our sequence. To do this we merely restrict ourselves to using primitive polynomials. But, of course, for this to be helpful we need to be sure that there are sufficiently many primitive polynomials. To determine the number of primitive polynomials of a given degree we need to introduce the Euler function. For any positive integer m the **Euler function $\phi(m)$** is the number of positive integers which are less than or equal to m but coprime to it. For any given positive integer n the number of primitive polynomials of degree n over $GF(2)$, which we denote by $\lambda(n)$, is given by the equation $\lambda(n) = \dfrac{\phi(2^n - 1)}{n}$. (This fact is by no means obvious. We will not prove it here, the interested reader should consult [16].) For any m, it is easy to compute $\phi(m)$, and thus we can evaluate $\lambda(n)$ for any n.

Table 5.3 gives the number of primitive polynomials over $GF(2)$ of degree n for $1 \leq n \leq 24$. In Appendix 3 we actually list all primitive polynomials for a few small degrees. From this table we can see that as n becomes reasonably large we have a wide choice of polynomials which we can use to generate sequences of maximum period. Note, by the way, that $\lambda(n)$ does not necessarily increase as n increases. It is, in general, true for the Euler function ϕ that $\phi(p)$, with p a prime, is greater than $\phi(n)$ for those composite n which are slightly larger than p. So we would expect $\lambda(n)$ to be larger (relative to n) whenever $2^n - 1$ is a prime. A prime number of the form $2^n - 1$ is called a **Mersenne prime** and it is well known that if $2^n - 1$ is prime then n must also be prime. It is not true, however, that if p is a prime then $2^p - 1$ is also a prime. In fact there are only 27 Mersenne primes $2^n - 1$ with $n < 45000$. The largest known Mersenne prime is $2^{44497} - 1$ (a very large number!). It is not known if there are any primes $2^n - 1$ with $n > 45000$.

n	$\lambda(n)$	n	$\lambda(n)$	n	$\lambda(n)$
1	1	9	48	17	7710
2	1	10	60	18	8064
3	2	11	176	19	27594
4	2	12	144	20	24000
5	6	13	630	21	84672
6	6	14	756	22	120032
7	18	15	1800	23	356960
8	16	16	2048	24	276480

Table 5.3
The number of primitive polynomials with degree at most 24

5.5 Randomness

We must now see if we can satisfy the second of our two objectives and obtain ciphertext which appears random. Since our ciphertext is obtained by adding the plaintext to the output sequence of the shift register, the randomness of the ciphertext will depend on the randomness of the register output sequence.

EXERCISE 5.12
 (*i*) *If the plaintext has a probability of 0·7 for producing a 0 and the register sequence has about 60% 0s, show that about 54% of the resulting output will be 0s.*
 (*ii*) *Show that, no matter what the probability of a 0 in the plaintext, if the sequence has an equal probability of producing a 0 or 1 then the same is true for the output.*

In our discussion of randomness in Section 4.6 we listed three random-ness properties suggested by Golomb, and defined any sequence satisfying them to be G-random. We will now show that any m-sequence is G-random which, of course, shows that we can meet simultaneously our requirements for **A1** and **A2**. A crucial observation to the argument is that during the generation of an m-sequence the shift register goes through each of its $2^n - 1$ non-null states before it repeats. Of these $2^n - 1$ states, 2^{n-1} have a 1 in the S_0 position while $2^{n-1} - 1$ have a 0 there. This shows that each cycle has 2^{n-1} 1s and $2^{n-1} - 1$ 0s and, consequently, an m-sequence satisfies **R1**.

Since the null state never appears in the register an m-sequence cannot have a gap of length n or more. There is certainly a block of length n in any cycle, but there cannot be a block of bigger length. (The reason for this is that a block of length $n + 1$ would mean two successive states of $111...1$ in the register.) The block of length n implies the existence of the following sequence of $n + 2$ consecutive bits: $011...10$. But these $n + 2$ bits give rise to the states 011...1 and 111...10 as they pass through the register. Since these two states only occur once, there cannot be a block of length $n-1$ in the cycle. (A block of length $n-1$ would give the $(n+1)$-bit sequence 011...10 in the sequence and again give rise to the states 01111...1 and 11...10.) There is, however, a gap of length $n-1$, which gives rise to the states 10...0 and 0...01. If $n=2$ then we have considered all possible blocks and gaps. If $n>2$, then let r be any integer $r \leq n-2$. Any block of length r implies the existence of the following $r+2$ consecutive bits: 0111...110. In order to count the number of blocks with length r it is sufficient to count the number of states which have these $r+2$ bits on the left hand side. (Because, as the sequence passes through the register, any $r+2$ consecutive bits must reach this position.) Since each state occurs exactly once, there is a state whose first $r+2$ positions are 011...10 with each possible sequence of 0s and 1s filling the remaining $n-r-2$ positions. There are 2^{n-r-2} ways of filling these $n-r-2$ stages, so the number of blocks of length r in a cycle is 2^{n-r-2}. Similarly, the number of gaps of length r is also 2^{n-r-2}. The total number of blocks in a cycle is

$$1 + \sum_{r=1}^{n-2} 2^{n-r-2} = 2^{n-2}.$$

Since this is also the total number of gaps we have shown that an m-sequence satisfies **R2**. Any sequence generated by an initial state of 000...01 is called an **indicator sequence**. Our calculations are summarized by:

THEOREM 5.10   If (s_t) is an indicator m-sequence of period 2^{n-1} then:

(i)   any cycle contains 2^{n-1} 1s and $2^{n-1}-1$ 0s,

(ii)   a generating cycle has 1 block of size n and no gaps of size n,

(iii)   a generating cycle has no blocks of size $n-1$ and 1 gap of size $n-1$,

(iv)   If $1 \leq r < n-1$ then a generating cycle has 2^{n-r-2} blocks and 2^{n-r-2} gaps of length r,

(v)   a generating cycle has 2^{n-2} blocks and 2^{n-2} gaps.   ◻

Note that, in the actual statement of the theorem, we have restricted ourselves to generating cycles of indicator m-sequences. The reader should convince himself that all the claims are true for any cycle of an m-sequence, provided that the first and last entries of that cycle are distinct.

Of course if (s_t) is generated on an n-stage register but is not an m-sequence then it is not so easy to count the blocks and gaps of each size. However we can say a little.

EXERCISE 5.13   If (s_t) is a non-null sequence generated by an n-stage shift register show that it cannot have a run of length $n+1$ or more. Show that *it has at most one block of size n, no gap of size n, at most one block of size n − 1 and at most one gap of size n − 1. Finally show that it cannot have a block of size n and a block of size n − 1.*

In order to show that an m-sequence satisfies **R3** we now find its out-of-phase autocorrelation function.

THEOREM 5.11 *The out-of-phase autocorrelation function of an m-sequence with period $2^n - 1$ is $\dfrac{-1}{2^n - 1}$.*

PROOF Let (s_t) be an m-sequence of period $2^n - 1$. For any τ with $0 < \tau < 2^n - 1$, the positions in which (s_t) and $(s_{t+\tau})$ agree are identical with those in which $(s_t) + (s_{t+\tau})$ has a 0. But, by Exercise 5.6, since $(s_t) \neq (s_{t+\tau})$, there is a ρ such that $(s_t) + (s_{t+\tau}) = (s_{t+\rho})$. So, to compute the out-of-phase autocorrelation $C(\tau)$, we count the number of 0s in the first $2^n - 1$ positions of $(s_{t+\rho})$, subtract the number of 1s and divide by $2^n - 1$. Thus, by Theorem 5.10:

$$C(\tau) = \frac{(2^{n-1} - 1) - 2^{n-1}}{2^n - 1} = \frac{-1}{2^n - 1}. \qquad \square$$

If we wish to compute the out-of-phase autocorrelation function of an arbitrary periodic binary sequence (u_i) with period p, it may be difficult to count the number of agreements and disagreements between (u_i) and $(u_{i+\tau})$. It is often easier to compute $\sum_{i=0}^{p-1} u_i$ (the number of 1s in a cycle) and $\sum_{i=0}^{p-1} u_i u_{i+\tau}$ (the number of positions in which the generating cycles of (u_i) and $(u_{i+\tau})$ both have 1s) and then use the following exercise.

EXERCISE 5.14 *Show that for a binary sequence (u_i) of period p the autocorrelation function $C(\tau)$ is given by:*

$$C(\tau) = \frac{1}{p}\left(p - 4\sum_{i=0}^{p-1} u_i + 4\sum_{i=0}^{p-1} u_i u_{i+\tau}\right).$$

Note that if (s_t) is an m-sequence of period $2^n - 1$ then, since by Theorems 5.10 and 5.11 we know

$$C(\tau) = \frac{-1}{2^n - 1} \quad \text{and} \quad \sum_{t=0}^{2^n - 2} s_t = 2^{n-1},$$

Exercise 5.14 implies that $\sum_{i=0}^{2^n - 2} s_t s_{t+\tau} = 2^{n-2}$.

We now know that m-sequence satisfy our randomness postulates, i.e. that they are G-random. Clearly, if (s_t) is any G-random then $(\bar{s}_t)$, the sequence obtained by interchanging 0s and 1s, is also a G-random. Thus $(\bar{s}_t)$ is a PN-sequence which, by Theorem 5.10 (ii), is not an m-sequence.

On page 170 we remarked that G-random sequences are often called PN-sequences. Unfortunately the term PN-sequence is even more commonly used for an m-sequence. As we have seen above these two uses of the term PN-sequence are inconsistent and, in fact, have led to some confusion in the literature. While recognising our inconsistency we will now 'drop' the term m-sequence and use PN-sequence to mean maximum length linear shift register sequence.

Since they satisfy all three of our randomness properties and give sequences of guaranteed period, PN-sequences appear to be good candidates for the sequences we need for our stream cipher. The diagram of the stream cipher is shown in Figure 5.7.

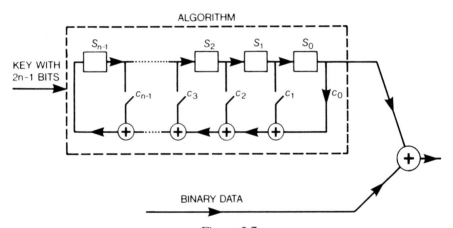

Figure 5.7
A stream cipher with a linear shift register as algorithm

Our algorithm is now a linear feedback shift register. The key defines the initial state of the register and the feedback function by setting the n switches $c_0, \ldots, c_{n-1}$. In fact, since we are prepared always to assume $c_0 = 1$, there are really only $n-1$ switches to set. If the function used is a primitive characteristic polynomial (as is the case for PN-sequences) then, since there are $\lambda(n)$ primitive polynomials of degree n and $2^n - 1$ possible initial states, the number of transformations available is $(2^n - 1)\lambda(n)$.

Furthermore the G-random sequence produced has period $2^n - 1$. All the indications are that our ciphertext sequence will have good randomness properties.

5.6 Security

5.6.1 Synopsis

We now wish to see if this system will remain secure under the worst possible conditions which were listed in Section 4.4, page 164. Consequently we assume that the cryptanalyst has:

(*i*)   *a complete knowledge of the cipher system,*
(*ii*) *a considerable length of ciphertext,*
(*iii*) *a certain amount of plaintext corresponding to part of his ciphertext.*

Given that the cryptanalyst knows the plaintext equivalent of some of the cryptogram and that he also knows the details of the cipher system, he can certainly discover some of the sequence being produced by the shift register. If, from this portion of the sequence, he can produce the entire sequence or uncover the key, then our system is obviously not secure. Clearly the length of the portion he knows is relevant. If, to go to a ridiculous (we hope!) extreme, he knows an entire generating cycle then, obviously, he knows the entire sequence. We will assume that what he knows is small in comparison with the period.

In order to decide how secure our system is we need to answer certain questions. One obvious one is: how much of a shift register sequence do we need to know in order to determine the sequence completely? A similar, almost equivalent, question is: in how many consecutive positions can two different shift register sequences agree? The answer to both these questions will depend on the periods of the sequences. We know that a shift register sequence is completely determined by a characteristic polynomial and an initial state. Different characteristic polynomials will give distinct sequences from the same initial state. So clearly we can get two distinct sequences from an n-stage shift register agreeing in at least n consecutive terms. These sequences must have period at most $2^n - 1$. A third natural question is: can the same sequence arise from two shift registers with different lengths by using different characteristic polynomials and initial states? As we shall soon see the answer to this last question is 'yes'; in Exercise 5.15, which all readers should attempt, we give an example of a sequence which can be generated on a four-stage shift register and also on a seven-stage register. Given this fact, then we need to know how to generate a given sequence on the smallest possible shift register.

The main concept of this section is that of the **linear equivalence** (or **recursion length**) of a sequence. This is defined as the length of the smallest linear shift register which can be used to generate the sequence. If the entire sequence is known, then Theorem 5.14 shows how to determine its linear equivalence and, in fact, how actually to generate the sequence on a register of that size. The exact formulation of the result is comparatively unimportant, but it is crucial to realize that it can be done. Having discussed linear equivalence we then go on to consider the problem of determining the entire sequence from a knowledge of part of it. In this discussion it is, not surprisingly, the linear equivalence of the sequence and not the size of the register used which is relevant. We show that, for a sequence with a known linear equivalence n, a straightforward matrix inversion gives the entire sequence if $2n$ consecutive bits are known. An example is given to show that $2n-1$ consecutive bits are not enough to determine the sequence uniquely. Finally in Section 5.6.5 we discuss the problem of determining the sequence from a knowledge of non-consecutive bits.

5.6.2   Linear equivalence

In order to discuss the linear equivalence of a sequence we must first establish some results about the relations between polynomials and their solution spaces.

THEOREM 5.12   *If $f(x)$ and $g(x)$ are two characteristic polynomials over GF(2) then $\Omega(f) \subseteq \Omega(g)$ if, and only if, $f(x) \mid g(x)$.*

PROOF   We again stress that all our characteristic polynomials have 1 as their constant terms.

Suppose $f(x) \mid g(x)$ and let $g(x) = f(x)h(x)$. If $(s_t) \in \Omega(f)$ and if $G(x)$ is its generating function $\sum_{i=0}^{\infty} s_i x^i$, we have, by Theorem 5.6, $G(x) = \dfrac{\phi(x)}{f^*(x)}$, where $\deg \phi(x) < \deg f(x)$. But, by Exercise 5.11, $f^*(x)h^*(x) = g^*(x)$ and thus $G(x) = \dfrac{\phi(x)h^*(x)}{g^*(x)}$ with $\deg \phi(x)h^*(x) = \deg \phi(x) + \deg h^*(x) < \deg f(x) + \deg h^*(x)$. Thus, since $\deg h^*(x) = \deg h(x)$ and $\deg g(x) = \deg f(x) + \deg h(x)$, $\deg \phi(x)h^*(x) < \deg g(x)$, and $G(x)$ is the generating function of a sequence in $\Omega(g)$, i.e. $(s_t) \in \Omega(g)$. (Note that, since both $f(x)$ and $g(x)$ have constant term 1, $h(x)$ had constant term 1 and thus $\deg f(x) = \deg f^*(x)$, $\deg g(x) = \deg g^*(x)$ and $\deg h(x) = \deg h^*(x)$.) Thus $\Omega(f) \subseteq \Omega(g)$.

Now suppose $\Omega(f) \subseteq \Omega(g)$. From Theorem 5.6 and the discussion following it, we know that, for any polynomial $\phi(x)$ over GF(2) with $\deg \phi(x) < \deg f(x)$, there is a sequence in $\Omega(f)$ with generating function $\dfrac{\phi(x)}{f^*(x)}$. Thus there is a sequence (s_t) in $\Omega(f)$ with generating function $G(x) = \dfrac{1}{f^*(x)}$. But since $\Omega(f) \subseteq \Omega(g)$, (s_t) is also in $\Omega(g)$. So there must exist a polynomial $h(x)$ over GF(2) with $\deg h(x) < \deg g(x)$ such that $G(x) = \dfrac{h(x)}{g^*(x)}$. Equating these two expressions for $G(x)$ and taking reciprocals gives $f(x)h^*(x) = g(x)$, i.e. $f(x) \mid g(x)$.   □

This theorem says that if we can generate a sequence on an n-stage linear shift register then we can generate it on one of any bigger size.

EXERCISE 5.15   Show that the sequence generated by $1 + x + x^3 + x^4$ on a four-stage shift register with initial stage 1101 has period 3, i.e. that it is $110110110\ldots$. Theorem 5.12 says that we can generate this sequence on a seven-stage shift register using, for example, $(1 + x + x^3)(1 + x + x^3 + x^4)$. Clearly, since the initial state gives the first seven terms of the sequence, the initial state must be 1101101. Check that this state and characteristic polynomial give the initial sequence.

EXERCISE 5.16   Show that the sequence generated by $1 + x^3$ on a three-stage register with 011 as initial state is the same as the sequence generated by $1 + x^2 + x^4$ on a four-stage register with 0110 as initial state. Note, however, that $1 + x^3 \nmid 1 + x^2 + x^4$.

Although Theorem 5.12 is interesting it is, in a way, another step in the 'wrong direction'. We need to know the smallest shift register we can use to generate a given sequence; rather than to know we can generate it on one as large as we please. For instance, in Exercise 5.15, we are clearly not using the seven-stage register efficiently if we use it to generate a sequence which we could have obtained from a four-stage register. In order to determine the minimum size shift register which can generate a given sequence, we need to find the smallest degree for a characteristic poly-nomial. Theorem 5.12 tells us that if we take any characteristic polynomial of a given sequence and multiply it by a polynomial with constant term 1 we get another characteristic polynomial for the same sequence. How-ever, Exercise 5.16 illustrates that if a sequence has two characteristic poly-nomials then neither one need divide the other.

To help us decide the minimum possible size of shift register to generate a given sequence we make a definition. A characteristic polynomial $f(x)$ of a non-null sequence (s_t) is called **minimal** if $(s_t) \in \Omega(h)$ with $h(x)|f(x)$ implies $h(x) = f(x)$; i.e. if no factor of $f(x)$ is also a characteristic poly-nomial for (s_t). Clearly if a characteristic polynomial of a given sequence is not minimal then it has a factor which is also a characteristic polynomial for the same sequence. Thus it must have a factor which is minimal. However it is not obvious from the definition that a sequence cannot have more than one minimal characteristic polynomial. We shall now show that each shift register sequence (s_t) has a *unique* minimal polynomial $f(x)$. Since every other characteristic polynomial of (s_t) must have $f(x)$ as a factor, deg $f(x)$ will then give the smallest size for a shift register to generate (s_t).

If (s_t) is a linear recurring sequence of period p we call the polynomial $s(x) = s_0 + s_1 x + \ldots + s_{p-1} x^{p-1}$ the **period polynomial** of (s_t). As we saw in the proof of Theorem 5.8, the generating function $G(x)$ of (s_t) is $\dfrac{s(x)}{1 + x^p}$.

But if $f(x)$ is any characteristic polynomial of (s_t) of degree n then, by Theorem 5.6, there is a polynomial $\phi(x)$ of degree at most $n-1$ with $G(x) = \dfrac{\phi(x)}{f^*(x)}$. Clearly different choices for $f(x)$ will give different polynomials $\phi(x)$. The next lemma, which we need for the following theorem, shows the relation between $\phi(x)$ and $f(x)$ when $f(x)$ is minimal.

LEMMA 5.13 *If $f(x)$ is a characteristic polynomial for the binary recurring linear sequence (s_t) with generating function $G(x) = \dfrac{\phi(x)}{f^*(x)}$, then $f(x)$ is minimal if, and only if $(\phi(x), f^*(x)) = 1$.*

PROOF We will prove this lemma by showing that $(\phi(x), f^*(x)) \neq 1$ if, and only if, $f(x)$ is not minimal.

Suppose $(\phi(x), f^*(x)) = d(x)$ where $d(x) \neq 1$, i.e. $\deg d(x) > 0$. If we write $\phi(x) = d(x)\phi_1(x)$ and $f^*(x) = d(x)f_1^*(x)$ then $\deg \phi_1(x) < \deg f_1^*(x)$ and since $f_1(x) \mid f(x)$, $f_1(x)$ has constant term 1. So

$$G(x) = \frac{\phi(x)}{f^*(x)} = \frac{\phi_1(x)}{f_1^*(x)}$$

and, by Theorem 5.6, $(s_t) \in \Omega(f_1)$. Since $f_1(x) \mid f(x)$ this implies that $f(x)$ is not minimal.

Suppose $f(x)$ is not a minimal characteristic polynomial for (s_t), i.e. there exists a characteristic polynomial $h(x)$ with $h(x) \mid f(x)$, $h(x) \neq f(x)$ and $(s_t) \in \Omega(h)$. Let $f(x) = d(x)h(x)$. By Theorem 5.6 there is a polynomial $\mu(x)$ such that $G(x) = \dfrac{\mu(x)}{h^*(x)}$ and $\deg \mu(x) < \deg h^*(x)$. Thus

$$\frac{\phi(x)}{f^*(x)} = \frac{\mu(x)}{h^*(x)}$$

or $\phi(x)h^*(x) = f^*(x)\mu(x)$. But, since $f(x) = h(x)d(x)$, $f^*(x) = h^*(x)d^*(x)$ which gives $\phi(x) = d^*(x)\mu(x)$. Hence, since $d^*(x) \mid f^*(x)$ and $d^*(x) \mid \phi(x)$, $(f^*(x), \phi(x)) \neq 1$.   □

THEOREM 5.14 *Let (s_t) be a binary linear recurring sequence with period p and period polynomial $s(x)$. Then (s_t) has a unique minimal characteristic polynomial $f(x)$ given by*

$$f^*(x) = \frac{1 + x^p}{(s(x), 1 + x^p)}.$$

Let us place ourselves in the role of the cryptanalyst and suppose that we have intercepted a cryptogram knowing that the cipher system of Figure 5.7 was used and that, by having the plaintext equivalent of some cipher-text, we know the subsequence $s_r, s_{r+1}, \ldots, s_{r+2n-1}$ of the shift register sequence (s_t) (where n is the linear equivalence of the sequence). From Lemma 5.15 we will know (s_t) completely if we can evaluate the feedback constants. If the feedback constants are $c_0 = 1, c_1, \ldots, c_{n-1}$ then we know

$$s_{t+n} = \sum_{i=0}^{n-1} c_i s_{t+i}$$

for $t = r, r+1, \ldots, r+n-1$. But, as in the last section, we can write this as a matrix equation $\mathbf{s} = \mathbf{Sc}$ where

$$\mathbf{s} = \mathbf{s}_{r+n} = \begin{pmatrix} s_{r+n} \\ s_{r+n+1} \\ \vdots \\ s_{r+2n-1} \end{pmatrix}, \quad \mathbf{c} = \begin{pmatrix} c_0 \\ c_1 \\ \vdots \\ c_{n-1} \end{pmatrix}$$

and $\mathbf{S} = (s_{ij})$ is the n by n matrix with $s_{ij} = s_{r+i+j-2}$ i.e.:

$$\mathbf{S} = \begin{pmatrix} s_r & s_{r+1} \ldots s_{r+n-1} \\ s_{r+1} & s_{r+2} \ldots s_{r+n} \\ \vdots & \vdots \quad \vdots \\ s_{r+n-1} & s_{r+n} \ldots s_{r+2n-2} \end{pmatrix}$$

We now observe that for any j with $1 \le j \le n$, column j of $\mathbf{S}$ is the state vector $\mathbf{s}_{r+j-1}$ and so, by Theorem 5.16, the columns of $\mathbf{S}$ are linearly independent. Thus $\mathbf{S}$ is non-singular and has an inverse. Hence $\mathbf{c} = \mathbf{S}^{-1}\mathbf{s}$ and we can determine the feedback constants by merely computing $\mathbf{S}^{-1}$. Although finding $\mathbf{S}^{-1}$ is not trivial, it is straightforward and many computers have a matrix inversion subroutine available. Later on we will discuss the time needed for such an operation.

To illustrate how straightforward this cryptanalysis is, and consequently to emphasize the insecurity of the system, we will work through a small example. Suppose that we know the cipher system of Figure 5.7 has been used with a five-stage shift register. To complete our knowledge of the system let us assume that we know that ITA2 (see Appendix 2) was used for coding the data. Thus the data, i.e. the plaintext message, was converted to a binary sequence with 5 bits representing each character. It was enciphered by adding it to a shift register sequence and then transmitted. The bits are enciphered, and transmitted using least significant bits first. We will also assume that, from past experience, we know the messages from this source normally begin 'DEAR', with the D occasionally preceded by a letter shift. Two plaintext letters define 10 consecutive bits of the binary data and thus enable us to work out 10 consecutive bits of the shift register sequence. This, by Theorem 5.16, is sufficient to determine the entire key.

Suppose that the ciphertext begins YVTNM E... which, using our knowledge of ITA2, means the binary output sequence was 10101 01111 00001 00110 00111 10000 . . . . If we assume that the first 10 bits of the plaintext message represent DE then, again using our knowledge of the alphabet used, the binary data begins 10010 10000. Since the shift register sequence is merely the modulo 2 sum of these two, this assumption implies that the shift register sequence begins 00111 11111. But, as we saw in Exercise 5.13, the sequence cannot have a block of size greater than 5. Thus either our information concerning the system was incorrect or the message does not begin DE. Hoping that our information was correct, we next assume that the plaintext begins with a letter shift and then D. This gives 11111 10010 for the first 10 bits of the binary data and implies that the shift register sequence begins 01010 11101.

We now form our matrix equation $s = Sc$, with $r = 0$, to get

$$
\begin{pmatrix} 1 \\ 1 \\ 1 \\ 0 \\ 1 \end{pmatrix} = \begin{pmatrix} 0 & 1 & 0 & 1 & 0 \\ 1 & 0 & 1 & 0 & 1 \\ 0 & 1 & 0 & 1 & 1 \\ 1 & 0 & 1 & 1 & 1 \\ 0 & 1 & 1 & 1 & 0 \end{pmatrix} \begin{pmatrix} c_0 \\ c_1 \\ c_2 \\ c_3 \\ c_4 \end{pmatrix}
$$

Straightforward verification shows that

$$
S^{-1} = \begin{pmatrix} 0 & 1 & 1 & 0 & 1 \\ 1 & 1 & 0 & 1 & 0 \\ 1 & 0 & 0 & 0 & 1 \\ 0 & 1 & 0 & 1 & 0 \\ 1 & 0 & 1 & 0 & 0 \end{pmatrix} \text{ and so } c = S^{-1}s = \begin{pmatrix} 0 & 1 & 1 & 0 & 1 \\ 1 & 1 & 0 & 1 & 0 \\ 1 & 0 & 0 & 0 & 1 \\ 0 & 1 & 0 & 1 & 0 \\ 1 & 0 & 1 & 0 & 0 \end{pmatrix} \begin{pmatrix} 1 \\ 1 \\ 1 \\ 0 \\ 1 \end{pmatrix} = \begin{pmatrix} 1 \\ 0 \\ 0 \\ 1 \\ 0 \end{pmatrix}
$$

Thus the feedback constants are $c_0 = c_3 = 1$, $c_1 = c_2 = c_4 = 0$ and the characteristic polynomial is $1 + x^3 + x^5$. Since $1 + x^3 + x^5$ is primitive (see Appendix 3 and Theorem 5.9), it is certainly a reasonable polynomial for the encipherer to use. Assuming we are correct, the recurrence relation gives the following for the first 30 terms of the shift register's sequence: 01010 11101 10001 11110 01101 00100. Adding this to the ciphertext we get 11111 10010 10000 11000 01010 10100 as the first 30 bits of the binary data. But this, decoding from ITA2, means that the plaintext begins: letter shift DEARS. Since this was the plaintext we were expecting we can confidently assume we are correct and proceed to decipher the rest of the message.

Our example was, of necessity, small. However, no matter how big the linear equivalence n is, it should be clear that the only work necessary to decipher a message is the matrix inversion. Even with a mini-computer the inversion of a 50 by 50 matrix with entries from $GF(2)$ takes about 1·5 seconds and a 100 by 100 matrix can be inverted in under 12 seconds. With a larger machine or a piece of purpose built equipment these times could be reduced to a few microseconds. The entire cryptanalysis can, therefore, be achieved remarkably quickly unless n is very large. (In fact the time taken to invert an n by n matrix over $GF(2)$ is proportional to n^3.)

If only $2n-1$ consecutive bits are known then, even for PN-sequences, this may not be enough to determine the entire sequence. As an illustration we give an example of two PN-sequences with $n=4$ which have identical subsequences which are 7 bits long.

EXERCISE 5.18   *Show that, for an initial state of* 1010, *the PN-sequence generated by* $1+x+x^4$ *has* 101011110001001 *for its first cycle while the PN-sequence generated by* $1+x^3+x^4$ *has* 101011001000111. *Note that the seven consecutive entries* 1101011 *occur in both sequences.*

Clearly, unless n is so large that inversion of an n by n matrix takes longer than the required cover time, the cipher system of Figure 5.7 is not secure when the cryptanalyst has the information listed at the beginning of this section. Unless n is very large, it is certainly highly likely that any interceptor will have this type of information and the system is not usable. Nevertheless, despite the now obvious ease with which their cryptograms can be cryptanalyzed, these systems were still being manufactured in the early 1970s. What is wrong with them? What makes the cryptograms so easily breakable? They certainly satisfy our conditions **A1** and **A2** concerning the guaranteed period and the randomness. The flaw is that a knowledge of a comparatively short part of the shift register sequence determines the entire sequence. The reason for this is, quite simply, the linearity of the feedback function. It is this property which enabled us to use matrix inversion to break the system. It is, then, natural to add a third requirement for our system to obtain the following:

A1   *The sequence must have a guaranteed minimum length for its period.*
A2   *The ciphertext must appear random.*
A3   *The equation describing any bit of the output sequence in terms of the key must contain terms that are non-linear in the key; i.e. for shift registers the equation must contain the product of at least two of the s_i.*

In the next chapter we will show that this extra condition is still not necessarily enough to provide adequate security.

5.6.5   Further cryptanalysis

In the last section we assumed that the cryptanalyst knew at least $2n$ consecutive bits of the sequence. We now consider the situation where he knows at least $2n$ bits of the sequence but where the bits are not necessarily consecutive. Not only does this situation represent a more realistic set of circumstances, but the techniques we develop will also be useful when we consider non-linear systems. Again placing ourselves in the role of crypt-analysts, we consider two possible methods of attack. In each case we discuss the general ideas behind the method and then apply it to a specific example. In the example we assume that the system uses a 5-bit linear feedback shift register and that we, as cryptanalysts, know 12 bits. Furthermore we assume they are spaced as follows: 1?101??0?1??0? 11??0?10. The question marks merely denote positions of the sequence for which we do not know the entry.

METHOD 1 This method uses the technique of the last section. The idea is to find $2n$ consecutive positions for which we know the maximum number of entries. We then try every possibility for filling the remaining positions. For each of these possibilities we begin to compute the rest of the sequence and try to find one which agrees with all our remaining known positions. If, for instance, the chosen $2n$ positions contain m question marks then there will be 2^m different possibilities to try. These will give us roughly 2^m possibilities for the initial state and feedback function. (There may be a few possibilities which do not result in a solution. For instance if we obtained a singular matrix but knew that a maximal length sequence was used, then we could immediately dismiss that possibility.) When trying to decide the correct one by comparing the sequence generated with our known bits, we expect about half the possibilities to be eliminated at each position. This is merely because each PN-sequence has roughly the same number of 0s and 1s. So we need of the order of a further m positions to obtain a unique solution. Thus for this method we still only need to know approximately $2n$ positions. However this time we cannot guarantee that $2n$ positions will be sufficient. Occasionally more may be required, but the number will very rarely be much larger than $2n$. Although this method does not require $2n$ consecutive bits it is clear that the smaller the value of m, the quicker the method works. Thus this method is particularly efficient when the known positions are close together.

In our example we must look for 10 consecutive positions which contain as few question marks as possible. Our best choice is the first 10 positions which contain only four question marks; 1?101??0?1. We now have $2^4 = 16$ possibilities to consider, and for each one we merely use the techniques of the last section. For our first guess we take the four unknown positions to be 0000 so that the first 10 positions are 1010100001. This leads to the matrix equation

$$
\begin{pmatrix} 0 \\ 0 \\ 0 \\ 0 \\ 1 \end{pmatrix} = \begin{pmatrix} 1 & 0 & 1 & 0 & 1 \\ 0 & 1 & 0 & 1 & 0 \\ 1 & 0 & 1 & 0 & 0 \\ 0 & 1 & 0 & 0 & 0 \\ 1 & 0 & 0 & 0 & 0 \end{pmatrix} \begin{pmatrix} c_0 \\ c_1 \\ c_2 \\ c_3 \\ c_4 \end{pmatrix}
$$

which, since

$$\begin{pmatrix} 1 & 0 & 1 & 0 & 1 \\ 0 & 1 & 0 & 1 & 0 \\ 1 & 0 & 1 & 0 & 0 \\ 0 & 1 & 0 & 0 & 0 \\ 1 & 0 & 0 & 0 & 0 \end{pmatrix}^{-1} = \begin{pmatrix} 0 & 0 & 0 & 0 & 1 \\ 0 & 0 & 0 & 1 & 0 \\ 0 & 0 & 1 & 0 & 1 \\ 0 & 1 & 0 & 1 & 0 \\ 1 & 0 & 1 & 0 & 0 \end{pmatrix} \text{ gives } \begin{pmatrix} c_0 \\ c_1 \\ c_2 \\ c_3 \\ c_4 \end{pmatrix} = \begin{pmatrix} 1 \\ 0 \\ 1 \\ 0 \\ 0 \end{pmatrix}$$

Thus we have an initial state of 10101 and feedback function $c_0 = c_2 = 1$, $c_1 = c_3 = c_4 = 0$. Generating the first few terms of the sequence gives: 1010100001001. So this sequence has a 1 in position 13 whereas our given sequence has a 0. Thus this possibility is eliminated. All that remains is to try every other possibility until we find the one which agrees with our given sequence in all the known positions.

EXERCISE 5.19   Consider the possibility 0001 for the unknown positions i.e. assume the sequence begins 1010100011. Write down the matrix equation $s = Sc$. Show that

$$S^{-1} = \begin{pmatrix} 1 & 0 & 1 & 0 & 1 \\ 0 & 0 & 0 & 1 & 0 \\ 1 & 0 & 0 & 0 & 1 \\ 0 & 1 & 0 & 1 & 0 \\ 1 & 0 & 1 & 0 & 0 \end{pmatrix}$$

and that $c_0 = c_1 = c_2 = c_3 = 1$, $c_4 = 0$. Finally show that this can be eliminated by considering the thirteenth position.

EXERCISE 5.20   Show that the possibility 0010 gives a singular matrix S which immediately eliminates it.

EXERCISE 5.21   Find the initial state and feedback function for the example. How many bits of plaintext were necessary to obtain a unique solution?

METHOD 2   This method also involves a mixture of guessing and solving simultaneous equations. Again we rely on Lemma 5.15 (page 205), but this time we try to guess the feedback function and use it to determine the initial state. Referring to the discussion before Lemma 5.15 and using the same notation we know that, for any i, $s_i = C^i s_0$. Thus, if we let c_i denote the first row of C^i, $s_i = c_i . s_0$. If we happen to know m bits of the sequence $s_{t_1}, s_{t_2}, \ldots, s_{t_m}$ then, for any given guess of the feedback function, we can build up a matrix equation $s' = C' s_0$ where

$$s' = \begin{pmatrix} s_{t_1} \\ s_{t_2} \\ \vdots \\ s_{t_m} \end{pmatrix} \text{ and } C' = \begin{pmatrix} c_{t_1} \\ c_{t_2} \\ \vdots \\ c_{t_m} \end{pmatrix}$$

Of course C' is an m by n matrix, but if we can find n linearly independent rows of $\mathbf{C}'$ then these n equations will determine $\mathbf{s}_0$ uniquely. This procedure can be carried out for each possible feedback function. Once again possibilities are eliminated by comparing later terms of the resulting sequence with the known terms of our sequence. This method is particularly useful if the number of possible feedbacks is small. For instance from Table 5.3 (page 195) we know that there are only six primitive polynomials of degree 5 which means, for our given example, we have only six possible feedback functions to try. We will consider one of them; namely $c_0 = c_2 = 1$, $c_1 = c_3 = c_4 = 0$ which gives:

$$\mathbf{C} = \begin{pmatrix} 0 & 1 & 0 & 0 & 0 \\ 0 & 0 & 1 & 0 & 0 \\ 0 & 0 & 0 & 1 & 0 \\ 0 & 0 & 0 & 0 & 1 \\ 1 & 0 & 1 & 0 & 0 \end{pmatrix}$$

The first few terms which we know of the sequence are $s_0 = 1$, $s_2 = 1$, $s_3 = 0$, $s_4 = 1$, $s_7 = 0$, $s_9 = 1$, so we must work out $\mathbf{c}_0$, $\mathbf{c}_2$, $\mathbf{c}_3$ etc. But this is straightforward.

EXERCISE 5.22   Compute $\mathbf{C}^i$ for $0 \le i \le 9$. Thus show that $c_0 = (10000)$, $c_2 = (00100)$, $c_3 = (00010)$, $c_4 = (00001)$, $c_7 = (00101)$. (When solving this exercise note that there is a systematic way of computing $\mathbf{C}^i$ and hence c_i.)

Before we continue to discuss Method 2 we will sidetrack slightly to consider Exercise 5.22. Look at the feedback shift register arrangement of Figure 5.8. It is rather different to those which we have discussed so far.

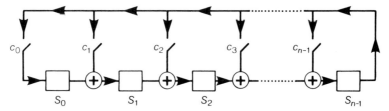

Figure 5.8
A dual shift register

However, any sequence which can be produced from the registers which we have discussed can also be produced from one of these arrangements. (Although the sequence of states for the two arrangements may be completely different.) An arrangement like Figure 5.8 is normally called a **Galois shift register** or **dual shift register** but, because they produce the same set of sequences, engineers often refer to them merely as linear feedback shift registers. For this reason the literature is occasionally slightly confusing and it is advisable to check the terminology used before reading articles.

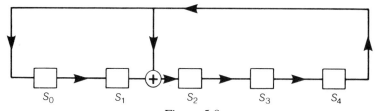

Figure 5.9
The dual shift register for this example

Suppose now that we have a five-stage dual shift register with $c_0 = c_2 = 1$, as shown in Figure 5.9. If we start with an initial state of 10000 the first ten states are 10000, 01000, 00100, 00010, 00001, 10100, 01010, 00101, 10110, 01011 which are the row vectors $c_0, c_1, \ldots, c_{10}$ of our example. This will always happen and so, by using the appropriate dual shift register, it will always be fairly easy to generate our matrix C'. Returning to our example and using our first five known positions we have:

$$\begin{pmatrix} 1 \\ 1 \\ 0 \\ 1 \\ 0 \end{pmatrix} = \begin{pmatrix} 1 & 0 & 0 & 0 & 0 \\ 0 & 0 & 1 & 0 & 0 \\ 0 & 0 & 0 & 1 & 0 \\ 0 & 0 & 0 & 0 & 1 \\ 0 & 0 & 1 & 0 & 1 \end{pmatrix} s_0.$$

But clearly row 5 of this matrix is the sum of rows 2 and 4. So we remove it and introduce s_9 and c_9 to replace s_7 and c_7. This gives:

$$\begin{pmatrix} 1 \\ 1 \\ 0 \\ 1 \\ 1 \end{pmatrix} = \begin{pmatrix} 1 & 0 & 0 & 0 & 0 \\ 0 & 0 & 1 & 0 & 0 \\ 0 & 0 & 0 & 1 & 0 \\ 0 & 0 & 0 & 0 & 1 \\ 0 & 1 & 0 & 1 & 1 \end{pmatrix} s_0.$$

EXERCISE 5.23   *Show that*

$$\begin{pmatrix} 1 & 0 & 0 & 0 & 0 \\ 0 & 0 & 1 & 0 & 0 \\ 0 & 0 & 0 & 1 & 0 \\ 0 & 0 & 0 & 0 & 1 \\ 0 & 1 & 0 & 1 & 1 \end{pmatrix}$$

is non-singular and that its inverse is

$$\begin{pmatrix} 1 & 0 & 0 & 0 & 0 \\ 0 & 0 & 1 & 1 & 1 \\ 0 & 1 & 0 & 0 & 0 \\ 0 & 0 & 1 & 0 & 0 \\ 0 & 0 & 0 & 1 & 0 \end{pmatrix}$$

Deduce that

$$\mathbf{s}_0 = \begin{pmatrix} 1 \\ 0 \\ 1 \\ 0 \\ 1 \end{pmatrix}$$

From Exercise 5.23 we now know that if the feedback function was $c_0 = c_2 = 1$, $c_1 = c_3 = c_4 = 0$ then the initial state must have been 10101. But this gives a sequence which begins 1010100001001.... Since this has the wrong entry in the thirteenth position our guess for the feedback function must be wrong. We must now try each of the other five possibilities until we find the correct one. Like Exercise 5.21, the following is worthwhile but lengthy.

EXERCISE 5.24   Use Method 2 to determine the initial state and feedback function for our example. How many bits of plaintext were necessary?

In practice the choice between Methods 1 and 2 is usually made by seeing which will require fewer trials. In our example, Method 1 needs 16 trials but Method 2 requires only 6, so we would use Method 2. On a reasonable computer both methods require approximately the same amount of time per trial since, in practice, determining a set of linearly independent rows (or columns) and then inverting the matrix requires very little extra time than simply inverting a matrix. The methods of this section will be used again in Chapter 6.

Further Reading

[20], [21] and [24] are algebra texts covering all the material needed for this chapter. [21] may be especially useful to the non-mathematician. [16], [22] and [27], between them, cover all the shift register theory that this chapter requires. They also include more detail concerning the case of non-maximal length sequences. [26] contains a list of primitive polynomials. [23] is an example of a paper, as recent as 1972, suggesting the use of linear feedback shift registers to secure communications. [25], published in the same year, points out the weaknesses of such a system.

[20]   Albert, A. A., *Fundamental Concepts of Higher Algebra*, 1st Edition, The University of Chicago Press, 1956.
[21]   Ayres, F. *The Theory and Problems of Matrices*, Schaum's Outline Series, Schaum Publishing Co.
[22]   Birdsall, T. G. and Ristenbatt, M. P., *Introduction to Linear Shift-Register Generated Sequences*, University of Michigan Research Inst., Technical Report No. 90, 1958.
[23]   Donn, E. S., 'Secure Your Digital Data', *Electronic Engineer*, 1972, 5–7.

[16] Golomb, S. W., *Shift Register Sequences*, Holden-Day, 1967.

[24] Herstein, I. N., *Topics in Algebra*, Xerox College Publishing, 1964.

[25] Meyer, C. H. and Tuchman, W. L., 'Pseudorandom Codes Can Be Cracked', *Elec. Des. 23*, 1972, 74–6.

[26] Peterson, W. W. and Weldon, E. J., *Error Correcting Codes*, 2nd Ed. M.I.T. Press, 1972.

[27] Selmer, E. S., *Linear Recurrence Relations over Finite Fields*, University of Bergen, 1966.

[28] Zierler, N., 'Linear Recurring Sequences', *J. Soc. Ind. Appl. Math. 7*, 1959, 31–48.

6.
Non-Linear Algorithms

6.1 Introduction

In Chapter 5 we considered the use of a linear feedback shift register as the algorithm for a stream cipher system. We saw that, under our worst-case conditions, such a system cannot be considered secure. Furthermore, we saw that no practically realizable linear system can provide sufficient security. It is certainly a requirement, therefore, that our algorithm contains some non-linearity.

It should be borne in mind that, no matter what form the encipherment algorithm takes, each bit of the output sequence can be represented by an equation in terms of a number of variables. The variables are of course determined by the key. Although it is always possible to obtain such equations, the amount of work involved depends on the complexity of the algorithm employed and may be large. Under our worst-case conditions we are assuming that the cryptanalyst knows some of the output sequence (since he knows some corresponding plaintext and ciphertext). Thus he has available to him a set of equations over $GF(2)$ whose solution will yield the key that the communicants are using. In Chapter 5 we saw that if these equations are linear, and their number is not exorbitantly large, they can be solved with relative ease. We must determine whether the complexity of solution is increased by the introduction of non-linearity.

In Section 6.2 we consider what makes a problem computationally difficult to solve. To this end we introduce the concepts of intractability and NP-completeness. In particular we see that at the present time a general solution to non-linear equations over $GF(2)$ does not exist. Furthermore, since finding such a solution would also imply the solution of many other 'difficult' mathematical problems, most mathematicians consider it unlikely that a general solution will ever be found! So it does appear that the introduction of non-linearity, into the algorithm, can increase the complexity of the cryptanalyst's problem.

However, although this is encouraging, the non-existence of a *general* solution does not guarantee that every particular configuration which we might use will automatically present the cryptanalyst with a set of equations he cannot solve. It only means that neither we nor the cryptanalyst can develop a general theory for handling non-linear systems.

Our first task will be to explore how we might be able to implement systems that do exhibit non-linearity. In order to analyze such systems we will need to consider each configuration individually and attempt to determine the difficulty of the cryptanalyst's job. So, with each individual system under consideration, we will begin by analyzing it with respect to our three criteria:

A1 *Periodicity*
A2 *Randomness*
A3 *Non-linearity*

It is worth emphasizing that although we may be able to determine explicit formulae for the periodicity and thus guarantee this property of our sequence, the same is not true for **A2**. In some of our examples we will be able to prove encouraging results regarding the 'global' randomness properties of the sequence produced. However, the sequences we are dealing with may, in practice, have periods of 10^{10} and more. We must therefore, as detailed in Chapter 4, pay great attention to statistical analyses of 'small' segments of the sequence. This part of the analysis will not be considered in this chapter.

Sections 6.3 and 6.4 consider a number of non-linear algorithms of increasing complexity. As well as discussing **A1** and **A2** we consider the determination of the equations linking the parameters of the algorithm to the sequence itself. Given that these equations are non-linear, and non-trivial, we then consider how difficult it might be to solve them. We shall see, repeatedly, that simply being non-linear does not imply that the system is good. Also, in this context, another important consideration is the linear equivalence of the sequence. However, again, it must not be forgotten that a large linear equivalence, although a necessary requirement, does not imply we have a good sequence. In fact we shall see many instances of non-linear systems, with large linear equivalences that can be broken relatively easily. Each system is considered in the light of our worst-case conditions. It should, by the end of this chapter, be clear that cryptography is not easy! It is not simple to design a secure cipher system. However, it should also be apparent that highly complex algorithms can be assembled using simpler, easier to analyze sub-systems as 'building blocks'.

6.2 Intractability and NP-completeness

In our discussion of shift registers with linear feedback we stated that the inversion of a non-singular matrix was a straightforward operation. This led us to the conclusion that it is 'easy' to determine the entire sequence once a comparatively small section of it is known. Our aim in this section is to be rather more precise about what we mean by an 'easy' problem. In particular, we will give the reader a general understanding of intractability and introduce the concept of NP-completeness. In this way we will be able to establish that our new systems can definitely be more secure than those we have already discussed. Our aim is solely to convey the general ideas behind these two concepts. We make no attempt to justify many of our statements and anyone interested in more detail should consult the excellent text of Garey and Johnson [30].

In our earlier chapters we used words like problem and algorithm without defining them. We relied on the reader's instinctive understanding of these terms and, within the context of those chapters, that was sufficient. However to introduce intractability we must now formally define these terms. A **problem** is a general question which must be answered. A problem will usually possess several parameters whose values are unspecified and it is described by giving:

(a)   a general description of all the parameters, and
(b)   a statement of those properties which the answer (or **solution**) must satisfy.

An **instance** of a problem is obtained by listing a particular set of values for all the problem's parameters.

As an example we consider one of the problems which is of particular interest to us; namely, the problem of solving polynomial equations over $GF(2)$. (We remind the reader that $GF(2)$ is merely the set $\{0, 1\}$ with addition and multiplication modulo 2.) The parameters of this problem are a set of polynomials in some indeterminates $x_1, x_2, \ldots, x_n$, with each coefficient equal to 0 or 1. In other words the parameters are a set of polynomials $f_i(x_1, \ldots, x_n)$, $(1 \le i \le m)$, over $GF(2)$. An instance of the problem is formulated by actually stating some particular choices for the polynomials. A solution is then a set $u_1, u_2, \ldots, u_n$ of n elements in $GF(2)$ such that $f_i(u_1, u_2, \ldots, u_n) = 0$ for each i with $1 \le i \le m$. This particular example is one of the problems which occurs repeatedly in many different contexts. For this reason it is given a specific label and is often referred to as **AN9** in the literature (the origin of this particular label is that it is **9**th in Garey and Johnson's list of **A**lgebra and **N**umber Theory problems). We will also adopt this convention.

An **algorithm** is, in general, a step by step procedure for solving a problem. We can think of it as simply being a computer program. An algorithm is said to solve a problem, if that algorithm can be applied to any instance of the problem and is *guaranteed* to produce a solution. For any given problem, there are likely to be many possible algorithms and, in general, it is usually desirable to find the most efficient one. Of course there are many criteria by which the efficiency of an algorithm can be measured. However, as we have already seen on many occasions, speed is likely to be crucial for us. (When faced with a cipher to break one could, in theory, systematically try all possibilities. As we saw in Chapter 4, in practice life is too short and some other, faster algorithm is needed.) Since time is so important to us we will concentrate solely on this one resource when determining the efficiency of an algorithm.

If we wish to compare the time requirement for various problems then we must adopt some uniform way for measuring it. One convenient way is to express the time requirement in terms of a single parameter, called the **size** of the problem instance. This is intended to measure the amount of input necessary to describe that particular instance. As an illustration, in **AN9** the size is often taken as the number of variables. If our concept of size is to reflect time requirements accurately, then we must take care to define the size of an instance in such a way that it takes account of all the parameters of the problem. To do this we note that, if a problem instance is provided as the input to a computer, it can be regarded as a single sequence of symbols chosen from a finite alphabet. The size of the instance is then reflected by the length of the sequence. Of course there are many ways in which a particular instance may be described. It does not really matter which way is chosen, so long as the same one is used for all problem instances. Let us assume that one particular method has been chosen and that each problem has associated with it a fixed **encoding scheme**, i.e. a fixed way of representing any instance as a sequence of symbols. The **input length** of any instance is simply the length of the corresponding sequence. As an example we will consider a small instance of **AN9** with $n = 3$ and $m = 3$,

$$f_1(x_1, x_2, x_3) = x_1 + x_2 x_3$$
$$f_2(x_1, x_2, x_3) = 1 + x_1 x_2$$
$$f_3(x_1, x_2, x_3) = 1 + x_1 + x_2 + x_3 + x_1 x_2 x_3.$$

One particular encoding scheme for **AN9** might be to use the alphabet $\{0, 1, 2, 3, 4, 5, 6, 7, 8, 9, /, +, *\}$. Each term of each f_i is then described by listing the subscripts separated by an asterisk, and using the symbol 0 to represent the term 1. So, for example, 1*2 represents $x_1 x_2$ while, when there are sufficient variables, 12 represents x_{12}. The various terms in a function are separated by + while the functions are separated by /. Finally // is used to signify the end of the last function. Using this particular encoding scheme our example is written:

$$1+2*3/0+1*2/0+1+2+3+1*2*3//$$

and the input length is 27.

Once we have agreed on an encoding scheme, the **time complexity function** for an algorithm expresses its time requirements by giving, for each possible input length, the maximum time which might be needed to use the algorithm to solve a problem instance of that given length. Of course, the precise value of this function depends on both the encoding scheme and on the type of computer used to execute the program. However, we are not really interested in attaching a precise value to the function. Our aim is merely to distinguish between problems which can be solved in a reasonable amount of time and those which are likely to take 'forever'. Within this context the choice of encoding scheme is irrelevant provided that the scheme obeys some simple (and reasonable) guiding principles. For instance it should be concise and not padded with unnecessary information or symbols.

In order to discuss the theory of computers we will make a rash generalization (or over-simplification) and divide them into two broad classes: deterministic and non-deterministic. By a **deterministic computer** we merely mean a realistic one, or one with properties that are actually achievable by a manufacturer. Any other computer is **non-deterministic**. So, for example, if we start talking about computers which are capable of performing arbitrarily many operations in parallel, we are talking about a non-deterministic computer. When discussing deterministic computers we need models with the basic properties shared by them all. The simplest such machine is an imaginary computer, suggested by A. M. Turing, and called a **Turing machine**. This is an automaton equipped with an infinite supply of paper tape divided into squares. The machine is capable of moving the tape, writing or erasing marks in the squares and halting. The remarkable thing about the Turing machine is that, in spite of its simplicity, it can, given enough time, solve any problem which the most sophisticated deterministic computer can solve. Like a Turing machine, a modern high-speed computer has a memory and a set of instructions for entering, processing and retrieving information. The memory is usually divided into individual cells that can be separately addressed. Because of this capability, the memory is called a **random-access memory** (RAM) and the computer, a **random-access machine**. Although the Turing machine may need to perform many steps to simulate a single action of the random-access machine, it has been proved that the latter can solve only those problems that can be solved by a Turing machine.

So if we choose an encoding scheme which obeys our general principles and keep to computers in one of the two classes (deterministic or non-deterministic) then the values obtained for the time complexity function of a given problem will be reasonably consistent.

It is now time to be a little more precise about what we meant by 'forever'. The usual way of distinguishing between solvable and unsolvable problems is by drawing a line between problems with polynomial time complexity functions and those with exponential functions. (Here we are regarding the time complexity function as having the input length as its variable.)

An algorithm is called a **polynomial time algorithm** if there is a polynomial $p(r)$ and a constant k such that its time complexity function $f(r)$ is always less that $kp(r)$. (Here, of course, r is the input length.) Any algorithm whose time complexity function is not bounded in this way is called an **exponential time function**. Table 6.1 and Figure 6.1 illustrate the vast difference between polynomial time algorithms and exponential time algorithms. In Table 6.1 the functions give the time in microseconds, i.e. 10^{-6} seconds. Even for an input length of 40 a problem with time complexity function 3^r is essentially unsolvable.

Time complexity function (microseconds)	Input length 10	20	30	40	50	60
r	10^{-5} secs	2×10^{-5} secs	3×10^{-5} secs	4×10^{-5} secs	5×10^{-5} secs	6×10^{-5} secs
r^2	10^{-4} secs	4×10^{-4} secs	9×10^{-4} secs	$1\cdot6\times10^{-3}$ secs	$2\cdot5\times10^{-3}$ secs	$3\cdot6\times10^{-3}$ secs
r^3	10^{-3} secs	8×10^{-3} secs	$2\cdot7\times10^{-2}$ secs	$6\cdot4\times10^{-2}$ secs	$1\cdot25\times10^{-1}$ secs	$2\cdot16\times10^{-1}$ secs
r^5	10^{-1} secs	$3\cdot2$ secs	$24\cdot3$ secs	$1\cdot7$ mins	$5\cdot2$ mins	$13\cdot0$ mins
2^r	10^{-3} secs	1 sec	$17\cdot9$ mins	$12\cdot7$ days	$37\cdot7$ years	366 centuries
3^r	$5\cdot9\times10^{-2}$ secs	$5\cdot2$ mins	$6\cdot5$ years	3855 centuries	2×10^{8} centuries	$1\cdot3\times10^{13}$ centuries

Table 6.1
Comparison of time complexity functions

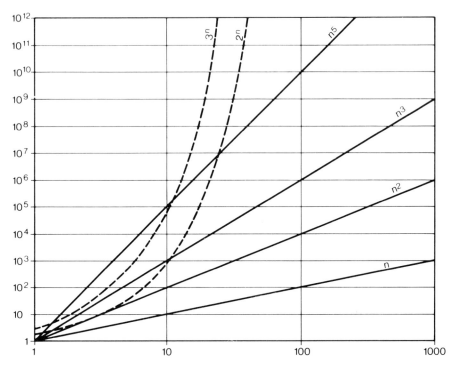

Figure 6.1
Comparison of time complexity functions

EXERCISE 6.1   Suppose we have a problem with time complexity function r^3, and that our computer can solve an instance of size n in an hour. If we are able to improve the speed of our computer by a factor of 100 show that the size of problem our new machine will be able to handle in an hour is 4·64 n. By using logarithms (or otherwise) show that if the time complexity function of our problem was 3^r our new machine would only be able to handle a problem of size n+4·19.

Exercise 6.1 is very revealing and illustrates the type of calculations needed to obtain Table 6.2. This table shows how any increase in the speed of computers will affect the time taken to solve problems. For each of the time complexity functions we considered in Table 6.1 the numbers n_1, n_2, ..., n_6 represent the size of the largest problem instances solvable in one hour. The last two columns show the effect on these numbers when the computer speed is increased. The relevant fact is that for polynomial functions the number is multiplied by a factor, i.e. is increased significantly, whereas for exponential functions they are merely increased by adding a small constant. The reader should note that the time complexity function for matrix inversion, mentioned in Section 5.6.4 was kr^3. Matrix inversion is thus a problem with a polynomial time algorithm.

Time complexity function	Largest size with present computer	Largest size with a computer which is 100 times faster	Largest size with a computer which is 1000 times faster
r	n_1	$100\ n_1$	$1000\ n_1$
r^2	n_2	$10\ n_2$	$31 \cdot 6\ n_2$
r^3	n_3	$4 \cdot 64\ n_3$	$10\ n_3$
r^5	n_4	$2 \cdot 5\ n_4$	$3 \cdot 98\ n_4$
2^r	n_5	$n_5 + 6 \cdot 64$	$n_5 + 9 \cdot 97$
3^r	n_6	$n_6 + 4 \cdot 19$	$n_6 + 6 \cdot 27$

Table 6.2
Effect of improved technology

From the point of view of problem solving, a polynomial time complexity function is obviously desirable. However the cryptographer has exactly the opposite wish. Clearly he wants the time complexity function for a cryptanalyst to discover his key to be exponential (at least on any deterministic computer). Once he has achieved this, Tables 6.1 and 6.2 show that he need not be too worried about the speed of the computer at the cryptanalyst's disposal. In practice, most exponential time algorithms are merely variations of an exhaustive search. Polynomial time algorithms, on the other hand, rely on an 'understanding' of the problem. There is wide agreement that a problem has not been 'well-solved' until a polynomial time algorithm is known for it. A problem is called **intractable** if no polynomial time algorithm can possibly solve it on a deterministic computer.

There are a number of points about intractable problems which need to be stressed (and we shall certainly do so on more than one occasion!). First it should not be assumed that polynomial time algorithms are efficient, whereas exponential algorithms are not. Time complexity functions are essentially a measure of the time needed to solve the 'worst' instance. If we are only concerned with instances of limited size, an exponential time algorithm may prove very efficient. To say that a problem is intractable means that there is at least *one instance* of the problem which requires exponential time. A number of problem instances may actually require far less time. The cryptographer must never forget this fact. The second point which we must stress is that there may be more than one cause of intractability. The obvious one is that the problem may be so difficult that an exponential amount of time is needed to solve it. Another is that the solution itself may be so extensive that it cannot be described with an expression whose length is bounded by a polynomial function of the input length. This latter form of intractability is normally apparent from the definition of the problem and is recognizable from the outset. We will concentrate on the former type.

Normally, when discussing problems in this context, one considers only **decision problems**, i.e. problems whose solution is either yes or no. We say that a decision problem belongs to **class P** if, under a particular encoding scheme, there is a polynomial time Deterministic Turing Machine program which solves the problem. (As explained earlier, provided we restrict ourselves to reasonable encoding schemes and deterministic computers, if we can find a polynomial time algorithm for one machine we will be able to find one for any machine.) Similarly we say that a decision problem belongs to **class NP** if, again under a particular encoding scheme, the problem can be 'solved' in polynomial time by a non-deterministic computer. Clearly any problem in class **P** is automatically in class **NP**. However, since it is a machine which can pursue an unbounded number of independent computational sequences in parallel, a non-deterministic computer is unrealistic and thus any problems in class **NP** but not class **P** are, in practice, unsolvable for large sizes. (We should point out that no-one has yet actually established the existence of a problem in class **NP** which is not in class **P**. However such problems may exist. Certainly there are a number of problems which, at present, are known to be in class **NP** for which there is no known polynomial time solution on a deterministic computer.)

We can think of the class **NP** as those problems for which possible solutions can be checked in polynomial time. For instance, in our problem **AN9**, if someone were to claim that a particular set of elements of $GF(2)$, $u_1, u_2, \ldots, u_n$ satisfied each of our m functions it would be a simple matter for us to verify the truth of their claim: simply by trying it out. So our polynomial time algorithm on a non-deterministic machine can be thought of as a parallel guessing procedure. We try out all possibilities and perform our polynomial time algorithm to check the possible validity of each one of these possibilities. (The reader should be aware that our definitions are very informal and our intention is to convey the flavour of problems in the class **NP**. For formal definitions [30] should be consulted.)

In the class **NP** there is one well known problem, called the 'satisfiability' problem, which is particularly significant. We will not even attempt to define the problem but merely state why it is so important. For any given problem in class **NP**, there is a polynomial time algorithm which reduces that particular problem to the satisfiability problem. Thus, if a polynomial time algorithm is ever found to solve the satisfiability problem, this will imply that every problem in class **NP** is also in class **P**. In other words if there are any intractable problems in class **NP** then the satisfiability problem must be one of them.

There are a number of other problems in class **NP** which share this property. They are called the **NP-complete problems**. Of course it is not known if an **NP**-complete problem is intractable, but the number of problems which are known to be **NP**-complete is increasing and it is important that this question be answered. (Note, in case it is not clear, that finding a polynomial time algorithm for a deterministic computer to solve any one of the **NP**-complete problems would imply that every problem in class **NP** is also in class **P**. Equivalently showing that one **NP**-complete problem is intractable would imply they are all intractable.)

Let us return to our problem **AN9**. As stated it is not a decision problem. However we can easily reword it to make it one. We can, for instance, ask: 'Does there exist a set $\{u_1, u_2, \ldots, u_n\}$ of n elements in $GF(2)$ such that, for $1 \leq i \leq m$, $f_i(u_1, u_2, \ldots, u_n) = 0$?' Clearly our original problem is at least as difficult as the equivalent decision problem, since a polynomial time solution to our initial problem immediately answers the decision problem. We already know, either from considering elementary Gaussian elimination, or from Chapter 5, that if each term of every f_i involves only one variable (i.e. if each f_i is linear), then there is a polynomial time solution. However it has been shown that without this restriction the decision problem form of **AN9** is **NP**-complete (see for instance [29]).

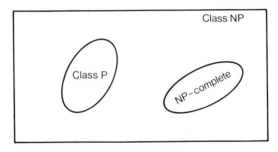

Figure 6.2
A Venn diagram for class NP

As can be seen from Figure 6.2 not all problems in **NP**, that are not known to belong to **P**, are **NP**-complete. An example of such a problem is the question of whether an integer is composite, i.e. whether it can be written as the product of at least two other integers. Notice that although there is no known efficient procedure for answering the question, if someone claims that a number is composite and supplies the factors there is a simple polynomial time algorithm to check their claim; namely to multiply the numbers together.

Although we have not included much detail in our discussion it should now be apparent that, by introducing non-linearity into our sequence generator, we may have made the cryptanalyst's task significantly harder. However we must stress (yet again!) that although we appear to be setting him an **NP**-complete problem we cannot be sure that the particular instances which he meets cannot be solved, in practice, by a polynomial time algorithm. All that intractability or **NP**-completeness guarantees is that there is at least one instance of the problem which is difficult. Thus any particular example must be individually assessed. As we shall repeatedly see in this chapter, some non-linear systems of equations can be solved very easily.

6.3   Shift Registers with Non-linear Feedback

In the light of the discussions in Section 6.2 and in Chapter 5, it now seems quite reasonable to consider the sequences generated by a shift register with a non-linear feedback. This means that we must reconsider the problems of determining which feedbacks give sequences with long periods and high degrees of randomness. Although we know we are considering an **NP**-complete problem, we must examine carefully the problem instances which will face the cryptanalyst under our worst case conditions **C1**, **C2** and **C3** of Chapter 4. In any given situation these conditions may give an easy instance for him to solve. There is one further point for us to consider. If we are going to have more complex feedback functions then we must pay some attention to the actual implementation of the function. Figure 5.7 illustrates that the implementation of a linear feedback is remarkably simple. But, as we shall see, non-linear systems can be considerably more complex and the actual complexity of implementation is relevant when deciding on the suitability of any given function.

Before tackling the above problems we must decide how we are going to describe shift registers with non-linear feedback, and how many such feedbacks exist. In order to do this we introduce the concept of a **truth table**. (Truth tables are widely used by electronic engineers and we will use them again in later chapters.) In general a truth table for a machine is merely a table which lists the output corresponding to each possible input. It must not be forgotten that each output is quite likely to depend on the state of the machine as well as the input. In fact for shift registers our input is normally null and so the output depends only on the state. Consequently we take the input as being the actual state of the register and the output is the entry which is fed back into stage S_{n-1}. Using the notation of Chapter 5, since state $(s_r, s_{r+1}, \ldots, s_{r+n-1})$ changes to $(s_{r+1}, s_{r+2}, \ldots, s_{r+n})$ the output corresponding to the state $(s_r, s_{r+1}, \ldots, s_{r+n-1})$ is s_{r+n}.

As an example we will list a possible truth table for a three-stage shift register and then show the corresponding state diagram. (When writing the table we put $r = 0$.) The states of an n-stage register may be regarded as the binary representation of the integers 0 to $2^n - 1$. It is customary to order the rows of the truth table according to the values of the integers they represent. We will adopt this convention. Note, by the way, that once this convention is adopted all the information is contained in the final column.

Note that in this example the zero state is followed by a non-zero state and that the sequence of states has period 8. This, of course, means that the shift register sequence we obtain also has period 8 and cannot, therefore, be generated by a three-stage register with linear feedback.

Since we have described the output for each possible input we have certainly defined a feedback function. We now wish to see how to represent it as a polynomial in s_0, s_1, s_2. To do this we consider the rows of our truth table individually. The expression $(s_0 + 1)(s_1 + 1)(s_2 + 1)$ is 1 if and

Input			Output
s_0	s_1	s_2	s_3
0	0	0	1
0	0	1	1
0	1	0	0
0	1	1	1
1	0	0	0
1	0	1	0
1	1	0	1
1	1	1	0

Table 6.3
A truth table for $n = 3$

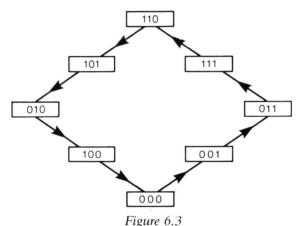

Figure 6.3
The state diagram for the above truth table

only if all three of s_0, s_1 and s_2 are 0; i.e. it is 1 for the first row and no other. Similarly the expressions $(s_0+1)(s_1+1)s_2, (s_0+1)s_1(s_2+1), (s_0+1)s_1s_2,$ $s_0(s_1+1)(s_2+1), s_0(s_1+1)s_2, s_0s_1(s_2+1), s_0s_1s_2$ take the value 1 for exactly one row. (The order of the rows is the same as the order in which the expressions are written.) If we now attach the value of the output of each row to the expression corresponding to that row, we obtain a function which reflects our truth table. Thus the function $f(s_0, s_1, s_2)$ which describes our truth table is given by $f(s_0, s_1, s_2) = (s_0+1)(s_1+1)(s_2+1).1 +$ $(s_0+1)(s_1+1)s_2.1 + (s_0+1)s_1(s_2+1).0 + (s_0+1)s_1s_2.1 + s_0(s_1+1)(s_2+1).0$ $+s_0(s_1+1)s_2.0+s_0s_1(s_2+1).1+s_0s_1s_2.0$. So $f(s_0, s_1, s_2)=s_0s_1s_2+s_0s_1+s_1s_2$ $+ s_2s_0 + s_0 + s_1 + s_2 + 1 + s_0s_1s_2 + s_0s_2 + s_1s_2 + s_2 + s_0s_1s_2 + s_1s_2 +$ $s_0s_1s_2 + s_0s_1$. But now it is important to remember that each of the s_i is either 0 or 1 and that $1+1=0$. Thus any expression added to itself must give 0. So, for example $s_0s_1s_2 + s_0s_1s_2 = 0$ for all possible values of s_0, s_1, s_2. This enables us to simplify our function to $f(s_0, s_1, s_2) = 1 + s_0 + s_1 + s_1s_2$.

Clearly any truth table will, by the type of argument given above, give a unique feedback function. Also, merely by writing $f(s_0, s_1, \ldots, s_{n-1})$ in the final column, any feedback function can be used to construct a truth table. No two functions can give rise to the same truth table and, thus, the number of feedback functions for an n-stage shift register is the same as the number of truth tables. But, as we have already observed, a truth table is completely determined by its last column. Since a truth table has 2^n rows, this last column has 2^n positions and, for each one, there are two possible entries, i.e. 0 or 1. Thus we have shown:

THEOREM 6.1   There are 2^{2^n} feedback functions for an n-stage shift register.   □

Since there are only 2^n linear functions it is clear that, for any reasonably large choice of n, we have significantly more choices when we do not restrict ourselves to a linear feedback. We will now begin to look at the problem of which of these non-linear feedbacks produce long sequences with good randomness properties. In order to see the type of situation which can occur we will consider another example. As before we illustrate the example by a truth table and a state diagram (Figure 6.4).

	Input		Output
s_0	s_1	s_2	s_3
0	0	0	1
0	0	1	0
0	1	0	0
0	1	1	0
1	0	0	0
1	0	1	0
1	1	0	0
1	1	1	1

Table 6.4
A truth table for our example

EXERCISE 6.2   Show that the feedback function of the above example is $1 + s_0 + s_1 + s_2 + s_0 s_1 + s_1 s_2 + s_2 s_0$.

Our example illustrates a number of important points. Firstly it has two cycles, one of length four and the other of length one. Secondly there are a number of states which do not occur in either of these cycles, two have more than one predecessor and two have no predecessor. A state vector with more than one predecessor is called a **branch point** and, clearly, the

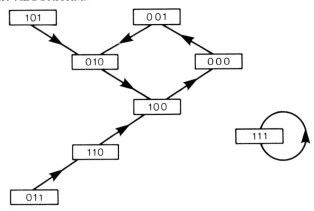

Figure 6.4
The state diagram for the example

existence of branch points means that the diagram cannot consist of one cycle of maximal length. Since each state has a unique successor, a branch point will exist precisely when there exists a state having no predecessor. Our first problem is to decide when branch points occur.

The successor to state $(\alpha_0, \alpha_1, \ldots, \alpha_{n-1})$ is $(\alpha_1, \alpha_2, \ldots, \alpha_{n-1}, f(\alpha_0, \alpha_1, \ldots, \alpha_{n-1}))$ while the successor to $(\beta_0, \beta_1, \ldots, \beta_{n-1})$ is $(\beta_1, \beta_2, \ldots, \beta_{n-1}, f(\beta_0, \beta_1, \ldots, \beta_{n-1}))$. Thus these two different states can have the same successor only if $\alpha_1 = \beta_1, \alpha_2 = \beta_2, \ldots, \alpha_{n-1} = \beta_{n-1}$, i.e. if they agree in every position except the first. Furthermore, since each entry is either 0 or 1, α_0 must equal $\bar{\beta}_0$ where, for $x = 0$ or 1, $\bar{x}$ denotes the complement of x in $GF(2)$. (Thus $\bar{0} = 1$ and $\bar{1} = 0$.) So $f(\alpha_0, \alpha_1, \ldots, \alpha_{n-1}) = f(\bar{\alpha}_0, \alpha_1, \alpha_2, \ldots, \alpha_{n-1})$. But this means that we can avoid branch points by choosing f so that it cannot have this last property for any choice of $\alpha_0, \alpha_1, \ldots, \alpha_{n-1}$. One way, then, is to choose f so that $f(s_0, s_1, \ldots, s_{n-1}) = s_0 + f'(s_1, s_2, \ldots, s_{n-1})$ where f' is some other feedback function for an $(n-1)$-stage shift register. It is in fact true that this is the only way to avoid branch points.

THEOREM 6.2   *A state diagram has no branch points if and only if the feedback function satisfies* $f(s_0, s_1, \ldots, s_{n-1}) = s_0 + f'(s_1, s_2, \ldots, s_{n-1})$.

Although we do not include a proof the reader with mathematical interests should provide one for himself.

EXERCISE 6.3   *Complete the proof of Theorem 6.2.*   ⏹

EXERCISE 6.4   *Show that the state diagram for a shift register with linear feedback has no branch points if and only if* $c_0 = 1$.

EXERCISE 6.5   *Show that a state diagram has no branch points if and only if the last column of the corresponding truth table has its bottom half* *equal to the complement of the top half.* (*Note that the top half corresponds to* $s_0 = 0$ *while the bottom corresponds to* $s_0 = 1$ *and then use Theorem 6.2.*)

Since the top half of the truth table corresponds to $s_0 = 0$ this means that, if there are no branch points, it is essentially the truth table for $f'(s_1, s_2, \ldots, s_{n-1})$. To see this look back at Table 6.3. As we saw in our discussion this is the truth table for $f(s_0, s_1, s_2) = 1 + s_0 + s_1 + s_1 s_2$. There are no branch points and we can write $f(s_0, s_1, s_2) = s_0 + f'(s_1, s_2)$, where $f'(s_1, s_2) = 1 + s_1 + s_1 s_2$. But if we look at the top half of the truth table in Table 6.3 and 'forget' s_0, we get Table 6.5 which is, of course, the truth table of $f'(s_1, s_2)$.

Input		Output
s_1	s_2	s_3
0	0	1
0	1	1
1	0	0
1	1	1

Table 6.5
A modified version of the top half of Table 6.3

Since we are mainly interested in sequences with large periods we will concentrate initially on functions which give branchless diagrams; a maximal length cycle will of course be branchless. Suppose that we have a truth table for a branchless function and that we change one of the output entries. By Exercise 6.5 we know that, if we wish our new truth table to represent a branchless function, we must also change an output entry in the other half of the table. Clearly each changed entry in the truth table amounts to the state of that row having a new successor. Thus, in the state diagram, the arrow coming from that state is redirected. Changing one entry in the truth table means changing the successor to one particular state. If we call this state s_1 then this change leaves the successor of s_1, which we will denote by s_2, with no predecessor. Since the second change, which we are forced to make, gives a new branchless diagram, it must 'create' a new predecessor for s_2 and, at the same time, not leave any other state without a predecessor. But, in our new diagram, the only state with

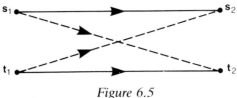

Figure 6.5
The changes in the state diagram

two predecessors is the new successor of s_1. If we call this t_2, then our second change must make s_2 a successor to the other predecessor, (t_1), of t_2. (See for instance Figure 6.5.) From this we can see that the two changes in the truth table alter the number of cycles in the state diagram by one.

EXERCISE 6.6 Show that the above two changes in the truth table increase the number of cycles by one if s_2 and t_1 are in the same cycle but decrease it by one otherwise. (*Draw diagrams.*)

As we have seen the top half of the truth table for a branchless function is, essentially, the table for $f'(s_1, s_2, \ldots, s_{n-1})$.

EXERCISE 6.7 Show that if f' is linear $(n>2)$ and $f' \neq 0$ then its truth table has an equal number of 1s and 0s.

From Chapter 5 we know that, if we take f to be linear with a primitive characteristic polynomial, f will have two cycles (namely one of length 2^n-1 and one of length 1) and, from Exercise 6.7, $f'(s_1, s_2, \ldots, s_{n-1})$ will have equally many 0s and 1s in its truth table. From Section 5.4 we know that there is always at least one such f. This means that, for $n>2$, there always exists a feedback which gives rise to a branchless state diagram with two cycles and an equal number of 1s and 0s in the top half of its truth table. We need this observation in order to prove:

THEOREM 6.3 In order to obtain a sequence of length 2^n from an n-stage shift register, $(n>2)$, the following are necessary:
  (*i*)   all n available tap positions must be used in the feedback function,
  (*ii*) the top half of the truth table must have an odd number of 1s.

PROOF We first show that the number of cycles into which a branchless shift register sequence is decomposed is even or odd according to whether the number of 1s in the truth table of $f'(s_1, \ldots, s_{n-1})$ is even or odd. Consider the truth table for any PN-sequence. Then, from the discussion preceding this theorem, for $n>2$, this has two cycles and an even number of 1s in the truth table of f'. By Exercise 6.6 and the discussion preceding it, we know that a single change to the truth table of f' changes the number of cycles by 1. Since, by making an even (odd) number of changes to f', we will always obtain an even (odd) number of cycles our claim is proved.

So, to obtain a single cycle of length 2^n we must have an odd number of 1s in the truth table of f'. Suppose that the feedback function $f'(s_1, \ldots, s_{n-1})$ does not use one of the variables, s_l say. Then whenever a 1 occurs in the right hand column of the truth table for state $(x_1, x_2, \ldots, x_l, \ldots, x_{n-1})$ there must always be a 1 for state $(x_1, x_2, \ldots, \bar{x}_l, \ldots, x_{n-1})$. Thus the number of 1s in the output column is even. So to obtain a single cycle (of length 2^n) every available tap position must be used. $\qquad\square$

It is important to realize that the conditions of Theorem 6.3 do not guarantee a sequence of length 2^n. (All that is guaranteed is that there will be an odd number of cycles.) Condition (i) has important practical consequences for our cipher system. It means that to get a maximal cycle we require a lot of hardware to supply the feedback functions. This is different from the linear case where (although we obtained a minimum of two cycles) on occasions we only needed two taps to provide the feedback.

Another important consideration before we decide whether non-linear feedback functions give 'suitable' sequences for our cipher system is the autocorrelation. We recall, from Chapter 4, that if the period is p and a is any integer with $0 \le a \le p-1$ then the autocorrelation $C(a) = \dfrac{A-D}{p}$ where A and D are respectively the number of agreements and disagreements between the first p terms of (s_t) and its translate (s_{t+a}). If the sequence is branchless then $s_r = f'(s_{r-n+1}, \ldots, s_{r-1}) + s_{r-n}$. So $s_r = s_{r-n}$ whenever $f'(s_{r-n+1}, \ldots, s_{r-1}) = 0$ and $s_r \ne s_{r-n}$ otherwise. Thus the autocorrelation is very dependent on the truth table of $f'(s_1, s_2, \ldots, s_{r-1})$. A branchless sequence will only have zero out-of-phase autocorrelation if the truth table of f' has equally many 1s and 0s. But by Exercises 6.6 and 6.7, this can only occur if the sequence has an even number of cycles. This short discussion of the autocorrelation is not particularly encouraging.

Despite our reservations, we will still consider how a cryptanalyst might tackle one particular example of a sequence which he knows is generated by a shift register with a special non-linear feedback. This example will also show how a sequence of length 2^n with linear equivalence $2^n - 1$, which is almost as large as possible, need not be secure. For any n we define a feedback function $f(s_r, s_{r+1}, \ldots, s_{r+n-1}) = f^*(s_r, s_{r+1}, \ldots, s_{r+n-1}) + \bar{s}_{r+1}\bar{s}_{r+2} \ldots \bar{s}_{r+n-1}$ where f^* is a linear feedback function corresponding to a primitive polynomial of degree n. The sequence generated always has period 2^n and linear equivalence $2^n - 1$. To see that the period is 2^n we merely notice that the successor to almost any state is the same as that given by the linear feedback function f^*. The only time, apart from the all 0 state, that a different successor occurs is when the state is 1 followed by $n-1$ zeros. (Because this is the only time that $\bar{s}_{r+1}\bar{s}_{r+2} \ldots \bar{s}_{r+n-1} = 1$.) This state is followed by the zero state. Thus the sequence generated by f is the same as that generated by f^*, except that an extra 0 is inserted after each run of $n-1$ zeros. The proof of the assertion about the linear equivalence is a little harder and we will not include it.

We now consider how, as a cryptanalyst, we might attack a system that is based on a feedback function of the above type. Of course, in some sense, we are 'cheating' by taking a function that is almost linear. However the point we wish to illustrate is that maximal period and linear equivalence are no guarantee of security. As in the linear case, we will assume that we know the plaintext equivalent of $2n$ consecutive bits of ciphertext, i.e. that we know $2n$ consecutive bits of the sequence. If the $2n$ bits do not include the extra 0 then we can break the system by the matrix inversion technique of Chapter 5. (To do this we merely note that we have $2n$ bits of the sequence generated by f^* and use the matrix inversion to determine the feedback coefficients of f^* which, of course, determine f.) Since the sequence has period 2^n, there are 2^n possible sections of $2n$ bits. Of these exactly $2n$ will contain the extra 0, which means that the probability that our $2n$ bits will not contain the extra 0 is $\dfrac{2^n - 2n}{2^n}$; i.e. is almost one for reasonably large n. Thus all the extra work in using a non-linear feedback has given us virtually no extra protection. This is, of course, an example of an instance of an **NP**-complete problem which can be solved in polynomial time.

Although we do not intend to say any more about non-linear feedbacks the reader should be aware that we have not fully explored the many possibilities for this function. This is not intended to imply that they might not prove of great use in specific situations.

6.4 Some Examples Using more than One Register

In this section we explore the possibility of introducing some non-linearity into our system by using more than one shift register (each one having a linear feedback function). As explained earlier no general algorithm is known which will solve all non-linear systems. But, as we shall repeatedly see, this does not mean we cannot solve many particular instances. In order to illustrate the theory we will merely examine a number of different examples. The reader may well see ways in which our examples can be generalized and may even see how to overcome some of the problems encountered. We do not intend to worry too much about questions of this type. Our aim is merely to introduce some of the techniques and ideas necessary to begin an analysis of non-linear systems. We shall, of course, frequently refer back to our three crucial requirements **A1**, **A2**, **A3** (see Section 6.1) for a sequence to be considered for use in a cipher system.

6.4.1 Multiplication

The first example we consider is simply to multiply together the outputs of two shift registers with linear feedback (Figure 6.6). Thus if shift register SR1 generates sequence (a_t) and SR2 generates (b_t) the output sequence will be (c_t) where, for each t, $c_t = a_t b_t$. Since we wish to have an output sequence with as large a period as possible it seems reasonable to concentrate on the situation where SR1 and SR2 both generate PN-sequences, i.e. sequences of lengths $2^m - 1$ and $2^n - 1$ respectively. Before we work out an actual example we note that as soon as both registers return simultaneously to their initial state, the output will begin to repeat itself. Thus the output sequence has period at most $(2^m - 1)(2^n - 1)$. In fact if $(m, n) = 1$ then the period is actually equal to $(2^m - 1)(2^n - 1)$. We set the proof of this as a difficult but worthwhile exercise.

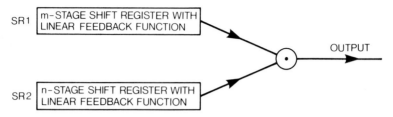

Figure 6.6
Multiplying two sequences

EXERCISE 6.8   *Show that if $(m, n) = 1$ and the sequences generated by SR1 and SR2 have periods $2^m - 1$ and $2^n - 1$ respectively then the output sequence of Figure 6.6 has period $(2^m - 1)(2^n - 1)$.*

For our worked example we will take $m = 4$, $n = 3$, $f(x) = x^4 + x^3 + 1$ and $g(x) = x^3 + x^2 + 1$. We will also assume that each register has an initial state of all 1s. By Exercise 6.8, the output sequence has period 105. So, in the following table, we list only the first 105 states for each machine with the corresponding entries for the output sequence. (The sequence is in the column headed 0.)

SR1	SR2	0	SR1	SR2	0	SR1	SR2	0	SR1	SR2	0	SR1	SR2	0
1111	111	1	0110	111	0	0001	111	0	1010	111	1	0010	111	0
1110	110	1	1100	110	1	0011	110	0	0101	110	0	0100	110	0
1101	101	1	1001	101	1	0111	101	0	1011	101	1	1000	101	1
1010	010	0	0010	010	0	1111	010	0	0110	010	0	0001	010	0
0101	100	0	0100	100	0	1110	100	1	1100	100	1	0011	100	0
1011	001	0	1000	001	0	1101	001	0	1001	001	0	0111	011	0
0110	011	0	0001	011	0	1010	011	0	0010	011	0	1111	011	0
1100	111	1	0011	111	0	0101	111	0	0100	111	0	1110	111	1
1001	110	1	0111	110	0	1011	110	1	1000	110	1	1101	110	1
0010	101	0	1111	101	1	0110	101	0	0001	101	0	1010	101	1
0100	010	0	1110	010	0	1100	010	0	0011	010	0	0101	010	0
1000	100	1	1101	100	1	1001	100	1	0111	100	0	1011	100	1
0001	001	0	1010	001	0	0010	001	0	1111	001	0	0110	001	0
0011	011	0	0101	011	0	0100	011	0	1110	011	0	1100	011	0
0111	111	0	1011	111	1	1000	111	1	1101	111	1	1001	111	1
1111	110	1	0110	110	0	0001	110	0	1010	110	1	0010	110	0
1110	101	1	1100	101	1	0011	101	0	0101	101	0	0100	101	0
1101	010	0	1001	010	0	0111	010	0	1011	010	0	1000	010	0
1010	100	1	0010	100	0	1111	100	1	0110	100	0	0001	100	0
0101	001	0	0100	001	0	1110	001	0	1100	001	0	0011	001	0
1011	011	0	1000	011	0	1101	011	0	1001	011	0	0111	011	0

Table 6.6
Worked example: multiplying two shift register outputs

When we count the entries in the output sequence of Table 6.6 we find that there are 32 1s and 73 0s. This is nowhere near the type of fifty-fifty split necessary for **A2**. This predominance of 0s is not really surprising and is an almost inevitable consequence of using a multiplier. Whenever either of our two sequences has a 0 in a given position then, since a multiplier is being used, the output will be 0. There are four possibilities for the pairs of entries in corresponding positions of our two sequences; i.e. $(0, 1)$, $(0, 0)$, $(1, 0)$ or $(1, 1)$. Since three out of these contain a 0 we 'expect' our output sequence to have three 0s for each entry of 1. In fact we can compute the precise number of 1s in any sequence when SR1 and SR2 both generate PN-sequences. Each register cycles through every one of its non-zero states and, during a complete cycle of the output sequence, each non-zero state of SR1 will appear exactly once with each non-zero state of SR2. There are 2^{m-1} states of SR1 which begin with a 1 and 2^{n-1} states of SR2 with the same property. Thus, since the output sequence has a 1 only if both shift registers have a 1 in their first stage, the number of 1s in the output sequence is 2^{m+n-2}. Thus the probability of finding a 1 in any given position is

$$\frac{2^{m+n-2}}{(2^m - 1)(2^n - 1)}.$$

But

$$\frac{2^{m+n-2}}{(2^m - 1)(2^n - 1)}$$

is approximately equal to

$$\frac{2^{m+n-2}}{2^m \cdot 2^n}, \text{ i.e. } \tfrac{1}{4}.$$

Clearly **A2** is not satisfied by this example and there is no need to even consider **A3**. This example is unsuitable.

6.4.2 J-K flip-flops
Figure 6.7 shows the block diagram for our second example. Again we assume that both registers generate PN-sequences and that the key will

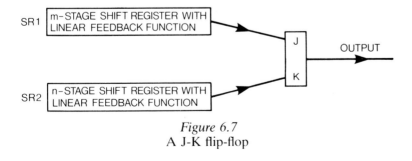

Figure 6.7
A J-K flip-flop

specify the initial states of the two registers. The mixer which we are using this time is known as a **J-K flip-flop** and is widely used in electronics circuits. It sometimes has more inputs than we are using here, but for the purposes of this example two inputs are sufficient. The action of a J-K flip-flop can best be described by giving its truth table (Table 6.7). For this table we let q_t denote the output at time t.

J	K	q_n
0	0	q_{n-1}
0	1	0
1	0	1
1	1	$\bar{q}_{n-1}$

Table 6.7
The truth table for a J-K flip-flop

Let the sequence of SR1 be (a_t) and that of SR2 (b_t). Since each entry of the output sequence (q_t) is dependent on the previous term, we cannot get a value for q_0 without assigning a value to q_{-1}. It is normal to put $q_{-1} = 0$ and this is what we will do. Using the methods of Section 6.3 we see that the equation relating q_{n-1}, a_n and b_n to q_n is:

$$q_n = (a_n + 1)(b_n + 1)q_{n-1} + (a_n + 1)b_n.0 + a_n(b_n + 1).1 + a_n.b_n(q_{n-1} + 1)$$
$$= (a_n + b_n + 1)q_{n-1} + a_n.$$

Thus the first few terms of the output sequence are:

$$q_0 = a_0, \; q_1 = (a_1 + b_1 + 1)a_0 + a_1, \; q_2 = (a_2 + b_2 + 1)[(a_1 + b_1 + 1)a_0 + a_1] + a_2.$$

Clearly these are non-linear equations which are becoming increasingly complex. Thus this system certainly appears to satisfy **A3**. If, as we normally do anyway, we restrict ourselves to the situation where $(m, n) = 1$ then the following exercise shows that **A1** is also satisfied. As with Exercise 6.8 this is not simple.

EXERCISE 6.9   If $(m, n) = 1$ show that the sequence produced by Figure 6.7 ultimately has period $(2^m - 1)(2^n - 1)$.

Regarding **A2**, it appears to be reasonably well satisfied although there are a number of results of the following type.

EXERCISE 6.10   Show that in the example of Figure 6.7 the probability of a transition in the output from q to $\bar{q}$ is greater than a half. (This, of course, means that consecutive entries of 0, 1 or 1, 0 are more likely than 0, 0 or 1, 1.)

In fact we need not be too concerned about **A2** since we will now show that, as soon as we know some of the sequence, these complex equations can be solved reasonably easily. If, for instance, for some value of r we know q_r and q_{r+1} then, by substituting these values in our equation for the truth table, we get:

if $q_r = 0$ and $q_{r+1} = 0$ then $a_{r+1} = 0$
if $q_r = 0$ and $q_{r+1} = 1$ then $a_{r+1} = 1$
if $q_r = 1$ and $q_{r+1} = 0$ then $b_{r+1} = 1$
if $q_r = 1$ and $q_{r+1} = 1$ then $b_{r+1} = 0$.

So from every pair of known consecutive entries in (q_t) we can deduce one value of either a_i or b_i for some i.

EXERCISE 6.11   Show that if the output from the system of Figure 6.7 is 0100011010110 then the corresponding output from SR1 must be ?1?001??1?1?? and that from SR2 is ??1???01?1?01.

Thus knowledge of a section of the output sequence enables us to deduce certain bits of the two sequences (a_t) and (b_t). These bits will almost certainly not be consecutive but, as soon as we know enough, we can use the results of Section 5.6.5 to deduce both the sequences. Thus this system certainly cannot be considered secure under our worst case conditions.

6.4.3   A more complex system
Our third example is a far more realistic type of algorithm which may be used to produce the pseudo-random sequence for our stream cipher. Its analysis is consequently rather more complex than our earlier examples, and we will discuss it in considerably more detail. This system, which relies heavily on the J-K flip-flops of Section 6.4.2, was first proposed by Pless [35]. It is designed to overcome the fundamental weakness of the J-K flip-flops but, nevertheless, fails to achieve a high level of security.

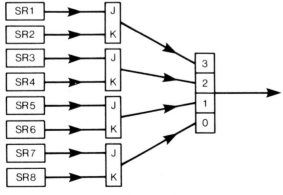

Figure 6.8
Pless's system

We will begin by describing the system, It consists of eight linear feedback shift registers, four J-K flip-flops and a recycling counter as shown in Figure 6.8. The recycling counter merely has the effect of changing the output box with each time pulse so that at time t it transmits the box $(t + c)$ modulo 4, where c is a constant between 0 and 3. The key for this system is the contents of the eight shift registers, their feedbacks (which are chosen to generate maximal length sequences), the initial states of the J-K flip-flops and the constant c. Clearly there are 2^4 possibilities for the initial states of the J-K flip-flops and 4 choices for c. We could, for such a system, choose shift registers of any sizes but Table 6.8 lists the actual sizes etc. proposed by Pless. The last column of the table lists the number of possible feedbacks which is the same as the number of primitive polynomials of the various degrees (see Table 5.3).

	Number of stages	Number of possible initial states	Number of possible feedbacks
SR1	5	31	6
SR2	19	524,287	27,594
SR3	7	127	18
SR4	17	131,071	7,710
SR5	9	511	48
SR6	16	65,535	2,048
SR7	11	2,047	176
SR8	13	8,191	630

Table 6.8
Parameters of Pless's system

The sizes of the shift registers have been carefully chosen so that each pair is relatively prime. This means that the final sequence has a period which is the product of all the individual periods, namely $1 \cdot 519 \times 10^{29}$. The randomness properties of this sequence have not, as far as we know, been studied in any great detail but, superficially, they appear reasonable. It is certainly difficult to see a simple way of using statistics on the cipher to gain an entry to the system. We will now consider a method, due to Rubin [37], for breaking this system. Before we start we observe that the number of keys is $2 \cdot 435 \times 10^{51}$ and so, as with most of the systems we discuss, an exhaustive search is out of the question.

Rubin's method involves some searching and the solving of some linear equations. It employs the techniques of method 2 in Section 5.6.5 and involves trialling a number of possibilities and trying to eliminate the incorrect ones.

We begin by redrawing Figure 6.8 and treating each sub-system of two shift registers and one J-K flip-flop as a separate block. The method

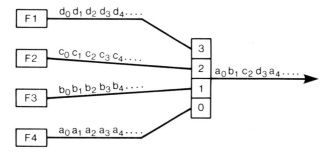

Figure 6.9
Figure 6.8 redrawn

depends on analyzing each block independently of the others. We need to assume a particular value for the constant c and so, for simplicity, we will assume $c = 0$. This means that if the output sequence is $x_0 x_1 x_2 x_3 x_4 \ldots$ and the sequence from F4 is $a_0 a_1 a_2 a_3 a_4 \ldots$. Then $x_0 = a_0$, $x_4 = a_4$ and so on.

We will start by considering F1. But before doing this we set a general exercise.

EXERCISE 6.12   Show that if the output of Fi is q and if, for the J-K flip-flop of Fi, the J-input, j, is such that $j \neq q$ (i.e. the J-input and output are different) then $j = k$, where k is the K-input. Hint: use Table 6.7.

If we now apply this exercise to F1, it tells us that if we know the sequence of its smaller register, i.e. SR1, then, on average, knowing $2n$ bits of the output of F1 will tell us n bits of the output from SR2. Since SR2 has a linear feedback producing a maximal sequence we can use method 2 of Section 5.6.5 to determine its initial state and feedback function. But SR2 has 19 stages and 27,594 possible feedbacks. So this will involve 27,594 trials and, by Exercise 6.12, we will need to know about 38 bits of the output of F1. Of course, the above argument only works if we know the initial state and feedback function of SR1. But there are only 31 possible initial states and 6 possible feedbacks. Thus there are 186 possibilities for the initial state and feedback function and we can consider all possibilities for SR1 by performing 5,132,484 ($= 27,594 \times 186$) trials. To obtain a unique possibility, we must compare the output of F1, for the particular solution we have obtained for the initial contents of SR2 together with the 'guess' for the remaining parameters, against the actual bits of known output from F1. So we expect a unique solution if approximately $19 + y$ bits of the output of F1 are known where $2^y = 5,132,484$. The reason for this is that, as we saw in Section 5.6.5, we would expect to lose half the possibilities for each further bit of the output against which we test. For this particular case $y \simeq 23$ so about 42 bits will yield a unique solution.

To summarize we see that to find both the initial states and feedback functions of SR1 and SR2 requires approximately 5,132,484 trials and about 42 bit of output from F1. If we carry out the same procedure for F2, F3, F4 we get Table 6.9.

	Approximate number of trials needed	Approximate number of output bits necessary
F1	5,132,484	42
F2	17,625,060	42
F3	50,233,344	42
F4	226,971,360	41

Table 6.9
Estimated number of bits required

In the above discussion we assumed that c was 0 and so, in order to consider all possibilities, we must multiply the number of trials by 4. This still means that if we know about 167 bits of output we can break the system after about $1 \cdot 2 \times 10^9$ trials. Rubin estimates that each trial can be performed in about $10 \mu S$ which gives the total time required as about 200 minutes. (To achieve this he assumes usage of a large mainframe computer and/or purpose-built hardware.)

In practice it may not be necessary to have as many as 167 bits of known plaintext. It is possible that the code for converting the data into binary has 'bad' properties which can be utilized. We will consider this type of problem in Chapter 8.

Finally we must note that increasing some of the parameters in this system might mean the particular attack we have just seen becomes impracticable. Thus the general scheme proposed by Pless might still prove reasonable. However, as we have said before, the cryptanalyst need only concern himself with breaking the system under consideration; not all generalizations of it.

6.4.4 Multiplexing

Our next example illustrates how the difficulty of analysis grows as the means for producing non-linearity becomes more complex. This system uses a standard electronic component called a multiplexer. A **multiplexer** is a many input, one output, system.

The set of inputs (often termed **select lines**), labelled **A**, provides an address for the multiplexer. (We may regard the elements of **A** as determining a binary number which gives the 'address'. Thus if $|\mathbf{A}| = h$ there will be 2^h addresses.) The output of the multiplexer is then merely the member of set **B** specified by the address. In order to see that a multiplexer is a non-linear device we will consider a small example. Let $\mathbf{A} = \{x_1, x_2, x_3\}$ and $\mathbf{B} = \{y_1, y_2, \ldots, y_8\}$ and assume that the elements

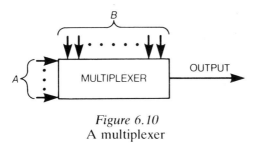

Figure 6.10
A multiplexer

of **B** are written in address order. Thus y_1 has address 000, y_2 has address 001, etc. The truth table is shown in Table 6.10. Thus, if we let q represent the output, the equation for q is $q = (x_1 + 1)(x_2 + 1)(x_3 + 1)y_1 + (x_1 + 1)(x_2 + 1)x_3 y_2 + (x_1 + 1)x_2(x_3 + 1)y_3 + (x_1 + 1)x_2 x_3 y_4 + x_1(x_2 + 1)(x_3 + 1)y_5 + x_1(x_2 + 1)x_3 y_6 + x_1 x_2(x_3 + 1)y_7 + x_1 x_2 x_3 y_8$. Clearly this is non-linear.

x_1	x_2	x_3	*output*
0	0	0	y_1
0	0	1	y_2
0	1	0	y_3
0	1	1	y_4
1	0	0	y_5
1	0	1	y_6
1	1	0	y_7
1	1	1	y_8

Table 6.10
Truth table for multiplexer

We will now define what we mean by a multiplexed system. Let SR1 and SR2 be two shift registers with m and n stages respectively, ($m > 1$, $n > 1$), such that each has a linear feedback function. We denote the stages of SR1 by $A_0, \ldots, A_{m-1}$ and those of SR2 by $B_0, \ldots, B_{n-1}$. Furthermore we let $a_i(t)$ and $b_j(t)$ denote the contents of A_i and B_j at time t. When discussing multiplexed sequences we usually assume that both shift registers have primitive characteristic polynomials, i.e. that SR1 generates a binary sequence (a_t) of period $2^m - 1$ and SR2 generates a binary sequence (b_t) of period $2^n - 1$. A multiplexer is used to produce a sequence, which we call a **multiplexed sequence**, related to the states of SR1 and SR2 in the following way. We first choose an integer h in the range $1 \leq h \leq m$. Then 2^h stages are chosen from the n stages of SR2 and one of these is output (via the multiplexer) at time t, depending upon the contents (at that time) of h of the m stages of SR1.

To state this more mathematically, we can only choose $h = m$ if

$$2^m - 1 \leq n$$

and if $h \neq m$ then h must also satisfy $2^h \leq n$. Having chosen h, we now choose h stages $a_{x_1}, a_{x_2}, \ldots, a_{x_h}$ of SR1 and, for convenience, we assume $0 \leq x_1 < x_2 < \ldots < x_h \leq m - 1$. These stages form the set $\mathbf{A}$ of Figure 6.10. At any time t, the binary h-tuple $(a_{x_1}(t), a_{x_2}(t), \ldots, a_{x_h}(t))$ is interpreted as the binary representation of a natural number which we denote by N_t. Clearly $0 \leq N_t \leq 2^h - 1$, but if $h = m$ then, since the binary m-tuple $(0, 0, \ldots, 0)$ is never a state, we can improve the inequality slightly to $1 \leq N_t \leq 2^m - 1$. If $h < m$ we choose a reversible mapping

$$\theta : \{0, 1, \ldots, 2^h - 1\} \to \{0, 1, \ldots, n - 1\}$$

while if $h = m$ we choose a reversible mapping

$$\theta : \{1, 2, \ldots, 2^h - 1\} \to \{0, 1, \ldots, n - 1\}.$$

Thus the integers $\theta(0), \theta(1), \ldots, \theta(2^h - 1)$ form the ordered set $\mathbf{B}$ of Figure 6.10. (Note that the restrictions on h guarantee the existence of such a mapping.) With these choices of h, $x_1, x_2, \ldots, x_h$ and θ we define a new sequence (u_t), called a multiplexed sequence, by $u_t = b_{\theta(N_t)}(t)$. Basically all that the multiplexer does is pick one of the stages of SR2 at each time t, namely $b_{\theta(N_t)}$. But, for any t and any i, $b_i(t) = b_0(t + i) = b_{t+i}$ which means $u_t = b_{t + \theta(N_t)}$ for every t.

AN EXAMPLE   Figure 6.11 is an illustration of a multiplexed sequence with $m = 3$ and $n = 4$.

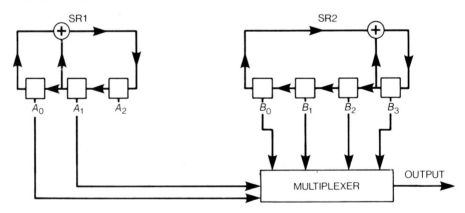

Figure 6.11
The diagram for our example

We will assume that the initial state of SR1 is 100 and that of SR2 is 1000. For this example we take $h = 2$, $x_1 = 0$, $x_2 = 1$ and let θ be the mapping $\{0, 1, 2, 3\} \to \{0, 1, 2, 3\}$ given by $\theta(0) = 2$, $\theta(1) = 3$, $\theta(2) = 0$, $\theta(3) = 1$.

The first seven states of each register are shown below

SR1			SR2			
1	0	0	1	0	0	0
0	0	1	0	0	0	1
0	1	0	0	0	1	1
1	0	1	0	1	1	1
0	1	1	1	1	1	1
1	1	1	1	1	1	0
1	1	0	1	1	0	1

From this we see that $N_0 = 2$, $N_1 = 0$, $N_2 = 1$, $N_3 = 2$, $N_4 = 1$, $N_5 = 3$ and $N_6 = 3$. Thus $\theta(N_0) = 0$, $\theta(N_1) = 2$, $\theta(N_2) = 3$, $\theta(N_3) = 0$, $\theta(N_4) = 3$, $\theta(N_5) = 1$, $\theta(N_6) = 1$ and, finally, $u_0 = b_0(0) = 1$, $u_1 = b_2(1) = 0$, $u_2 = b_3(2) = 1$, $u_3 = b_0(3) = 0$, $u_4 = b_3(4) = 1$, $u_5 = b_1(5) = 1$ and $u_6 = b_1(6) = 1$. Straightforward computation gives the first 120 terms of (u_t) as 1 0 1 0 1 1 1 1 0 1 0 0 0 0 0 0 1 0 1 1 1 1 1 1 1 0 1 0 0 0 0 0 1 1 1 1 0 0 0 1 1 1 1 1 0 1 1 0 1 1 1 1 1 1 0 1 1 0 0 0 0 0 0 0 1 0 1 0 1 0 0 0 1 0 0 0 0 0 1 1 1 1 0 1 1 1 0 1 0 1 0 0 1 1 1 0 1 0 0 1 0 1 1 0 1 1 0 1 0 1 1 1 1 0 1 0 0 0 0 0.

In any multiplexed sequence each entry depends on the previous states of both registers. So as soon as the two states repeat simultaneously the multiplexed sequence must begin to repeat itself. Thus we have:

LEMMA 6.4   The multiplexed sequence is periodic with period $p \le (2^m - 1)(2^n - 1)$.   □

Straightforward verification shows that our example has period at least 105. So, since $105 = (2^3 - 1) \cdot (2^4 - 1)$, its period must be 105 and so, for at least some m and n, Lemma 6.4 is the best possible. A great deal is known about the period of multiplexed sequences and, more importantly, about their linear equivalences. We will restrict our attention to the situation where the multiplexed sequence is longer than that which can be obtained from either register. For reasons which we will not even begin to explain this means we will assume $n \nmid m$.

Lemma 6.4 can obviously be improved to say that

$$p \le l.c.m(2^m - 1, 2^n - 1).$$

The following result, which we will not prove, shows precisely when p is as large as possible.

THEOREM 6.5   If $n \nmid m$ and

$$\left(2^m - 1, \frac{2^n - 1}{2^{(m,\, n)} - 1}\right) = 1$$

then the period of a multiplexed sequence is $l.c.m.(2^m - 1, 2^n - 1)$. So, in particular, if $(m, n) = 1$ the period is $(2^m - 1)(2^n - 1)$.

Theorem 6.5 is rather powerful. It implies that the period of a multi-plexed sequence does not depend on either the characteristic polynomial, the value of h or the choice of θ. If we write $p = 2^m - 1$ and $e = 2^n - 1$ then analysis of the statistics of a multiplexed sequence yields:

THEOREM 6.6   If $(m, n) = 1$ the mean value of the out-of-phase autocorrelation is

$$\frac{p - e}{e(pe - 1)} \simeq \frac{1}{e^2} - \frac{1}{pe}. \qquad \qquad \square$$

Since $\dfrac{1}{e^2} - \dfrac{1}{pe}$ is small this is encouraging but, of course, the mean itself gives no information about specific values of $C(a)$. It is desirable to have $C(a)$ close to zero for all a in the range $1 \leq a \leq pe - 1$. It is fairly straightforward to show that, if n is large in comparison with m,

$$C(a) \simeq \frac{-1}{2^n - 1}$$

for most values of a.

We are now in the situation where we can generate a sequence with a large period and with reasonable statistical properties. However we do not yet know if it is suitable for our purposes. To help us decide this we need to know its linear equivalence. (Again we stress that a large linear equiva-lence is necessary, but not sufficient, for a good sequence generator.) The following result is due to Jennings [31]. We state it without proof.

THEOREM 6.7   If $(m, n) = 1$ the linear equivalence d of a multiplexed sequence is related to the h stages selected from $SR1$ in the following way:
(a) $d = n(1 + m)$ if $h = 1$.

(b) $d = n\left(1 + m + \binom{m}{2}\right)$ if $h = 2 < m$.

(c) $d \leq n\left(1 + \sum\limits_{i=1}^{h} \binom{m}{i}\right)$ if $2 < h < m - 1$, with equality if the h stages are spaced at equal intervals.

(d) $d = n(2^m - 1)$ if $h = m - 1$ or m. $\square$

It should be noted that if the h stages are unevenly distributed then equality need not occur in (c). Although Theorem 6.7 does not tell us d for all possible situations, it does mean that, by suitable choices of m, n and h, we can use two linear shift registers to obtain a sequence which appears to have reasonable properties. Furthermore the linear equivalence varies exponentially with the parameter sizes. Nevertheless it must be remem-bered that although the linear equivalence may be large the system is not necessarily secure. A large linear equivalence is a necessary but not sufficient condition for a good sequence generator. For instance if some or all of the parameters m, n or h are not large enough the system may prove to be insecure. All we have shown is that conditions **A1**, **A2** and **A3** can be reasonably well satisfied. A lot more work would be necessary to decide whether such a system might indeed be suitable and if so what parameters should be used.

6.4.5 Some other possibilities

In this section we have considered four different non-linear systems. There are, of course, many others and many variations on the ones we have discussed. We can, for instance, replace the multiplexer of Section 6.4.4 by a device called a **Binary Rate Multiplier (BRM)**. Like the multiplexer a BRM has h inputs which define a number from 0 to $2^h - 1$. The BRM then supplies this number of clock pulses to another machine. The BRM might take its h inputs from the stages of a shift register, SR1, and deliver the extra clock pulses to a second register, SR2. In this example each shift register is 'clocked' in the normal way but, in order to obtain an output, SR2 is then 'clocked' an extra N times, where $0 \le N \le 2^h - 1$ and N is the integer determined by the h positions in SR1.

The possibilities, both for the actual electronic devices and for the methods of implementation, are almost endless. We can, of course, also build up much larger and more complicated systems by using a number of 'building blocks' of the type discussed in this chapter. However the temptation to use as many non-linear devices as possible to build a large, complex system must be resisted. Although we might design a hypothetical engineering masterpiece, if we make it too 'random' and cumbersome we will not be able to analyze it and, consequently, will have no idea of the level of security it offers. It is absolutely crucial that we have some idea of the level of security, and thus we must be careful that we do not complicate the system beyond our capability to analyze it. The safest method seems to be to begin with a small number of building blocks (like the examples discussed in this chapter) which we can analyze completely. Any of the small systems we have discussed in this chapter might be suitable. Even though they were not sufficiently secure in their own right, when used as a small 'cog' within a larger system they may have very desirable properties. Once we know their advantages and disadvantages, we then use them as 'sub-systems' to build up our complete system. In this way we should, hopefully, end up with a system which we understand. With practice, it is possible to achieve a complex system that will thwart the attempts of a determined cryptanalyst. Similarly anyone faced with the problem of analyzing a system which he has not designed, should try to break it into smaller sub-systems and analyze each component separately. This was the approach we used in Section 6.4.3.

The history of cryptography contains surprisingly many examples of extremely complex systems which have been shown to be insecure. Despite the fact that the solution of non-linear equations is an **NP-**

complete problem, the cryptographer should never be complacent. There is comfort to be drawn from the **NP**-completeness. Nevertheless we must always ensure that the particular instances of the problems set by our system are not solvable in a reasonably short time. Furthermore we must never forget that our own inability to find a short time algorithm for breaking a system does not necessarily mean that such an algorithm does not exist.

Further Reading

[30] is an excellent introduction to the theory of **NP**-completeness. [16] may serve as a useful introduction to non-linear feedbacks of shift registers. [31]-[38] are a cross-section of papers on the subject of non-linear sequences and their generation. In particular, [32] gives an algorithm for finding the linear equivalence of a given sequence and [36] is an interesting survey of the work that has been done on non-linear feedbacks.

[29]   Fraenkel, A. S. and Yesha, Y., *Complexity of problems in games, graphs and algebraic equations,* unpublished manuscript, 1977.

[30]   Garey, M. R. and Johnson, D. S., *Computers and Intractability: A guide to the Theory of NP-completeness,* W. H. Freeman & Co., 1979.

[16]   Golomb, S. W., *Shift Register Sequences,* Holden-Day, 1967.

[31]   Jennings, S. M., *A Special Class of Binary Sequences,* Ph.D Thesis, University of London, 1980.

[32]   Massey, J. L., 'Shift Register Synthesis and BCH Decoding', *IEEE Trans. on Inform. Theory,* Vol. IT–15, No. 1, 1969, 122–127.

[33]   Nyffeler, P., *Binaere Automaten und ihre Linearen Rekursionen,* Ph.D. Thesis, University of Bern, 1975.

[34]   Pless, V. S., 'Mathematical Foundations of Interconnected J-K Flip-Flops', *Inform. and Control,* 30, 1976, 128–42.

[35]   Pless, V. S., 'Encryption Schemes for Computer Confidentiality', *IEEE Trans. Comput,* Vol. C-26, 1977, 1133–6.

[36]   Ronse, C., 'Non-linear Shift Registers: A Survey', *MBLE Research Report R430,* 1980.

[37]   Rubin, F. 'Decrypting a Stream Cipher Based on J-K Flip-Flops', *IEEE Trans. on Comput,* Vol. C-28, No. 7, 1979, 483–87.

[38]   Zierler, N. and Mills, W. H., 'Products of Linear Recurring Sequences', *J. Algebra,* 27, 1973, 147–51.

7.
Some Block Cipher Systems

7.1 Introduction

In the last two chapters we have concentrated on the development of stream cipher systems. These ciphers are characterized by the property that the encipherment of each bit of data is independent of the rest of the message. This means that if an error occurs during the transmission of any single bit, the rest of the message will be unaffected. Thus errors are not propagated and, as we shall see in Chapters 8 and 9, in many situations this is a highly desirable property. There are, however, occasions when we might need to reject an entire message if it contains even one bit in error. In such a situation, error propagation will certainly not bother us and, since it may make it more likely that the processor will notice the error, might even be an advantage. For instance, one single error may cause a number of other bits to be in error, formatting information etc. may be lost and the processor will readily realize that errors have occurred. One example of a case when a single error may be completely unacceptable is a computer network where information is entered on a remote terminal, enciphered for transmission to the main processor, deciphered at the processor and then stored in a file. In this situation it is quite likely that the information will not be examined for a long time, and it is conceivable that the original source of the information will have disappeared before then. Thus any errors in the data have to be deleted and corrected before filing. However if a stream cipher is used and only one error occurs, it is quite likely that the receiver will not detect it. This illustrates that there are certainly uses for cipher systems which do propagate errors. Such a system will be characterized by the fact that the encipherment of a bit of data depends not only on the key but also on some of the other bits of data. These systems are usually broken down into two classes: block cipher systems and cipher feedback systems. We have already introduced block ciphers in Chapter 4 and, as we saw, they use a fixed number of bits of plaintext plus all, or part of, the key to encipher each block of plaintext. A cipher feedback system, on the other hand, uses a fixed number of bits of ciphertext plus all, or part of, the key for enciphering each individual bit. Figure 7.1 illustrates a

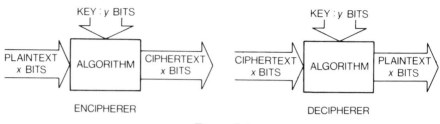

Figure 7.1
A block cipher system

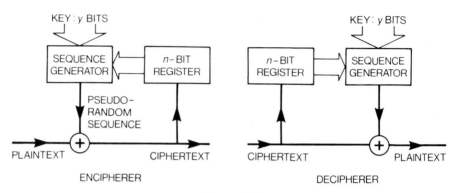

Figure 7.2
A cipher feedback system

typical block cipher system which uses an algorithm to 'mix' x bits of plaintext with y bits of key to produce a block of x bits of ciphertext. Thus the plaintext is broken down into equal blocks of x bits. The plaintext is then fed, block by block, into the cipher algorithm and each block yields x bits of ciphertext.

Figure 7.2 illustrates an example of a cipher feedback system which is based on the type of sequence generator used in our earlier stream cipher systems. In this example the last n bits of ciphertext are continually affecting the sequence generator and, consequently, the resulting cipher. Although we will not exhibit one until later, cipher feedback systems can also be based on block cipher type algorithms.

There are various advantages and disadvantages to each of these systems. One advantage of a block cipher is that it can also be used as a sequence generator or even as a cipher feedback system. Although we are not yet in a position to appreciate it, we mention that a great advantage of the cipher feedback system is that it can be self-synchronizing. We will discuss synchronization in this and the next two chapters. For the moment we merely note that synchronization is an important, and often expensive, part of any system.

In the next section we introduce some examples of cipher feedback systems. We then introduce block ciphers and examine, in detail, one particular block cipher algorithm made public by the U.S. National Bureau of Standards.

7.2 Some Examples of Cipher Feedback Systems

Cipher feedback systems can take many forms and, in particular, may be based on either block ciphers or stream ciphers. However, as we have already stressed, their essential property is that the ciphertext is actually fed back into the system and influences subsequent enciphering. As an illustration of an extremely simple cipher feedback system we will modify slightly the Vigenère cipher system of Chapter 1.

EXAMPLE 7.1   In Section 1.3.1 we used a Vigenère cipher with key word 'radio' to encipher the message **codebreaking**. The result was:

Keyword: r a d i o r a d i o r a
Plaintext: **c o d e b r e a k i n g**
Ciphertext: **T O G M P I E D S W E G**

To obtain a cipher feedback system we merely allow the ciphertext to determine the shift immediately the entire keyword has been utilized. Thus, for this particular example, we have

Key: r a d i o T O G M P K S
Plaintext: **c o d e b r e a k i n g**
Ciphertext: **T O G M P K S G W X X Y**

If, as in earlier chapters, we represent **a** by 1, **b** by 2, etc., (so that $z = 0$), and if the key, ciphertext and message characters are denoted by κ_i, μ_i and λ_i respectively then we have $\mu_i \equiv \kappa_i + \lambda_i - 1 \pmod{26}$. But, if the keyword has length h then, in this modified system, we also have $\kappa_{h+i} = \mu_i$ for all $i \geq 1$. Clearly such a system is rather ineffective since, as soon as we know h, we can decipher all but the first h letters. One advantage however is that the ciphertext no longer exhibits the type of periodicity which enabled us to break it by using the Kasiski and index of coincidence tests.

EXAMPLE 7.2   A slightly more effective system is obtained by using a combination of ciphertext plus keyword to determine the key (after the keyword has 'run out'). For instance if the characters of the keyword are $\kappa_1 \kappa_2 \ldots \kappa_h$ then we have: $\mu_i \equiv \kappa_i + \lambda_i - 1 \pmod{26}$ for $1 \leq i \leq h$ and $\mu_i \equiv \kappa_j + \mu_{i-h} + \lambda_i - 1 \pmod{26}$ for all $i > h$ where $j \equiv i \pmod{h}$ and $1 \leq j \leq h$. If we use this further modification we obtain:

Key: r a d i o r+T a+O d+G i+M o+P r+C a+T
Plaintext: **c o d e b r   e   a   k   i   n   g**
Ciphertext: **T O G M P C   T   K   F   M   H   A**

This method has many advantages over the basic Vigenère cipher and Example 7.1. As it stands it is also not vulnerable to the Kasiski or index of coincidence tests. We do not wish to spend time discussing the cryptanalysis of this example, but instead we will proceed to a rather more sophisticated one. Nevertheless the reader should try the following exercise.

EXERCISE 7.1   Suppose a cipher feedback system like Example 7.2 is in use with a keyword of length h. On the assumption that a reasonable length of ciphertext is known, discuss possible methods of cryptanalysis when:
  (*i*)   *We have h consecutive characters of plaintext corresponding to h characters of ciphertext;*
  (*ii*)   *We have about $\dfrac{h}{2}$ consecutive characters of plaintext corresponding to the same number of ciphertext characters;*
  (*iii*) *We have no known plaintext.*

EXERCISE 7.2   Try to find possible methods for the cryptanalysis of Example 7.2 when the keyword length is not known.

EXAMPLE 7.3   Figure 7.3 illustrates a cipher feedback system using a linear shift register.

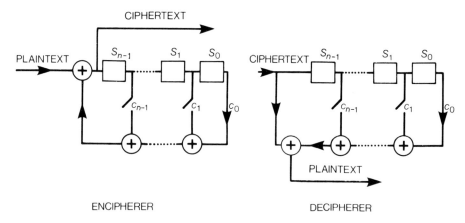

Figure 7.3
A cipher feedback system using a linear shift register

We will suppose that we have such a system; that, for $i = 0, 1, \ldots, n-1$, the initial content of stage S_i is s_i and that our key determines the feedback constants in some way. (Note that, as always, $c_0 = 1$.) If we let our plaintext be $m_0 m_1 m_2 \ldots$ and the ciphertext be $e_0 e_1 e_2 \ldots$ then we can see how the system works. Initially, when m_0 is 'fed in', the output e_0 will simply be

$$m_0 + \sum_{i=0}^{n-1} c_i s_i.$$

But now s_0 is no longer in the register and e_0 is in S_{n-1}. Thus, when m_1 is the input, we get

$$e_1 = m_1 + \sum_{i=0}^{n-2} c_i s_{i+1} + c_{n-1} e_0.$$

Note that the earlier ciphertext is already influencing the encipherment and that the summation of $c_i s_{i+1}$ ranges only from 0 to $n-2$. At each of the first n outputs, one of the initial stage entries disappears from the register. So after n outputs each e_j depends only on m_j and the n previous ciphertext characters. The precise equations are:

$$e_0 = m_0 + \sum_{i=0}^{n-1} c_i s_i$$

$$e_1 = m_1 + \sum_{i=0}^{n-2} c_i s_{i+1} + c_{n-1} e_0$$

$$e_j = m_j + \sum_{i=0}^{n-j-1} c_i s_{i+j} + \sum_{i=n-j}^{n-1} c_i e_{i-(n-j)} \text{ for each } j \text{ with } 1 < j < n-1$$

$$e_{n-1} = m_{n-1} + c_0 s_{n-1} + \sum_{i=1}^{n-1} c_i e_{i-1}$$

$$e_n = m_n + \sum_{i=0}^{n-1} c_i e_i$$

$$e_{n+1} = m_{n+1} + \sum_{i=0}^{n-1} c_i e_{i+1}$$

$$e_{n+h} = m_{n+h} + \sum_{i=0}^{n-1} c_i e_{i+h} \text{ for each } h > 1.$$

We can do a similar calculation for the deciphering.

We will denote the initial state of the receiver's register by $s_0^*, s_1^*, \ldots, s_{n-1}^*$. Naturally we assume that the receiver has the correct key and the same feedback constants as the encipherer. The receiver's input will be $e_0 e_1 e_2 \ldots$ and we denote his output by $m_0^* m_1^* m_2^* \ldots$. Clearly at each of the first n inputs, one of the initial entries disappears from the register and plays no further role in the decipherment. Thus, apart from the first n bits, each m_i^* depends only on the input sequence and the feedback constants.

EXERCISE 7.3   *Show that* $m^*_{n+h} = e_{n+h} + \sum_{i=0}^{n-1} c_i e_{i+h} = m_{n+h}$ *for all* $h \geq 0$.

Thus we see that, after at most n bits, the plaintext is reproduced, i.e. the system works! The first n bits of the deciphered message depend on the initial states of both registers. We could, of course, include the initial contents of each register as part of the key and, in this way, all the plaintext would be recovered. However these particular bits are irrelevant after the first n time pulses and so to include them in the key would be a poor utilization of key material. It is usually better to accept that the first n bits transmitted are always lost and simply not start the message until the $(n+1)^{st}$ bit.

EXERCISE 7.4   *Explain why it would not be wise to clear the encipherer's register to the zero state before transmission.*

In Exercise 7.4 we rule out the possibility of always starting with the encipherer's register set with all 0s. In fact it is inadvisable to start with the same sequence of 0s and 1s for each encipherment (no matter which one is chosen). The reason for this will be explained in Chapter 8 when we define message keys and discuss their purpose. When that chapter has been read it will be clear that the initial contents of the register can act as an automatic message key. For the moment we merely observe that, if we were to use the same initial state repeatedly, this would convey information for a cryptanalyst to utilize. It is definitely better to have a random state at the start of each encipherment.

When using a stream cipher, if a bit is lost or gained (as opposed to being altered) during transmission the two sequence generators at the transmitting and receiving ends may drop out of step. This would result in the decipherer using the wrong sequence element from that step onwards, and the rest of the cryptogram would probably be deciphered incorrectly. If, however, a cipher feedback is used then, provided that the recipient receives the next n bits without any problems, the two registers will be back in step and all but at most $n+1$ bits will be received correctly. This is an illustration of what we mean by saying that a cipher feedback system is self-synchronizing and shows one big advantage of the system. Unfortunately, as always, there is a price to be paid for this advantage. In this instance it is, as we have already mentioned, the error propagation which inevitably accompanies all cipher feedback systems.

EXERCISE 7.5   *For Example 7.3 discuss the relation between the number of feedback taps used (i.e. the number of non-zero feedback constants) and the propagation of a single error incurred in the transmission path.*

In Chapters 5 and 6 we tried to develop the habit of considering three important properties of our sequence generators: periodicity, randomness and non-linearity. In Chapter 5 we also saw that if the input to a finite state machine is ultimately periodic then so is the output. In a cipher feedback system the input is the plaintext and, since there is no reason why plaintext should be ultimately periodic, there is no reason why our ciphertext should be. Normally with cipher feedback systems the period of the sequence generator is considered to be the period obtained from an all zero input. Note that in Example 7.3 an all zero plaintext input means that the ciphertext corresponds to the linear shift register sequence of Chapter 5 (with of course the corresponding initial state). For particular applications we may be interested in the response of our system to certain other specific inputs. For instance, as we shall see in Chapter 9, for digital voice systems we will often be interested in the period of the sequence produced by an input of 01010101 ....

Similar remarks to the above apply to the randomness properties of the ciphertext of a cipher feedback system.

EXERCISE 7.6 Consider the period and randomness of the sequence obtained by an all 1 plaintext input to Example 7.3.

As in earlier chapters the question of non-linearity poses the hardest problem. For this particular example, however, the situation is very similar to that in Chapter 5. Although the system of Example 7.3 is linear, we can generalize it to introduce non-linearity in ways similar to those discussed in Chapter 6. To ensure our self-synchronization capability (which may in fact be the only reason for using a cipher feedback system), we must simply make certain that all registers have ciphertext as their input. The 'delay' before plaintext produced by the receiver will then correspond to the number of clocks necessary for the first bit of ciphertext to reach the end of the largest register whose infill is not part of the key.

EXERCISE 7.7 Devise a non-linear system with cipher feedback by modifying one of the systems in Section 6.4.

We shall return to cipher feedback systems in Section 7.4. Meanwhile we introduce block ciphers.

7.3 Block Cipher Systems

7.3.1 Introduction

Since, as the list of further reading at the end of the chapter indicates, the researchers at IBM have been responsible for most of the recent published work on block ciphers, we will spend a large part of this section considering systems which they have designed. However we begin by looking at a few simple examples. Much of what follows is very similar to the material in Chapter 1; the difference being that the characters of Chapter 1 are now replaced by blocks of bits. As we have seen, two ways of achieving this are by using either one of the codes ITA2 or ITA5 in Appendix 2 (page 401).

Let **m** denote a block of bits of plaintext, **k** the key for encipherment and **c** the corresponding block of ciphertext. Then there is an enciphering function f_k, depending on the particular key **k** chosen, such that $c = f_k(m)$.

Furthermore, since we have a cipher system, **m** is uniquely recoverable from **c** which means there is a deciphering function f_k^{-1} such that $m = f_k^{-1}(c)$. Suppose that our plaintext blocks have size s and that the ciphertext blocks have size t. Since one essential property of our cipher system is that distinct messages must encipher to different ciphertexts, the size of a ciphertext block must be at least as large as the size of a plaintext block i.e. $t \geq s$. It is certainly possible to have $t > s$, but this leads to message extension which, as we saw in Section 4.3, is normally considered undesirable. So, unless clearly stated otherwise, we will assume $s = t$. (Note, in fact, that we even built this assumption into our definition of a block cipher in Section 4.2.)

In a block cipher each block of message is replaced by another block. Thus a block cipher is nothing more than a simple substitution cipher. However, in general, this substitution cipher is considerably more complex than those we met in Chapter 1. (In fact the discussion in Chapter 1 is merely the special case when each block is identified with a character. So, for instance, if we use ITA2 we have $s = 5$.) Because of this similarity with Chapter 1 we will often omit proofs and merely set exercises.

When the block size is s there are 2^s possibilities for a block. Thus we may think of our substitution cipher as a uniquely reversible transformation from the 2^s possible input messages to the 2^s possibilities for the output. Clearly we may represent each of these sets of possible blocks by the integers 0 to $2^s - 1$. This means we may regard our transformations as having the same message and cryptogram spaces; i.e. as being endomorphic. Any uniquely reversible transformation from any set into itself is called a **permutation** and it should be clear that the key for our cipher merely selects one of the permutations on $\{0, 1, \ldots, 2^s - 1\}$. One such possibility with $s = 3$ is shown in Figure 7.4. In this example suppose, for instance, that the input is 100. Then, since 100 corresponds to 4 and 4 is mapped to 7, the output is 111.

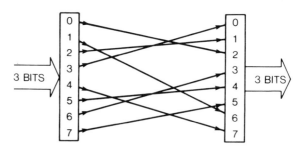

Figure 7.4
One of the possible permutations when $s = 3$

Since there are 2^s possible message blocks a repetition of the argument used in Chapter 1 shows there are $(2^s)!$ possible permutations. Obviously it would be nice to have a key which enabled us to use any one of them but, as we shall see, there will normally only be a comparatively small number available to us.

Before we attempt to analyze block cipher systems we need a way to describe them mathematically. One such way is to regard our system as a look-up table (or truth table), similar to those discussed in Chapter 6. If we try this for our example in Figure 7.4, we obtain Table 7.1 where each output is a 3-bit sequence. But we can get nearer to the situation of Chapter 6 by constructing three separate tables; one for each output position. These are shown in Table 7.2 where it is assumed that $\mathbf{c} = c_1 c_2 c_3$.

$$\mathbf{m} = m_1 m_2 m_3 \qquad \mathbf{c} = c_1 c_2 c_3$$

m_1	m_2	m_3	$\mathbf{c}$
0	0	0	010
0	0	1	110
0	1	0	001
0	1	1	000
1	0	0	111
1	0	1	100
1	1	0	011
1	1	1	101

Table 7.1

m_1	m_2	m_3	c_1
0	0	0	0
0	0	1	1
0	1	0	0
0	1	1	0
1	0	0	1
1	0	1	1
1	1	0	0
1	1	1	1

m_1	m_2	m_3	c_2
0	0	0	1
0	0	1	1
0	1	0	0
0	1	1	0
1	0	0	1
1	0	1	0
1	1	0	1
1	1	1	0

m_1	m_2	m_3	c_3
0	0	0	0
0	0	1	0
0	1	0	1
0	1	1	0
1	0	0	1
1	0	1	0
1	1	0	1
1	1	1	1

Table 7.2
The truth tables corresponding to Figure 7.4

EXERCISE 7.8   Show that:
  (i) $c_1 = m_1 + m_3 + m_1 m_2 + m_2 m_3 + m_1 m_3$
  (ii) $c_2 = 1 + m_2 + m_1 m_2 + m_1 m_3$
  (iii) $c_3 = m_1 + m_2 + m_1 m_2 + m_2 m_3 + m_1 m_3$.

In general these truth tables enable us to write each output as a function of the bits in the corresponding input block.

There are two fundamental problems with all simple substitution ciphers. Firstly they are vulnerable to statistical attacks involving the analysis of cipher blocks. (Such attacks are similar to those carried out on the message characters in our monoalphabetic examples of Chapter 1.) Secondly an interceptor is often able to compile a directory of corresponding plaintext/ciphertext blocks. The size of such a directory obviously depends on the number of possibilities for the plaintext block and, consequently, on the block size. Both these methods of attack can be thwarted by making the value of s sufficiently large. With this in mind Meyer [54] suggests that the minimum block size used should be equivalent to four characters. This means that if, for instance, an 8-bit character code is used s should be at least 32. But if $s = 32$ then, when we attempt to draw the diagram equivalent to Figure 7.4, our transformation would require 2^{32} links. This is a daunting possibility. Such a system would also require a key space capable of producing any of the $(2^{32})!$ permutations. Clearly this is out of the question and a system with $s = 32$ is impracticable unless a severe restriction is placed on the available permutations. The number $(2^{32})!$ is so large that we obviously cannot 'handle' it. But even for much smaller values of s, $(2^s)!$ may still be too large. The following exercise illustrates how quickly the size of the key space grows with s if all possible permutations are to be allowed.

EXERCISE 7.9   *Show that even with $s = 6$ we require a 296-bit key to be able to attain all possible permutations.*

One nice way to restrict our permutations is to use only those which are defined by certain simple, mathematical functions. When we do this, it means that any given key determines a mathematical function which, in turn, gives an appropriate permutation. We begin by choosing those functions which are, essentially, the 'block analogues' of the mono-alphabetic ciphers encountered in Chapter 1.

For our first example we merely let each key $\mathbf{k}_i$ determine a unique binary s-tuple $\mathbf{t}_i$, and then define our simple substitution by $\mathbf{c} = \mathbf{m} + \mathbf{t}_i$ and call it **translation by $\mathbf{t}_i$**. The simplest way to do this is to identify $\mathbf{k}_i$ with $\mathbf{t}_i$; i.e. to take each key as having s bits. Such a system is often called a **translation cipher system** and is the block analogue of the additive cipher system in Chapter 1. As an illustration let us take $s = 3$ and consider translation by 010. If we regard this as a permutation of $0, 1, \ldots, 7$ then the image of 4 is $100 + 010 = 110$ i.e. 6.

EXERCISE 7.10   *Draw a diagram like Figure 7.4 to illustrate translation by 010.*

Clearly when $s = 3$ the translation cipher system has only 8 keys out of the total of $8! = 40320$ possibilities.

EXERCISE 7.11   Compare the translation cipher system with the additive cipher system of Chapter 1. Discuss how, given a reasonable amount of ciphertext, statistical methods might be employed to attack a translation cipher system.

EXERCISE 7.12   If it is known that a translation cipher was used, show that knowledge of one block of plaintext and corresponding ciphertext is sufficient to decipher the entire cryptogram.

Since, in a translation cipher, a constant s-tuple t is added to each message block m, each output bit depends only on the corresponding bit of plaintext. Thus no real use is made of the fact that it is a block cipher. One system which overcomes this defect is a **linear cipher system**. In this case each key k_i determines a non-singular s by s matrix A_i and the encipherment rule is $c = A_i m$.

EXERCISE 7.13   If $s = 3$ and the particular key chosen gives rise to

$$A = \begin{pmatrix} 1 & 0 & 0 \\ 1 & 1 & 0 \\ 0 & 1 & 1 \end{pmatrix},$$

show that this corresponds to the substitution cipher:

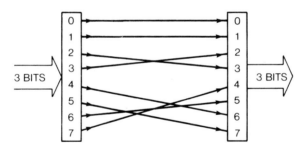

EXERCISE 7.14   Compare the linear block cipher with the multiplicative cipher of Chapter 1. Explain why the matrix A_i has to be non-singular and show that a plaintext block of all 0s is left unchanged after encipherment.

In Chapter 1 we were able to combine the additive and multiplicative ciphers to get affine ciphers. Now, in a similar way, we can combine translation block ciphers and linear block ciphers to get affine block ciphers. Thus an **affine block cipher** is one where the key specifies a non-singular s by s matrix A and an s-tuple t to define the **affine transformation** $c = Am + t$ where, as always, m is a block of plaintext and c is the corresponding ciphertext. (Note that when A is the identity matrix we have a translation block cipher, while $t = 0$ gives a linear block cipher.)

Since $\mathbf{A}$ is non singular, $\mathbf{A}^{-1}$ exists and decipherment is given by

$$\mathbf{m} = \mathbf{A}^{-1}(\mathbf{c} + \mathbf{t}).$$

If we are going to use these affine transformations then we must determine the size of our key space; i.e. the number of affine block transformations. We will count this number when $s = 3$ and leave the general case as an exercise. This restriction to $s = 3$ enables us to avoid vector space terminology. However for $s > 3$ it is necessary to use the concept of linear independence. Even if the reader does not wish to attempt the exercise, its result is important and should be noted.

When $s = 3$ then, since any 3-tuple will do, there are $8 \, (= 2^3)$ choices for $\mathbf{t}$. We must now determine the number of non-singular 3 by 3 matrices at our disposal. We first note that a singular 3 by 3 matrix over $GF(2)$ has either:

    (i)   a column of 0s,
    (ii) two identical columns, or
    (iii) one of its columns equal to the sum of the other two.

We will determine the number of possible $\mathbf{A}$ by counting the number of ways in which we can choose its columns. Since $\mathbf{A}$ is non-singular it cannot have a column of 0s. But any other 3-tuple can be the first column and thus we have seven choices for the first column of $\mathbf{A}$. If we choose a 3-tuple $\mathbf{a}_1$ for the first column then our second column can be any non-zero 3-tuple except $\mathbf{a}_1$ itself. Thus, after choosing the first column, we have six choices for the second. If we choose $\mathbf{a}_2$ for the second column then our final column can be any 3-tuple except $\mathbf{0}, \mathbf{a}_1, \mathbf{a}_2, \mathbf{a}_1 + \mathbf{a}_2$. This means that any one of the remaining four 3-tuples may be chosen as our final column and the total number of possibilities for $\mathbf{A}$ is $7 \times 6 \times 4 = 168$. Combining each of these matrices with every one of the eight choices for $\mathbf{t}$ gives a total of $8 \times 168 = 1344$ affine block ciphers.

EXERCISE 7.15   *If the block size is s show that there are* $2^s(2^s - 1)$ $(2^s - 2)(2^s - 2^2)\ldots(2^s - 2^{s-1})$ *affine transformations.*

EXERCISE 7.16   *If* $f(\mathbf{m}) = \mathbf{Am} + \mathbf{t}$ *show that*
    (i) $f(\mathbf{m}_1 + \mathbf{m}_2) = f(\mathbf{m}_1) + f(\mathbf{m}_2) + \mathbf{t}$,
    (ii) $f(\mathbf{m}_1 + \mathbf{m}_2 + \mathbf{m}_3) = f(\mathbf{m}_1) + f(\mathbf{m}_2) + f(\mathbf{m}_3)$, *and*
    (iii) $f\left(\sum_{i=1}^{n} \mathbf{m}_i\right) = \sum_{i=1}^{n} f(\mathbf{m}_i) + \mathbf{t}\delta_n$
where $\delta_n = 0$ *if n is odd and* 1 *if n is even.*

When we discussed affine ciphers in Chapter 1 we saw that knowledge of just two bits of plaintext/ciphertext equivalent was sufficient to determine the entire linear transformation. Affine block ciphers have a similar defect.

Suppose that we know that an affine block cipher system with block size s is being used. Suppose also that $\mathbf{m}_1, \mathbf{m}_2, \ldots, \mathbf{m}_u$ are any u blocks for which we know the corresponding ciphertext $\mathbf{c}_1, \mathbf{c}_2, \ldots, \mathbf{c}_u$. Then, by Exercise 7.16

(iii), we know the ciphertext of any block which is the sum of an odd number of the $\mathbf{m}_i s$. In order to know the ciphertext of any block which is the sum of an even number of the $\mathbf{m}_i s$ we need to know $\mathbf{t}$. But, again by Exercise 7.16 (iii), knowledge of the ciphertext equivalent of any single block·which is the sum of an even number of the $\mathbf{m}_i s$ will give us $\mathbf{t}$. Thus knowledge of the ciphertext equivalents of a small number of message blocks is likely to give the cryptanalyst knowledge of a lot more. This makes affine block cipher systems particularly weak whenever there is a possibility that corresponding plaintext and ciphertext are known. The following exercise is an illustration of this weakness.

EXERCISE 7.17 Suppose we know that an affine cipher block system with $s = 3$ is being used and that, in the notation of Figure 7.4, $1 \rightarrow 3, 3 \rightarrow 0, 4 \rightarrow 1$ and $7 \rightarrow 5$. Find $\mathbf{A}$ and $\mathbf{t}$, thereby determining the rest of the transformation.

An obvious question to ask is how large u must be before the cryptanalyst can be certain of deducing the ciphertext equivalent of every message i.e. of finding $\mathbf{A}$ and $\mathbf{t}$. The answer depends on the particular messages $\mathbf{m}_1, \mathbf{m}_2, \ldots, \mathbf{m}_u$, but the smallest possibility for u is s. (Any reader who has studied vector spaces will realize that this happens when $\mathbf{m}_1, \ldots, \mathbf{m}_s$ are linearly independent and form a basis for the vector space of all possible messages of size s.)

Before leaving affine block ciphers we note that superencipherment using two affine transformations results in another affine transformation.

EXERCISE 7.18 Show that if $\mathbf{f}(\mathbf{m}) = \mathbf{A}_1 \mathbf{m} + \mathbf{c}_1$ and $\mathbf{g}(\mathbf{m}) = \mathbf{A}_2 \mathbf{m} + \mathbf{c}_2$ then $\mathbf{f}(\mathbf{g}(\mathbf{m})) = \mathbf{A}_1 \mathbf{A}_2 \mathbf{m} + \mathbf{A}_1 \mathbf{c}_2 + \mathbf{c}_1$.

Mathematically, affine block ciphers are very 'neat' in the sense that they are easy to describe and have many interesting properties. However, as we have seen many times before, a neat mathematical description of a system often makes it easy to break. Our earlier exercises have shown that affine block cipher systems are no exception and, once again, we need to make our system more complex so that, in order to break it, a cryptanalyst

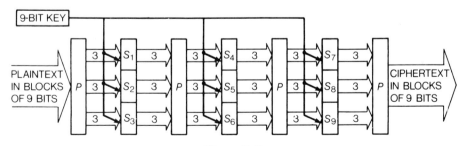

Figure 7.5
A diagram for Example 7.4

will have to solve non-linear equations. As a step in this direction we now consider an example which involves repeated superencipherment. We begin our discussion of this type of system by looking at a specific small example which is shown in Figure 7.5.

EXAMPLE 7.4   In this diagram each of the boxes S_1, S_2, ..., S_9 is a substitution cipher of the type shown in Figure 7.4. The boxes labelled P are permutations of the nine positions. For this particular example we will assume that each P is the same permutation although, of course, in general this need not be the case. We will assume that if the input bits are i_0, i_1, ..., i_8 then the output bits are i_0, i_3, i_6, i_1, i_4, i_7, i_2, i_5, i_8 (see Figure 7.6).

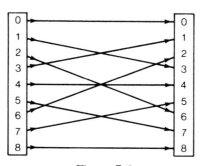

Figure 7.6
The permutation in the boxes labelled P in Figure 7.5

In this example our key has nine bits which we denote by k_1, k_2, ..., k_9. Each k_i determines a transformation S_i in the following way: if $k_i = 0$ then, for any block **x** of three input bits,

$$S_i(\mathbf{x}) = \begin{pmatrix} 110 \\ 011 \\ 100 \end{pmatrix} \mathbf{x} + \begin{pmatrix} 1 \\ 1 \\ 1 \end{pmatrix} \text{ and if } k_i \neq 0, S_i(\mathbf{x}) = \begin{pmatrix} 011 \\ 101 \\ 100 \end{pmatrix} \mathbf{x} + \begin{pmatrix} 0 \\ 1 \\ 1 \end{pmatrix}.$$

Thus in this particular example we have chosen to let each of the nine transformations be affine. In general we need not be restricted in this way. Our example is now completely defined. We wiil not include a description of a general system of this type. (Basically we can change the number of bits in each block, the size of each S_i and the length of the system. We can also vary it by using different permutations P at different stages and also allow ourselves more choice for the transformations S_i.) We now set a few exercises to familiarize the reader with this system.

EXERCISE 7.19   *If the key is* 110100001 *show that the output is* 100111111 *when* 101110001 *is fed into Example 7.4.*

EXERCISE 7.20   *Draw a diagram, similar to Figure 7.5, for the decipherment process of this system. Determine the appropriate permutations and transformations for decipherment. Check that this procedure works by deciphering the cryptogram of Exercise 7.19.*

EXERCISE 7.21   If our example has key $k_1, k_2, \ldots, k_9$ and if $q_1 q_2 \ldots q_9$ is the output corresponding to an input of $00\ldots0$ show:

$q_1 = (k_1 + k_2 + k_4 + k_1 k_4 + k_3 k_4 + k_5 + 1)(k_7 + 1) + (k_5 + k_6)k_7$

$q_2 = (1 + k_2 + k_3 + k_2 k_4 + k_1 k_4)(k_8 + 1)$

$q_3 = 1 + k_1 + k_9 + k_1 k_9$

$q_4 = (k_5 + k_6 + 1)(k_7 + 1) + (k_1 + k_2 + k_4 + k_1 k_4 + k_3 k_4 + k_6 + 1)k_7$

$q_5 = 1 + k_8(k_2 + k_3 + k_2 k_4 + k_1 k_4)$

$q_6 = 1 + k_1 k_9$

$q_7 = k_1 + k_2 + k_4 + k_1 k_4 + k_3 k_4$

$q_8 = k_2 + k_3 + k_2 k_4 + k_1 k_4$

$q_9 = 1 + k_1.$

(Hint: remember that a decision of the type 'use $f(x)$ or $g(x)$ depending on whether $h(x) = 0$ or 1 respectively' can be represented by $(h(x) + 1)f(x) + h(x)g(x)$.)

EXERCISE 7.22   If it is known that the ciphertext block output corresponding to an all zero input is 100111001, use Exercise 7.21 to show that the key must take one of the following four possibilities:

000000011

000010111

010100011

010110111.

From solving these exercises it should be clear that, in general, the complexity of the equations can be increased by introducing extra sets of transformations and permutations. It should also be clear that the equations were kept reasonably simple by us restricting ourselves to affine transformations. In fact, because of this restriction, the only non-linearity in Example 7.4 came from the key bits used to determine the transformations and not from the transformations themselves. If the transformation boxes themselves had contributed some non-linearity, our final equations would probably have been much more complex. Of course we must not forget that our equations in Exercise 7.21 relate to an all-zero input. A different input will give different equations. The following exercise is very long but worthwhile.

EXERCISE 7.23   Find a set of equations, similar to those in Exercise 7.21, for a general data input $d_1 d_2 \ldots d_9$. (Remember that putting $d_i = 0$ for all i in your solution should give the equations of Exercise 7.23.)

For the more general system of this type we have seen that the complexity is increased by each transformation stage. Thus in a realistic system we would like to have rather more stages. We would also, of course, need a much larger block size. But this all means that to build a realistic system of this type requires a great deal of hardware. The hardware can be kept to a minimum by using the permutation stage and transformation stage a number of times. To do this we simply feed the output from our transformation stage back into the permutation box and proceed to iterate as many times as we choose.

EXERCISE 7.24 *If the input is* 110101100 *find the output after 2 iterations in the system of Figures 7.7 and 7.8 where*

$$S_1(\mathbf{x}) = \mathbf{x} + \begin{pmatrix} 1 \\ 0 \\ 1 \end{pmatrix}, \; S_2(\mathbf{x}) = \begin{pmatrix} 1 & 0 & 0 \\ 1 & 1 & 0 \\ 1 & 1 & 1 \end{pmatrix} \mathbf{x} + \begin{pmatrix} 0 \\ 0 \\ 1 \end{pmatrix}, \; S_3(\mathbf{x}) = \begin{pmatrix} 1 & 0 & 1 \\ 0 & 1 & 1 \\ 1 & 0 & 0 \end{pmatrix} \mathbf{x}.$$

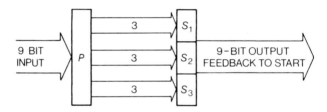

Figure 7.7
The diagram for Exercise 7.26

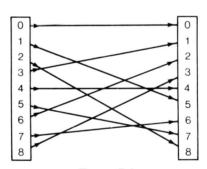

Figure 7.8
The permutation for Figure 7.7

Adoption of this iterative technique certainly eases the hardware problem. Our only practical constraint now is that of time; i.e. the amount of time available until the next block of data arrives.

It may appear that if we continue to iterate in the above manner then our output equations will continue to increase in complexity. This is not necessarily so. The reason is that we have to use a finite key. This means that during a very large number of iterations some bits of the key will almost certainly be used a number of times. This, in turn, implies that if we iterate indefinitely our equations may well settle into a recurring pattern (which might of course be very long) or there may be stages at which the equations simplify considerably.

Another point to notice is that, as we have seen in previous exercises, the equations we obtain are functions of both the input data and the key. Thus it may be possible to choose particular input data for which the equations simplify. From the cryptographer's point of view this is highly undesirable and should be avoided. Even if our system appears to be clear of such problems it is still possible that a known plaintext attack, where the plaintext is actually chosen by the cryptanalyst, may be very successful. One such system is the NDS (**New Data Seal**) which we will discuss shortly. First, however, we must describe the Feistel Cipher.

7.3.2 The Feistel Cipher

In a **Feistel Cipher** the block size has to be even. If we have block size $2n$ then each message block $\mathbf{m}$ is divided into two halves and written

$$\mathbf{m} = (\mathbf{m}_0, \mathbf{m}_1).$$

Each key $\mathbf{k}$ defines a set of 'subkeys' $\mathbf{k}_1, \mathbf{k}_2, \ldots, \mathbf{k}_h$ for some fixed integer h, and each subkey $\mathbf{k}_i$ determines a transformation $\mathbf{f}_{\mathbf{k}_i}$ on the set of blocks of length n into itself. Any message $\mathbf{m}$ is enciphered in h 'rounds' using the following rule:

At round 1: $\boldsymbol{\mu}_0 = (\mathbf{m}_0, \mathbf{m}_1) \rightarrow \boldsymbol{\mu}_1 = (\mathbf{m}_1, \mathbf{m}_2),$

$\quad \vdots \qquad\qquad\qquad\qquad \vdots$

At round i: $\boldsymbol{\mu}_{i-1} = (\mathbf{m}_{i-1}, \mathbf{m}_i) \rightarrow \boldsymbol{\mu}_i = (\mathbf{m}_i, \mathbf{m}_{i+1})$

$\quad \vdots \qquad\qquad\qquad\qquad \vdots$

At round h: $\boldsymbol{\mu}_{h-1} = (\mathbf{m}_{h-1}, \mathbf{m}_h) \rightarrow \boldsymbol{\mu}_h = (\mathbf{m}_h, \mathbf{m}_{h+1})$

where $\mathbf{m}_{i+1} = \mathbf{m}_{i-1} + \mathbf{f}_{\mathbf{k}_i}(\mathbf{m}_i)$ for each i. The ciphertext is then the $2n$ bit block $\mathbf{m}_h \mathbf{m}_{h+1}$.

To decipher we note that, since all addition is modulo 2, the equation $\mathbf{m}_{i+1} = \mathbf{m}_{i-1} + \mathbf{f}_{\mathbf{k}_i}(\mathbf{m}_i)$ can also be written as $\mathbf{m}_{i-1} = \mathbf{m}_{i+1} + \mathbf{f}_{\mathbf{k}_i}(\mathbf{m}_i)$. Thus if we reverse the two halves of the ciphertext block and apply the encipherment procedure, but using the subkeys, and hence the $\mathbf{f}_{\mathbf{k}_i}$s, in reverse order, we have:

$\bar{\boldsymbol{\mu}}_h = (\mathbf{m}_{h+1}, \mathbf{m}_h) \rightarrow \bar{\boldsymbol{\mu}}_{h-1} = (\mathbf{m}_h, \mathbf{m}_{h-1})$ at round 1

$\quad \vdots$

$\bar{\boldsymbol{\mu}}_i = (\mathbf{m}_{i+1}, \mathbf{m}_i) \rightarrow \bar{\boldsymbol{\mu}}_{i-1} = (\mathbf{m}_i, \mathbf{m}_{i-1})$ at round $h+1-i$

$\quad \vdots$

$\bar{\boldsymbol{\mu}}_1 = (\mathbf{m}_2, \mathbf{m}_1) \rightarrow \bar{\boldsymbol{\mu}}_0 = (\mathbf{m}_1, \mathbf{m}_0)$ at round h.

Thus we can decipher provided that we can reproduce each of the $\mathbf{f}_{\mathbf{k}_i}$ at the appropriate moment. It is important to note that we do not require that the functions have any special properties. In particular they do not need to be reversible. The basic principle behind the Feistel cipher is not only fundamental to the NDS system but is also the basis of the **Data Encryption Standard** (DES). It is clearly important and the reader should convince himself that he understands the system. The following simple exercise may help.

EXERCISE 7.25   Take $n = 1$ and $h = 3$. Assume a key k has been chosen so that f_{k_1} maps $0 \to 0$ and $1 \to 1$, f_{k_2} maps $0 \to 0$ and $1 \to 0$ while f_{k_3} maps $0 \to 1$ and $1 \to 0$. Show that the message $(1, 0)$ is enciphered as $(0, 0)$ which is then deciphered correctly.

7.3.3   The NDS system

The NDS system, which was analyzed by Grossman and Tuckerman [50], uses a Feistel cipher. Thus, in order to describe it, we must state the values of n and h and define all the $\mathbf{f}_{k_j}$. For our discussion we will take $n = 64$ and $h = 16$. (Note this means that our blocks have size 128.) The key for an NDS system is an arbitrary transformation from the set of all 256 possible 8-bit blocks into itself. We denote this transformation by S_k.

The system also contains two fixed transformations S_0 and S_1 which map the set of all 16 possible 4-bit blocks into themselves. These transformations are chosen to be non-affine.

For the ith encipherment, i.e. the ith round, the 64 bits of $\mathbf{m}_i$ are divided into eight 8-bit blocks. If $\mathbf{m}_i^*$ represents the block consisting of the first bit of each of these 8-bit blocks then $\mathbf{m}_i^*$ is input to S_k. Each of the eight 8-bit blocks of $\mathbf{m}_i$ is then divided into two 4-bit blocks. The first of these is transformed by S_0 and the second by S_1. After these transformations the left and right halves of each of the resulting 8-bit blocks are interchanged, or not, depending on the bit in the appropriate position of the 8-bit vector $S_k(\mathbf{m}_i^*)$. To make our illustration precise we will say that if the jth bit of $S_k(\mathbf{m}_i^*)$ is 1 then the two halves of the jth block will be interchanged. Otherwise no change takes place. Finally the resulting 64-bits are permuted amongst themselves; where once again this permutation is fixed. As with our earlier examples, the purpose of this permutation is merely to prevent the system from consisting of eight independent smaller systems. This permutation is taken as $(u, v) \to (v, u)$ where the first parameter determines which of the eight blocks the bit comes from and the second parameter identifies its position in that block. See Figure 7.9.

Although we have previously mentioned the possibility of a planted plaintext attack we have not yet made specific use of one. In this discussion we will actually assume that the cryptanalyst is able to choose some plaintext for which he would particularly like to know the ciphertext. He might be able to obtain this knowledge, for instance, by having brief access to the enciphering equipment.

In the NDS system the encipherment key being used is independent of the round. If we write $\mathbf{f}$ for $\mathbf{f}_{k_j}$ then a single round of the encipherment can be described by the transformation

$$\mathbf{T}(\mathbf{m}_{i-1}, \mathbf{m}_i) = (\mathbf{m}_i, \mathbf{m}_{i-1} + \mathbf{f}(\mathbf{m}_i)).$$

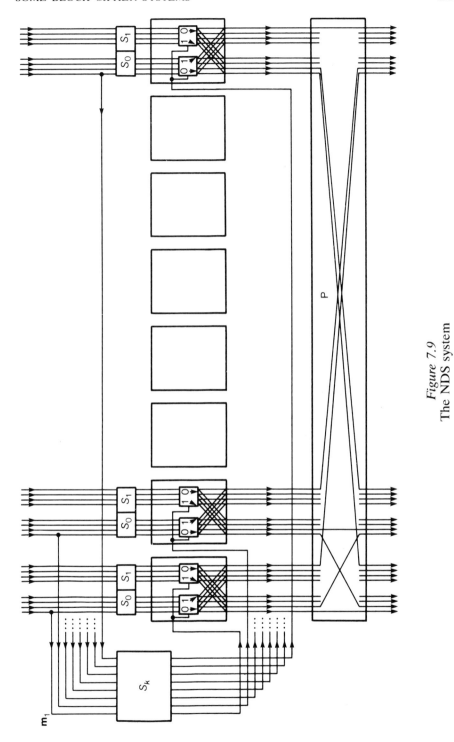

Figure 7.9
The NDS system

Then if $\mathbf{F}$ denotes the enciphering function we have $\mathbf{F} = \mathbf{T}^h$. But this implies that, for any $\boldsymbol{\mu}$, $\mathbf{F}(\mathbf{T}(\boldsymbol{\mu})) = \mathbf{T}(\mathbf{F}(\boldsymbol{\mu}))$. (To prove this we merely note

$$\mathbf{F}(\mathbf{T}(\boldsymbol{\mu})) = \mathbf{T}^h(\mathbf{T}(\boldsymbol{\mu})) = \mathbf{T}^{h+1}(\boldsymbol{\mu}) = \mathbf{T}(\mathbf{T}^h(\boldsymbol{\mu})) = \mathbf{T}(\mathbf{F}(\boldsymbol{\mu}))$$

for all $\boldsymbol{\mu}$.)

Now suppose that we have a known plaintext block $\boldsymbol{\mu}$ and that we encipher it to obtain $\boldsymbol{\varepsilon} = \mathbf{F}(\boldsymbol{\mu})$. Suppose we make a guess for $\mathbf{T}(\boldsymbol{\mu})$ which we denote by $\mathbf{T}^*(\boldsymbol{\mu})$. If our guess happens to be correct, i.e. if

$$\mathbf{T}^*(\boldsymbol{\mu}) = \mathbf{T}(\boldsymbol{\mu}), \text{ then } \mathbf{F}(\mathbf{T}^*(\boldsymbol{\mu})) = \mathbf{F}(\mathbf{T}(\boldsymbol{\mu})) = \mathbf{T}(\mathbf{F}(\boldsymbol{\mu})) = \mathbf{T}(\boldsymbol{\varepsilon}).$$

In other words enciphering a correct guess for $\mathbf{T}(\boldsymbol{\mu})$ is the same as a one-round encipherment of the ciphertext $\boldsymbol{\varepsilon}$. But this means that the left half of our enciphered guess should equal the right half of the enciphered plaintext. What are the chances of this happening? The machine under discussion is sufficiently complex that we can assume that, for various guesses $\mathbf{T}^*(\boldsymbol{\mu})$, the bits $\mathbf{F}(\mathbf{T}^*(\boldsymbol{\mu}))$ are randomly distributed amongst the 2^{128} possible 128-bits, and thus there is a probability of 2^{-64} of coincidence between its left half and the right half of $\boldsymbol{\varepsilon}$. So, whenever we are fortunate enough to have a 'match', we can be virtually certain that our guess is correct.

But whenever $\boldsymbol{\mu}$ is known, i.e. whenever we have a known block of plaintext, then under our worst case conditions, the only part of $\mathbf{T}(\boldsymbol{\mu})$ which is unknown is whether or not the interchange of halves has taken place. This interchange depends on $S_k(\mathbf{m}_1^*)$, which is unknown. However since $\mathbf{m}_1$ is known we certainly know $\mathbf{m}_1^*$. Our objective then is to determine S_k. Regarding each 8-bit block as the binary representation of an integer from 0 to 255 we can then think of S_k as an 8 by 256 array of 0s and 1s with the property that if $\mathbf{i}$ is the binary representation of i, the ith column is $S_k(\mathbf{i})$. There are now a number of ways in which we can proceed to determine S_k. We begin by giving an obvious, but not particularly efficient, method and will then refine it to more subtle methods.

Suppose we pick an integer q, from 0 to 255. We can then choose a message $\boldsymbol{\mu} = (\mathbf{m}_0, \mathbf{m}_1)$ such that $\mathbf{m}_1^* = \mathbf{q}$. Using our basic elimination test described above, we then systematically try each possible guess of $S_k(\mathbf{q})$. Each guess for $S_k(\mathbf{q})$ is equivalent to a guess for $\mathbf{T}(\boldsymbol{\mu})$ and after at most 256 trials we will know $S_k(\mathbf{q})$. In other words if we know 256 corresponding pairs of chosen plaintext and ciphertext then we can determine $S_k(\mathbf{q})$ for any appropriate q. Often considerably fewer than 256 pairs will be sufficient.

It is worth noting that a little care must be taken when choosing $\boldsymbol{\mu}$ to ensure that only the correct guess passes our test. All that we need to do is to make sure that each of the 8-bit blocks within $\boldsymbol{\mu}$ have two unequal halves. If we fail to do this there will be some ambiguity over whether or not the halves have been interchanged. Our aim is to achieve a situation where, for any block $(\boldsymbol{\lambda}, \boldsymbol{\rho})$, $S_0(\boldsymbol{\lambda}) \neq S_1(\boldsymbol{\rho})$. Unless S_0 and S_1 have properties which will make the system useless, we can certainly choose our blocks to ensure this. Provided this care is taken then, if we have freedom to choose the plaintext for which we require the ciphertext, we need at most $256 \times 256 = 65536$ such pairs to deduce the whole of S_k.

Having described the obvious methods we now look for ways to 'speed it up'. Suppose that, for any given $\mathbf{q}$, we choose our $\mathbf{m}_1$ so that $S_0(\boldsymbol{\lambda}) = S_1(\boldsymbol{\rho})$ on each of its blocks except one, the jth block say, and then ensure that $S_0(\boldsymbol{\lambda}) \neq S_1(\boldsymbol{\rho})$ for the jth block. This means that we almost know $\mathbf{T}(\boldsymbol{\mu})$. Our only doubt is whether or not interchanging occurs in the jth block. When we guess this we have a fifty-fifty chance of being right. So we make a guess, which amounts to guessing the jth bit of $S_k(\mathbf{q})$, and this gives us $\mathbf{T}^*(\boldsymbol{\mu})$. One encipherment should then be enough to decide whether or not we guessed correctly. If we guessed correctly then all is well. If not then we must merely complement the jth bit of $S_k(\mathbf{q})$. To determine $S_k(\mathbf{q})$ for the whole of $\mathbf{q}$ we only have to repeat the process for all 8 possible values of j. Thus, since for each bit we will have required encipherments for $\boldsymbol{\mu}$ and $\mathbf{T}^*(\boldsymbol{\mu})$, we need only 16 encipherments to determine $S_k(\mathbf{q})$ for any $\mathbf{q}$. Using this improvement we can determine S_k in $256 \times 16 = 4096$ encipherments.

We can make still further improvements by determining the entries of S_k in a less systematic manner. (In other words if we allow ourselves not to concentrate on any particular column.) We will not discuss this but set two exercises which are intended to give an indication of how this can be achieved.

EXERCISE 7.26   Show that if S_0 and S_1 have at least one 4-bit block common to both their output truth tables then we can choose a message $\boldsymbol{\mu}$ such that $\mathbf{T}(\boldsymbol{\mu})$ is known.

EXERCISE 7.27   Suppose we have a $\boldsymbol{\mu}$ for which $\mathbf{T}(\boldsymbol{\mu})$ is known. Then with one encipherment, we can obtain $\mathbf{F}(\boldsymbol{\mu}) = (\mathbf{m}_h, \mathbf{m}_{h+1}) = (\mathbf{c}_0, \mathbf{c}_1)$. If $S_k(\mathbf{c}_1^*)$ is not completely known discuss how one more chosen encipherment will yield every bit of $S_k(\mathbf{c}_1^*)$ for which the corresponding block of $\mathbf{c}_1$ has $S_0(\boldsymbol{\lambda}) \neq S_1(\boldsymbol{\rho})$.

A number of further refinements on the above method can be found in [50]. The same paper contains the results of an experiment in which the best method tried yielded S_k in 556 trial encipherments.

7.3.4   Data Encryption Standard (DES)

The fundamental trouble with the NDS system is that the key used is independent of the round. The next system uses a Feistel Cipher but with a key which is used in a way which depends on the round. This system is the National Bureau of Standards (NBS) Data Encryption Standard (DES). The reader should now be in a position that he can read and understand the Federal Publication that describes the Standard. The following few pages are taken from this Federal Publication, reprinted with the permission of the U.S. Department of Commerce, National Technical Information Service.

We cannot overstress the importance of this publication. Apart from its practical usage it is one of the very few published realistic algorithms. It is therefore important that the reader should acquaint himself with DES and we strongly recommend that he reads the entire article. Of course (as always!) it may be necessary to skip some of the details during the first reading. We will discuss some of the strengths and weaknesses of DES following its description.

**Federal Information
Processing Standards Publication 46**

1977 January 15

ANNOUNCING THE

DATA ENCRYPTION STANDARD

Federal Information Processing Standards are issued by the National Bureau of Standards pursuant to the Federal Property and Administrative Services Act of 1949, as amended, Public Law 89-306 (79 Stat 1127), Executive Order 11717 (38 FR 12315, dated May 11, 1973), and Part 6 of Title 15 Code of Federal Regulations (CFR).

Name of Standard: Data Encryption Standard (DES).

Category of Standard: Operations, Computer Security.

Explanation: The Data Encryption Standard (DES) specifies an algorithm to be implemented in electronic hardware devices and used for the cryptographic protection of computer data. This publication provides a complete description of a mathematical algorithm for encrypting (enciphering) and decrypting (deciphering) binary coded information. Encrypting data converts it to an unintelligible form called cipher. Decrypting cipher converts the data back to its original form. The algorithm described in this standard specifies both enciphering and deciphering operations which are based on a binary number called a key. The key consists of 64 binary digits ('0's or '1's) of which 56 bits are used directly by the algorithm and 8 bits are used for error detection.

Binary coded data may be cryptographically protected using the DES algorithm in conjunction with a key. The key is generated in such a way that each of the 56 bits used directly by the algorithm are random and the 8 error detecting bits are set to make the parity of each 8-bit byte of the key odd, i.e., there is an odd number of '1's in each 8-bit byte. Each member of a group of authorized users of encrypted computer data must have the key that was used to encipher the data in order to use it. This key, held by each member in common, is used to decipher the data received in cipher form from other members of the group. The encryption algorithm specified in this standard is commonly known among those using the standard. The unique key chosen for use in a particular application makes the results of encrypting data using the algorithm unique. Selection of a different key causes the cipher that is produced for any given set of inputs to be different. The cryptographic security of the data depends on the security provided for the key used to encipher and decipher the data.

Data can be recovered from cipher only by using exactly the same key used to encipher it. Unauthorized recipients of the cipher who know the algorithm but do not have the correct key cannot derive the original data algorithmically. However, anyone who does have the key and the algorithm can easily decipher the cipher and obtain the original data. A standard algorithm based on a secure key thus provides a basis for exchanging encrypted computer data by issuing the key used to encipher it to those authorized to have the data. Additional FIPS guidelines for implementing and using the DES are being developed and will be published by NBS.

Approving Authority: Secretary of Commerce.

Maintenance Agency: Institute for Computer Sciences and Technology, National Bureau of Standards.

Applicability: This standard will be used by Federal departments and agencies for the cryptographic protection of computer data when the following conditions apply:
   1. An authorized official or manager responsible for data security or the security of any computer system decides that cryptographic protection is required; and
   2. The data is not classified according to the National Security Act of 1947, as amended, or the Atomic Energy Act of 1954, as amended.

However, Federal agencies or departments which use cryptographic devices for protecting data classified according to either of these acts can use those devices for protecting unclassified data in lieu of the standard.

In addition, this standard may be adopted and used by non-Federal Government organizations. Such use is encouraged when it provides the desired security for commercial and private organizations.

Data that is considered sensitive by the responsible authority, data that has a high value, or data that represents a high value should be cryptographically protected if it is vulnerable to unauthorized disclosure or undetected modification during transmission or while in storage. A risk analysis should be performed under the direction of a responsible authority to determine potential threats. FIPS PUB 31 (Guidelines for Automatic Data Processing Physical Security and Risk Management) and FIPS PUB 41 (Computer Security Guidelines for Implementing the Privacy Act of 1974) provide guidance for making such an analysis. The costs of providing cryptographic protection using this standard as well as alternative methods of providing this protection and their respective costs should be projected. A responsible authority then should make a decision, based on these analyses, whether or not to use cryptographic protection and this standard.

Applications: Data encryption (cryptography) may be utilized in various applications and in various environments. The specific utilization of encryption and the implementation of the DES will be based on many factors particular to the computer system and its associated components. In general, cryptography is used to protect data while it is being communicated between two points or while it is stored in a medium vulnerable to physical theft. Communication security provides protection to data by enciphering it at the transmitting point and deciphering it at the receiving point. File security provides protection to data by enciphering it when it is recorded on a storage medium and deciphering it when it is read back from the storage medium. In the first case, the key must be available at the transmitter and receiver simultaneously during communication. In the second case, the key must be maintained and accessible for the duration of the storage period.

Hardware Implementation: The algorithm specified in this standard is to be implemented in computer or related data communication devices using hardware (not software) technology. The specific implementation may depend on several factors such as the application, the environment, the technology used, etc. Implementations which comply with this standard include Large Scale Integration (LSI) 'chips' in individual electronic packages, devices built from Medium Scale Integration (MSI) electronic components, or other electronic devices dedicated to performing the operations of the algorithm. Micro-processors using Read Only Memory (ROM) or micro-programmed devices using microcode for hardware level control instructions are examples of the latter. Hardware implementations of the algorithm which are tested and validated by NBS will be considered as complying with the standard. Procedures for testing and validating equipment for conformance with this standard are available from the Systems and Software Division, National Bureau of Standards, Washington, D.C. 20234. Software implementations in general purpose computers are not in compliance with this standard. Information regarding devices which have been tested and validated will be made available to all FIPS points of contact.

Export Control: Cryptographic devices and technical data regarding them are subject to Federal Government export controls as specified in Title 22, Code of Federal Regulations, Parts 121 through 128. Cryptographic devices implementing this standard and technical data regarding them must comply with these Federal regulations.

Patents: Cryptographic devices implementing this standard may be covered by U.S. and foreign patents issued to the International Business Machines Corporation. However, IBM has granted nonexclusive, royalty-free licenses under the patents to make, use and sell apparatus which complies with the standard. The terms, conditions and scope of the licenses are set out in notices published in the May 13, 1975 and August 31, 1976 issues of the Official Gazette of the United States Patent and Trademark Office (934 O. G. 452 and 949 O. G. 1717).

Alternative Modes of Using the DES: The 'Guidelines for Implementing and Using the Data Encryption Standard' describe two different modes for using the algorithm described in this standard. Blocks of data containing 64 bits may be directly entered into the device where 64-bit cipher blocks are generated under control of the key. This is called the electronic code book mode. Alternatively, the device may be used as a binary stream generator to produce statistically random binary bits which are then combined with the clear (unencrypted) data (1-64 bits) using an 'exclusive-or' logic operation. In order to assure that the enciphering device and the deciphering device are synchronized, their inputs are always set to the previous 64 bits of cipher that were transmitted or received. This second mode of using the encryption algorithm is called the cipher feedback (CFB) mode. The electronic codebook mode generates blocks of 64 cipher bits. The cipher feedback mode generates cipher having the same number of bits as the plain text. Each block of cipher is independent of all others when the electronic codebook mode is used while each byte (group of bits) of cipher depends on the previous 64 cipher bits when the cipher feedback mode is used. The modes of operation briefly described here are further explained in the FIPS 'Guidelines for Implementing and Using the Data Encryption Standard.'

Implementation of this standard: This standard becomes effective six months after the publication date of this FIPS PUB. It applies to all Federal ADP systems and associated telecommunications networks under development as well as to installed systems when it is determined that cryptographic protection is required. Each Federal department or agency will issue internal directives for the use of this standard by their operating units based on their data security requirement determinations.

NBS will provide assistance to Federal organizations by developing and issuing additional technical guidelines on computer security and by providing technical assistance in using data encryption. A data encryption testbed has been established within NBS for use in providing this technical assistance. The National Security Agency assists Federal departments and agencies in communications security and in determining specific security requirements. Instructions and regulations for procuring data processing equipment utilizing this standard will be provided by the General Services Administration.

Specifications: Federal Information Processing Standard (FIPS 46) Data Encryption Standard (DES) (affixed).

Cross Index:
 a. FIPS PUB 31, 'Guidelines to ADP Physical Security and Risk Management'
 b. FIPS PUB 39, 'Glossary for Computer Systems Security'
 c. FIPS PUB 41, 'Computer Security Guidelines for implementing the Privacy Act of 1974'
 d. FIPS PUB—, 'Guidelines for Implementing and Using the Data Encryption Standard' (to be published)
 e. Other FIPS and Federal Standards are applicable to the implementation and use of this standard. In particular, the American Standard Code for Information Interchange (FIPS PUB 1) and other related data storage media or data communications standards should be used in conjunction with this standard. A list of currently approved FIPS may be obtained from the Office of ADP Standards Management, Institute for Computer Sciences and Technology, National Bureau of Standards, Washington, D.C. 20234.

Qualifications: The cryptographic algorithm specified in this standard transforms a 64-bit binary value into a unique 64-bit binary value based on a 56-bit variable. If the complete 64-bit input is used (i.e., none of the input bits should be predetermined from block to block) and if the 56-bit variable is randomly chosen, no technique other than trying all possible keys using known input and output for the DES will guarantee finding the chosen key. As there are over 70,000,000,000,000,000 (seventy quadrillion) possible keys of 56 bits, the feasibility of deriving a particular key in this way is extremely unlikely in typical threat environments. Moreover, if the key is changed frequently, the risk of this event is greatly diminished. However, users should be aware that it is theoretically possible to derive the key in fewer trials (with a correspondingly lower probability of success depending on the number of keys tried) and should be cautioned to change the key as often as practical. Users must change the key and provide it a high level of protection in order to minimize the potential risks of its unauthorized computation or acquisition. The feasibility of computing the correct key may change with advances in technology. A more complete description of the strength of this algorithm against various threats will be contained in the Guidelines for Implementing and Using the DES.

When correctly implemented and properly used, this standard will provide a high level of cryptographic protection to computer data. NBS, supported by the technical assistance of Government agencies responsible for communication security, has determined that the algorithm specified in this standard will provide a high level of protection for a time period beyond the normal life cycle of its associated ADP equipment. The protection provided by this algorithm against potential new threats will be reviewed within five years to assess its adequacy. In addition, both the standard and possible threats reducing the security provided through the use of this standard will undergo continual review by NBS and other cognizant Federal organizations. The new technology available at that time will be evaluated to determine its impact on the standard. In addition, the awareness of any breakthrough in technology or any mathematical weakness of the algorithm will cause NBS to re-evaluate this standard and provide necessary revisions.

Comments: Comments and suggestions regarding this standard and its use are welcomed and should be addressed to the Associate Director for ADP Standards, Institute for Computer Sciences and Technology, National Bureau of Standards, Washington, D.C. 20234.

Waiver Procedure: The head of a Federal agency may waive the provisions of this FIPS PUB after the conditions and justifications for the waiver have been coordinated with the National Bureau of Standards. A waiver is necessary if cryptographic devices performing an algorithm other than that which is specified in this standard are to be used by a Federal agency for data subject to cryptographic protection under this standard. No waiver is necessary if classified communications security equipment is to be used. Software implementations of this algorithm for operational use in general purpose computer systems do not comply with this standard and each such implementation must also receive a waiver. Implementation of the algorithm in software for testing or evaluation does not require waiver approval. Implementation of other special purpose cryptographic algorithms in software for limited use within a computer system (e.g. encrypting password files) or implementations of cryptographic algorithms in software which were being utilized in computer systems before the effective date of this standard do not require a waiver. However, these limited uses should be converted to the use of this standard when the system or equipment involved is upgraded or redesigned to include general cryptographic protection of computer data. Letters describing the nature of and reasons for the waiver should be addressed to the Associate Director for ADP Standards as previously noted.

Sixty days should be allowed for review and response by NBS. The waiver shall not be approved until a response from NBS is received; however, the final decision for granting the waiver is the responsibility of the head of the particular agency involved.

Where to Obtain Copies of the Standard:

Copies of this publication are for sale by the National Technical Information Service, U.S. Department of Commerce, 5285 Port Royal Road, Springfield, Virginia 22161. Order by FIPS PUB number and title. Prices are published by NTIS in current catalogs and other issuances. Payment may be made by check, money order, deposit account or charged to a credit card accepted by NTIS.

**Federal Information
Processing Standards Publication 46**

1977 January 15

SPECIFICATIONS FOR THE

DATA ENCRYPTION STANDARD

The Data Encryption Standard (DES) shall consist of the following Data Encryption Algorithm to be implemented in special purpose electronic devices. These devices shall be designed in such a way that they may be used in a computer system or network to provide cryptographic protection to binary coded data. The method of implementation will depend on the application and environment. The devices shall be implemented in such a way that they may be tested and validated as accurately performing the transformations specified in the following algorithm.

DATA ENCRYPTION ALGORITHM

Introduction

The algorithm is designed to encipher and decipher blocks of data consisting of 64 bits under control of a 64-bit key. Deciphering must be accomplished by using the same key as for enciphering, but with the schedule of addressing the key bits altered so that the deciphering process is the reverse of the enciphering process. A block to be enciphered is subjected to an initial permutation IP, then to a complex key-dependent computation and finally to a permutation which is the inverse of the initial permutation IP^{-1}. The key-dependent computation can be simply defined in terms of a function f, called the cipher function, and a function KS, called the key schedule. A description of the computation is given first, along with details as to how the algorithm is used for encipherment. Next, the use of the algorithm for decipherment is described. Finally, a definition of the cipher function f is given in terms of primitive functions which are called the selection functions S_i and the permutation function P. S_i, P and KS of the algorithm are contained in the Appendix.

The following notation is convenient: Given two blocks L and R of bits, LR denotes the block consisting of the bits of L followed by the bits of R. Since concatenation is associative $B_1 B_2 \ldots B_8$, for example, denotes the block consisting of the bits of B_1 followed by the bits of $B_2 \ldots$ followed by the bits of B_8.

Enciphering

A sketch of the enciphering computation is given in figure 1.

The 64 bits of the input block to be enciphered are first subjected to the following permutation, called the initial permutation IP:

$$IP$$

58	50	42	34	26	18	10	2
60	52	44	36	28	20	12	4
62	54	46	38	30	22	14	6
64	56	48	40	32	24	16	8
57	49	41	33	25	17	9	1
59	51	43	35	27	19	11	3
61	53	45	37	29	21	13	5
63	55	47	39	31	23	15	7

That is the permuted input has bit 58 of the input as its first bit, bit 50 as its second bit, and so on with bit 7 as its last bit. The permuted input block is then the input to a complex key-dependent computation described below. The output of that computation, called the preoutput, is then subjected to the following permutation which is the inverse of the initial permutation:

$$IP^{-1}$$

40	8	48	16	56	24	64	32
39	7	47	15	55	23	63	31
38	6	46	14	54	22	62	30
37	5	45	13	53	21	61	29
36	4	44	12	52	20	60	28
35	3	43	11	51	19	59	27
34	2	42	10	50	18	58	26
33	1	41	9	49	17	57	25

That is, the output of the algorithm has bit 40 of the preoutput block as its first bit, bit 8 as its second bit, and so on, until bit 25 of the preoutput block is the last bit of the output.

The computation which uses the permuted input block as its input to produce the preoutput block consists, but for a final interchange of blocks, of 16 iterations of a calculation that is described below in terms of the cipher function f which operates on two blocks, one of 32 bits and one of 48 bits, and produces a block of 32 bits.

Let the 64 bits of the input block to an iteration consist of a 32-bit block L followed by a 32-bit block R. Using the notation defined in the introduction, the input block is then LR.

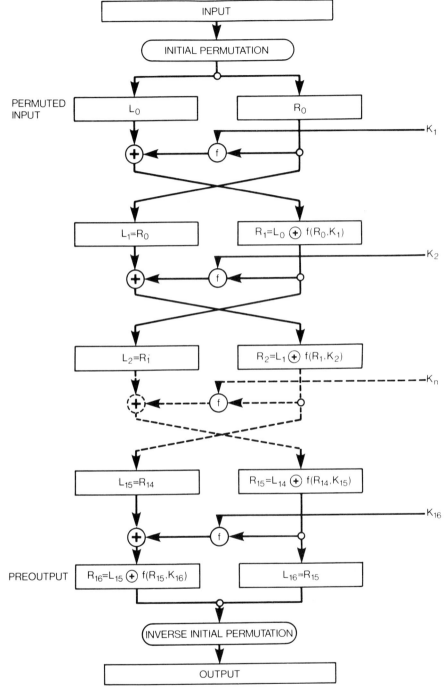

Figure 1   Enciphering computation

Let K be a block of 48 bits chosen from the 64-bit key. Then the output $L'R'$ of an iteration with input LR is defined by:

(1)
$$L' = R$$
$$R' = L \oplus f(R, K)$$

where $\oplus$ denotes bit-by-bit addition modulo 2.

As remarked before, the input of the first iteration of the calculation is the permuted input block. If $L'R'$ is the output of the 16th iteration then $R'L'$ is the preoutput block. At each iteration a different block K of key bits is chosen from the 64-bit key designated by KEY.

With more notation we can describe the iterations of the computation in more detail. Let KS be a function which takes an integer n in the range from 1 to 16 and a 64-bit block KEY as input and yields as output a 48-bit block K_n which is a permuted selection of bits from KEY. That is

(2)
$$K_n = KS(n, KEY)$$

with K_n determined by the bits in 48 distinct bit positions of KEY. KS is called the key schedule because the block K used in the n'th iteration of (1) is the block K_n determined by (2).

As before, let the permuted input block be LR. Finally, let L_0 and R_0 be respectively L and R and let L_n and R_n be respectively L' and R' of (1) when L and R are respectively L_{n-1} and R_{n-1} and K is K_n; that is, when n is in the range from 1 to 16,

(3)
$$L_n = R_{n-1}$$
$$R_n = L_{n-1} \oplus f(R_{n-1}, K_n)$$

The preoutput block is then $R_{16}L_{16}$.

The key schedule KS of the algorithm is described in detail in the Appendix. The key schedule produces the 16 K_n which are required for the algorithm.

Deciphering

The permutation IP^{-1} applied to the preoutput block is the inverse of the initial permutation IP applied to the input. Further, from (1) it follows that:

(4)
$$R = L'$$
$$L = R' \oplus f(L', K)$$

Consequently, to *decipher* it is only necessary to apply the *very same algorithm to an enciphered message block*, taking care that at each iteration of the computation *the same block of key bits K is used* during decipherment as was used during the encipherment of the block. Using the notation of the previous section, this can be expressed by the equations:

(5)
$$R_{n-1} = L_n$$
$$L_{n-1} = R_n \oplus f(L_n, K_n)$$

where now $R_{16}L_{16}$ is the permuted input block for the deciphering calculation and L_0R_0 is the preoutput block. That is, for the decipherment calculation with $R_{16}L_{16}$ as the permuted input, K_{16} is used in the first iteration, K_{15} in the second, and so on, with K_1 used in the 16th iteration.

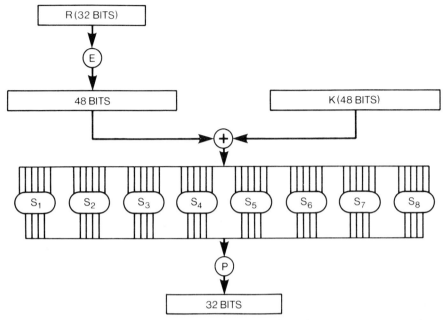

Figure 2   Calculation of $f(R, K)$

The Cipher Function f

A sketch of the calculation of $f(R, K)$ is given in figure 2.

Let E denote a function which takes a block of 32 bits as input and yields a block of 48 bits as output. Let E be such that the 48 bits of its output, written as 8 blocks of 6 bits each, are obtained by selecting the bits in its inputs in order according to the following table:

E BIT-SELECTION TABLE

32	1	2	3	4	5
4	5	6	7	8	9
8	9	10	11	12	13
12	13	14	15	16	17
16	17	18	19	20	21
20	21	22	23	24	25
24	25	26	27	28	29
28	29	30	31	32	1

Thus the first three bits of $E(R)$ are the bits in positions 32, 1 and 2 of R while the last 2 bits of $E(R)$ are the bits in positions 32 and 1.

Each of the unique selection functions $S_1, S_2, \ldots, S_8$, takes a 6-bit block as input and yields a 4-bit block as output and is illustrated by using a table containing the recommended S_1:

$$S_1$$

Column Number

Row No.	0	1	2	3	4	5	6	7	8	9	10	11	12	13	14	15
0	14	4	13	1	2	15	11	8	3	10	6	12	5	9	0	7
1	0	15	7	4	14	2	13	1	10	6	12	11	9	5	3	8
2	4	1	14	8	13	6	2	11	15	12	9	7	3	10	5	0
3	15	12	8	2	4	9	1	7	5	11	3	14	10	0	6	13

If S_1 is the function defined in this table and B is a block of 6 bits, then $S_1(B)$ is determined as follows: The first and last bits of B represent in base 2 a number in the range 0 to 3. Let that number be i. The middle 4 bits of B represent in base 2 a number in the range 0 to 15. Let that number be j. Look up in the table the number in the i'th row and j'th column. It is a number in the range 0 to 15 and is uniquely represented by a 4 bit block. That block is the output $S_1(B)$ of S_1 for the input B. For example, for input 011011 the row is 01, that is row 1, and the column is determined by 1101, that is column 13. In row 1 column 13 appears 5 so that the output is 0101. Selection functions $S_1, S_2, \ldots, S_8$ of the algorithm appear in the Appendix.

The permutation function P yields a 32-bit output from a 32-bit input by permuting the bits of the input block. Such a function is defined by the following table:

$$P$$

16	7	20	21
29	12	28	17
1	15	23	26
5	18	31	10
2	8	24	14
32	27	3	9
19	13	30	6
22	11	4	25

The output $P(L)$ for the function P defined by this table is obtained from the input L by taking the 16th bit of L as the first bit of $P(L)$, the 7th bit as the second bit of $P(L)$, and so on until the 25th bit of L is taken as the 32nd bit of $P(L)$. The permutation function P of the algorithm is repeated in the Appendix.

Now let $S_1, \ldots, S_8$ be eight distinct selection functions, let P be the permutation function and let E be the function defined above.

To define $f(R, K)$ we first define $B_1, \ldots, B_8$ to be blocks of 6 bits each for which

$$(6) \qquad\qquad B_1 B_2 \ldots B_8 = K \oplus E(R)$$

The block $f(R, K)$ is then defined to be

$$(7) \qquad\qquad P(S_1(B_1) S_2(B_2) \ldots S_8(B_8))$$

Thus $K \oplus E(R)$ is first divided into the 8 blocks as indicated in (6). Then each B_i is taken as an input to S_i and the 8 blocks $S_1(B_1), S_2(B_2), \ldots, S_8(B_8)$ of 4 bits each are consolidated into a single block of 32 bits which forms the input to P. The output (7) is then the output of the function f for the inputs R and K.

APPENDIX

PRIMITIVE FUNCTIONS FOR THE DATA ENCRYPTION ALGORITHM

The choice of the primitive functions $KS, S_1, \ldots, S_8$ and P is critical to the strength of an encipherment resulting from the algorithm. Specified below is the recommended set of functions, describing $S_1, \ldots, S_8$ and P in the same way they are described in the algorithm. For the interpretation of the tables describing these functions, see the discussion in the body of the algorithm.

The primitive functions $S_1, \ldots, S_8$, are:

$$S_1$$

14	4	13	1	2	15	11	8	3	10	6	12	5	9	0	7
0	15	7	4	14	2	13	1	10	6	12	11	9	5	3	8
4	1	14	8	13	6	2	11	15	12	9	7	3	10	5	0
15	12	8	2	4	9	1	7	5	11	3	14	10	0	6	13

$$S_2$$

15	1	8	14	6	11	3	4	9	7	2	13	12	0	5	10
3	13	4	7	15	2	8	14	12	0	1	10	6	9	11	5
0	14	7	11	10	4	13	1	5	8	12	6	9	3	2	15
13	8	10	1	3	15	4	2	11	6	7	12	0	5	14	9

$$S_3$$

10	0	9	14	6	3	15	5	1	13	12	7	11	4	2	8
13	7	0	9	3	4	6	10	2	8	5	14	12	11	15	1
13	6	4	9	8	15	3	0	11	1	2	12	5	10	14	7
1	10	13	0	6	9	8	7	4	15	14	3	11	5	2	12

$$S_4$$

7	13	14	3	0	6	9	10	1	2	8	5	11	12	4	15
13	8	11	5	6	15	0	3	4	7	2	12	1	10	14	9
10	6	9	0	12	11	7	13	15	1	3	14	5	2	8	4
3	15	0	6	10	1	13	8	9	4	5	11	12	7	2	14

$$S_5$$

2	12	4	1	7	10	11	6	8	5	3	15	13	0	14	9
14	11	2	12	4	7	13	1	5	0	15	10	3	9	8	6
4	2	1	11	10	13	7	8	15	9	12	5	6	3	0	14
11	8	12	7	1	14	2	13	6	15	0	9	10	4	5	3

$$S_6$$

12	1	10	15	9	2	6	8	0	13	3	4	14	7	5	11
10	15	4	2	7	12	9	5	6	1	13	14	0	11	3	8
9	14	15	5	2	8	12	3	7	0	4	10	1	13	11	6
4	3	2	12	9	5	15	10	11	14	1	7	6	0	8	13

$$S_7$$

4	11	2	14	15	0	8	13	3	12	9	7	5	10	6	1
13	0	11	7	4	9	1	10	14	3	5	12	2	15	8	6
1	4	11	13	12	3	7	14	10	15	6	8	0	5	9	2
6	11	13	8	1	4	10	7	9	5	0	15	14	2	3	12

$$S_8$$

13	2	8	4	6	15	11	1	10	9	3	14	5	0	12	7
1	15	13	8	10	3	7	4	12	5	6	11	0	14	9	2
7	11	4	1	9	12	14	2	0	6	10	13	15	3	5	8
2	1	14	7	4	10	8	13	15	12	9	0	3	5	6	11

The primitive function P is:

16	7	20	21
29	12	28	17
1	15	23	26
5	18	31	10
2	8	24	14
32	27	3	9
19	13	30	6
22	11	4	25

Recall that K_n, for $1 \leq n \leq 16$, is the block of 48 bits in (2) of the algorithm. Hence, to describe KS, it is sufficient to describe the calculation of K_n from KEY for $n = 1, 2, \ldots, 16$. That calculation is illustrated in figure 3. To complete the definition of KS it is therefore sufficient to describe the two permuted choices, as well as the schedule of left shifts. One bit in each 8-bit byte of the KEY may be utilized for error detection in key generation, distribution and storage. Bits 8, 16, ..., 64 are for use in assuring that each byte is of odd parity.

Permuted choice 1 is determined by the following table:

$$PC-1$$

57	49	41	33	25	17	9
1	58	50	42	34	26	18
10	2	59	51	43	35	27
19	11	3	60	52	44	36
63	55	47	39	31	23	15
7	62	54	46	38	30	22
14	6	61	53	45	37	29
21	13	5	28	20	12	4

The table has been divided into two parts, with the first part determining how the bits of C_0 are chosen, and the second part determining how the bits of D_0 are chosen. The bits of KEY are numbered 1 through 64. The bits of C_0 are respectively bits 57, 49, 41, ..., 44 and 36 of KEY, with the bits of D_0 being bits 63, 55, 47, ..., 12 and 4 of KEY.

With C_0 and D_0 defined, we now define how the blocks C_n and D_n are obtained

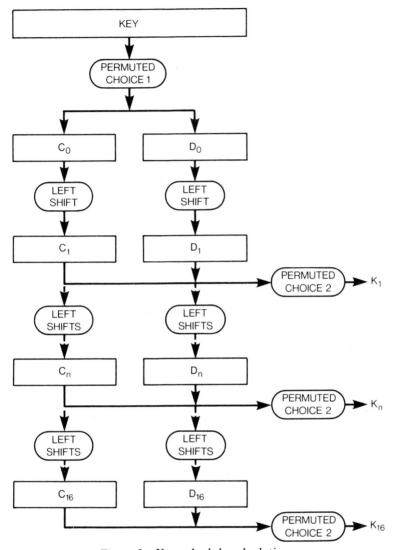

Figure 3   Key schedule calculation

from the blocks C_{n-1} and D_{n-1}, respectively, for $n = 1, 2, \ldots, 16$. That is accomplished by adhering to the following schedule of left shifts of the individual blocks:

Iteration Number	Number of Left Shifts
1	1
2	1
3	2
4	2
5	2

6	2
7	2
8	2
9	1
10	2
11	2
12	2
13	2
14	2
15	2
16	1

For example, C_3 and D_3 are obtained from C_2 and D_2, respectively, by two left shifts, and C_{16} and D_{16} are obtained from C_{15} and D_{15}, respectively, by one left shift. In all cases, by a single left shift is meant a rotation of the bits one place to the left, so that after one left shift the bits in the 28 positions are the bits that were previously in positions 2, 3, ..., 28, 1.

Permuted choice 2 is determined by the following table:

PC−2

14	17	11	24	1	5
3	28	15	6	21	10
23	19	12	4	26	8
16	7	27	20	13	2
41	52	31	37	47	55
30	40	51	45	33	48
44	49	39	56	34	53
46	42	50	36	29	32

Therefore, the first bit of K_n is the 14th bit of $C_n D_n$, the second bit the 17th, and so on with the 47th bit the 29th, and the 48th bit the 32nd.

The DES has had a very mixed reception. It poses two controversial questions. The first is whether or not there should be a 'standard'. The next is, given that there is one, should it be DES? This second question relates to the security level attained by the DES. We will consider each of these issues in turn and try to present some relevant points for each 'side' in the controversy. However we do not intend to make any judgement on either question. We prefer to leave the reader to make up his own mind. (The list of further reading at the end of the chapter gives a number of further references on DES.)

The idea of a standard in cryptography is revolutionary. The reader will recall that, when we discussed our worst-case conditions for the cryptographer, we assumed that the cryptanalyst knew all about the system used. In particular it was assumed that he knew the algorithm, and all equipment should be designed under this assumption. However, prior to DES, we know of no publication containing a complete algorithm for practical usage. In fact, despite making the assumptions claimed above, most cryptographers went to great lengths to try to conceal the details of their algorithm. The DES is the first example where an algorithm has actually been published and the 'world' has been challenged to break it. In trying to break the DES the cryptanalyst will have to solve numerous non-linear systems of equations over $GF(2)$, i.e. he will have to solve instances of the problem **AN9** stated in Chapter 6. Thus the problem involved is certainly **NP**-complete. However, as we stressed in Chapter 6, it is, as far as we know, absolutely impossible to guarantee that this particular instance is not solvable in polynomial time. Consequently there is always a danger, hopefully very small, that someone will find a way to break the system. If the standard is accepted on a nationwide (or even worldwide) basis and someone does find a solution then the standard will have to be changed. This will be a mammoth and exceedingly expensive task.

There is another obvious disadvantage to a standard. If a standard is widely used then the cryptanalyst knows that, by breaking it, he will gain access to many users' messages. Thus, if he finds a method of attack which works, it will be worth his while to implement it no matter what the cost. If, on the other hand, he were trying to break a cipher system adopted by a single user he might consider certain implementations too expensive. The adoption of a standard also focuses the attention of all cryptanalysts on the same system and must therefore increase the chances of it being broken.

One of the main advantages associated with the existence of a standard relates to the cost for the user. If a chip, or set of chips, is designed to implement the standard, then it can be produced in sufficient quantity that the cost to the user will be low. However we must point out that, in practice, the algorithm is only a comparatively small part of a system and so the overall saving will not be as significant as it might appear. Despite this, the existence of a standard might increase considerably the number of users of cipher systems. The reason is simple. Throughout history there have been many examples of custom built cipher systems which have been very insecure. Thus people who do not have the resources and/or ability to assess systems may be reluctant to use them. Unless they have a great deal of confidence in the designers of their systems, these people may feel much more inclined to use a standard which many people have both used and studied. Another obvious advantage of using the standard is the compatibility which can be attained between various systems. Although, as we have said before, the risk remains that if one network is broken then they all are.

Before we attempt to analyze the actual algorithm of the DES we include a brief discussion of its history. The development leading to DES started in 1973 with the initiation of a search for a common method of encryption which could be economically employed in a variety of computer security applications. The NBS wanted the method of encryption selected as a standard to be amenable to various types of equipment built by the many vendors of computer and terminal equipment. They also required that all information relating to this project should be publicly available. Their first search was unsuccessful but the second, begun in August 1974, produced an algorithm which showed sufficient merit to warrant further consideration. After undergoing U.S. Government review for acceptability as a federal standard this algorithm was published for public comment in March 1975. (The patents for the algorithm are held by IBM, and the terms and conditions of the agreement by IBM to grant non-exclusive, royalty free licences under these patents are given in [59].) After the publication, many comments, both for and against, were forthcoming.

The first interesting points came from a workshop held at Stanford University in 1976. Since they provide the non-linearity, the S-boxes are very important. The workshop claimed that, although they had the definite advantages of being non-affine, the S-boxes were not random and appeared to be designed for some specific (albeit unknown) purposes. They also observed the possible weakness noted in the next exercise.

EXERCISE 7.28   *Let* $c = f(m, k)$ *denote the ciphertext obtained from plaintext* m *and key* k. *If, for any block* a, $\bar{a} = a + (1, 1, \ldots, 1)$ *show that, for the DES algorithm,* $\bar{c} = f(\bar{m}, \bar{k})$.

Despite the points made at the Stanford workshop we know of no method of breaking the system other than an exhaustive search. Furthermore it is not even possible for us to attempt to estimate the likelihood for a better method being found. So we will now explore the possibilities of an exhaustive key search.

Diffie and Hellman [44] have put forward the concept of a purpose-built machine to exhaust all key possibilities. This special equipment would search through all the 2^{56} ($\simeq 10^{17}$) keys at a rate of 10^{12} keys per second and would, therefore, require about one day for the entire search. The machine itself would consist of about 10^6 chips, each searching a different portion of the keyspace at a rate of one key per microsecond. Their estimate is that the chips could be produced at $10 each which, allowing 100% overhead for power supply, boards, racks, control logic, etc., leads to a machine cost of about $20 million. It is further argued that the cost of processing has decreased by a factor of ten every five years since 1940 and that it is likely to continue at this rate for the next decade.

However, in contrast to Diffie and Hellman, others have estimated the cost of the machine to be nearer $200 million. We have no way of making a sensible estimate but, no matter which of the two figures is correct, it is clear that a key of 56 bits for DES allows no real safety margin. If the key is chosen badly then the number of possibilities decreases rapidly. For instance if the key is eight ITA5 characters, as opposed to 56 random bits, then allowing a realistic 64 possibilities per character the number of distinct keys is only $64^8 \simeq 2 \cdot 8 \times 10^{14}$. Even worse, if the key is eight alphabetic characters then there are only $26^8 \simeq 2 \cdot 1 \times 10^{11}$ possibilities.

Having said all this we must now add that the NBS are well aware of these problems. Ruth Davis [42], formerly of the NBS, says: 'Keys should be random; keys should be independent; keys should never have any part predetermined. Failure to follow these rules or compromises in their achievement will compromise the security equivalently.'

There are many people who, in line with the Stanford working party, would like further information on how the particular S-boxes were chosen. There has also been considerable discussion on the number of rounds required and, for instance, in [55] it is claimed that there should be at least 32.

With something as revolutionary as the DES it is hardly surprising that there was, and still is, a wide spectrum of public opinion. After considering the various reactions to their proposals, NBS held two workshops to consider DES. According to Davis [42, (1978)] both workshops resulted in a consensus that the DES was satisfactory as a cryptographic standard for the next 10–15 years.

Given that a standard is to be used, the block cipher system's great versatility makes it very useful. In the next section we describe how the DES (and in fact any block cipher) can be used in various ways; including stream cipher or cipher feedback modes.

7.4   Applications of a Block Cipher

Throughout this section we assume that we have designed a block cipher system which has an input of an n-bit block of data and an m-bit key to produce an output of an n-bit block of ciphertext. We will discuss various ways of using it.

7.4.1   The codebook method

The natural way of using a block cipher is often called the codebook method and is illustrated in Figure 7.10.

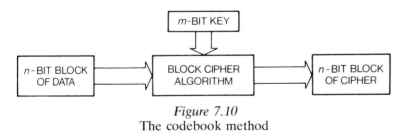

Figure 7.10
The codebook method

One of the major disadvantages of this system is that inputting a given n-bit block of data always results in the same n-bit block of cipher; i.e. it acts exactly like a codebook. Of course the consequence of this can be reduced by making n sufficiently large. Nevertheless, with highly formatted data, the same n-bit blocks may still occur relatively frequently with the obvious consequences. Increasing n introduces another disadvantage. No matter how short our message may be we always have to produce an n-bit block of ciphertext and so, for short messages, increasing n might lead to message extension. Another possible disadvantage is the error propagation. We have already mentioned that a single error in transmission is likely to cause a complete block of data to be in error. This is certainly not always a disadvantage but there are many situations where it is undesirable.

7.4.2 The stream cipher mode

There are many ways in which a block cipher can be used to produce a pseudo-random sequence of digits. Figure 7.11 illustrates one.

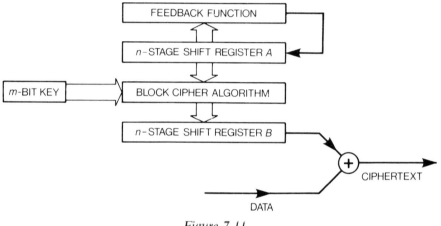

Figure 7.11
The stream cipher mode

In Figure 7.11 the n-stage shift register A has a feedback function which is determined by some polynomial. We have considered this situation in Chapter 5 and know, for instance, that by taking the feedback to be linear and the polynomial to be primitive we obtain a sequence of states of period $2^n - 1$. At any given time pulse the state of A is used as the input to the block cipher, replacing what is normally a block of data. The m-bit key is also input to the block cipher. (Depending on the use of the system, the feedback function and initial state of A might be part of the key or simply transmitted to the receiver as part of the message. In this latter case they might, as we shall see in Chapter 8, be used as a message key.) The block cipher algorithm then produces an n-bit block which is held in register B. Thus each time the state of A changes we obtain a new n-bit block in B. By outputting i of these n bits each time, $(1 \le i \le n)$, we obtain a sequence that can then be modulo-2 added to the data to produce the ciphertext. It should be clear from this description that we are using the block cipher algorithm to produce a pseudo-random sequence of i-bit blocks.

To have any confidence in this type of system the periodicity, randomness and non-linearity of the sequence must meet our usual requirements. We state, without justification, some relevant facts about them. If the block cipher is reasonable then the periodicity will almost certainly be determined by the periodicity of the states of A. The non-linearity and randomness of the sequence are closely related to those of the block cipher, and if either are inadequate the same is also certainly true for the block cipher itself. The number of bits, i, which are output each time will depend mainly on the format of the data and the speed at which it is arriving. For example if the data is at a very low bit rate and arriving bit by bit we can probably take $i = 1$. If, on the other hand, it is arriving somewhat faster in 8-bit blocks we may take $i = 8$ or even a greater multiple of 8.

7.4.3 The cipher feedback mode
Figure 7.12 illustrates one of the many ways in which a block cipher may be used to produce a cipher feedback system. This is very similar to the

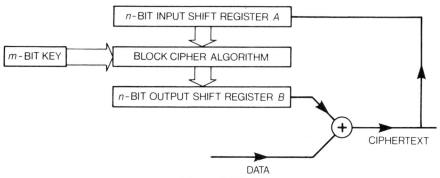

Figure 7.12
The cipher feedback mode

stream cipher system in Figure 7.11. We begin with an n-bit input register A filled with an arbitrary set of n bits. (If we are prepared to lose the first n bits of data then these contents can be ignored, but if not then they must be transmitted to the receiver at the start of the message.) These n bits are then presented to the block cipher algorithm in place of data and an n-bit output block is produced. Finally, as before, we take i of these bits and modulo-2 add them to i bits of data. This time, however, in addition to being transmitted the resulting i bits of ciphertext are also fed back to become the last i bits of shift register A, i.e. on the right as we look at it. To 'make room' for these new bits in the register the original n bits are moved i places to the left.

This new block of n bits is then presented to the block cipher algorithm and the process continues in this way. Since, after the first few rounds, the input to the algorithm depends only on the ciphertext this system is self-synchronizing.

7.4.4   The block chaining mode

The block chaining mode is an alternative feedback method and is shown
in Figure 7.13. In this method all data is handled in n-bit blocks. To begin
encipherment an n-bit initializing block **v** is modulo-2 added, bit by bit, to

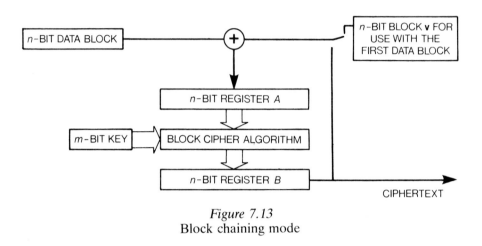

Figure 7.13
Block chaining mode

the first n-bit data block. The result is presented to the block cipher
algorithm and an n-bit ciphertext block is produced in B. As well as being
transmitted this ciphertext is fed back for by-by-bit modulo-2 addition with
the second data block. The result of this addition passes through the block
cipher algorithm as before and it should now be clear how the system
continues. To decipher, the first block is presented to the block cipher
algorithm and the resultant n-bit block is added to **v** to produce the
plaintext. From then onwards each ciphertext block is deciphered and
then added to the previous ciphertext block.

Block chaining is particularly useful if the cryptographer is seeking
protection against deletions or the insertion of spurious information (see,
for example, Exercise 8.5).

We have devoted these last three chapters to the development of
algorithms for use in determining the transformation, from message space
to cryptogram space, of a cipher system. In the next two chapters we
consider ways of incorporating these algorithms into equipment to
produce complete systems. As we shall see, although it is essential, having
a good algorithm is certainly not the only requirement for a secure cipher
system.

Further Reading

[46]–[48], [50] and [53]–[54] are general papers on block cipher techniques. The rest of the references are about DES and the discussions as to whether the security level it can offer is sufficient. [45] and [49] are concerned with the implementation of DES.

[39]   Branstad, D. K., *Draft Guidelines for Implementing and Using the NBS Data Encryption Standard*, NBS, 1975.

[40]   Branstad, D. K., 'Encryption Protection in Computer Data Communications', *Proc. 4th Data Communications Symp.*, Quebec City, Canada, 1975.

[41]   Branstad, D. K. (Editor), 'Computer Security and the Data Encryption Standard', *Proceedings of the conference at Gaithersburg, Maryland*, 1977.

[42]   Davis, R., 'The Data Encryption Standard in Perspective', *IEEE Comms. Soc. Mag.*, Vol 16, No. 6, 1978, 5–10.

[43]   Diffie, W. and Hellman, M. E., 'A critique of the proposed Data Encryption Standard', *Communications ACM*, 19, 1976, 164–5.

[44]   Diffie, W. and Hellman, M. E., 'Cryptanalysis of the NBS Data Encryption Standard', *Stanford University Report MEH-76-2*, 1976.

[45]   Erickson, Chuck, 'Encryption – An Ancient Art Enhanced by LSI', *Fairchild Journal of Semiconductor*, Vol 7, No. 1, 1979, 4–11.

[46]   Feistel, H., 'Cryptography and computer privacy', *Scientific American*, 228, 1973, 15–23.

[47]   Feistel, H., 'Block Cipher Cryptographic System', *U.S. Patent No. 3, 798, 359*, 1974.

[48]   Feistel, H., Notz, W. A. and Smith, J. L., 'Some Cryptographic Techniques for Machine-to-Machine Data Communications', *Proc. IEEE*, 63, 1975, 1545–54.

[49]   Gebler, P. 'Implementations of the DES Algorithm', *Elect. Product Design*, 1980, 52–4.

[50]   Grossman, E. K. and Tuckerman, B., 'Analysis of a Feistel-like cipher weakened by having no rotating key', *IBM Thomas J. Watson Research Center Report*, 1977.

[51]   Hellman, M. E. *et al.*, 'Results of an initial attempt to cryptanalyse the NBS Data Encryption Standard', *Stanford University Report SEL 76–042*, 1976.

[52]   Hindon, H. J., 'Cipher-Shifters fight it out', *Electronics*, 1979, 81–2.

[53]   Meyer, C. H., 'Design Considerations for cryptography', *AFIPS Conf. Proc. 42*, 1973, 603–606.

[54]   Meyer, C. H., 'Enciphering Data for Secure Transmission', *Computer Design*, 1974, 129–34.

[55]   Morris, R., Sloane, N. J. A. and Wyner, A. D., 'Assessment of the National Bureau of Standards Proposed Federal Data Encryption Standard', *Cryptologia*, Vol 1, 1977, 281–306.

[56]   Morris, R., 'The Data Encryption Standard – Retrospective and
       Prospects', *IEEE Comms. Soc. Mag.*, Vol 16, No. 6, 1978, 11–14.
[57]   National Bureau of Standards, 'Encryption Algorithm for computer
       data protection: Requests for comments', *Federal Register*, 40,
       No. 12134, 1975.
[58]   National Bureau of Standards, 'Notice of a proposed Federal
       Information Processing Data Encryption Standard', *Federal
       Register*, 40, No. 12607, 1975.
[59]   *Official Gazette of the U.S. Patent and Trademark Office*, 13 May,
       1975 and 31 August, 1976.
[60]   Proposed Federal Standard 1026, 'Telecommunications: Inter-
       operability and Security Requirements for use of the Data
       Encryption Standard in Data Communication Systems', 1980.
[61]   Yasaki, E. K., 'Encryption Algorithm: Key size is the thing',
       Datamation, 22, No. 3, 1976, 164–6.

8.
Applying Cipher Systems

8.1 Introduction

In the last four chapters we have considered the problem of designing a pseudo-random sequence generator and have considered many helpful techniques. We have also seen a number of ways in which such a generator can be used to encipher data. However we have not yet looked at any real examples and have not demonstrated how these algorithms can form part of modern cipher equipment. In the next two chapters we will try to put the role of the sequence generator into perspective. For this chapter we restrict our attention to data networks and in Chapter 9 we consider the important task of securing speech systems.

One of our main aims is to illustrate how a particular situation may make certain types of algorithms preferable to others, and how an entire system might fit together. Although it is certainly the heart of the system, the sequence generator is only a comparatively small part and there are many aspects to be considered when designing any secure communications ·system. Every facet of its intended use is important and influences not only the choice of algorithm but also the design of the peripheral components. These two chapters should convince the reader that there is much more to the protection of communications than simply designing a sequence generator. In particular they should illustrate that the assessment of a cipher system is only possible if the entire network is considered.

We begin the chapter by discussing the central problem of key management and concentrate on a number of important questions. How large should the key be? How often should it be changed? Can it be changed automatically? How should it be generated and transmitted? The rest of the chapter is then devoted to the problems involved in the security of three particular types of communications systems. The implications and requirements of the three examples vary considerably and they have been chosen to emphasize how practical considerations affect the design of the system.

The third of these examples is an on-line electronic fund transfer system. Such systems are very important and are likely to influence the lives of almost everyone in the western world. Their requirements highlight a number of very interesting problems.

8.2   Key Structure

Throughout this book we have emphasized that the security of a cipher system should depend solely on the choice of the key. This point was highlighted when we specified our worst case conditions for the cryptographer. There we asserted that the cryptographer must be prepared for the cryptanalyst to have full details of the entire system and, in particular, completely understand the algorithm. Given the importance of the key, it is obviously crucial that we pay great attention to the problems of choosing and changing keys. We must also consider how the encipherer can tell the receiver the fact that he is changing to a new key.

Before we attempt to discuss these problems it is probably worthwhile restating exactly what we are trying to achieve. We are now discussing practical, realistic systems which means that they are theoretically breakable. This must be accepted as a premise. Our problem is to determine how long it would take to break a particular system and/or to estimate the cost involved. If the time or expense is excessive then, for all practical purposes, we may regard our system as secure. This means we must attempt to quantify the word 'excessive' in the last sentence.

As we saw in Chapter 4 if, to break our system, a cryptanalyst requires storage for 10^{50} elements then we can safely regard it as absolutely unbreakable. A similar conclusion holds if 10^{50} operations are needed. In fact, given current technology, far fewer than 10^{50} storage elements or operations make a system unbreakable in practice. Thus, for any given system, we must determine the number of operations or storage elements needed to break it, and then decide if this is large enough for our purposes. This, of course, is one of the main problems which we have discussed repeatedly and, as we have seen, with today's sophisticated systems the solution is by no means simple. However we do know that, if the cryptanalyst is able to try every key, he will be able to break our system. Thus one estimate for the maximum number of operations needed by a cryptanalyst is the number necessary to try all possible keys. Although this gives us an upper bound for the number of operations, in practice far fewer will usually suffice. In order to increase the number of operations needed by a cryptanalyst, we must increase the number of possibilities for the key. But this implies increasing the actual size of the key. Unfortunately, as we increase the size of our key, it may make it more difficult to ensure secure distribution and quick, accurate entry. There are many practical situations where these latter constraints are very important and, on these occasions, the smallest possible key is advantageous.

As on so many previous occasions, we find ourselves with two conflicting requirements. It is therefore necessary to find a compromise. We must keep our key as small as possible, while still ensuring that nobody can try every possibility in a reasonable time interval. As an attempt to quantify these sizes we can look at the recent work on the DES described in Chapter 7. There has been much discussion on whether the key, which is 56 bits, is sufficiently large. Diffie and Hellman claim that a 56-bit key is inadequate to resist a 'brute force' attack using a purpose built computer costing about $20 million. Others claim a more realistic estimate of the cost is $200 million. Whoever is right, it is clear that a key size of 56 bits is marginal. But it is widely agreed that 64 bits would be sufficient to stop the 'brute force' attack using present day equipment. We should not, of course, forget that any system being built is expected to last for a few years. Thus it should be adequate to resist not only today's attack but one using any likely 'new' equipment developed in the system's projected life span. We end this brief discussion of key size choice by noting that one way of reaching our compromise might be to incorporate a two-part key, in such a way that only one part needs changing at any given time. We will explore this idea in detail when we discuss customer option keys later in the chapter.

8.2.1 The need for key change
In order to illustrate the problem of determining how often we need to change the key we will consider a specific example. Suppose that our system employs the stream cipher of Figure 8.1.

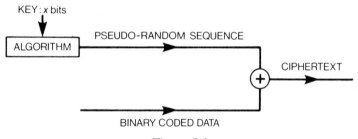

Figure 8.1
The stream cipher for this system

Assume that we have selected a key of x bits which initializes the algorithm, i.e. gives the algorithm a starting point, and that we then use this key to encipher n different messages $\mathbf{m}_1, \mathbf{m}_2, \ldots, \mathbf{m}_n$. If we let $|\mathbf{m}_i|$ denote the number of characters in the message $\mathbf{m}_i$ then, for any j satisfying $1 \le j \le |\mathbf{m}_i|$, we will let a_{ij} represent the jth ciphertext character of $\mathbf{m}_i$. In order to encipher $\mathbf{m}_1$ we first enter the key. The algorithm, using the key as an initializing process, then produces a pseudo-random sequence which determines the sequence of transformations. Similarly for each subsequent message, we enter the same key and, as a consequence, obtain the same pseudo-random sequence and the same sequence of transformations.

If an interceptor obtains n enciphered messages he will be able to arrange them in the kind of array shown in Table 8.1. (Note that the method of superimposing messages of Section 1.3.3 will enable him to check that these messages employed the same enciphering sequence.)

$$
\begin{array}{llllllll}
a_{11} & a_{12} & . & . & . & . & . & . & a_{1\,|\,\mathbf{m}_1\,|} \\
a_{21} & a_{22} & . & . & . & . & . & . & . & . & . & . & a_{2\,|\,\mathbf{m}_2\,|} \\
. & . & & & & & & . \\
. & . & & & & & & . \\
. & . & & & & & & . \\
. & . & & & & & & . \\
a_{n1} & a_{n2} & . & . & . & . & . & . & . & . & a_{n\,|\,\mathbf{m}_n\,|}
\end{array}
$$

Table 8.1
The interceptor's array

Once he has done this he knows that, for any given column, the same section of the enciphering sequence has been used. Thus he can restrict his attention to the columns in turn. But if we let m_{ik} be the kth plaintext letter of $\mathbf{m}_i$, then $m_{ik} = m_{jk}$ if and only if $a_{ik} = a_{jk}$, and this means that the system used for any given column is merely a monalphabetic substitution. Furthermore it is essentially additive which, of course, guarantees that knowing the ciphertext equivalent of one character determines the entire substitution.

The amount of use which the cryptanalyst can make of this observation depends on the size of n. If n is large then clearly he can utilize it, but for small n it is not at present clear how much it helps him. Certainly if $n = 1$ then the cryptanalyst has learnt nothing. If n is greater than 1, however, he has further information. Since each column comes from a substitution which is essentially additive and each row represents a message, he can attempt to break each column and use the extra fact that each row must be meaningful to settle any ambiguous positions. The precise way of doing this depends on n. If n is large he can use the statistics relating to the frequency of occurrence of each letter to determine the most likely substitutions for each column. The fact that each row must be meaningful should soon enable him to make firm decisions about any columns where the frequencies leave any room for chance. But if n is small then there will not be sufficient characters in each column for the frequency statistics to be reliable. In this case he might find it advantageous to concentrate on the rows and use them to try to determine the substitution alphabets. As an illustration, we will consider a specific situation and begin by restricting ourselves to the first two columns.

Suppose that the code used is ITA 2 as listed in Appendix 2. Then, since there are 32 possibilities for each of the substitutions in the first two columns, there are $32^2 = 1024$ possibilities for the pair of substitutions. By trying each of these 1024 possibilities he would obtain the corresponding first two plaintext characters for each message. But, since each of the n

messages is assumed to be meaningful, this will enable him to consult a table of bigram frequencies for ITA 2 and thereby assign probabilities to each of the 1024 possibilities. We saw in Chapter 1 that, for the English language, a very small number of bigrams occur with a non-negligible frequency. The number of these 1024 possibilities with non-negligible probabilities obviously depends on both n and the language used but, due to the high redundancy in most languages, will be very small even with n as low as 5. The cryptanalyst then proceeds by taking each of the 'likely' possibilities and coupling it with each of the 32 possibilities for column 3. Continuing to later columns and using frequencies of bigrams, trigrams and n-grams, if they are available, the number of possibilities decreases rapidly and eventually words begin to appear. Even with $n = 2$ this method has a remarkably high success rate, and the reader has only to refer back to Exercise 1.1 to get some indication why. It is, of course, precisely this high success rate which causes the one-time-pad to demand that $n = 1$; i.e. that the key (which in this case is the enciphering sequence) is used only once to guarantee perfect secrecy.

In most practical situations the cryptanalyst will not even need to try all 32 possibilities for each column. For instance if the ITA 2 is used he can be reasonably sure that no message will contain null characters. This is simply because most teleprinter systems do not have the null characters available from the keyboard. But this means that the five bits of the enciphering sequence can never be the same as the corresponding ciphertext; otherwise the corresponding plaintext character would have been a null. So, if n_i is the number of distinct characters in column i of Table 8.1, there are only $32-n_i$ possible substitution alphabets for that column. Once again the value of this type of information depends on the size of n. But for large values of n it can reduce the number of trials considerably.

So far our discussion seems to indicate that, irrespective of the algorithm used, the key should be changed after each individual message. But, if this is so, then it is hard to see what genuine advantages our stream cipher has over the one-time-pad. If, with both systems, the key must be changed after every single message, then all we appear to have done is managed to arrange for the key to be of fixed size. To counteract this, we have gone from a theoretically unbreakable system to one that is theoretically breakable. Fortunately, the situation can be remedied and we can avoid having to change our key so frequently. To do this we introduce the concept of a **message key**. As is suggested by the title of this section, we shall be introducing various types of key. To avoid confusion from now on we shall refer to our fundamental key i.e. that key which is kept secret and can easily be changed on a regular basis, as the **base key**. The same key is often referred to as the **primary key**.

8.2.2 The message key
In order to demonstrate the essential function of a message key, we consider an analogy with the one-time-pad system. In the traditional

'picture' of the system, a pad is used and each page of this pad contains a random sequence of numbers. Each page is then used once as a key. However, if each page is numbered then there is no reason why the pages should be used in consecutive order. Each message could, for instance, be prefixed with a number telling the receiver which page to turn to. Thus these numbers would randomize the starting point for the enciphering sequence. This illustrates the role of our message key; it will alter the starting point of the pseudo-random sequence we are producing. To achieve this effect within a stream cipher, we generate a message key at the start of each message. For the moment we will not worry about the method of generation; it may be random, pseudo-random or even depend on the message itself. The base key is then mixed with the message key in some way to produce a new key which is used to initialize the encipherment algorithm of that particular message only. At the start of the next message a new message key is generated and mixed with the base key in the same way. In this manner the algorithm for each message is initialized by its own individual key. The system is shown in Figure 8.2.

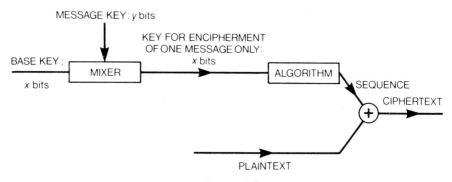

Figure 8.2
The introduction of a message key

It is important to remember that if we wish to use a message key then that message key must be transmitted to the receiver. Furthermore it is crucial that it be transmitted correctly, because if the receiver uses the wrong message key he will almost certainly decipher the ciphertext incorrectly. (This incorrect decipherment would obviously imply a reduction in the effectiveness of the communications network.) Also, in many instances, the message key will be randomly and automatically generated for each individual message. When this happens, if the message key is corrupted during transmission and the receiver has to ask for a retransmission, the key used for retransmission could, depending on the system, be different from the original. Thus, with an exceptionally bad transmission link, an interceptor may obtain several different encipherings of the same message. Although this may not enable him to break the system immediately, it will almost certainly prove helpful. So, to avoid having to retransmit, it is obviously advantageous to apply an error-correcting code to the message key. This code can then be chosen so that, for the type of link being used, it is highly unlikely that any errors will remain after the message has been transmitted and the error correction applied. (We do not want to get side-tracked into the many interesting problems associated with error correction and refer the reader to [67] or [26].)

Another problem associated with the transmission of the message key is deciding in what form it should be sent. For instance, is it necessary to conceal it, or is it safe to transmit the message key in clear? If we return to our analogy comparing the message key of a stream cipher system with page numbering for a one-time-pad, then we might be tempted to conclude that there is no real disadvantage in transmitting it in clear. Certainly in the one-time-pad situation it is absolutely irrelevant whether or not the interceptor knows the message key. In this case, knowing which page is used is of no advantage to him since he does not know the contents of the pages. It is also obviously true that, no matter how the message key is transmitted, it will still be effective in nullifying the type of attack discussed in the last section. (This is simply because there will no longer be a number of different messages using the same key.) However we must not draw too many conclusions from our analogy with the one-time-pad. There is one absolutely fundamental difference between the one-time-pad and a stream cipher or, in fact, any other cipher. Within the one-time-pad each bit of the random enciphering sequence is completely independent of all other bits. In our stream cipher this is not the case; all bits are a function of the key. Many cryptographers have forgotten this, looked at the analogy with the one-time-pad and assumed that knowledge of the message key will not help the interceptor. This is not necessarily true. Although use of a message key has prevented a certain type of attack, knowledge of the message key may, depending on how the base and message keys are mixed together, enable the interceptor to reduce the complexity of the equations he must solve. Thus knowledge of the message key may open up new avenues of attack. To illustrate this we give an extremely simple, and consequently unrealistic, example.

Suppose that we have a cipher system with a two bit base key and that the system employs a message key which is also two bits. Before loading into the algorithm, the message key is modulo 2 added bit-by-bit to the base key. The first bit of sequence produced is the product of these two bits of key. Thus if the base key chosen is k_1, k_2 and the message key for the first message is r_1, r_2, then the first bit of the sequence will be $s_0 = (k_1 + r_1)(k_2 + r_2)$. In terms of Figure 8.2, $x = y = 2$, the algorithm is non-linear (at least for the first bit) and the mixer is a bit-by-bit modulo 2 adder.

Suppose now that we encipher a second message with this base key and that the message key for this second message is r_3, r_4. So in this case the first bit of the sequence produced is $s_0' = (k_1 + r_3)(k_2 + r_4)$. To complete our knowledge of the system we assume that the message keys are transmitted in clear which, of course, makes them readily available to any interceptor. Under our worst case conditions we must assume that the interceptor also knows the plaintext equivalent of some ciphertext. But knowledge of, for instance, the first bit of the ciphertext and its plaintext equivalent determines the first bit of the enciphering sequence. Thus in our example we will suppose he knows s_0 and s_0'. This means that to determine k_1 and k_2 he must solve the following two non-linear equations in k_1 and k_2; $s_0 = k_1 k_2 + k_1 r_2 + k_2 r_1 + r_1 r_2$ and $s_0' = k_1 k_2 + k_1 r_4 + k_2 r_3 + r_3 r_4$. But notice that $s_0 + s_0' = k_1 (r_2 + r_4) + k_2 (r_1 + r_3) + r_1 r_2 + r_3 r_4$ and, since we know r_1, r_2, r_3, r_4, this equation is linear in k_1 and k_2. Although, in this small example, our original equations were straightforward, the principle we are illustrating is that, depending upon how the base key and message key are mixed, it may be possible to reduce the complexity and degree of non-linearity of the equations characterizing the algorithm; the usual way for achieving this being to combine known bits of the sequence from several different messages. It is therefore clear that, in many situations, there will be a considerable advantage in enciphering the message key for transmission. This can be achieved either by using a completely separate sequence generator or, more usually, the same generator as is used for the encipherment of the data. If, on the other hand, the encipherer still chooses to transmit the message key in clear then the mixing process must be carefully examined to ensure against the type of attack we have just discussed.

Another choice which has to be made is whether to use a message key which is random, pseudo-random or part of the message. This decision depends largely on the use being made of the cipher system. Although all keys should be as unpredictable as possible, it is not true that keys need to be randomly generated. There are in fact many situations where there exist overriding reasons for choosing a non-random message key. We will look at a few examples.

For our first example we consider a system where a mixture of random and pseudo-random message keys might be used. As we shall see, there are situations where it is advantageous to allow late entry into a secure communications network. For instance, in Chapter 9 we discuss the encipherment of speech and we will need to ensure that if, in that context, two people are engaged in a secure conversation it should be possible for a third person to join in the discussion after it has started. Now, because the ciphering involves a sequence generator, the third person must be able to synchronize his own generator; i.e. he must produce the correct sequence element at the right time. A common way of enabling him to do this is to transmit frequent synchronization updates and to include, with each, some extra details which indicate how far the sequence generator has advanced from the start of the message. If, as is certainly advantageous, a message key is employed then this must also be transmitted each time any updating information is sent. The great disadvantage of this system is obvious; an interceptor who obtains the message, after the beginning, can easily deduce how much he has missed. This can be avoided by using an alternative method for obtaining synchronization and making use of the message key. This time, a new message key is sent with every synchronization update and, within each encryption equipment, the sequence generator is then reloaded with the base key mixed with this new message key. An added advantage of this system is that fewer bits of the enciphering sequence are used for each key loaded. Any third person joining the network simply extracts the message key from the synchronization information, and mixes it with his own base key before loading a key into the sequence generator. But now we have introduced the disadvantage that if, after joining the network, a synchronization update is missed (perhaps because of a poor quality link), the new message key may also be missed, and the receiver will not be able to load the correct key into his sequence generator. However this can, in turn, be overcome by transmitting pseudo-random message keys. If this is done then, as soon as one correct message key is known, all later ones used by the transmitter can be generated. This means that if, at any update time, the receiver misses the new message key, he can deduce what it should have been under the assumption that the previous one used was correct. If his assumption is correct then he will stay in synchronization, if it is wrong then he will, of course, lose synchronization but is no worse off than he was. This process is known as **flywheeling**.

In this system just discussed, the transmitter uses a random message key for the start of his message but then changes to a pseudo-random sequence generator to obtain his subsequent message keys.

As an example where it might be advantageous to have a message key which is part of the message, we consider any data system which uses poor links. Perhaps, for instance, the link suffers badly from fading, in which case blocks of information will be lost quite often. As we mentioned earlier in our discussion of the need for error protection of the message key, it is undesirable to retransmit the same message several times if, on each occasion, it has been enciphered using different keys. But this is likely to happen if we use either random or pseudo-random message keys. So in this situation a message key which is part of the message may be advantageous. Certainly it will guarantee that all retransmissions are identical and, consequently, give no extra information to the interceptor.

Our third example, where again it may be best to have a message key which is part of the message, illustrates how practical necessity can influence the choice. Suppose we have to design a small, portable, encryption unit for tactical military usage. Here, although of course security is very important, it may only be necessary to ensure that the message is secure for a short while. In this case, once the minimal necessary security is ensured, the overriding factors are likely to be size, weight and cost. But to have a good random, or even pseudo-random, message key may involve increasing the hardware in the unit and so, for purely physical and economic reasons, it may be best to use a message key which is simply part of the message.

So far we have restricted our attention to message keys with respect to stream ciphers. Within any stream cipher system which is employed in a cipher feedback mode there is an enciphering sequence, in the same way as with the stream cipher itself. However, in this case, the enciphering sequence is dependent on not only the initial states of the registers employed but also on previous ciphertext. Thus, in some sense, we have an automatic message key. Furthermore it may not be possible to control the initial contents of all the registers, which means that repetitions of the same message may employ different initializations and, hence, have different enciphering sequences. Block ciphers, which are essentially large substitution ciphers, do not have the same problems associated with an enciphering sequence. However when using a block cipher it is important to prevent an interceptor who knows portions of plaintext from building up a 'directory' of the substitutions used. One way of doing this is by frequently changing the base key. Another way is to use one of the block chaining methods described in Chapter 7. The idea of a message key can be included by initializing the first block with some random data.

We will now return to the problem of trying to decide how often the base key should be changed. Since our aim is to avoid the interceptor having two cryptograms which used the same enciphering sequence, the answer must depend on the number of possibilities and hence the size of the message key. For instance, to take a ridiculously small example, if we had a message key with just two bits then the messages enciphered using a given base key would employ at most four different enciphering sequences. Thus if an interceptor obtained five enciphered messages he could be certain that at least two employed the same enciphering sequence. So, in this case, we would need to change our base key after at most four messages. Clearly, to avoid changing our base key too often, we need a reasonably large message key. But we must not forget that the message key also has to be transmitted to the receiver and will cause a significant message extension. Within many networks a message extension of more than a few bits is unacceptable. In such circumstances, there is no option but to let the maximal length permitted for message extension determine the size of the message key and, as a consequence, the frequency with which the base key is changed. In practice one normally begins by deciding the size of message key acceptable to the system, and then considers whether or not this allows the transmission of enough messages for the base key to remain unchanged. Thus we must consider how, for a message key with m possibilities, the probability of using the same message key more than once varies as we increase the number of messages transmitted. This is a routine statistical problem. To solve it we assume that r messages are transmitted and evaluate the probability that each one employs a different message key. For our first message we have m choices for the key. However, once we have made that choice, there will be only $m-1$ choices for the second. Since any one of the original m choices can be followed by any of the remaining $m-1$, the total number of choices for the first two message keys is $m(m-1)$. Similarly there will now be $m-2$ choices for the third message key and, by repeated use of the same argument, we see that the total number of ways of choosing our r keys is $m(m-1)(m-2) \ldots (m-r+1)$. On the other hand if we do not insist that no key·is used more than once then there are m^r ways of choosing r message keys. The ratio of these two numbers shows the proportion of the total number of possibilities which have all the message keys distinct i.e. it is precisely the probability that all r message keys are different. But this ratio is

$$\frac{m(m-1) \ldots (m-r+1)}{m^r} = \left(\frac{m}{m}\right)\left(\frac{m-1}{m}\right) \ldots \frac{m-r+1}{m}$$
$$= \left(1 - \frac{1}{m}\right)\left(1 - \frac{2}{m}\right) \ldots \left(1 - \frac{r-1}{m}\right),$$

and thus, if we let p denote the probability that all r message keys are distinct, we have

$$p = \left(1 - \frac{1}{m}\right)\left(1 - \frac{2}{m}\right) \ldots \left(1 - \frac{r-1}{m}\right).$$

To get some idea of what this means, suppose we use an 8-bit message key and transmit five messages employing the same base key. Then $r = 5$ and $m = 256$ which give a value for p of about 0.96. Thus the probability of two of our messages using the same message key is 0.04. This means that, if we changed our base key after five messages, for about four base keys in every hundred we could expect to find a repeated message key. In practice, of course, the values for r and m will be much larger. However r is also likely to be small compared with m and, on this assumption, we can use the approximation $\ln(1-x) \approx -x$, for small x to obtain a quick way of estimating p. Since

$$p = \left(1 - \frac{1}{m}\right)\left(1 - \frac{2}{m}\right) \ldots \left(1 - \frac{r-1}{m}\right),$$

$$\ln p = \ln\left(1 - \frac{1}{m}\right) + \ln\left(1 - \frac{2}{m}\right) + \ldots + \ln\left(1 - \frac{r-1}{m}\right)$$

$$\approx -\frac{1}{m} - \frac{2}{m} \ldots - \frac{(r-1)}{m} = -\left(\frac{1}{m}\frac{r(r-1)}{2}\right).$$

Thus

$$\ln p \approx -\frac{r(r-1)}{2m} \quad \text{or} \quad p \approx e^{-(r(r-1))/2m}.$$

EXERCISE 8.1   *Show that if we use a 32-bit message key and transmit 1000 messages with the same base key then the probability that they all use different message keys is virtually one. (On our calculator, the approximation*

$p \simeq e^{-(r(r-1))/2m}$ *to ten decimal places gives* $p \simeq 0{\cdot}9998837079$ *whereas the exact formula* $p = \left(1 - \dfrac{1}{m}\right)\left(1 - \dfrac{2}{m}\right)\ldots\left(1 - \dfrac{r-1}{m}\right)$ *gives* $p = 0{\cdot}9998837074\,!$)

EXERCISE 8.2   Show that if we use a 16-bit message key and transmit more than 301 messages using the same base key then it is probable that we will have used at least one message key twice.

Although obviously important, the size chosen for the message key is certainly not the only decision to be taken. Other factors have to be considered. For instance, one practical consideration is that it is often physically impossible to send a new base key within a certain time interval. Another relevant factor is the amount of use made of the system. Clearly, for any single base key, we want to keep the length of ciphertext available to an interceptor as small as possible. An absolutely crucial consideration is that we must ensure that any base key is changed before it has been used for the duration of its break time. By this we mean that, for any given base key, we will have our own estimate of the time needed to discover it, and we must not use it for anywhere approaching this length of time. If, for instance, we believe we have a system with a break time of one year and we change the key weekly, a would-be cryptanalyst trying to read all our communications will very quickly be hopelessly behind.

To conclude this section, we mention the problems involved in the physical changing of keys within a network. If, for example, it is decided to change all the keys in a given network at midnight this will almost certainly result in the disruption of all transmissions in a short time interval around midnight. As an illustration, all messages *en route* at midnight are likely to be lost because by the time they reach their destinations the key may have changed. Furthermore any errors incurred during the change of keys may be catastrophic. Not only will they lead to confusion, but they may also offer the interceptor useful information. Each of the above problems can be partially overcome by allowing the equipment to store a small number of base keys. We can then include an identifier at the start of each message to signify which store is being used. If, when this is done, the key is changed during a transmission it can be ensured that the old key is still available in the receiving equipment. In practice the storage of too many keys can lead to confusion and about ten keys are usually considered sufficient to overcome these problems.

8.2.3   Customer option keys
As well as the base key and message key there is a third type of key in common usage. This key has many names, e.g. **customer option key**, **family key** or **algorithm changing key**. Its main function is to extend the key size of a system without increasing the work involved in changing the

keys. As we have already stressed, the base key needs changing frequently and is, consequently, normally easily accessible. It may, for instance, be changed by means of front panel switches or a front panel keyboard. It is usually anticipated that the customer option keys will be changed much less frequently and they are usually only accessible by means of wire links, plug-in modules or switches within the equipment. Whereas the base key is normally mixed with the message key and then used to initialize an algorithm, the customer options usually change the algorithm in some way. Of course if they are used to change the algorithm they must ensure that the complexity is in no way affected.

As an example we will consider the multiplexed sequences described in Chapter 6. Here, whereas the base key might be used to provide the initial contents of each register, the customer option key might be a number of primitive polynomials for the tap settings of the registers. Provided that the polynomials are carefully selected, the complexity of the system will be unaffected by the choice of customer option key. However the existence of the customer option key has undoubtedly made the cryptanalyst's task more difficult.

Finally we note that the customer options give the user some confidence that the algorithm he is using is unique to him. This may be particularly important if he is employing a commercially designed system which is likely to have many other users. The problem of deciding the likelihood of another user adopting the same algorithm is similar to that of determining the likelihood of two messages employing the same message key.

EXERCISE 8.3   Suppose that a user has a system with a 12-bit customer option key. Estimate how many other users of the same system there would have to be before the probability that he was the only one using his algorithm became less than 0·95.

8.3   Key Management

In the last section we described the key structure which is employed by most current systems. It consists of the customer option key which is changed infrequently, the base key which is changed quite often and the message key which is automatically altered for every message. Within most systems there is no need for any further keys and it is left to the user to determine his own key management procedure, i.e. to determine his own way of generating and distributing the keys. The generation and distribution of the customer option keys tend to be on a much smaller scale than the others, so most concern is shown for the base key.

As far as the generation is concerned it is, as we have stressed many times, important that the keys be unpredictable to any interceptor. This means that, ideally, a random number generator, which is usually a purpose-built hardware device, should be used. In this case tests must be performed regularly to test the randomness of the generation. For this, one can develop a series of tests similar to those which we introduced in Chapter 4 to assess the randomness properties of a sequence generator. In many tactical situations, when the key is entered via an alphanumeric keyboard, there are obvious advantages in using phrases for the key. Although this significantly reduces the number of possible keys available to the user, the advantage that he can easily remember it without writing it down is likely to be the overriding factor. Since the secrecy of the key phrases are so important, their choice must not be left to the user. Just as we did in Section 1.2.4, he too is likely (without realizing it) to choose a key which has a special relevance to him, e.g. an address, telephone number or name. Such an association between the key phrase and the user is likely to be noticed by a clever cryptanalyst.

The distribution of key information is probably the hardest problem in key management. Traditionally the safest method is by using couriers. Another popular technique is the use of a second cipher system, perhaps even using a technique similar to the one-time-pad.

With skilled operators and good management procedure, the key structure described is sufficient for the establishment of a cipher system. However in many commercial systems and computer networks it is essential that the operators do not even know there is a cipher system. Furthermore the changing of keys on a regular basis may be impracticable. We will discuss one such example when we consider Electronic Fund Transfer later in this chapter. We will then go even further with our key structure and actually produce as complete a key management procedure as we can.

If we cannot rely on the operator to change the keys, then we must look for ways to change the base key automatically. Before considering the possibilities, we note that any automatic changes will involve the loss of some security. Perhaps the most obvious method is simply to encipher the new base key using the previous key, and then to transmit it to the rest of the network. This is obviously feasible but has the great disadvantage that, once an interceptor has deduced one base key, he will be able to decipher all later keys as they are transmitted. A better method, which is used in many computer networks, involves the concept of **key-encrypting keys** and **data-encrypting keys**. The base key becomes our key-encrypting key and at the start of each session a master equipment somewhere within the network (often the central processor) generates a key. This key is then enciphered under the control of the base key, and is transmitted to all other equipments and initializes a sequence generator. This is now the only purpose which our base key has: to encrypt other keys. This new key, often called the **session key**, is then decrypted by the receiving equipments and loaded into a store to be used for the encryption and decryption of data until the end of that session. Thus our base key is a key-encrypting key, while the session key is a data-encrypting key. (We have not formally defined a **session**. It can be defined in a number of ways, e.g. in terms of a fixed number of characters or messages or as a certain time interval.)

If our base key is only used for enciphering session keys then, if session keys are generated randomly, it is only used to encipher random information. Thus the only way in which a cryptanalyst can obtain plaintext for an attack on the base key is by discovering a number of session keys. By carefully designing the key-encrypting sequence generator, we can ensure that the number of session keys which must be discovered, in order to mount such an attack, will be large. Furthermore, despite the automatic change of keys, even if after a certain amount of work a cryptanalyst manages to discover one session key, he will almost certainly need to do the same amount of work to discover the next one. Note, by the way, that apart from hardware constraints there is no reason why the key-encrypting sequence generator and data-encrypting sequence generator should be the same.

We could now go on to complicate our system by extending the key hierarchy and introduce further key-encrypting keys. In this way we could ensure that, apart from inside a secure area within the equipment, unenciphered keys are never stored. This should certainly increase the security. For a fuller account of this, and of automatic key management systems in general, we refer the reader to [63] and [68].

No matter how complex and apparently secure we make our system, it must never be forgotten that an automatic key management system is not as secure (theoretically!) as a system employing individually generated and distributed keys. However in practice, as we have seen, it is not usually possible for the generation and distribution of base keys to be totally secure and, if this is the case, an automatic system may be advantageous. Even within an automatic system, the base key will, of course, need changing occasionally. The frequency with which it is changed depends not only on the amount of traffic within the network but also the difficulties involved in the actual change.

In the next three sections we consider a few examples of secure communications systems. We assume that we are actually trying to design a system and look at some of the special problems which need to be considered. Since Chapter 9 includes a fairly detailed discussion of speech systems we will restrict our attention to data systems.

8.4 Example 8.1: A Strategic Asynchronous Telegraph System

8.4.1 The requirements

Before going into any detail we must consider some of the implications of such a communications system on the cipher. In particular we must be quite sure what type of communications system we have.

First we note that we are considering a **strategic** system. This means that the highest priority must be given to obtaining the maximum possible security. Its size, weight, cost, etc. will all be of secondary importance except, of course, that the cost must always be kept to a realistic level. So we may assume that there is sufficient space available for a highly complex sequence generator, a random message key (if we decide to use a stream cipher system) and virtually anything else we need to increase the level of security offered by the device.

Secondly it is specified as an asynchronous telegraph system. We have already mentioned the concept of synchronization and seen that, within digital systems, lack of synchronization can be a potential source of confusion. Within any such system, it is necessary not only to be able to identify a received signal correctly but also to know where in the sequence any given signal belongs. As a small example suppose we are transmitting octal numbers, i.e. numbers in the range 0 to 7, using the code $0 = 000$, $1 = 001, \ldots, 7 = 111$. Let us suppose that we transmit the octal sequence 31602 which, in binary, is 011 001 110 000 010. Provided there is not too great a noise problem, the receiver will be able to reconstruct this sequence but, to illustrate the problems, we will assume that for some reason the receiver missed the leading 0. Then he would assume he had received 110 011 100 000 10. From this he would deduce that the first four octal digits were 6340 and that the last one, which is incomplete, was either 4 or 5. By missing the first 0 the receiver is essentially out of step with the transmitter, and this little example shows quite clearly that being just one bit out of step can completely corrupt a message. With a cipher system we will also have the added problem of keeping the bits of sequence generation exactly in step. Thus we may even need two forms of synchronization to keep the transmitter and receiver in step.

There are many ways in which synchronizing information can be added to a signal, but for data systems two methods dominate. The first is known as a **synchronous system**. This achieves synchronization by sending an initial, agreed pattern of digits. On seeing this agreed pattern the receiver knows a message will immediately follow. This system is widely used for high data rates where, as in the above example, the data is in the form of a continuous sequence. One advantage of this method is that it does not require large numbers of extra bits per code word. It is a 'once and for all' process carried out before the transmission of actual data. One disadvantage however is that it cannot cope so effectively with data sources which are sporadic in nature, e.g. a human generating data on a teletypewriter. So, to meet the need for a system which can handle low rates of rather sporadic data more effectively, we use the asynchronous system. In an **asynchronous system**, a number of synchronizing bits are inserted into the code equivalent of each character. In a typical example the transmitter sends a 1 continuously throughout the spaces between data transmissions. Each character is then preceded by a change of level from 1 to 0 for one bit period. The 1s are known as the **stop-bits** and the 0s as the **start-bits**. The code equivalent of the character is then sent. If ITA5 is used the character is usually sent for eight periods followed by the 1 level again for a minimum of one or sometimes two bit periods. (With ITA5 the first seven bit periods are the relevant code combinations and the eighth bit is usually a parity check, on the preceding seven bits, to offer the user some error protection. Thus, for instance, an **even parity check** would mean choosing the eighth bit so that the modulo 2 sum of all eight bits is zero.) Figure 8.3 gives a diagramatic illustration.

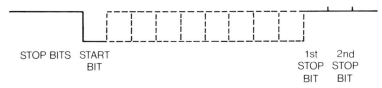

STOP BITS   START   1st   2nd
            BIT   STOP   STOP
                                                        BIT   BIT

Figure 8.3
An asynchronous system for ITA5

EXERCISE 8.4   Using the 8-character code for ITA5 complete the diagram of Figure 8.3 to show the 11 bit periods used to transmit a P.

Unlike the synchronous system, the clocks at the receiver and transmitter do not have to be matched to a high tolerance. Since retiming occurs at each start bit, they merely have to remain synchronized long enough to ensure the correct sampling of a single character. This system is widely used to connect teletypewriters to computers, and is virtually always used for telegraph systems.

8.4.2   The choice of equipment

Now that we know what is meant by a strategic asynchronous telegraph system, let us return to the problem of trying to build one. The first decision to be taken is which type of cipher system to utilize. A telegraph system may have to operate over relatively poor links and, as in a telex system which many readers may have used, the type of messages sent are not highly formatted. Furthermore, since the majority of messages will be in standard language and consequently highly redundant, we do not mind the occasional error. As we have seen, the redundancy of the language will almost certainly ensure that we still understand the message correctly. Thus we are prepared to accept the occasional error, but would prefer there to be no error propagation. This suggests that a stream cipher is the most desirable method to use for such a system. So now we need base and message keys whose sizes must be decided. Since this device is to be designed as a strategic system, we are free to choose a large base key. Also, since we do not expect to be sending messages continuously and can tolerate some additional delay at the start of each message, we can afford to introduce a reasonable length of message key. It should also be possible to include a truly random message key but, if we do, this will mean we must also include some error protection for it. We must also decide whether or not the message key should be enciphered. The system, so far, may be shown in Figure 8.4. The dotted line shows that there may be some

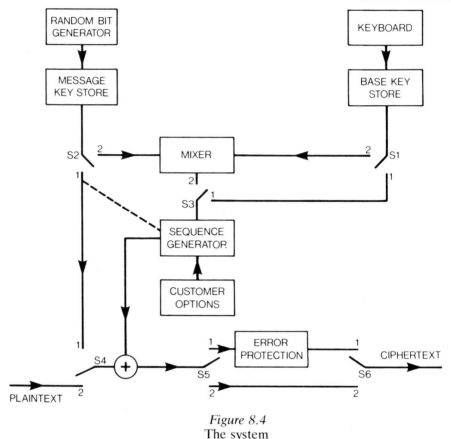

Figure 8.4
The system

algorithmic dependence of the message key during its encipherment; i.e.
the sequence generator may be altered from its normal running mode.

For message key encipherment, switches $S1$–$S6$ are all in position 1. For
data encipherment the switches are all set in position 2. In this particular
system we have used a single sequence generator for both message key
encipherment and data encipherment. In practice they may well be
different. We have included error protection for the message key but not
for the message. We could, of course, have included error protection for
the message as well. However, if we decide to include such protection it is
crucial that it comes after the message has been enciphered, since
otherwise we will effectively be adding even more redundancy to the
language. It is also worth noting that our customer option key is an input to
the sequence generator and could be used to alter the algorithm. We have
also drawn our message key/base key mixer as a separate entity from the
sequence generator. In practice it is possible to combine them.

So far we have not really considered the character coding in any
analytical sense. As we have observed, many systems employ ITA5. They
use the first seven bits for actually encoding and then include an eighth bit

as a parity check. In this way they incorporate some error detection into the system; the receiver checks the parity bit on the received character and if it is not correct he knows at least one error has occurred during transmission.

As we have already seen, any error protection within this type of system should take place after encipherment. Otherwise we are adding unnecessary redundancy to our plaintext. Thus the enciphering procedure is: first encode using ITA5, then encipher the seven-bit codeword and finally add the parity bit.

Let us now look more critically at ITA5 to see if it is suitable as a code in an enciphering system. If we refer to the look-up table for ITA5 in Appendix 2, we notice that all the capital letters lie in one of two columns. Because of the format of the table, this means that they all have bits 01 in positions 6 and 7. With many teletypewriters there are no lower case letters available and only upper case letters can be used. This, of course, means that for textual messages almost all characters will have 01 in positions 6 and 7 which means that any interceptor automatically knows about 2/7 of the binary plaintext. Of course the plaintext will not be quite so regular as at first appears. Other characters such as space, numbers, carriage return, line feed will appear and help to confuse the interceptor when he is guessing the precise location of these parts of the plaintext. Our statistics in Appendix 1 suggest that non-alphabetic characters account for about 24% of the plaintext. So, to give an example, let us suppose that a cryptanalyst needs to know 50 bits of the sequence, and hence of plaintext, in order to deduce the key. We will also assume that if any of the 50 sequence bits he is using are wrong he will almost certainly discover the fact during his trials. On the assumption that his only means of guessing plaintext is by knowing that positions 6 and 7 of each letter are 01, we now want to know how many trials we expect a cryptanalyst to make before he discovers our key. If he simply looks at positions 6 and 7 of each character there is a probability of about $0 \cdot 76$ that they are 01. (Remember that about 76% of the plaintext consists of actual letters.) In order to obtain his 50 bits of sequence, the interceptor needs 25 such pairs, i.e. he must find 25 blocks such that positions 6 and 7 are 01. But the probability of 25 blocks chosen at random all having 01 in positions 6 and 7 is about $(0 \cdot 76)^{25} \simeq 0 \cdot 001$. Thus we would expect him to have to make $1/0 \cdot 001 \simeq 1000$ trials until he obtains the required 50 bits of sequence.

The problem of virtually presenting the cryptanalyst with known plaintext can be overcome by avoiding the use of a standard character coding system and using source coding instead; i.e. designing a code to randomize the distribution of 0s and 1s in the plaintext. Unfortunately most teletypewriters are designed to work with particular coding systems which, of course, means that the coding is part of the teletypewriter and not part of the cipher system. It may therefore be considered necessary to include a second character conversion within the cipher system. The system then looks like Figure 8.5.

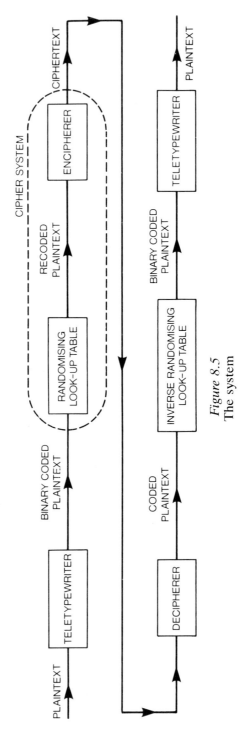

Figure 8.5
The system

When choosing our randomization look-up table we must remember that, as well as the overall distribution of 0s and 1s being random, the distribution of 0s and 1s for the bits in any given position of each character must be unpredictable.

Another important factor which must be considered is precisely how the characters are transmitted. Since this system is asynchronous, as each character is typed on the teletypewriter and processed by the enciphering system it is ready to be sent. A typical speed used is 110 bits per second which, for the 11 bits per character implementation of the ITA5 code, means 10 characters per second. If the operator is able to type at 10 characters per second this is no problem but, of course, a slower speed is more likely. This means that the transmission must go into an idling state while it waits for the next character. If we use the asynchronous system discussed earlier then this idling state is all 1s. One consequence of this is that, from an interceptor's point of view, there is a continuous transmission in which he is easily able to distinguish between enciphered characters and the pauses between them.

The mere fact that there is a particular operator typing out a message can also give information to an interceptor. When watching a typist at work, it is usually apparent that there are a number of distinctive characteristics about the typing rhythm. For instance, when typing a string of small, well-known words the typist usually proceeds quite quickly. However, when faced with unusual words or names, the speed drops considerably. There are also often pauses after typing a carriage return, while the typist waits for the machine to settle itself at the start of a new line. In addition, there are often uniform pauses between sentences and a further distinctive interval between paragraphs. All such facts are well known to the cryptanalyst, and the typing rhythm which he observes while intercepting some text may prove very useful as an aid to guessing some plaintext. Furthermore, he might even begin to recognize the distinguishing characteristics of certain operators. This could prove invaluable, as operators definitely tend to adopt particular formats for messages. Since it is obviously dangerous to give an interceptor any information or assistance, we need to seek ways in which all the above information can be concealed.

8.4.3 Padding characters

One way to avoid the long periods of idling is to insert padding characters into the text whenever there is no character available from the teletypewriter. The idea is that, whenever a character is needed, the device looks to see if one is available from the teletypewriter. If no such character is available, it selects one of the padding characters and processes it exactly as if it had come from the teletypewriter. Thus the system transmits precisely the maximum number of characters per second and the interceptor sees a continuous stream of ciphertext. Furthermore, since the padding characters are enciphered, the interceptor cannot distinguish between real text and padding. This means he cannot detect any pauses. Clearly the introduction of these padding characters makes life harder for an interceptor. But, of course, we have not yet said how we can generate these padding characters. Furthermore we must not forget that they need to be recognized by the receiver and then removed, so that they are not printed as part of the message.

Since nulls are non-printing characters, they are certainly candidates to be padding characters. However, pauses occur frequently in any text and, consequently, using any one fixed character for padding will almost certainly affect the statistics of the plaintext. It is usually very difficult to compensate for this. In fact, in a small sample of tests conducted within a system operating at 10 characters per second and using competent typists, we found that it was not unusual for 40% of the text to be padding characters. This illustrates just how dramatically the choice of padding characters might affect the statistics of the plaintext. Certainly we need a fairly large number of padding characters. One possibility is to use a pseudo-random source for the padding characters. Of course we cannot let the source be completely random as our receiver must be able to recognize all padding characters. However, if the source is pseudo-random, it is possible for the receiver to monitor the input continually and then compare it with what he would expect if the characters were padding. There are dangers involved in this. The system must be carefully designed so that the receiver does not delete part of the text by accident. It must also be designed so that it is not disrupted by errors occurring in transmission. One possible way of guarding against these hazards is to insert padding strings rather than single characters. This will automatically increase the probability of recognition by the receiver.

We will not develop this theme any further since we would now have to start considering likely error patterns for particular channels etc. This is beyond the scope of this book. Nevertheless the reader should be aware of the problems and the type of solution.

There are still further problems to be considered, but we will only consider one of them. Once we have fixed our transmission medium, there may be certain characters which cannot be transmitted. For instance some of the control characters of ITA5 may affect the transmission equipment between sender and receiver. In particular, if this cipher system is to be used in conjunction with a message switch, there may be particular combinations of letters, unlikely to occur naturally in text, which are used to give the message switch instructions. Although these characters are likely to be banned from all plaintext, they have a reasonable probability of occurring in the transmitted ciphertext. (This is simply because ciphertext characters can take all possibilities.) This problem can be overcome by using a literalizer. The role of a **literalizer** is to watch for 'illegal' characters and replace them by legitimate ones. For instance, if in ITA5 the characters representing TC1–TC10 are illegal, the literalizer may replace them by *XA–XJ*. (This particular implementation is our own

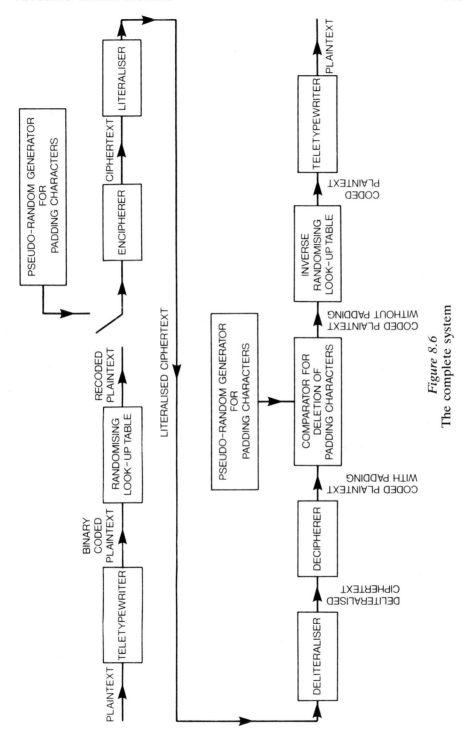

Figure 8.6
The complete system

choice. Any ten bigrams with the same first letter will do.) The letter X, which prefixes each of the replacements, is called the **flag** and, in order to avoid confusing the receiver, it must also be declared an illegal character. Thus we must find a replacement for it whenever it occurs as a ciphertext letter; one common way is to follow it by another fixed letter, e.g. XK. But now we have replaced one character by two and have caused message extension. This, as we have stressed before, is undesirable and should be kept to a minimum. Any system which employs any form of literalizer before encipherment will extend the plaintext. This might mean that knowledge of one plaintext character plus the fact that it was literalized gave the interceptor two plaintext characters. To avoid this it is advantageous to do all literalization after encipherment. Literalizing may also be used if we want the output to be a restricted set of characters in a particular format, e.g. groups of five alphabetic characters.

We have now built a complete system which is shown in Figure 8.6. Note that we now regard the circuit of Figure 8.4 as a single enciphering module. In both the transmitter and receiver, the pseudo-random sequence generator for padding characters may be initialized by a function of base key and the message key. It may also be dependent on the customer option key.

We conclude our description of Example 8.1 by emphasizing that there are a number of other problems which we have ignored. Our discussion is in no way complete, but merely serves as an illustration of the number of decisions facing a system designer and the many problems that can effect a cipher system and the way it is deployed.

8.5 Example 8.2: A Portable Tactical On/Off Line System

A system is said to be **off-line** if the equipment is not directly connected to any transmission media. In such a system the operator will normally prepare his cryptogram and then transmit it by some unspecified medium. In an **on-line** system it is assumed that the machine is connected to a transmission path, for instance radio or line, and the cryptogram can be transmitted immediately. The requirements for Example 8.2 are completely different from those for Example 8.1. We will not go into any details, but merely include it to provide a contrast with the last system and to show how various requirements place totally different constraints on the design.

As we have already explained, with a tactical system a few hours, or at most a few days, is normally the maximum security which needs to be guaranteed. Provided this is achieved, the major constraints are cost (as always!), size, weight, simplicity and reliability of operation. For these reasons it may be decided to omit many of the desirable, but not essential, components of our earlier systems. For instance, if we decide to use a stream cipher system, which may well be the case as the device may have to work on-line using bad transmission media, then we may feel it is adequate to let our message key be dependent on the message itself or be pseudo-random. This might, if the amount of space is critical, have the advantage of requiring less hardware than providing a random bit generator. It may also be more efficient, in a system like this, not to operate in real time but to allow messages to be entered, edited and then for the ciphertext to be output if in an off-line mode or, if in an on-line mode, to be transmitted as a burst of information. This permits the use of a synchronous, as opposed to an asynchronous, method of synchronization.

Since this type of device normally has its own keyboard and does not rely on a separate teletypewriter, a binary coding method may be specifically designed for its cipher system. When this occurs great care must be taken to build into the coding scheme an even distribution of 0s and 1s.

We will not say any more about Example 8.2. We merely stress that the cryptographic design of such a system will not normally be as ambitious or complex as that for a strategic system.

8.6 Example 8.3: An On-Line Electronic Fund Transfer System

This third example is very different from the others and we will consider it in detail.

An **electronic fund transfer system** (EFTS) is designed to offer an alternative to the growing problem of paper-based transactions. Many articles have appeared discussing both the economics and ergonomics of EFTS (see for instance [62] and [70]). But here we shall restrict our discussion to the security aspects of EFTS in its role as an on-line fund transfer system. Here, by an on-line system we mean that all verification and authorisation takes place within a computer network that is remote from the terminal.

8.6.1 General description and security problems

In order to examine the type of security threats with which an EFTS might have to cope, let us first consider the way in which a typical EFTS works. Suppose our typical system consists of terminals at the point of sale in a retail outlet and that these terminals communicate, via a communications network, with a central computer, whose function it is to ratify the transaction and return a signal to the terminal which may either authorize it or not.

A customer wishing to use this system is normally issued with a plastic card bearing a magnetic stripe. The magnetic stripe contains some identification of the customer, for example an account number together with various other information; typically some card-issuer identification and an expiry date. In addition the customer is issued with some **Personal Identification data** (PID) that should be kept secret. Ideally this data is known only to the customer and the card-issuer (better still if it is only the card-issuer's computer that has this information). When using the system the following sequence of events takes place. First the retailer enters, on the EFT terminal, the amount of the transaction. The customer's card is then read by the terminal. The customer, on agreeing the amount, enters his PID which should ideally be via a separate keyboard. Thus the terminal now knows the amount of the transaction, the customer identification and the PID as well as other information such as the card expiry date, terminal identification, etc. It must now, via the communications network, communicate with the **card-issuer's computer** (CIC). The CIC has a record of this customer's PID, which can be accessed via the customer identification, and can thus verify that the user has entered the correct PID corresponding to his magnetic card. In this way the PID acts as a signature. So, provided the CIC's records show that the funds are available, the transaction can be authorized. This authorization (or non-authorization) information is communicated to the terminal and the CIC then awaits a confirmation that the transaction has taken place, upon which it can make the transfer of funds. Within some systems, the transfer of funds may not take place immediately, but might be recorded by the CIC and carried out when the terminal is logged-off and some auditing is carried out.

It is immediately clear that the EFTS transmissions require some form of protection, since otherwise they could easily be tampered with or monitored. For instance monitoring the line could, if there is no protection of the data, give the interceptor corresponding customer identification and PID pairs. He could then either steal cards for which he knows the PID or, more profitably, manufacture his own cards. In this case he could record, on the magnetic stripe, a customer identification for which he knows the PID. On the other hand, tampering with the line could be just as profitable, since he could change the amount of a transaction being made by a collaborator. Thus large amounts being transferred from his collaborator to a retailer could be substituted by much smaller ones, whilst refunds from the retailer could be made to show much larger values. In addition, by impersonating a terminal, he could cause funds to be diverted to his own account. Thus it is essential that the data be protected from change and, furthermore, that at least some of the data being transferred between the terminal and CIC should be enciphered.

As usual, when discussing the security of any system, we must adopt the attitude that things are as bad as possible and that an interceptor has the maximum possible information. But, of course, in this situation a possible interceptor is not our only worry. We must also assume that, at a point of interception, a computer can be interposed in the communications path to alter or copy parts of the message, replay messages or even emit false material. The prospect of an interceptor tampering with messages is far more critical in this type of situation than in any of our earlier examples. This is because the messages will almost certainly be highly formatted and received by a computer, which is normally far less discriminating in its acceptance of properly formatted messages than a human operator.

8.6.2 The encipherment procedure

Now that we have highlighted the objectives of our intended system and the security problems, we can start trying to design one. We turn first to the encipherment procedure and, for this, there are many possibilities. Since our messages are likely to use the same format, there is some advantage in using a cipher system which will destroy this formatting. If we do not do this, an intruder into the system will be able to tamper with our messages and know precisely which part of the message he is changing. At present most card issuers seem to be in favour of using the DES as the basis for this cipher system. As we saw in Chapter 7, this is a block cipher which uses a 56 bit key to encipher each block of 64 bits of data. Also in Chapter 7, we observed the error propagation properties of this type of block cipher. These properties mean that with any reasonable block cipher, and so certainly with DES, if a single bit of data is altered after it has been enciphered it may cause the entire block of data to be deciphered as a meaningless jumble of information. Thus alterations which occur during transmission, whether intentional or not, can be more easily detected.

As always, we must remember that our cipher system is theoretically breakable. We must, therefore, take all possible steps to avoid giving any helpful information to a would-be cryptanalyst. As an example, one way in which an attack might be made harder is by introducing, into every block of information to be ciphered, a number of purely random bits. This would necessitate the existence of a random bit generator within both the terminal and the CIC. The effect would be that the interceptor could never be certain of obtaining corresponding blocks of plaintext and ciphertext. As we shall see when discussing authentication, we will be able to utilize this random information advantageously.

8.6.3 Some possible methods of attack

In order to decide which other security features we should incorporate into our system, we discuss some of the other ways in which an EFTS might be compromised. We will assume that the data, or at least part of it, is enciphered prior to transmission and that the interceptor does not know the key being used. Of course, if the interceptor does know the key, he can mount the type of attack described earlier. Even if he does not, he may still be able to inflict considerable damage on the system.

The most obvious way of attacking the network is by discovering, or guessing, PIDs. The ease with which the PID may be discovered is largely the responsibility of the card-issuer and user. Both these parties should be aware of their responsibility and take steps to keep the PID secret. The best way for the user to do this is to memorize it. Unfortunately, this must restrict the amount of data contained within the PID. In practice it appears that the most convenient amount of data that people can easily memorize is four decimal digits; i.e. a number between 0000 and 9999. The PID is thus often termed a PIN (**Personal Identification Number**). The implication of a small PID is that an unauthorized user with a fraudulently obtained card may be able to try all possibilities until he discovers the correct one, and thus obtain an authorization. One way of stopping this type of exhaustive search is for the CIC to keep track of the number of non-authorized transactions made with a card and, if this number exceeds a predetermined threshold, for the card to be automatically declared invalid for all future transactions.

Regarding the part played by the card-issuers in keeping the PIDs secure, there are a number of precautionary steps that can be taken. For instance, if the PID is randomly generated for each system user, an unauthorized person will be unable to deduce the user's PID, either from extra information relating to the user or knowledge of when the PID was generated. This is also a good reason for not allowing the user to choose his own PID. (As we have repeatedly stressed, it is a fact that people tend to select numbers that are already familiar to them, for example telephone numbers, birthdays, addresses, etc.) The CIC could further protect PIDs by keeping only an enciphered version of them within the computer file. The key used for this encipherment could be protected far more easily than all the PID files.

A more sophisticated attack against an EFTS might be to 'impersonate' either the terminal or the CIC. For instance, if someone can monitor the line whilst a legitimate refund to a collaborator is being made by a retailer, he will then be able to 'impersonate' this terminal and continually send this same message up the line. Unless the system has been designed to be secure against this type of attack, the CIC will recognize this as a valid transaction (which it originally was) and transfer funds each time as requested, until of course the retailer runs out of money. On the other hand we could spend our time just as profitably by 'impersonating' the CIC. In this case, we may be able to record a legitimate authorization from the computer and then send it to the retailer's terminal whenever we wish to make a purchase. Thus the terminal would record an authorized transaction when in fact no transfer of funds has taken place.

This type of attack by 'impersonation' can be carried out without any knowledge of the encipherment procedure or the key used. It can only be adequately overcome by ensuring that each transaction includes a full two-way authentication procedure between the terminal and CIC. We will describe a possible method of authentication later.

Returning to the encipherment of the data, if we do not encipher all the data then we must at least protect the remaining data from change; either deliberate or accidental. There are a number of reasons why it might not be advantageous to encipher all the data; the most important of these being that the more information that is enciphered, the greater the message extension. (This is simply because the ciphered information may need literalizing before transmission.) This in turn increases the response time for the system and diminishes one of the great attractions of EFTS: namely its speed in ratifying transactions.

Also, information such as the terminal identity cannot be enciphered since, as we shall see, this identity tells the network which decipherment key to employ. If all the information is not protected, however, the system could be compromised. As an example, if the amount of the transaction is not enciphered this could be altered and the transaction might still appear valid. Another reason for protecting all the data is that an unauthorized person might remove a block of information (whether or not it be enciphered) and replace it with a different block. Unless the entire message is protected from change, this may result in the redirection of funds. We will return to these problems later.

There is yet another means of attacking the enciphered message. Apart from actually breaking the cipher system to discover its keys, an unauthorized person might try to discover the keys from the terminal by direct physical means. To combat both these types of attack we need to establish a key hierarchy.

8.6.4 A possible key hierarchy

The EFTS terminal must contain a key to encipher the data prior to transmission. Since so much of the security of the system is dependent on this key, it is desirable that, at any given time, each key should be assigned to at most one terminal. In other words, no two terminals should ever apply the same key simultaneously. Of course, in practice, it may be unrealistic to *guarantee* this but, since the number of available keys is so large compared with the number of terminals, the probability of achieving this aim is virtually one.

One of our first considerations must be how to enter the key into the terminal. If the entire key is simply stored in the terminal's memory then, since making the terminal completely tamper proof is almost impossible, there is a reasonably high risk that the key may be obtained by an unauthorized person, without anyone even being aware of it. For instance, any maintenance engineer will have easy access to the key. Alternatively if the retailer uses a magnetic card to insert the key at log-on time, the risk is even higher because the card might be lost, stolen or copied.

Thus it appears desirable to use a two part key. Each half could consist of 56 bits, for example if DES were used, and the complete key would be the modulo 2 sum of the two parts. One half could then be resident in the terminal, ideally loaded at the network management site, while the other half could be on a magnetic card to be read by the terminal at log-on time.

Using this arrangement it would be very simple to meet our requirement that each terminal should have a key which is not currently being used by any other. Even in the context of a large retail outlet with many terminals, this could be achieved easily since the half of the key on the magnetic card could be common to all these terminals (to facilitate the log-on procedure) whilst the half of the key resident in each terminal could be different from all the others.

The locations and physical distribution of the terminals in an EFTS make it difficult to change the key, and thus it is advantageous to use a key hierarchy involving base keys and session keys. The only role of the base key is to enable secure log-on and simultaneously to decipher a session key transmitted to the terminal from the network (i.e. at log-on time the network transmits a session key to the terminal, enciphering it using that terminal's base key). All data encipherment then uses the session key.

Such a system has two definite advantages. Firstly, should an interceptor gain knowledge of the session key by breaking the cipher system using a known-data attack, he will only be able to read the traffic until the terminal logs-on again. A new session key then comes into operation and the interceptor is back where he started. Secondly, this system only needs the base key during log-on time. The base key (or at least the half entered by the retailer) can, therefore, be deleted from memory as soon as the terminal has logged-on. This implies that the entire base key is in the terminal only during log-on time.

Ideally within such a key hierarchy the session key should be generated randomly so that the base key is used only to encipher random information. This greatly increases the complexity of a cryptanalytic attack to discover the base key.

The EFTS key hierarchy may be extended to include further keys within the network and CIC in order to encipher both these base and session keys as well as PIDs etc. It may also be necessary to have a hierarchy of keys between certain nodes of the network where management and auditing might take place. Again, the session keys should be changed regularly, perhaps during the early hours of the morning when the system is presumably at its quietest.

8.6.5 Authentication

We now come to the problem of authentication. We have already pointed out that, to ensure a high level of security, each transaction must be fully authenticated. If we let $X \rightarrow Y$ mean that X has authenticated Y then, for a full authentication between two nodes, we require $X \rightleftarrows Y$. In the EFTS the two end nodes are the terminal and the CIC. Normally there are three transmissions between these end nodes: a request for authorization from the terminal to the CIC, an authorization (or not) from the CIC to the terminal and finally a 'transaction completed' signal from the terminal to the CIC. Since we have these three transmissions we are able to operate a so-called **full handshake authentication** process. We will describe this process in general terms and then relate it to EFTS.

We suppose that a session key Sk_{XY} has been set up between X and Y, and that X now wants to communicate with Y in such a way that full authentication will be established. In the first transmission X sends a message to Y to include X's identification x plus a unique identifier I_X which has been encrypted using Sk_{XY}. Ideally this identifier should be different to all other identifiers that X has used in previous messages to Y.

When Y receives the message, the information x tells him that the message is from X and that he must therefore use key Sk_{XY} for decipherment. When he deciphers the message, he finds I_X and then returns a message which includes a unique identifier of his own, I_Y say, together with a known function of I_X, which we will denote by $g(I_X)$. Both must be encrypted using Sk_{XY}. When X receives this message, he compares the $g(I_X)$ contained in the message with the correct version of $g(I_X)$, which he knows since he chose I_X. If they agree then he has authenticated Y. The reason that he can safely authenticate Y lies in the fact that he chose I_X and so the only way in which Y could have returned the correct function of I_X was by knowing Sk_{XY}. At this stage Y has not yet authenticated X and, for this to happen, X must return a message which depends on I_Y. In practice he will send a message involving $g(I_Y)$ and, once this is deciphered correctly, Y will have authenticated X and we will have $X \rightleftharpoons Y$ in three communications. We should add that this is only one of a number of variations of full handshake authentication; for extra details see [64] and [69].

We now relate this procedure to our EFTS example using DES and its encryption function. For $X \rightarrow Y$, X sends a random block of information enciphered, for example, within the first half of a 64-bit block of data. Y deciphers this block to obtain the random information. He re-enciphers it within a different part, the second half, say, of a block of data to be returned to X. When X receives the data he compares it against that which he sent. If they agree he has authenticated Y. For $Y \rightarrow X$, Y can include in the other half of his message some random information. So all that is necessary now, for $X \rightleftharpoons Y$, is for this to be enciphered by X and transmitted back to Y.

Notice that we only insist that the identifiers are random but not that they are unique. This is because each transmission will contain other enciphered information, part of which may include a transaction number which, obviously, will alter from transaction to transaction. The session key will also change fairly frequently. Thus the probability of using the same identifier twice can be made very low, and even if the same identifier were used twice there is no way for an interceptor to know. (The other information within an enciphered block of data would be different and this would cause the entire ciphertext to be different.)

The advantages of this system over the commonly used methods of a password and/or transaction number are that every authentication is independent of all others and, further, that random information is being enciphered with the data. This eliminates the possibility that an interceptor knows a block of corresponding plaintext and ciphertext.

In practice an on-line EFTS may include more than one card issuer and/or a number of processors at various physical locations. In this case the data will normally be transmitted between a number of nodes. Some of these nodes may also need to be included in any authentication procedure. For instance there may be a terminal control node, a network management node, etc.

The system of authentication described above can easily be generalized to include more nodes.

Consider the situations of Figure 8.7 with three nodes. Let us take (a) first. There is a directed path, in each direction, between any two nodes, and this implies that every two nodes have authenticated each other. Thus this system gives complete authentication. (Note that for X to authenticate Y he relies on Z's authentication of Y. This means that X is showing great faith in Z's 'integrity'!)

Consider (b) now. Here there is actually an edge in each direction, between any two nodes, so this system also offers complete authentication. However, it is also clear that (a) requires less authentication procedures than (b) and hence is more efficient (in terms of the number of transmissions).

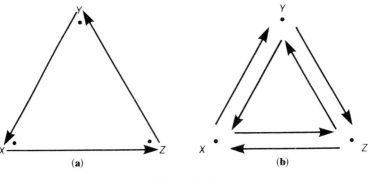

Figure 8.7
Authentication

In practice the system should normally be designed for as efficient an authentication procedure as possible, although the efficiency that can be obtained depends on the exact layout of the network. Within such a network, where there may be several thousand nodes, it is important to ensure that it is possible to authenticate fully every pair of nodes for which it is considered necessary.

As previously discussed, it is not necessary, and indeed not possible, to encipher the entire block of data being transmitted at each stage of a transaction. (Clearly we cannot encipher everything since the terminal identity, for instance, is needed by the network to identify the key needed for decipherment.) We must, however, protect all the data from change, both intentional and otherwise. We must also ensure that the entire message is protected so that it is not possible for an interceptor to remove blocks of information and replace them with other information. So, what information should be enciphered and how can the remainder of the information be protected? The PID must be enciphered and preferably on an end-to-end basis; i.e. it should never appear unenciphered anywhere except the terminal and CIC, both of which are unavoidable. Also authentication information must be enciphered. It appears that nothing else, i.e. customer identification, amount of transaction etc., need be enciphered provided that it is protected. In much of the literature a check sum has been suggested as an appropriate way of protecting the unenciphered data. If one is used then the method chosen must be very carefully analyzed.

8.6.6. Examples of check sums

Below we give two examples of check sums currently in use. These *cannot* guarantee that the message has not been changed in some way, even though the added protection of both adding random information to the check sum and also enciphering the check sum have been included.

(i) *A standard cyclic redundancy check* Essentially a cyclic redundancy check expresses the message as a polynomial and divides that polynomial by a 'small' fixed polynomial, $f(x)$. The remainder after this division is the cyclic redundancy check, and when this is also transmitted the effect is that the entire message (including the check bits) is perfectly divisible by $f(x)$. The receiver checks that this is the case and, if not, knows that the message he has received is incorrect. If, during the transmission, a perfect multiple of the fixed polynomial is inserted into the message, the receiver will find that his cyclic redundancy check shows no errors.

It may well be that this can be done in such a way as to alter the amount of a transaction or terminal identity. In these cases the CIC will not spot the changes either, because the account number and PID still match.

(ii) *A modulo arithmetic sum of the data* One example of this is a longitudinal parity check. Even not knowing the modulus used, part of the information can be altered so that the check does not pick up the changes made. For instance, a simple transposition of digits has this effect. The consequences are the same as those outlined under (i) above.

The essential point illustrated in the above two examples is that most check sums are designed to detect errors. They cannot detect all error patterns. Although they are designed so that the error patterns which they do not detect have a very low probability of occurring naturally, these error patterns are predictable and can be inserted quite easily by an unauthorized active interceptor. In fact there is a relatively high probability of being able to insert such error patterns so that the message still makes sense but huge funds are diverted into the wrong accounts.

Two ways of overcoming the problem are outlined below:

(i) Encipher more of the message – in particular the complete amount and as much of the terminal identity as possible. This method is generally unsatisfactory.
(ii) Use a check sum method that is dependent on either a key or some random information that is enciphered.

EXERCISE 8.5 Suggest ways in which the block chaining method of Section 7.4.4 may be used to generate check sums.

It must be appreciated that methods like the above *cannot guarantee* that all error combinations will be discovered. (The more check bits that are used the more error combinations it is possible to detect.) An unauthorized interceptor, however, will not know how to alter the message so that it will not be detected. Thus regular attempts to alter messages will be detected by the system operators.

The check sum described above does not, of course, replace any error detection included to reduce the chances of an unwarranted refusal of authorization for a transaction.

From the discussion on possible methods of attacking an EFTS, it should be apparent that security features for the transmission path are very necessary, especially in the light of how enormous a fraud might take place if funds could be easily redirected. Furthermore, if the system is not constantly on the alert, it may take some time before the fraud is even discovered – if it ever is!

We must also bear in mind that the security of the system rests ultimately within the PID, and no matter how secure the transmissions of data are made the system is still vulnerable at the two ends of the link, namely the terminal and card-issuer's computer. Both the card-issuer and user must be made aware of the importance of keeping the PID confidential. Within the computer there is the problem of securing files and programs. This can be achieved by storing them in ciphered form and restricting the distribution of the ciphering key. The terminal may be vulnerable to so simple an attack as someone spying on a user as he enters his PID. The latter method of attacking the system can be at least partially dealt with in the careful design of the terminal. In any case, this type of attack should not result in the huge illegitimate transfer of funds which might occur if it were possible to tamper with the transmission path.

In this discussion we have primarily restricted ourselves to a particular type of EFTS and to the security features employed to protect the transmission of data. We have not concerned ourselves with the physical security of the system. Despite having limited our discussions to a particular type of EFTS, most, if not all, of the comments we have made are applicable to virtually all types of EFTS. It is however vital that the security features necessary within a system be viewed within the context of how that system is to be deployed.

In this chapter we have considered a few examples of complete cipher systems. Our discussions have by no means been exhaustive. However, hopefully, we have illustrated how each system must be examined carefully before deciding how the cipher system is to be designed and used. It is not enough to decide that we have a good sequence generator or block cipher system. It cannot be ensured that the system provides an adequate level of security unless every aspect of its operation has been investigated. Furthermore the system should, as far as possible, be operator proof. In other words it should remain secure no matter what mistakes the operator makes. It becomes apparent when reading books such as Kahn [2], that many systems in the past have been broken through operator carelessness and error. Thus it is essential that the device be simple and reliable. In many situations it is desirable that the cipher system be completely transparent, since, in the computer or EFTS environment, there is no need for the operators even to be aware that there is a cipher system.

Further Reading

[63] and [68] are concerned with key management; [64] and [69] with authentication. For more details about the economics and ergonomics of EFTS [62], [66] and [70] are interesting papers. [67] and [26] are general books on error-correction codes.

[62] Benton, J. B., 'Economics and use of electronic fund transfer', *Telecommunications*, Vol. 12, No. 5, 1978, 35–41.

[63] Ehrsam, W. F., Matyas, S. M., Meyer, C. H. and Tuchman, W. L., 'A cryptographic key management scheme for implementing the Data Encryption Standard', *IBM Sys. Journal*, Vol. 17, No. 2, 1978, 106–25.

[64] Evans, A., Kantrowitz, W. and Weiss, E., 'A user authentication scheme not requiring secrecy in the computer', *Comms. of ACM*, Vol. 17, No. 8, 1974, 437–42.

[65] Feistel, H., 'Cryptographic coding for data-bank privacy', *Research Report RC-2827*, T. J. Watson Research Center, IBM, 1970.

[66] Houghton, M. R., 'An introduction to electronic fund transfer techniques', *Commun. Int.*, Vol. 17, No. 8, 1980, 32–3.

[[2]] Kahn, David, *The Codebreakers, The Story of Secret Writing*, New York, Macmillan, 1967.

[67] MacWilliams, F. J. and Sloane, N. J. A., *The Theory of Error-correcting Codes*, North-Holland Publishing Co., 1978.

[68] Matyas, S. M. and Meyer, C. H., 'Generation, distribution and installation of cryptographic keys', *IBM Sys. Journal*, Vol. 17, No. 2, 1978, 126–37.

[69] Needham, R. M. and Schroeder, M. D., 'Using encryption for authentication in large networks of computers', *Comms. of ACM*, Vol. 21, No. 12, 1978, 993–9.

[70] Pease, D. L., 'EFT systems are evolving', *Telecommunications*,
      Vol. 12, No. 5, 1978, 51–64.
[26] Peterson, W. W. and Weldon, E. J., *Error-correcting Codes*,
      2nd Ed., MIT Press, 1972.

9.
Speech Security Systems

9.1 Introduction

Today's communications systems can be roughly divided into two classes depending on the type of signal they process: digital or analogue. In Chapter 8 we concerned ourselves, primarily, with digital signals, i.e. signals that are made up from a finite number of discrete levels. Our main interest was with binary systems which use two levels corresponding to 0 and 1. **Analogue signals** can vary continuously over their dynamic range and, for our purposes, the principal example of an analogue signal is speech.

Speech is probably the most fundamental form of communication available to us. The majority of people are very familiar with the most common forms of speech communication; i.e. the telephone and radio. These forms of communication are very widely used. We must therefore examine how such signals might be enciphered. As we shall see, there are a variety of methods available; some clearly better (at least in theory) than others.

In order to understand why particular methods are chosen we must, at the very least, gain a superficial knowledge of some of the problems facing the communicator and the electronic engineer. Whereas the majority of the chapters in this book have required that the electronic engineer learn some mathematics, in this chapter it is the turn of the mathematician to be presented with new concepts. In particular, he will need to appreciate something of the way in which the highly complex acoustic signal that we recognize as human speech is formed. He will also need to appreciate the characteristics of the resulting, equally complex, electrical waveform produced when this acoustic signal is applied to a microphone. Furthermore, when dealing with 'scrambled' speech signals, we will need to take into account the relevant features of human perception in order to consider the question: how much intelligibility remains in a 'scrambled' speech signal? We will not be concerned with any precise 'information theoretic' quantification of residual intelligibility. We will simply try to decide if an interceptor is likely to be able to understand more of a scrambled message than we would expect him to obtain from guesswork. At times we will quote experimental results which the reader will either have to verify for himself or simply accept.

For the purposes of this book it is not necessary to develop a detailed theory of the response of electronic circuits to analogue signals, and the interested reader is referred to [88]. We merely concentrate on those topics necessary to enable us to understand why speech signals are restricted to certain bandwidths, and how our particular scrambling techniques work.

The reader must, at all times, remain aware that we should always avoid degrading our communications network. Almost all speech security systems reduce, at least to some extent, the audio quality of a voice transmission. Clearly, security will not be enhanced if the link has been so badly degraded that we have to repeat the same message a number of times. There is, therefore, a need to take into consideration the type of transmission link to be used and, for any particular security requirement, to choose an encryption system that will give the least degradation of audio quality. There is no point in having a very high security level if it is no longer possible to communicate!

After a discussion of the properties of certain types of communication channel and the make-up of speech signals, we consider the merits and defects of various scrambling methods. We then consider the advantages and disadvantages associated with digital speech security.

9.2   Basic Concepts

As we mentioned in the introduction it is now the turn of the mathematician to be faced with electronic concepts and terminology which are probably unfamiliar. We begin by defining some special properties of electronic components and/or circuits.

Suppose we have a circuit with input signals $\mathbf{X}=\{x_1, x_2, \ldots\}$ which produce outputs $\mathbf{Y}=\{y_1, y_2, \ldots\}$ where y_i is the output corresponding to x_i. The circuit is said to satisfy the **principle of homogeneity** if, whenever any x_i is 'multiplied' by a constant and input to the circuit, the output signal is y_i 'multiplied' by the same constant (Figure 9.1(a)). The **principle of superposition** says that, for any two input signals x_i and x_j, the input signal which is the superposition (or **sum**) of the two signals x_i and x_j will produce an output signal which is the sum of y_i and y_j (Figure 9.1(b)). A **linear circuit** satisfies both the principles of homogeneity and superposition.

Many of the components and circuits of telecommunication systems are either linear or may be considered as such, at least over a limited range of values for input and output. This range is normally referred to as the **dynamic range.**

A circuit modifies the electronic signal at its input to produce a different electronic signal at its output. If we are interested in analyzing the response of our circuit to all possible input signals (our **input space**) then it is clearly not desirable (or practicable) to consider each individual signal in our input

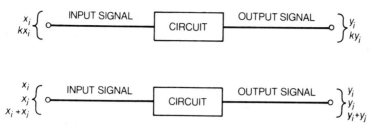

Figure 9.1
(a) Principle of homogeneity
(b) Principle of superposition

space. We can make use of the linearity of our circuit by considering its response to a subset of the input space, called a **generating set**. This is any subset of signals such that, by multiplying them by constants and/or adding together appropriate combinations of them, we can form any signal in the space. Thus if we have a linear circuit and can find a generating set for our input space then, as soon as we know the output corresponding to each of our generating signals, we can use the homogeneity and superposition principles to determine the output of any possible input signal.

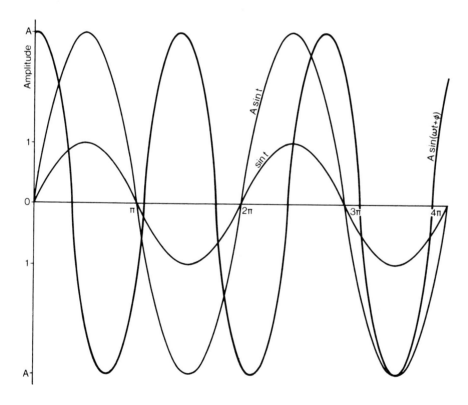

Figure 9.2
Graphs of $\sin t$, $A\sin t$ and $A\sin(\omega t + \varphi)$

There are many sets of signals which can, and do, act as generating sets for input spaces, the most convenient and widely used being the sinusoids. (We should point out that the term 'signal' usually refers to varying currents and voltages which convey information. **A sinusoid** does not convey information in the same sense as a signal does. However, it is nevertheless customary to refer to sinusoids as signals.) A sinusoid is a waveform which is represented by either of the following: $A\cos(\omega t + \phi)$ or $A\sin(\omega t + \phi)$ where A, ω, ϕ are constants and t represents time. The constant A is called the **amplitude** of the wave and, since both $\cos x$ and $\sin x$ have a maximum value of 1, it is the height of the peak of the waveform above its average value. The functions $\sin x$ and $\cos x$ are both periodic with period 2π. Thus a sinusoid must also be periodic with period $2\pi/\omega$. However, instead of referring to the period of a waveform, it is customary to talk about its **frequency**, which is the number of periods (or **cycles**) in one second. Clearly, for any waveform, if the period is T seconds and f is the frequency then $f = 1/T$. This means that, for a sinusoid, $f = \omega/2\pi$ or $\omega = 2\pi f$. The unit of frequency is the **hertz** (Hz); one hertz is one cycle per second. Since f is the frequency and ω is f multiplied by 2π, ω is called the **angular frequency** of the sinusoid. (There are, we must add, more convincing reasons for the terminology, but they need not concern us now.) The constant ϕ, which determines the height of the wave when $t = 0$, is called the **phase** of the sinusoid. If two sinusoids have different phases then we say that they are **out-of-phase** and refer to the difference of their ϕs as the **phase difference**.

Clearly multiplying the sinusoid $A\sin(\omega t + \phi)$ by k gives the sinusoid $kA\sin(\omega t + \phi)$; i.e. it produces another sinusoid with the same phase and frequency but with the amplitude multiplied by k.

9.3 Fourier Analysis

9.3.1 Definitions

Since both the sine and cosine waves are periodic, we will begin by discussing periodic signals i.e. considering signals which can be represented by periodic functions. If $f(t)$ is a periodic function then its **Fourier series** is its representation as a sum of sinusoids, and the process of determining the Fourier series of given functions is called **Fourier Analysis**. If $f(t)$ is a periodic function of t with frequency f_1 then $f(t)$ has a Fourier series of the form

$$f(t) = a_0 + \sum_{n=1}^{\infty} a_n \cos(n\omega_1 t) + \sum_{n=1}^{\infty} b_n \sin(n\omega_1 t)$$

where $\omega_1 = 2\pi f_1$. Since f_1 is the frequency of $f(t)$, it is called the **fundamental frequency** of the series. The terms $a_n \cos n\omega_1 t$ and $b_n \sin n\omega_1 t$ represent the **harmonic frequencies** $(n\omega_1)$ of the fundamental angular frequency ω_1. They occur at frequencies $n\omega_1$ for all positive integers n. To determine the **Fourier coefficients** a_n, b_n we have to integrate over any complete cycle i.e.

over any interval of length $\dfrac{1}{f_1}$. Adopting the standard notation that $\oint$ represents integration over one complete cycle and writing T for the period we have:

$$a_0 = \frac{1}{T} \oint f(t)\, dt$$

$$a_n = \frac{2}{T} \oint f(t) \cos(n\omega_1 t)\, dt$$

$$b_n = \frac{2}{T} \oint f(t) \sin(n\omega_1 t)\, dt$$

We will not establish these formulae here and the reader wishing to see a proof can consult [72]. However, we must point out that there are some restrictions on the type of signals to which these formulae apply. Fortunately we can ignore them as they do not apply to the type of signals considered in this book.

For a non-periodic signal we can no longer use a Fourier series. Heuristically, if we consider a non-periodic signal as having an infinite period, then it must have an infinitesimally small fundamental frequency. Thus multiples of the fundamental frequency no longer take discrete values. Instead they take all possible values and the summations in the Fourier series become integrals. When we introduced the Fourier series of a periodic function $f(t)$, we wrote it as

$$f(t) = a_0 + \sum_{n=1}^{\infty} a_n \cos(n\omega_1 t) + \sum_{n=1}^{\infty} b_n \sin(n\omega_1 t)$$

which means, as we have seen, that to determine the series one has to determine the constants a_n and b_n, for all n. But any expression of the form $a \cos x + b \sin x$ can be written in the form $k \cos(x + y)$ (where k and y are determined by a and b). Thus, for any n, we can write $a_n \cos(n\omega_1 t) + b_n \sin(n\omega_1 t)$ as $k_n \cos(n\omega_1 + \phi_n)$ where k_n and ϕ_n are constants which are determined by a_n and b_n. Hence an alternative form for the Fourier series of a periodic function is

$$f(t) = \tfrac{1}{2}k_0 + \sum_{n=1}^{\infty} k_n \cos(n\omega_1 t + \phi_n).$$

If we now replace $f(t)$ by a non-periodic function and change the summation to integration then we obtain:

$$f(t) = \frac{1}{\pi} \int_0^{\infty} k(\omega) \cos(\omega t + \phi(\omega))\, d\omega.$$

(Note: the integration is 'with respect to' ω because instead of regarding n

as the variable of the summation we are taking the variable as $\omega_1 n$. This also accounts for the $1/\pi$.) Instead of determining constants, as in the periodic case, it is now necessary to determine the functions $k(\omega)$ and $\phi(\omega)$ in order to characterize $f(t)$.

9.3.2 An illustration of the use of the Fourier series
To illustrate the use of the Fourier series we will now determine the **spectrum**, (i.e. the various frequency components), of a square pulse train. The graph of a square pulse train is shown in Figure 9.3.

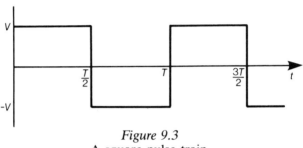

Figure 9.3
A square pulse train

In our example $f(t)$ has period T and, during any interval of T seconds, it takes the value of V for $T/2$ seconds and $-V$ for $|T/2$ seconds. We have chosen our time interval so that $t = 0$ is at the start of a pulse. To determine the Fourier coefficients we must choose an interval of length T over which to integrate. We select the interval from 0 to T which gives

$$f(t) = \begin{cases} V \text{ for } 0 \le t \le T/2 \\ -V \text{ otherwise} \end{cases}.$$

Using our formulae for the Fourier coefficients and putting $\omega_1 = \dfrac{2\pi}{T}$ we now obtain:

$$a_0 = \frac{1}{T}\int_0^T f(t)\,dt = 1/T\left[\int_0^{T/2} V\,dt + \int_{T/2}^T -V\,dt\right] = 0$$

$$a_n = \frac{2}{T}\int_0^T f(t)\cos(n\omega_1 t)\,dt$$

$$= \frac{2}{T}\left[\int_0^{T/2} V\cos(n\omega_1 t)\,dt + \int_{T/2}^T (-V\cos(n\omega_1 t)\,dt)\right] = 0$$

$$b_n = \frac{2}{T}\int_0^T f(t)\sin(n\omega_1 t)\,dt$$

$$= \frac{2}{T} \left[\int_0^{T/2} V \sin (n\omega_1 t) dt + \int_{T/2}^T (-V) \sin (n\omega_1) dt \right]$$

$$= \frac{2}{T} \left(\frac{VT}{n\pi} + \frac{VT}{n\pi} \right) = \frac{4V}{n\pi} \quad \text{if } n \text{ is odd. (Recall that } \omega_1 T = 2\pi$$

or

$$= \frac{2}{T} (0+0) = 0 \quad \text{if } n \text{ is even.}$$

Thus

$$f(t) = \sum_{\substack{n=1 \\ n \text{odd}}}^{\infty} \frac{4V}{n\pi} \sin (n\omega_1 t).$$

For each of the frequency components, i.e. for each of n, $\sin (n\omega_1 t)$ represents the sinusoidal variation at an angular frequency of $n\omega_1$. The coefficient of this term, i.e. $4V/n\pi$ is the amplitude corresponding to the harmonic frequency $n\omega_1$. Figure 9.4 shows the amplitude-frequency spectrum of this periodic square wave, Figure 9.5 (a) shows the first four Fourier components of the square wave, and Figure 9.5 (b) gives the successive approximations formed by successively adding the components.

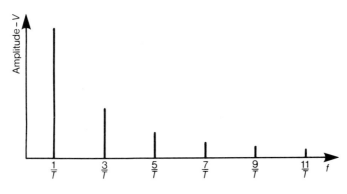

Figure 9.4
The amplitude-frequency spectrum of the square wave

9.3.3 Non-periodic signals

The determination of spectra for non-periodic signals is much more difficult than for periodic ones. The graph spectrum will no longer consist of discrete lines, as in our last example, but will be continuous.

The mathematics involved is often difficult, but we can resolve the problems by appealing to the physics of our situation. Our signals are, essentially, varying voltages and currents. This means that, at any given instance, we can calculate the electrical power of our signal. Let us first

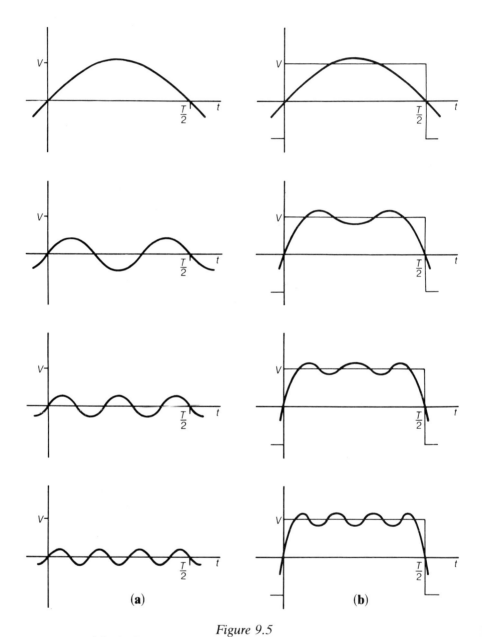

Figure 9.5
(a) The first four Fourier components of the square wave
(b) The effect of successively adding the components

explain what is meant by power. **Power** is defined as the rate of doing work, or, equivalently, the rate of change of energy. The unit of electrical power is the **watt**. If the voltage across a network is v volts and the current is i amps then the power in watts is given by $p=vi$. (Thus one watt is the work done in one second when a current of one amp passes through a network with a voltage of one volt across it.) If the voltage and current are varying then the product of the instantaneous current and voltage is the **instantaneous power**. Thus the instantaneous power is the rate at which energy is being transferred at a particular instant and is independent of the waveforms of the voltage and current. If z ohms is the impedance of the network then, by Ohm's Law, $v=iz$ which implies that p is proportional to v^2. It is far more convenient to consider power than either voltage or current. It is this fact which motivates us to talk about the **power density spectrum**. We shall see that the mathematics is simplified by working with powers in small frequency bands.

The power density spectrum of a signal can be measured by using an instrument called a **wave analyzer** or **spectrum analyzer**. The main part of a wave analyzer consists of a number of band-pass filters. Each of these filters has a 'central frequency' and allows through only those frequency components of the signal which lie in a narrow band centred at that central frequency. Attached to each of these filters is a meter which averages the squares of the voltages for those components which passed through its filter. An example of such an instrument is shown in Figure 9.6. Since the machine measures the mean square voltages $\bar{v}_i^2$, it enables us to plot power density against frequency. The accuracy obtained clearly depends on the number of band-pass filters and their bandwidths. (Note that the bandwidth of a filter determines the range of frequencies which pass through that filter.)

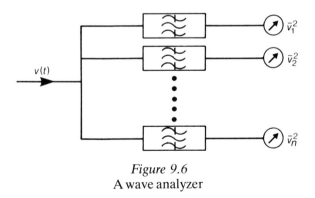

Figure 9.6
A wave analyzer

Figure 9.7 is a simple example of a power density spectrum and represents the case when the power density is independent of frequency. This is one of the principal characteristics of **'white' noise**. A 'white' noise source is generally regarded as a source of truly random information.

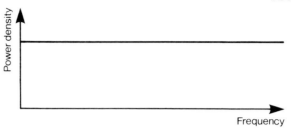

Figure 9.7
The power density spectrum of white noise

9.4 Some Properties of Speech

As we said in the introduction the aim of this chapter is to discuss the special problems associated with the encipherment of speech signals. We have now introduced enough concepts and terminology that we can consider the relevant properties of speech. Such a consideration will be necessary in order for us to understand the intricate problems involved in the design of secure speech systems.

9.4.1 Spectral analysis

In Figure 9.8 a 'typical' speech spectrum is illustrated. By 'typical' we mean that the power density at each part of the spectrum is that obtained by averaging a relatively large number of conversations over a relatively long time. (One obvious example of a speech signal is that obtained from a microphone when someone speaks into it.)

There are several observations to make about this graph. The first is that the frequency uses a logarithmic scale and that the power density is measured in μWHz^{-1}, ($1\mu WHz^{-1}$ being 10^{-6} watts per Hz). The second is that for frequency components higher than 3 to 4kHz, ($1kHz=10^3Hz$), the power density is falling rapidly. Consequently very high frequency components make a much smaller contribution to the signal than, for example, frequencies in the range 500-3000Hz. Finally we note that frequencies of less than about 300Hz contribute very little to the overall signal.

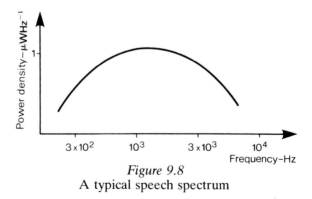

Figure 9.8
A typical speech spectrum

If we restrict ourselves to frequencies of up to 3kHZ and use a very sensitive analyzer we should obtain a jagged curve like the one shown in Figure 9.9. This shows the spectrum obtained when a particular sound is made. The diagram shows clearly that there are a number of peaks, called **formants**. These formants are produced as a result of the way in which speech is formed and Figure 9.10 illustrates how these frequency components change with time. It should be noted that the change is fairly slow. (In Figure 9.9 the three formants are marked F_1, F_2, F_3, to enable comparison with Figure 9.10.)

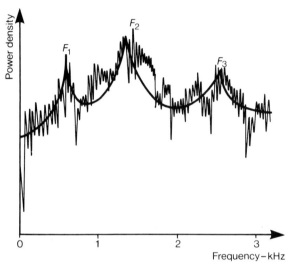

Figure 9.9
The result of using a sensitive analyser

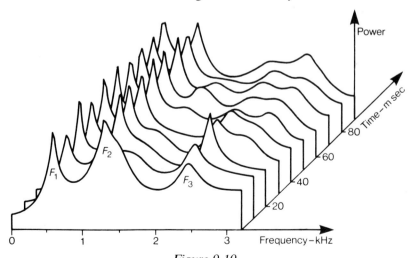

Figure 9.10
How frequency components change with time

9.4.2 Phonemes and pitch frequency

In order to analyze speech we break it down into its individual component sounds, called **phonemes**. (We will now give a very brief discussion of different phonemes for the English language and how they arise. However an understanding of the details is not necessary. The important fact to realize is that various different letters or sounds give rise to completely different waveforms.) Phonemes vary considerably from language to language and we will restrict our attention to English. In the English language there are about forty phonemes which fall into three classes; the vowels forming one complete family while the consonants and some other single syllable phonetic sounds, e.g. *st, ch,* form two classes called **plosives** and **fricatives**.

Vowels are produced by movements of the vocal chords which convert the stream of air passing through the larynx into a series of pulses. The airstream then passes into a number of cavities of which the most dominant are the nose, mouth and throat. This results in modifying the frequency spectrum in a way which is rather similar to the effect that a series of bandpass filters has on a rectangular pulse train. Clearly the sound which emerges depends on the shape and size of these cavities, but it is usually characterized by a large low-frequency content. A vowel sound builds up gradually and, typically, takes about 100 milliseconds to reach its peak amplitude. Figure 9.11 shows typical cavity shapes and amplitude spectra for two vowel sounds.

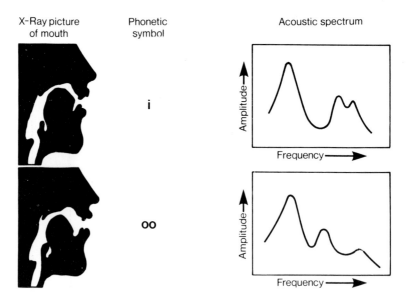

Figure 9.11
The amplitude spectra for two vowel sounds

Plosives are produced by shutting off the airstream and then releasing it with an explosive effect. There are various points at which the airstream may be blocked, e.g. the palate, tongue or lips. One obvious example of a plosive produced by blocking the airstream with the lips is a '*p*'. We will not give a list of plosives but merely note that they tend to be characterized by their high frequency components and typically reach 90% of their peak amplitude in less than 5mS.

Fricatives are produced by partially shutting off the airstream to produce a sound like 'white' noise. This sound is then filtered by the vocal tract cavities. A fricative sound typically reaches its peak amplitude in 20-50mS and most of its power density is concentrated between 1 and 3kHz. One example of a fricative is '*sss. . .*'.

We realize that the above discussion is extremely brief and is probably insufficient to enable the reader to distinguish between some of the plosives and fricatives. However, hopefully it will make the reader realize that his vocal system performs different operations to produce various different sounds, and that the difference in these operations is reflected in various distinguishing properties of the resulting signal.

A further characteristic of human speech which needs mentioning is the **pitch-frequency**. This is the frequency of the vibration of the vocal chords. The middle value of this frequency varies from individual to individual, and each particular speaker then has a range of about an octave above and below this central frequency (i.e. if the pitch-frequency is f, the range will be about $f/2$ to $2f$). For a typical male the pitch-frequency is about 130Hz while the average female is about twice as high.

Another significant point should be emerging from this discussion. As well as conveying the spoken message, a speech signal also contains considerable information about the vocal characteristics of the speaker. As far as the message itself is concerned this information is largely redundant but does of course contain information relating to the 'personality' of the speaker. (By the personality of the speaker we merely mean those slight variations of frequency, pitch etc. which enable us to identify him.)

For any given speech signal, we could use the pitch, formants, timing and so on, to form another signal to convey the same spoken message. This reproduction might sound rather unnatural and some of the 'personality' of the speaker would almost certainly be lost. How much of this information is lost would depend on the precise parameters employed in the formation of our new signal. This principle of reproduction is the basic idea behind vocoders and we shall discuss them a little later. For the moment we merely emphasize that a voice message contains two types of information, i.e. the content of the message and the personality of the speaker. We stress that, ideally, a ciphered message should conceal both types of information from an interceptor. Before we discuss the various ways of achieving this objective it is worth discussing briefly the various ways in which speech signals are transmitted.

9.5   Voice Message Transmission

As we saw earlier, most of the information in a speech signal has a
frequency between roughly 300Hz and 4kHz. For most practical purposes
the range may be taken to be even smaller and, for instance, telephone
speech signals are normally band-limited to the range 300–3400Hz, i.e. to
a bandwidth of 3100Hz. However a transmission link can carry signals with
a much wider bandwidth than 3100Hz. Thus, by taking the signals for
individual telephone calls and 'frequency shifting' them, the bandwidth
limitations imposed on the speech signals enable a channel to carry several
thousand telephone calls simultaneously. (This process is called **frequency
division multiplexing**.) This produces a considerable reduction in the
transmission costs. (It is interesting to note that, although a bandwidth of
3·1kHz is sufficient for speech recognition, the human ear can recognize
sound at much higher frequencies. It is often possible to hear sounds at up
to 20kHz and, indeed, for high quality transmissions a bandwidth of at
least 15kHz is considered necessary.)

There are similar restrictions on the bandwidth when speech signals are
transmitted by radio waves. For instance the **high frequency (h.f.)** band of
3MHz–30MHz is extremely overcrowded and liable to a great deal of
interference. In this situation the speech signal may be restricted to about a
2·4kHz bandwidth. In the **very high frequency (v.h.f.)** wave-band of
30–300 MHz and the **ultra high frequency (u.h.f.)** wave-band of
300MHz–3GHz wider bandwidths are permissible, possibly even greater
than 10kHz. (Note: $1\text{MHz} = 10^6\text{Hz}$ and $1\text{GHz} = 10^9\text{Hz}$.) It is absolutely
crucial that the cryptographer is aware that there are limitations such as
these permissible bandwidths for the various forms of transmission. The
reason should be clear after the following discussion.

There are essentially two different ways to encipher a speech signal. The
first is to scramble the signal in some way. This is done by changing the
relationships between time, amplitude and frequency. This method, if
carefully engineered, should not have any significant effect on the
bandwidth of the signal. For the second method the analogue signal is
converted into a digital one, i.e. the speech signal is represented as a series
of digits. Once this has been achieved the signal may be enciphered using
the techniques which have been discussed in the earlier chapters. The
recipient deciphers the cryptogram in its digital form and then the
analogue signal is recovered from these digits. The problem with this
method is that most digitization techniques increase the bandwidth of the
signal. From the last paragraph it should now be clear that this might mean
we can no longer use the same transmission channel. It is, in fact, possible
to digitize speech signals without increasing the bandwidth. This is
achieved by using vocoder techniques but, at present, the devices needed
are extremely expensive and destroy many important properties of the
signal. They may also be very susceptible to errors incurred during
transmission.

We will discuss these digital techniques later in the chapter but first we turn our attention to some scrambling techniques.

9.6   Voice Scrambling

One important factor in trying to determine the security level of a scrambling process is that of human perception. In other words it is crucial, when trying to assess the strength of a scrambling system, simply to listen to the resultant signal and see how much can be understood. Of course such a process is highly subjective and some people will understand more than others. When doing this it is advisable to scramble many different messages and to let a number of people listen to them many times. Often someone will hear a scrambled message and understand absolutely nothing. But the human brain tends to adjust and learn very quickly and, after two or three more hearings, the listener may begin to 'recognize' odd words and/or syllables. Eventually, by a mixture of careful listening and intelligent guessing, he may well understand the entire message. In fact he may even actually 'hear' the correct message. It must also not be forgotten that, just as parents can understand their children's 'speech' long before anyone else, there are experts at understanding scrambled messages. On no account should the cryptographer ignore or underestimate the ability of the human brain to unscramble certain messages, even if the listener does not have access to any sophisticated electronic equipment. For this reason, when we discuss scrambling methods, we will usually relate them to experiments carried out on human listeners, as well as discussing the various mathematical weaknesses they possess.

9.6.1   Speech inverters

One of the earliest forms of frequency scrambler was a device known as a speech inverter. Suppose we have a speech signal which is band-limited to the 300–3000Hz range as in Figure 9.12.

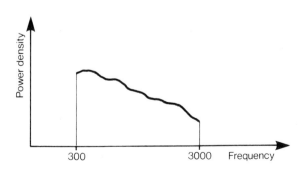

Figure 9.12
A speech signal band-limited to 300–3000 Hz

The basic idea of an inverter is to interchange the high and low frequencies. This can be achieved rather easily and, since most frequency domain scramblers rely on the same basic technique, it is worth seeing how it is done. First we consider the individual sinusoidal components of our speech signal. If one such component is $V_m \cos \omega_m t$ and if this signal together with a second signal $V_c \cos \omega_c t$ is fed to a device called a **balanced modulator** then the output is $V_c V_m \cos \omega_m t \cos \omega_c t$. (This essentially defines the action of a balanced modulator.) But, using the elementary trigonometric identity, $\cos A \cos B = \frac{1}{2} \cos (A + B) + \frac{1}{2} \cos (A - B)$, we can express the output of our balanced modulator as

$$\tfrac{1}{2} V_c V_m \cos (\omega_c + \omega_m) t + \tfrac{1}{2} V_c V_m \cos (\omega_c - \omega_m) t.$$

When using a balanced modulator, the operator is free to choose V_c and ω_c. From now on we assume that $V_c = 1$ and that ω_c is larger than ω_m. So we now have an amplitude-angular frequency spectrum as in Figure 9.13. If

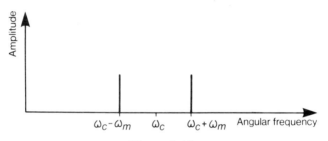

Figure 9.13
Amplitude-angular frequency spectrum

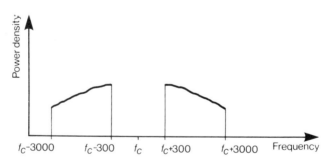

Figure 9.14
Power density spectrum of balanced modulator output

we were to consider each sinusoidal component of our speech signal and the corresponding output from the balanced modulator, we would obtain a power density spectrum as in Figure 9.14. In this figure the value f_c, which is equal to $\omega_c/2\pi$, is called the **carrier frequency**. The two bands of 'side' signals above and below the carrier frequency are called the **upper** and **lower side-bands** respectively. Clearly the upper side-band is similar to the original signal but translated up in frequency, i.e. each frequency component has had f_c added to it. Notice that the spectrum of the lower side-band is the mirror image of our original signal spectrum; in other words it is the original spectrum with the high and low frequencies interchanged. Thus, by a suitable choice of the carrier frequency, and by filtering the output of the balanced modulator to remove the upper side-band we can obtain the inverted speech signal of Figure 9.15. In practice the actual filtering may prove difficult and circuits other than the balanced modulator may be used to produce only the lower side-band. It is perhaps worth pointing out that the method described here is very similar to the frequency division multiplexing used to transmit telephone calls. By choosing carrier frequencies for different signals each signal can be shifted to a different frequency space and several thousand calls can be carried on a single transmission link.

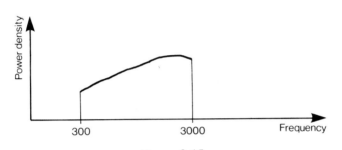

Figure 9.15
Power density spectrum of inverted speech signal

So far, in our description of inversion, we have not introduced a key. Thus the system is simply a code which, as such, is not secure against any interceptor with a similar piece of equipment to reinvert the signal. Some improvement on this basic inversion code is obtained by using a device known as a **band-shift inverter**. Once this device is introduced we at least have a genuine cipher system in the sense that the concept of varying keys is introduced. One theoretical way of considering band-shift inversion is the following.

When we discussed inversion we began with a signal which was bandwidth-limited to 300–3000Hz. If our inverted signal is to be in the same band then, clearly, our carrier frequency must be 3300Hz. If instead we let our carrier frequency be, say, 4000Hz then we obtain an inverted signal whose spectrum is shown in Figure 9.16 (a). This signal is no longer in the same band as our original one, but we can arrange for it to be in this band by taking that part of the signal above 3000Hz and putting it at the low frequency end. (Note that although the signal of Figure 9.16 (a) has a different frequency range it has, of necessity, the same bandwidth as our original signal.) This is the principle of band-shift inverting and is illustrated in Figure 9.16 (b).

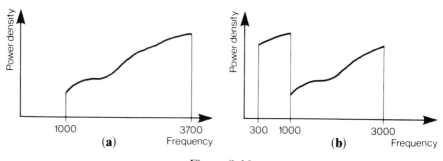

Figure 9.16
The principle of band-shift inversion

A typical inverter has between 4 and 16 different carrier frequencies which result in the same numbers of different 'shifts'. There are two ways in which a key may operate. The simple way is to select the carrier frequency to be used. Alternatively it may be used to initialize a pseudo-random number generator (this may be similar in construction to the sequence generators discussed in earlier chapters), which will then select a different carrier frequency every so often. A typical time interval for each carrier frequency might be 10 or 20mS. This latter arrangement is often referred to as a **cyclical band-shift inversion**.

Systems relying on band-shift inverters have two obvious failings. Firstly since, at any given time, there are only a limited number of possibilities for the carrier frequency, the original signal can be recovered reasonably easily by using 'trial and error' methods with relatively simple equipment. Secondly, and perhaps more importantly, the residual intelligibility in the output signal is unacceptably high. The **residual intelligibility** of an output signal is that proportion of the original signal which can be understood directly when listening to the enciphered message. In this case, this is especially high after the message has been reinverted.

9.6.2 Bandscramblers

In this section we consider a third speech scrambler in the frequency domain: the **bandscrambler** or **bandsplitter**. In this case the spectrum is divided into a number of equal sub-bands and the signal is then scrambled by rearranging their order. In some of the more sophisticated systems certain of the sub-bands may also be inverted. Figure 9.17 illustrates a simple example with five sub-bands. The sub-bands 1, 2 and 5 have been inverted as well as displaced. For this particular example there are 5! possible reorderings and 2^5 ways of deciding which, if any, sub-bands to invert. Thus there are $5! \times 2^5 = 3840$ possible ways of rearranging the sub-bands. Unfortunately the residual intelligibility is unacceptably high for most of these arrangements, and it is generally agreed that, if one is forced to rely on reordering alone and not use inversion, less than 10% of the possibilities provide reasonable security. Some of the reasons for the high residual intelligibility are easy to understand. For instance, experiments have shown that reorderings which leave some of the sub-bands in their original positions tend to have high residual intelligibility. Since these reorderings leave part of the signal unaltered this is not completely surprising.

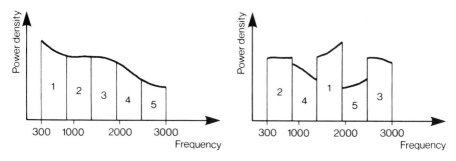

Figure 9.17
Band scrambling technique

There is another disadvantage to this type of system. As we saw in Figures 9.8 and 9.9, it is usual for more than 40% of the energy to lie in the first two sub-bands corresponding to the first formant. So, in our example, no matter which reordering is used, as soon as the cryptanalyst finds the new positions of the first two sub-bands and translates them back, he will have recovered sufficient of the content of the signal to have a good chance of 'understanding' the message. We can improve matters slightly by having a number of different rearrangements and using a pseudo-random number generator sequence to select a new one every few hundred milliseconds. For many practical systems, the 'better' reorderings, i.e. those with small residual intelligibility, are stored in a ROM (**read only memory**) within the equipment. For our example the system may work as follows. In a five sub-band system the number of stored reorderings is typically about 32 and consequently, since there are still 2^5 ways of inverting some or all of the sub-bands, there are 1024 rearrangements available. Each rearrangement needs 10 bits of the sequence to define it; five to determine the reordering and five to decide on the inversions. The sequence generator itself may have a period of many millions of bits so that the cycle of rearrangements used does not repeat itself for days. Clearly, then, the size of the key may be chosen so that it is large enough to deter an interceptor from trying all possibilities. Nevertheless, no matter what is done, the residual intelligibility of a large proportion of the arrangements is so high that this system cannot be considered fully secure.

In general, scramblers which affect only the frequency domain are regarded more as privacy devices than as fully secure systems. Their use tends to be limited to situations where the aim is to prevent a casual listener from understanding a conversation or possibly even a determined interceptor who does not have any reasonably sophisticated equipment. But, as we shall see, the majority of the more secure systems either increase the bandwidth necessary for the signal or introduce a time delay in transmission. Both of these changes introduce their own problems and so, when the strictest security is not essential, the systems just discussed are often preferable.

Before discussing these new systems we must say something about the number of sub-bands in a bandscrambler. In our example we had five sub-bands and, clearly, if this number were significantly increased there would be a considerable increase in the number of reorderings available and we might expect that this would increase the security. However, the introduction of too many sub-bands would introduce too many practical difficulties. We must not forget that the input signal has to be reconstructed at the receiver's end of the transmission link. The filters and other components used introduce noise into the signal and are not truly linear in their operation. Any modification of the signal results in the introduction of imperfections and degrades the final quality of the signal. Bandscramblers are particularly susceptible to these types of imperfection. Thus introducing a larger number of sub-bands would, for most practical transmission links, render the system either unusable or so expensive as to be uneconomical.

9.6.3 Time division multiplexing (t.d.m.)
We will now look at scramblers which affect the time element of a signal. These **time element scramblers** are often referred to as **time division multiplexing** (t.d.m.) systems and they usually employ the following basic principle. The analogue signal is first divided into (equal) time periods called **frames**. Each frame is then sub-divided into small equal time periods called **segments**. Once this has been done the input is scrambled by permuting the segments within each frame. The process is illustrated diagrammatically in Figure 9.18 where we have divided the frame into eight segments.

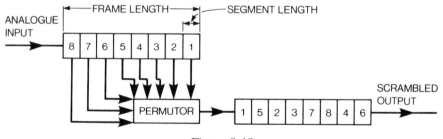

Figure 9.18
Time division multiplexing

When setting up a t.d.m. system it is necessary to decide upon values for the lengths of the frames and segments. Clearly the message within a segment is not distorted in this type of scrambling. Furthermore the segment length decides how much information is contained within that segment. This makes it desirable to keep the segments as short as possible and, obviously, they must be short enough that whole words cannot be contained within a segment. On the other hand, the segment length has a significant bearing on the audio quality of the transmitted message, and the quality decreases as the segment lengths get smaller. Thus, because of difficulties in implementation, there is a delicate balance to be made when choosing a segment length.

In order to choose a frame length we need to see how this choice affects the delay between the analogue signal being fed into the equipment and the signal being reconstructed as 'clear speech'. To understand this time delay we will look back at our example in Figure 9.18. Let us suppose that, in this example, the segment length is T seconds. Thus it takes $8T$ seconds for our eight speech segments to enter the scrambler. Although it is not so in our example, we may wish to permute the segments so that segment 8 is transmitted first. Consequently we will not start to transmit until all 8 segments are in the device and consequently, delays have already occurred. (For instance segment 1 must be delayed by at least $8T$ seconds). Once the transmission is begun it takes another $8T$ seconds to complete it. This, of course, causes further delays. If we wish to allow all permutations then, as in the case of our example, the last segment to reach the receiver may be the first that he must output. This means that the receiver cannot begin to decipher until he has received all 8 segments. So, even if we assume negligible time for the actual transmission, there is a time delay of $16T$ seconds for each speech segment. In general for a system with m segments per frame the time delay is $2mT$. This, of course, is provided no restriction is placed upon the permutations to be used. Figure 9.19 shows which segment is being processed during each of the first 24 T-second periods of transmission, for our example.

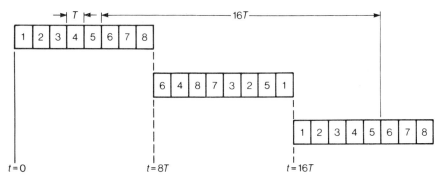

Figure 9.19
A timing diagram for the t.d.m. process

The effect of this delay is similar to that experienced on international telephone calls which are transmitted via satellite. From the user's point of view they are undesirable and present a case for making the frame as short as possible. Unfortunately (yes, you've guessed it!) from the security point of view we need long frames. One reason for this is that, as we saw when discussing phonemes, a speech 'sound' can last for quite a long time. To see this we merely have to look back at Figure 9.10 which shows how slowly the speech spectrum changes. To illustrate how disastrous short frames can be, let us suppose that we have a frame which is so short that it consists of a single tone. No matter how we scramble it the result will still be a single continuous tone (but almost certainly degraded in quality as a result of our tampering). Although this example is extreme, it nevertheless shows that if we make our frames too short we may not be able to achieve sufficient dispersement of the segments. This may result in significant parts of words being unaltered and allow a listener to guess part, or all, of the message. Furthermore it is clear that increasing the numbers of segments in a frame increases the number of permutations.

There is no obvious mathematical way for choosing optimal values for the lengths of the segments or frames. In practice it is necessary to test any given choice experimentally. One good, and very demanding, test for a t.d.m. system is to read out, in an arbitrary order, some numbers between one and ten, and for some listeners to write down the numbers which they believe they 'hear'. Our reason for claiming that this test is demanding is that the listener is only trying to distinguish between ten possible sounds. This is considerably easier than trying to understand what is being said when he has no idea of the context. Experiments show that, unless the frame length is sufficiently large, most t.d.m. systems perform badly against this test. One interesting point about this particular test is that most of the listeners' mistakes arise from confusing 5 and 9. This is because they are the only two of the numbers with the same vowel sound and, as explained earlier, vowel sounds are far longer than consonant sounds. Thus the listener tends to identify the vowel sounds and then guess the final word from them.

As a general rule the frame length should be as long as the user will accept. Within most of these types of equipment currently available a frame comprises between 8 and 16 segments, and each segment has a duration of, typically, between 20 and 60mS.

Once the lengths of the segments and frames are chosen the final 'ingredient' for a t.d.m. is the permutation. Clearly some permutations are better than others and we must now try to decide precisely which ones are 'good'. We must also decide how to use the permutations. As in the case of band-shift inverters or bandscramblers there are a number of ways in which we can use our basic t.d.m. system. We can, for instance, have a key which selects one fixed permutation and then use this given permutation for every frame. Another alternative is to let our key select several permutations and then repeatedly use them in some fixed order. However, as before, a better system is to employ some form of sequence generator to select a 'different' permutation for each frame. (Here, when we say 'different' we merely mean that the permutations are not chosen in any fixed order. Two distinct frames may well use the same permutation if the output of the sequence generator, which makes the selection, is the same.) With eight segments in a frame the total number of permutations is $8! = 40320$. So, if each segment has a duration of 40mS, after about 3·6 hours of continuous usage we must be using permutations for at least the second time. However, the pattern of permutations used will not begin to repeat until the sequence repeats, i.e. the period of the sequence determines the period of repetition of the sequence of permutations used. Although we have said that there are a maximum of 40320 permutations on eight symbols, we may not wish to use them all. As an illustration, consider the following two permutations. For these and future permutations, the top line represents the original order of the segments and the second line represents the order after scrambling. Thus the permutation representing the example of Figure 9.18 is:

$$1\ 2\ 3\ 4\ 5\ 6\ 7\ 8$$
$$6\ 4\ 8\ 7\ 3\ 2\ 5\ 1$$

Example 1 $\quad 1\ 2\ 3\ 4\ 5\ 6\ 7\ 8$
$$\qquad\quad 1\ 3\ 2\ 4\ 5\ 7\ 6\ 8$$

Example 2 $\quad 1\ 2\ 3\ 4\ 5\ 6\ 7\ 8$
$$\qquad\quad 3\ 6\ 2\ 5\ 8\ 4\ 7\ 1.$$

If we were able to listen to the effects of each of these two permutations we would find that the first has a very high residual intelligibility. In fact, after a few repetitions, we would probably begin to understand the message. The second permutation would have a far lower residual intelligibility and it is doubtful whether our understanding would increase after the first few hearings. If we now look closely at our two examples we can see the reason for this. In Example 1 four segments remain unmoved and each of the others is only moved one place. Thus the permutation does not do much to distort the input signal. However, in the second example most of the segments have been displaced much further.

If, for any permutation α, we let $\alpha(i)$ represent the position to which α moves the ith segment then the displacement of i is merely $|i - \alpha(i)|$. (For instance, in Example 2, $\alpha(2) = 3$ and the displacement of 2 is $|2-3| = 1$.) We can then easily compute the average displacement of α by computing

$$\tfrac{1}{8} \sum_{i=1}^{8} |i - \alpha(i)|.$$

For Example 1 this average is $\tfrac{1}{2}$ whereas for Example 2 it is $2\tfrac{1}{2}$. The value of this average displacement is called the **shift factor** of the permutation and a high shift factor is essential if a permutation is to result in low residual intelligibility. But a high shift factor certainly offers no guarantees about the residual intelligibility. The following is an example, with a shift factor of 4, which could perform very badly in listening tests. As this discussion progresses some of the reasons for this will become clear.

Example 3   1 2 3 4 5 6 7 8
               5 7 6 8 3 2 4 1

Apart from its low shift factor, Example 1 has a number of other undesirable properties. Consider, for instance, the consecutive segments 4 and 5. In the scrambled frame they appear in the same consecutive order. Thus if segments are approximately 40mS long, this gives about 80mS of the original speech signal. As we have already observed, most phonemes can be clearly recognized within this sort of time interval. Now look at the segments 6 and 8. In both Examples 1 and 3 they appear as consecutive elements and, although it is not immediately apparent, this is also undesirable. Perception trials have established that if the scrambled signal has two consecutive segments of the type i and $i+2$, for some i, then the listener will usually be able to deduce the corresponding part of the message; the human brain is able simply to improvise and 'fill in' the missing segment. (The reader should not find this too surprising. If we hold a telephone conversation on a 'noisy' line then we are usually able to understand the entire conversation although we do not actually hear every syllable.) As well as being able to 'fill in' missing segments the brain also naturally rejects superfluous segments. Thus patterns like $i?(i+1)$ in the scrambled signal also lead to a high residual intelligibility. To a lesser extent the patterns $i?(i+2)$, $i?(i+3)$, $i??(i+2)$ and $i??(i+3)$ also yield some residual intelligibility. (In case it is not clear, when we say that the scrambled signal has a pattern like $i??(i+3)$ for some i we mean that it contains two segments which, in both the original and scrambled message, are only separated by two other segments. For instance in Example 3 the scrambled frame contains 5768 which is of the form $i??(i+3)$ with $i=5$. Similarly 324 is of the form $i?(i+1)$ with $i=3$.)

EXERCISE 9.1   Find three permutations of $\{1, 2, 3, \ldots, 8\}$ which have no patterns of any of the following types: $i(i+1)$, $i?(i+1)$, $i(i+2)$, $i?(i+2)$, $i??(i+2)$, $i?(i+3)$, $i??(i+3)$. Choose them so that they also have a shift factor of at least $2\frac{1}{2}$, and do not fix the first segment. (This last condition ensures that two consecutive segments which occur at the end and beginning of consecutive frames are not consecutive in the scrambled message.)

Exercise 9.1 is not difficult. But if we try to solve it by merely writing down permutations and then checking to see if they have all the desired properties, we will probably find ourselves writing down a lot of permutations. This is because a very small proportion of permutations satisfy them. Even when we have a permutation which meets the demands of Exercise 9.1, we still have no guarantee that it will give a scrambled signal with low residual intelligibility. The extra conditions which must be imposed are highly subjective and different people use different criteria. This results in considerable discrepancies in values for the number of 'good' permutations. For instance in [91] it is claimed that about half of the 40320 permutations on eight segments are useful, whereas MacKinnon [82] puts the number as low as about 3000. If there is any reasonable doubt about a permutation then, since his aim is to guarantee security, the cryptographer should not use it. For this reason we feel it is safer to adopt MacKinnon's figure.

Having agreed upon our conditions for good permutations, we must now decide how our key is going to select them. Basically we have two choices. One alternative is to allow the sequence generator to produce arbitrary permutations and then 'screen' them in some way to see which ones meet our requirements. The other is to select some (or all) of the 'good' permutations, store them in a ROM within the equipment and then let the sequence generator select pseudo-randomly from the ROM. We will consider the relative merits of each alternative.

The main disadvantage of the first alternative is the time factor. If a frame lasts for 320mS, say, then at the end of that time we must have selected the next 'good' permutation. But if we merely let our sequence generate permutations at random then, although statistically the probability is very high, we cannot guarantee that it will produce a 'good' one in time. So we need to incorporate some contingency plan to protect ourselves from this possibility. This could, for example, allow the use of a previous permutation for a second time. Other possibilities include relaxing the screening conditions as time runs out or simply allowing extra time to wait for a 'good' permutation. But all are undesirable. On the other hand the system has one big advantage. This is that, once we have a reasonable sequence generator and algorithm for generating permutations from that sequence, all the good permutations can be used. In contrast the ROM method only allows the use of those permutations which are stored. If our store is not big enough then this will not be all the good permutations. Furthermore we must assume that a determined interceptor will know the contents of our ROM. When there are only eight segments per frame then, if we take the 'strictest' definition of 'good', the number of such permutations is small enough that we can probably store them all. When this happens the ROM method is usually considered preferable. But, as soon as we start using more than eight segments per frame, the limitation on the number of permutations which can actually be used is a definite disadvantage of our second method.

In order to understand another of the advantages of the ROM method we must remind ourselves of some properties of the inverses of permutations. For a permutation γ on a given set (we will take our set as $\{1, 2, 3, 4, 5, 6, 7, 8\}$), the inverse permutation, which we denote by γ^{-1}, is the permutation which 'undoes' the scrambling i.e. it is that permutation which must be performed on the segments of a scrambled frame to reproduce the original signal. The following exercises indicate that various properties are shared by any permutation and its inverse.

EXERCISE 9.2   Show that the inverses of Examples 1, 2 and 3 are respectively:
    12345678,   12345678,   12345678
    13245768   83164275   86571324

EXERCISE 9.3   Show that, for any γ, the permutations γ and γ^{-1} have equal shift factors.

EXERCISE 9.4   Show that if there are two consecutive elements which have consecutive images under γ, then there are also two consecutive elements which have consecutive images under γ^{-1}.

So far, in our discussion of residual intelligibility, we have concentrated on a listener as opposed to an interceptor with a similar piece of equipment. Clearly any receiver needs to have the inverse of all possible 'good' permutations, so we must assume that any interceptor has the same knowledge. We can now illustrate one type of 'accident' which may occur when the interceptor has similar equipment. Suppose that one of the permutations in our ROM is Example 2 and that we have used it to scramble a frame. An interceptor will not know precisely which permutation was used and may be guessing by trying certain inverses on the scrambled frame. If our ROM also contains

                        1 2 3 4 5 6 7 8
                        3 6 2 5 8 4 1 7

then the interceptor might try the inverse of this instead of the correct inverse. But the effect of scrambling using Example 2 and then unscrambling by using the inverse of this last permutation is

                        1 2 3 4 5 6 7 8
                        1 2 3 4 5 6 8 7

This is so near to being the actual frame that he will almost certainly be able to predict the correct signal. There are, of course, many other permutations that are so 'similar' to Example 2 that unscrambling by using them will lead to 'correct' decipherment. If we are using the 'screening' method to obtain our good permutations, i.e. using our sequence generator to generate the permutations directly, then there is nothing we can do to eliminate this possibility. All we can do is rely on the fact that the number of permutations is so large that the probability of a 'success' of this type is small. However with only eight segments per frame, the total number of 'good' permutations is, in our view, not large enough for us to trust to 'luck' and the system is liable to be broken by straightforward trial and error. If, on the other hand, we are only using permutations which we have chosen and stored in a ROM then, at the cost of further reducing the number of usable 'good' permutations, we can protect ourselves. To do this we simply avoid putting any pair of permutations λ, μ in our ROM before first testing that $\mu^{-1}\lambda$ is sufficiently bad; i.e. so that scrambling by λ and then unscrambling by μ does not give a signal which is too similar to our original one. We build up this store by testing any new entry with all the existing ones until either our ROM contains sufficient permutations for our purposes or the list of 'good' permutations is exhausted. (This process of testing permutations against each other is often referred to as testing **mutual security**).

In Figure 9.20 we give a block diagram for a typical time-division multiplexing scrambler. If the sequence generator is used to generate patterns in real time then the n-bit register and ROM must be replaced by a processor (or complex piece of hardware) to determine permutations and 'screen' them for low residual intelligibility.

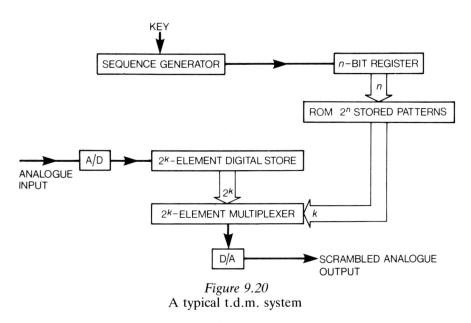

Figure 9.20
A typical t.d.m. system

The A/D converts the analogue input to a digital form to make the actual storing and processing easier, and later in the chapter we will discuss ways of achieving this conversion. Once it is converted to a digital form, the signal is fed into a store of 2^k elements, where 2^k is the number of segments in a frame. (So, in our example, where we have been using eight segments per frame, $k = 3$.) Each element of this store contains the number of digital elements appropriate to a particular segment. The segments are then removed from the store by a multiplexer addressed from the ROM containing the permutation. Finally the signal is reconverted to an analogue form for transmission.

9.6.4 The security of a t.d.m. system

Having described the t.d.m. scrambler we must now look at the security it offers. We begin by considering the level of security against a listener. We have seen that, from the designer's point of view, the problem is to strike a balance between minimizing the residual intelligibility and satisfying the operator's need for a negligible time delay. We will now discuss three possible options for reducing the residual intelligibility. The first option is simply to reverse the order in which bits are taken from an element of the 2^k element digital store in Figure 9.20. This more or less reverses the order of a segment of speech. (The sequence generator can be used to decide which segments should be reversed in this way.) Superficially it may appear that reversing in this way will have a significant effect on the residual intelligibility. However, as we have already seen, a typical segment is 20–60mS and, in comparison, most phonemes are reasonably long. This means that this type of reversing is often ineffective. In practice use of the numbers test suggests that the success rate of a listener is reduced by about 10% if inversion is used in this way.

The second method of reducing residual intelligibility is to vary the clock rate of the A/D and D/A converters. This method, which is a form of frequency modulation, will be discussed when we consider these converters later in the chapter. The clock may either vary in some fixed way or be dependent on the sequence generator. In either case varying the clock rate has the effect of changing the signal in the frequency domain. Use of the numbers test indicates that this method reduces the success rate of a listener by about 15%.

The third alternative also depends on the frequency domain. This time we use a bandscrambler and a t.d.m. simultaneously to obtain a two-dimensional system. Although such a method reduces the success rate of a listener by about 20% it has a number of disadvantages when compared to the other two. To start with it is considerably more expensive to implement. Secondly, it requires a frequency-stable, noise-free transmission path for good audio performance. (We have already observed that every modification to the signal reduces the audio quality and that frequency distortions are particularly susceptible to noise and non-linearities in the transmission path.)

By using one or more of these three methods, the residual intelligibility can be reduced to a low enough level that an interceptor is unlikely to be able to understand any of the message merely by listening to it. However we must now consider the security of our system against more sophisticated attacks. One such attack might, for example, involve trying to unscramble the speech frame by frame. This task is simplified by the use of a piece of equipment called a **sonograph** which is used to produce a sonogram of each frame. A **sonogram** is a three-dimensional graph with time on the horizontal axis, frequency on the vertical axis and amplitude displayed using a 'grey scale'. In this scale black represents the maximum amplitude and white the minimum. The other amplitudes are represented by various shades of grey; the lighter the shade the smaller the amplitude. (Thus, although a sonogram has three variables and is, consequently, three-dimensional it is actually represented in two dimensions.) Figure 9.21 gives an example.

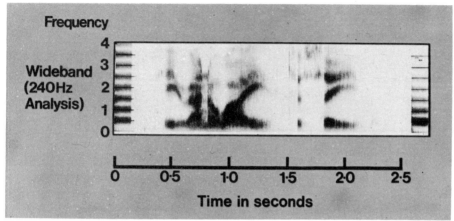

Figure 9.21
A typical Sonogram

A possible approach for the cryptanalyst is to unscramble enough frames that, with an assumed knowledge of the ROM or screening process, he can deduce sufficient output from the sequence generator to determine the key used. But this is precisely the situation we have discussed in Chapters 5–7. To counteract this we need a sequence generator that is difficult to break; i.e. one for which knowledge of a section of the sequence does not enable the cryptanalyst to determine the key within any reasonable time. It should also be noted, by the way, that a real-time screening process automatically introduces non-linearity into the system, thereby rendering it even more difficult for the interceptor to deduce the key.

Let us assume that our system is secure against this approach. This means that the only way in which the cryptanalyst can deduce our message is by unscrambling each individual frame. Clearly, then, the time required to obtain the message is directly proportional to the number of frames. Having said that we must stress that it is often possible to determine the information within a frame without a perfect unscrambling. Furthermore if the cryptanalyst knows the ROM contents or screening process, then he knows precisely which permutations he needs to try for the unscrambling. He might even be able to build an automatic system to try each possibility and analyze which possibilities give a signal most like speech. (To determine which are most like speech he might, for example, examine the sonogram.) To guard against this possibility we need as large a number of 'good' permutations as possible which, in turn, requires a larger frame. But, as we have already seen, this type of time division system can cause a time delay which is twice the frame length. Thus when we increase the frame we also have the undesirable effect of increasing the delay. But, if we now look back to Figure 9.19 and the accompanying discussion, we see that a time delay of twice the frame length was only necessary because every permutation was allowed and, as a consequence, a segment could be delayed for the entire duration of the frame. Thus if we limit our permutations so that no segment is delayed for 'too long' we can reduce the delay time. This is called a **sliding window system**. Before we discuss sliding window systems we must make one important observation. In our discussion, and in the earlier one, we are regarding the segments as being indivisible. Consequently we are assuming that we cannot transmit a segment until we have received it all. In practice, of course, this is not necessarily true. However our aim is merely to illustrate the type of considerations involved and so, since it simplifies the discussion considerably, we will continue to make this assumption. Referring back to Figure 9.19 we see that there were two causes for the delay. First the transmitter had to wait for all segments to arrive before he could start his transmission (this was to allow for the possibility that the permutation might 'shift' the last segment to the first position). Then the recipient had to wait for all of them to be received before he could start to decipher (this was in case the permutation had 'shifted' the first segment to the last position). The principle behind a sliding window system is to choose only those permutations which do not shift any segment too far and, in this way, the time is reduced.

Before moving on from t.d.m. systems we must return to Figure 9.20 and note that an important part of the system is missing from our diagram: the synchronization. Some form of synchronization signal is required by the receiver so that he can recognize when a message is beginning to arrive and start his sequence generator. He must also ensure that his sequence remains in step with that of the transmitter. There are two standard techniques for doing this. In the first, known as **initial synchronization only**, the receiver relies on the initial synchronization and then uses a quartz crystal oscillator (i.e. a type of clock) to keep them in step. The alternative, known as **continuous synchronization**, is simply to look for frequent updatings of the synchronization. Some of the properties of continuous synchronization have already been mentioned in Section 8.2.2 (page 298). We now compare it with the method of initial synchronization only.

Continuous synchronization has two obvious advantages over initial synchronization. First it permits late entry; i.e. it allows someone to start receiving the message even if he has missed the beginning. In the system of Figure 9.20, or in any initial synchronization only system, there is no way in which someone can join a secure conversation after it has begun. He will simply be unable to determine how far the sequence generator has moved from its initial position. With continuous synchronization, late entry is possible by signalling, at each synchronization update, how far the sequence generator has progressed. Another (preferable) possibility is to reload the sequence generator at each update with a combination of key and a **time of day** (TOD) signal which is part of the synchronization. (The signal is called 'time of day' because it changes each time that synchronization information is transmitted.) The TOD can also act as the message key. This reloading of the sequence generator gives the system the added advantage that the sequence generator repeatedly starts in different places and thus uses a different pseudo-random sequence of permutations.

The second advantage of continuous synchronization is that, by only inserting it in enciphered messages, a machine which allows both enciphered and 'clear' messages can deduce for itself whether a message is enciphered by simply locating the synchronization information. It then switches-in the sequence generator and deciphers the cryptogram.

Despite these two obvious advantages, continuous synchronization is not always the better alternative. The reason for this is that in order to decipher a cryptogram the synchronization signal must be received. But, if the channel is poor or if there is a possibility of someone trying to **jam** the signal, i.e. actively trying to prevent the receiver from getting the transmission, then the initial synchronization only method may be more suitable. From the practical viewpoint, no matter which method is used, the synchronization information is often transmitted with the speech signal. This can be achieved by removing a portion of the signal in a small frequency band, typically 1800–2000Hz, and using this band to insert the synchronization information.

Before moving on to digital systems we summarize what we have established about scramblers. They are characterized by their analogue output which is of the same bandwidth as the original sequence. Furthermore they usually contain the distinctive syllabic rhythms, plus the frequency/power distribution patterns and phonemic sequences, of clear speech (but, of course, in a distorted form). The security depends both on the type of scrambling and on the way in which it is implemented. In particular, the use of a key-dependent sequence generator to pseudo-randomize the scrambling can considerably increase the security level. The particular method chosen for scrambling depends largely on the type and quality of the transmission channel and on the threat considered likely. (This latter consideration affects the likely investment in machinery.) Scramblers range from cheap inverters, which are merely privacy devices, right through to sophisticated t.d.m. systems which offer a high level of security and force any would-be cryptanalyst to invest a great deal of time and money before he can have any hope of breaking the system. Nevertheless all scramblers must be considered purely as tactical security systems. (As we saw in Chapter 8 this means that we are prepared to assume that, eventually, any scrambled analogue message may be broken if the cryptanalyst has sufficient determination. Increasing the sophistication merely delays the inevitable. But, in practice, it may be possible to delay it for as long as the situation demands.)

9.7 Analogue to digital (A/D) converters

Digital methods depend on the conversion of the analogue signal to a digital one. There are many ways in which this can be achieved and, in order to appreciate some of the difficulties encountered with this type of encipherment, we will consider three analogue to digital converters.

9.7.1 Pulse code modulation (p.c.m.)

In **pulse modulation** the signal is converted into a series of pulses. The message signal is sampled at frequent intervals and the value of each sample used to determine a property (e.g. amplitude or width) of a corresponding pulse. In this way the transmitted information corresponds to the values of the message signal at discrete instants in time. The process of sampling is illustrated in Figure 9.22. The vertical lines show the values of the signal at regular time intervals, and it is these values which determine the transmitted information. Naturally it is important that these sample values are sufficiently close together that they completely determine the original signal. (If we cannot recover the original signal from our transmission then we are in trouble!) This raises an important question; how often should the message signal be sampled? The aim is to have as few samples as possible provided that the original signal is recoverable. The number of samples per second is known as the **sampling rate** and the following theorem, (whose proof is in [88]), gives a precise value for the minimal sampling rate.

THEOREM 9.1 (**The Sampling Theorem**) *Suppose a function $f(t)$ is limited to a bandwidth of B Hz between frequencies f_1 and f_2 Hz ($f_2 > f_1$). The minimum sampling rate required to characterize the function is $\dfrac{2f_2}{m}$ samples per second, where m is the largest integer not exceeding $\dfrac{f_2}{B}$.*   □

This means that, as a rough approximation, a band-limited signal of bandwidth B Hz can be characterized by about $2B$ samples per second. To obtain some idea of the numbers involved we set a simple exercise.

EXERCISE 9.5 *What is the minimum sampling rate for a speech signal extending from (i) 0–4kHz, (ii) 300–3400 Hz?*

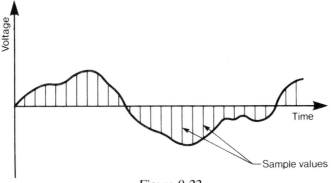

Figure 9.22
Sample values of a signal

In practice, in order to determine the minimum sampling rate of a speech signal, it is assumed to occupy a 4kHz bandwidth as in (i). This allows the use of simpler filters within the communications systems which form the route of the signal.

In **pulse code modulation** (p.c.m.), the message sample values are sent as a code formed by a pattern of binary pulses. A scheme is used whereby each sample value is transmitted as a sequence of bits, called a **word**. For speech a word is often eight bits which means that it can take 256 ($= 2^8$) different values. However if the distance between the maximum and minimum values is divided into 256, it is extremely unlikely that each sample will have exactly one of these values. It is customary to use the value closest to that of the sample. (This does of course introduce an error termed the **quantization error**.) Figure 9.23 shows the action of a p.c.m. encoder with 16 levels, i.e. with 4 bits per sample. In this example the first of the 4 bits is used to indicate whether the signal value is above or below the axis and the last 3 indicate the 'distance' from the axis. For this reason, the levels 0000 and 1000 both represent the fact that the signal is on the axis and, consequently, coincide.

In order to obtain a binary code to represent a signal, we take the sample value for each of the prescribed times. At time 0 we have 0000, for time t we have 1001, for $2t$ the sample value seems marginally nearer to 1001 than 1010 so we get 1001 again. Continuing in this way the p.c.m. signal is 0000 1001 1001 1011 1100 1110 1101 1010 0010. (Note that in practical systems the codewords will not be evenly spaced. It is normal to have a concentration of them near the axis in order to increase the dynamic range.)

Any p.c.m. signal has a pattern of 0s and 1s corresponding to the sample values of its message signal. Thus the shape of its spectrum depends on the sequence of sample values. We can, however, estimate the required bandwidth for a p.c.m. signal. In Figure 9.24 we illustrate the relation between the p.c.m. code and p.c.m. signal. Since the receiver only needs to distinguish between 0s and 1s, any block or gap, in the p.c.m. signal,

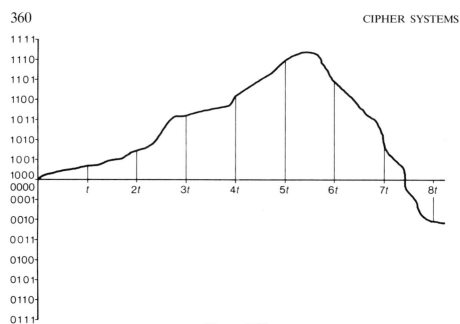

Figure 9.23
The action of a p.c.m. encoder

requires a bandwidth just sufficient to pass a sinewave with a frequency which is inversely proportional to the length of the run. Thus it should be clear that a pattern of digits which contains alternate 1s and 0s, i.e. has only runs of length one, will contain the highest frequency components of the signal; this frequency is in fact half the rate at which the digits are generated by the p.c.m. encoder.

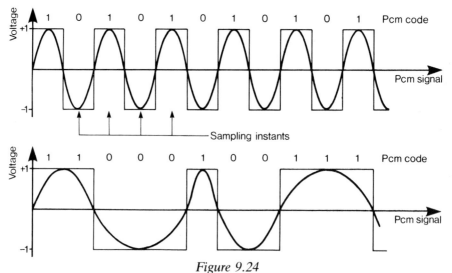

Figure 9.24
Bandwidth necessary to transmit a p.c.m. signal

EXERCISE 9.6 What is the bit rate of an 8-bit p.c.m. signal used to encode the signal of Exercise 9.5 (i)? Show that the minimum bandwidth for this p.c.m. signal is 32kHz.

This exercise shows that our signal with a band of 4kHz actually requires 32kHz for transmission. Clearly, then, we can never use this system if we have a transmission path with a narrow band.

9.7.2 A linear delta modulator system (l.d.m.)

An l.d.m. is another A/D converter. If a band-limited signal $f(t)$ is the input for an l.d.m. then the output, which we denote by $Q(t)$, consists of pulses which are equally spaced and have amplitudes $\pm v$ volts, for some v. The interval between these pulses is denoted by T seconds, so that the pulses occur with frequency $f_p = 1/T$. One crucial fact is that T is chosen to make f_p larger than the minimum sampling rate given in the sampling theorem. Rather than discuss the relation between $f(t)$ and $Q(t)$ in general, we will illustrate it by the example shown in Figure 9.25. In this diagram the graph of $f(t)$ is drawn. We pick an arbitrary point with voltage a and use it as a starting point to determine $x(t)$ in the following way. For the first T seconds $x(t) = a$. At $t = T$, (i.e. at the point A), since $x(t) < f(t)$, we increase $x(t)$ by v_1 volts (where v_1 is a fixed number chosen by us). For the next T seconds $x(t)$ remains constant again (this time at $a + v_1$ volts), and then when $t = 2T$ we look again at the relative values of $x(t)$ and $f(t)$. In our example we still have $x(t) < f(t)$, so we add another v_1 volts to $x(t)$. The shape of $x(t)$ should now be clear. At each multiple of T seconds it either increases or decreases by v_1 volts, depending upon whether $x(t) < f(t)$ or $x(t) > f(t)$. In our example we do not have $x(t) > f(t)$ until $4T$ seconds (i.e. at the point marked B). So the first three steps are all upwards. Each time $x(t)$ increases, $Q(t)$ assumes a positive value while $Q(t)$ is negative when $x(t)$ decreases. The pulse $Q(t)$ is shown at the foot of the diagram.

When the input signal is increasing the pulse $Q(t)$ tends to have more 1s than 0s, while a negative step for $f(t)$ produces the opposite effect. At times when $f(t)$ is more or less constant, for instance near its maxima and minima, $Q(t)$ tends to oscillate between 1 and 0. This is referred to as the **idling state** of $Q(t)$, since it is the condition of $Q(t)$, which in turn defines $x(t)$, for no input signal.

The quality of speech recovered from the digital signal $Q(t)$ is directly related to the efficiency of the A/D converter, the D/A converter of the receiver and the sampling rate of the clear voice input. Voice quality can be improved by using rather more complex delta modulators than the linear system described above. For instance it is possible to adapt the **step height** (i.e. voltage v_1) of $x(t)$ depending on the number of successive 1s or 0s in $Q(t)$ and this enables $x(t)$ to follow $f(t)$ more closely. Recent advances have enabled the bit-rate to be reduced to as low as 9.6 kbits/sec. (while still preserving a reasonable speech quality) to satisfy

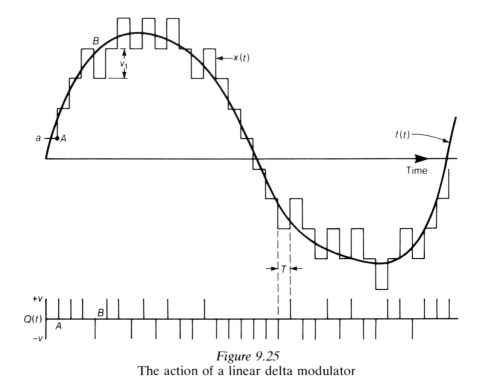

Figure 9.25
The action of a linear delta modulator

certain channel bandwidth limitations. The bandwidth required for this signal can be estimated in a similar way to that used for a p.c.m. It is approximately half the maximum rate at which digits are generated by the delta modulator.

9.7.3 Vocoders

In the last two A/D converters, the input signal is sampled at regular time intervals and a digital 'approximation' is then transmitted. Furthermore the minimum possible sampling rate is determined by the Sampling Theorem (page 358). There is, however, another way of transmitting the information. If, for example, our input signal is a sinusoid with frequency f then, instead of sending our digital approximation, we could merely tell the receiver that the input is a sinusoid with frequency f and leave him to build up his own signal. This is the principle behind **vocoders**. They are essentially speech synthesis systems which produce low bit-rate output signals, typically 1·2–4·8kbits/sec. As we saw in Exercise 9.5 (ii), to characterize a speech signal we need a sampling rate of at least 6·8kbits/sec. However the aim is not to characterize the speech signal but merely to send enough information that the receiver can build his own signal and understand the message. For instance, in **linear predictive coders** a filter is continuously modified to provide an approximation of the filtering action of the vocal tract cavities. This modifying information, together with pitch information, is transmitted to the receiver. (In practice the filter is usually implemented using digital rather than analogue techniques.) It has been found that the transmission then contains enough information for the receiver to construct a signal and understand the message. But, depending on the precise parameters of the system, some of the elements of speech which allow recognition of the voice or personality of the speaker may be lost. In a 'bad' case (where the use of the word 'bad' is subjective) the result may be a rather monotonous single-pitch noise resembling the voice of a 'dalek' or any other 'voice' which film directors attribute to talking computers. This fact has proven unpopular with most users, and the more recent vocoders attempt to preserve more of this 'personality' information.

There are other definite disadvantages of vocoder systems. For instance, since we are dispensing with so much of the redundant information, the system becomes considerably more sensitive to noise on the transmission path. In fact in some vocoder systems it has been found advantageous to make the bit-rate as low as possible and then introduce some extra redundancy to allow the receiver to carry out certain error correction methods; the idea is to choose the added redundancy so that the receiver can discover and correct certain error patterns. (Although we do not discuss error correction systems in this book, we must stress again that error detection and correction circuits are extremely important in cipher systems (see [67] and [26]).) Another major disadvantage of vocoder systems arises from the physiological differences between various races. For instance, without going into any details, a vocoder designed for a European speaker is likely to be much less effective when used by an Oriental. Yet another disadvantage of vocoders is that their complexity implies high cost and large size. However the use of microelectronics is quickly reducing the effect of both these parameters.

The reader should not assume that any one of the A/D converters we have described is necessarily superior to the others for all communication links. In practice the type of converter selected by a user will depend on the precise parameters of the communication circuits being used.

9.8 Use of A/D and D/A converters

There are many other digitization techniques besides the three discussed in the last section and any one of them may be used. However delta modulators are the converters which are currently most popular in encryption units, and consequently we will always assume that our A/D converter is one. One reason for this popularity is that a delta modulator performs well in noisy conditions. In fact, because of the high redundancy in speech, it is possible to understand a message even if a high proportion of errors has arisen in transmission. Even in a transmission medium with an average error rate of one in ten, 16kbit/sec delta modulated speech can still be understood. (This is in direct contrast with what occurs for data. As we have seen in Chapter 8 a single error can, in that case, change the entire sense of the message.)

There are a number of aspects of the system to discuss and we begin with the more common encipherment techniques.

9.8.1 Encipherment

Figure 9.26 illustrates a system using a cipher feedback system as defined in Chapter 7. This is the system which, at the present time, seems to be in most common use; the main reason being that, as described in Chapter 7, it is self-synchronizing and hence, since less additional circuitry is required, the cost of the equipment is minimized. But, as we also saw in Chapter 7, one of the biggest practical problems with this system is that it propagates errors. Suppose, for instance, that we are transmitting over a noisy channel with a 10% mean error rate. The deciphering process of Figure 9.26 will propagate errors, increase the error rate and may, as a consequence, result in an unintelligible output. The effect of this on radio systems, for example, is to reduce significantly the distance from the transmitter, at which the transmission can be successfully received. A possible improvement is shown in Figure 9.27. This is the straightforward stream cipher system. But now we have reintroduced the disadvantage that we require some extra form of synchronization to keep the 'send' and 'receive' sequence generators in step. (We note that block cipher systems, in their codebook form, are not used for voice systems as the error propagation would lead to enormous problems.) We must consider the method of synchronization but first we mention briefly the 'form' in which an intercept will appear. If we assume that the sequence generator produces a 'good' psuedo-random sequence, i.e. one which has good randomness properties, the intercept will sound like white noise. This prompts many users to employ what has become known as traffic flow security. With **traffic flow security**, noise is sent down the line whenever no message is being transmitted. This means that, since he is always intercepting a stream of pulses which resemble white noise, the interceptor does not know if a message is being transmitted or not. So it is crucial that any synchronization signal which is sent over the channel must be recognized by the receiver but not the interceptor. Thus, ideally, the synchronization signal should not be a fixed sequence of digits which everyone could recognize as the start of a message.

As in the case of scramblers there are two types of synchronization in normal use: initial synchronization only and continuous synchronization. Furthermore the same advantages and disadvantages of the two systems still apply. There is, however, one important difference. The continuous synchronization may be sent in a block at certain time intervals as opposed to being transmitted continuously and interleaving it with data. If this is the case then the temptation to synchronize at regular time intervals has to be resisted since the existence of predictable time intervals facilitates

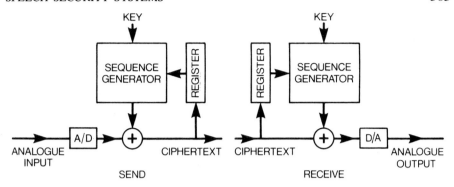

Figure 9.26
A typical cipher feedback system

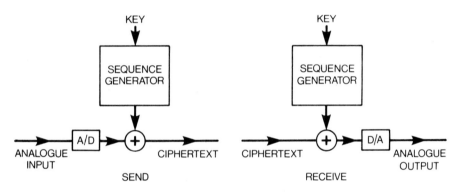

Figure 9.27
A typical stream cipher system

jamming. So, ideally, continuous synchronization should be sent at pseudo-random time intervals and should itself be pseudo-random. All this can be achieved by using a sequence generator to determine both the synchronization information and the time at which it is to be sent. A further consideration is the need to protect the TOD information against transmission errors. There must be a high probability of it being received correctly even in a noisy channel. The reason is clear; if the sequence generator in a receiver is reloaded incorrectly complete sections of the transmitted message will be lost. Since the digital speech can be understood at noise levels such as a 10% mean error rate, it is typically required that there be a probability of at least 0.9 that the synchronization block and TOD information will be correctly received in these conditions.

With many of these systems (and also in many scramblers) a flywheel is operated. The TOD information, both for digital voice cipher systems and for scramblers, can also be used as the message key and is of the utmost importance.

How does a digital voice system measure up against the worst case conditions of Chapter 4? Clearly the first two conditions are no problem. We have assumed throughout that any interceptor will have complete knowledge of our equipment and a number of ciphered messages (although we sometimes try to confuse him on the latter by traffic flow security). The third condition states that the interceptor may know a reasonable amount of plaintext corresponding to the ciphertext. First of all we must decide if this is a reasonable assumption in this setting. What does it mean? Given the way the system is set up, even the encipherer does not know the plaintext for his message; i.e. he does not know the sequence of binary digits being enciphered. However we must not forget that the digital encoder is a fixed process and will, consequently, produce a fixed output pattern of bits for any fixed input pattern (apart, perhaps, from a few bits at the beginning of the message while the machine is stabilizing). Now suppose, for instance, that there is an air-conditioning whine, or some other well-known noise, in the background while someone is speaking. Whenever they pause in their speech the bit pattern produced will be the response of the A/D converter to this noise. But this is likely to be recognized, particularly in a long speech with many pauses, and illustrates one way in which known plaintext may be obtained. There is, however, another and much more important source of plaintext.

Throughout this chapter we have highlighted the extent of the redundancy in human speech. Although this is an advantage when considering transmission errors it has the disadvantage of enabling the interceptor to utilize the statistical tests described in Chapter 4. Rather than give a detailed discussion we merely record some of the results of applying them to a portion of digitized speech from a delta modulatoı. The input to the delta modulator consisted of English speech with rather exaggerated pauses and relatively little background noise. The modulator sampled at 16,000 bits per second and the sample contained 7,110,496 bits.

First we applied the frequency test which, in this example, means nothing more than counting the number of 0s (n_0) and the number of 1s (n_1). The results were: $n_0 = 3,546,356$ and $n_1 = 3,564,131$. This gives 95% confidence intervals for the probability of occurrence of a 0 or 1 (p_0 and p_1 respectively) as: $0·4984 \leq p_0 \leq 0·4991$ and $0·5009 \leq p_1 \leq 0·5016$. From this we see that there is a reasonably even distribution of 0s and 1s and that the probabilities are 'roughly' as expected.

Next we consider a serial test considering every consecutive pair of bits. The results are shown below.

Pair	Frequency
00	1,086,972 $(= n_{00})$
01	2,459,393 $(= n_{01})$
10	2,459,392 $(= n_{10})$
11	1,104,739 $(= n_{11})$

These give 95% confidence intervals for the probabilities p_{ij} (where p_{ij} is the probability that j follows i):

$$0\cdot3060\leq p_{00}\leq0\cdot3070 \qquad 0\cdot3095\leq p_{11}\leq0\cdot3104$$
$$0\cdot6930\leq p_{01}\leq0\cdot6940 \qquad 0\cdot6896\leq p_{10}\leq0\cdot6905.$$

These probabilities p_{ij} are called the **transition probabilities**. It is clear that there is a far greater probability of making a transition than of remaining in the same state. For instance if the last bit produced was a 0 the next one is much more likely to be a 1 than a 0.

0	6004.0	22	34928.0	44	18435.0
1	7276.0	23	7526.0	45	21168.0
2	2345.0	24	10859.0	46	7334.0
3	11781.0	25	24094.0	47	3109.0
4	2456.0	26	34235.0	48	10314.0
5	7550.0	27	5286.0	49	20831.0
6	11758.0	28	20726.0	50	19688.0
7	18574.0	29	5816.0	51	17310.0
8	2466.0	30	8215.0	52	14964.0
9	5256.0	31	6699.0	53	24830.0
10	23462.0	32	7425.0	54	4992.0
11	17055.0	33	6576.0	55	2857.0
12	16540.0	34	7626.0	56	20562.0
13	18211.0	35	18196.0	57	12834.0
14	19356.0	36	5253.0	58	5675.0
15	11525.0	37	32656.0	59	2284.0
16	3624.0	38	23320.0	60	12410.0
17	5240.0	39	12212.0	61	2369.0
18	18383.0	40	6348.0	62	6458.0
19	18334.0	41	31441.0	63	5804.0
20	22525.0	42	182459.0		
21	183784.0	43	25453.0		

Expected Character Total = 18516.9
5% Confidence Interval = 18252.3–18781.5
1% Confidence Interval = 18169.1–18864.7
Total No. of Characters = 1185082.0

Table 9.1
Results of poker test for $k=6$

Next we consider a particular case of the poker test. For the poker test the bits are arranged in blocks of some fixed length, k say, and the observed frequencies of occurrence of the different possibilities for the k-bit blocks are recorded. Each block of k bits can be regarded as a binary number in the range 0 to $2^k - 1$ and this gives us a natural way in which to order the possibilities. For our test we take $k = 6$ and the results are shown in Table 9.1.

With a random sequence each of the 2^k possibilities is equally likely, but the distribution we obtain is obviously not uniform and has two definite peaks corresponding to 010101 and 101010 which are, of course, the idling patterns for the modulator. What appears to happen is that, since there was virtually no background noise, each time the speaker pauses the delta modulator reverts to its idling state. Although these pauses are hardly perceptible to a listener, the relatively high sampling rate means that even a pause of only 2 or 3mS can lead to a 30–50 bit idling pattern. Of course there will be some background noise and the pattern may not be perfect every time, but it certainly means that guessing some plaintext is much easier than we might have expected. As we saw in Section 4.4 the break time for a system is highly dependent on the number of trials necessary to guess some plaintext. Part of the cryptanalyst's task is to decide how many bits of plaintext are required to minimize his break time. Clearly this will involve him in carrying out tests like the poker test for various values of k and deciding which is best.

Obviously this property of delta-modulators is undesirable from the cryptographer's point of view. However delta modulators are not the only A/D converters which yield information when subjected to some simple statistical tests. In fact all three of the digitization techniques which we have discussed have this weakness. The main reason is the highly redundant nature of speech. For our particular example these properties were rather exaggerated by including reasonably long pauses in the speech and reducing the background noise. Nevertheless users of digital speech cipher systems must be aware of both the highly redundant nature of the plaintext being ciphered and also of the vast quantities of ciphertext that the cryptanalyst is obtaining for analysis. For instance our 7,000,000 bit sample used earlier represents only about seven minutes of speech! So, unless great confidence is held in the sequence generator being used, digitized speech cipher systems cannot be considered fully secure.

Since all the systems we have met in this chapter are theoretically breakable, we would obviously have more confidence in a system that was not so redundant. For this reason, at the present time, most messages of strategic importance, i.e. those which require long term security, are preferably transmitted over the type of data system we discussed in the last chapter (Example 8.1, page 305). At the present time speech systems of any kind, i.e. digital or scramblers, tend to be used primarily for tactical security.

Further Reading

[72], [75], [86], [88] and [90] are general texts on telecommunications, signal analysis and speech analysis. [74] covers the subject of pulse code

modulation; [81] and [89] are concerned with delta modulators and [77], [78], [83], [85] and [87] with vocoder techniques. [73], [76], [80], [82], [84] and [91] are interesting surveys of speech encipherment techniques. [79] is an interesting comparison of four different techniques. [71] covers digital voice encryption.

[71] Beker, H. J., 'Cryptographic requirements for digital secure speech systems', *Electronic Engineering*, Vol. 52, No. 634, 1980, 37–46.

[72] Brown, J. and Glazier, E. V. D., *Telecommunications*, Chapman and Hall, 1964.

[73] Brunner, E. R., *Speech Security Systems Today and Tomorrow*, Gretag Ltd., 1980.

[74] Cattermole, K. W., *Principles of Pulse Code Modulations*, Iliffe, 1969.

[75] Flanagan, J. L., *Speech Analysis; Synthesis and Perception*, Springer-Verlag, 1972.

[76] Gallois, A. P., 'Communication privacy using digital techniques', *Electronics and Power*, Vol. 22, 1976, 777–80.

[77] Gold, B. and Rader, C. M., 'The channel vocoder', *IEEE Trans. Audio and Electroacoustics.* Vol. AU–15, No. 4, 1967, 148–60.

[78] Gunawardana, R., 'Using the LPC speech synthesis circuits', *Elect. Product Design*, 1980, 35–7.

[79] Jayant, N. S., McDermott, B. J., Christensen, S. W. and Quinn, A. M. S., 'A comparison of four methods for analog speech privacy', *IEEE Trans. on Comms.*, Vol. COM–29, No. 1, 1981, 18–23.

[80] Kirchhofer, K. H., 'Secure voice communication-cryptophony', *Int. Def. Rev.*, Vol. 9, 1976, 761–7.

[81] Lamba, T. S. and Faruqui, M. N., 'Intelligible voice communication through adaptive delta modulation at bit rates lower than 10 k bits/s', *Radio and Electronic Engineer*, Vol. 48, No. 4, 1978, 169–75.

[82] MacKinnon, N. R. F., 'The development of speech encipherment', *Radio and Electronic Engineer*, Vol. 50, No. 4, 1980, 147–55.

[67] MacWilliams, F. J. and Sloane, N. J. A., *The Theory of Error-correcting Codes*, North-Holland Publishing Co., 1978.

[83] Markel, J. D. and Gray, A. H., *Linear Prediction of Speech*, Springer-Verlag, 1976.

[84] McCalmont, A. M., 'Communication security for voice techniques systems and operations', *Telecommunications*, 1973, 35–42.

[85] Meier, P., 'Die menschliche spracke digital analysiest und optisch dargestellt', *Krieg im Aether*, Folge XVII, 1978.

[86] Papoulis, A., *Signal Analysis*, McGraw Hill, 1977.

[26] Peterson, W. W. and Weldon, E. J., *Error-correcting Codes*, 2nd Ed., MIT Press, 1972.

[87] Pickuance, R., 'Speech synthesis; the new frontiers', *Electronic Engineering*, 1980, 37–52.

[88] Rosie, A. M., *Information and Communication Theory*, 2nd Ed., Van Nostrand Reinhold, 1973.

[89] Steele, R., *Delta Modulation Systems*, Pentech Press, London, 1975.

[90] Taub, H. and Schilling, D. L., *Principles of Communication Systems*, McGraw-Hill, 1971.

[91] Telsy Systems, *Secure Voice: Reality and Myth*, 1979.

10.
Public-Key Cryptography

10.1 Introduction

In the first nine chapters we have outlined the historical development of cipher systems up to, and including, some current commercially available systems. As we saw in Chapter 1, the security of many of the 'paper and pencil' systems was minimal and relied on the secrecy of both the key and the ciphering algorithm. As systems improved and became more secure it became feasible to allow the cryptographer to make the assumptions **C1**, **C2**, **C3** of Chapter 4. In particular this meant that the designer assumed that his algorithm was known and that all security lay within the key. We then showed in Chapters 6 and 7 that, although not simple, it was possible to design systems with a good chance of remaining secure under these basic assumptions. But so far each system, whether good or bad, has had the requirement that, prior to the transmission of each message, the sender and receiver must have agreed upon the key to be used and that this key must remain secret. This requirement, of course, poses many problems and a number of them were discussed in Chapter 8.

In this final chapter we attempt to take cipher systems one step further. We discuss systems where it is theoretically possible to make public the encipherment key as well as the enciphering algorithm. This is another revolutionary idea. The first published article to suggest that such a system might be possible was written in 1976 by Diffie and Hellman [97] and called 'New Directions in Cryptography'. In this chapter we make considerable use of that excellent article. The systems under discussion are called **public-key cryptosystems** and the fundamental concept on which they are based is the simple and obvious (with hindsight!) observation that there is no need for the encipherment procedure and key to be the same as the decipherment procedure and key. In fact we have already met examples where they differ. In the DES, for instance, the deciphering procedure is different from the enciphering one. But in the early commercially available electronic systems these two procedures were usually identical. This was merely to make the implementation of the machine easier and so, as electronics advanced, it became recognized as less important. We have also seen examples where the two keys are different. For instance, if we have a cipher that simply permutes the n characters in a block, then the inverse permutation is required for decipherment. So, if the permutation is the key, the decipherment key is the inverse of the encipherment key. But of course, in this case, knowledge of the encipherment key immediately tells us the decipherment key and so, although they are different, we dare not publicize our encipherment key. What we require is a cipher system such that given the encipherment procedure and key and, perhaps, the decipherment procedure it is impossible, or at least computationally infeasible, to deduce the decipherment key. Once we have such a system, anyone wishing to use it will be assigned an encipherment key which will be published in a directory. Anyone wishing to send a message to one of the users merely consults the directory to see which encipherment key he should use. In this way a user, who will of course have his own secret decipherment key, will be able to decipher any cryptogram sent to him without even needing to know the identity of the sender.

In this chapter we suggest a few possibilities. Some of the arguments to justify our claims involve a little number theory. Although the results used will normally appear in an elementary undergraduate course, the reader should, as always, be prepared to skip the mathematical justifications and merely attempt to get the overall picture.

10.2   Formal Definition

Before we attempt to construct any examples we will make a more formal statement of our requirements. Our system is illustrated in Figure 10.1. In it there are two distinct keys, e and d, plus two distinct algorithms, g and h. The enciphering key e, the enciphering algorithm g and deciphering algorithm h are all made public. Only the deciphering key d is secret and the only person who needs to know it is the receiver. Anyone may send a message to the receiver. To send a message $\mathbf{m}$, the encipherer merely uses g and e to generate the cryptogram $\mathbf{c} = g_e(\mathbf{m})$. When the receiver gets $\mathbf{c}$, he applies h in conjunction with d to obtain the message $\mathbf{m}$. Thus $\mathbf{m} = h_d(\mathbf{c})$ and h_d is the inverse of g_e. This means that we need general procedures g and h for which pairs of inverse keys e and d are easily generated, but for which it is, in practice, impossible to deduce d from a knowledge of e, g and h.

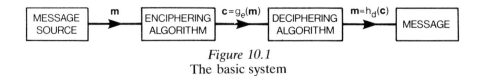

Figure 10.1
The basic system

As a simple illustration of the principles involved we discuss a possible system. This system is insecure and, consequently, totally unsuitable, but we include it to demonstrate the basic concepts. Let us suppose that we have a system where, for encipherment, each message $\mathbf{m}$ is broken down into blocks of n bits. Our encipherment procedure is to choose an n by n non-singular matrix, $\mathbf{E}$, and to encipher each n-bit block by 'multiplying' it by the matrix. Thus, in this case, our enciphering keys are non-singular n by n matrices and, if $\mathbf{c}$ is the cryptogram vector corresponding to an n-bit message $\mathbf{m}$ after the matrix $\mathbf{E}$ has been chosen, the encipherment procedure is given by $\mathbf{c} = \mathbf{Em}$. Since $\mathbf{E}$ is non-singular, its inverse $\mathbf{D}$ exists and the decipherment procedure is $\mathbf{m} = \mathbf{Dc}$.

Since both the enciphering and deciphering operations are multiplication of a vector and a matrix, they each require about n^2 operations. It is also conceptually easy to generate pairs of inverse matrices. To do this we merely start with the identity matrix and perform a sequence of elementary row and column operations to obtain an arbitrary non-singular matrix $\mathbf{E}$. By carrying out the inverses of these same elementary operations in reverse order on the identity matrix we obtain $\mathbf{D}$. Thus we have defined a system in which both encipherment and decipherment are simple, the enciphering and deciphering keys are different but it is easy to obtain two suitable keys. 'All' (and, of course, this is always where the problems will be!) that we need to do now is to see if it is possible for a cryptanalyst to deduce the decipherment key from a knowledge of the encipherment key used. But, in this case, this means he has to deduce $\mathbf{D}$ from $\mathbf{E}$. Unfortunately, as we saw in Chapter 5, n by n matrix inversion only needs about n^3 operations. Thus, although he has a significantly harder task than the decipherer, it will not take an interceptor an unreasonably long time to decipher a cryptogram, and we do not have a suitable public key system. What we need is a system where the enciphering and deciphering operations, as well as the generation of inverse keys, all take polynomial time, but the deduction of d from e needs exponential time.

10.3 A System due to Merkle and Hellman

Our first realistic example is based on a famous problem which is known as the **Knapsack Problem** (or the **subset sum problem**). This problem may be stated as follows: Given a knapsack of length t and a set of n rods, each with the same diameter as the knapsack but with various lengths $a_1, a_2, \ldots, a_n$, can one find a subset of the rods which completely fills the knapsack? An alternative formulation of the problem is: Given an integer t and a set $\mathbf{A}$ of positive integers $a_1, a_2, \ldots, a_n$, is there a subset of $\mathbf{A}$ whose elements add up to t?

This problem has been shown to be **NP**-complete. Thus there is no known polynomial time solution. Furthermore if a polynomial time algorithm is ever found to solve the general problem this will imply that the classes **P** and **NP** are equivalent. It is essentially the conviction that the classes **P** and **NP** are distinct which encourages people to assume that the solution of the knapsack problem (or any other **NP**-complete problem) needs exponential time and that no-one is going to suddenly produce a polynomial time algorithm to solve it (*cf* Chapter 6).

Since it forms the basis of Merkle and Hellman's public key system, we now investigate how it may be used. We suppose that any data to be enciphered has already been converted to binary. The sender who wishes to transmit his binary message will consult a public directory to find the enciphering key for the proposed recipient of his message. This enciphering key will take the form of an n-tuple $\mathbf{a} = (a_1, a_2, \ldots, a_n)$ where each a_i is a positive integer. In order to encipher the message the sender divides it into blocks of n bits, thus forming binary n-tuples $\mathbf{x}_1, \mathbf{x}_2, \ldots, \mathbf{x}_u$. Each block of the message is now enciphered by taking the inner product of $\mathbf{a}$ with each of the n-bit blocks $\mathbf{x}_i$ in turn. (Recall that the inner product of $(a_1, a_2, \ldots, a_n)$ with $(b_1, b_2, \ldots, b_n)$ is $a_1b_1 + a_2b_2 + \ldots + a_nb_n$.) Since each entry in $\mathbf{x}_j$ is either 1 or 0, the inner product of $\mathbf{x}_j$ with $\mathbf{a}$ is an integer c_j which is the sum of a subset of the set $\mathbf{A} = \{a_1, a_2, \ldots, a_n\}$. It is the sequence of numbers $c_1, c_2, c_3, \ldots$ which is transmitted to the receiver. Thus at a given instant an interceptor will have a number c_j plus knowledge of the set $\mathbf{A} = \{a_1, a_2, \ldots, a_n\}$ which, like the encipherer, he can obtain from the public directory. In order to discover the block of data $\mathbf{x}_j$ he must find a subset of $\mathbf{A}$ which adds up to c_j. The security of the system lies in the difficulty of this problem. However, from what we have said so far, it appears that the receiver is faced with the same problem. This system does, of course, need to be designed so that this is not so but, before we discuss the receiver, we will consider a small example.

We suppose that the enciphering key for a particular receiver is the set $\mathbf{A} = \{2106, 880, 1320, 974, 2388, 1617, 1568, 2523, 48, 897\}$ and that we wish to encipher the word **cipher**. First we must convert **cipher** to a binary form. Since, in our example, $n = 10$ it seems convenient to use a code which converts each character into five bits. The ITA2 of Appendix 2 is adequate for our purposes. Thus our message becomes 0111001100011010010110000001010. Breaking this down into message blocks of 10 bits we have:

$$\mathbf{x}_1 = 0111001100$$
$$\mathbf{x}_2 = 0110100101$$
$$\mathbf{x}_3 = 1000001010$$

Thus to encipher our first block we must take $\mathbf{a} \cdot \mathbf{x}_1 = 2106 \times 0 + 880 \times 1 + 1320 \times 1 + 974 \times 1 + 2388 \times 0 + 1617 \times 0 + 1568 \times 1 + 2523 \times 1 + 48 \times 0 + 897 \times 0 = 7265$.

EXERCISE 10.1 Show that our other two message blocks $\mathbf{x}_2$ and $\mathbf{x}_3$ become 8008 and 3722 respectively.

Thus our complete message becomes 7265, 8008, 3722. An interceptor is faced with the task of determining subsets of **A** that sum to these numbers. Of course this example is unrealistically small and an interceptor might try each possibility.

EXERCISE 10.2   The number of subsets (including the empty set) of a set of n elements is 2^n. If $|A| = n$, how big must we take n in order to necessitate 10^6 trials?

In practice we might take n to be several hundred and since the number of subsets increases exponentially with n, attempting to trial every possible subset will be out of the question.

Now, what about the genuine receiver? How can he decipher the message?

The idea proposed by Merkle and Hellman is to make use of the fact that not all instances of the knapsack problem are hard enough to require exponential time for their solution. As we stressed in Chapter 6, the whole concept of **NP**-completeness is one that refers to worst-case situations. In other words a problem being **NP**-complete only means that there is at least one instance of the problem that is hard. There may be numerous instances of the problem that can easily be handled in polynomial time. In fact, we saw many such examples in Chapter 6.

Now consider the following set of instances of our knapsack problem. If we are given a set of positive integers $A' = \{a_1', a_2', \ldots, a_n'\}$ such that

$$a'_{k+1} > \sum_{i=1}^{k} a'_i$$

for all k in the range $1, \ldots, n-1$ and a number t', can we find a subset of A' whose members sum to t'?

The difference between this and the more general knapsack problem is that we have now put some conditions on our set **A**. These extra conditions are sufficient to make the problem solvable and the following crude algorithm provides a solution.

Step 1   Put $k = n$ and put $t'' = t'$.
Step 2   Compare t'' and a_k'. If $t'' \geq a_k'$ then a_k' must be one of the numbers in the required subset of A'. If $t'' < a_k'$ then a_k' is not one of the numbers in our required subset of A'.
Step 3   If $t'' \geq a_k'$ put $t'' = t'' - a_k'$.
Step 4   Decrease k by 1.
Step 5   If $k = 0$ then stop, otherwise go to Step 2.

When $k = 0$ we will have identified a subset of A' and we will have a value of t'' remaining. If $t'' = 0$ then the answer to the problem is yes and in fact the particular subset of A' has been determined.

It is not too difficult to see why this algorithm works and, in doing so, we shall also see the crucial role played by our extra condition. At Step 2 of the first round we are comparing t' and a'_n. If $t' \geq a'_n$ and if a subset of $\mathbf{A}'$ does exist whose members sum to t' then, since the sum of $a'_1, a'_2, \ldots, a'_{n-1}$ is less than a'_n, a'_n must be a member of that subset. On the other hand if $t' < a'$ then obviously a'_n cannot belong to any subset whose sum is as small as t'. If a'_n is in the set then we subtract it from t', otherwise we leave t' alone, and we then compare the new value with a'_{n-1}. A repetition of our earlier reasoning now determines whether or not a'_{n-1} is in the set. Continuing in this way we will eventually know whether or not such a subset of $\mathbf{A}'$ exists. Furthermore a slight modification of the algorithm will record the subset for us.

As an example of the use of the algorithm we will let $\mathbf{A}'$ be the set $\{2, 6, 9, 19, 41, 79, 159, 320, 643, 1310\}$. (Note that $6 > 2$, $9 > 6 + 2$, $19 > 2 + 6 + 9$, etc. so that $\mathbf{A}'$ satisfies our extra condition.) We will try $t' = 513$. First, since $513 < 643 < 1310$, neither 643 nor 1310 can be in our subset. However, 320 is the largest member of $\mathbf{A}'$ which is less than 513 and consequently must be in the subset. Since $513 - 320 = 193$ and $193 > 159$ we know that, if such a subset exists, 159 must also be in it. We now see that $193 - 159 = 34$ and so the next largest member of $\mathbf{A}'$ which must belong to our subset is 19. Continuing in this way we see that there is, in fact, a subset with the desired properties and it is $\{6, 9, 19, 159, 320\}$. This means that if we had used $\{2, 6, 9, 19, 41, 79, 159, 320, 643, 1310\}$ as our set $\mathbf{A}$ and 513 was a cryptogram formed by $\mathbf{a} \cdot \mathbf{x}$, where $\mathbf{a}$ is the 10-tuple corresponding to $\mathbf{A}$ and $\mathbf{x}$ is a block of data, then we would know that $\mathbf{x} = 0111001100$.

Clearly the algorithm described above requires polynomial time and, thus, is suitable as a decipherment procedure for a receiver. However, equally clearly, we cannot use a set like $\mathbf{A}'$ (i.e. a set satisfying our extra condition) as our public enciphering key, since any interceptor could deduce the message as easily as we could. Instead we try to transform our set $\mathbf{A}'$, for which a polynomial time decipherment algorithm exists, into a set $\mathbf{A}$ which is complex enough to be placed in the public directory. Then, through knowledge of this transform and its inverse, we can transform any cryptogram intended for us into a form where $\mathbf{A}'$ can be used for decipherment. The intention is that, since he does not know the necessary transformation, an interceptor will not be able to change the cryptogram into a form for which he knows a polynomial time deciphering algorithm. In other words we want to select a set $\mathbf{A}$, and therefore an instance of the knapsack problem, for which a polynomial time algorithm exists but for which, hopefully, the algorithm will not be deducible by any interceptor. The general name given to this type of function (i.e. a function for which there does not appear to be a polynomial time algorithm but for which there is one so long as the method of application is known) is a **trapdoor function**. In our situation it is intended that the genuine receiver should be the only person who knows how to 'open' the trapdoor. We will illustrate how this can be achieved by using the above example. Thus we take $\mathbf{A}'$ as

$\{2, 6, 9, 19, 41, 79, 159, 320, 643, 1310\}$. Our method for constructing **A** depends upon choosing two large random numbers w and m whose greatest common divisor is 1. In order to enable us to work through our example 'by hand' we will take $w = 1053$ and $m = 2719$. But, and this needs emphasizing, this is merely to clarify this example. In practice **A'** will, of course, be a much larger set and our two numbers will also be greater. Our rule for generating **A** from **A'** is given by $a_i \equiv a_i'w \pmod{m}$ for each i with $1 \le i \le n$. So, in this case, $a_1 \equiv 2 \times 1053 \pmod{2719}$, i.e. $a_1 \equiv 2106 \pmod{2719}$, and $a_2 \equiv 6 \times 1053 \pmod{2719}$, i.e. $a_2 \equiv 880 \pmod{2719}$.

EXERCISE 10.3   Show that **A** = $\{2106, 880, 1320, 974, 2388, 1617, 1568, 2523, 48, 897\}$. (*Note that this was our original choice for* **A** *earlier in this section.*)

Once **A'** has been transformed to **A**, it is the set **A** which is published in the public directory. This means that, for our example, anyone wishing to send a message to us will use the set of Exercise 10.3 as his encipherment key. Suppose that someone sends us a message and that we receive 7265, 8008, 3722. In order to decipher we must, from our knowledge of w and m, transform these cryptograms into a form which will enable us to use **A'** rather than **A**. When we introduced w and m we said that the only restriction placed on them was that $(w, m) = 1$. However we must point out that certain choices of w and m are 'bad'. (We do not want to get involved in determining all the bad possibilities, but will merely list a couple; various reasons why certain pairs are bad will probably occur to the reader during the rest of this section. If, for instance, m happens to be the difference of two elements of **A'** then the set **A** will be smaller than **A'**. Another bad situation occurs if $wa_n' < m$; in this case every element of **A** will have w as a factor.) As we shall see in a moment, the condition $(w, m) = 1$ guarantees the existence of an integer w^{-1} such that

$$ww^{-1} \equiv 1 \pmod{m}.$$

In order to justify our claim about the existence of w^{-1}, we will use a variation of Euclid's algorithm to show how to evaluate 1053^{-1} with $m = 2719$. The basic reasoning behind the algorithm is that if r is the remainder when x is divided by y, then any integer which divides x and y must also divide y and r. Thus $(x, y) = (y, r)$. (For more detail see [101].) The algorithm is essentially in two halves; the first part being a general algorithm for computing the g.c.d. of two integers. This is done by computing a series $r_0, r_1, r_2, \ldots$, where $r_0 = m$, $r_1 = w$ and $r_{i+1} \equiv r_{i-1} \pmod{r_i}$, until an r_k equal to 0 is found. Then r_{k-1} is the g.c.d. of r_0 and r_1. We then compute, for each r_i, numbers a_i and b_i such that $r_i = a_i r_0 + b_i r_1$. If $r_{k-1} = 1$ then

$$r_{k-1} = 1 = a_{k-1}m + b_{k-1}w.$$

But this means that $b_{k-1}w \equiv 1 \pmod{m}$, i.e. that $b_{k-1} = w^{-1}$.

We will carry out this procedure for $m = 2719$, $w = 1053$.

$$r_0 = 2719, \; r_1 = 1053$$

$2719 =$	$1053 \cdot 2 + 613$	so r_2	$= 613$
$1053 =$	$613 \cdot 1 + 440$	so r_3	$= 440$
$613 =$	$440 \cdot 1 + 173$	so r_4	$= 173$
$440 =$	$173 \cdot 2 + 94$	so r_5	$= 94$
$173 =$	$94 \cdot 1 + 79$	so r_6	$= 79$
$94 =$	$79 \cdot 1 + 15$	so r_7	$= 15$
$79 =$	$15 \cdot 5 + 4$	so r_8	$= 4$
$15 =$	$4 \cdot 3 + 3$	so r_9	$= 3$
$4 =$	$3 \cdot 1 + 1$	so r_{10}	$= 1$
$3 =$	$1 \cdot 3 + 0$	so r_{11}	$= 0.$

The fact that $r_{10} = 1$ merely confirms that $(2719, 1053) = 1$.

Now, $r_2 = r_0 - 2r_1$

$$r_3 = r_1 - r_2 = r_1 - (r_0 - 2r_1) = 3r_1 - r_0$$
$$r_4 = r_2 - r_3 = r_0 - 2r_1 - (3r_1 - r_0) = 2r_0 - 5r_1$$
$$r_5 = r_3 - 2r_4 = 3r_1 - r_0 - 2(2r_0 - 5r_1) = 13r_1 - 5r_0$$
$$r_6 = r_4 - r_5 = 2r_0 - 5r_1 - (13r_1 - 5r_0) = 7r_0 - 18r_1$$
$$r_7 = r_5 - r_6 = 13r_1 - 5r_0 - (7r_0 - 18r_1) = 31r_1 - 12r_0$$
$$r_8 = r_6 - 5r_7 = 7r_0 - 18r_1 - 5(31r_1 - 12r_0) = 67r_0 - 173r_1$$
$$r_9 = r_7 - 3r_8 = 31r_1 - 12r_0 - 3(67r_0 - 173r_1) = 550r_1 - 213r_0$$
$$r_{10} = r_8 - r_9 = 67r_0 - 173r_1 - (550r_1 - 213r_0) = 280r_0 - 723r_1$$

therefore $b_{k-1} = b_{10} = -723$ therefore $w^{-1} \equiv +1996 \pmod{2719}$.

It should be noted that the above algorithm is still feasible even if w and m are large numbers having the order of 50 digits.

As soon as we know the value of w^{-1}, deciphering a cryptogram becomes easy. Suppose that the plaintext block $\mathbf{x} = (x_1, x_2, \ldots, x_n)$ was enciphered to give $c = \mathbf{a}.\mathbf{x} = a_1 x_1 + a_2 x_2 + \ldots + a_n x_n$. then we compute

$$c' \equiv c w^{-1} \pmod{m}$$
$$\equiv (a_1 x_1 + a_2 x_2 + \ldots + a_n x_n) w^{-1} \pmod{m}$$
$$\equiv a_1 w^{-1} x_1 + a_2 w^{-1} x_2 + \ldots + a_n w^{-1} x_n \pmod{m}.$$

But our transformation from $\mathbf{A}'$ to $\mathbf{A}$ was $a_i \equiv a_i' w \pmod{m}$ for all i. Thus $a_i' \equiv a_i w^{-1} \pmod{m}$ and c' is nothing more than

$$a_1' x_1 + \ldots + a_n' x_n \pmod{m}.$$

But this means that, modulo m, c' is the cryptogram we would have received if $\mathbf{A}'$ had been used. So deciphering c' is merely solving the special case of the knapsack problem and we can do it. Of course, in order to ensure that our special case has the same solution as the original one, we need c' to be equal to $a_1' x_1 + \ldots + a_n' x_n$ rather than just being congruent to it modulo m. We can guarantee this by always choosing m large enough.

Returning to our example with $w = 1053$ and $m = 2719$, we know that $w^{-1} = 1996$ and so, for our first cryptogram number 7265, we have

$$c' \equiv c_1 w^{-1} \ (\mathrm{mod}\ m) \equiv 7265 \times 1996 \ (\mathrm{mod}\ 2719) \equiv 513 \ (\mathrm{mod}\ 2719).$$

But we have already deciphered this and obtained $\mathbf{x} = (0111001100)$.

EXERCISE 10.4   Decipher the remainder of our example.

EXERCISE 10.5   Assume that we have a secret key $\mathbf{A}' = \{3, 4, 10, 21, 43,$ $87, 192, 375, 810, 1607\}$ with $w = 1185$ and $m = 3407$:
  (*i*)   *Deduce w^{-1}.*
  (*ii*) *Find the public enciphering key $\mathbf{A}$ which can be published.*
  (*iii*) *Decipher $14135, 5995, 6055, 6856, 3550$ on the assumption that it has been encrypted using our public enciphering key, and, as in our earlier example, that ITA2 was used for encoding.*

To clarify this particular public-key cryptosystem we will summarize the basic ideas which we have used. We took a particular instance of an **NP**-complete problem which we know can be solved in polynomial time; i.e. the knapsack problem with our extra condition. We then used two large, randomly chosen integers to transform it to another instance of the problem. However, although there is obviously still a polynomial time solution, this second instance does not satisfy our extra condition and consequently, despite the fact that one exists, a polynomial time algorithm is not so readily found. Clearly to guess our values for w and m is, in all practical circumstances, virtually impossible. Because of this the security of the system depends upon the inability of any interceptor to calculate the transformation which 'simplifies' $\mathbf{A}$ to $\mathbf{A}'$. But this highlights one of the dangers associated with this system. Although we can be fairly confident that an interceptor will not determine our values for w and m, we cannot be sure that he cannot apply some other transformation to $\mathbf{A}$ to produce another easily solvable instance of the knapsack problem. In other words it might be possible to apply a transformation to $\mathbf{A}$ to produce another set $\mathbf{A}''$ which satisfies our extra condition. In fact Herlestam [99] claims that the numerous simulations he has carried out suggest this will occur. He even outlines a scheme which, he claims, might have a 'pretty good chance of success'. If $\mathbf{A} = \{a, a_2, \ldots, a_n\}$ is the public enciphering key, let p be any prime satisfying $p > a_1 + a_2 + \ldots + a_n$ and let j be an integer with $1 \leq j \leq n$. He then suggests we compute w so that $wa_j \equiv 1 \ (\mathrm{mod}\ p)$. (Note that we can do this by using the variation of Euclid's algorithm. Note also that this is a convenient way of obtaining pairs of coprime integers; in this case w and p.) We then let $\mathbf{A}'' = \{a_1'', a_2'', \ldots, a_n''\}$ be the set obtained from $\mathbf{A}$ by the rule $a_i'' \equiv wa_i \ (\mathrm{mod}\ p)$ for $1 \leq i \leq n$, and transform the cryptogram c so that $c'' \equiv wc \ (\mathrm{mod}\ p)$. If, with a suitable reordering, if necessary,

$$a_n'' > a_1'' + a_2'' + \ldots + a_{n-1}'' \quad \text{and} \quad c'' + p > a_1'' + a_2'' + \ldots + a_n''$$

then $(c'', \mathbf{A}'')$ is called a **reduction** of $(c, \mathbf{A})$ and x_n, *the nth bit* of plaintext, is easily determined from $(c'', \mathbf{A}'')$. The reduced knapsack problem

$$c'' - a_n'' x_n = a_1'' x_1 + \ldots + a_{n-1}'' x_{n-1}$$

can then be handled by choosing another prime and using the same technique. If, for each j, a given choice for p does not produce any reduction of $(c, \mathbf{A})$, then we merely choose another initial prime and start again. Herlestam claims that this technique has proved successful in practical experiments on both systems obtained by transforming sets with our special condition and on randomly chosen ones. Of course there is no proof that the above method will always work. However there is a possibility that, at least in the special case of sets which have been obtained by a transformation from one with our special property, the above method, or one similar to it, may be successful.

We end our discussion of this system by observing that there is no reason why we should restrict ourselves to using one transformation when obtaining $\mathbf{A}$ from $\mathbf{A}'$. In a practical system, where n may be of the order of several hundred, it may be advantageous to use several transformations. We also note that, with respect to implementation, the only real problems arise from the size of the integers concerned. But for computer systems this should present no real difficulties and, even within small stand-alone equipments, such a system should be feasible.

10.4   The RSA System

Our next public-key cryptosystem was invented by Rivest, Shamir and Adleman [107] and is named after them. Its security lies in the difficulty of the problem of factoring large integers. Although it is not an **NP**-complete problem it certainly belongs to that subclass of **NP** problems which are not known to be in the class **P**. This, of course, is in complete contrast to the generation of large numbers with, say, few prime factors, which merely involves a few multiplications. For instance consider the relatively small number 27641. To factor this we could start with 2 and then try each prime less than or equal to $\sqrt{27641}$. There are quite a few such primes and we eventually find that $27641 = 131 \times 211$. On the other hand starting with 131 and 211 it is a trivial operation to multiply them and obtain 27641. As the size of the integer to be factored increases, the amount of work to factor it using any known algorithm grows dramatically.

We will now describe the RSA system. To encrypt a message m we use a public encryption key (h, n), where h and n are a pair of positive integers. As with the last system, the message must be split up into blocks, although in this case there is no need for the message to be encoded in binary. All we need is that, regarded as an integer, each block of the message must lie between 0 and $n - 1$. The reason for this is that we are going to perform an encryption function modulo n and, without this restriction on the blocks, our system would be unable to distinguish between messages which were congruent modulo n. Having chosen h and n, the block m_i of the message is encrypted by raising it to the hth power modulo n. Thus, if c_i is the corresponding ciphertext block, $c_i \equiv m_i^h \pmod{n}$. To decipher, we raise it to another power d such that $m_i \equiv c_i^d \pmod{n}$. (It may not be clear that we can find an integer d for deciphering. However a justification will automatically be given when we illustrate a method for finding it.)

Note that in this system each message block and ciphertext block is an integer between 0 and $n-1$. Thus, by choosing n and the encoding scheme sensibly, we can avoid any message extension. One typical coding system which we have already used is simply to put A = 01, B = 02, ..., Y = 25, Z = 26. In practice, other systems may be used. Note also that it is the deciphering key d which is kept secret. As usual with public-key systems, each user will have his own set of keys n, h, d and, for this particular system, only n and h will appear in the directory. Thus each user will publish his own particular values for n and h. In order to obtain an RSA system we must be able to generate pairs of integers h and d with the required properties modulo n. To ensure that we can do this we restrict ourselves to some special values for n.

To generate a pair of keys d and h for this system we first select two large primes, p and q. For the moment we will ignore the problem of how to find such pairs of primes, and assume we have them. We then put $n = pq$. Although n is made public it is important to remember that p and q remain secret. In fact the security of the entire system depends on it being extremely unlikely that anyone will be able to deduce the two primes which are the factors of any particular n appearing in the directory. Having chosen n, we then choose d to be a large random integer satisfying $(d, (p-1)(q-1)) = 1$. It should be clear that there are many suitable choices for d. We could, for instance, merely choose a prime which is greater than $p-1$ and $q-1$. Finally we then compute h so that

$$dh \equiv 1 \pmod{(p-1)(q-1)}.$$

(We point out that the variation of Euclid's algorithm shows how to calculate h.) Now that we have values for d, h and n we must show that they do, in fact, work. To do this we need some very elementary number theory, involving the Euler function $\phi(m)$. We have already met the Euler function in Chapter 5, but we remind the reader that $\phi(m)$ is the number of positive integers which are less than m and coprime to it. Thus, for instance, since every integer less than a prime is coprime to it, for any prime p, $\phi(p) = p-1$. A slight extension of that reasoning will solve the following:

EXERCISE 10.6   If $n = pq$, where p and q are distinct primes, show that $\phi(n) = (p-1)(q-1)$.

Our justification that the chosen values for d, h and n will work depend on the following theorem. Since it is number theoretic we will not include a proof here and the interested reader can consult [101].

THEOREM 10.1 (**Euler's Theorem**)   *If a and m are positive integers with $(a, m) = 1$ then $a^{\phi(m)} \equiv 1 \pmod{m}$.*   □

In our system d was chosen so that it was coprime to $(p-1)(q-1)$ and so, since $\phi(n) = (p-1)(q-1)$, we certainly have $(d, \phi(n)) = 1$. Furthermore, h was chosen so that $hd \equiv 1 \pmod{\phi(n)}$ and this means there exists an integer k such that $hd = 1 + k\phi(n)$. When we enciphered a message m_i the rule was $c_i \equiv m_i^h \pmod{n}$ and then to decipher c_i we raised it to the power d. Thus the deciphered message is c_i^d which is congruent to $m_i^{hd} \pmod{n}$. To show that our system works we must show that c_i is deciphered correctly; i.e. that $c_i^d \equiv m_i \pmod{n}$ or $m_i^{hd} \equiv m_i \pmod{n}$. But $hd = 1 + k\phi(n)$, so $m_i^{hd} = m_i^{1+k\phi(n)}$. From Theorem 10.1, if $p \nmid m_i$ then $m_i^{p-1} \equiv 1 \pmod{p}$ which, since $p-1 \mid \phi(n)$, implies $m_i^{1+k\phi(n)} \equiv m_i \pmod{p}$. If $p \mid m_i$ then $m_i \equiv 0 \pmod{p}$ and so, trivially, $m_i^{1+k\phi(n)} \equiv m_i \pmod{p}$. Thus $m_i^{1+k\phi(n)} \equiv m_i \pmod{p}$ for all m_i. Similarly, $m_i^{1+k\phi(n)} \equiv m_i \pmod{q}$ for all m_i. The following exercise completes the proof of our assertion that, at least in theory, the system works.

EXERCISE 10.7   *Show that if $x \equiv a \pmod{p}$ and $x \equiv a \pmod{q}$, with p and q distinct primes, then $x \equiv a \pmod{pq}$.*

In practice, however, we still need to clarify a few points. For instance, our encryption and decryption procedures look rather difficult and we must make sure we can implement them. In order that p and q may remain secret, n must be rather large, perhaps involving 200 decimal digits. In this case d and h will probably be of the same magnitude and to raise the number representing a message block to a power involving 200 decimal digits appears a horrific task. (Especially since the number itself may be equally large.) This highlights only one of our practical problems. We also need to find two large 'random' primes p and q and to decide how to choose d. We will discuss each of these problems in turn.

There are various algorithms for computing $m^h \pmod{n}$; some of which can be found in [18]. Although it is not the most efficient known, we will illustrate the algorithm often referred to as **exponentiation by repeated squaring and multiplying**. This algorithm has only a few steps and is comparatively simple.

Step 1   Let $h_k h_{k-1} \ldots h_1 h_0$ be the binary representation of h.

Step 2   Set $c = 1$.

Step 3   Set $i = k$.

Step 4   Set c equal to the remainder when c^2 is divided by n.

Step 5   If $h_i = 1$ then set c equal to the remainder when cm is divided by n.

Step 6   Decrease i by 1.

Step 7   If $i < 0$ stop, otherwise go to Step 4.

To illustrate this algorithm we will calculate $(122)^{27}(\bmod\,391)$. The binary representation of $27 = 11011$ so we put $c = 1$ and $i = 4$. This means we first set $c \equiv c^2 \equiv 1(\bmod\,391)$ and then, since $h_4 = 1$, we put

$$c \equiv 122c(\bmod\,391) \equiv 122(\bmod\,391).$$

Taking $i = 3$, we get

$$c \equiv (122)^2(\bmod\,391) \equiv 26(\bmod\,391)$$

and then, since $h_3 = 1$,

$$c \equiv 26 \times 122(\bmod\,391) \equiv 44(\bmod\,391).$$

With $i = 2$,

$$c \equiv (44)^2(\bmod\,391) \equiv 372(\bmod\,391)$$

and, since $h_2 = 0$, it remains at this value. Now, for $i = 1$,

$$c \equiv (372)^2(\bmod\,391) \equiv 361(\bmod\,391)$$

and since $h_1 = 1$ we then get

$$c \equiv 361 \times 122(\bmod\,391) \equiv 250(\bmod\,391).$$

Finally, putting $i = 0$,

$$c \equiv (250)^2(\bmod\,391) \equiv 331(\bmod\,391)$$

and, since $h_0 = 1$,

$$c \equiv 331 \times 122(\bmod\,391) \equiv 109(\bmod\,391).$$

Thus $(122)^{27} \equiv 109(\bmod\,391)$.

There is no doubt that this algorithm is far more efficient than merely multiplying m by itself h times and it is certainly feasible for powers of the order of 200 decimal digits. Anyone wishing to see why it works should follow through the steps in our example and note that we have actually computed

$$(((((1^2 \times 122)^2 \times 122)^2)^2 \times 122)^2 \times 122)(\bmod\,391)$$

which is clearly $(122)^{27}(\bmod\,391)$.

When choosing d we must be sure that it is chosen from a large enough set that a cryptanalyst will not find it by direct search. We require only that $(d, \phi(n)) = 1$, which means that there are

$$\phi(\phi(n)) = \phi((p-1)(q-1))$$

possibilities to choose from. We also need some method for finding such numbers, but this presents no problem. As we have already remarked, any prime greater than p and q will do, provided it is less than $\phi(n)$. Thus if we can find large 'random' prime numbers, we will be able to find d. This will also enable us to find suitable choices for p and q. One way of generating large primes is the following probabilistic algorithm due to Solovay and Strassen [109]. This algorithm relies on the properties of a particular number theoretic function called the Jacobi symbol. We shall make no attempt to show that this algorithm works and any interested reader should consult [101] for details of the Jacobi symbol and the associated Legendre symbol. Before we actually give the algorithm we must stress two crucial points. First this is a probabilistic algorithm, which means that we have absolutely no guarantee that the number which we test for primality is actually a prime, even if it passes all our tests. We can, however, make the probability that it is not a prime extremely small, and, in practice, a probability of 2^{-100} that we are wrong is considered acceptable. The second point is that the algorithm makes no attempt to factor the number being tested. If the algorithm did this it would be unusable, since it would be as expensive as a system built to break our cipher system.

The Jacobi symbol is defined for two integers a and b such that b is odd, $a \leq b$ and $(a, b) = 1$. It is denoted by $\mathbf{J}(a, b)$ and always has a value of $+1$ or -1. It can be evaluated by using the following algorithm. If $a = 1$, then $\mathbf{J}(a, b) = 1$. If a is even then

$$\mathbf{J}(a, b) = \mathbf{J}(\tfrac{1}{2}a, b) \times (-1)^{(b^2-1)/8},$$

otherwise

$$\mathbf{J}(a, b) = \mathbf{J}(b(\bmod a), a) \times (-1)^{(a-1)(b-1)/4}.$$

As an example we will compute $\mathbf{J}(6, 13)$. Since 6 is even,

$$\mathbf{J}(6, 13) = (-1)^{(13^2-1)/8}\mathbf{J}(3, 13) = (-1)^{21}\mathbf{J}(3, 13) = -\mathbf{J}(3, 13).$$

But

$$-\mathbf{J}(3, 13) = -\mathbf{J}(13(\bmod 3), 3) \times (-1)^{(3-1)(13-1)/4} = -\mathbf{J}(1, 3) \times (-1)^6$$
$$= -\mathbf{J}(1, 3) = -1.$$

Suppose now that we wish to decide whether or not a large number b is a prime. We pick an integer a at random from $(1, 2, \ldots, b-1)$ and test whether

$$(a, b) = 1 \text{ and } \mathbf{J}(a, b) \equiv a^{(b-1)/2} \pmod{b}.$$

If b is a prime then both these equalities will hold for every choice of a. If, on the other hand, b is not a prime then they will fail for at least half the choices of a, i.e. the probability of their not holding for a given a is more than $\frac{1}{2}$. So, if we were to choose randomly 100 different values of a, and if the equalities held for each of them, then the probability that b is a prime would be about $1-2^{-100}$. In these circumstances, we would then assume that b is prime. Rivest *et al.* claim that, using the above algorithm, a high speed computer can test a 100-digit number for primality in a few seconds, and needs only a couple of minutes to find the first prime after any designated number of this order.

We are now in a position where we can encipher a message using the RSA system. For our example, we will take $p=61$ and $q=53$, which gives $n=3233$, and

$$\phi(n)=60\times52=3120.$$

We must now choose a value for d so that $(d, 3120)=1$. We will take $d=37$.

EXERCISE 10.8   Show that $h=253$.

Given these values of d, h and n we will now encipher the message **cipher**. Assigning integers to letters by our rule $A=01$, $B=02$, etc., we get $C=03$, $I=09$, $P=16$, $H=08$, $E=05$ and $R=18$. The enciphering key, which can be obtained from the public directory, is $(253, 3233)$ and we need each message block to give an integer less than 3233. Given this restriction, it seems natural to take our message blocks as two characters each. Thus they become $m_1=309$, $m_2=1608$ and $m_3=518$.

The binary representation of 253 is 11111101 and use of our earlier algorithm gives

$$(309)^{253}\equiv1971(\mathrm{mod}\ 3233)$$

and this will be our first cryptogram block.

EXERCISE 10.9
   (i)   *Encipher m_2 and m_3.*
   (ii)   *Using the secret key $d=37$, show that the message deciphers correctly.*

In order to get a true picture of the RSA system we must now consider how the cryptanalyst might attack it. The most obvious way, of course, is to factor n. If the cryptanalyst knows p and q he can calculate d from h in exactly the same way that we obtained h from d. As we have stressed many times, there is no known polynomial time algorithm for factoring integers, and the security of the system is closely related to the difficulty of this problem. To justify our confidence in the inability of the cryptanalyst to factor n we list the time required to factor integers of various sizes. The assumption made in obtaining Table 10.1 is that the method used is that of R. Schroeppel [unpublished], and that each operation takes one micro-second. By allowing a safety margin for improving algorithms and faster

No. of decimal digits in n	No. of operations to factor	Time needed
50	$1 \cdot 4 \times 10^{10}$	3·9 hours
75	$9 \cdot 0 \times 10^{12}$	104 days
100	$2 \cdot 3 \times 10^{15}$	74 years
200	$1 \cdot 2 \times 10^{23}$	$3 \cdot 8 \times 10^9$ years
300	$1 \cdot 5 \times 10^{29}$	$4 \cdot 0 \times 10^{15}$ years
500	$1 \cdot 3 \times 10^{39}$	$4 \cdot 2 \times 10^{25}$ years

Table 10.1
The time needed for factoring integers

computers, the cryptographer can choose the integer n to correspond to any security level required. However, it must not be forgotten that any increase in n produces an increase in the complexity of implementation, which concerns not only the hardware, but also the time for encryption/decryption. Thus we should not choose n any larger than we feel necessary.

Another possible method of attack for the cryptanalyst is to try to determine $\phi(n)$. Clearly, this would then enable him to compute d from h and thus break the system. However, as the next exercise shows, the determining of $\phi(n)$ implies the factorization of n and is no easier than actually factoring n.

EXERCISE 10.10   If $n = pq$ then, from Exercise 10.6 (page 381),

$$\phi(n) = (p-1)(q-1) = n - (p+q) + 1.$$

Use this observation to show that if both n and $\phi(n)$ are known then p and q can be determined.

Similarly it can be shown that computing d is no easier than factoring n. Thus we see that a number of the more obvious methods of attacking this system are not any easier than factoring n which, of course, is encouraging for the cryptographer. However, it may be that there is a method of deducing the message from the cryptogram without first deducing the secret deciphering key. Such a method would almost certainly not involve factoring n.

In [99], [108] and [110] further discussion takes place regarding the security of the RSA system and the first of these papers actually suggests a possible cryptanalysis algorithm. We do not give the details here nor do we attempt to discuss how successful the algorithm might be in practice, although we note that this method attempts to decipher messages without determining the deciphering key.

It should be clear from our brief description and discussion that further research is needed before the RSA system can be considered absolutely secure. It exhibits many of the characteristics of block ciphers and, as a consequence, may need adapting for use in certain communication systems. Nevertheless it still appears very promising.

Finally, to complete our consideration of the practical implementation of such a system, we must pay some attention to the time necessary for some kind of processor to perform the main encipherment/decipherment operations (i.e. the exponentiation). Davies *et al.* [96] assert that the effort necessary to compute a number of the form a^b, (where a and b are of roughly the same size), is about $3zw^2$ multiplications, where z is the number of bits in the binary representation of a or b and w is the number of computer words necessary to contain one of them. For instance with $z = 100$ and an 8-bit processor, (8, 16 or even 32 bits per word are common for a microprocessor), then $w = 13$ and the number of multiplications is about $300 \times 169 = 50700$. If the time for one multiplication is about five microseconds then the computation required for two 100-bit numbers is about 250 mS.

EXERCISE 10.11
   (i)   *Estimate the time required if a and b are*
         (a)   *200-bit numbers, and*
         (b)   *200 decimal digit numbers*
         with an 8-bit processor needing five microseconds for one multiplication.
   (ii) *Repeat the calculation for a 36-bit word machine which performs a multiplication in about one microsecond.*

At the time of writing the machine in Exercise 10.11 (i) corresponds to a typical microprocessor, while that in (ii) might represent a mainframe computer. Since in the latter case only a few mS are required for the calculation, the system does appear feasible. On the other hand, the microprocessor requires a few seconds to process each block, which may make it impracticable.

10.5   Another System

This third system, which was suggested by Lu and Lee [102], also relies on the difficulty of factoring large numbers. However, its implementation is far easier than the RSA system. Once again we need a number n which is the product of two distinct primes p and q. As usual for any realistic system both p and q will be large but, to illustrate the system, we will consider an example with small values. Having chosen p and q, we next choose four integers a_{11}, a_{12}, a_{21} and a_{22} such that $a_{11}a_{22} - a_{12}a_{21} \neq 0$. Since p and q are both primes, $(p, q) = 1$ and so, using Euclid's algorithm, we can find integers b_1 and b_2, such that $b_1p + b_2q = 1$. Once we have determined b_1 and b_2 we compute c_1, c_2 such that

$$c_1 \equiv ((a_{21} - a_{11})b_1p + a_{11})(\bmod n)$$

and

$$c_2 \equiv ((a_{22} - a_{12})b_1p + a_{12})(\bmod n).$$

The following exercise gives some important properties of c_1 and c_2.

EXERCISE 10.12   Show that $a_{11} \equiv c_1 (\text{mod } p)$, $a_{12} \equiv c_2 (\text{mod } p)$ $a_{21} \equiv c_1$ $(\text{mod } q)$ and $a_{22} \equiv c_2 (\text{mod } q)$.

In the system we are going to describe the public encryption key will be (c_1, c_2, n), plus two integers s_1 and s_2 which satisfy:

$$s_1 \leq \left[\tfrac{1}{2} \min \left\{ \frac{r}{a_{11}}, \frac{r}{a_{21}} \right\} \right] \quad \text{and} \quad s_2 \leq \left[\tfrac{1}{2} \min \left\{ \frac{r}{a_{12}}, \frac{r}{a_{22}} \right\} \right],$$

where r is the smaller of p and q and, as usual, $[t]$ denotes 'the greatest integer less than or equal to t'. The secret deciphering key will be $(a_{11}, a_{12}, a_{21}, a_{22}, p, q)$. If a message m is to be encrypted then it is divided into two parts so that it is represented by a pair of numbers (m_1, m_2) satisfying $0 < m_1 < s_1$ and $0 < m_2 < s_2$. The cryptogram c is then given by

$$c \equiv c_1 m_1 + c_2 m_2 (\text{mod } n).$$

In order to obtain a deciphering rule we first put $c' \equiv c (\text{mod } p)$ and $c'' \equiv c (\text{mod } q)$. Since $c \equiv c_1 m_1 + c_2 m_2 (\text{mod } n)$ and $n = pq$, it is clear that $c' \equiv c_1 m_1 + c_2 m_2 (\text{mod } p)$. But $a_{11} \equiv c_1 (\text{mod } p)$, and $a_{12} \equiv c_2 (\text{mod } p)$ which gives $c' \equiv a_{11} m_1 + a_{12} m_2 (\text{mod } p)$. If we now look at the restrictions on our choice of s_1 and s_2, we see that $a_{11} s_1 + a_{12} s_2 < r$ which, since $r \leq p$, implies $a_{11} s_1 + a_{12} s_2 < p$. Finally, we note that $m_1 < s_1$ and $m_2 < s_2$ so that $a_{11} m_1 + a_{12} m_2 < p$; i.e. $c' = a_{11} m_1 + a_{12} m_2$. Similarly, $c'' = a_{21} m_1 + a_{22} m_2$. Solving these last two equations gives the following decryption rule:

$$m_1 = \frac{c' a_{22} - c'' a_{12}}{a_{11} a_{22} - a_{12} a_{21}} \quad \text{and} \quad m_2 = \frac{c'' a_{11} - c' a_{21}}{a_{11} a_{22} - a_{12} a_{21}}.$$

In order to consider a small example we will take $p = 89$ and $q = 97$. Thus $n = 8633$. We will let $a_{11} = 2$, $a_{12} = 3$, $a_{21} = 3$ and $a_{22} = 4$, which gives $a_{11} a_{22} - a_{12} a_{21} = -1 \neq 0$. Using Euclid's algorithm we find that

$$1 = 12 \times 89 - 11 \times 97.$$

Thus

$$c_1 \equiv 1 \times 12 \times 89 + 2 (\text{mod } 8633) \equiv 1070 (\text{mod } 8633)$$

and

$$c_2 \equiv 1 \times 12 \times 89 + 3 (\text{mod } 8633) \equiv 1071 (\text{mod } 8633).$$

Also the restrictions on s_1 and s_2 are given by

$$0 < s_1 \leq \left[\frac{1}{2} \min \left\{ \frac{89}{2}, \frac{89}{3} \right\} \right] \quad \text{and} \quad 0 < s_2 \leq \left[\frac{1}{2} \min \left\{ \frac{89}{3}, \frac{89}{4} \right\} \right].$$

Thus

$$0 < s_1 \leq \left[\frac{89}{6} \right] = 14 \quad \text{and} \quad 0 < s_2 \leq \left[\frac{89}{8} \right] = 11.$$

Now suppose that, after using some code to convert alphanumeric characters into the appropriate form, the first two blocks of our message have $m_1 = 8$ and $m_2 = 5$. Then

$$c \equiv 1070{\times}8 + 1071{\times}5 \equiv 13915 \equiv 5282 (\mathrm{mod}\ 8633),$$

i.e. the cryptogram is 5282.

EXERCISE 10.13   Check that the deciphering rule works.

At first sight this system is very similar to the RSA system. Certainly both are based on a composite number which is the product of two large unknown primes p and q. For the RSA system the security appears to lie in the fact that it is very difficult to determine p and q from a knowledge of n. As we saw, we do not know how to attack the system without first determining p and q. The same is not true of the Lu-Lee system. Despite the obvious similarities, three recent papers [92, 100, 98] have demonstrated considerable weaknesses in this system which do not appear to be shared by the RSA system. We will, in a moment, give a very brief summary of these papers. For the moment, however, we will discuss the lesson to be learned from this example which, incidentally, is our main reason for including it. The point to be stressed is the fact that basing a cipher system on a difficult problem is no guarantee that the particular problem must be solved before the system can be broken. Both the RSA and Lu-Lee systems appear to rely on the difficulty of factoring large numbers. As far as we know the RSA is relatively secure. However, the Lu-Lee system is comparatively insecure because, as we shall see, successful attacks have been found which do not require the factoring of n. In other words, attacks have been found which avoid solving the difficult problem on which the system is based. Of course there is no guarantee that similar successful attacks will not be found for the RSA system. But if they are this will merely strengthen our point, not weaken it. We must also stress that we can never be completely confident that the breaking of a given system will require the solution of a particular problem. There may be some ingenious way of replacing the particular problem by others which can be solved. This is one of the obvious hazards facing the adoption of any public system and helps to explain why any proposed system must be fully exposed and discussed before it can be adopted.

  We will now give a very brief indication of how the Lu-Lee system may be attacked without factoring n. Our explanations are in no way complete and the interested reader should consult the three papers referred to earlier. In the first two papers an attack is devised using only the fact that the cryptogram c, to be deciphered, has a unique corresponding pair of integers m_1, m_2 satisfying $c \equiv c_1 m_1 + c_2 m_2$ (mod n) with $0 < m_1 < s_1$ and $0 < m_2 < s_2$. (Of course the public part of the key, i.e. (c_1, c_2, n, s_1, s_2), is assumed to be known.) In the third paper a method is given of finding p and q without actually factoring n. It relies on the observations that, for $j = 1$ or 2, $c_j - a_{1j} \equiv 0$ (mod p) and $c_j - a_{2j} \equiv 0$ (mod q) which imply $(c_j - a_{1j}, n) = p$ and $(c_j - a_{2j}, n) = q$. But since s_1 and s_2 need to be reasonably large it is normally desirable to pick the a_{ij} to be quite small. Thus, in principle, we could simply try all possibilities for the a_{ij}, and use Euclid's algorithm to compute $(c_j - a_{ij}, n)$ for $i = 1$ and 2. Since $n = pq$, as soon as $(c_i - a_{ij}, n)$ has a value other than 1 we know it must be p or q. In fact in [98] it is shown there are simpler, more systematic, ways for determining the a_{ij} and consequently of finding p and q.

10.6   Authentication

With the standard systems discussed in the earlier chapters, one of the main problems was that of distributing keys in such a way that no unauthorized person had the opportunity to see them. With public key systems the situation is totally different. For these, a directory of enciphering keys is published and readily available. But this poses an extra problem. It is now necessary to ensure that no one can tamper with the directory and change one of the keys. (Since the keys are likely to be large, an electronic directory may be more convenient than, for example, a book.) If this precaution is not taken, an unauthorized person might substitute an enciphering key of his own for that of someone whose messages he wants to read. Once he has done this all messages intended for that source will be intelligible to the unauthorized person but not to the intended recipient. Thus some caution must be exercised in the compilation and distribution of the public directories.

There is another fundamental difference between the classical systems and public systems. With a classical system, unless the system has been compromised, any intelligible received message may be assumed to have originated from a sender who is privy to the key. But with a public-key system the reception of an intelligible message gives no information about its source. Consequently, it is crucial that some form of message authentication is included in the system. It must at least contain a signature system which allows the recipient of a message to identify the sender. It might even be advantageous to organize the signature so that even the correct recipient cannot forge it; a facility not generally present in the classical cipher systems.

One method for full authentication is the full handshake described for single key systems in Chapter 8. The reader should look back at the description in Chapter 8 (page 320) and modify it to apply to a public key system. The advantage of the full handshake is that it works for any public key system. Some of the neater methods which we will consider shortly are only valid for certain types of public key systems. Before we look at some of these other methods we must consider the fact that, even if the start of a message is authenticated, an active interceptor could tamper with later parts of the message. Unless they are linked in some way he could, for instance, delete and/or insert message blocks. One way to prevent this, which also has the added advantage of inhibiting a known plaintext attack, might be to include a portion of random data in the first message block and then take consecutive functions of this data in subsequent blocks. For instance, if a random number r is included in the first block then, for some relatively simple function g, $g(r)$ might be included in the second block, $g^2(r)$ in the third and so on. Note that, because anyone can encipher messages for a particular recipient, the block chaining method discussed in Section 7.4 should not be used.

10.6.1 Signatures

We now turn our attention to signatures. Ideally the aims of a signature are that the receiver should not be able to forge a received message and that the sender should not be able to deny transmitting one. One main advantage of a signature system is that it enables a third party to resolve certain disputes between receiver and sender. We begin by giving an example of a signature system which is only valid when the message and cryptogram spaces coincide. In this system, in order to sign (i.e. to authenticate) a message the sender transforms a message m by operating on it using his secret deciphering key d. Thus the sender puts $c = h_d(m)$. This is then transmitted and the receiver applies the public enciphering key e of the anticipated sender to obtain $g_e(c) = g_e(h_d(m)) = m$. (Note that if the cryptogram and message spaces did not coincide we could not be sure that these two operations were possible.) Since m is a meaningful message, perhaps even with a check sum or similar feature built in, the sender is uniquely defined. No-one else could have been in possession of the secret key d, so no-one could have generated c. Thus the message has been signed and the sender may now proceed to transmit any information he wishes. Notice, however, that the initial message m was not enciphered for transmission. Thus this signature system provides only one-way authentication, not encipherment. Anyone who intercepts the message and knows the identity of the sender will, by consulting the directory, be able to comprehend the message. However the message has been identifiably signed by the sender, since only he knows his secret deciphering key, and so only he could have used h_d to transform the message. This type of system might be used if, for instance, the receiver needed a decision from the sender as to whether or not to proceed with a business deal. He would be able to prove that he had followed the sender's instructions correctly, providing the entire message is signed.

EXERCISE 10.14   Show that the above signature system can be applied to the RSA public-key cryptosystem.

EXERCISE 10.15   Sign, independently, each of the blocks m_1, m_2, m_3 of Exercise 10.9 employing the RSA system with public key $(253, 3233)$ and secret key 37.

EXERCISE 10.16   Show that the above signature system cannot be applied directly to the knapsack public-key cryptosystem.

In theory this system can easily be extended to include encipherment as well as signature. The sender first applies his own deciphering key to the message and then enciphers using the receiver's public enciphering key. The receiver first deciphers using his own secret key and then applies the anticipated sender's enciphering key. Of course this only makes sense if the message and cryptogram spaces of both the communicants coincide. So, for instance, this latter system as it stands may not work for the RSA system. The reason is simple. For any individual user the message and cryptogram spaces are the integers modulo n. But two different users may have different values for n and, consequently, have distinct message spaces. If there are two users X and Y with respective integers n_X and n_Y, and if $n_X > n_Y$ then messages from X to Y may need 'reblocking' (i.e. dividing into shorter blocks) between signing and enciphering. This problem could be overcome by choosing a threshhold value, r say, for the entire RSA system and then equipping each user with two public key pairs (h_1, n_1) and (h_2, n_2). By always having $n_1 < r < n_2$, using (h_1, n_1) only for signature and (h_2, n_2) only for encipherment, the reblocking would be unnecessary. This is simply because any user's message space for encipherment will always be larger than that for signature. A likely value for r is of the order of 10^{199}.

One other possibility is to separate completely the encipherment and authentication procedures. We could, for instance, use the following method which relies on a function f such that, for any message x in its domain, $f(x)$ can be computed relatively easily. The particular domain of f will be clear from the following discussion. If we have a message m made up of message blocks $m_1, m_2, \ldots$, we put $x_1 = f(m_1)$ and let $x_i = f(m_i + x_{i-1})$ for every i with $2 \leq i \leq n$. However the $+$ sign here indicates addition of entries in corresponding positions (i.e. addition without carries) and not addition as binary numbers. Now to sign a message m the sender not only sends the enciphered m but also $s = h_d(x_n)$. To check the signature s the receiver can compute $x_n = g_e(s)$ and any receiver who deciphers m correctly can use his m in clear to compute what x_n should be. If the two values for x_n agree the message is authenticated. The multiple use of the function f is to prevent an unauthorized person making changes to the message which do not affect x_n. If f is sufficiently complex he will find this very difficult.

In this way all message blocks can be authenticated simultaneously and whether or not the message is separately enciphered is no longer relevant. In fact it has been suggested that the RSA system should be used in conjunction with DES. The idea is that DES provides the message encryption, whilst the RSA system is employed to provide authentication as well as key exchange. (Note also that, if necessary, this signature method can be used to provide two-way authentication.)

In this chapter we have considered the relatively new idea of public-key cryptosystems. We have presented two of the best known public-key cryptosystems, namely the knapsack based system and the RSA system. We have also demonstrated a third system that has been proven to be insecure. The two former systems have also been criticized, but, as yet, none of the suggested attacks against them has been demonstrably successful. Of the two, the RSA system appears to be withstanding attacks rather better than any of the other proposed systems. (Details of other suggested public-key systems can be found in [93] and 103].)

Public-key cryptosystems have two important advantages over the classical systems, notably easier key distribution and, in some cases, a simple method of signature authenticity. However it should now be clear that, even within a public-key network, key distribution must be handled very carefully, and that some form of authentication is almost always essential. We must also point out that, at the present time, implementation of the most promising public-key cryptosystems appears to cause problems to anything other than mainframe computers or large mini-computers.

Whether or not these particular public-key systems will stand the test of time we cannot say. They do appear very promising, but this has been true of many proposed systems throughout history. Very few systems have, in practice, stood this most difficult of tests.

Further Reading

Public-key cryptosystems are introduced in [93], [102], [103], [104] and [107]. We recommend [101] as a suitable introduction to Number Theory. [18] and [109] provide algorithms that are needed for this chapter. The remaining references are discussions on the security and usages offered by the various systems that have been proposed.

[92]   Adleman, L. M. and Rivest, R. L., 'How to break the Lu-Lee public-key cryptosystem', *MIT Lab. for Comp. Sci.*, 1979.

[93]   Arazi, B., 'A trapdoor multiple mapping', *IEEE Trans. Inform. Theory*, Vol. IT-26, No. 1, 1980, 100–102.

[94]   Blakley, B. and Blakley, G. R., 'Security of number theoretic public-key cryptosystems against random attack, I, II and III', *Cryptologia*, 1978, 305–321; 1979, 29–42 and 105–118.

[95]   Davies, D. W. and Price, W. L., 'The application of digital signatures based on public-key cryptosystems', *NPL Report DNACS 39/80*, 1980.

[96]   Davies, D. W., Price, W. L. and Parkin, G. I., 'An evaluation of public-key cryptosystems', *NPL Report CTU 1*, 1980.

[97]   Diffie, W. and Hellman, M. E., 'New directions in cryptography', *IEEE Trans. Inform. Theory*, Vol. IT-22, No. 6, 1976, 644–54.

[98]   Goethals, J. M. and Couvreur, C., 'A cryptanalytic attack on the Lu-Lee public-key cryptosystem', *Phillips J. Res.*, 35, 1980, 301–306.

394   CIPHER SYSTEMS

[99]   Herlestam, T., 'Critical remarks on some public-key crypto-
         systems', *BIT 18*, 1978, 493–6.
[100]   Kochanski, M. J., 'Remarks on Lu and Lee's proposals for a
         public-key cryptosystem', *Cryptologia*, Vol. 4, No.   1980,
         204–207.
[18]   Knuth, D. E., *The Art of Computer Programming, Volume 2:
         Seminumerical Algorithms*, Addison-Wesley, 1973.
[101]   LeVeque, W. J., *Fundamentals of Number Theory*, Addison-
         Wesley, 1977.
[102]   Lu, S. C. and Lee, L. N., 'A simple and effective public-key
         cryptosystem', *Comsat. Tech. Rev.*, Vol. 9, 1979, 15–24.
[103]   McEliece, R. J., 'A public-key cryptosystem based on Algebraic
         Coding Theory', *DSN Report*, 1978, 42–4.
[104]   Merkle, R. C. and Hellman, M. E., 'Hiding information and
         signatures in trapdoor knapsacks', *IEEE Trans. on Inform.
         Theory*, Vol. IT-24, No. 5, 1978, 525–30.
[105]   Rivest, R. L., 'Remarks on a proposed cryptanalytic attack on the
         MIT public-key cryptosystem', *Cryptologia*, Vol. 2, No. 1, 1978,
         62–5.
[106]   Rivest, R. L., 'Critical remarks on "Critical remarks on some
         public-key cryptosystems" by T. Herlestam', *BIT 19*, 1979,
         274–5.
[107]   Rivest, R. L., Shamir, A. and Adleman, L., 'A method for
         obtaining signatures and public-key cryptosystems', *Comms. of
         ACM*, Vol. 21, No. 2, 1978, 120–26.
[108]   Simmons, G. J. and Norris, M. J., 'Preliminary comments on the
         MIT public-key cryptosystem', *Cryptologia*, Vol. 1, No. 4, 1977,
         406–414.
[109]   Solovay, R. and Strassen, V., 'A fast Monte-Carlo test for
         primality', *SIAM J. Computing*, Vol. 6, 1977, 84–5.
[110]   Smith, D. R. and Palmer, J. T., 'Universal fixed messages and the
         Rivest-Shamir-Adleman Cryptosystem', *Mathematika*, 26,
         1979, 44–52.
[111]   Williams, H. C. and Schmid, B., 'Some remarks concerning the
         MIT public-key cryptosystem', *BIT 19*, 1979, 525–38.

Appendix 1

In this appendix we include some statistics of the English language. To obtain them we took passages from various newspapers and novels. The total sample contained 132,597 characters of which 100,362 were alphabetic and 23,922 were 'space'.

Table S1 is concerned with the frequency of single characters and contains three columns. The first contains the relative frequencies of all characters, the second those of the alphabetic characters and space while the third is concerned with alphabetic characters only. Each value listed gives the number of appearances of the appropriate character as a percentage of the total number of characters. The values for the letter probabilities which we used in Chapter 1 are found in the third column. At the foot of each column we give the corresponding value for I_c.

In Tables S2a and S2b we give the bigram frequencies for alphabetic characters plus space and alphabetic characters only respectively (as if, for instance, we wrote our text as a continuous stream of alphabetic letters). To read these tables our first character of the bigram is in the left hand column. Thus, for example, in Table S2a the number corresponding to AC is 381 while that for CA is 394. Similarly from Table S2b the number of occurrences of E followed by a space is 4621. (Note that we can use Table S2b to get the most frequent first and last letters of words by considering the last row and column respectively. So, for instance, T is the most common initial letter of a word.)

Finally we include in Table S3 and S4 lists of the 50 most frequent bigrams and trigrams (in each case for alphabetic characters only). The figures quoted for the bigrams are merely taken from Table S2a.

Character	Relative Frequencies of all Characters	Relative Frequencies of Alphabetic Characters and Space	Relative Frequencies of Alphabetic Characters only
TAB	0·002		
LINE FEED	1·604		
CARRIAGE RETURN	1·600		
SPACE	18·041	19·248	
!	0·008		
·	0·312		
£	0·004		
$	0·005		
&	0·001		
'	0·302		
(	0·007		
)	0·007		
,	0·914		
-	0·208		
.	0·956		
0	0·044		
1	0·053		
2	0·017		
3	0·016		
4	0·017		
5	0·020		
6	0·014		
7	0·013		
8	0·009		
9	0·015		
:	0·023		
;	0·041		

Table S1

Character	Relative Frequencies of all Characters	Relative Frequencies of Alphabetic Characters and Space	Relative Frequencies of Alphabetic Characters only
?	0·058		
A	6·182	6·595	8·167
B	1·129	1·205	1·492
C	2·106	2·246	2·782
D	3·219	3·434	4·253
E	9·614	10·257	12·702
F	1·686	1·799	2·228
G	1·525	1·627	2·015
H	4·612	4·921	6·094
I	5·272	5·625	6·966
J	0·116	0·124	0·153
K	0·584	0·624	0·772
L	3·047	3·251	4·025
M	1·821	1·943	2·406
N	5·108	5·450	6·749
O	5·682	6·062	7·507
P	1·460	1·558	1·929
Q	0·072	0·076	0·095
R	4·532	4·835	5·987
S	4·789	5·109	6·327
T	6·855	7·313	9·056
U	2·088	2·227	2·758
V	0·741	0·790	0·978
W	1·787	1·906	2·360
X	0·114	0·122	0·150
Y	1·494	1·594	1·974
Z	0·056	0·060	0·074
I_c	0·07078	0·07976	0·06550

Table S1 (*cont.*)

Total number of bigrams (excludes all non alpha chars): 100361

	A	B	C	D	E	F	G	H	I	J	K	L	M	N	O	P	Q	R	S	T	U	V	W	X	Y	Z
A	16	186	381	462	25	117	197	43	425	8	110	684	247	1419	12	239	3	827	942	1117	101	204	119	11	278	24
B	132	3	1	1	531	1	0	0	51	7	0	145	1	1	158	1	0	103	30	15	191	4	0	0	121	0
C	394	3	59	4	491	9	2	404	175	2	139	120	2	1	561	63	3	80	27	231	69	1	5	0	9	1
D	432	213	75	99	543	112	53	217	471	13	8	108	84	107	367	63	5	141	276	517	101	32	165	0	66	0
E	993	195	584	1305	471	299	151	346	404	35	54	566	451	1141	339	348	23	1860	1170	851	74	207	474	115	285	7
F	201	16	33	13	269	140	14	61	220	3	3	117	31	6	389	30	1	179	44	302	88	4	48	0	24	0
G	219	23	24	18	304	54	28	279	162	6	0	76	37	69	186	19	2	110	83	186	80	3	42	0	11	1
H	1070	22	27	9	3004	19	10	55	741	4	0	16	36	27	505	26	2	88	46	242	88	4	44	0	31	0
I	169	54	436	333	237	206	194	36	6	2	73	413	238	1872	350	70	5	328	858	842	4	173	57	18	2	15
J	7	0	0	0	21	0	0	0	0	0	0	0	0	0	74	0	0	0	0	0	52	0	0	0	0	0
K	43	10	6	3	270	9	7	14	152	2	0	28	8	57	38	6	0	2	47	45	3	0	17	0	0	0
L	415	44	32	312	644	67	20	34	594	7	24	489	39	15	397	39	1	20	143	187	55	34	39	0	389	0
M	469	86	16	9	634	11	3	25	235	5	0	8	66	9	306	128	0	50	80	83	84	3	26	0	79	0
N	436	89	324	1040	594	113	968	121	362	16	53	98	70	90	470	52	9	40	392	1105	44	37	124	4	119	3
O	104	118	141	167	46	694	81	93	110	9	132	293	496	1182	325	203	4	902	334	473	1037	168	392	3	23	4
P	282	7	3	0	402	4	1	96	114	2	1	179	8	1	261	146	0	198	61	84	63	0	11	0	11	0
Q	0	0	0	0	0	0	0	0	0	0	0	0	0	0	0	0	0	0	0	0	95	0	0	0	0	0
R	569	73	135	229	1353	89	53	118	563	8	92	74	204	150	601	69	5	167	487	483	85	54	112	0	232	4
S	662	140	184	81	767	115	40	615	507	10	47	106	145	86	451	213	24	55	406	1147	223	26	245	0	55	0
T	628	94	124	51	805	76	25	3015	891	6	21	142	110	35	1111	68	5	322	360	513	206	14	267	0	195	4
U	83	52	102	61	92	19	146	16	102	0	6	312	68	384	8	120	1	479	313	383	0	2	17	0	1	1
V	84	0	1	0	676	0	0	0	171	0	0	0	0	0	43	1	0	0	1	1	0	0	0	0	2	0
W	565	7	4	19	376	8	3	438	374	0	2	13	0	92	278	11	0	21	56	45	6	2	16	0	17	1
X	10	0	15	0	7	2	0	6	15	0	0	0	4	0	3	34	0	1	1	43	1	0	7	0	0	0
Y	199	62	85	51	170	72	26	83	132	9	9	50	55	29	291	50	2	36	193	194	14	7	141	0	20	1
Z	15	0	0	1	16	0	0	0	14	0	0	3	0	0	8	0	0	0	0	0	4	2	0	0	3	8

Table S2a

Total number of bigrams (includes space): 124283

	A	B	C	D	E	F	G	H	I	J	K	L	M	N	O	P	Q	R	S	T	U	V	W	X	Y	Z	SP
A	0	138	312	432	23	77	168	15	418	3	105	635	200	1400	3	184	0	798	856	1062	100	195	75	11	274	22	691
B	129	3	1	1	531	1	0	0	49	7	0	145	1	1	157	0	0	103	27	11	191	4	0	0	121	1	14
C	389	0	55	0	490	0	1	403	170	0	139	118	0	0	560	0	3	77	17	226	69	0	0	0	9	0	65
D	159	5	1	59	504	9	23	2	281	0	0	35	5	24	222	155	1	95	120	3	60	20	7	0	40	0	2593
E	557	15	299	1135	360	101	45	32	142	2	17	440	251	1059	64	155	12	1715	764	310	35	166	102	115	228	6	4621
F	126	0	0	1	255	125	0	0	190	0	0	102	2	0	375	0	0	161	0	88	82	0	1	0	4	0	726
G	119	3	8	1	284	0	23	239	99	0	0	62	57	57	130	2	0	104	42	12	72	0	0	5	5	1	757
H	985	5	1	4	2998	0	1	0	702	0	0	1	3	19	464	4	0	83	15	143	83	1	1	0	18	0	581
I	142	51	409	318	236	198	189	0	0	0	62	405	232	1868	348	69	5	313	817	825	3	172	0	18	1	15	295
J	7	0	0	0	21	0	0	0	0	0	0	0	0	0	74	0	0	0	0	0	52	0	0	0	0	0	0
K	3	0	1	0	268	2	3	0	124	0	0	24	0	56	8	1	0	0	36	1	1	0	1	0	6	0	240
L	362	4	3	301	633	44	5	1	545	0	22	479	21	1	367	14	0	7	91	109	51	29	8	0	385	0	558
M	426	73	2	0	631	4	1	0	217	0	0	4	56	4	283	118	0	43	52	4	82	0	0	0	78	0	337
N	163	7	246	1007	536	35	943	5	250	13	46	68	15	73	348	6	7	2	259	694	30	31	6	4	93	3	1884
O	40	47	93	127	17	662	53	19	78	3	118	263	437	1168	301	178	2	870	244	334	1029	164	339	3	14	4	927
P	264	1	0	0	401	0	0	88	102	0	0	177	6	1	252	143	0	195	53	62	62	0	1	0	9	0	119
Q	0	0	0	0	0	0	0	0	0	0	0	0	0	0	0	0	0	0	0	0	95	0	0	0	0	0	0
R	411	14	60	194	1316	27	40	21	481	2	86	41	116	132	503	16	0	137	366	258	75	45	12	0	218	3	1435
S	302	37	98	12	710	15	4	486	329	0	42	53	61	17	258	146	18	3	242	795	201	0	42	0	33	0	2446
T	377	3	59	0	767	9	4	2844	693	0	1	94	19	2	951	0	0	284	209	165	189	1	67	0	162	0	2186
U	58	42	89	54	91	17	143	6	98	0	0	305	64	381	5	119	0	477	303	375	0	0	0	0	0	1	144
V	84	0	0	0	676	0	0	0	171	0	0	0	0	0	43	0	0	0	1	4	4	0	0	0	2	0	4
W	541	1	0	10	374	1	1	418	355	0	1	9	0	87	271	0	0	21	37	40	4	0	0	6	2	0	228
X	7	0	15	0	7	1	0	6	14	0	1	0	2	0	3	34	0	0	82	40	4	0	0	0	6	0	21
Y	10	6	4	3	139	8	4	0	30	1	1	9	13	5	225	11	0	3	82	15	4	0	4	0	0	0	1408
Z	14	0	0	0	16	0	0	0	14	0	0	3	0	0	8	0	0	0	0	0	4	0	0	0	0	0	5
SP	2522	1036	609	464	896	371	0	1536	1439	123	134	568	911	418	1311	736	47	518	1717	3553	197	152	1702	0	274	8	1637

Table S2b

TH	3015	EN	1141	OR	902	AL	684	EC	584
HE	3004	AT	1117	TI	891	VE	676	RA	569
IN	1872	TO	1111	IS	858	SA	662	EL	566
ER	1860	NT	1105	ET	851	LE	644	WA	565
AN	1419	HA	1070	IT	842	ME	634	RI	563
RE	1353	ND	1040	AR	827	TA	628	CO	561
ED	1305	OU	1037	TE	805	SH	615	DE	543
ON	1182	EA	993	SE	767	RO	601	BE	531
ES	1170	NG	968	HI	741	NE	594	DT	517
ST	1147	AS	942	OF	694	LI	594	TT	513

Table S3

THE	2032	FOR	306	TTH	249	TIO	213	ONE	190
ING	747	DTH	304	TER	249	ITH	212	ULD	189
AND	667	HAT	298	HES	248	TIN	207	REA	189
HER	547	SHE	281	EDT	244	FTH	206	RTH	187
ERE	448	ION	277	EST	237	AST	206	EAR	187
ENT	376	INT	274	THI	236	OME	202	NGT	184
THA	353	HIS	264	HAD	232	ONT	199	OUN	183
NTH	353	STH	257	OTH	218	YOU	195	ATT	183
WAS	336	ERS	252	ALL	216	OUL	192	WIT	179
ETH	312	VER	249	ATI	215	OFT	191	RES	175

Table S4

Appendix 2

In this appendix we exhibit two of the most common codes used to convert teletypewriter characters to binary.

Combination no.	Code bits					British teleprinter keyboard	
	1	2	3	4	5		
1	1	1	0	0	0	A	–
2	1	0	0	1	1	B	?
3	0	1	1	1	0	C	:
4	1	0	0	1	0	D	WHO ARE YOU WRU
5	1	0	0	0	0	E	3
6	1	0	1	1	0	F	%
7	0	1	0	1	1	G	@
8	0	0	1	0	1	H	£
9	0	1	1	0	0	I	8
10	1	1	0	1	0	J	BELL
11	1	1	1	1	0	K	(
12	0	1	0	0	1	L	)
13	0	0	1	1	1	M	.
14	0	0	1	1	0	N	,
15	0	0	0	1	1	O	9

Table C1

A version of
International Telegraph Alphabet No. 2 (ITA2)

Combination no.	Code bits					British teleprinter keyboard	
	1	2	3	4	5		
16	0	1	1	0	1	P	0
17	1	1	1	0	1	Q	1
18	0	1	0	1	0	R	4
19	1	0	1	0	0	S	'
20	0	0	0	0	1	T	5
21	1	1	1	0	0	U	7
22	0	1	1	1	1	V	=
23	1	1	0	0	1	W	2
24	1	0	1	1	1	X	/
25	1	0	1	0	1	Y	6
26	1	0	0	0	1	Z	+
27	0	0	0	1	0	CARRIAGE RETURN	
28	0	1	0	0	0	LINE FEED	
29	1	1	1	1	1	LETTERS	
30	1	1	0	1	1	FIGURES	
31	0	0	1	0	0	SPACE	
32	0	0	0	0	0	NULL	

Table C1 (*cont.*)

A version of
International Telegraph Alphabet No. 2 (ITA2)

Bits

b7 →					0	0	0	0	1	1	1	1
b6 →					0	0	1	1	0	0	1	1
b5 →					0	1	0	1	0	1	0	1
b4	b3	b2	b1	Row/Col	0	1	2	3	4	5	6	7
0	0	0	0	0	NUL	(TC₇)DLE	SP	0	(@)	P	`	p
0	0	0	1	1	(TC₁)SOH	DC₁	!	1	A	Q	a	q
0	0	1	0	2	(TC₂)STX	DC₂	"	2	B	R	b	r
0	0	1	1	3	(TC₃)ETX	DC₃	£	3	C	S	c	s
0	1	0	0	4	(TC₄)EOT	DC₄	$	4	D	T	d	t
0	1	0	1	5	(TC₅)ENQ	(TC₈)NAK	%	5	E	U	e	u
0	1	1	0	6	(TC₆)ACK	(TC₉)SYN	&	6	F	V	f	v
0	1	1	1	7	BEL	(TC₁₀)ETB	'	7	G	W	g	w
1	0	0	0	8	FE₀(BS)	CAN	(	8	H	X	h	x
1	0	0	1	9	FE₁(HT)	EM	)	9	I	Y	i	y
1	0	1	0	10	FE₂(LF)	SUB	*	:	J	Z	j	z
1	0	1	1	11	FE₃(VT)	ESC	+	;	K	[	k	{
1	1	0	0	12	FE₄(FF)	IS₄(FS)	,	<	L	/	l	—
1	1	0	1	13	FE₅(CR)	IS₃(GS)	–	=	M	]	m	}
1	1	1	0	14	SO	IS₂(RS)	.	>	N	⌐	n	~
1	1	1	1	15	SI	IS₁(US)	/	?	O	–	o	DEL

Table C2

A version of International Telegraph Alphabet No. 5 (ITA5)

Appendix 3

Here we exhibit all Primitive Polynomials of degree at most 8 over GF(2).

Degree	Polynomial
2	$1+x+x^2$
3	$1+x+x^3$
	$1+x^2+x^3$
4	$1+x+x^4$
	$1+x^3+x^4$
5	$1+x^2+x^5$
	$1+x^3+x^5$
	$1+x^2+x^3+x^4+x^5$
	$1+x+x^2+x^3+x^5$
	$1+x+x^2+x^4+x^5$
	$1+x+x^3+x^4+x^5$
6	$1+x+x^6$
	$1+x^5+x^6$
	$1+x+x^2+x^5+x^6$
	$1+x+x^4+x^5+x^6$
	$1+x^2+x^3+x^5+x^6$
	$1+x+x^3+x^4+x^6$
7	$1+x^3+x^7$
	$1+x^4+x^7$
	$1+x+x^2+x^3+x^7$
	$1+x^4+x^5+x^6+x^7$
	$1+x^2+x^3+x^4+x^7$
	$1+x^3+x^4+x^5+x^7$
	$1+x+x^2+x^4+x^5+x^6+x^7$
	$1+x+x^2+x^3+x^5+x^6+x^7$
	$1+x+x^2+x^3+x^4+x^5+x^7$
	$1+x^2+x^3+x^4+x^5+x^6+x^7$
	$1+x^2+x^4+x^6+x^7$
	$1+x+x^3+x^5+x^7$
	$1+x+x^2+x^7$
	$1+x^5+x^6+x^7$

Degree	*Polynomial*
	$1+x+x^3+x^6+x^7$
	$1+x+x^4+x^6+x^7$
	$1+x^2+x^5+x^6+x^7$
	$1+x+x^2+x^5+x^7$
8	$1+x^2+x^3+x^4+x^8$
	$1+x^4+x^5+x^6+x^8$
	$1+x^3+x^5+x^6+x^8$
	$1+x^2+x^3+x^5+x^8$
	$1+x+x^2+x^5+x^6+x^7+x^8$
	$1+x+x^2+x^3+x^6+x^7+x^8$
	$1+x+x^3+x^5+x^8$
	$1+x^3+x^5+x^7+x^8$
	$1+x^2+x^5+x^6+x^8$
	$1+x^2+x^3+x^6+x^8$
	$1+x+x^5+x^6+x^8$
	$1+x^2+x^3+x^7+x^8$
	$1+x+x^2+x^3+x^4+x^6+x^8$
	$1+x^2+x^4+x^5+x^6+x^7+x^8$
	$1+x+x^6+x^7+x^8$
	$1+x+x^2+x^7+x^8$

Bibliography

The rapid advancement of cryptology in recent years makes it very difficult to assemble a complete bibliography. We have included all the more important mathematical and electronics papers of which we know but deliberately neglected many of the historical works. We apologize for any inaccuracies or omissions.

Abene, P. V., 'Secure commercial digital communications', master's thesis, Air Force Inst. of Tech., July 1977.

Adleman, L. M., 'A subexponential algorithm for the discrete logarithm problem with applications to cryptography', *Proc. 20th IEEE Symp. on Foundations of Computer Science*. 55–60, October 1979.

Adleman, L. M. and Rivest, R. L., 'The use of public key cryptography in communication system design', *IEEE Communications Soc. Magazine*, 20–23, November 1978.

Alanen, J. D. and Knuth, D. E., 'Tables of finite fields', *Sankhya, Ser. A.*, 26, 305–328, 1964.

American Bankers Association (ABA), *Report No. 207213*, 1979.

American National Standards Institute (ANSI), USA Standard Method for Measurement of Monosyllabic Word Intelligibility, New York, *ANSI, USAS 53.2*, 1960.

American National Standard Institute (ANSI), ANSI DEA Standard, *ANSI x 3.92*, July 1981.

Anderson, J. P., 'Information security in a multi-user computer', *Advances in Computers*, Vol. 12, Academic Press, New York, 1–35, 1972.

Andrew, A. M., 'Counting to 1099508482050 without carries', *Elect. Eng.*, 172–175, 1966.

Arazi, B., 'Decimation of m-sequences leading to any desired phase shift', *Elect. Lett.*, 13, 7, 213–215, 1977.

Arazi, B., 'A trapdoor multiple mapping', *Trans. IEEE Inform, Theory*, IT–26, 1, 101–102, January, 1980.

Asmuth, C. A. and Blakley, G. R., 'An efficient algorithm for constructing a cryptosystem which is harder to break than two other cryptosystems', *Comp. and Maths. with Appls.*, 7, 6, 447–450, 1981.

Bach, G. G. F., 'Data privacy', *Telecommunications*, 14, 5, 43–48, 1980.

Baker, H. C., 'Voice privacy transmission techniques', *Communication News*, 38–42, June 1972.

Ball, J. R. and Spittle, H. T., 'High speed m-sequence generation: a further note', *Elect. Lett.*, 11, 107–108, 1975.

Balza, C., Fromageot, A. and Moniere, M., 'Four level pseudo-random sequences', *Elect. Lett.* 3, 313–315, 1967.

Baran, P., 'On distributed communications: 1X security, secrecy and tamper-free considerations', The Rand Corporation, Santa Monica, CA RM-3765-PR, 1964.

Barker, W. G., *Cryptanalysis of the Hagelin Cryptograph*, Aegean Park Press, 1977.

Barker, W. G., 'Solving a Hagelin, type CD–57, cipher', *Cryptologia*, 2, 1, 1–8, 1978.

Bartek, D. J., 'Encryption for data security; *Honeywell Comp. J.*, 8, 2, 86–89, 1974.

Beard, J. T. B. Jr., 'Computing in GF (q)', *Mathematics of Computation*, 28, 128, 1159–1168, 1974.

Beaston, J. 'One-chip data-encryption unit accesses memory directly', *Electronics*, 52, 16, 126–129, August, 1979.

Beker, H. J., 'Some mathematical and cryptographical aspects of modern cipher systems', *Proc. Mecom.*, 4.1.1.-4.1.3., 1979.

Beker, H. J., 'Cryptographic requirements for digital secure speech systems', *Elect. Eng.*, 52, 634, 37–46, 1980.

Beker, H. J., 'Cryptography for radio communications applications', *Comms. Eng. Int.*, 2, 4, 36–41, 1980.

Beker, H. J., 'Security in an electronic fund transfer system., *Inform. Privacy*, 2, 5, 185–189, 1980.

Beker, H. J., 'Cryptography – what is a cipher system', *New Elect.* 13, 23, 29–31, 1980.

Beker, H. J., 'Cryptography – modern cipher systems, *New Elect.*, 13, 24, 29–33, 1980.

Beker, H. J., 'Digital secure speech systems', *Proc. No. 50 IERE*, 237–246, 1981.

Beker, H. J. and Piper, F. C., 'Shift Register sequences', *Proc. 8th British Comb. Conf.*, 56–79, 1981.

Beker, H. J. and Piper, F. C., 'Communications security: a survey of cryptography', *Proc. IEE*, to appear.

Bentham, R., 'Security in banking', *Inform. Priv.*, 2, 1, 17–20, 1980.

Berson, T. A. and Barksdale, G. L., 'KSOS – development methodology for a secure operating system', *Proc. NCC*, 365–371, 1979.

Birdsall, T. G. and Ristenbatt, M. P., 'Introduction to linear shift-register generated sequences', *Cooley Elect. Lab. Tech. Rep. 90*, Univ. of Michigan, 1958.

Blakley, B. and Blakley, G. R., 'Security of number theoretic public key cryptosystems against random attack parts 1–3', *Cryptologia*, 2, 4, 305–321, October, 1978; *Cryptologia*, 3, 1, 29–42, January, 1979; *Cryptologia*, 3, 2, 105–118, April, 1979.

Blakley, G. R., 'Safeguarding cryptographic keys', *Proc. AFIPS NCC*, 48, 313–317, 1979.

Blakley, G. R., 'One-time pads are key safeguarding schemes, not cryptosystems. Fast key safeguarding schemes (threshold schemes) exist', *Proc. 1980 Symp. on Security and Privacy*, 108–113, 1980.

Blakley, G. R. and Borosh, I., 'Rivest-Shamir Adleman Public-key cryptosystems do not always conceal messages', *Comp. and Maths. with Appls.*, 5, 169–176, 1979.

Blakley, G. R. and Purdy, G. B., 'A necessary and sufficient condition for fundamental periods of cascade machines to be products of the fundamental periods of their constituent finite state machines', *Inform. Sciences*, 24, 71–91, 1981.

Blakley, G. R. and Swanson, L., 'Security proofs for information protection systems', *Proc. 1981 Symp. on Security and Privacy*, 75–88, 1981.

Branstad, D. K., 'Privacy and protection in operating systems', *Operating Sys. Rev. 7*, 1973.

Branstad, D. K., 'Security aspects of computer networks', *AIAA Conf. Proc.*, Huntsville, Alabama, Paper No. 73–427, 1973.

Branstad, D. K., 'Encryption protection in computer data communications', *Proc. 4th ACM/IEEE Data Communications Symposium*, Quebec, 8.1–8.7, October, 1975.

Branstad, D. K., 'Computer security and the Data Encryption Standard', *National Bureau of Standards*, Special Publication, 500–527, February, 1978.

Branstad, D. K., 'Security of computer communication', *IEEE Communications Soc. Magazine*, 26, 6, Special issue on communications privacy, 33–40, November, 1978.

Branstad, D. K., Gait, J. and Katzke, S., 'Report of the workshop on cryptography in support of computer security', *National Bureau of Standards*, Report NBSIR77-1291, September, 1977.

Brassard, G., 'A note on the complexity of cryptography', *Trans. IEEE Inf. Theory*, IT-25, 2, 232-234 (1979 (Mar)).

Brassard, G., 'Relativized cryptography', *Proc. 20th Annual IEEE Symp. on Foundations of Computer Science*, 383-391, 1979.

Brassard, G., 'A time-luck tradeoff in cryptography', *Proc. 21st Annual IEEE Symp. on Foundations of Computer Science*, 380-386, 1980.

Brawley, J. V. and Levine, J., 'Equivalences of Vigenère systems over finite groups', *Clemson Univ. Tech Rep.* 177, 1974.

Breeze, M., 'Turpin on the line', *Systems. Int.*, 8, 8, 47-49, 1980.

Briggs, P., and Godfrey, K. R., 'Autocorrelation function of a 4-level sequence', *Elect. Lett.* 4, 232-233, 1963.

Bright, H. S., 'Information content authentication using cryptographic algorithms', *Proc. Trends and Applications*, 1980, Computer Network Protocols, Gaithersburg, 128-131, 1980.

Bright, H. S. and Enison, R. L.,'Cryptography using modular software elements', *Proc. AFIPS NCC*, 45, 113-123, 1976.

Bright, H. S. and Enison, R. L., 'Quasi-random number sequences from a long-period TLP generator with remarks on application to cryptography', *ACM Computing Surveys*, 11, 4, 357-370, 1979.

Brunner, E. R., 'Efficient speech scrambling: an economic solution to the secure voice communication problem', *Proc. Int. Conf. on Comms. Equip. and Sys. Brighton*, 336-339, 1976.

Brunner, E. R., 'Speech security systems today and tomorrow', *Gretag Report*, 1980.

Bryant, P. R., 'Theory of feedback shift registers with invertors', *Proc. IEE*, 116, 9, 1599-1605, 1969.

Budzinski, R., 'Single-chip computer scramblers for security', *Electronics*, 52, 15, 140-144, July, 1979.

Burris, H. R., 'Computer network cryptography engineering', *Proc. AFIPS NCC*, 45, 91-96, 1976.

Burris, H. R., 'Microprogrammed tamper detection for network processors: preliminary results', *National Bureau of Standards/IEEE Trends and Applications Symposium, Computer Security and Integrity*, 83-85, May, 1977.

Callas, N. P., 'An application of computers to cryptography', *Cryptologia*, 2, 4, 350-364, 1978.

Callimahos, L. D., 'Cryptography', *Colliers Encyclopedia*, 7, 513-530, 1973.

Callimahos, L. D., 'Cryptology', *Encyclopedia Britannica*, 15th Ed., Macropaedia, 5, 322-333, 1976.

Campbell, C. M., 'Design and specification of cryptographic capabilities', *IEEE Communications Soc. Magazine*, 16, 6, Special Issue on Communications Privacy, 15-19, November, 1978.

Campbell, D., 'Whose eyes on secret data', *New Scientist*, 593-595, 1978.

Campbell, R. P. and Sands, G. A., 'A modular approach to computer security risk management', *Proc. NCC*, 293-303, 1979.

Carleial, A. B. and Hellman, M. E., 'A note on Wyner's wiretap channel', *IEEE Trans. on Inform. Theory*, IT-23, 3, 387-390, 1977.

Carlson, R. L., Telley, J. M. and Schreiber, W. L., 'Privacy of voice communication', *Security World*, 49-53, May, 1972.

Carroll, J. M. and McLelland, P. M., 'Fast "Infinite-key" privacy transformation for resource sharing systems', *Proc. Fall Joint Computer Conf.*, Houston, 223–230, November, 1970.

Carter, D. E., 'On the generation of pseudo-noise codes', *IEE Trans. Aerospace Elect. Sys.*, 10, 898–899, 1974.

Charters, J. S. T., 'Structured magnetic materials for data security', *Proc. Int. Conf. on Video and Data Recording (IERE)*, Southampton, 261–266, July, 1979.

Chesson, F. W., 'Computers and cryptology', *Datamation*, 19, 1, 62–64, January, 1973.

Chin, F. Y., 'Security in statistical data bases for queries with small counts', *ACM Trans. on Database Sys. 3*, 1, 92–104, 1978.

Chu, W. W. and Neat, C. E., 'A new computer cryptography the expanded character set cipher', *Advances in Computer Communications Sect. XIII*, 442–453, Artech House, 1976.

Cole, G. D., 'Design Alternatives for computer network security', *National Bureau of Standards*, Special Publication 500–21, Vol. 1, January, 1978.

Conway, R. W., Maxwell, W. L. and Morgan, H. L., 'On the implementation of security measures in information systems', *Comm. ACM*, 15, 4, 211–220, 1972.

Cooper, R. H., 'Linear transformations in Galois fields and their applications to cryptography', *Cryptologia*, 4, 3, 184–188, 1980.

Coppersmith, D. and Grossman, E., 'Generators for certain alternating groups with applications to cryptography', *Siam J. Appl. Math*, 29, 4, 624–627, 1975.

Costas, J. P., 'Cryptography in the field', *Byte*, 4, 3, 56–64, 1979.

Coven, E. M., Hedlund, G. A. and Rhodes, F., 'The commuting block maps problem', *Trans. AMS*, 249, 1, 113–138, 1979.

Cover, T. M. and King, R. C., 'A convergent gambling estimate of the entropy of English', *IEEE Trans. Inform. Theory*, IT–23, 289–294, 1977.

Cumming, I. G., 'Autocorrelation function and spectrum of a filtered pseudo-random binary sequence', *Proc. IEE 114*, 1360–1362, 1967.

Davies, A. C., 'Probability distribution of pseudo-random waveforms obtained from m-sequences', *Elect. Lett. 3*, 3, 115–117, 1967.

Davies, A. C., 'Calculations relating to delayed m-sequences', *Elect. Lett. 4*, 14, 291–292, 1968.

Davies, D. W. and Bell, D. A., 'Protection of data by cryptography', *Information Privacy 2*, 3, 106–126, 1980.

Davies, D. W. and Price, W. L., 'The application of digital signatures based on public key cryptosystems', *Proc. 5th ICCC*, Atlanta, Ga., October 1980.

Davies, D. W. and Price, W. L., 'Selected papers in cryptography and data security', *NPL Report DNACS 38/80*, 1980.

Davies, D. W., Price, W. L. and Parkin, G. I., 'An evaluation of public key cryptosystems', *National Physical Lab. Rep. CTU 1*, 1979 and *Information Privacy 2*, 4, 138–154, 1980.

Davis, R. M., 'The data encryption standard in perspective', *IEEE Comms Soc.* 16, 6, 5–10, 1978.

Deavours, C. A., 'The Kappa test', *Cryptologia*, 1, 3, 223–231, 1977.

Deavours, C. A., 'Unicity points in cryptanalysis', *Cryptologia*, 1, 1, 46–68, 1977.

De Lellis, 'Linear prediction techniques for digital secure voice systems', *GTE Sylvania Inc. Rep.*

Denning, D. E., 'Secure personal computing in an insecure network', *Comm. ACM*, 22, 8, 476–482, August, 1979.

Denning, D. E. and Denning, P. J., 'Data security', *ACM Computing Surveys*, 11, 4, 227–249, September, 1979.

Denning, D. E. and Schneider, F. B., 'Personal keys, group keys and master keys', *Dept. of Comp. Science, Cornell Univ. Report TR80–409*, 1980.

Diffie, W., *Data Security for EFT and Automated Business, SBS Publishing*, San Jose, CA, 1978.

Diffie, W., 'The outlook for computer security', *Mini-Micro Sys.*, 2, 9, 42–44, October, 1978.

Diffie, W., *A Technical Bibliography of Cryptography*, private compilation, 1982.

Diffie, W. and Hellman, M. E., 'Cryptanalysis of the NBS Data Encryption Standard', *Stanford Univ. Report*, MEH – 76 – 2, 1976.

Diffie, W. and Hellman, M. E., 'A critique of the proposed Data Encryption Standard', *Comm. ACM*, 19, 3, 164–165, March, 1976.

Diffie, W. and Hellman, M. E., 'Multiuser cryptographic techniques', *Proc. NCC*, New York, 109–112, 1976.

Diffie, W. and Hellman, M. E., 'New directions in cryptography', *Trans. IEEE Inform. Theory*, IT–22, 6, 644–654, November, 1976.

Diffie, W. and Hellman, M. E., 'Exhaustive cryptanalysis of the NBS Data Encryption Standard', *Computer*, 10, 6, 74–84, 1977.

Diffie, W. and Hellman, M. E., 'Privacy and authentication: an introduction to cryptography', *Proc. IEEE 67*, 3, 397–427, 1979.

Donn, E. S., 'Secure your digital data', Elect. Eng., 5–7, 1972.

Dunham, J. G., 'Bounds on message equivocation for simple substitution ciphers', *IEEE Trans. Inform. Theory*, IT–26, 5, 522–527, 1980.

EDP Analyzer, 'Data encryption: is it for you?', Vol. 16, No. 22, 1–13, December 1978.

Edwards, D. J., 'OCAS – on-line cryptanalytic aid system', *MIT Project Mac*, Tech. Report 27, 1966.

Ehrsam, W. F., Matyas, S. M., Meyer, C. H. and Tuchman, W. L., 'A cryptographic key management scheme for implementing the Data Encryption Standard', *IBM Sys. J.*, 17, 2, 106–125, 1978.

Erickson, C., 'Encryption – an ancient art enhanced by LSI', *Progress 7*, 1, 4–11, 1979.

Evans, A., Kantrowitz, W. and Weiss, E., 'A user authentication scheme not requiring secrecy in the computer', *Comms. ACM 17*, 8, 437–442, 1974.

Everett, D., 'Periodic digital sequences with pseudo noise properties', *GEC journal 33*, 3, 115–126, 1966.

Feiertag, R. J. and Neumann, P. G., 'The foundation of a provably secure operating system', *Proc. NCC*, 329–334, 1979.

Feistel, H., 'A survey of problems and systems in authenticated communication and control', *MIT Lincoln Lab.*, May, 1958.

Feistel, H., 'Cryptographic coding for data-bank privacy', *IBM Research Report RC 2827*, March, 1970.

Feistel, H., 'Cryptography and computer privacy', *Scientific American*, 228, 5, 15–23, May, 1973.

Feistel, H., Notz, W. A. and Smith, J. L., 'Some cryptographic techniques for machine-to-machine data communications', *Proc. IEEE*, 63, 11, 1545–1554, 1975.

Fillmore, J. P. and Marx, M. L., 'Linear recursive sequences', *SIAM Rev. 10*, 342–353, 1968.

Fischer, E., 'Language redundancy and cryptanalysis', *Cryptologia 3*, 4, 233–235, 1979.

Flynn, R. and Campasano, A. S., 'Data dependent keys for a selective encryption terminal', *Proc. AFIPS NCC*, 47, 1127–1129, 1978.

Fredrickson, H., 'The lexicographically least de Bruijn cycle', *JCT 9*, 1–5, 1970.

Fredrickson, S., 'A class of non-linear de Bruijn cycles', *JCT A*, 19, 192–199, 1975.

Fredrickson, S., 'Pseudo-randomness properties of shift register sequences', *IEEE Trans. Inform. Theory*, IT–21, 115–120, 1975.

French, R. C., 'Speech scrambling', *Electronics and Power*, 263–264, July, 1972.

Friedman, W. F., 'Military cryptanalysis', *US Government Printing Office*, Washington DC, 1944.

Friedman, W. F., 'Codes and ciphers (cryptology)', *Encyclopedia Britannica*, 1956.

Friedman, W. F., 'Cryptology', *Encyclopedia Britannica*, 6, 844–851, 1967.

Gaines, H. F., *Cryptanalysis, a study of ciphers and their solution*, New York: Dover, 1956.

Gait, J., Validating the correctness of hardware implementations of the NBS Data Encryption Standard', *NBS Publication*, 500–520, 1977.

Gait, J., 'Encryption standard: validating hardware techniques', *NBS Dimensions*, 62, 22–23, 1978.

Gait, J., 'Maintenance testing for the Data Encryption Standard', *NBS Publication*, 500–61, 1980.

Gallois, A. P., 'Communication privacy using digital techniques', *Electronics and Power*, 777–780, 1976.

Gardner, M., 'A new kind of cipher that would take millions of years to break', *Scientific American*, 237, 2, 120–124, August, 1977.

Gebler, P., 'Implementations of the DES algorithm', *Elect. Prod. Design*, 1, 3, 52–54, June, 1980.

Geffe, P. R., 'An open letter to communications engineers', *Proc. IEEE*, 55, 2173, 1967.

Geffe, P. R., 'How to protect data with ciphers that are really hard to break', *Electronics*, 46, 1, 99–101, 1973.

General Services Administration, 'Telecommunications: security requirements for use of the Data Encryption Standards', *Federal Standard 1027*, May, 1981.

General Services Administration, 'Telecommunications: Compatibility requirements for use of the Data Encryption Standards', *Federal Standard 1026*, June, 1981.

Gilbert, E. N., MacWilliams, F. J. and Sloane, N. J. A., 'Codes which detect deception', *Bell Sys. Tech. J.*, 53, 3, 405–424, 1974.

Girdansky, M. B., 'Cryptology, the computer and data privacy', *Comput. Automation*, 21, 4, 12–19, 1972.

Goethals, J. M. and Couvreur, C., 'A cryptanalytic attack on the Lu-Lee public-key cryptosystem', *Phillips J. Res.* 35, 301–306, 1980.

Gold, B., 'Digital speech networks', *Proc. IEEE*, 65, 1636–1638, 1977.

Gold, B. D., Linde, R. R., Peeler, R. J., Schaefer, M., Scheid, J. F. and Ward, P. D., 'A security retrofit of VM/370', *Proc. NCC*, 335–344, 1979.

Gold, R., 'Characteristic linear sequences and their coset functions', *J. Siam Appl. Math.*, 14, 5, 980–985, 1966.

Goldberg, L. L., 'Computers and crime', *Telecommunications*, 14, 5, 19–26, 1980.

Golomb, S. W., *Shift Register Sequences*, Holden-Day, San Francisco, 1967.

Golomb, S. W., 'On the classification of balanced binary sequences of period 2^n-1', *IEEE Trans. Inform. Theory*, IT–26, 6, 730–732, 1980.

Gordon, J. A., 'Very simple method to find the minimum polynomial of an arbitrary non zero element of a finite field', *Elect. Lett. 12*, 25, 663–664, 1976.

Gordon, J. A., 'Recent trends in cryptology', *Electronics and Power*, 26, 2, 162–165, February, 1980.

Gordon, J. A. 'The use of intractable problems in cryptography', *Information Privacy*, 2, 5, 178–184, 1980.

Gordon, J. A. and Retkin, H. 'Are big S-boxes best?', *IEEE Workshop on Comms. Security*, Santa Barbara, 1981.

Graham, G. S. and Denning, P. J., 'Protection – principles and practice', *Proc. Spring Comp. Conf.*, 417–429, 1972.

Green, D. H. and Dimond, K. R., 'Polynomial representation of non linear feedback shift registers', *Proc. IEE*, 117, 1, 56–60, 1970.

Green, D. H. and Dimond, K. R., 'Non-linear product-feedback shift registers', *Proc. IEE*, 117, 4, 681–686, 1970.

Grossman, E. K., 'Group Theoretic remarks on cryptographic systems based on two types of addition', *IBM T. J. Watson Research Center*, RC4742, 1974.

Grossman, E. K. and Tuckerman, B., 'Analysis of a Feistel-like cipher weakened by having no rotating key', *IBM Research Rep. RC 6375*, 1977.

Groth, E. J., 'Generation of binary sequences with controllable complexity', *IEEE Trans on Inform. Theory*. IT–17, 3, 288–296, 1971.

Gudes, E., Koch, H. S. and Stahl, F. A., 'The application of cryptography for data base security', *Proc. NCC.*, New York, 97–107, June, 1976.

Guillen, M., 'Automated cryptography', *Science News*, 110, 12, 188–190, September, 1976.

Guillou, L. and Lorig, B., 'The impact of cryptography in the design of data services', *Proc. 4th ICCC*, Kyoto, 303–308, September, 1978.

Halsey, J. C., *Finite automata admitting inverses with some applications to cryptography*, PhD Thesis, North Carolina State Univ., 1970.

Heinrich, F., 'The network security center: A system level approach to computer network security', *NBS Pub.* 500–21, Vol. 2., 1978.

Heinrich, F. R. and Kaufman, D. J., 'A centralised approach to computer network security', *Proc. AFIPS NCC*, 45, 85–90, 1976.

Helleseth, T., 'A note on the cross-correlation function between two binary maximal length sequences', *Discrete Math. 23*, 3, 301–307, 1978.

Hellman, M. E., 'The information theoretic approach to cryptography', *Stanford University Rep. MEH–76–1*, 1974.

Hellman, M. E., 'An extension of the Shannon theory approach to cryptography', *IEEE Trans on Inform. Theory IT–23*, 3, 289–294, 1977.

Hellman, M. E., 'An overview of public-key cryptography', *IEEE Comms. Soc. 16*, 6, 24–32, 1978.

Hellman, M. E., 'Security in communication networks', *Proc. NCC*, 1131–1134, 1978.

Hellman, M. E., 'The mathematics of public-key cryptography', *Scientific American*, 214, 2, 146–157, August, 1979.

Hellman, M. E., 'A cryptanalytic time-memory trade off', *Trans. IEEE Inform. Theory*, IT–26, 4, 401–406, 1980.

Hellman, M. E., 'The mathematical theory of secrecy systems', *Proc. of Internat. Conf. on Communications*, Minneapolis, 40D/1–4, June 1974.

Hellman, M. E., Merkle, R., Schroeppel, R., Washington, L., Diffie, W., Pohlig, S. and Schweitzer, P., 'Results of an initial attempt to cryptanalyse the NBS Data Encryption Standard', *Stanford Univ. Report Sel. 76–042*, 1976.

Herlestam, T., 'Critical remarks on some public-key cryptosystems', *BIT*, 18, 493–496, 1978.

Hindin, H. J., 'Cipher-shifters fight it out', *Electronics*, 81-82, February, 1979.

Hindin, H. J., 'LSI-based data encryption discourages the data thief', *Electronics*, 52, 13, 107–120, June, 1979.

Hindin, H. J., 'Encryption chips sort themselves out', *Electronics*, 96–97, July, 1980.

Hodgart, M. S., 'A revolution in cryptography – privacy and authentication', *Comms. Eng.*, 32–39, December, 1979.

Hoffman, L. J., *Modern Methods for Computer Security and Privacy*, Prentice-Hall, Englewood Cliffs, New Jersey, 1977.

Houghton, M. R., 'Protecting data by encryption techniques', *Comms. Int.*, 6, 3, 20–26, March, 1979.

Houghton, M. R., 'Developments in speech security', *Comms. Int.*, 7, 2, 22–23, February, 1980.

Houghton, M. R., 'An introduction to electronic fund transfer techniques', *Comms. Int.*, 32–33, August, 1980.

Humphrey, T. and Toth, F. L., 'Two-chip data-encryption unit supports multi-key systems', *Electronics*, 53, 2, 136–139, January, 1980.

Hurd, W. J., 'Efficient generation of statistically good pseudo noise by linearly interconnected shift registers', *IEEE Trans. Comp. C-23*, 2, 146–152, 1974.

Ingemarsson, I. 'Analysis of secret functions with application to computer cryptography', *Proc. AFIPS NCC*, 45, 125–127, 1976.

Inman, B. R., 'The NSA perspective on telecommunications protection in the non governmental sector', *Cryptologia*, 3, 3, 129–135, 1979.

Jayant, N. S., McDermott, B. J., Christensen, S. W. and Quinn, A. M. S., 'A comparison of four methods for analog speech privacy', *IEEE Trans. on Communications*, COM–29 1, 18–23, 1981.

Jeffrey, S., 'Data integrity and security in the EFT interchange environment', *Institute for Computer Sciences and Technology*, National Bureau of Standards, 1977.

Jennings, S. M., *A special class of binary sequences*, PhD Thesis, University of London, 1980.

Jones, B., *The Secret War*, New York, Methuen, 1978.

Kahn, D., 'Modern cryptology', *Scientific American*, 215, 1, 38–46, 1966.

Kahn, D., *The Codebreakers, The Story of Secret Writing*, Macmillan, New York, 1967.

Kahn, D., 'Cryptology', *Encyclopedia Americana*, 8, 276–285, 1976.

Kahn, D., 'Secret writings: selected works on modern cryptology', *Bulletin of the New York Public Library*, Vol. 73, No. 5, 315–327, May 1969.

Kaufman, D. and Averbach, K., 'A secure, national system for electronics funds transfer', *Proc. AFIPS NCC*, 45, 129–138, 1976.

Kent, S. T., 'Encryption-based protection protocols for interactive user-computer communication', *MIT Tech. Report 162*, 1976.

Kent, S. T., 'A comparison of some aspects of public-key and conventional cryptosystems', *Proc. 15th Internat. Communications Conf.*, Boston, Mass., 4.3.1–4.3.5, June, 1979.

Key, E. L., 'An analysis of the structure and complexity of non-linear binary sequence generators', *IEEE Trans. on Inform. Theory*, IT–22, 6, 732–736, 1976.

Keys, R. R. and Clamons, E. H., 'Security architecture using encryption', *Proc. NBS Conf. 1974 (March) called 'Approaches to Privacy and Security in Computer Systems'*, 37–41, 1974.

Keys, R. R. and Clamons, E. H., 'File encryption as a security tool', *Honeywell Comp. J.*, 8, 2, 90–93, 1974.

Kinnucan, P., 'Data Encryption Gurus: Tuchman and Meyer', *Mini-Micro Sys. 2*, 9, 54–60, October, 1978

Kirchhofer, K. H., 'Cryptology: Part 1 – users, principles and methods', *Int. Def. Rev.*, 9, 2, 281–286, 1976.

Kirchhofer, K. H., 'Crytology: Part 2 – the unbreakable system', *Int. Def. Rev.*, 9, 3, 389–394, 1976.

Kirchhofer, K. H., 'Cryptology: Part 3 – crypto communication', *Int. Def. Rev.*, 9, 4, 585–589, 1976.

Kirchhofer, K. H., 'Secure voice communication – cryptophony', *Int. Def. Rev.*, 9, 5, 761–767, 1976.

Kirchhofer, K. H., 'Cryptography in perspective', *Comms. Int.*, 7, 2, 24–26, February, 1980.

Kjeldsen, K., 'On the cycle structure of a set of non linear shift registers with symmetric feedback functions', *JCT (A)*, 20, 154–169, 1976.

Kochanski, M. J., 'Remarks on Lu and Lee's proposals for a public-key cryptosystem', *Cryptologia*, 4, 4, 204–207, 1980.

Kohnfelder, L. M., 'On the signature reblocking problem in public-key cryptosystem', *Comsat. Tech. Rev.*, 9, 15–24, 1979.

Kolata, G. B., 'Computer encryption and the national security agency connection', *Science*, 197, 438–440, 1977.

Kolata, G. B., 'Cryptography: on the brink of a revolution?', *Science*, 197, 747–748, 1977.

Kolata, G. B., 'Prior restraints on cryptography considered', *Science*, 208, 1442–1443, June, 1980.

Konheim, A. G., *Cryptography, a Primer*, John Wiley and Sons, 1981.

Konheim, A. G., Mack, M. H., McNeill, R. K., Tuckerman, B. and Waldbaum, G., 'The IPS cryptographic programs', *IBM Systems Journal*, Vol. 19, No. 2, 253–283, 1980.

Kreindler, R. J., 'Password protection for your computer', *Byte*, 194–195, March, 1979.

Krum, L., 'The Hagelin cryptographer, type C–52', *Cryptologia*, 3, 2, 78–82, 1979.

Kullback, S., *Statistical Methods in Cryptanalysis*, Aegean Park Press, 1976.

Lampson, B. W., 'A note on the confinement problem', *Comm. ACM*, 16, 10, 613–615, 1973.

Lempel, A., 'Cryptology in transition', *ACM Computing Surveys*, 11, 4, 285–303, 1979.

Lempel, A. and Ziv, J., 'On the complexity of finite sequences', *Trans. IEEE Inform. Theory*, IT–22, 1, 1976.

Lennon, R. E., 'Cryptography architecture for information security', *IBM Sys. J.*, 17, 22, 138–150, 1978.

Lennon, R. E., 'Putting data encryption to work', *Mini-Micro Systems*, 11, 84, 84–88, December, 1978.

Leung-Yan-Cheong, S. K., 'On a special class of wire-tap channels', *Trans. IEEE Inform. Theory*, IT–23, 625–627, 1977.

Leung-Yan-Cheong, S. K. and Hellman, M. E., 'The Gaussian wire-tap channel', *Trans. IEEE Inform. Theory*, IT–24, 451–456, 1978.

Levine, J. and Brawley, J. V., 'Some cryptographic applications of permutation polynomials', *Cryptologia*, 1, 1, 76–92, 1977.

Lewin, R., *Ultra Goes to War*, Hutchinson and Co., 1978.

Lindholm, J. H., 'An analysis of the pseudo-randomness properties of subsequences of long m-sequences', *Trans. IEEE Inform. Theory*, IT–14, 4, 1968.

Lu, S. C., 'Random ciphering bounds on a class of secrecy systems and discrete message sources', *Trans. IEEE Inform. Theory*, IT–25, 4, 405–414, 1979.

Lu, S. C., 'On secrecy systems with side information about the message available to a cryptanalyst', *Trans. IEEE Inform. Theory*, IT–25, No. 4, 472–475, 1979.

Lu, S. C., 'The existence of good cryptosystems for key rates greater than the message redundancy', *Trans. IEEE Inform. Theory*, IT–25, 4, 475–477, 1979, and *Trans. IEEE Inform. Theory*, IT–26, 1, 129, 1980.

Lu, S. C. and Lee, K. N., 'A simple and effective public-key cryptosystem', *COMSAT Technical Review*, Vol. 9, No. 1, 15–24, 1979.

Lu, S. C. and Lee, K. N., 'Message redundancy reduction by multiple substitution: a pre-processing scheme for secure communications', *COMSAT Technical Review*, Vol. 9, No. 1, 37–47, 1979.

Mackinnon, N. R. F., 'The development of speech encipherment', *Radio and Elect. Eng.*, 50, 4, 147–155, 1980.

McMaster, G. E., 'On a Canadian Data Encryption Standard', *Proc. of Conf. of the Canadian Information Processing Society (CIPS)*, the *Data Processing Managers Association of Canada (DPMA Can)* and the *Federation de l'Information du Quebec (FIQ)*, Montreal, Que, 276–9, June, 1979.

MacWilliams, F. J. and Sloane, N. J. A., 'Pseudo-random sequences and arrays', *Proc. IEEE*, 64, 12, 1715–1729, 1976.

Maritsas, D. G., 'On the statistical properties of a class of linear feedback shift registers', *IEEE Trans. Computers*, C–22, 961–962, 1973.

Massey, J. L., 'Shift register synthesis and BCH decoding', *Trans. IEEE Inform Theory*, IT–15, 1, 122–127, 1969.

Matyas, S. M., 'Digital signatures – an overview', *Computer Networks*, 3, 2, 87–94, 1979.

Matyas, S. M. and Meyer, C. H., 'Generation, distribution and installation of cryptographic keys', *IBM Sys. J.*, 17, 2, 126–137, 1978.

McCalmont, A. M., 'Communications security for voice-techniques, systems and operations', *Telecommunications,* 35–42, April, 1973.

McCalmont, A. M., 'How to select and apply various voice scrambling techniques', *Commun. News*, 34–37, January, 1974.

McEliece, R. J., 'A public-key cryptosystem based on algebraic coding theory', *DSN Progress Report*, 42–44, 1978.

Mellon, G. E., 'Computers, cryptography and common sense', *Proc. NCC*, New York, 569–579, 1973.

Merkle, R. C., 'Secure communications over insecure channels', *Comm. ACM*, 21, 4, 294–299, 1978.

Merkle, R. C., 'Secrecy, authentication and public-key systems', *Stanford Univ. Tech. Report No. 1979–1*, 1979.

Merkle, R. C., 'A certified digital signature', *IEEE Elect. and Aerospace Systems Conf*, 663, 1979.

Merkle, R. C. and Hellman, M. E., 'Hiding information and signatures in trapdoor knapsacks', *Trans. IEEE Inform. Theory*, IT–24, 5, 525–530, 1978.

Meushaw, R. V., 'The standard data encryption algorithm', *Byte*, 4, 3, 66–74, March, 1979.

Meyer, C. H., 'Voice scramblers in two-way systems', *Communications News*, 32–33, August, 1972.

Meyer, C. H., 'Design considerations for cryptography', *Proc. NCC*, New York, 603–606, 1973.

Meyer, C. H., 'Enciphering data for secure transmission', *Computer Design*, 129–134, April, 1974.

Meyer, C. H., 'Ciphertext/plaintext and ciphertext/key dependence via number of rounds for the Data Encryption Standard', *Proc. AFIPS NCC*, 47, 1119–1126, 1978.

Meyer, C. H. and Tuchman, W. L., 'Pseudorandom codes can be cracked', *Elect. Design*, 23, 74–76, 1972.

Meyer, C. H. and Tuchman, W. L., 'Putting data encryption to work', *Mini–Micro Sys.*, 11, 9, 46–52, 1978.

Michelman, E. H., 'The design and operation of public-key cryptosystems', *Proc. NCC*, 305–311, 1979.

Monier, L., 'Evaluation and comparison of two efficient probabilistic primality testing algorithms', *Informatics Research Lab. Era 452*, Univ. of Paris-Sud. Report 20, June, 1978.

Morris, R., 'The Hagelin cipher machine (M209) reconstruction of the internal settings', *Cryptologia*, 2, 3, 267–289, 1978.

Morris, R., 'The Data Encryption Standard – retrospective and prospects', *IEEE Communications Soc. Magazine*, 16, 6, 11–14, 1978.

Morris, R., Sloane, N. J. A. and Wyner, A. D., 'Assessment of the National Bureau of Standards proposed Federal Data Encryption Standard', *Cryptologia*, 1, 281–306, 1977.

Morris, R. and Thompson, K., 'Password security: a case history', *Comm. ACM*, 22, 11, 594–597, 1979.

Mykkeltveit, J., 'Non-linear recurrences and arithmetic codes', *Inform. and Control*, 33, 193–209, 1977.

Mykkeltveit, J., 'On the cycle structure of some non-linear shift register sequences', *Inform. and Control*, 43, 2, 202–215, 1979.

Nakamura, K. and Iwadare, Y., 'Data scramblers for multi-level pulse sequences', *NEC Res. and Develop.*, 26, 53–63, 1972.

National Bureau of Standards, 'Report of the 1976 workshop on estimation of significant advances in computer technology', *Report NBSIR*, 76–1189, December, 1976.

National Bureau of Standards, 'Data Encryption Standard', *Federal Information Processing Standard (FIPS) Publication No. 46.*, January, 1977.

National Bureau of Standards, 'Computer security and the Data Encryption Standard', *NBS Pub. 500–7*, 1978.

National Bureau of Standards, 'Guidelines for implementing and using the DES', *FIPS Pub. 74*, April, 1981.

National Security Agency, 'Public Cryptography', *Signal*, 67–77, April, 1981.

Needham, R. M. and Schroeder, M. D., 'Using Encryption for authentication in large networks of computers', *Comms. ACM*, 21, 12, 993–999, 1978.

Nelson, R. E., 'A guide to voice scramblers for law enforcement agencies', *NBS Pub. 480–12*, 1979.

Noll, M. A., 'The interactions of computers and privacy', *Honeywell Computer J.*, 163–172, 1973.

Norman, A. R. D., 'Computer fraud', *Electronics and Power*, 1978.

Nye, J. M., *Who, what and where in communications security*, Marketing Consultants Int., 1981.

Nyffeler, P., *Binaere Automaten und ihre linearen Rekursionen*, PhD Thesis, Univ.of Bern, 1975.

O'Brien, M. J., 'Technical specification of a proposed federal information processing standard on the modes of operation for the Data Encryption Standard', Institute of Computer Sciences and Technology, National Bureau of Standards, *Report NBSIR 20–2019*, April, 1980.

Orceyre, M. and Courtney, R. H., 'Considerations in the selection of security measures for automatic data processing systems', *NBS Pub.*, 500–33, 1978.

Orceyre, M. and Heller, R. M., 'An approach to secure voice communication based on the Data Encryption Standard', *IEEE Comms. Soc.*, 16, 6, 14–52, 1978.

Ostermann, B., 'Security for data and information', *Electrotechnik* (Germany), Vol. 58, No. 23, 16–21, December, 1976.

Padlipsky, M. A., Snow, D. W. and Karger, P. A., 'Limitations of end-to-end encryption in secure computer networks', *Mitre Corporation Report No. MTR–3592*, 1978.

Perlman, M., 'Generation of key in cryptographic system for secure communications', *NASA Tech. Brief 75–10278*, 1976.

Pieprzyk, J., 'Random Vigenère ciphers and their applications in computer systems', *Arch, Automat. Telemech*, 25, 2, 237–256, 1980.

Pless, V., 'Two encryption schemes for computer confidentiality', *Colloquia Mathematica Societatis Janos Bolyai, Topics in Information Theory, Keszthaly*, 521–526, 1975.

Pless, V.'Mathematical foundations of interconnected J–K flip-flops', *Inform. and Control*, 30, 128–142, 1976.

Pless, V., 'Encryption schemes for computer confidentiality', *IEEE Trans. Computers*, C–26, 11, 1133–1136, 1977.

Pohlig, S. C., *Algebraic and combinatoric aspects of cryptography*, PhD Thesis, Stanford Univ., Sel–77–038, 1977.

Pohlig, S. C. and Hellman, M. E., 'An improved algorithm for computing logarithms over GF(p) and its cryptographic significance', *Trans. IEEE Inform. Theory*, IT–24, 1, 106–110, 1978.

Popek, G. J., 'Protection structures', *Computer*, 7, 6, 22–33, 1974.

Popek, G. J. and Kline, C. S., 'Encryption and secure computer networks', *ACM Computing Surveys*, 11, 4, 331–356, 1979.

Pratt, F., *Secret and Urgent*, Blue Ribbon Books, 1942.

Price, W. L., 'A fourth annotated bibliography of recent publications on data security and cryptography', *NPL Report DNACS 33/80*, 1980.

Price, W. L. and Davies, D. W., 'Issues in the design of a key distribution centre', *NPL Report DNACS 43/81*, 1981.

Pritchard, J. A. T., Computer security: security software', *National Computing Centre Report*, 1980.

Purdy, G. B., 'A high security log-in procedure', *Comms. ACM*, 17, 8, 442–445, 1974.

Quarendon, S. and Everett, D., 'Data transmission security', *Telecommunications*, 15, 6, 34E–34F, 1981.

Rabin, M. O., *Algorithm and Complexity, New Directions and Recent Results*', Academic Press, 21–24, 1971.

Rabin, M. O., 'Digitalised signatures and public-key functions as intractable as factorisation', *MIT Report MIT/LCS/TR–212*, 1979.

Reed, I. S. and Turn, R., 'A generalisation of shift register sequence generators', *J. ACM*, 16, 3, 461–473, 1969.

Reeds, J., '"Cracking" a random number generator', *Cryptologia* 1, 1, 20–26, 1977.

Reeds, J., 'Rotor algebra', *Cryptologia* 1, 2, 186–194, 1977.

Reeds, J., 'Entropy calculations and particular methods of cryptanalysis', *Cryptologia*, 1, 3, 235–254, 1977.

Rejewski, M. E., 'How Polish mathematicians deciphered the enigma', *An. of the History of Computing*, Vol. 3, No. 3, 213–234, July, 1981.

Rhodes, F., 'The sum of powers theorem for commuting block maps, *Private Comm.*, 1980.

Rhodes, F., 'The principal part of a block map', *Private Comm.*, 1980.

Rhodes, F., 'Polynomial presentations of block maps', *Private Comm.*, 1980.

Rhodes, F. 'Regular mappings of sequence over finite fields', *Private Comm.*, 1980.

Richter, M., 'A note on public-key cryptosystems', *Cryptologia*, 4, 1, 20–22, 1980.

Ristenbatt, M. P., Daws, J. L. and Pearce, H. M., 'Crack resistant sequences for data security', *Cooley Elect. Lab. Tech. Report*.

Ritts, R. R., 'Data encryption basics', *Telecommunications*, 15, 6, 39–44, 1981.

Rivest, R. L., 'Remarks on a proposed cryptanalytic attack on the MIT public-key cryptosystem', *Cryptologia*, 2, 1, 62–65, 1978.

Rivest, R. L., 'The impact of technology on cryptography', *ICC*, 1978, 46.2.1.–46.2.4.

Rivest, R. L., 'Critical remarks on "Critical remarks on some public-key cryptosystems" by T. Herlestam', *Bit*, 19, 274–275, 1979.

Rivest, R. L., 'A description of a single-chip implementation of the RSA cipher', *Lambda*, 1, 3, 14–18, October, 1980.

Rivest, R. L., Shamir, A. and Adleman, L., 'A method for obtaining digital signatures and public key cryptosystems', *Comms ACM*, 21, 2, 120-126, 1978.

Roberts, P. and Davis, R. H., 'Statistical properties of smoothed maximal-length linear binary sequences', *Proc. IEE*, 113. 190–196, 1966.

Rohrbach, H., 'Mathematical and mechanical methods in cryptography', *Cryptologia*, 2, 1, 20–37, 1978.

Rondon, E. E. C., *Digital encoding for secure data communications*, Thesis, Naval Postgrad. School, Monterey, CA, 1976.

Ronse, C., 'Non-linear shift registers: a survey', *MBLE Report R430*, 1980.

Ronse, C., 'Substitution networks', *MBLE Report R444*, October, 1980.

Rubin, F., 'Computer methods for decrypting random stream ciphers', *Cryptologia*, 2, 3, 215-231, 1978.

Rubin, F., 'Cryptographic aspects of data compression codes', *Cryptologia*, 3, 4, 202–205, 1979.

Rubin, F., 'Solving a cipher based on multiple random streams', *Cryptologia* 3, 3, 155–157, 1979.

Rubin, F., 'Decrypting a stream cipher based on J-K flip-flops', *IEEE Trans. on Computers*, C-28, 7, 483–487, 1979.

Saltzer, J. H. and Schroeder, M. D., 'The protection of information in computer systems', *Proc. IEEE*, 6, 3, 9, 1278–1308, 1975.

Sambur, M. R. and Jayant, N. S., 'Speech encryption by manipulations of LPC parameters', *Bell Syst. Tech. J.*, 55, 9, 1373–1388, 1976.

Savage, J. E., 'Some simple self-synchronising digital data scramblers', *Bell Sys. Tech. J.*, 449–487, 1967.

Schanning, B. P., 'Data encryption with public-key distribution', *IEEE Elect. and Aerospace Sys. Conf.*, 653–660, October, 1979.

Schatz, B. R., 'Automated analysis of cryptograms', *Cryptologia*, 1, 2, 116–142, 1977.

Scherf, J. A., 'Computer and data security: a comprehensive annotated bibliography', *MIT Project Mac, Tech. Report 122*, 1974.

Schicker, P., 'Seals and signatures in a computer-based mail environment', *Bell-Northern Research Ltd. Report WP31249*, 1979.

Schiff, A., 'Ultrasecure communications for commercial alarm systems', *Proc. of 1977 Internat. Conf. on Crime Countermeasures – Science and Engineering*, Oxford, England, 135–140, July, 1977.

Schmid, P. E., 'Review of ciphering methods to achieve communication security in data transmission networks', *Proc. IEEE*, 76, 1054–1056, 1976.

Schroepel, R. and Shamir, A., 'A T $*$ (S $**2$) $= 0$ (2$**$n) time/space trade off for certain NP-complete problems', *Proc. 20th IEEE Symposium on Foundations on Computer Science*, 328–336, 1979.

Selmer, E. S., *Linear recurrence relations over finite fields*, Dept. of Math., Univ. of Bergen, 1966.

Sendrow, M., 'Key management in EFT environments', *Proc. Compcon*, 351–354, September, 1978.

Sendrow, M., 'A method of authentication in EFT networks using DES without downline loading of working keys', *IEEE Trends and Appl. Symp.*, 168–175, May, 1980.

Shamir, A., 'A fast signature system', *MIT Report MIT/LCS/TM-107*, 1978.

Shamir, A., 'How to share a secret', *Comm. ACM 22*, 11, 612–613, 1979.

Shamir, A., Rivest, R. and Adleman, L., 'Mental poker', *MIT Report TM-125*, 1979.

Shamir, A. and Zippel, R. E., 'On the security of the Merkle-Hellman Cryptographic Scheme', *Trans. IEEE Inform. Theory*, IT–26, 3, 339–340, 1980.

Shannon, C. E., 'Communication theory of secrecy systems', *Bell Sys. Tech. J.*, 28, 657–715, 1949.

Shannon, C. E., 'Prediction and entropy of printed English', *Bell Sys. Tech. J.*, 30, 50–64, 1951.

Shulman, D., *An Annotated Bibliography of Cryptography*, Garland Publishing, New York and London, 1976.

Simmons, G. J., 'Cryptology: the mathematics of secure communication', *Math. Intelligencer*, 1, 4, 233–246, 1979.

Simmons, G. J., 'Symmetric and asymmetric encryption', *ACM Computing Surveys*, 11, 4, 305–330, 1979.

Simmons, G. J., 'Message authentication without secrecy: a secure communications problem uniquely solvable by asymmetric encryption techniques', *IEEE Elect. and Aerospace Sys. Conf.*, 661–662, October, 1979.

Simmons, G. J., 'A system for point-of-sale or access user authentication and identification', *IEEE Workshop on Comms. Security*, Santa Barbara, 1981.

Simmons, G. J. and Norris, M. J., 'Preliminary comments on the MIT public-key cryptosystem', *Cryptologia*, 1, 4, 406–414, 1977.

Simpson, H. R., 'Statistical properties of a class of pseudo-random sequences', *Proc. IEEE*, 113, 12, 2075–2080, 1966.

Sinkov, A., *Elementary Cryptanalysis: a Mathematical Approach*, New York, Random House, 1978.

Skatrud, R. O., 'A consideration of the application of cryptographic techniques to data processing', *Proc. Fall Joint Computer Conf.*, Las Vegas, 111–117, November, 1969.

Sloane, N. J. A., 'Error-correcting codes and cryptography', in *The Mathematical Gardner*, edited by D. A. Klarner, Prindle, Webster and Schmidt, Boston, 346–382, 1981.

Smid, M. E., 'A key notarization system for computer networks', *NBS Pub.*, 500–54, 1979.

Smith, D. R. and Palmer, J. T., 'Universal fixed messages and the Rivest-Shamir-Adleman Cryptosystem', *Mathematika*, 26, 44–52, 1979.

Smith, J. L., 'The design of Lucifer, a cryptographic device for data communications', *IBM T. J. Watson Research Center, RC3326*, 1971.

Smith, J. L., 'Hardware implementation of a cryptographic system', *IBM Tech. Disclosure Bull.*, 13, 3, 1004–1008, 1971.

Smith, J. L.,Notz, W. A. and Osseck, P. R., 'An experimental application of cryptography to a remotely accessed data system', *Proc. ACM Nat. Conf.*, 282–297, August, 1972.

Snow, D. W., 'The application of cryptography to information security in EFTS', *Proc. 1977 Canadian Conference on Crime Countermeasures*, Lexington, KY, USA, 121–132, April, 1977.

Solomon, R. J., 'The encryption controversy', *Mini-Micro Systems*, Vol. 11, No. 2, 22–26, February, 1978.

Solovay, R. and Strassen, V., 'A fast Monte-Carlo test for primality', *Siam J. Computing*, 6, 1, 84–85, 1977.

Soreng, J., 'Symmetric shift registers', *Pacific J. Math.*, 85, 1, 201–229, 1979.

Stahl, F. A., 'A homophonic cipher for computational cryptography', *Proc. NCC*, New York, 565–568, June, 1973.

Stephan, E., 'Communication standards for using DES', *Proc. Compcon.*, 348–350, September, 1978.

Sugarman, R., 'On foiling computer crime', *IEEE Spectrum*, 16, 7, 31–41, 1979.

Tausworthe, R. C., 'Random numbers generated by linear recurrence modulo 2', *Math. Computation*, 19, 201–209, 1965.

Torrieri, D. J., 'Cryptographic digital communication', *NRL Report 7900*, 1975.

Tuchman, W. L. and Meyer, C. H., 'Efficacy of DES in data processing', *Proc. Compcon.*, 340–347, September, 1978.

Tuckerman, B., 'A study of the Vigenère-Vernam single and multiple loop enciphering systems', *IBM Research Rep. RC-2879*, 1970.

Tuckerman, B., 'Solution of a substitution-fractionation-transposition cipher', *IBM T. J., Watson Research Centre*, RC 4537, 1973.

Turn, R., 'Privacy transformations for data banks', *Proc. NCC*, New York, 589–600, 1973.

Turn, R., 'Privacy and security in transnational data processing systems', *Proc. NCC*, 283–291, 1979.

Turn, R., 'Technical implications of privacy protection requirements', *Information Privacy*, 2, 1, 2–6, 1980.

Turn, R. and Shapiro, N. Z., 'Privacy and security in data bank systems: measures of effectiveness, costs and protection – intruder interactions', *Proc. AFIPS*, 41, 435–444, 1972.

Twigg, T., 'Need to keep digital data secure', *Elect. Design*, 23, 68–71, November, 1972.

United States Senate Select Committee on Intelligence, 'Unclassified summary: involvement of NSA in the development of the Data Encryption Standard', *IEEE Comms. Soc.*, 16, 6, 53–55, 1978.

Vernam, G. S., 'Cipher printing telegraph systems for secret wire and radio telegraphic communications', *J. AIEE*, 45, 109–115, 1926.

Verriest, E. and Hellman, M. E., 'Convolutional encoding for Wyner's wire-tap channel', *Trans. IEEE Inform. Theory*, IT-25, 234–237, 1979.

Wall, R. S., 'Decryption of simple substitution ciphers with word divisions using a content addressable memory', *Cryptologia*, 4, 2, 109–115, 1980.

Watson, E. J., 'Primitive polynomials (mod 2)', *Math. Computation*, 16, 368–369, 1962.

Widmer, W. R., 'Message authentication, a special identification requirement in one-way digital data transmission', *Proc. INT. Zurich Seminar on Digital Comms.*, March, 1976.

Willett, M., 'Deliberate noise in a modern cryptographic system', *Trans. IEEE on Inform Theory*, IT-26, 102–105, 1980.

Williams, D. and Hindon, H. J., 'Can software do encryption job?', *Electronics*, 53, 15, 102–103, July, 1980.

Williams, H. C., 'A modification of the RSA public-key encryption procedure', *Trans. IEEE Inform. Theory*, 26, 6, 726–729, 1980.

Williams, H. C. and Schmid, B., 'Some remarks concerning the MIT public-key cryptosystem', *BIT*, 19, 525–538, 1979.

Wood, H. M., 'The use of passwords for controlled access to computer resources', *NBS Pub 500-9*, 1977.

Wood, H. M., 'On-line password techniques', *Proc. NBS/IEEE Trends and Applications symp. Computer Security and Integrity*, 27–31, 1977.

Woodward, J. P. L., 'Application for multilevel secure operating systems', *Proc. NCC*, 319–328, 1979.

Wyner, A. D., 'The wire-tap channel', *Bell Sys. Tech. J.*, 54, 8, 1355–1387, 1975.

Wyner, A. D., 'An analog scrambling scheme which does not expand bandwidth, Part 1', *Trans. IEEE Inform. Theory*, IT–25, 3, 261–274, 1979.

Wyner, A. D., 'An analog scrambling scheme which does not expand bandwidth, Part 2: continuous time', *Trans. IEEE Inform. Theory*, IT-25, 4, 415–425, 1979.

Yardly, H. O., *The American Black Chamber*, Indianapolis, Bobbs-Merrill, 1931.

Yasaki, E. K., 'Encryption algorithm: key size is the thing', *Datamation*, 22, 3, 164–166, 1976.

Yuval, G., 'How to swindle Rabin', *Cryptologia*, 3, 187–189, 1979.

Zierler, N., 'Linear recurring sequences', *J. Soc. Ind. Appl. Math.*, 7, 1, 31–48, 1959.

Zierler, N. and Mills, W. H., 'Products of linear recurring sequences', *J. Algebra*, 27, 1, 147–151, 1973.

Index

Page numbers in bold are those on which the definition of the entry appears.